THE ENCYCLOPEDIA
OF
JUDAISM

THE ENCYCLOPEDIA

OF

JUDAISM

VOLUME IV

SUPPLEMENT ONE

Edited by

JACOB NEUSNER

ALAN J. AVERY-PECK

WILLIAM SCOTT GREEN

PUBLISHED IN COLLABORATION WITH
THE MUSEUM OF JEWISH HERITAGE
NEW YORK

CONTINUUM • NEW YORK

2002

The Continuum International Publishing Group, Inc.
370 Lexington Avenue
New York, NY 10017

Distribution in the United States and Canada by The Continuum International
Publishing Group Inc., 370 Lexington Avenue, New York, NY 10017-6503, USA

Distribution in the rest of the world by Brill, Plantijnstraat 2, P.O.Box 9000,
2300 PA, Leiden, The Netherlands

This book is printed on acid-free paper.

Printed in The Netherlands

Library of Congress Cataloging-in-Publication Data

The Encyclopedia of Judaism, Supplement / edited by Jacob Neusner, Alan J. Avery
-Peck, and William Scott Green.
     p.   cm.
    "Published in collaboration with the Museum of Jewish Heritage, New York."
    Includes index.
    ISBN 0-8264-1460-5 (set : alk. paper)
    1. Judaism—Encyclopedias.   I. Neusner, Jacob, 1932–   .
II. Avery Peck, Alan J. (Alan Jeffery), 1953–   III. Green, William
Scott. IV. Museum of Jewish Heritage (New York, N.Y.)
BM50.E63   2002
296'.03—dc21   2002014145
                                    CIP

TABLE OF CONTENTS

ADDITIONAL CONSULTING EDITORS

FOR SUPPLEMENT ONE

PREFACE TO SUPPLEMENT ONE

When we completed the initial three volumes of THE ENCYCLOPAEDIA OF JUDAISM, we found satisfaction in having covered the more than one hundred topics to which we devoted entries. But we realized that many other important topics remained to be set forth in a systematic way. At the suggestion of William Scott Green, we approached our publisher, Brill, with the proposal of a Supplement-series, which would permit us to continue to search for scholars to write on a variety of problems and subjects not addressed in the first three volumes of THE ENCYCLOPAEDIA OF JUDAISM. Brill's positive response led to new inquiries into the history, practices, and theology of the religion, Judaism, and, as a result of these inquiries, we are very pleased to have been able to identify specialists on the practice of Judaism in locations not treated in the initial three volumes, on problems of ethics in the halakhic setting, and on aspects of the history of Judaism neglected in our opening presentation. The result is more than ninety new studies, of which the first thirty-two are in the present volume. Supplement Two is anticipated for 2003, and Supplement Three, for 2004.

The consulting editors for this part of the work encompass those listed in the original ENCYCLOPAEDIA OF JUDAISM, under the chairmanship of David Altshuler, then director of the New York Museum of Jewish Heritage, as well as the additional colleagues added here. We take pride in having elicited the collaboration of a vast cross-section of those who work on the academic study of Judaism, the religion, its history and theology, literature and ethics and philosophy, definition and practice, and a range of special problems as well. We consider the success of THE ENCYCLOPAEDIA OF JUDAISM to stand for an entire generation of scholars, representing the State of Israel and the Exilic communities, philosophers, theologians, historians, ethicists, literary and textual scholars, not to mention those interested in attempting constructive and systematic accounts of the religion that calls itself "the Torah," in all its formulations, expressions, modulations, and systems. We take it as a compliment that they have participated in this on-going project under our leadership and management.

The Editors

JACOB NEUSNER
Bard College
ALAN J. AVERY-PECK
College of the Holy Cross
WILLIAM SCOTT GREEN
University of Rochester

PREFACE

[Reproduced from THE ORIGINAL ENCYCLOPAEDIA OF JUDAISM]

THE ENCYCLOPAEDIA OF JUDAISM provides a full and reliable account of the religion, Judaism, beginning in ancient Israelite times and extending to our own day. About Judaism, the religion, its diverse history, literature, beliefs past and present, observances, practices and world-view, and place in the context of society and culture, this is what we know. In context and proportion, here is how we think we know it. All principal topics required for the systematic description of any religion—[1] the world view, [2] way of life, [3] theory of the social entity constituted by the faithful—are addressed here. In all cases information is set forth in historical and systemic context. Therefore facts take on meaning and produce consequences.

These systematic entries are essays written both to be read for enlightenment and also to be used for ready-reference to on-the-spot facts. The table of contents identifies the topical program, and two elaborate indices make the volumes immediately useful for finding quick definitions of facts, persons, places, things, events, practices, and the like. The work speaks to anyone interested in religion, in understanding what religion—viewed through the example of Judaism—is, and in comprehending the difference religion makes in general. It is written for people of all ages and backgrounds and not only for specialists in the subject or practitioners of Judaism or any other religion. No special pleading for or against religion in general or for Judaism or any particular viewpoint therein finds a place in the pages of this work. Nor is there room here for partisanship within Judaism. The religion, Judaism, is represented by the entire range of Judaic systems of belief and behavior put forth over time and in our own times.

For our highly qualified editorial board of specialists, we have sought as broad and representative a variety of viewpoints within the faith and about the faith as we could assemble. The editorial consultants advised us on the entire range of topics to be covered, not only their own, and each wrote the principal entry in his or her area of specialization. The program of THE ENCYCLOPAEDIA OF JUDAISM therefore responds to the viewpoints of a great many scholars of Judaism, not only of the editors. Objectivity and academic authority characterize the presentation throughout. Numerous editors from universities and other centers of learning and enterprises of culture, originating in every place where Judaism is practiced and studied today—North America, South Africa, Great Britain, Eastern, Central, and Western Europe, the State of Israel, and elsewhere—helped plan the program and executed it. In identifying our co-workers, we imposed no conditions concerning religious belief or practice. We therefore claim to offer a consensus of responsible and objective learning on each topic and to cover nearly all subjects required systematically to describe, analyze, and interpret the religion, Judaism.

Judaism deserves such full-scale treatment because of its place among the great religions of human civilization. It is practiced throughout the world, both in the State of Israel, where it is the majority-religion, and throughout Europe, South Africa, Australia, New Zealand, the Western hemisphere, North and Latin America, and elsewhere. It is an indispensable example of a religion for all who study religion, exemplifying as it does the power of religion to speak to diverse settings of history and culture over nearly the whole of recorded history. Additionally, Judaism has exercised profound influence on, and engaged in dialogue with, the two other monotheist religions, Christianity and Islam. Its relationships with those kindred religions prove complex and illuminating. But of still more interest: Judaism has retained the loyalty of its practitioners over nearly the entire course of recorded history and under duress as in times of ease. Even though, through most of the history of the Jews, abandoning the faith and people of holy Israel promised worldly advantages, Jews affirmed their religion and, at great personal sacrifice, adhered to its way of life and community. The power of the faith over long centuries to retain the commitment of those that kept the faith attracts attention. More important, still, in an era of challenges of another sort, Judaism provides a fine case of a vital contemporary religion, showing how an ancient, continuous tradition makes a compelling statement to the contemporary world. In concrete everyday terms, Judaism shapes the community of the faithful, and it defines in various systems a distinctive way of life and world-view. So by reason of its antiquity, influence on other world religions, power to persuade the faithful of its truth, and contemporary vitality, Judaism demands sustained attention.

THE ENCYCLOPAEDIA OF JUDAISM focuses in a comprehensive way upon Judaism the religion, presenting accounts of the history, literature, practices and beliefs, theology and philosophy, and contemporary practice of that faith. The history of Judaism is laid out both by periods and by regions, that is, Judaism in Christian Europe and in the Muslim Middle East and North Africa. The important holy books of Judaism, from ancient Israelite Scripture ("Tanakh," meaning, Torah, or Pentateuch, Nebi'im or Prophets, and Ketubim or Writings, called by Christianity "the Old Testament"), to the Dead Sea Scrolls, the writings of the sages of ancient times, including the Mishnah, Midrash, and Talmuds, writings of theology, philosophy and mysticism—all are introduced. The liturgy of the synagogue is spelled out, as well as synagogue architecture, art, and material culture. The practice of Judaism in important centers of the religion, the U.S.A., Britain, Russia, France, South Africa, the State of Israel, and elsewhere, is described. So too is the practice of Judaism in significant times and circumstances, e.g., in the time of the Holocaust, in the circumstance of life in central and eastern Europe, in Muslim countries, in medieval Christendom.

Besides the normative Judaism defined by the ancient rabbis and called Classical or Rabbinic or—in the world today—Orthodox, other Judaisms are described, including the Essene Judaism of Qumran, Karaite Judaism, Reform, Conservative, and Reconstructionist Judaisms, and the like. Jewish mysticism and Kabbalah in particular receive systematic treatment. Philosophy, numerous theological topics within the paramount, Rabbinic Judaism, ethics, law, and other normative components of the religion are explained in detail. The life cycle of Judaism is spelled out, as are the components of everyday piety, religious observance, and liturgy and worship. The material culture of Judaism, synagogue architecture, and other concrete matters are presented.

How Judaism relates to other religions and the views upon Judaism expressed by outsiders, ancient Greek and Latin historians and philosophers, Christian and Muslim theologians both in ancient times and in the world today, are covered. How Judaism makes its impact upon politics, the relationship of Judaism to natural science, psychology, and economics, all are expounded. Numerous special topics of religious thought and theological systemization of religious ideas, such as theological anthropology, sin, the soul, evil, suffering, tradition, death and afterlife, are set forth. Topics of acute contemporary interest, such as medical ethics, women and Judaism, Zionism and Judaism, are treated in a thorough and objective manner. In all, the table of contents shows a comprehensive and thorough treatment of a complex religion, revealing what we believe is required in the systematic and descriptive study of a religion.

The articles serve two purposes, reading and reference. In this way we have learned from the excellent idea of the Encyclopaedia Britannica, which presents a macropaedia, with long, readable articles, and a micropaedia, ready reference for basic facts of various topics. Our entries are meant to accomplish the same double purpose. First, they are written to be read, so that anyone in search of a systematic account of a topic will find here a cogent and comprehensive statement. The editors hope that readers will find many occasions to follow a topic from beginning to end, as the many contributors to these pages organize knowledge of their respective subjects.

Second, the articles are meant for ready reference in looking up facts, so that people in search of specific information will find it conveniently via the index at the end. Alongside names, places, and concepts, this index includes topical references, so that each individual topic covered in a protracted entry is made accessible. Through these references, readers may locate the individual paragraphs that form the counterpart to the brief entries of dictionaries and quick-reference encyclopaedias. To take a simple example, a reader who wants to know about the Sabbath, the Festival of Sukkot, or Passover will be directed by the index to the relevant references in the long article, Calendar of Judaism. There concrete information is available on each of the holy times and seasons of Judaism. But that information is put in a context in which the Sabbath or the Festival of Sukkot or Passover forms part of a larger picture, the system of keeping time, of celebrating holy days and festivals, of an entire religion. The advantage of seeing details in their larger contexts is formidable.

The editors hope in this way both to inform by providing information and also to enlighten by placing facts into the setting in which they take on meaning, and forming out of them significant generalizations about the religion, Judaism. Above all, by seeing things whole and in context, readers may form a judgment concerning matters of proportion and significance, assigning to some matters appropriate weight, to others a lesser priority in the assessment of the whole.

In providing both ready-references and large-scale, comprehensive statements, THE ENCYCLOPAEDIA OF JUDAISM differs from all other dictionaries and encyclopaedias of Judaism to date. These have tended to supply short entries, containing facts and defining words, but to neglect the larger framework in which facts take on meaning. But to describe the religion, Judaism, as we propose to do in these pages, facts out of context do not illuminate, and information without an effort at interpretation yields knowledge of only limited consequence. We cannot know a religion without mastering the facts that religion generates, but we also cannot understand a religion without some broader conception of its principal points of emphasis and contention. These impart to the whole that shape and structure that turn information into knowledge and produce insight for purposes of comparison and contrast.

While the knowledge we convey in these pages rests on a detached and objective foundation, one bias does dictate proportion and structure, defining our priorities throughout. This bias is to insist that Judaism is a living religion, not only a phenomenon out of the past. That is why many articles are devoted to the practice of Judaism in various parts of the world today, and many others to how Judaism is practiced in general, its piety, liturgy, calendar, and other practices. We wish Judaism to emerge in these pages as a set of vivid religious systems, all of them capable of sustaining and maintaining communities of "Israel," however defined, and every one of them rich in nourishment of individual and family life as well.

From the very beginning we signal our bias. Every contributor to The Encyclopaedia of Judaism, whether a practitioner of Judaism, some other religion, or no religion at all, whether of Jewish origin or otherwise, writes about Judaism with respect for a living religious community, its world view and way of life as these cohere, respectively, to form a self-evidently valid response to an urgent and paramount question. If we may use the word "passion" in speaking of learning, what the contributors bear in common is a passion for their subject, which they treat with respect and unfailing dignity. But the statements made in each of the more than one hundred entries are objective, factual, and non-partisan. No particular position within Judaism dominates, and every group and viewpoint is covered in a manner we believe to be fair and balanced. The list of contributors includes specialists from the major universities of the State of Israel, Europe, and the U.S.A. and Canada, as well as other parts of the world; scholars of Orthodox and Reform and Conservative and Reconstructionist origin; Jews and gentiles, women and men, a wide range of convictions and engagements. Judaism is set forth as both a religious tradition and also a living religion, practiced by large and cogent communities of the faithful today. The editors mean not only to inform and enlighten, but to advance understanding of Judaism in its own terms and in the framework of the study of religion generally. That is why, among the articles, approaches of social science and comparative religion are represented, as well as studies of Judaism in its own terms and setting.

To understand the plan of the Encyclopaedia overall, its inclusions and omissions, a particular complication in studying Judaism requires attention. Judaism, the religion, bears intimate relations with a particular nation-state, the State of Israel, on the one side, and a trans-national ethnic group, the Jewish people, on the other. We here take account of the confusion of the national, ethnic, and political with the religious that complicates the study of Judaism as a religion. Take the national first of all. The State of Israel recognizes Judaism and supports that religion. But Judaism the religion is trans-national and does not tie itself to any secular political entity, even with the State of Israel. Then there is the ethnic, often a matter of individual self-definition or identification, called "Jewish identity." The ethnic may or may not engage with the religious at all. In the ethnic framework the Jews, viewed individually as defining themselves in some way or another as Jewish, by reason of shared history, sentiment, and culture claim to constitute a group formed around shared history and memory. Finally, among Judaic religious communities are those that reject the nationality offered by the State of Israel and also dismiss the ethnic ties that to many Jews are binding. These categories— national, ethnic, political, religious—complicate the work of defining the task of THE ENCYCLOPAEDIA OF JUDAISM.

Clearly, the border between the religion, Judaism, and the secular, ethnic group, the Jews, or between that religion and the State of Israel, cannot be drawn very rigidly or with much precision. But it is obvious that, because of its intimate tie to the Jews as individuals and the Jewish people, an ethnic group, Judaism also helps to define the secular culture of Jews wherever they live, whether or not they practice the religion, Judaism, no religion, or some other religion altogether. And the religion, Judaism, further contributes many of the critical mythic and symbolic elements of Zionism and shapes many aspects of the cultural life of the State of Israel. We have tried to take account of the interplay of the national, the ethnic, and the religious dimensions of Jewish existence, while focusing upon the religion in particular. Accordingly, while paying most attention to Judaism, the religion, THE ENCYCLOPAEDIA OF JUDAISM presents the entire range of contexts in which that religion affects human life and culture. These include areas often deemed essentially secular, such as the impact of Judaism upon systems of politics and economics, psychology, and the supposedly secular life of contemporary Jews living in conditions of religious freedom. Given the rich and diverse religious heritage of Judaism, from ancient Israel to the modern State of Israel, such descriptions claim a central position within the analysis of Judaism, the religion.

* * *

The Editors take special pride that THE ENCYCLOPAEDIA OF JUDAISM finds a place as one of the first major educational projects under the sponsorship of the new MUSEUM OF JEWISH HERITAGE, in New York City. The ENCYCLOPAEDIA reached its final stages just as the Museum opened its doors. Through the Museum's collaboration with our work from the very beginning and through the participation of its director, Dr. David Altshuler, as chairman of the editorial board, the Museum helped both to create THE ENCYCLOPAEDIA OF JUDAISM and also to define its educational program and scholarly mission. It is the link between THE ENCYCLOPAEDIA OF JUDAISM and its editors and publishers, on the one side, and the educational mission of the organized Jewish community, on the other. Just as the MUSEUM OF JEWISH HERITAGE speaks to the entire public world of learning and culture, so we mean in these pages to do the same.

Special thanks are owed to Dr. Altshuler for opening to us the Museum of Jewish Heritage's extensive photo-archives. We benefited as well from the help of the Museum's staff, in particular, Louis Levine, Director of Collections and Exhibitions, and from the painstaking work of Shari Segel, Curator of

Photography, who identified appropriate materials in the Museum's collection. Identification and acquisition of photos from other collections was the result of the hard work of our photo-researcher, Rhoda Seidenberg, who also prepared all of the captions and photo credits. We benefitted tremendously from her expertise and great dedication to this project.

For a companion to this ENCYCLOPAEDIA, providing easy access to facts and definitions, the editors call attention to their now-complete and in-print reference-work, Dictionary of Judaism in the Biblical Period, from 450 B.C. to 600 A.D. (N.Y., 1995: Macmillan Publishing Co.). That systematic work facilitates ready-reference to persons, places, events, and the like in the period in which Judaism took shape.

The editors found much pleasure in the professionalism of the scholarly executives of Brill, who sustained the project from the moment it was proposed to them. These are Elisabeth Erdman-Visser, now retired, the first, and Elisabeth Venekamp, the second, of Brill's editors assigned to THE ENCYCLOPAEDIA OF JUDAISM. Both not only supported every proposal and initiative aimed at producing a still more ambitious work than originally contemplated. They also identified with the project and took as much pleasure in the results as have the editors, noting the excellent quality of the entries as they made their appearance and appreciating the ever-expanding range of coverage of the work. Among the European and international academic imprints in the field of Judaism, Brill has long taken the principal position as the leading publisher. Our uniformly positive experience with the firm explains why. The editors also enjoyed the counsel and acumen of Werner Mark Linz and Justus George Lawler and the staff of Continuum. We take special pride in the participation in this project of two such formidable publishers.

The editors express their thanks to their respective universities, which sustain their research and scholarly projects. The University of South Florida and Bard College, The College of the Holy Cross, and the University of Rochester make possible the work and careers of the three, respectively, including the rather considerable enterprise that reaches fruition here. Along with the collaboration of the MUSEUM OF JEWISH HERITAGE in the largest Jewish community in the world, this diverse mixture of academic sponsors—a huge, municipal and public university, a tiny private college, a Catholic college, and a major private research university— matches the mixture of personalities and viewpoints comprised by the entire editorial board.

To the Board of Consulting Editors, who advised on the planning of the project and produced the articles, is owed the credit for the successful completion of THE ENCYCLOPAEDIA OF JUDAISM. Given the vast range encompassed by the history and contemporary practice of Judaism, the diversity that characterizes the Board of Consulting Editors proves entirely appropriate to the subject and the task of elucidating it. Many talents contributed to the project. That explains why the editors also owe their genuine gratitude to the dozens of contributors. Each a principal expert in his or her field, they not only did their work as assigned and on time but turned in their best work and produced first rate scholarship in literate and interesting articles. THE ENCYCLOPAEDIA OF JUDAISM forms a felicitous indicator of where we now stand in the study of Judaism within the academic study of religion today. To the many contributors to these pages we pay tribute for the excellence that their entries evince and express our thanks for the learning, wit, intelligence, and responsibility that they brought to this collaborative project. It is hardly necessary to say we could not have done it without them!

The Editors

JACOB NEUSNER
University of South Florida, Tampa, Florida, and Bard College,
Annandale-upon-Hudson, New York
ALAN J. AVERY-PECK
College of the Holy Cross, Worcester, Massachusetts
WILLIAM SCOTT GREEN
University of Rochester, Rochester, New York

A

AGGADAH IN THE HALAKHAH: Aggadic discourse comments on a received text, tells a story, or advocates an attitude or a proposition of normative conviction and conscience. Halakhic discourse expounds and analyzes a topic of normative conduct. How does narrative or theological discourse participate in the presentation of the halakhic norms of conduct? The two modes of discourse, Aggadah and Halakhah, are quite different from one another. Each organizes its presentation in large building blocks or category-formations, and the halakhic ones do not match the aggadic ones in morphology or structure, nor do the aggadic invoke halakhic composites, let alone category-formations, within their own. Occasionally the halakhic presentation will invoke aggadic facts, less commonly vice versa. But the respective composites of building blocks or category-formations do not intersect. Since, however, within the halakhic structure of category-formations, aggadic compositions and composites occasionally figure, we may ask about the cogency of the Halakhah and the Aggadah at those points. For the intersection indicates markers of inner unity between the Halakhah and the Aggadah. It signals the point at which Rabbinic Judaism as a unitary construct emerges out of its diverse, distinctive sectors and their building blocks.

At issue is not the very occasional reference to a halakhic fact in an aggadic exposition, or the somewhat more commonplace resort to an aggadic datum in a halakhic one, e.g., for purposes of illustration. What is at stake is the context of thought and expression established by systematic composites, compilations of many discrete facts in the service of a coherent argument. We occasionally find the intersection of large aggregates of well-composed aggadic data in a halakhic composite or of halakhic ones in an aggadic setting—not discrete texts but articulated contexts of thought. Where and why do these intersect when they do?

Overall, the category-formations of the Aggadah and those of the halakhah are indeed incompatible. The aggadic documents rarely introduce halakhic materials in their exposition of aggadic propositions. And the contrary is also the case. The exposition of the halakhic components of the halakhic documents, meaning, nearly the entirety of the Mishnah, Tosefta, and Yerushalmi, and the greater part of the Bavli, only rarely requires aggadic complements or supplements. Yet while the aggadic documents rarely resort to halakhic materials to make the case they wish to set forth, in some of the Rabbinic documents of the formative age the presentation of the Halakhah is accompanied by a massive aggadic component.

The Uses of the Aggadah by the Halakhah: Halakhic discourse seldom invokes Aggadah to accomplish its purposes. In Rabbinic literature, rarely indeed does a fully articulated halakhic category-formation encompass and utilize a fully articulated aggadic category-formation. To be sure, an aggadic composition may find a place in proximity to a halakhic exposition. But the Halakhah within its own categorical bounds will not then exploit the aggadic discourse for its purpose, e.g., allude to the aggadic fact to make the halakhic point. That is so, even though the rare exceptions to that rule show that the halakhic discourse could have done so. Conversely, when the aggadic category-formation defines the primary discourse, e.g., in a Midrash-compilation, the Halakhah in its cogent category-formations still more rarely occurs in aggadic composites. That is the case, moreover, even though when it does, the halakhic composition serves to render the aggadic exhortation more compelling and concrete. But the actual occasions prove remarkably few in number and negligible in proportion. Aggadic discourse rarely asks Halakhah to contribute norms of practical conduct to its expositions of its propositions of an other-than-concrete character, e.g., the moral rules and their consequences. So how do the two media of Rabbinic discourse, halakhic and aggadic, with their two distinct bodies of data, form a complete and cogent whole: the statement of Rabbinic Judaism as a coherent structure and system?

A simple fact makes possible an answer to the question of the unity of the Aggadah and the Halakhah. It is that, despite the rule that in the halakhic documents the halakhic category-formations rarely intersect with aggadic category-formations and vice versa, there is a substantial point at which Aggadah and Halakhah do meet. That is in some of the halakhic documents of Rabbinic literature. There, aggadic compositions and composites take a position side by side with halakhic ones. And when a halakhic exposition, within the halakhic category-formation, is juxtaposed to aggadic compositions that articulate the categorical constructions of the Aggadah viewed whole, we sometimes see a remarkable fact. It is how the Aggadah makes the halakhic discourse more profound and encompassing. Then who has seen the implicit correspondence of the halakhic and the aggadic category-formations and so effected the juxtaposition, if not the union, of the two? Clearly, the framer of the document, not the author of the composition or composite, whether halakhic or aggadic, conceived that the Aggadah intersects with, and vastly enriches, the halakhic discourse.

These established facts carry us to the problem at hand. Since in the halakhic documents—Mishnah, Tosefta, Yerushalmi, Bavli—we find aggadic compositions and composites, we want to know how the aggadic contribution affects the halakhic discourse: what holds them together? These aggadic components of halakhic documents stand on their own. But since, at some points, while the aggadic discourses are free-standing, they contribute to the halakhic exposition within the category-formations defined by the Halakhah, an interesting question arises. It is one that is systematic and not merely episodic in character, as follows:

> In halakhic discourse viewed in its entirety what does the Aggadah provide that the Halakhah cannot say in its own terms but that nevertheless the compositor of the document deemed essential to the presentation of the halakhic statement?

The answer to that question carries us deep into the profound unities of halakhic and aggadic discourse. These unities define Rabbinic Judaism at its core. This study explores that generative conception behind the juxtapositions, reconstructing its principles by working back from the data to the premises and presuppositions. What I wish to find out is, case by case, what connections did the compiler of the halakhic documents perceive between the halakhic and the aggadic category-formations that he has juxtaposed, often with great effect?

For the Halakhah is normative in deed, definitive in practice. The Aggadah, people generally maintain, allows for greater latitude in conviction than the Halakhah does in conduct. So when we find that a compositor has encompassed in his halakhic repertoire an aggadic corpus, we identify elements of the Aggadah that participate in the normative statement of the Halakhah. Accordingly, given the issue at hand, when we assess the role of the Aggadah in the Halakhah, it is the Halakhah that defines the basis for coherent discourse, the governing category-formation. Therein, aggadic compositions occasionally find a place. So it is for the Halakhah to explain why the selected aggadic composite belongs. But then, with that explanation, the Halakhah also encompasses the aggadic selection within its penumbra of what is authoritative and obligatory, thus, once more, Judaism.

Mere proximity of an aggadic to a halakhic composition by itself does not settle the matter. The occurrence of a free-standing sentence here or there hardly suggests that to the Aggadah in that context is assigned a role in the halakhic discourse. Only when we can establish a large-scale intrusion of the one into the other does the question before us arise. That is to say, we have to establish that into the halakhic context, an aggadic construction, itself fully cogent, has entered. But that is not always self-evident.

Why the uncertainty about whether the presence of an aggadic composite in a halakhic context makes a difference? That is because the category-formations of the Aggadah and those of the Halakhah are incompatible. Both the Halakhah and the Aggadah select data and construct of them coherent statements within category-formations that impart cogency and context for the discrete pieces of information. But the very model of category-formations of the one bears little in common with those of the other. The halakhic topics and the aggadic ones do not intersect or even correspond in formal expression, let alone in principles of coherence. The fundamental theory of category-formation governing for halakhic data does not explain the construction of the category-formations that serve for the aggadic, and the opposite is also the case. If the halakhic category-formations define the model of discourse that imparts sense and coherence to data, then the Aggadah yields no larger constructions that qualify as category-formations at all—and vice versa. It is therefore noteworthy when the category-formation of the one accommodates the presence of a cogent composition of the other. And in the pages of this study and its companions, we address those noteworthy occasions and ask the question that stands at the head: what does the Aggadah uniquely provide for halakhic discourse that the Halakhah requires but cannot supply on its own?

Aggadic and Halakhic Incompatibility in Category-Formations: Let us dwell on the incompatibility of the category-formations that function in the respective modes of discourse. The Halakhic category-formations, topical, analytical, and cogent, are defined for us on documentary grounds. That is, they are framed by the documents that convey the Halakhah: their divisions and the basis therefor. They are comprised, specifically, by the tractates of the Mishnah, which are topical and propo-sitional in character. The Mishnah (ca. 200 C.E.) identifies the five dozen of these topical category-formations that govern the Halakhah in its formative age. These then are explored by the continuation-documents of the Mishnah, which are the Tosefta (ca. 300 C.E.), Yerushalmi (Talmud of the Land of Israel, ca. 400 C.E.) and Bavli (Talmud of Babylonia, ca. 600 C.E.). The respective halakhic category-formations include nearly everything that a given document wishes to say on the specified topic and nothing that does not pertain to that topic. They organ-ize the data in a rational and coherent way. Not only so, but in many, though not all, category-formations, a particular focus of interest, a problem repeatedly posed for solution, dictates what, concerning a given topical category-formation, the Halakhah will wish to investigate. So the category-for-mations match literary divisions, tractates, with the classification of data by topic and problematic.

Not so the Aggadah. While the Halakhah announces its category-formations for us, the Aggadah requires us to define them on our own, as best we can. But they do not emerge out of the aggadic documents, and, so far as they are topical, the topics derive from an a priori expectation of how aggadic discourse should take shape. That is to say, given the character of aggadic discourse in the Midrash-compilations, we have no problem in proposing obvious aggadic cat-egory-formations, e.g., God, Torah, Israel, idolatry, sin, the gentiles, and so on. Then the lines of definition of the Aggadic cate-gory-formations do not coincide with the documentary limits that present the Agga-dah, e.g., Genesis Rabbah (ca. 400), Levi-ticus Rabbah (ca. 450), Pesiqta deRab Kahana (ca. 500), Song of Songs Rabbah and Lamentations Rabbati (of no clear date), and their subdivisions.

None of these constitutes a category-for-mation or is topically divided into category-formations that correspond in function to those of the Halakhah. The documents are organized according to the Scriptural books on which they comment (Genesis Rabbah) or large themes, theological or ethical pro-positions for example (Leviticus Rabbah, Song of Songs Rabbah, Pesiqta deRab

Kahana). But these composites do not match in formal cogency or analytical rigor the indicative traits of the halakhic ones. The aggadic discourses certainly do not coalesce into topical-analytical units. We now address a specific case, on the basis of which generalizations may be constructed.

Aggadah in the Halakhah of Taanit, the law of fasting in times of crisis and of the village cohort that participates in the Temple cult: We come now to the case of Mishnah-Tosefta-Yerushalmi-Bavli Tractate Taanit, taking up the four documents one by one in succession, and systematically answering the same questions out of the resources of each one.

a. Aggadic Compositions in Mishnah-Tosefta Taanit

MISHNAH TAANIT 3:8

A. On account of every sort of public trouble (may it not happen) do they sound the shofar,

B. except for an excess of rain.

C. M'SH S: They said to Honi, the circle drawer, "Pray for rain."

D. He said to them, "Go and take in the clay ovens used for Passover, so that they not soften [in the rain which is coming]."

E. He prayed, but it did not rain.

F. What did he do?

G. He drew a circle and stood in the middle of it and said before Him "Lord of the world! Your children have turned to me, for before you I am like member of the family. I swear by your great name—I'm simply not moving from here until you take pity on your children!"

H. It began to rain drop by drop.

I. He said, "This is not what I wanted, but rain for filling up cisterns, pits, and caverns."

J. It began to rain violently.

K. He said, "This is not what I wanted, but rain of good will, blessing, and graciousness."

L. Now it rained the right way, until Israelites had to flee from Jerusalem up to the Temple Mount because of the rain.

M. Now they came and said to him, "Just as you prayed for it to rain, now pray for it to go away."

N. He said to them, "Go, see whether the stone of the strayers is disappeared."

O. Simeon b. Shatah said to him, "If you were not Honi, I should decree a ban of excommunication against

you. But what am I going to do to you? For you importune before the Omnipresent, so he does what you want, like a son who importunes his father, so he does what he wants.

P. "Concerning you Scripture says, 'Let your father and your mother be glad, and let her that bore you rejoice' (Prov. 23:25)."

1) The Context, in Halakhic Discourse, of the Aggadic Composition or Composite: The aggadic narrative illustrates the rule, A-B, that the alarm is sounded for every crisis except an excess of rain. But the narrative does not qualify as a legal precedent; the incident is treated as exceptional in every way. On the basis of the aggadic narrative, we could not have reconstructed the halakhic ruling. But with that ruling in hand, we are informed by the Aggadah how exceptional a case would have to be to trigger the exception to the rule just now given.

2) What links do we discern between the aggadic composition and the halakhic composite in which it has been situated? The link between the aggadic composition and the halakhic composite is intimate. The Aggadah, as noted, contradicts the rule, giving a case in which the alarm is sounded for an excess of rain.

3) Does the Aggadah play a role in the documentary presentation of the Halakhah, and if so, what task does it perform? So far as the Halakhah requires an expression of the remission of the law, the Aggadah provides that expression. On the basis of this instance, we may say, the Halakhah states the rule, the Aggadah, the exception.

4) Can we explain why the compositor of the halakhic document (or its main components) found it necessary to shift from halakhic to aggadic discourse to accomplish his purposes? Hence the function of the Aggadah is to illustrate, in extreme terms, the working of the Halakhah: where the Halakhah is remitted. It is not possible to frame a case for the union of the Halakhah and the Aggadah more fitting than this one. Now to Tosefta:

T. TAANIYYOT 2:12-13

2:12 A. *A town which gentiles besieged, or a river* [M. Ta. 3:7B]—

B. and so too, a ship foundering at sea,

C. and so too, an individual pursued by gentiles or by thugs or by an evil spirit—

D. they are not permitted to afflict themselves in a fast, so as not to break their strength [but only to sound the shofar].

E. And so did R. Yose say, "An individual is not permitted to afflict himself in a fast,

F. "lest he fall onto the public charity, and [the community] have to support him."

2:13 A. M'SH B: To a certain pious man did they say, "Pray, so it will rain."

B. He prayed and it rained.

C. They said to him, "Just as you have prayed so it would rain, now pray so the rain will go away."

D. He said to them, "Go and see if a man is standing on Keren Ofel [a high rock] and splashing his foot in the Qidron Brook. [Then] we shall pray that the rain will stop [cf. M. Ta. 3:8].

E. "Truly it is certain that the Omnipresent will never again bring a flood to the world,

F. "for it is said, 'There will never again be a flood' (Gen. 9:11).

G. "And it says, 'For this is like the days of Noah to me: as I swore that the waters of Noah should no more go over the earth, so I have sworn that I will not be angry with you and will not rebuke you' (Is. 54:9)."

H. R. Meir says, "A flood of water will never be, but a flood of fire and brimstone there will be, just as he brought upon the Sodomites.

I. "For it is said, 'Then the Lord rained on Sodom and Gomorrah brimstone and fire from the Lord out of heaven' (Gen. 19:24)."

J. R. Judah says, "A flood affecting all flesh there will never be, but a flood affecting individuals there will yet be.

K. "How so?

L. "[If] one falls into the sea, and he drowns, or if one's ship sinks at sea, and he drowns, lo, this is his [particular] flood."

M. R. Yose says, "A flood affecting everything there will not be, but a flood of pestilence there will be for the nations of the world in the days of the Messiah,

N. "as it is said, 'And I took my staff, and I broke it, annulling the covenant which I had made with all the peoples' (Zech. 11:11).

O. "What does it say? 'So it was annulled on that day' (Zech. 11:12)."

1) The Context, in halakhic Discourse, of the aggadic composition or Composite: Here is a case in which the Tosefta has its version of the Mishnah's story, but the halakhic setting is lost.

We may then say, the Tosefta contains a formulation of the tale that is prior to the Mishnah's version, and the Mishnah's version improves by supplying details; or the Mishnah's version has been removed from the halakhic setting that affords context and meaning and has been treated in a generalized way by its heirs in the Tosefta; or we have two independent formulations of the same theme, but we need not waste time on petty historical questions that in the end cannot be definitively settled.

2) What links do we discern between the aggadic composition and the halakhic composite in which it has been situated? In Tosefta's version, there is no connection between the halakhic statement at T. 2:12 and the Aggadah of T. 2:13; that is explicit.

3) Does the Aggadah play a role in the documentary presentation of the Halakhah, and if so, what task does it perform? No.

4) Can we explain why the compositor of the halakhic document (or its main components) found it necessary to shift from halakhic to aggadic discourse to accomplish his purposes? The documentary program of the Tosefta is different from that of the Mishnah. The halakhic focus of the Mishnah has secured a halakhic reference-point for the story as set forth by the Mishnah. The Tosefta's compositor had no such interest, at least, not at this point.

MISHNAH-TAANIT 4:5

A. The time of the wood offering of priests and people [comes on] nine [occasions in the year]:

B. on the first of Nisan [is the offering of] the family of Arah b. Judah [Ezra 2:5, Neh. 2:10];

C. on the twentieth of Tammuz [is the offering of] the family of David b. Judah;

D. on the fifth of Ab [is the offering of] the family of Parosh b. Judah [Ezra 2:3, Neh. 2:8];

E. on the seventh of that month [is the offering of] the family of Yonadab b. Rekhab [Jer. 35:1ff.];

F. on the tenth of that month [is the offering of] the family of Senaah b. Benjamin [Ezra 2:35, Neh. 7:38I];

G. on the fifteenth of that month [is the offering of] the family of Zattu b. Judah [Ezra 2:8, Neh. 7:13];

H. and with them [comes the offering of] priests, Levites, and whoever is uncertain as to his tribe, and the families of the pestle smugglers and fig pressers.

I. On the twentieth of that same month [is the offering of] the family of Pahat Moab b. Judah [Ezra 2:6, Neh. 7:11].

J. On the twentieth of Elul [is the offering of] the family of Adin b. Judah [Ezra 2:15, Neh. 7:20].

K. On the first of Tebet the family of Parosh returned a second time [with another wood offering].

L. On the first of Tebet [Hanukkah] there was no delegation,

M. for there was Hallel on that day, as well as an additional offering and a wood offering.

T. TAANIYYOT 3:5

3:5 A. Why did they set aside [special times for] the wood-offering of priests and people [M. Ta. 4:5A]?

B. For when the exiles came up, they found no wood in the wood-chamber.

C. These in particular went and contributed wood of their own, handing it over to the community.

D. On that account prophets stipulated with them, that even if the wood-chamber should be loaded with wood, even with wood belonging to the community, these should have the privilege of contributing wood at this time, and at any occasion on which they wanted,

E. as it is said, "We have likewise cast lots, the priests, the Levites, and the people, for the wood-offering, to bring it into the house of our God, according to our fathers' houses, at times appointed, year by year, to burn upon the altar of the Lord our Cod, as it is written in the law" (Neh. 10:34).

F. And it says, "For Ezra had set his heart to study the law of the Lord and to do it, and to teach his statutes and ordinances in Israel" (Ez. 7:10).

3:6 A. Those days [of the wood-offering, M. Ta. 4:5] it is prohibited to conduct the rite of mourning or to have a fast,

B. whether this is after the destruction of the Temple or before the destruction of the Temple.

C. R. Yose says, "After the destruction

of the Temple it is permitted [to lament or to fast], because it is an expression of mourning for them."

D. Said R. Eleazar b. R. Sadoq, "I was among the descendants of Sana'ah [M. Ta. 4:5F, Ezra 2:35] of the tribe of Benjamin. One time the ninth of Ab coincided with the day after the Sabbath, and we observed the fast but did not complete it."

3:7 A. What was the matter having to do with the families of the Pestle-Smugglers and the Fig-Pressers [M. Ta. 4:5H]?

B. Now when the Greek kings set up border-guards on the roads, so that people should not go up to Jerusalem, just as Jeroboam the son of Nebat did, then, whoever was a suitable person and sin-fearing of that generation—what did he do?

C. He would take up his first fruits and make a kind of basket and cover them with dried figs,

D. and take the basket with the first-fruits and cover them with a kind of dried figs,

E. and he would put them in a basket and take the basket and a pestle on his shoulder and go up.

F. Now when he would come to that guard, [the guard] would say to him, "Where are you going?"

G. He said to him, "To make these two rings of dried figs into cakes of pressed figs in that press over there, with this pestle which is on my shoulder."

H. Once he got by that guard, he would prepare a wreath for them and bring them up to Jerusalem.

3:8 A. What is the matter having to do with the family of Salmai the Netophathites [cf. I Chr. 2:54: "The sons of Salma: Bethlehem, the Netophathites"?

B. Now when the Greek kings set up guards on the roads so that the people should not go up to Jerusalem, just as Jeroboam the son of Nebat did,

C. then whoever was a suitable and sin-fearing person of that generation would take two pieces of wood and make them into a kind of ladder and put it on his shoulder and go up.

D. When he came to that guard, [the guard] said to him, "Where are you going?"

E. "To fetch two pigeons from that dovecote over there, with this ladder on my shoulder."

F. Once he got by that guard, he

would dismantle [the pieces of wood of the ladder] and bring them up to Jerusalem.

G. Now because they were prepared to give up their lives for the Torah and for the commandments, therefore they found for themselves a good name and a good memorial forever.

H. And concerning them Scripture says, "The memory of a righteous person is for a blessing" (Prov. 10:17).

I. But concerning Jeroboam son of Nebat and his allies, Scripture says But the name of the wicked will rot (Prov. 10:17).

3:9 A. R. Yose says, "They assign a meritorious matter to a day that merits it, and a disadvantageous matter to a day of disadvantage."

B. When the Temple was destroyed the first time, it was the day after the Sabbath and the year after the Sabbatical year.

C. And it was the watch of Jehoiarib, and it was the ninth of Ab.

D. And so in the case of the destruction of the Second Temple.

E. And the Levites were standing on their platform and singing, "And he has brought upon them their own iniquity, and he will cut them off in their own evil" (Ps. 94:23).

F. Now tomorrow, when the Temple-house will be rebuilt, what will they sing?

G. "Blessed be the Lord, the God of Israel, from everlasting to everlasting" (I Chr. 16:36).

H. "[Blessed be the Lord, the God of Israel] who alone does wondrous things. Blessed be his glorious name [forever; may his glory fill the whole earth! Amen and Amen]" (Ps. 72:18–19).

1) The Context, in Halakhic Discourse, of the Aggadic Composition or Composite: The Halakhah, M. Ta. 4:5A, refers to particular times for wood offerings presented to the Temple by priests and people, as catalogued. The Tosefta's aggadic amplification then provides a narrative account of the origin of those details of the cult. We have found counterpart instances at which aggadic tales explain the origins of cultic regulations, broadly construed. To this point we have not found, in aggadic compositions, etiologies, in the form of narrative, of the origin of other than Temple-rites and procedures. The explanation is not only gen-

eric, but particular and detailed, as T. 3:7-8 show. T. 3:9 is tacked on.

2) What links do we discern between the aggadic composition and the halakhic composite in which it has been situated? The link concerns not the detail of the Halakhah to be explained, but the occasion for the making of the Halakhah in general terms. The bias of the Aggadah favors a narrative explanation for cultic rites, as noted.

3) Does the Aggadah play a role in the documentary presentation of the Halakhah, and if so, what task does it perform? The Mishnah's presentation of the Halakhah does not require the aggadic picture of historical, one-time origins, but derives support from it.

4) Can we explain why the compositor of the halakhic document (or its main components) found it necessary to shift from halakhic to aggadic discourse to accomplish his purposes? The framer of the Tosefta fills out the picture given by the Mishnah in the manner set forth above. What about the Yerushalmi's use of aggadic compositions within its halakhic composites?

b. Aggadic Compositions in Yerushalmi Taanit

YERUSHALMI TAANIT 3:9 III.1–2

III:1. A. And he prayed, but it did not rain [M. 3:9E]:

B. Why did the rain not come properly?] Said R. Yose b. R. Bun, "Because he did not come before God with humility."

III:2. A. Said R. Yudan Giria, "This is Honi the circle drawer [of M. 3:9], the grandson of Honi the circle drawer. *Near the time of the destruction of the Temple, he went out to a mountain to his workers. Before he got there, it rained. He went into a cave. Once he sat down there, he became tired and fell asleep.*

B. *"He remained sound asleep for seventy years, until the Temple was destroyed and it was rebuilt a second time.*

C. *"At the end of the seventy years he awoke from his sleep. He went out of the cave, and he saw a world completely changed. An area that had been planted with vineyards now produced olives, and an area planted in olives now produced grain.*

D. *"He asked the people of the district, 'What do you hear in the world?'*

E. *"They said to him, 'And don't you know what the news is?'*

F. *"He said to them, 'No.'*

G. *"They said to him, 'Who are you?'*

H. *"He said to them, 'Honi, the circle drawer.'*

I. *"They said to him, 'We heard that when he would go into the Temple courtyard, it would be illuminated.'*

J. *"He went in and illuminated the place and recited concerning himself the following verse of Scripture*: 'When the Lord restored the fortune of Zion, we were like those who dream'" (Ps.)

1) The Context, in Halakhic Discourse, of the Aggadic Composition or Composite: The point of halakhic intersection is attenuated; it is at III:1, which is then expanded at III:2.

2) What links do we discern between the aggadic composition and the halakhic composite in which it has been situated? None.

3) Does the Aggadah play a role in the documentary presentation of the Halakhah, and if so, what task does it perform? No.

4) Can we explain why the compositor of the halakhic document (or its main components) found it necessary to shift from halakhic to aggadic discourse to accomplish his purposes? The Yerushalmi's final compositor has provided a topical appendix on the figure of Honi. The story does not bear on the Halakhah in any direct way. I have omitted from the repertoire a large mass of Honi-stories and counterparts set forth by the Bavli; these connect to the Halakhah only via the name of Honi (!).

c. Aggadic Compositions in Bavli Taanit

B. TO M. TAANIT 2:12 XII.1, 3 17B-18A

XII.1. A. As to any [day concerning which] in the Fasting Scroll [Megillat Taanit] it is written [in Aramaic:] "not to mourn"— on the day before, it is prohibited to mourn. On the day after, it is permitted to mourn:

XII.3. A. The master has said: *from the eighth of Nisan until the close of the Festival of Passover, during which time the date for the Festival of Pentecost was reestablished, fasting is forbidden:*

B. *Why say, "until the close of the Festival of Passover"? Why not say simply, until the Festival, and since the Festival itself is a festival period, mourning is forbidden at that time anyhow.*

C. Said R. Pappa, "It is in line with what Rab said, **[18A]** 'That for-

mulation was required only to extend the prohibition to the preceding day.' Here too, that formulation was required only to extend the prohibition to the preceding day."

D. *In accord with the view of what authority does that position conform?*

E. *It conforms to the position of R. Yose, who has said, "It is forbidden to mourn both on the day prior and on the day following the specified occasions."*

F. *If that is the rule, it should be forbidden to mourn also on the twenty-ninth day of Adar also—why do you determine to focus on the consideration that it is the day before the Daily Offering was established, when you can derive the rule governing that day from the fact that it is the day after the twenty-eighth of Adar.*

G. *For it has been taught on Tannaite authority:*

H. *On the twenty-eighth of that [month, that is, Adar], good news came to the Jews, that they need not separate themselves from [practice of] the law.'* For the government had decreed that they may not involve themselves with [study and practice of] Torah, that they may not circumcise their sons, and that they must profane the Sabbath. What did Judah b. Shammua and his associates do? They went and took council with a certain matron with whom all of the notables of Rome were familiar. She said to them, "Tonight, come and cry [to the Roman government] for help!" That night, they came and cried out: 'In the eyes of [God in] heaven, are we not your brothers? And are we not all the children of a single father? And are we not all the children of a single mother? How are we different from every other people and language that you enact harsh decrees upon us?' Now, as a result [the government] annulled those [decrees], and [as for] that same day—they designated it a feast.

I. Said Abbayye, "That formulation was required only to deal with the case of a month that is full [that has thirty days, not twenty-nine]. [In that case the thirtieth of Adar would be the last day of the month and could only be included in the restriction on the ground that it precedes the first of Nisan and not that it follows the twenty-ninth of Adar, since a day, the twenty-eight, intervenes]."

J. R. Ashi said, "You may even maintain that it pertains to a month that is lacking [and is only twenty-nine days]. On a day following a festival day fasting alone is forbidden, but mourning is permitted, but as for the twenty-ninth of Adar, situated between two festival days, it is treated as though it were a festival day itself, with mourning forbidden on that day too."

1) The Context, in Halakhic Discourse, of the Aggadic Composition or Composite: The Aggadah, H, is essential to the argument of F, which makes reference to the clause of the mourning scroll that pertains. Then the aggadic narrative explains the background of the celebratory occasion. We note the very favorable representation of Roman government, accessible as it is alleged to have been to rational argument on humanitarian grounds!

2) What links do we discern between the aggadic composition and the halakhic composite in which it has been situated? The aggadic narrative forms evidence in the halakhic argument and makes a contribution to the corpus of facts on which the argument is built.

3) Does the Aggadah play a role in the documentary presentation of the Halakhah, and if so, what task does it perform? The Aggadah is integral to the halakhic presentation.

4) Can we explain why the compositor of the halakhic document (or its main components) found it necessary to shift from halakhic to aggadic discourse to accomplish his purposes? Only by appeal to the Aggadah at hand (or a comparable story) can the case have been made for the position that is maintained by a party to the discussion.

M. TAANIT 3:1-2

3:1. A. The conduct of these fast days which have been described applies in the case of the first rainfall.

B. But in the case of crops that exhibit a change [from their normal character]

C. they sound the shofar on their account forthwith.

D. And so [if] the rain ceased between one rainstorm and the next for a period of forty days,

E. they sound the shofar on that account forthwith,

F. for it represents the blow of famine.

3:2 A. If the rain fell sufficient for crops but not for trees,

B. for trees but not for crops,

C. for this and that, but not for [filling up] cisterns, pits, or caverns,

D. they sound the shofar on their account forthwith.

B. TO M. TAANIT 3:1-2 III.1-6 19B-20A

III.1. A. If the rain fell sufficient for crops but not for trees, for trees but not for crops, for this and that, but not for [filling up] cisterns, pits, or caverns, they sound the shofar on their account forthwith:

B. *Now it is so that rain sufficient for crops but not for trees does happen, when it rains gently and not heavily; so too, rain that is good for trees but not for crops happens, when it rains heavily and not gently; and there can be rain that is good for both crops and trees but not fill up cisterns, ditches, and caves, if it falls heavily and gently but not yet sufficiently. But how is it possible for sufficient rain to fall to fill cisterns, ditches, and caves, yet not to be good for crops and frees, in accord with the Tannaite formulation?*

C. *It would be a case of torrential rain.*

III.2. A. *Our rabbis have taught on Tannaite authority*:

B. They sound an alarm for rain for trees if it has not rained by half a month prior to Passover [that is, the new moon of Nisan], and for cisterns, ditches, and caves even half a month prior to Tabernacles; and whenever there is not sufficient water for drinking, it is done at once.

C. What is the definition of "at once"?

D. On the following Monday, Thursday, and Monday.

E. They sound the alarm only in their own province [T. Ta. 2:8C-F].

F. In the case of croup, they sound the alarm only if deaths result. If no deaths result, they do not sound the alarm.

G. They sound the alarm in case of locusts, however small the sample.

H. R. Simeon b. Eleazar says, "Even on account of grasshoppers [do they sound the alarm]" [T. Ta. 2:9D-E, 2:10A-B].

III.3. A. *Our rabbis have taught on Tannaite authority*:

B. They sound the alarm on account of the condition of the trees [needing rain] through the other years of the Sabbatical cycle [but not in the Seventh Year], and for cisterns, ditches, and caves, even in the Sabbatical Year.

C. Rabban Simeon b. Gamaliel says, "Also on account of trees in the Sabbatical Year [do they sound the alarm], because they provide support for the poor [who then are permitted freely to take the fruit]."

C. *It has further been taught on Tannaite authority*:

D. They sound the alarm on account of the condition of the trees [needing rain] through the other years of the Sabbatical cycle [but not in the Seventh Year], and for cisterns, ditches, and caves, even in the Sabbatical Year.

E. Rabban Simeon b. Gamaliel says, "Also on account of trees in the Sabbatical Year [do they sound the alarm]."

F. For the scrub in the field they sound the alarm even in the Seventh Year because it provides support for the poor."

III.4. A. *It has been taught on Tannaite authority*:

B. From the day on which the house of the sanctuary was destroyed, rains have turned irregular for the world: there is a year in which the rain is abundant, and there is a year in which the rain is scanty; there is a year in which the rain falls at the anticipated time, and there is a year in which the rain does not fall at the anticipated time.

C. To what is a year in which the rain falls at the anticipated time to be compared? To the case of a worker who is given his week's food in advance on Sundays: the dough is well baked and edible.

D. To what is a year in which the rain does not fall at the anticipated time to be compared? To the case of a worker who is given his week's food at the end of the week on Fridays: the dough is not well baked and is inedible.

E. To what is a year in which the rain is abundant to be compared? To the case of a worker who is given his week's food all at once. The waste in grinding a qab [thirty seahs] is no more than the water in grinding a qab [a sixth of a seah], and the waste in kneading a kor is no more than the waste in kneading a qab.

F. To what is year in which the rain is scanty to be compared? To the case of a worker who is given his food bit by bit. The waste in grinding a qab is no less than the waste in grinding a kor, so too with kneading a qab, it is no less than kneading a kor.

G. Another matter: to what is a year in which the rain is abundant to be compared?

H. To the case of a man kneading clay. If he has plenty of water, then the clay is well kneaded, but not all of the water is used up; if he has only a little water, then the water will be used up, but the clay still won't be well kneaded.

III.5. A. *Our rabbis have taught on Tannaite authority*:

B. One time all Israel ascended to Jerusalem for the festival, and they didn't have enough water to drink. Naqedimon b. Gurion went to a certain lord. He said to him, "Lend me twelve wells of water for the pilgrims, and I shall pay you back with twelve wells of water, and if I don't do it, then I'll give you instead twelve talents of silver," with a fixed time for repayment.

C. When the time came for repayment and it did not rain, in the morning, he sent him a message, "Send me the water or the money that you owe me."

D. He sent word, "I still have time, for the rest of the entire day belongs to me."

E. At noon he sent him word, "Send me the water or the money that you owe me."

F. He sent word, "I still have time, for the rest of the entire day belongs to me."

G. At dusk he sent him word, "Send me the water or the money that you owe me."

H. He sent word, "I still have time today."

I. That lord ridiculed him. He said to him, "The whole year it hasn't rained, [20A] and now is it going to rain?"

J. He cheerfully went off to the bath-house.

K. While the lord was cheerfully going to the bath house, Naqedimon sadly went to the house of the sanctuary. He wrapped himself in his cloak and stood up in prayer, saying before him, "Lord of the world, it is obvious to you that it was not for my own honor that I acted, not for the honor of my father's house did I act, but I acted for your honor, to provide ample water for the pilgrims."

L. At that moment the skies darkened with clouds and it rained until water filled twelve wells and more.

M. As the lord was going out of the bath-house, Naqedimon b. Gurion was leaving the house of the sanctuary. When the two met, he said to him, "Pay me the cost of the extra water that you owe me."

N. He said to him, "I know full well that the Holy One, blessed be he, has disrupted his world only on your account. But I still have a legitimate gripe against you to collect the money that is owing to me! The sun has already set, so the rain has fallen in the time that belongs to me [after the end of the specified time limit]."

O. He once more went into the house of the sanctuary, wrapped himself in his cloak, and stood up in prayer, saying before him, "Lord of the world, let people know that you have loved ones in your world."

P. At that instant the clouds scattered and the sun shone at that moment.

Q. The lord said to him, "Had the sun not broken through, I still would have had a legitimate gripe against you to collect the money that is owing to me."

R. A Tannaite statement:

S. His name wasn't Naqedimon, it really was Boni, and why was he called Naqedimon? For the sun broke through [niqedera] on his account.

III.6. A. *Our rabbis have taught on Tannaite authority*:

B. In behalf of three persons the sun broke through: Moses, Joshua, and Naqedimon b. Gurion.

C. *As to Naqedimon b. Gurion, we have a tradition.*

D. *As to Joshua, there is a verse of Scripture*: "And the sun stood still and the moon stayed" (Josh. 10:13).

E. But how do we know that that is so of Moses?

F. Said R. Eleazar, *"It derives from the use of the words*, "I will begin," *in the two instances. Here we find*, 'I will begin to put the dread of you' (Deut. 2:25), and in connection with Joshua, 'I will begin to magnify you' (Josh. 3:7)."

G. R. Samuel bar Nahmani said, *"It derives from the use of the word 'put' in both cases. Here we find*, 'I will begin to put the dread of you' (Deut. 2:25), and in connection with Joshua, 'In the day when the Lord put the Amorites' (Josh. 10:12)."

H. Said R. Yohanan, *"From the verse itself the lesson is to be derived*: 'The peoples that are under the whole heaven who shall hear the report of you and shall tremble and be in anguish because of you' (Deut. 2:25): And when did they tremble and feel anguish on account of Moses? This is when the sun stood still for him."

1) The Context, in Halakhic Discourse, of the Aggadic Composition or Composite: The theme of the Mishnah-rule, M. 3:2, and the Bavli's compositions in amplification of that rule, III.1-2, is sounding the alarm for a dearth of rain, which accounts for the formation of the composite, III.1-5. In that composite, what is the role of the Aggadah? The story translates the general allusions to a situation of drought into a particular case and how Israelite ingenuity, resting on divine grace, solved the problem. The miracles compound, as the story unfolds. Then, III.6 adds, the exceptional situation is comparable to occasions involving Moses and Joshua. Then the whole, III.5-6, is formed around Naqedimon's name, and inserted because of the general thematic interest in drought. But while the Halakhah deals with routine response to the crisis, the Aggadah explicitly deals with the one-time and extraordinary.

2) What links do we discern between the aggadic composition and the halakhic composite in which it has been situated? The links are attenuated and merely thematic,

but placing the aggadic narrative into this context bears a theological implication of considerable weight.

3) Does the Aggadah play a role in the documentary presentation of the Halakhah, and if so, what task does it perform? The Aggadah articulates what is implicit in the Halakhah, which is, in the end, Israel has to make itself worthy of Heaven's provision of miracles.

4) Can we explain why the compositor of the halakhic document (or its main components) found it necessary to shift from halakhic to aggadic discourse to accomplish his purposes? The Halakhah prescribes certain activities to that end, but the decision remains in the hands of God and is not to be coerced. That is the message involving both Naqedimon and Honi. Joining the aggadic stories to the halakhic rules allows the compositor to make a statement that the Halakhah, on its own, cannot make; and to correct an impression that the Halakhah, willy-nilly, might leave.

B. TO M. TAANIT 3:11 XVI.1-4 25B-26A

XVI.1. A. If they were fasting and it rained for them before sunrise, they should not complete the fast. [If it rained] after sunrise, they should complete the day in fasting:

B. *Our rabbis have taught on Tannaite authority:*

C. "If they were fasting and it rained for them before sunrise, they should not complete the fast. [If it rained] after sunrise, they should complete the day in fasting," the words of R. Meir.

D. R. Judah says, "It if rained before noontime, they need not complete the fast. If it rained after noontime, they should complete the day in fasting."

E. R. Yose says, "If it rained before the ninth hour, they need not complete the fast, if after the ninth hour, they must complete it. For lo, we find in the case of Ahab, king of Israel, that he did fast from the ninth hour onwards: 'See you how Ahab humbles himself before me' (1 Kgs. 21:29)."

XVI.2. A. R. Judah the Patriarch decreed a fast and it rained after dawn. He considered that people should complete the fast.

Said to him R. Ammi, "We have learned: 'before noontime . . . after noontime.'"

XVI.3. A. Samuel the Younger decreed a fast and it rained before down. The people thought that it was a gesture of praise for the community. He said to them, "I shall tell you a parable: to what is the matter to be compared? To a slave who asked his master for a favor, and the master said to them, 'Give it to him, so I don't have to hear his voice.'"

XVI.4. A. Again Samuel the Younger decreed a fast, and it rained after sunset. The people thought that it was a gesture of praise for the community. He said to them, "This is not a gesture of praise to the community. But I shall tell you a parable: to what is the matter to be compared? To a slave who asked his master for a favor, and the master said, 'Let him wait until he is submissive and upset and then give him his favor.'"

B. And then, from the viewpoint of Samuel the Younger, *what would represent a case that involved a gesture of praise to the community at all?*

C. He said, "[a case in which they recited the prayer, 'he causes the wind to blow,' and the wind blew; 'he causes rain to fall' and rain fell."

1) The Context, in Halakhic Discourse, of the Aggadic Composition or Composite: The Halakhah, XVI.1, provides for the occasion of Heaven's immediate response to prayers for rain: do the people have to complete the fast day that has early on accomplished its purpose? I should distinguish between the precedent, XVI.2, and the aggadic narratives, XVI.3-4. The former involves the law as articulated, the latter moves beyond the Halakhah and raises exactly the point paramount elsewhere in the halakhic exposition: does Israel coerce Heaven by these rites? The answer is, not only does Israel not have the power to coerce Heaven, but even though Israel's prayers for rain are answered, that is not a mark that Israel enjoys special favor in Heaven. So here, as is often the case, the Aggadah moves beyond the this-worldly limits of the Halakhah.

2) What links do we discern between the aggadic composition and the halakhic composite in which it has been situated? The Aggadah directly addresses the facts of the Halakhah but changes the focus of analysis.

3) Does the Aggadah play a role in the documentary presentation of the Halakhah, and if so, what task does it perform? The power of the Aggadah to disclose a deeper layer of theological thinking provoked by the Halakhah could not be more dramatically articulated.

4) Can we explain why the compositor of the halakhic document (or its main components) found it necessary to shift from halakhic to aggadic discourse to accomplish his purposes? The Halakhah permitted him to raise the deeper question that, in his view, the Aggadah resolves. Only together, in their counterpoint relationship, do the Aggadah and the Halakhah make the entire statement that the compositor had in mind for the topic at hand.

The Aggadic Role in the Halakhic Discourse of Taanit: At each point in the unfolding of Mishnah-Tosefta-Yerushalmi-Bavli Taanit, the Aggadah and the Halakhah work together, each carrying out its particular task, to present a cogent and proportionate picture for the topic before us. The topic, fasting in times of crisis in order to win Heaven's favor, bears within itself the obvious dilemma: does God respond automatically when Israel fasts? Or does God exercise mercy as an act of grace, in which case, why fast? The Halakhah then sets the stage, defines the activity, and so raises the question, and the Aggadah responds, time and again, to that deeper question implicit in the very provisions of the Halakhah for human activity in response to evidences of divine displeasure. In this context, the Mishnah's story about Honi underscores the uncertainty of importuning Heaven. That is something Honi could accomplish, but not many others. The secondary expansion of the Honi-materials in the Tosefta and Yerushalmi need not detain us. A still more explicit statement emerges in the compositors' union of M. Ta. 3:1-2, with their secondary exposition at B. to M. Ta. 3:1-2 III.2-4, at III.5-6: such events of divine

intervention are exceedingly rare. And then, at the end, comes the explicit response to the challenge of the Halakhah in the aggadic narratives of B. to M. Ta. 3:11 XVI.1-4.

A more familiar role of the Aggadah is to account for the origin of halakhic rules for the Temple cult and its extensions in the village and household, so B. to M. Ta. 2:12 XII.1, 3.

How the Halakhah and the Aggadah Relate in Shared Discourse: The four documents, through the Aggadah that intersects with the Halakhah, in the native-category-formation, Taanit, do make a single, coherent statement, one in which the Halakhah sets the norm, the Aggadah the exception. Here, the Halakhah details with the ordinary, the Aggadah the extraordinary. A single religious system of the world order comes to expression, for the particular halakhic system at hand, only when the Aggadah and the Halakhah are permitted to make each its distinctive contribution. Separately they produce cacophony, together, coherence and cogency—Judaism, whole and complete.

JACOB NEUSNER

ANCIENT JUDAISMS—MODERN SYNTHESES: Every scholar of ancient Judaism has to deal with the many "Judaisms" that existed in antiquity. That is because during its formative period, the first seven centuries C.E., no unified monolithic religion called "Judaism" flourished in Palestine, Babylonia, Alexandria, and other places in the Roman Empire. Rather, the texts from these centuries give evidence of many different Judaic religious systems, each of which saw itself and none other as Israel and claimed that it and none other kept Torah in the way that God intended it to be kept. For example, the framers of the Mishnah exclude Sadducees and Samaritans from the world to come (M. San. 10:1), while authors of the Community Rule of the Dead Sea Scrolls pronounce a curse on everyone who does not submit to the sons of Zadok (1QS V).

Before scholars can speak of a single "Judaism," they must therefore explain how they will treat multiple "Judaisms" as a coherent whole. Because academic disciplines first taxonomize what they study, we should expect to see scholars of Judaism begin by delimiting the smallest coherent taxonomic units of study—individual religious systems or "Judaisms"—an exercise in contrast. Only then, as a second step, can they construct a larger classification, within which the individual Judaisms form subspecies—an exercise in comparison. This enterprise should produce a matrix, built in the order of smallest unit to largest, of subspecies, species, and genus. Thus, in the case of E.P. Sanders, as we shall see below, Rabbinic Judaism, the Dead Sea Scrolls, and the books of the Apocrypha and Pseudepigrapha comprise subspecies, "Judaism" the species, and (were he to continue to construct the taxonomy) "Judaism," "Christianity," and "Islam" the species of the genus "monotheisms."

In this article we will examine five authors, three of the past generation (Solomon Schechter, George Foot Moore, and Ephraim E. Urbach) and two of the current one (E.P. Sanders and Jacob Neusner), in order to perceive how recent scholarship has produced syntheses of ancient Judaism. We want to know, first, how scholars understand the problem of many and different ancient Judaisms, second, if they propose a solution to the problem, and, third, whether each solution is sustainable. We can answer this last question, knowing that a synthesis is arguably correct, if the matrix the author produces allows us to understand how diverse Judaisms can be classified as subspecies of a single religion: "Judaism."

Solomon Schechter compiled the first systematic theology of Judaism of the past century.[1] The bulk of his work (17 chapters) he devotes to laying out and systematizing theological ideas contained in Rabbinic sources: "the Talmudic and the recognized Midrashic literature," or the "great Midrashim" (p. xxx; cf., p. 3), but also the Medieval *Sifrè Mussar* and *Piyutim* (pp. xxxiii-xxxiv). Given the diversity of these documents, we want to know how Schechter arrives at a homogeneous Judaism whose thought he can systematize. He provides an answer in his Preface (p. xxx):

> This literature covers ... many centuries and was produced in widely differing climes amid varying surroundings and ever-changing conditions, and was interrupted several times by great national catastrophes and by the rise of all sorts of sects and schisms.

Here Schechter lays out the problem of the diversity of the sources: we should expect the varying circumstances in which the documents were produced to yield manifold opinions on different theological subjects. His solution follows (p. xxxi):

> Notwithstanding, however, all these excrescences which historic events contributed towards certain beliefs and the necessary mutations and changes of aspects involved in them, it should be noted that Rabbinic literature is, as far as doctrine and dogma are concerned, more distinguished by the consensus of opinion than by its dissentions.

The language indicates that Schechter adopts a model used by historians of Christianity: orthodoxy (which he calls "Catholic Israel," pp. xxviii, 9, versus "heresy" (see, esp., p. 10)). In this matrix, a core set of beliefs held by the majority of people ("the religious consciousness of the bulk of the nation," p. xxviii) constitutes the theology of Judaism. Whatever makes up various minority opinions Schechter discards as extraneous or superfluous. Schechter passes the same judgment on what he calls "mere legend and fancy, falling within the province of folk-lore and apocalypse" (p. xxviii), which could constitute a reference to components of the Apocryphal, Pseudepigraphic, or midrashic literature. By what criterion does Schechter reckon one idea to be "Catholic" and another incidental? That which leaves "almost no mark on Jewish thought" (p. 7)—by which we must surmise that he means an idea that appears infrequently in the literature and not at all in the liturgy (pp. 10-11)—Schechter does not treat in his study.

Hence Schechter presents a coherent solution to the problem of many ancient Judaisms: he examines what is orthodox and leaves aside what he judges to be heretical or marginal. But does this solution work? The classic Christian orthodoxy-heresy paradigm introduces the problem of how to produce history using Rabbinic texts: we do not know whether what we label orthodox or "Catholic" in the sources reflects what the majority of people actually believed and practiced at any given time. We simply cannot verify what people did or did not do.

More importantly, Schechter asserts the homogeneity of Rabbinic sources but fails to provide the grounds for doing so. He claims that "widely differing climes" made their impact on Rabbinic literature but that these had only superficial effects, producing no real change in the great stream of Jewish thought from beginning to end. Schechter never demonstrates how he can treat such different texts, produced centuries apart, as products of a single, monolithic religion.

George Foot Moore was the first Christian scholar to study Judaism on its own terms. In the introductory "Historical" section of his landmark work,[2] he acknowledges the many "parties and sects" that existed during the long stretch of these centuries. How does he deal with these many Judaisms? We explains in the opening lines of his work (vol. I, p. vii):

> [S]ources of various kinds disclose not only the continuity of development in the direction of the normative Judaism of the second century, but many divergent trends—the conflict of parties over fundamental issues, the idiosyncrasies of sects, the rise of apocalyptic with its exorbitant interest in eschatology—a knowledge of all of which is necessary to a historical understanding of the Judaism which it is the principal object of this work to describe.

Moore's language implies that he proposes an evolutionary model in which initial diversity yields to conformity. How so? We may conceive of Moore's model as a tree consisting of a main trunk from which many limbs diverge, each in a different direction. The trunk symbolizes what Moore calls "normative" (also "Tannaitic") Judaism, with its roots in the time of Ezra and becoming the most common or representative type of Judaism in the late first century c.e. From this trunk many branches—the several and varied "divergent trends" of Judaism—sprouted as offshoots. The Judaism of Ezra (vol. I, pp. 29ff.), the Scribes (vol. I, pp. 37ff.), Pharisees (vol. I,

pp. 56ff.), and the schools of Shammai and Hillel (vol. I, pp. 83ff.) constitute the early development of Judaism that becomes "normative," while the colony at Elephantine (vol. I, p. 23), Samaritans (vol. I, pp. 23ff.), "apocalyptic" (vol. I, pp. 127-130), Sadducees (vol. I, pp. 68ff.), and the authors of the Damascus Document (vol. I, pp. 200ff.)[3] make up the divergent trends. Normative Judaism eventually yields the Mishnah, which includes the work of scholars from preceding generations, the Tannaim. What of other Judaisms? In Moore's model, these become evolutionary dead-ends; they do not survive the First Jewish Revolt, and they produce no continuators that exist side by side with normative Judaism.

Having summarized Moore's understanding of Judaism, we ask whether he constructs a coherent solution to the problem. Moore's argument encounters difficulties when he moves from his historical section to a description of the tenets and practices of the Tannaitic Judaism of the first centuries c.e. The problem is that Moore adduces for his claims evidence from documents that in no way match the criteria for this Judaism.[4] A single example suffices. In his chapter on "Motives for Moral Conduct" (vol. II, pp. 89ff.), Moore discusses the idea of "merit laid up for the hereafter" (vol. II, p. 90). We are surprised, however, to see him cite Jesus' words in Matt. 19:21, Mark 10:21, and Luke 18:22 as his first examples, and then 4 Esdras and 2 Baruch as corroborating evidence. Later in the same discussion he will draw examples from the much later Rabbinic midrash Tahnhuma and Sifre Deut. Nowhere does Moore explain how he can adduce these texts as data in an argument about Tannaitic Judaism.

In the end, Moore produces a work of harmonization much like that of Schechter. His initial solution to the problem of many Judaisms accounts for both diversity and unity,[5] but he then abandons that solution, treating so-called Jewish documents as if all were produced by a single, monolithic religion in which differences in place and century of origin have no bearing.

Ephraim E. Urbach was the first student of Judaism to produce a monumental synthesis of ancient Judaism in Hebrew.[6]

Unlike Schechter or Moore, however, Urbach does not begin by explaining and resolving the problem of diverse ancient Judaisms. Rather, he ignores the problem from the start, dissolving all distinctions between different Judaisms into a single religious system that exists unchanged for nearly a millennium. This Urbach makes explicit at the outset (vol. I, p. 1):

> The term "Sages" is customarily used to denote the Sages of the Oral Law, who are mentioned in its literary sources: the Mishnah, Tosefta, Halakhic Midrashim, Talmuds and Haggadic Midrashim. The earliest of the scholars lived in the era preceding the Maccabean revolt, and the last, when the Mediterranean countries were conquered by the Arabs—that is, their activities extended over a period of more than nine hundred years.

This is how Urbach asserts the longevity and permanence of Rabbinic Judaism: he places its first sages in the third or second century B.C.E., two hundred years or so earlier than any other scholar dates them.[7] Their homogeneity he alleges with the following language (vol. I, p. 2):

> On the one hand it is clear that the events enumerated [from Alexander to the ascension of Christianity]—and many others besides—left their mark on the thought and doctrines of their times; but on the other, the Sages, in each generation, introduced, by their beliefs and concepts, a ferment into the ranks of the nation, and by waging a constant struggle they achieved the crystallization and formulation of ideas and sentiments that were accepted as credal principles and were held in common by the scholars and the nation as a whole.

That is to say, although the world around them changed, the sages themselves did not. This assertion marks a return to Schechter's work of sixty years ago. But Urbach goes even further than Schechter had: he maintains that the sages were able to enforce a uniformity of belief on all Jews everywhere. Where we envisioned Moore's construction of Judaism as a tree with many limbs, we can conceive of Urbach's as a wide and tranquil river, neither admitting tributaries into its flow nor permitting forks to diverge from it, indistinguishable at its mouth from what it was at its source. Urbach posits a monolithic Judaism that survived unchanged for almost a thousand years.

We cannot say, therefore, that Urbach produces a matrix that allows us to understand both how many Judaisms differ from one another and how they nevertheless can be classified as subspecies of the same religion, for he ignores all the data that point to the existence of a variety of Judaisms during this period. He does not address the problem of the various collections of documents, such as the Apocrypha, Dead Sea Scrolls, and the sources of the "Oral Law." Nor does he account for differences within the collections themselves, such as variations in language, place of origin, purpose, topical program, logic of coherent discourse, worldview, and construal of the social order, for example. As with Schechter and Moore before him, differences in the parts have no bearing on the whole.

E.P. Sanders: Each scholar that we have surveyed presents a work of history in the guise of theology, by which I mean that he attempts to show, through a study of theological ideas found in literary sources, what Jewish people believed in antiquity. Each wanted to know what people did and when. In his monumental work *Paul and Palestinian Judaism*,[8] E.P. Sanders, by contrast, does not address the historical question. Rather, he asks what systems of thought the Jewish sources reveal without claiming to deduce what the majority of people in a given time or place believed. He is the first to produce a comprehensive study of ancient Judaism working primarily from ideas.

Sanders compares two religious systems that he calls "Palestinian Judaism" and "Paulinism," but he seeks to avoid the errors of past studies, nearly all of which based their comparisons on superficial similarities between religious "motifs" (pp. 2-16). His solution is to compare one "pattern of religion" with another. This allows Sanders (p. 16):

> . . . to compare an entire religion, parts and all, with an entire religion, parts and all; to use the analogy of a building, to compare two buildings, not leaving out of account their individual bricks.

Thus Sanders indicates that he recognizes a problem: how to synthesize many different data into a single "pattern," which he can then compare with another pattern, similarly synthesized. Sanders then defines what he means by "pattern of religion" (p. 17):

> A pattern of religion, defined positively, is the description of how a religion is perceived by its adherents to *function*. "Perceived to function" has the sense not of what an adherent does on a day-to-day basis, but of *how getting in and staying in are understood*: the way in which a religion is understood to admit and retain members is considered to be the way it "functions."

By a "pattern of religion," therefore, Sanders indicates the mechanism by which a religion works out its view of the social order: who makes up the community of the faithful and who does not.

In order to get at the pattern for Judaism, Sanders examines three collections of writings, produced between 200 B.C.E. and 200 C.E. (p. 24), which he calls "Tannaitic Literature," "Dead Sea Scrolls," and "Apocrypha and Pseudepigrapha." He finds in all three a single pattern, which he names "covenantal nomism" (p. 422):

> (1) God has chosen Israel and (2) given the law. The law implies both (3) God's promise to maintain the election and (4) the requirement to obey. (5) God rewards obedience and punishes transgression. (6) The law provides for means of atonement, and atonement results in (7) maintenance or re-establishment of the covenantal relationship. (8) All those who are maintained in the covenant by obedience, atonement and God's mercy belong to the group which will be saved.

This is how Sanders synthesizes many different Judaisms into one: he discovers the least common denominator shared by the three bodies of literature he has identified.

Sanders' solution to the problem of many Judaisms encounters two difficulties. First, he never explains how all sources of a given collection—the Rabbinic literature, Dead Sea Scrolls, and Apocrypha-Pseudepigrapha—constitute a coherent whole. Sanders does not demonstrate by what logic, except fortuitous accident, we should read the *Manual of Discipline* and the *Habakkuk Commentary*, or *Ben Sirach* and *4 Ezra*, as documents that express the same religious system (pp. 24-25). Second and most important, Sanders never finds "covenantal nomism" whole in any one text (p. 423). Rather, he takes one component of the pattern from this document and another from that one. The result is a pattern cobbled together from many different sources, but existing complete in none.

It is this last problem that shows how Sanders, like those who preceded him, homogenizes many Judaisms into one Judaism. He asserts, but never demonstrates, how many different texts comprise the documents of one religion.

Jacob Neusner is the first scholar of ancient Judaism to produce an extended exposition of Rabbinic literature, presenting a detailed taxonomy of how each source is organized, how it makes its argument, how it sustains a particular world-view, understanding of the social order, and way of life, and how these components may be compared and contrasted with those of any other source. Indeed, it was he who coined the term "Judaisms," in the plural, to denote the variety of Judaic systems that existed in antiquity. While this labor of analysis and differentiation has taken shape over many decades, recently Neusner has addressed the second task of taxonomy, that of synthesis or comparison, of stating how the different religious systems (i.e., Judaisms) of the many sources are held together in a coherent whole. Neusner suggests that the key to reading the Rabbinic texts all together lies in discerning the theological system they all express. We examine a single work of that project, *The Theology of the Oral Torah*.[9] Because Neusner presents a methodical response to the problems laid out at the beginning of this article, his work requires an extended exposition.

In his first chapter ("Prologue: Imagining Eden") Neusner presents a detailed report of both the problem of producing what he calls a "descriptive theology" of Judaism and the methodology that he employs. While he uses language familiar from our previous study, he redefines terms and reconfigures the concepts. Like Schechter, he maintains that he sets forth the "orthodox" or "catholic" views of the rabbis; from Moore he borrows the language "normative" to indicate those sayings or stories that are representative of the rabbis' ideas; like Urbach, he claims to "portray *the* sages and *their* beliefs and opinions" (pp. 34-35). How, then, does the synthesis Neusner presents avoid recapitulating what these others have done? Neusner lays out his program as follows (pp. 34-35):

> By what is representative I mean not what stands for broadly held opinion, but rather what embodies the ubiquitous governing rational modes of thought, on the one side, and what sets forth the necessary and sufficient and integral doctrines generated by that rationality, on the other. By that criterion of what is "representative," therefore, the former—the modes of thought— are alleged to define rationality, and the latter—the logically consequent propositions—are claimed to define the *logos*, the principle that pervades the whole. This takes from in the idea that creation reveals God's justice, defined in terms man comprehends, and appears in many forms.

Neusner indicates that unlike the other authors cited in this study, he does not begin by setting forth ideas at all. The result would be an account of scattered and disconnected thoughts, found here and there in the Rabbinic sources, which he could then systematize. On the contrary, he intends first to discover the "*logos*" that lies behind the thought of those who compiled the Rabbinic sources. By *logos* Neusner means a principle that governs both the ideas that are set forth and the system that animates those ideas. Once he has discovered this governing principle, Neusner proposes that he can identify the normative propositions of Judaism and that he can present them in the only order in which they make sense. If he were to state these propositions in any other order, changing the position of only one, the entire system would collapse. By that same token, propositions presented in proper order represent no less than Judaism's theology, a complete system, needing no further systematization (p. 37). Here is how Neusner states what I have summarized (p. 36):

> In my view, what represents the structure and system that sustains a variety of kindred writings emerges in positions that logically hold together among them all. These positions, whether concerning doctrine or correct modes of thought, will ... form a

tight fabric, of gossamer weight to be sure, spread over the whole, a thin, translucent tent that holds within everything that belongs and keeps out everything that does not. As with philosophy, so here too, consistency with the first-established givens, beginning with the principle of one, sole, omnipotent, just God, opens the way for inclusion, while contradiction among parts, failure to form a seamless whole, excludes.

In these passages, Neusner reveals that the governing principle of Judaism's theology is the justice of God. It is this idea that generates the worldview and understanding of the social order that we find in the Rabbinic documents, the world and society, both as God intended them to be and as they are now. And it is in the difference between the two that we discover the system inherent in Judaism's theology: because God is just, he created an ordered world; humanity's will, in opposition to God's, constitutes the cause of disorder, the present state of things; God will one day restore the order that he built at the beginning (xii-xiii).

Although Neusner employs the technical language of "structure" and "system," he also uses the metaphor of story to explain the theology that he sets forth (p. xiv), and this is exactly what he reproduces: the story of God's creation of the world, humanity's fall, God's redemptive and ongoing activity of justice and mercy in the world, and his intention to restore it to the perfected state he intended at the beginning. I say "reproduces" because this story recapitulates the story of Scripture. This is why Neusner argues that Judaism's theology constitutes a system, and that each component can occupy one position and no other. If God were not just, we should not expect creation to be ordered and perfect; if creation were not perfect, we should not regard disorder as a problem; if disorder posed no threat to God's justice, we should not expect, either that he would involve himself in the dealings of humankind, or that he would one day restore the perfection of Eden. It is due to the coherence of this system/story, and because of its familiarity (that is, it exactly repeats the story of creation, fall, and redemption which we already know from the Hebrew scriptures), that Neusner regards as schismatic any proposition found in the Rabbinic sources that runs contrary to the principle parts he lays out here.[10] Furthermore, according to Neusner, anyone who wishes to argue that he has misrepresented Judaism's theological system must show how the opposite principle (God is not just) and the schismatic idea (creation is imperfect by design, God has no intention of restoring the perfection of the created order), and therefore an entirely different system/story, governs the thinking of the rabbis (pp. xvi, 37).

Finally, it is this recapitulation of the story of Scripture that provides an answer to the question, what texts of Judaism does Neusner synthesize? He does not spell this out at the outset, but the *aggadic* texts constitute his evidence, primarily the great scripture commentaries (Genesis and Leviticus Rabbah, Sifra, Sifre to Deuteronomy and Numbers), but also the *aggadic* sections of the *halakhah* (the Mishnah, Tosefta, the two Talmuds), and other *midrashim*. Thus Neusner argues, "the sages'" is the only possible system that the Hebrew Scriptures sustain (p. 645, n. 2). The story that the sages tell re-presents the story that Scripture tells.

The only question left for us to ask is whether Neusner accomplishes what he sets out to do. Neusner organizes the book, not topically by idea or dogma, but into four sections that reveal the logic of the system: "Sources of World Order," "Perfecting World Order," "Sources of World Disorder," "Restoring World Order." In each section Neusner reproduces large sections of his translations of the primary texts in order to allow readers to judge for themselves whether he provides "an accurate account of the meaning of matters" (p. xvi). Because the story's "plot" states that at the end of time God will restore the perfection that existed at the beginning, both the sections and the individual chapters naturally take on chiastic form. Sources of world order in the first section (the moral and political orders, and the anomaly of private lives) find their counterparts in the chapters of the last ("Restoring Private Lives: Resurrection" and "Restoring the Public Order: The

World to Come"). In the same way, the chapters of the two center sections balance one other.

The result of this presentation of matters matches what Neusner proposes to do. The book sets forth nothing less than a matrix for reading the many and different Rabbinic texts whole. In Neusner's synthesis the logic of the system, rather than the frequency with which ideas are discussed in the texts, reveals both the normative shank of the theology and what is beside the point.

Bibliography

Moore, George Foot, *Judaism in the First Centuries of the Christian Era: The Age of the Tannaim* (Cambridge, MA, 1950).

Neusner, Jacob, *The Theology of the Oral Torah: Revealing the Justice of God* (Montreal and Kingston, 1999).

Sanders, E.P., *Paul and Palestinian Judaism: A Comparison of Patterns of Religion* (London, 1977).

Schechter, Solomon, *Some Aspects of Rabbinic Theology* (Woodstock, 1993).

Urbach, Ephraim E., *The Sages: Their Concepts and Beliefs* (Jerusalem, 1975).

Vermes, Geza, *The Complete Dead Sea Scrolls in English* (New York, 1997).

Notes

[1] Solomon Schechter, *Aspects of Rabbinic Theology* (Woodstock, 1993; originally published in 1909 as *Some Aspects of Rabbinic Theology*).

[2] George Foot Moore, *Judaism in the First Centuries of the Christian Era: The Age of the Tannaim*, 3 vols. (Cambridge, 1950; originally published in 1927).

[3] When Moore completed his work the Dead Sea Scrolls had not been discovered. Hence he made no connection between the Damascus Document and the Essenes.

[4] "The recognized Palestinian scholars . . . from about the beginning of the Christian era [to the completion of the Mishnah], as transmitters of the unwritten law, are called *Tannaim*, 'Traditioners,' or, more generally, 'Teachers'" (vol. I, p. 4).

[5] Space does not permit us to debate whether the data bear out Moore's picture of a single, homogeneous Judaism from the second century onward. I merely argue that he presents a logical and coherent solution to the problem.

[6] Ephraim E. Urbach, *The Sages, Their Concepts and Beliefs*, 2 vols. (Jerusalem, 1975; translated from the second Hebrew edition, 1971; originally published in 1969).

[7] Urbach's hazy dating prevents us from being any more precise in ours.

[8] E.P. Sanders, *Paul and Palestinian Judaism: A Comparison of Patterns of Religion* (London, 1977).

[9] Jacob Neusner, *The Theology of the Oral Torah:*

Revealing the Justice of God (Montreal & Kingston, 1999). For a brief history of the work that led up to the writing of this particular book see pp. 42-47.

[10] Neusner goes on, pp. 38-39, to spell out the specific ways that the sages themselves signify what is normative.

James Riley Strange

ASTROLOGY AND MAGIC IN MEDIEVAL JEWISH THOUGHT: Astral magic was a type of sorcery popular among Jewish intellectuals beginning in the early twelfth century. Its basic idea was that humans are capable of harnessing the celestial bodies for their use and benefit. The stars and the constellations produce a constant stream of influence or emanation, known as spirituality (*ruhaniyyat* in the original Arabic), and they are a source of powerful forces. The nature of the emanation and the qualities of the forces depend on the heavenly bodies from which they derive and on their location in the heavens. Both emanation and powers may be received and purposefully directed in the terrestrial world, conditional on the proper preparation or disposition (Hebrew: *hakhanah*). Such reception of heavenly emanation or supernal forces is referred to as "bringing (or drawing) down" (Hebrew: *horadah*). The magician brings down spirituality for practical reasons, such as modifying nature, foretelling the future, or healing the sick. The emanation or supernal forces cannot be used to advantage without detailed, accurate knowledge of the position of the sources of emanation, that is, of the heavenly bodies (planets, constellations) and, correspondingly, of the necessary disposition. To achieve the proper disposition, the practitioner must fashion or procure some image, effigy, or amulet, symbolizing the emanating source, that is, the star or constellation, at a certain well-defined time. Underlying this procedure is the concept of sympathy and interaction between heaven and earth, between the symbol and what it symbolizes. In many cases the form of the emanating star or constellation is actually fashioned on the image.

There are several stages in the magician's actions:

a) First comes a careful examination of the configuration of stars and constellations that may yield the desired result. For example, if the object is to heal an invalid, the magician will examine the astrological and magical sources at his disposal to determine which configuration of the stars guarantees the proper emanation for healing that particular sickness. Possible configurations might be the sighting of a given constellation on the horizon, the position of a certain planet (*mesharet*, "servant") within the constellation (referred to in this context as a *bayit*, "house"), or the conjunction (*mahberet*) of two or more planets within that constellation. In many cases, the configuration is elementary, involving a single constellation or star.

b) An image or effigy symbolizing the emanating configuration is prepared.

c) The effigy is produced at the time the stars and constellations actually form the required configuration. In the above example, the magician might place the effigy on the diseased part of the body at the time the star or constellation is active.

d) Various secondary techniques may be necessary, such as burning incense, offering prayers to the stars, invocations, use of magical names, and the like.

Systematic manifestations of astral magic appear in the Hermetic writings, which date to the three first centuries C.E. These writings were concerned with the secrets of the god Hermes, who was identified with the Egyptian god of wisdom, Thoth. For the Greco-Roman world, the ancient Egyptian religion, still being practiced in Egypt, was a kind of "ancient truth" and therefore of singular importance. The earliest systematic articulations of astral magic date, therefore, to the waning years of the mythological idolatry of the Ancient East and the Hellenistic world. The philosophical worldview expressed in Hermetic literature is a mixture of Neoplatonic, Stoic, and oriental elements, presented together with astrological concepts and detailed astral-magical techniques. These techniques were intended to help achieve the theoretical and ecstatic goals envisaged by the Hermetic writings.

Another area in which magical and theurgical conceptions were formulated was Neoplatonic philosophy, in the writings of

Proclus and Iamblichus. The Hermetic worldview was a major factor in the development of philosophical alternatives to the Aristotelian picture of the world. The bearers of the Hermetic heritage sought to ascribe physical processes in some degree to stellar influence on the material world. That stellar emanation exerted an essential influence on processes in the terrestrial world was the fundamental principle informing astral-magical activity.

While the popularity of the Hermetic writings and of magical techniques aroused the disapproval of official church circles, they continued to influence the cultural and scientific world. One expression of this influence was the revival of Hermetic ideas in Harran, Mesopotamia, in the ninth and tenth centuries, where a religious group, known as the Sabians, emerged. They had internalized the elements of the original Hellenistic pattern: besides adopting Neo-platonic, Neo-Pythagorean, and Hermetic concepts, they formulated a broad range of astral-magical techniques and made a major contribution to the development of Hermetic concepts in the Arab world. The source of all wisdom and science, they believed, was Idris, identified with the ancient Enoch, though many identified him with Hermes Trismegistus. In time, the Sabians left their mark on the Muslim world. Hermetic influence may be detected in the writings of Al-Kindi (the letter *De Radiis*), the Brethren of Purity (*Ikhwān al-Safā'*), Al-Biruni, and other circles. These philosophers, as a whole, continued to favor an alternative to the purely scientific Aristotelian view of the world, at the same time teaching that the supernal world was intimately involved in establishing order in the sublunar world.

As in other areas, medieval Jewish thought in the area of astral magic was influenced by Muslim thought. Astral magic played an important role in shaping systematic Jewish theology beginning in the twelfth century. Many thinkers argued that Judaism possessed a superior ability to attract stellar emanation. Almost all the commandments of the Torah were explained as instruments for bringing down influence from the stars.

Beginnings: Definite astral-magical convictions were first expressed in the twelfth century by three poet-thinkers who were in personal contact: Moses ibn Ezra, Judah Halevi, and Abraham ibn Ezra; astral magic was in fact a distinct theological element in the writings of the last-named two. The process of internalization, however, was far from easy. Their older contemporary, Abraham bar Hiyya, and their younger contemporary, Maimonides, regarded the fashioning of effigies and the attraction of spirituality as idolatry; and Maimonides even launched an all-out attack on all branches of astrology. This stage of development may be described in greater detail as follows.

Judah Halevi, in *Sefer ha-Kuzari* (I, 77), describes the purpose of the golden calf (Exod. 32) as a vehicle to bring down the spirituality of the stars. The Israelites, fearful of being abandoned in the wilderness after Moses' disappearance, fashioned the golden calf as an amulet to attract stellar emanation. According to Judah Halevi, the people sinned in devising the amulet themselves, rather than waiting for God to supply one, as God did later, in form of the cherubim. In *Sefer ha-Kuzari*, the system of the commandments is seen at least in part as an effective way to derive benefit from stellar influence. The Hermetic writings are mentioned with respect in the book (I, 1), and it is therefore clear that Judah Halevi had admitted their content to Jewish theology. Being the first to do so, he disguised those ideas through techniques of esoteric writing. In view of their resemblance to idolatry, his reluctance to articulate them openly is certainly not surprising.

Abraham ibn Ezra. Judah Halevi and Abraham ibn Ezra were personally acquainted, and the latter's theological writings considerably expand the technique of astral-magical interpretation. Here are a few examples:

a) Ransom. Ibn Ezra lays down a rule: "For the edict of the constellation will not be removed save by the giving of ransom, and that is a great secret (*sod*)" (short commentary to Exod. 12:7). Sacrifices channel the negative astral powers emanated by the stars to the animals or birds being sacrificed (*ad* Lev. 1:1). The command to smear blood on the doorpost in Egypt, just before the Exodus, is readily understood on that basis (long commentary to Exod. 12:7).

b) Sanctuary and Temple. On several occasions, Ibn Ezra alludes in his Bible commentary to the role of the sanctuary and its appurtenances as talismans to bring down spirituality. For example: "Here is the rule: each cherub was fashioned to receive supernal power" (long commentary to Exod. 26:1).

c) Sacrifices. The role of sacrifice as an instrument capable of accelerating or obstructing the action of stellar powers is already alluded to in relation to offerings made before the theophany on Mount Sinai (*ad* Gen. 8:21).

d) Festivals. The times of the festivals are conditioned by astrological configurations (*ad* Lev. 23:24); it is hard to imagine that Ibn Ezra was unaware of the magical and theurgical significance of these times.

e) When Ibn Ezra likens the order of the tribes in the desert to a definite stellar configuration (*ad* Num. 1:19), he clearly is taking for granted the reception of stellar influence.

Ibn Ezra's astral-magical exegesis also figures in his treatment of certain negative aspects, such as the *teraphim*, the sin of the golden calf, the brass serpent, and the Balaam episode. He in fact perfected esoteric techniques to conceal astral-magical ideas, sometimes evading the use of astral-magical terms and only hinting at them, at others ostensibly rejecting astral-magical concepts but actually embracing them in their entirety. In his scientific writings, unlike his Bible commentaries, Ibn Ezra unreservedly expresses astral-magical ideas; the difference may be attributed to the difference between the prospective readers of the commentaries—the general public—and the astrologers, whether professional or novices, who read scientific literature.

Besides his extensive astral-magical exegesis of the commandments and of biblical events, Ibn Ezra occasionally describes the attraction of stellar spirituality as idolatry. It would appear that the distinction between worshiping a star and a permissible astral-magical practice was not necessarily a ques-

tion of technique: Stellar forces were brought down both in idolatrous ceremonies, when the stars were actually worshiped, and in procedures aimed at bringing down spirituality, unrelated to idolatry. The prohibition of such practices, therefore, was theological. The distinction depended on the celebrant's intent and the similarity of the practice to astral worship proper, not on the mere fact that stellar powers were being invoked. For the astral worshiper, attraction of heavenly powers was a necessary condition of idolatrous religion, or an intermediary agent in the worship of the deity; for the man of science, healer, or person observing a commandment, it was merely a utilitarian act, a source of benefit in the material and religious realm.

Maimonides' opposition. Maimonides produced an uncompromising assault on the validity of astrology and the reality of magic. Maimonides describes different levels of magic and sorcery, distinguishing between "folk" magic and "learned," that is, astral magic. While denying the reality of magical acts of any sort, he considers it a special challenge to divest "learned" magic of its pseudo-scientific cloak and demonstrate its falsehood. In *The Guide of the Perplexed* (III, 33), he divides those forms of magic whose reality he denies into different categories: (a) practices deriving from the use of forces inherent in existing objects, inanimate or animate; (b) acts whose supposed significance derives from their performance at certain prescribed times (*bitaḥdīd zamān*, i.e., "by determination of the time"); and (c) practices deriving from the use of forces inherent in human actions, such as burning incense. Maimonides goes on to classify magical practices into two categories: (a) those that possess all three of the above-mentioned characteristics; (b) those based on only one of the three characteristics. In his view, there is a qualitative difference between the two, as he associates those practices based on only one characteristic (the second category) with women, as a sign of contempt and limited intellectual value; while practices of the first category are not limited in that regard.

Furthermore, Maimonides distinguished between magic and two areas related directly or indirectly, justly or unjustly, to magic. One is astral magic and the other is the doctrine of *segullot* (special properties; sing.: *segullah*), which was based upon experimental verification. According to this doctrine, the activities of the visible form of an object constitute only a small part of the possibilities embodied in that object. There is a wondrous world of regularity in the hidden forms, which may be revealed by experience and experimentation alone. Such regularity, manifested in a *segullah*, such as the efficacy of remedies in pharmacology or the action of the magnet, cannot be explained in terms of Aristotelian causality but depends entirely on experience. Maimonides mentions numerous *segullot* in his medical writings. In *the Guide of the Perplexed* (III, 37) he lays down a rule: association of *segullot* with astrology renders them invalid and halakhically prohibited. In themselves, however, *segullot* are efficacious and halakhically permitted. This distinction rests on Maimonides' scientific method and his conception of nature.

Astral Magic in Fourteenth-Century Rationalism—Causes: In the first half of the thirteenth century astral magic more or less disappeared from the writings of the rationalists; one might say that it went underground. Maimonides' attack was therefore effective. The later thirteenth century and the fourteenth century, however, witnessed a significant shift in the position and prestige of astral magic in Jewish thought. Hitherto an enigmatic element, allusive and covert, it became a powerful exegetical and theological tool. Numerous works were written offering astral-magical exegesis, consistent and overt, of biblical and midrashic sources. The roots of this revival lay in various social-professional, exegetical-authoritarian and ideological-theological processes. In the social context, many rationalists were healers who used astrologically based amulets. In the exegetical context, fourteenth-century thinkers "rediscovered" Ibn Ezra's Torah commentary and composed a variety of supercommentaries to it. As far as ideology was concerned, astral magic profited from the onset of another phenomenon that emerged and took root during the fourteenth

century—"astrological theology." This term denotes a process in which the most fundamental tenets of Jewish theology were explicated in light of astrology, as if the Torah had been given on Mount Sinai in order to point man in directions guided by astrological calculations. If a person observed the commandments, he would be saved from adverse astrological judgment and enjoy success; but if he disobeyed them, he would be left to the fate predicted for him by the stars. This principle found expression in a variety of areas:

a) Biblical and midrashic exegesis explaining whole chapters on an astrological basis. For example, the Exodus from Egypt took place at the time of "the grand conjunction," that is, when "Saturn and Jupiter were in conjunction with the Zodiac, it was then that their constellation was taken and He took them out of their exile in Egypt" (Shem Tov ibn Mayor, late fourteenth century, *Ha-Ma'or ha-Gadol*, Ms. Oxford, Bodl. 228, fol. 103a).

b) Prophecy based on accurate knowledge of the ways of heaven, in regard to both the prophet's "disposition" to receive prophecy and the content and nature of that prophecy. For example, according to Solomon Alconstantin (mid fourteenth century), the prophets timed their actions to correspond with astrological events "on certain days" (*Megalleh 'Amuqot*, MS. Vat. 59, fol. 7a).

c) A person could not achieve perfection without familiarity with inter-stellar relationships, a precise knowledge of stellar influences and an ability to rise above such influences. Thus, Solomon ibn Ya'ish (first half of fourteenth century) declared that "man's wisdom and intelligence are dependent on the heavenly hosts" (supercommentary to Ibn Ezra's Torah commentary, Ms. Vat. 54, fol. 240a).

d) Definition of the Jewish people's uniqueness in light of their affinity with the astrological system or their complete independence therefrom. According to Solomon ibn Ya'ish, "Israel were born under the planet Saturn, which indicates and dictates exile" (*ibid.*, fols. 274b-275a). This is representative of views expressed by many thinkers explaining the historical fate of the

Jewish people in terms of their heavenly disposition.

All these thinkers were members of a well-defined philosophical circle which combined intensive study of *The Guide of the Perplexed* and its heritage with the intensive disclosure of Ibn Ezra's "secrets." However, astrological theology and astral-magical interpretation of the sources could also be found among other Spanish thinkers of the time, such as Hasdai ibn Crescas and his disciples. The echoes of astrological theology reached as far as Byzantium, where we find such figures as Judah Mosconi and Elnathan Kalkish applying astrological and astral-magical exegesis to the Bible.

Astral Magic in Fourteenth-Century Rationalism—Applications: In the fourteenth century, consequent to the above-mentioned causes, astral magic became a powerful exegetical and theological tool. Many thinkers accepted it without question as ancient, esoteric lore. An import super-commentator on Ibn Ezra, Joseph Bonfils (Tov Elem), wrote:

> . . . That is the way of the wise men of India, who make metal effigies at certain times to bring down the power of the stars, and that is a great science, of which there are many books, and I am acquainted with Ishmaelites who are conversant with it. And I myself know some of it, but theoretically and not practically, for it is in truth idolatry (*Zafenat Pa'aneah*, ed. D. Herzog, I, p. 245).

The definition of astral magic as idolatry was intended to conceal the author's adherence to it. Bonfils explained the use of the staff during the Ten Plagues as an amulet to bring down stellar forces. Solomon Alconstantin also attributed at least some of the plagues to the use of astral magic, portraying Moses as a magician. Astral magic found its main application in explaining the reasons for the commandments. Many details of the commandments were explained as techniques for the attraction of stellar spirituality. But astral-magical exegesis was at its best in providing a compelling explanation for the operation of the Sanctuary and the Temple, as talismans whose task was to bring down stellar forces. The point of departure of all these commentators was the analogy between the Sanctuary and the world of the heavenly bodies: the Sanctuary and its accessories symbolized the stars and the constellations. Once that principle was accepted, it was almost natural to present the various Temple utensils as tools for attracting stellar forces and "bringing down abundance and emanation" (a common phrase in Alconstantin's work).

In parallel, "demons" were explained as negative spirituality from the stars. Members of this circle had occasion to mention demons in sources of two types. In the first type, they denied demons any reality, describing them as products of diseased imagination or hallucination, not as actually existing. In the second type of source, demons are identified with heteronomic forces originating in the stellar world (spirituality); as such, they were indeed real and not imaginary. The difference between these two categories of sources actually represents a developmental process. At first, demons were described as mere figments of the imagination. Only at a later stage did these thinkers discover a translation, ascribed to Ibn Ezra, of a Hermetic work (*Sefer ha-'Azamim*), in which demons were portrayed as forces coming from the stars. Shem Tov ibn Shaprut (Spain, late fourteenth century) and Shem Tov ibn Mayor explicitly claimed that they had changed their minds after discovering *Sefer ha-'Azamim* (Book of the Substances), this being the reason they now identified demons with real negative stellar spirituality.

Fourteenth-century Spanish rationalists postulated a clear distinction between astral magic, which was real and valid, and other forms of magic. Astral magic was not included in the biblical and talmudic definitions of sorcery (except in its negative manifestations), and it thus became an important exegetical and theological tool. Sorcery, however, in its diverse forms, was considered as fraudulent, an illusion, and therefore forbidden. Here again one has the distinction between "learned magic," which is in effect not considered magic, and "primitive magic" which is unreal and prohibited.

Thirteenth- and Fourteenth-Century Disputes over Astral Magic: Toward the end of the thirteenth century, a fierce dispute broke out in Provence between traditionalists and rationalists. While the main bone of contention was radical rational-allegorical exegesis of the Bible, the dispute actually flared up over the rationalist practice of healing with astral magic. The traditionalists, headed by Abba Mari of Lunel, accused them of idolatry. Abba Mari tried to drag R. Solomon b. Adret (Rashba) into the argument, but failed. Rashba noted that he himself, before the anti-philosophical controversy had arisen, had unhesitatingly permitted the fashioning of effigies for medical purposes, and even while the controversy was still raging refused to issue an absolute prohibition of the medical use of astral magic. As against Maimonides' approach, denying the reality of sorcery, Rashba pointed out that both Talmuds contain an abundance of magical material which violates no religious precept. Moreover, Rashba accused the opponents of sorcery of denying the possibility of miracles. To support his acceptance of the possibility that spirituality might descend upon amulets, he wrote:

> And I say that it was the kindness of the Supreme Being at the start of Creation to create in his world things that would ensure the health of the created beings, that if the existents happen to fall ill or for any other reason deviate from their natural perfection, these [things] are ready to restore them to their realm or to make them healthy. And He placed these forces in the essence of things found in nature, as may be attained by study, such as medications and aids known to scholars of medicine, or in nature based on properties but not attainable by study . . . And it is not impossible that such a power should also be in speech, as in the case of amulets and similar things (*Minhat Qena'ot*, in Rashba, *Responsa*, ed. H.Z. Dimitrovsky, p. 302).

The possibility that stellar forces could be used to heal the sick was provided for in advance by God. Whether such practices were permissible or not depended, according to Rashba, on the magician's innermost intention: it was his awareness that God was the primary cause of recovery that legitimized the astral-magical practice. Thus, Abba Mari was unable to persuade Rashba to join him in condemnation of astral magic.

Through the fourteenth century, the dispute became increasingly acrimonious; at least four positions can be distinguished with regard to the status of astral magic:

a) False and forbidden: The moderate rationalists rejected astral magic of any kind and therefore also considered it halakhically prohibited. They thus accepted Maimonides' firm negation of any reality of astral magic and his prohibition of its practices. These thinkers, then, took up Maimonides' approach in content, style and language (Menahem ha-Meiri, David ha-Kokhavi). Some rationalists chose almost to ignore the issue, probably because they attached no reality whatever to astral magic (Joseph ibn Kaspi).

b) Dubious and forbidden: This was the view of the traditionalists, who consistently battled the radical rationalists and in fact defined the latter group, *inter alia*, in terms of their employment of astral magic for medical purposes (Abba Mari, Jacob b. Solomon ha-Zarfati). They, too, prohibited the practice absolutely, as did the moderate rationalists, although they did not entirely deny the possible reality of astral magic. Their most characteristic trait was the tie they perceived between the practice of astral magic and the magician's affinity for philosophy: in their view, a rationalist philosophy was bound to lead to the practice of astral magic.

c) False in respect of its reality but psychologically effective, and forbidden: Some circles denied that astral magic could actually bring down stellar forces, but believed that there was some psychological benefit in the practice. Nevertheless, they, too, prohibited its use from the standpoint of Halakhah (Gersonides, Jedaiah ha-Penini of Béziers). In a sense, this might be considered an intermediate position, though it is closer to that of the moderate rationalists and its proponents were essentially a subgroup of the latter.

d) Real and permitted: Certain thinkers believed in the absolute reality of astral magic (Nissim of Marseilles, Frat Maimon) and even considered it halakhically legitimate (Levi b. Abraham). For such thinkers, astral magic was a theological principle that could be used in interpreting various biblical passages.

The Provençal controversy left its mark in Spain as well, but in a much weaker form. While Isaac Pulgar entirely rejected astrology and astral magic, his was a lone voice. A more common position among the disciples of Rashba and R. Asher b. Jehiel (Rosh) was the following: Astral magic is real, but its use as a theological foundation should be limited. The limitation was on two counts: astral-magical exegesis of the sources was clearly circumscribed, being replaced by the traditional rationalist exegesis; and astral magic could not be considered an autonomous realm, recognized and permitted by the Torah and in fact supporting the Torah. The proponents of this stand were apprehensive about the dangerous affinity between astral magic and idolatrous cultic practices. This position aroused a lively dispute, with Abraham Altabib bitterly criticizing Solomon Franco, author of a supercommentary on Ibn Ezra's Torah commentary. The main targets of his attack were astral-magical interpretations of the following chapters: (a) the materials of the Sanctuary; (b) the reason for the scapegoat; (c) the reasons for the festivals; (d) the reasons for ritually forbidden foods; (e) the reasons for forbidden sexual unions. Solomon Franco's excuse was that he was not expressing his own opinions but merely revealing Ibn Ezra's intentions; but this feigned innocence did not avert the dispute. The debate may be found in MS Oxford, Bodl. 1258.

Astral Magic in Fifteenth-Century Rationalism—Applications: The prevailing fifteenth-century attitude toward astrology and astral magic was exemplified by the circle of R. Judah, son of the Rosh. Having been formulated in response to the controversies over the status of those two areas, it came to the fore in the century preceding the expulsion from Spain. Many thinkers, while critical of the considerable theological influence of astrology, nevertheless recognized the validity of astrological laws as a *fait accompli*. Astral magic, however, was different, and it was approached with some uncertainty. The influence on the dynamics of Spanish-Jewish philosophy exerted by those rationalists who had embraced astral-magical views had dwindled by the beginning of the fifteenth century, as

may be discerned in the work of Vidal Joseph de la Cabaliria, who was strongly influenced by Salomon Alconstatin. From that time on, the taditional approach which questioned the reality of astral magic, again came to the fore.

Thus, Isaac Arama criticized the consistent astrological interpretation of Jewish history that could be found, e.g., in the writings of Abraham bar Hiyya; but at the same time he, too, recognized the validity of astrology in itself, as is evident from many examples. His attitude to astral magic was similar: it was, he believed, a variety of idolatry. In his lengthy explanation of the golden calf episode he expressed profound doubts as to the reality of effigy worship, but was unwilling to reject it out of hand. On the contrary, Arama had proposed that the Israelites had chosen the form of the ox "in order to bring down the emanation from the heavenly forms," because the ox is "the king of animals." Why, then, did they not use the form of a lion? The answer was clear: "According to the path of truth, although we do not wholly accept such things, we nevertheless take them into consideration, for it was precisely in the month of Av, when the zodiacal constellation of *Leo* rises every morning, that the crown of our splendor fell and our magnificent Temple was burned twice" (*'Aqedat Yizhaq*, Gate 53). In other words, while Arama is dubious about astrological and astral-magical principles, they must nevertheless be heeded. A similarly ambiguous attitude was taken by Abraham Bibago, for whom the main characteristics of astral magic were esotericism ("one of a city and two of a family") and dependence upon place and time. Bibago, too, was doubtful of the existence of what he called "this science" and in fact carefully delineated its shortcomings, but did not reject it outright. Finally, some moderate astral-magical interpretations may be detected at this time in Isaac Abravanel's commentary on the sacrifices. Clearly, then, astral-magical doctrines were in a decline and had been ideologically marginalized. Rational works systematically explaining biblical chapters on an astral-magical basis were no longer common, and the situation was no different among

Spanish rationalist thinkers after the expulsion. There was, indeed, a revival of astral magic in Renaissance Italy, but that topic merits separate consideration.

Astral Magic in Kabbalah: Central schools of kabbalistic thought readily wove astral-magical principles into their doctrines, except that the kabbalists spoke of the influence not of the stars but of the *sefirot*. Thus, various commandments were interpreted as vehicles for attracting sefirotic emanation. The first kabbalist who powerfully and clearly adopted the astral-magical mode of thought was Nahmanides. One of the earliest theosophical kabbalists, although his relationship with the circle of Gerona kabbalists is a matter of scholarly controversy, Nahmanides was a healer who employed astral-magical techniques. His astral-magical inclinations are most obvious in his explication of sacrifices. Commenting on the midrashic dictum, "To till it and tend it [Genesis 2:15]—this refers to sacrifices," Nahmanides writes:

> The intent of the Rabbis in this interpretation is that plants and all living beings are in need of primary forces from which they derive the power of growth and that through the sacrifices there is an extension of the blessing to the higher powers. From them it flows to the plants of the garden of Eden [= the *sefirah* of *Malkhut*, Kingship], and from them it comes and exists in the world in the form of "rain of goodwill and blessing," through which they will grow. This conforms to what the Rabbis have said [*Gen. Rabba* 15,1]: "The Trees of the Lord drink their fill, the cedars of Lebanon, His own planting [Ps. 104:16]. R. Hanina said: Their life shall have its fill; their waters shall have their fill; their plantings shall have their fill. 'Their life' refers to their higher foundations; 'their wastes' refer to His good treasure which brings down the rain; and 'their plantings' refer to their force in heaven, just as the Rabbis have said: There is not a single blade of grass below that does not have a constellation in heaven that smites it and says to it, 'Grow.' It is this which Scripture says, 'Do you know the laws of heaven or impose its authority (*mishtarah*) on earth?' [Job 38:33]—[*mishtarah* being derived from the same root as] *shoter* (executive officer)" [*Gen. Rabba* 10,6; Nahmanides' commentary to Gen. 2:8].

This passage, which is replete with kabbalistic symbolism, postulates the active influence of the sacrifices on attracting or "extending" the heavenly emanation to both the *sefirot* ("higher foundations") and the stars ("their force in heaven"). Nahmanides' portrayal of the emanation that can be brought down and used has two aspects: a supernal one, as the divine emanation originating in the sefirotic world; and an inferior one, as astral emanation. The work of Nahmanides' kabbalist disciples, though following in his footsteps, exemplifies four different reactions:

a) Synthesis, combining theurgy and astral magic in Nahmanides' formulation (David Cohen, Shem Tov ibn Gaon, Menahem Recanati, Judah Canpanton).

b) Ignoring the astral-magical dimension or combining the theosophical and astral aspects in the definition of the descending influence, but without the magical emphasis (Bahya b. Asher, Jacob Sikili, Isaac of Acre).

c) Suppressing the astral-magical element (author of *Sefer ha-Hinnukh*, author of sermons from the school of Jonah of Gerona).

d) Suppressing the entire discussion, most probably because it was considered esoteric lore and not to be committed to writing (Rashba, Ritba).

The astral-magical model also penetrated kabbalistic circles other than that of Nahmanides. The *Zohar*, for example, expands the negative aspects of astral magic. However, scholars are divided as to the degree to which astral magic influenced the formulation of Zoharic thought. While some consider it highly significant, others belittle its role. The astral-magical model appeared in the fourteenth century among the members of the circle of *Sefer ha-Temunah*, and with amazing vigor in Spain just before the expulsion, in *Sefer ha-Meshiv*. It was resuscitated during the Renaissance in the teachings of various Italian thinkers, primary Johanan Allemanno.

Summary: The astral-magical model entered Jewish thought beginning in the twelfth century and soon became an important factor, shaping and molding that thought. One could in fact rewrite the history of late medieval Jewish philosophy from the standpoint of astral magic (as indeed done by Dov Schwartz in his *Astral*

Magic in Medieval Jewish Thought, BIU Press, Ramat-Gan, 1999). As a theological and exegetical factor (in relation to the reasons for the commandments and other issues), it derived its power from medical practice, as many doctors made their livings by healing with astrological amulets. In sum, astral magic became a distinct tool for interpreting Jewish theology in medieval times.

DOV SCHWARTZ

B

BIOLOGY AND THE LAW OF JUDAISM: Contrary to the statements of scholars in the field of history of biology or its special disciplines, Judaism requires deep biological knowledge from its followers. The Israelite Scriptures, however, were not composed as textbooks of biology. They are theological documents, written and edited to convey certain theological messages. Thus, the wisdom of the authors of the Torah concerning biological concepts can be deducted only indirectly from passages in which biological concepts are transmitted and from a comparison of these texts with the mainstream development of the science of biology. The high degree of advanced biological knowledge can be seen in the outlined examples, derived from Scripture and later Judaic sources.

The sequence of the Egyptian plagues: The background story is well known: Moses desperately wanted to free his people from Egyptian bondage. To persuade the ruler of Egypt, adhering to God's command, Moses announced a series of plagues that would occur if the request was not granted. The sequence of the plagues was as follows: (1) The turning to blood of the Nile; (2) The plague of frogs; (3) The plague of gnats on man and beasts; (4) The plague of flies; (5) The plague of the cattle diseases; (6) The plague of boils; (7) The plague of hail; (8) The plague of locusts; (9) The plague of darkness; (10) The death of the firstborn children.

Without ignoring the fact that this is primarily a theological text with a specific message concerning God's power and glory, it has certain intriguing features that may give it a deeper dimension: the order of the plagues and the role of the Egyptian magicians in the story. Of the ten plagues, seven, 1-6 and 8, are "biological." From a theological point of view, the order of the plagues would not matter. The message is always clear: Moses and Aaron were able to predict the disasters, but the Pharaoh did not give in until the last and worst of the plagues actually took place. There would be no theological need for a certain order, except that the worst plague, the death of the firstborn, would have to be at the end.

The order in which the plagues are recorded, however, does make biological sense. It describes the exact sequence of events expected when ponds or lakes and even a slow flowing river are disturbed in their nutrient and oxygen balance. Until the building of the Aswan Dam in the 1960s, the ecology of Egypt's main territory of settlement, the Nile delta, was governed by the annual rhythm of the rising and falling of the Nile's water levels. With our present knowledge of limnology, we are able to imagine scenarios in which deviations from this rhythm would inevitably lead to a disturbance of the nutrient and finally of the oxygen balance of the Nile water. Even more important, the balance in the numerous lakes, ponds, and the ground water would be affected as well. The first step would be an enhanced supply of minerals, a situation in which certain reddish algae would grow very fast. These algae grow on the surface of the water, and when the supply of nutrients is depleted they stop growing. At this point their autolysis and degradation by micro-organisms sets in. Since the algae concentrate at the surface of the water, the mineralization of their biomass leads to a quick complete depletion of oxygen in the water. It turns anoxic, becomes foul, and smells due to the formation of reduced organic sulphur compounds. The fish in these waters lack oxygen for breathing and die. An ecologically experienced person would certainly be able to predict such a development, i.e., the algal bloom, by observing the rise of the Nile and the concomitant changes in the ponds and lakes of the Nile delta. It is therefore not surprising that the Egyptian magicians could predict this event too, thus hardening the heart of the Pharaoh.

If such an anoxic episode in a certain body of water becomes severe, even the frogs will leave these waters and migrate to the land, in this case to the villages of the Egyptian peasants. Since the frogs cannot survive in the hot air and low humidity during the day, they will die quite fast, producing millions of dead bodies, adding to the foul smell. Since this is predictable with a certain amount of basic ecological knowledge, it is once again not surprising that the Egyptian magicians were able to foresee this development (Exod. 8:7). When the frogs leave the water and die, the most important natural enemies of insects, which lay their eggs and spend their larval stadium in shallow waters, are gone. Thus, the larvae of flies, mosquitoes, and gnats can develop in large quantities, and after they leave the water the land becomes flooded with them. So, with today's knowledge, it is not surprising that different waves of flying insects plagued the country (plagues 3 and 4). Since all these insects sting cattle or man, or even both, they can transmit skin and other diseases (plagues 5 and 6).

It is surprising, however, that the magicians were not able to follow the sequence further at this point and so predict future events. They were so taken by surprise by the insect plague that they urged the Pharaoh to give in, stating: *"This is the finger of God."* After the magicians' failure to comprehend the situation, they no longer interfered with the actions of Moses and Aaron. Obviously, their ecological background was not as developed as Moses' and therefore did not allow them to cope with the subsequent predictions of Moses and Aaron.

The last plague with an ecological background is the invasion of the locusts. A person with ecological insight could again have predicted this after the first two plagues. If the water of the Nile turns so poisonous that the fish die and the frogs leave the ponds and lakes, the birds will also suffer greatly, especially the bigger species that prey on fish and frogs. They will either leave the region or die from the poisonous diet, which transmits botulism. This means that the area will be deserted by herons, storks, and ibises. Thus, the most powerful biological control agents of locusts, the big wading birds, would be absent when a locust invasion occurred. The ibis species are especially effective in controlling this plague and are idolized for this ability in ancient Egypt. Any locust invasion, which occurred in Egypt on a fairly regular base, would thus be a much bigger disaster in the absence of these birds than in their presence.

The question is why the authors of Scripture chose to arrange the Egyptian plagues in the mentioned order. The chance that this sequence was random is very low. The probability that any order of seven events is not given by chance is $1/7! = 1/5040 = 0.002$. In biometrics, a probability of the alternative lower than 0.05 is considered evidence that the hypothesis is not falsified, that is, that it is valid. On the other hand, there would be no theological reason against a change in the sequence of events. The basic theological message of this pericope—God leads the Israelites out of Egyptian bondage by forcing the Pharaoh to release them by means of the plagues—does not depend on the order of events. In the Apocalypse of St. John 16, the seven plagues of wrath are listed in an order that does not make any ecological sense at all: (1) Boils on humans; (2) The sea turns to blood; (3) Streams and springs of water turn to blood; (4) The overheated sun turns the land to a desert; (5) Darkness; (6) The Euphrates runs dry, followed by an invasion of frogs; (7) Earthquake. Although exegetes agree that these plagues have their counterpart in the Egyptian ones, nothing here indicates an understanding of ecology. God has the power to do anything he wants and is not required to adhere to ecological or other rules. Thus the fact that the sequence of Egyptian plagues would be expected by a person with training in ecology seems important. It is the first precise description of such a sequence of events in world literature. In the ecological literature such events were not dealt with again until some 2,400 years later.

The earliest report of a deliberate botanical experiment: One way to facilitate observance of the Sabbath and festivals was creation of an *Eruv hatserot*, which permitted neighbors better social communication by allowing free movement and carrying between the areas of the two adjacent households. A food item that posed a problem for the blessing recited when the *eruv* was created was the fruit of the dodder (*Cuscuta spec.*). Dodder is a parasitic plant that grows on a host with threads that have no contact to the soil. In the spring, it can be found on a variety of host plants, including all kinds of shrubs. The fruit stands of the dodder were considered a food and, in case of need, one handful was sufficient for two meals (B. Erub. 28b). Since any food was likely to be used in the *Eruv*-ceremony, dodder could be also used for this purpose. The question was, which blessing was the correct one for dodder. According to B. Erub. 28b, two possibilities existed, the general blessing ("Everything is created by his word") and or the blessing for fruits of the soil ("He who creates the fruit of the soil"). For determine which blessing was correct, people had to know the origin of this plant, that is, whether it was a fruit of the soil or whether it obtained nourishment elsewhere. Translated into the language of modern biology, the question was whether it was an epiphyte (which uses the host plant as a mechanical support only, without receiving nutrient from it) or a true parasite. The Talmud reports that when the the host plant was cut, the dodder died too. From this it was possible to conclude that the dodder, although not being directly connected to the soil, is indeed a fruit of the soil and consequently the correct blessing could be chosen. The Talmud thus reports a typical scientific experiment, and, by proceeding in this manner, the sages were more than one millennium ahead of mainstream biology.

The right way to grow plants in pots: Due to the high respect that the Dual Torah pays to any type of life, it was forbidden on the Sabbath to remove anything from its base of growth. At B. Shab. 107b and 108a, several examples of this type of offence are given. Among these, one precept is very interesting with regard to the development of biological concepts: A person picking plant in a planting pot with holes is guilty of a Sabbath offence; a person picking a plant in a planting pot without holes is not guilty. The reason is that the latter does not count as natural growth, while the first does (B. Shab. 107b). A more detailed analysis of the pericope reveals two things. First, it shows that in the talmudic times, plants used for food were grown in pots. This displays a high level of gardening techniques, which were unique in the antique world. The passage also shows that the Israelites knew that in order to grow plants in pots, it is necessary for the pots to have at least one hole in the bottom, through which excess water may drain. If the pot has no hole, the contents might get waterlogged, preventing oxygen from passing through the soil and, over a period of time, preventing the plant from growing well. The sages termed this type of growth non-natural, and allowed picking such plants on the Sabbath. This corresponds exactly to the opinion held by every biologist and gardener on this subject today.

Nourishment of fungi: "Abayye said: 'The one who tears a mushroom from the edge of a bucket is guilty, because he tears a matter away from its base of growth.'" (B. Shab. 108a). The basic facts behind this statement are clear to any biologist: in the rather warm climate of Israel, fungi grow fairly quickly on wood, especially if they are at times in contact with water, supplying the moisture necessary for growth. The obvious thing for the owner of such a bucket to do was quickly to remove the fruiting body of a fungus in order to avoid the messy spores discharged by the fungi and to delay the process of deterioration. Such an action, however, was not allowed on the Sabbath because the fruiting body was torn away from its basis of growth.

How difficult it was for scientists to understand that fungi receive nourishment from wood can be seen from the development of the concept that fungi degrade wood in the history of forest pathology,[1] which started in nineteenth century Germany. At the beginning of the nineteenth century, German science, including plant and forest pathology, was dominated by romantic natural philosophy, which had developed as a reaction to Enlightenment and the French Revolution and tried to exclude rational experiments and understanding from science. The rotting of wood, either living or dead, was at this time considered to be a completely natural event that occurs spontaneously. German forest pathologists adhered quite closely to Justus von Liebig, who saw the cause for decay in the "ability which a chemical substance possesses, when in the process of decomposition or combination, to cause or enable another substance which is touching it to undergo the same change which it itself is undergoing." Rotting of wood caused by fungi was considered to be a special example of this principle, which he considered universal in organic chemistry. Liebig was such a powerful figure in German science that he influenced by his sheer prestige a number of lesser scientists. Because of his authority, the controversy over spontaneous generation was extended for another generation.[2] Liebig's view was challenged only by Pasteur in his papers on fermentation. These very conclusive studies, however, were only very reluctantly accepted in Germany, especially by Liebig.

This is another example that shows how carefully the Jews thought about nature. The question whether or not they are allowed to tear a fungal fruiting body away from the edge of a bucket forced them to spend time thinking about where the fungus received nutrients. They derived the right conclusions some 1,400 years before mainstream Western Science.

Human reproduction and embryology: The questions "how do humans reproduce?" and "when does human life start?" are extremely important not only for human curiosity but also for the life of the community. It makes a huge difference to a society whether both parents contribute equally to the newly born child or whether one parent dominates; the point at which human life starts is also extremely important when it comes to questions like abortion or modern biotechnology.

Looking at human embryogenesis with the eyes of a developmental biologist, we see a continuous development from a fertilized egg to a fully developed baby. The question is at what point we consider the developing embryo to be a human being, and the answer to this question cannot be drawn from biological facts. On the one hand, one might argue from the perspective of biology of human reproduction that a fertilized egg cell may not be a good candidate to be considered a human being, since it might be duplicated in its early development so that monozygotic twins, which will definitely be two separate human beings, will develop. In addition, the chance that a fertilized egg will actually develop to an embryo is not really high. About fifty percent of fertilized eggs do not develop to a fetus. On the other hand, the fact that a developing organism is completely dependent on another cannot be seriously taken as an argument to deny it any identity. The situation of an embryo developing in the uterus, completely nourished by its mother, is similar to numerous cases of parasitic and symbiotic relations, in which the different partners are considered autonomous individual entities.

So the answer to the question of when human life starts during the development of a fertilized egg must be given on a basis other than simple biology. It has much more to do with the value human life has in a given society. In the Hebrew Bible, the question at which time after conception life begins is not an important issue. Pregnancy and the premature death of an embryo due to a miscarriage is only dealt with in terms of compensation for damages: (Exod. 21: 22-25). This passage does not make any statements about the time at which the developing embryo is considered a human being. That question was first dealt with in the Talmud. As usual, the matter was not brought up as such but in connection with an apparently very remote problem. In B. Yeb. 69b, different cases are listed with regard to the right of a priest's daughter to eat heave-offering, the priests' share of agricultural produce. This privilege was accorded only to an unmarried daughter of a priest or a widowed daughter who had no children. What about the daughter of a priest widowed shortly after marriage with an Israelite? On the one side, the widow might be pregnant; on the other side, she would be deprived of her right to food if she was not pregnant. Hisda argued that if the widow was not pregnant, there would be no impediment to her partaking of heave-offering. If she was pregnant, the embryo was considered to be "mere water" until after the fortieth day of pregnancy. So she was allowed to continue to eat heave-offering for at least forty full days after her wedding. Hisda's ruling implies that the fetal development within the initial forty days of gestation was insufficient to warrant independent status of the embryo. This view is also taken at B. Nid. 30a, which declares that a fetus aborted less than forty days following cohabitation does not engender the impurity connected with the birth of a child as stated by Lev. 12:2-5. Furthermore, in the opinion of many authorities, a fetus cannot be considered a human with its own rights prior to the fortieth day of gestation.[3]

At M. Nid. 3:7, there is a very surprising discussion (translation: Jacob Neusner):

A. She who miscarries on the fortieth day does not take account of the possibility that it is a human fetus.
B. [If this takes place] on the forty-first day [after intercourse], let her sit [out the days of uncleanness] for a male, for a female, and for menstruation.
C. R. Ishmael says, "[If it takes place] on the forty-first day, let her sit [out the days of uncleanness] for the male and for menstruation.
D. "If it takes place on the eighty-first day, let her sit [out the days of uncleanness] for male, for female, and for menstruation.
E. "for the male is completed on the fortieth day, and the female on the eighty first."
F. And sages say, "All the same is the process of the formation of the male and female—both are completed on the forty-first day."

The concept that a male embryo is completed after forty days of gestation and a female embryo is completed only forty days later is clearly Aristotelian (His. Anim. VII, 3). Although Aristotle's view was brought up by a prominent sage, the majority of the rabbis obviously did not agree with him. The high degree of biological knowledge from which the sages refuted Aristotle's view becomes more clear from the pertinent discussion of this issue at B. Nid. 30b. First the sages discuss an "experiment" supposedly conducted at Queen Cleopatra's court to prove the point Aristotle had made. Female slaves who were sentenced to death were first treated with an abortive concoction, so that any fetus from a current pregnancy would be lost. They were then forced to mate with male slaves and killed a certain number of days after this forced conception. From the outcome of this experiment, it was concluded that male fetuses indeed were visible forty days after conception and female fetuses not before eighty days. For Ishmael, this "proof" was so convincing that he tried to introduce the Aristotelian concept of human development into the Oral Law. In the discussion recorded in the Babylonian Talmud, however, Ishmael and, with him, Aristotle were ridiculed. The sages blatantly declared that the proof he brought up for his view was simply a "proof of fools." To underline their point, they carefully analyzed the "experiment" quoted above and came up with all the arguments a modern scientist would have against the design of this experiment: first, the abortive concoction might not have worked, and, second, the female slave who carried a girl might have been fertilized forty days after the first forced mating (which might not have been successfull) by a watchman (i.e., against the protocol of this "experiment" and in a way that the people who carried out the "study" could not notice). So, rightly, the sages came to the conclusion that even such an experiment cannot be taken as evidence against the view that male and female embryos develop with the same speed.

From these statements of the Talmud, it can be concluded that a certain knowledge of human embryogenesis was available to the sages of the Talmud. Only an embryo that was more than 10 mm. long, tits size after forty days, was recognized as a human being in its own right; smaller embryos were probably not detected. It is not very clear from the talmudic texts how the sages actually attained that knowledge. However, this is also not clear from the writings of Aristotle. In his *Historia animalium* he simply states the facts without giving any information concerning the way he obtained this knowledge (His. Anim. VII, 3).

The fact that the issue of human ontogeny was discussed sincerely and eruditely in the Talmud once again shows the high standard of independence and scientific concepts of the sages. They did not simply adopt a view brought up by no one less than Aristotle, but even challenged a supposed experiment. To really appreciate the boldness of this talmudic passage, we should imagine a group of contemporary theologians discussing important results of a scientific hero of our time and rightly concluding that the controls in his or her experiments were not valid and, thus, that the whole experiment was meaningless.

Who contributes to the child: father, mother, or both? The Talmud makes a very clear statement concerning the contribution of the two parents to the developing child (B. Nid. 31a):

> Three parties participate in the (creation of a) human: The holy one, blessed be he, his father, and his mother. His father sows the white in him, from which the bones, the sinews, the nails, the brain in his head and the white of his eyes develop. His mother sows the red in him, from which the skin, the flesh, the hair and the black in the eyes develop. And the holy one, blessed be he, donates him spirit and soul, the form of the face, the vision of the eyes, the hearing of the ears, the speaking of the mouth, the walking of the feet, knowledge, judgement, and understanding. When the time comes to for man to part from this world, the holy one, blessed be he, takes his part and leaves him the parts man got from his father and his mother.

This pericope indicates that the sages had a concept of human reproduction very much different from any of the concepts put forward by the pre-Aristotelian Greek philosophers and Aristotle himself. In principle, the pre-Aristotelian philosophers had three different theories: the preformistic view—the body is preformed in the seed (mainly male semen) and nourished by the womb of the female; the theory that there is a competition between the seeds of the two parents; and the idea that both parents contribute in an unspecified way. Aristotle approached the problem philosophically and on the basis of his concept of form and matter. According to him, the male seed initiates the development of the embryo by transferring form and movement to the female matter. Under the influence of the male developmental program, the material of the female womb starts to produce the embryo in such a way that the male seed still determines the form developing from the female material. Aristotle compares this process to the production of a chair by a carpenter. The idea of a chair, which exists in an immaterial form in the carpenter's brain, is transferred, via the hands of the craftsman, to the wood, which is then transformed into the final product. In Aristotle's view, the only female contribution to embryogenesis is the crude undifferentiated material from which the master program of the male semen forms the new human being. The new human was perfect if the program of the male seed was transferred to the fetus completely, i.e., if the baby was a male. An imperfect transfer of the developmental program of the male seed resulted in a female baby.

Aristotle's view was taken up by Thomas Aquinas, who, in the thirteenth century, declared women to be imperfect beings with deficiencies, accidentally made and thus deformed men (I, qu. 92, a.3.). He stated that a man has a more perfect intellect and is stronger in his virtues (*ratione perfectior et virtute fortior*, C. Gent. III. 123). Thus, the view on human embryogenesis and the contribution of the different parents to the fetus held by the most influential Hellenistic natural philosopher, Aristotle, became the ideological basis for discrimination against women in our civilization.

The women of ancient Israel were held in much higher esteem than in the surrounding countries,[4] and during the first centuries C.E., for instance, had more civil rights than women in Germany until 1918.

This certainly has its roots in the better biological knowledge of the ancient Israelites.

The concept of biological species in the Dual Torah. The degree of the Mishnaic rabbis' knowledge of species is evident in an analysis of Tractate Kilayim, a commentary on Lev. 19:19 (= Deut. 22:9-11): "You shall not let your cattle breed with a different kind; you shall not sow your field with two kinds of seed." The sages saw several problems connected with this precept. When was a field to be considered sown with diverse kinds of seed? Which crop plants could be sown together without violating the precept? Which variants of animals were allowed to be crossbred?

The first problem was not as easy to solve as it would appear today with our system of intense agriculture, in which seeds are genetically designed to yield ripe produce exactly on the same day, and fields the size of several acres are tilled with highly sophisticated machinery. In ancient Israel, plots were small, and plants did not produce their crops so synchronously. Thus, at the time of the harvest of a given field there were always plants that had produced fully mature seeds, some which were already shed, while others were not fully ripe. When a different crop was sown the next year, some plants of the previous year's crop also appeared unavoidably on the field. Therefore, the sages had to make compromises. They came up with a reasonable definition of "different seeds:" only when more than 4% of the additional crop was present in a field was it considered a violation of the law and had to be forfeited (Y. Kil. 2:1). This shows that the sages were setting up rules that were pragmatic and practicable.

To solve the next two problems, the sages had to formulate precise definitions of the species of all agricultural crop plants and animals used for husbandry. Thus, from a biological viewpoint, it is of interest to look at the pertinent mishnaic tractate. Since the sages listed what were to be considered similar species of diverse kinds, they revealed their precise concept of a biological species (M. Kil. 1:1; translation: Irving Mandelbaum):

Different Annual Plants

A. (1) Wheat and tares
B. are not [considered] diverse kinds with one another.
C. (2) Barley and two-rowed barley,
   (3) rice wheat and spelt,
   (4) a broad bean and a French vetch,
   (5) a red grasspea and a grasspea,
   (6) and a hyacinth bean and a Nile cowpea,
D. are not [considered] diverse kinds with one another.

The logic of this and the following lists of species is that they make a clear statement concerning the diversity of the species pair within one line and whether they are compatible, i.e., of the same species, or not. Species listed in different lines are always considered to belong to diverse kinds.

The first part deals with cereals, beans, and peas. With regard to cereals, the first pair of species is very surprising, since it deals with two species that were definitely easy to tell apart: wheat and tares (i.e., rye grass, *Lolium temulentum*). Every farmer knew that these were different species; the pertinent discussion at Y. Kil. 1ff. leaves no doubt about this. Wheat was a crop and rye grass was a weed that was never sown intentionally. On the other hand, the seeds of rye grass, although being poisonous for humans, could be used as fodder for pigeons and therefore were a potential crop. So the problem was to decide the status of a field contaminated with more than the allowed portion of rye grass. By deciding against the known biological facts, the sages came up with a reasonable solution. Regardless of how much of this weed was growing in the field, permission was given to harvest and use the crops. In addition, the ruling left the option that, in the case of a high proportion of rye grass in the field, its seeds could be harvested for feeding pigeons. It was a wise move not to increase the burden on a farmer whose fields were already overgrown with weeds, allowing him to use the seeds of the weed at least as a crop for feeding pigeons.

The translation of the second pair of cereals, barley and two-rowed barley, is somewhat controversial and should be translated as (wild) oats.[5] As in the case of rye grass, wild oats could be harvested—this gave the farmers at least a little bit of crop.

Thus, the same rationale the sages put forward in the case of wheat and rye grass may have also been applied to tolerating oat in barley fields, where we can expect it to grow in abundance as a weed. Very surprising is that Kilayim differentiates between wheat and spelt, which are of the same genus and thus rather similar. The same is true for several species of beans and peas, where only very few were not considered to be different species.

In M. Kil. 1:2, wild species are paired with their cultivated offspring, which might look different. The sages thus knew about the domestication process of plants to crops and grouped them together in a very logical and biological way. With regard to trees (M. Kil. 1:4), the issue was not whether to plant them in the same field but about grafting, as was stated at Y. Kil. 1. Here the rules are rather strict. Pears can only be grafted with crustaminum pears, which are a variety of pears developed in Crustaminum, in the country of the Sabines (Italy). The school of Shammai even rejected this possibility but was overruled by the sages from the school in Yavneh (cf., Y. Kil. 1:4). And even wild apples (Syrian pear) cannot be grafted with cultivated apples. In M. Kil. 1:5, the sages come to the same conclusions as in modern taxonomy. The pairs of plants (mustard with wild mustard and Greek gourd with Egyptian gourd) are from the same genus but not closely related species and therefore the decision to consider them diverse kinds is logical.

The species concept the Mishnah follows with animals (M. Kil. 1:6) is again very strict. Even a wolf and a dog (which in fact is a domesticated wolf) are not allowed to interbreed.

Is the rule of diverse kind targeted against genetic engineering? One might conclude that Lev. 19:19 is clearly directed against interbreeding of different species as such. If one took the precept verbatim, one could indeed conclude that the authors of the Torah could foresee methods of genetic engineering, which were unthinkable until thirty years ago. Genetic engineering allows genes to be transferred from one plant to another, thus breeding plants with novel properties much faster than was possible

before. But Maimonides' commentary on this precept (Book of Agriculture, chapter IX; see further Guide for the Perplexed, chapter XLIX) suggests, rather, that its target is to prevent people from needing to carry out humiliating work. The point is that the interbreeding of animal species like horses and donkeys may require that a person actually inserts the male member into the vagina of the female. Therefore this precept is not mainly a ban on crossbreeding, which Maimonides regards as unnecessary anyway, but as a means to protect the lower class from work that is in any way humiliating.

From the principles of this commandment and the basic philosophy of the Torah as a whole, however, "it is clear that the Torah requires us to approach genetic engineering with great caution."[6] This technique should be applied with great care and only in a case of certainty that its implementation would eventually result in the saving of life.

Jewish theology and advanced scientific knowledge: Biological wisdom in ancient Israel is unparalleled in the contemporary literature of the neighboring countries and the Graeco-Roman Mediterranean. The question is how the ancient Israelites became so much more advanced than the world around them. The answer is thta their unique theology gave them the intellectual freedom to study nature in a much more advanced way than their contemporaries.

This unique concept of creation can be observed best by an analysis of the first verses of the Torah. Gen. 1 continues the breathtaking statement "In the beginning God created..." with a list of the items God created. Thus the first crucial point of this text is that it describes the *creatio ex nihilo*, the creation from nothing.[7] All cultures in antiquity were in no intellectual position to accept the fact that there might have been a real beginning before which there was nothing. The fear of a void was so great that Christian scholars tried to fix the Bible to match Aristotle rather than vice versa.[8] The creation from nothing is unique to religious texts, especially when compared to its counterparts in this geographic region, the Hellenistic, Egyptian, or Mesopotamian texts or the mythology of the Vedes, the holy Hinduistic scriptures from India, the creation myths from China, or the origin myths of the various tribes of the American Indians. Unlike Genesis, all these texts lack a precise and definite statement about the origin of creation. The Germanic mythology lacks a creation myth entirely: the world was already created when the first gods came into the picture.

Gen. 1 also shows the paramount importance that the Hebrew Bible gives to nature. The listing of the many things God created leaves absolutely no doubt about one fact: all items to be found in the universe are made by God and cannot be gods themselves. This is strongly emphasized in the Book of Wisdom (13:1-5) and is of extreme importance to the development of Western science, establishing the conditions for a rational study of nature. Max Weber calls this process the "disenchantment of nature," the beginning of a rationalization with regard to the conception of the world and the philosophical structures of life.

The feeling that there was a difference between the Jewish view of the world and the neighboring countries was present among the Jews in ancient times (The Book of Wisdom 7:21-23).

> And all such things as are hid and not foreseen, I have learned: for wisdom, which is the worker of all things, taught me. For in her is the spirit of understanding: holy, one, manifold, subtle, eloquent, active, undefiled, sure, sweet, loving that which is good, quick, which nothing hindereth, beneficent, Gentle, kind, steadfast, assured, secure, having all power, overseeing all things, and containing all spirits, intelligible, pure, subtle.

This is the *Magna Charta* of the intellectual approach, which scientists take regardless of their faith and whether or not they believe in God. Scientists need to be curious and open, to have the intellectual capacity to understand facts and the power to put these facts together into cogent theories. For scientists at the beginning of modern times, the exploration of nature was a legitimate way to demonstrate the greatness of the creator ("To show the greatness of the creator in the anatomy of a louse").[9] The complicated intellectual situation of Medieval Jewish scientists, which—apart from the special Jewish situation—more or less also applied to the Christian scientists of that time, can be described in the following way:

> Most of all, certain rabbis, interpreting and embellishing key biblical passages, assigned religious meaning to the quest to understand nature, both celestial and earthly, as a direct means of understanding God and of fulfilling his revealed commandments. The Jewish encounter with the dynamic intellectual life of medieval Islam in such centers as Baghdad, Cairo, and Cordova, and later in stimulating Christian territories such as Spain, Sicily, Italy, and Provence, provided an impetus for perpetuating the rabbinic approaches to nature while deepening their religious and intellectual significance. With the translation of the philosophical and scientific corpus of classical antiquity into Arabic, several influential Jewish figures in the Muslim world recast the Jewish Tradition into a philosophic key, elevating the quest for an understanding of God and his natural creation to the ultimate ideal of Jewish religiosity. Hand in hand with this newly articulated religious aspiration went an intellectual appreciation of the intrinsic worth of understanding the cosmos, as well as an awareness of the pragmatic value such knowledge could yield in terms of social and economic status. In the relatively open intellectual and social setting of medieval Islamic cities, Jews consumed the classic texts of philosophy and science, studied the contemporary Islamic modifications and elaboration's, and produced a philosophical and scientific literature of their own in Arabic and Hebrew.[10]

Not only did many founders of our modern science, such as Kepler and Newton take their motivation to do scientific research from their religion,[11] the same spirit can be found with leading scientists of our time also.[12]

The second important feature of the Jewish religion with regard to scientific research is its utterly holistic view of creation: Since all things have been created by God, there were only small hierarchical differences between the different strata of nature. The best example for this is given by Jacob Neusner,[13] who quotes tractate Berakhot in the Mishnah and Talmud. M. Ber. 8:6 states simply:

> A. They may not recite a blessing [at the conclusion of the Sabbath] over a lamp or spices of gentiles.

B. Ber. 52b-53a gives a breathtaking explanation of this precept:

> *Our rabbis have taught*:
> One may bless a light which has rested on the Sabbath, but one may not bless a light which has not rested on the Sabbath.

The commandment to keep the Sabbath applied not only to all members of the household, guests, cattle, and all other farm animals. It also included things or processes that we would today classify as inorganic or lifeless. For us, the lighting of a candle is a chemical process in which wax reacts with oxygen to yield carbon dioxide and water. The sages viewed this process differently. The candles on the Sabbath table were not regarded as simple wax-ester compounds. The decorated Sabbath table replaced the altar of the Temple, and the candles and bread were substitutes for the candles and the showbread of the Temple. So the candle also had to be in the correct cultic state—it had to have had a Sabbath rest. The molecules that undergo the reaction, the wax-esters that react with the oxygen, also had a right to rest. Thus the Israelite religion's holistic view of creation included not only all living creatures but also the chemical reactions of non-living things. The pronounced barrier between the living and the non-living parts of creation, which is prevalent in our way of thinking, did not exist for the Israelites. For them the burning of a candle was simply regarded as work, and work was forbidden on the Sabbath.

This holistic view of creation, together with the fact that no part of creation was of a godly nature, gave the Israelites the intellectual and spiritual freedom carefully to observe nature's functioning around. This observation was even a way to show God their appreciation of creation. The Israelites thus were bound by their religious tradition to watch nature carefully and eruditely. This feature of their religion enabled them to achieve scientific insights that our Western civilization obtained only some two thousand and more years later.

Bibliography

Hüttermann, A., *The Ecological Message of the Torah—Knowledge, Concepts, and Laws which made Survival in a Land of "Milk and Honey" Possible* (Atlanta, 1999).

Notes

[1] A. Hüttermann and S. Woodward, "Historical Aspects," in S. Woodward, J. Stenlid, R. Karjalainen, and A. Hüttermann, eds., *Heterobasidion Annosum: Biology, Ecology, Impact and Control* (Oxon, 1999), pp. 1-25.

[2] T.D. Brock, *Milestones in Microbiology* (Washington, 1975), p. 27.

[3] For more details see J.D. Bleich, "Abortion in Halachic Literature," in F. Rosner and J.D. Bleich, eds., *Jewish Bioethics* (New York, 1979), pp. 134-177.

[4] J. Hauptman, *Rereading the Rabbis, A Woman's Voice* (Boulder, 1998).

[5] Löw, the most important scholar of biblical and Talmudic botany so far, who was followed by Goldschmidt (1929), translates this line: barley and oats. Barley was the second most important cereal in ancient Israel, and oats were present in Israel both as a cultivated species (*Avena sativa*) and as a weed (*Avena sterilis*). According to Pliny (Hist. Nat. 18, 17, 44), the wild oat, *Avena sterilis*, was the second most important weed in cereal fields in the whole Mediterraneis and was especially frequent in barley fields.

[6] A. Carmell, *Masterplan: Judaism, Its Program, Meanings, Goals* (Jerusalem, 1991), p. 60.

[7] Cf. W. Eichrodt, "In the Beginning: A Contribution to the Interpretation of the First Word of the Bible," in B.W. Anderson, ed., *Creation in the Old Testament* (Philadelphia, 1984), pp. 65-73.

[8] C. Seife, *Zero: The Biography of a Dangerous Idea* (New York, 2000).

[9] See D.B. Ruderman, *Jewish Thought and Scientific Discovery in Early Modern Europe* (New Haven, 1995); R. Patai, *The Jewish Alchemists* (Princeton, 1994).

[10] Rudermann, loc. cit.

[11] F. DiTrocchio, *Newtons Koffer: Geniale Außenseiter, die die Wissenschaft blamierten* (Frankfurt, 1998).

[12] D.F. Noble, *The Religion of Technology* (New York, 1997).

[13] J. Neusner, *Invitation to the Talmud, A Teaching Book* (San Francisco, 1984).

ALOYS HÜTTERMANN

C

CHINA, PRACTICE OF JUDAISM IN:
Judaism in China is unique, as China is the only country in the Oriental world in which Jews have continually lived for over one thousand years. Within this long history, a significant distinction must be made between Jews in pre-modern China, before 1840, and those in modern China, since 1840. Those who came before modern times became part of Chinese society without distinct features; those who have come since modern times have remained aliens. The beginnings of Judaism in China are buried in the dim past and are as obscure as the beginnings of the Jewish people. With few reliable documents, various theories and much speculation have arisen. The beginning of the Judaism in China has been dated to different periods, ranging from biblical times to the Tang Dynasty in the seventh to tenth centuries.

The Biblical Period: Theories that place Jewish migrations to China in the biblical period derive from myths or wild guesses, based on vague or misunderstood scriptural references. For instance, some scholars accept a host of speculations related to the whereabouts of the Ten Lost Tribes or focus on Isa. 49:12: "Behold, these shall come from far; And, lo, these from the north and from the west, And these from the land of Sinim."

Hieromonach Alexei Vinogradoff, a nineteenth-century Russian churchman, was convinced that commercial ties existed between the Middle East and Orient in the reigns of David and Solomon. Once this thesis is allowed, it becomes reasonable to assume that the Phoenicians, then the outstanding maritime people of the Mediterranean littoral, transported cargo to and from China, and that their Hebrew friends and neighbors, who in the time of Solomon already possessed a substantial navy and merchant marine, participated in the same activity. Moreover, even if the merchandise was carried overland between the Levant and the Far East, by caravan rather than by sea, the trading nations of the Mediterra-

nean, the Jews among them, would scarcely have failed to carve out a niche in the presumably lucrative enterprise. Of course, Vinogradoff's view is highly subjective. Nowadays, most scholars ignore it because his assumptions are scarcely convincing and lack any supporting evidence. The word "Sinim," in fact, does not mean "China," but refers to Syene in Upper Egypt.

The Talmudic Era: Hypotheses suggesting that Jews arrived in China during the talmudic period are logical but unsupported. This was when the Silk Road was opened as a trade route between East and West. There is evidence that numerous merchants and traders from places where there was a heavy Jewish presence used the Silk Road to travel to China, including Western Asian countries. While mainly Arabs and Persians conducted this trade, there is every reason to believe that Jewish merchants or traders also involved themselves in such a profitable business, since they lived among these peoples. Indeed, many scholars believe that Jewish merchants played a leading part in trade after the fall of the Roman Empire, and there were Jewish traders known as "Radanites," a name probably from a Persian phrase meaning "knowing the way." Jews were undoubtedly involved in the comings and goings between East and West. Still, assumptions or hypotheses without evidence remain only assumptions or hypotheses.

The Tang Dynasty: In 618-907, we begin to have documentary evidence proving the presence of Jews in China. The earliest evidence is from the beginning of the eighth century: a business letter written in the Judeo-Persian language, discovered by Sir Marc Aurel Stein, the Hungarian-born British Jewish Orientalist and archaeologist. This letter (now housed in the British Museum) was found in Dandan Uiliq in Northwest China in 1901, an important post along the Silk Road. The thirty-seven line text was written on paper, a product then manufactured only in

China. It was dated by David Samuel Margoliouth to 718 C.E. From this fragment, we learn that a Persian-speaking Jew was trading commodities. He wrote to a fellow Jew who was obviously also a trader, asking his help in disposing of some sheep of inferior stock he had the misfortune to own.

Another bit of evidence proving the presence of Jews in China around this time is a page of Hebrew penitential prayers extracted by Paul Pelliot in 1908 from a massive trove of documents in the Cave of the Thousand Buddhas of Dunhuang, which was also collected by Stein. It consists of passages from the Psalms and the Prophets and also dates to the eighth century.

The earliest historical references to Jews in China are by Arab geographers and travelers of the ninth and tenth centuries. Abu-Zaid, a well-known Arab geographer and traveler in medieval times, described the massacre in 877 (or 878) of the foreign residents of the city of Khanfu conducted by the Chinese rebel Banshu. Among those killed he specifically mentions Jews.

All this evidence and more tells us that there were Jews in China no later than the Tang dynasty. From 1280 on, a few Chinese sources also mention the Jewish presence in China. *The Statutes of the Yuan and Official History of the Yuan* mention Jews several times. Westerners who were in China in this period also repeatedly mention Jews. For example, Marco Polo says there were Jews in Beijing in 1286. Olschki writes of an organized Jewish community, which was granted official recognition. The Franciscan John of Monte Corvino notes that there were Jews in China around 1300. Andrew of Perugia mentioned Jews in China in 1326. Jean de Marignolli asserts that he had disputes with Jews in Khanbaliq, China, in 1342. The Arab Ibn-Battuta mentions a "Jews' Gate" in Hangzhou in 1346.

Many Jews came to China for commercial and business purposes. They came from a variety of places, by whatever routes seemed most expedient. They traveled to China by land and by sea. Some went back and forth. Others stayed and eventually settled down. Inevitably, some fair-sized Jewish communities appeared in the cities in which Jews had businesses and resided. Other Jews were brought to China as captives taken by the Mongols during their march of conquest through Central Asia and Eastern Europe in the thirteenth and fourteenth centuries. The presence of Jews in China obviously brought the practice of Judaism in China. To trace specific practices, we need to further address the history of Jewish communities in China.

Kaifeng: The most documented Jewish community in China is Kaifeng. According to their own document, an inscription the Jews here erected in their synagogue compound in 1489, they came to China in the Song dynasty (960-1279). It is almost unanimously agreed that Jews came to Kaifeng, the capital city of the Song, between 960 to 1126. In 1163, after they felt very comfortable with the city and were better off economically, they constructed a building specifically to be used as a synagogue. Since the focus of our study of the practice of Judaism is on this community, we will come back to it after addressing Jewish communities in other Chinese cities.

Hangzhou: Hangzhou is located in East China and became prominent when the Sui dynasty (581-618) made it the southern terminus of the Grand Canal, which runs from north to south, joining several major rivers to provide China with an extensive inland waterway system. After 1126, Hangzhou served as the capital for the Southern Song dynasty (1127-1279). It has always been known as an important trade and handicrafts center. Its direct access to major sea routes made it convenient for merchants and traders.

Hangzhou is one of the few Chinese cities we are certain had a Jewish community. Although the arrival of the first settlers cannot be precisely dated, it would not be unreasonable to assume the presence of a Jewish community as early as the twelfth century, when the Northern Song was defeated by the Tartars and forced to move its capital from Kaifeng to Hangzhou. Chinese documents show that a large part of Kaifeng's populace moved with the royal court. Quite likely some of Kaifeng's Jews were among them.

Ai Tien, a Jew from Kaifeng who met Matteo Ricci in Beijing in 1605, told him that many Jews had once lived in Hangzhou, forming a large Jewish community with a synagogue of its own. He did not say how he knew this (or perhaps Ricci did not mention it in his reports to Rome). Scholars assume that at least some of the Hangzhou Jews had their roots in Kaifeng and were descended from people who came to the city around 1127 when the Song court moved there from Kaifeng. Obviously the Hangzhou and Kaifeng Jews had some kind of connection that made Ai Tien's knowledge possible.

An Arab traveler, Ibn Battuta, incidentally attests the existence of the Hangzhou Jewish community in the fourteenth century. Ibn Battuta visited Hangzhou in 1346. When he and his companions entered the city, they immediately became aware of a Jewish presence because of the name of the gate, the "Jews Gate," through which they passed. For some reason, the Jewish community of Hangzhou ceased to exist sometime before the seventeenth century.

Ningpo: Ningpo has been a seaport in East China for many centuries. Before modern times, it was the most important port connecting that part of China to Southeast Asia and beyond. It was one of the five treaty ports opened to foreign trade in 1842. The Jewish presence in the city began early. The Ningpo Jews established ties with Kaifeng Jewry by the fifteenth century if not before. In 1461 the Jews in Kaifeng obtained two Torah scrolls from Ningpo. The 1489 inscription tells the story: when the synagogue was rebuilt, Shi Bin, Li Rong, and Gao Jian, and Zhang Xuan went to Ningpo and brought back a scroll of the Scriptures. Zhao Ying of Ningpo brought another scroll to Kaifeng and presented it to the synagogue. Based on the availability of Torah scrolls, we may assume that there was a vibrant Jewish community in Ningpo. The fact that two scrolls were obtained there may also indicate the presence of a fairly large Jewish community in the city at that time. They must have had many more Torah scrolls if they could spare two for the Jews of Kaifeng.

Pan Guangdan, a Chinese historian, believes that the Jews in Ningpo probably arrived very early because it is a river port quite near the sea. The fact that they had many Torah scrolls indicates that the Jews and Judaism of Ningpo probably had a history no shorter than their Kaifeng counterparts, plus a considerable prestige. The existence of the Ningpo Jewish community gave much support, at least spiritually, to the Kaifeng Jewish community.

Yangzhou: Yangzhou was originally a seaport, but in the seventh to ninth centuries, as the course of the Yangtze River changed and its delta extended further into the ocean, it became a river port. Because of its location on the Grand Canal, a major inland transportation route, Yangzhou was an important hub from which one could travel south to Fujian and Canton and north to Kaifeng. There was a very large Muslim community in the city. According to the Fujian Chronicles, Western Region Notes, Islam was transmitted to Yangzhou thirteen centuries ago. Today, the Muslim population of the city numbers about four thousand.

It is reasonable to assume that there was also a Jewish community in Yangzhou. The 1512 inscription describes the connection between Kaifeng Jewry and the Yangzhou Jews, for it states that An, Li, and Gao of Kaifeng and Jin Pu of Yangzhou "contributed a scroll of the Torah and constructed a second gateway of the synagogue." In fact, the 1512 inscription was written by Zhu Tang, who was a resident of Yangzhou. Leslie believes that it was also feasible that the 1512 inscription of the Kaifeng synagogue was first written in Yangzhou and that it is definitely possible to say that there was a Jewish community in Yangzhou.

Ningxia: Ningxia, an important post city in Northwest China, also had Jewish residents and a historical connection with the Kaifeng Jewish community. Both the 1489 and 1512 inscriptions testify to their presence and their connection with Kaifeng Jewry. The 1489 inscription tells how Jin Xuan, a native of Ningxia, contributed an altar, a bronze censer, vases, and candlesticks to the Kaifeng synagogue when it was rebuilt after a flood. His younger brother, Jin Ying, contributed to the funds used to purchase land for the synagogue and pay for inscribing and erecting the 1489 stele. The 1512 inscription states that Jin Run built the kiosk in which it was housed. All three Jins were from Ningxia. The 1489 inscription also mentions that one of the ancestors of Jin Xuan and Jin Ying had been court president of state banquets and that their great-uncle had been a high military officer. Ningxia is located on the Silk Road and had served as a way-station. Merchants or traders who wanted to enter China from Central Asia via the Silk Road had to pass it. This makes the existence of Jews in the city even more probable.

Practice of Judaism of Kaifeng Jewry: Except for the Kaifeng Jewish community, we have almost no idea how Judaism was practiced in Chinese Jewish communities. Therefore, we have to concentrate on Kaifeng Jewry and their religious practices, which, no doubt, were the most important part of their inner life and which make us aware of their very existence as a community. The great devotion of the Kaifeng Jews to their religion can be seen from the enthusiasm they showed in building, rebuilding, and renovating their house of worship.

Synagogue History and Structure: Jewish records state that the congregation began to build the synagogue in 1163. Prior to this, it may have rented a place as a house of worship. Presumably special permission to build the synagogue was requested and granted. The synagogue was rebuilt during the reign of the Yuan emperor Kublai Khan in 1279. The name of the synagogue is given as "Ancient Temple of Purity and Truth." Fang Chao-ying points out the coincidence of these dates with the peaks of foreign influence in China.

The next major reconstruction was in 1421, under the sponsorship of the Prince of Zhou, posthumously called Ding, who was the younger brother of Ming emperor Chen Zu. During the Hong Wu period (1368-1399), he was appointed Governor of Kaifeng prefecture and had contacted the Kaifeng Jewish community. The third rebuilding was in 1445. The fourth was in 1461, after a flood. The fifth was in the Cheng Hua period (1465-1488), when a

Hall of Scriptures was added. The sixth was in 1489, which was the time of the first inscription. The seventh was in 1512, and the eighth in 1663, for both of which there were inscriptions. The synagogue was rebuilt for the ninth time in 1679. The tenth and final rebuilding was in 1688, a fact attested to by many new plaques. Thus the synagogue was repaired or rebuilt at least nine times since 1163, based on Chen Yuan's account. The funds and efforts devoted to this were enormous. For instance, more than 100,000 gold pieces were spent for the construction of the synagogue in 1512.

No doubt, the synagogue became the symbol of the Jews' identity and served as the focal point of their spiritual and communal life. That is why each construction and dedication of the synagogue became so important an event, with several large stone columns made to mark the occasions. Much of what we know of the community comes from three of these columns: the 1489 stele, the 1512 stele, and the 1663 stele.

The synagogue was enormous, although we have very little idea of the exact layout or structure of the earlier buildings. However, the stele of 1489 mentions that the synagogue compound reconstructed in 1279 was about thirty-five to forty *chang* (350 feet) long on each of its four sides. Thanks to the stele of 1663 and the written descriptions and drawings of Jesuits who visited in this period, we are fortunate to know the exact size of the synagogue that stood on the same site in the seventeenth and eighteenth centuries. The 1663 inscription states:

> There were the Hall for the Holy Patriarch, three sections; the Hall for the Patriarch of the Religion, 3 sections; North Lecture Hall, three sections; south Lecture Hall, 3 sections; Great Gateway, three sections; Second Gateway, three sections; kitchen, 3 sections; one Memorial Archway; Corridor, nine sections; the Imperial Tablet of the Ch'ing, in its dragon pavilion, set up in the Hall; two pavilions for the inscribed stones; two shrines for incense and devotion; and finally the painting in vermilion and the lacquering in black . . . the pattern of the synagogue was finally completed, and compared with the former one it was more completed.

The magnificence of the synagogue of Kaifeng Jewry can be appreciated if it is compared with synagogues in India around the same period. For instance, the largest synagogue in Cochin in the 1600s was thirty-five or forty feet in length and about one-third less in breadth.

While important, synagogue buildings are only external evidence of religion. The internal evidence—what goes on in people's lives and practices—is far more significant an indicator of their religion. Therefore, we turn now to examine the ritual life of Kaifeng Jewry.

The Annual Liturgical Cycle: Use of the Jewish calendar in a community's daily life reveals much about its piety. Although we do not have an actual calendar used by the Kaifeng Jewish community, observations by visitors tell us not only that they maintained a Jewish calendar but that they used it accurately, for instance, observing festivals on the correct dates. Thus, during his visit to Kaifeng in the early eighteenth century, Domenge, a missionary, was invited to participate in the service for Tabernacles on the twenty-third day of the eighth Chinese month, which was Saturday, October 3, 1722, or 22 Tishri 5483 on the Jewish calendar. This coincided with Shemini Azeret, the final day of the eight-day Tabernacles festival.

Not only did the community keep the Jewish calendar, they also publicly spelled out the rules for observing the Jewish holidays. For instance, the 1489 inscription clearly states that to observe Yom Kippur, the solemn Day of Atonement, Jews should

> close their doors for a whole day, and give them up to the cultivation of purity, and cut themselves off entirely from food and drink, in order to nourish the higher nature. On that day the scholar interrupts his reading and study; the farmer suspends his work of plowing or reaping; the tradesman ceases to do business in the market; and the traveler stops on his way. Desires are forgotten, attainments are put aside, and all apply themselves to preserving the heart and nourishment of the mind, so that through direction there may be a restoration of goodness. In this wise it is hoped that while man remains at rest, his heavenly nature will reach perfection, and, his

desire abating, his reasoning faculty will develop.

Similarly, the 1663 inscription states: "The seventh day is specially for the cultivation of the virtues of purity and enlightenment. On the day of purification, food should not be cooked."

Strict observance of the laws and commandments that comprise the halakhah was considered vital to the preservation of the nation and the faith. Kaifeng Jewry adopted a yearly circle for the reading of the Torah. It is clear that these readings of the Law were very close to those known elsewhere. Here is a description of the ceremonial reading of the Torah reading compiled from the inscriptions:

> First they washed their bodies, and changed their garments.
>
> Before performing acts of worship, he purifies himself and bathes, he dulls the ardor of sensual desire, he quiets his spirit, and he adjusts his robes and his headdress, and adopts a dignified deportment.
>
> During the acts of worship, the Law which is recited is sometimes chanted aloud, and in this the honoring of the Way is manifested. Sometimes there is silent prayer, and thus the Way is honored in secret . . . Advancing, the worshipper sees It in front of him; receding, It is suddenly behind him. Turning to the left, It seems to be to the left; turning to the right, It seems to be to the right.

The congregation's religious devotion can also be seen from the respect given the rabbis. Their names and merits are inscribed on the stele. The 1489 inscription, for instance, says: ". . . thanks to their [rabbis] efforts, today all of our people observe the law, worship God, venerate their ancestors, and are loyal to their sovereign and filial to their parents."

Kaifeng Jews' worship included daily and Sabbath worship, the Day of Atonement, New Year, Tabernacles, Passover, and Pentecost, Purim, Hanukkah, and the Ninth of Av. They also included the recitation of Grace after Meals, Kiddush, the Haggadah, and the Hazkarat Neshamot. There were special prayers and ceremonies for circumcisions, marriages, interments, and other events.

The Kaifeng community was unquestionably Rabbinic in its outlook. Indeed, in 1713, Gozani compiled a list that includes the titles of most of the talmudic tractates, perhaps testifying that the community even possessed a printing of the Talmud. In any case, the prayer books that survive are full of the theosophical values of the Talmud, indicating that the congregation's practice was in line with the traditions of Rabbinic Judaism. In particular, they followed Sephardic custom, reflected in their form of Grace after Meals (so A. Neubauer) and in their following of several variations associated with the Sephardic prayer book.

Jewish Education: The Kaifeng community, like communities in the western world, emphasized learning, which made a difference in continuity and development. Perhaps the traditional emphasis on learning was strengthened by Kaifeng Jews' isolation from Jewish communities outside of China. Without education, they would have been unable to practice their religion and maintain their heritage. Training "men learned in Torah" was crucial, for they depended on these sages to guide them in prayer and religious practice, instruct their children, and administer justice. In addition, and equally important, education enhanced their social status in Chinese society, which also greatly valued learning.

We lack materials that could tell us about the activities of talmudic academies in Kaifeng. Very little is known about how teachers for the children were selected. However, the community must have had a yeshivah, or perhaps just a class, for the few elite students needed to be rabbis when they grew up, since it was unlikely that the community would have been able to hire rabbis from elsewhere. Of course, a place to study Torah was also provided for lay people.

The basic Jewish education of Kaifeng Jews was most likely knowledge of enough Hebrew to recite the prayers and the weekly Torah portion, as has been true worldwide. Hebrew seems to have been taught orally from the older to the younger generation. The Hebrew knowledge of the Kaifeng Jews apparently varied at different times, and as a result the sources are contradictory. Some say that their Hebrew was poor in the seventeenth century; others say it was still good in the eighteenth century. It appears there was a fairly good knowledge of Hebrew in the seventeenth century, at least good enough to conduct services, copy the Torah scroll, and write prayer books. However, by the nineteenth century, after the community's last rabbi died, Jews knew very little Hebrew. This may explain why they sold their Hebrew texts. In the twentieth century, none of them could read or write Hebrew.

A more extensive education was provided as part of the training for the rabbinate. We see from the number of rabbis listed in the Memorial Book that rabbinical education was very active. From 1600 to 1670, the community trained eight rabbis: Rabbi Jacob, of the Li clan; the Master, representative (of the community), and teacher, Rabbi Shadai, of the Li clan; the representative, Rabbi Jeremiah, of the Li clan; the scribe, teacher, and representative, Rabbi Akibah, of the Ai clan; a scribe, Rabbi Mordecai, of the Kao clan; a scribe, Rabbi Judah, of the Shi clan; and a scribe, Rabbi Jacob, of the Kao clan.

Rabbis Jacob and Shadai were father and son. Jacob was the son of Rabbi Abishai, who was the son of Rabbi Eldad. Their family tree can be traced three more generations back in the Memorial Book (Nos. 343-350) to Rabbi Moses, the physician. All of them were members of the Li clan. Rabbi Jacob of the Li clan was the teacher as well as the representative of the community. If we take into consideration the fact that the early rabbis of the Kaifeng Jewish community were mostly from the Li clan, we may well assume that it was a tradition of this clan to serve in the synagogue. The Li clan in Kaifeng were believed to be Levites, so that it may not be a coincidence that they carried on the religious traditions of the Jewish people.

According to the 1663 inscription, Zhao Yingcheng wrote a book called *The Vicissitudes of the Holy Scriptures*. His brother Zhou Yingdou also wrote a work, *Preface to Clarifying the Law*, in ten chapters. Most likely those were works of biblical commentary. Had there existed no rabbinical education in Kaifeng, these men would not have been able to write such books.

Kashrut: Kaifeng Jews had special foods for the Sabbath and holidays, including fish on the Sabbath and matzot and lamb for Passover. Gozani, in 1704, mentions the unleavened bread and paschal lamb. Additionally, kashrut was important. The 1512 stele makes clear that "in their meat and drink they are careful to observe the distinction between what is permitted and what is not." Indeed, keeping kosher is the community's longest-observed tradition, and, even today, their descendants do not eat pork, the main meat for the Chinese. Documentary evidence indicates that the dietary laws were carefully observed and that communal authorities maintained strict discipline in this sphere. Ai Tien, the Kaifeng Jew who met Matteo Ricci in 1605, said that the chief rabbi had prohibited the members of the community from eating the meat of any animal not killed by his own hand. Strikingly, in the early 1600s, when the Kaifeng community offered the position of chief rabbi to Father Ricci (!), the condition they set was that he abstain from pork. In contrast, his Christian belief in Jesus as messiah was regarded as a personal idiosyncrasy of little consequence.

The community trained skilled slaughterers familiar with the approved method of slaughter and inspecting the carcass. The Memorial Book lists five ritual butchers around the seventeenth century. The skill was handed down from generation to generation. Slaughter took place in a courtyard on the south side of the synagogue compound.

While, generally speaking, the dietary laws were followed, not everyone in the community observed them since this was, at times, particularly difficult, especially for those who became Chinese officials, assigned to posts far away from Kaifeng. Those who were invited to attend imperial banquets had to eat Chinese food. What is amazing is not that some broke the dietary laws but that so many obeyed them. This adherence is illustrated by one of the names the Chinese applied to Kaifeng Jewry, Tiao Jin Jiao, "The Sect That Plucks out the Sinews," referring to the prohibition against eating the sciatic nerve. Rather than resent-

ing this designation, Kaifeng Jews appreciated it, because it differentiated them from their Muslim neighbors, who also abstained from pork and claimed Abraham and other biblical figures as patriarchs.

Burial: According to the 1489 inscription, the Jews' burial ritual was Chinese. However, Gozani reported in the early eighteenth century that they still followed traditional Jewish burial laws. The *Memorial Book*, which closed in the late seventeenth century and which chiefly records the names of deceased members of the community in both Hebrew and Chinese includes a form of the Kaddish prayer for the dead. Part of the text follows:

> a) May his great name be magnified and sanctified in the world (which he hath created according to his will); and in the world that he will create anew, where he will quicken the dead, and save the living; will rebuild the city of Jerusalem, and establish his holy temple; and will uproot all alien worship from the earth and restore the worship of Heaven to its place;
> b) For his name's sake, for his word's sake, and for the sake of the survivors of the exile, our brethren, may he remember us for our good, as in the days of old, may he bring near our end time, may he give (us) our messiah, may he save us, and may he be gracious to our dead ones, in his comparison, during the lives of the sons of his temple, and during the life of all the exile of Israel,
> c) (even speedily?) and at a near time, and say ye, Amen.
> d) Let his great name be blessed for ever and to all eternity. Blessed, praised, and glorified, exalted, magnified and extolled, honored and lauded be the name of the Holy One, blessed he; though he be high, high above all the blessings and hymns, praises and consolations, which are uttered in the world; and say ye, Amen.

It seems quite likely that this prayer would have been recited at burial services.

The worship rituals of Kaifeng Jewry remained close to those of Jews in other places. The 1489 inscription outlines the procedure followed in the ceremonial worship of venerating God:

> At first, the worshipper bends his body to honor the God, and the God is present in the act of bending the body. Then he stands erect, without leaning, to honor the God, and the God is present in the act of

standing erect. In response, he preserves his quietude of mind, and by silent praise he honors the God, for that which should not be forgotten is heaven. In movement, he examines his conduct, and by vocal praise he honors the Way, for that which should not be substituted for is Heaven. . . . The worshipper recedes three paces, and immediately the God is behind him, and in consequence he honors the God, which is behind him. He advances five steps, and perceives [the God] before him, and in consequence he honors the God before him. Turning to the left he bends his body to honor the God, which is good, for the God is then on his left. Turning to the right he bends his body to honor the God, which is not so good, for the God is then on his right. He lifts his head to honor the God, the God is above him; he lowers his head to honor the God, and the God is near him. Finally he worships the God, and it is honored in this act of worship.

For those who are familiar with Jewish rituals, this practice of Kaifeng Jewry brings to mind the genuflections in the Amidah, a central element in every Jewish service. The essence and spirit of the practices are the same, even if there is some difference in the external expression.

The writings of Kaifeng Jewry share many ideas and concepts with other Jewish works. For instance, Ai Shi-de presented an inscription to the synagogue that says, "Its presence is not impeded by visible form, its absence does not imply an empty void; for the Way is outside the limits of existence or non-existence." Compare what the great medieval philosopher Maimonides said in his Thirteen Principles of the Faith: "I believe with perfect faith that the Creator, blessed be his name, is not a body, and that he is free from all the accidents of matter, and that he has not any form whatsoever." In another example, we look at a prayer in the *Memorial Book*:

> May God remember the soul of my respected father, ____ son of ____, who has gone to his eternal home; on whose behalf I vow as alms ____; may his soul be bound up in Abraham, Isaac, and Jacob, Sarah, Rebekah, Rachel, and Leah, and all other righteous men and women who are in the Garden of Eden, and let us say, Amen.[27]

The similarity of this to the Yizkor prayer is striking. Another example is the Kaddish

DeRabbanan found at the front of the *Memorial Book*, close to the version of Maimonides and the Yemen.

By the mid-nineteenth century, however, the last rabbi of the community had died without a successor. The synagogue was unattended and it virtually ceased to exist. Although individual Jewish descendants still lived in Kaifeng, Judaism was no longer practiced in the city.

Judaism in Modern China: Judaism in modern China has a much clearer beginning, starting in the second half of the nineteenth century when China was forced to open its doors to western powers. From 1725, when the Chinese emperor decided to order all foreign missionaries to leave, to 1840, China was more or less a closed society in which foreign people were not allowed to live. The major cause of a change was the First Opium War between China and Great Britain in 1839-1842. China was defeated by Britain and forced to sign the Treaty of Nanjing. According to the Treaty and its supplementary protocols (1843), China agreed to surrender Hong Kong to the British and open five major port cities to British trade and settlements, which soon led to the establishment of territorial enclaves under the British flag. Other imperial powers followed suit, so that many foreign adventurers subsequently came to China, among them, Jews. In the following hundred years, Hong Kong, Shanghai, and later Harbin, Tientsin (now spelled Tianjin), and many other cities became centers of Jewish communal life in China.

Jews came in several waves. In the second half of the nineteenth century, Sephardic Jews, originally from Baghdad and Bombay, came, looking for business opportunities in the newly-opened cities. By the beginning of the twentieth century, they had built up solid Jewish communities in Shanghai and Hong Kong. The second wave was the arrival of Ashkenazic Jews from Russia and other East European countries. Most of them arrived in Harbin and the contiguous zone in Northeast China. Later many moved to the southern regions. Although a few came in search of better economic opportunities, the majority were fleeing pogroms or revolutions. The third wave was European Jewish refugees. During 1937-1940, about twenty thousand Jewish refugees fleeing the Nazis swarmed into Shanghai. The last wave was the arrival of some thousand Jews from Poland and other Eastern European countries in the early 1940s. Overall, in 1845-1945, more than forty thousand Jews came to China for business opportunities or safe haven. The arrival of Jews in modern China greatly strengthened the practice of Judaism there, as more than a dozen synagogues were constructed in the cities in which Jews resided.

The Jewish Communities in Shanghai: In the second half of the nineteenth and first half of the twentieth century, four separate Jewish communities were established in Shanghai, based on the different origins, customs, and traditions of the Jews who arrived.

The Sephardic Jewish Community of Shanghai: Sephardic Jews were the forerunners of the Jewish community in modern China. They came to the International Settlement of Shanghai via India shortly after the Opium War. In the wake of the Treaty of Nanjing, economic potential was the main attraction. The Shanghai Sephardim had British passports, which ensured that they could travel freely and enjoy extraterritorial rights. They were shopkeepers, importers and exporters, retailers, property and estate agents, and stockbrokers. With economic development of the city, the size of the community grew steadily. By 1895, there were about one hundred seventy-five Baghdadi Jews in the foreign enclave in Shanghai.

The Shanghai community is closely bound with the Sassoon family, which had built a dynasty in India in the first half of the nineteenth century, though their origin was Baghdad. David Sassoon together with his eight sons built an extensive business in Shanghai. The family was orthodox and conducted its life according to strict Jewish laws, ensuring the preservation of the traditions of the Baghdadi Jews. Until the mid-1870s, the Sassoons provided their staff with living accommodation and facilities for the observance of Judaism. No work or business was conducted on the Sabbath and festivals, and religious services were organized according to Baghdadi tradition. A legend holds that all family members and employees were required to learn how to slaughter poultry so that they would have kosher meat when they traveled in China.

The Sephardic community had a historic encounter with the Kaifeng Jews in the beginning of the twentieth century solely because of their common faith. The Shanghai Sephardim were saddened to learn of the miserable life and sad situation of the Kaifeng Jews. They invited the Kaifeng Jews to send a delegation to Shanghai and promised that they were willing to collect money to rebuild the synagogue and send a teacher to instruct them.

Sephardic Jews were permanent residents of Shanghai and built their homes as well as their business there. Thy made fortunes and became the most wealthy and influential Jewish community in Shanghai, though their members probably never exceeding eight hundred. Their contribution to the development of modern Shanghai is felt even today.

The Ashkenazic Community in Shanghai: The Ashkenazic Jewish community took shape at the beginning of the twentieth century, when Russian Jews started to arrive in relatively large numbers. Fleeing pogroms and revolutions, they first traveled via Siberia to cities in Northeast China, such as Harbin, Dalian, or Tianjin. In the early 1930s, their number in Shanghai already surpassed five thousand, making this a larger community than the Sephardic one. The Shanghai Ashkenazic Jewish Communal Association was established in June, 1931. It was an essentially secular Jewish community with strong Zionist and nationalist leanings.

The Ashkenazic community was the best organized and most active of all the Shanghai Jewish communities, represented by many and diverse communal institutions. Charitable societies, such as a relief society and shelter house, provided aid to the needy and indigent. The educational aid society assisted young people in the Jewish school with tuition. The burial society maintained a cemetery and provided free burial for the indigent. The clinic and hospital society provided a free dispensary to the poor. The Jewish Club, which was founded in the French concession in 1931, was the center of cultural, political, and social activities. It provided various activities such as concerts, lectures, and theatrical performances.

Zionism played an important role in the community's life. Alongside all kinds of Zionist groups, it was Ze'ev Jabotinsky's movement that captured the imagination of the young people. The Betar branch became very active. Among some two hundred soldiers in the Jewish Company, most were Betar members.

Central European Jews: Beginning in 1938, some twenty thousand Jewish refugees from Central Europe, chiefly from Germany and Austria, escaped to Shanghai, the only place in the world that did not demand documents (e.g., visa, health certificate, financial statement). Among them were Michael Blumenthal, who later became U.S. Secretary of the Treasury in the Carter Administration, and Shaul Eisenberg, who founded and ran the Eisenberg Group of Companies in Israel. Refugees received assistance from two existing Jewish communities upon their arrival. The International Committee for Granting Relief to European Refugees was established in Shanghai on August 7, 1938, to manage the flood of refugees. The Joint Distribution Committee provided help so that a large number of the refugees achieved economic independence.

The refugees assumed that the Shanghai experience would be temporary, and none expected that most refugees would stay in Shanghai for a decade or longer. Coming from Central Europe, they were ill-prepared for the radically different economic, cultural, and even environmental conditions in Shanghai. However, most finally settled in the heavily Chinese- and Japanese-populated Hongkou area of the Shanghai International Settlement, north of Suzhou Creek. Later on, this area became known as the "Hongkou Ghetto." Through initiative and creativity, the Jews made the most of an extremely difficult situation.

The refugees reflected German Jewish society in general, containing Orthodox, Reform, and secular Jews. Despite this wide range of religious practice, a single organization, the Community of Central European Jews, united them and provided comprehensive services, including religious education, a women's league, a cemetery and burial society, kosher slaughtering, and an arbitration board to resolve disputes.

Polish Jewish Community: In 1941, about a thousand Jews chiefly from Poland arrived in Shanghai from Japan. They obtained permission to move to the city through the excellent work of Zerah Wahrhafting, who had come to Shanghai in 1941 and who later became an influential leader of the Mizrahi Movement and member of the Israeli Cabinet (1962-1974). Among the Jews who came in 1941 were all the teachers and students of the *Mirre Yeshivah*, some four hundred people. They escaped Lesovelia, Poland, through Vilna, and obtained transit visas to Japan from Sugihara Chiune, the Japanese consul in Kovno. After a short stay in Kobe, Japan, they made their way to Shanghai.

The *Mirre Yeshivah* was the only talmudic academy of Eastern Europe to survive the Holocaust intact. In Shanghai, they printed their own books in Yiddish and Hebrew. Together with remnants of several other yeshivot, throughout the war, they continued their studies in the Beth Aharon Synagogue. Some students were also invited to teach at Jewish schools in Shanghai.

Communal Life and Practice of Judaism: Jewish communal life in Shanghai started with the Sephardic Jews in 1862, when the Sassoons endowed land for use as a cemetery, Shanghai's first Jewish communal project. As Orthodox Jews, the Sephardim were serious in their religious practice. Their observances and use of Judeo-Arabic, written in a cursive Hebrew script, reflected their radically separate ethnicity. To meet their religious needs, the community set up its first synagogue, Beth El, in 1887. In 1900, a second synagogue, Shearith Israel, was established.

By the 1910s, as the growing size of the congregation warranted a larger place for worship, Sir Jacob Sassoon and his brother Sir Edward endowed the Ohel Rachel

Synagogue, named after Jacob's late wife. Consecrated on January 23, 1921, with a sanctuary capacity of seven hundred people, it was the first edifice built specifically for divine worship in Shanghai. Marble pillars flanked a walk-in ark, and wide balconies overlooked the sanctuary. As many as thirty Torah scrolls were held in the ark. The synagogue was considered "second to none in the East." The site hosted the Shanghai Jewish School, library, and mikveh. With the completion of the Ohel Rachel, the Sephardic community appointed Rabbi Hirsch its first rabbi.

Beth Aaron Synagogue was built in 1927 on Museum Road (today's Hu Qiu Road), as a gift to the community from Silas Aaron Hardoon, a wealthy Jewish entrepreneur in Shanghai, to replace Shearith Israel synagogue. In the 1940s, it became the house of worship and study for the students and rabbis of the *Mirre Yeshivah*. The synagogue was demolished in 1985.

In 1932, the Sephardic community appointed an Ashkenazic rabbi, implying a reduced commitment to the preservation of Sephardic tradition. Innovations such as a choir, a few Ashkenazic melodies, a sermon, and prayer books with the English translation alongside the Hebrew were introduced. Otherwise, there was no intrinsic change in the form of worship.

The Ashkenazic community followed its own traditions and rituals in its own house of worship. In 1902, a synagogue committee was formed by Russian Jews and inaugurated in 1907 in a rented premise, named Ohel Moshe after Moshe Greenberg, a leading Russian Jewish personality.

In 1925, Meir Ashkenazi, a Lubavicher rabbi, was invited to become the Shanghai Russian Jews' spiritual leader. He served as Chief Rabbi of Shanghai from 1926-1949 and was the spokesman for the Ashkenazic community, directing its many relief, educational, and religious affairs. He found the small rented synagogue inadequate for the growing community's requirements. With his efforts, in 1927, a building was remodeled into a synagogue. The second floor was removed and pillars were erected to support its roof. A mezzanine was constructed for women. This Ohel Moshe Synagogue served as the religious center for the Russian Jewish community for many years. In April, 1941, a modern Ashkenazic synagogue was built, which seats a thousand people. Russian Jews called it the New Synagogue. Worship in this synagogue continued until 1956.

In Shanghai, Jews initially used the traditional method of a father's personally teaching his son or hiring a private tutor. As their numbers grew, the Shearith Israel Synagogue incorporated in 1902 a *Talmud Torah*, in which six boys were taught Hebrew and Jewish studies in Judeo-Arabic. Later, when European refugees came, the school was attended by many refugees' children. In 1944, the school had as many as three hundred students and sub-campuses in different districts. The Shanghai Jewish Youth Association, better known as the Kadoorie School, was founded especially for the refugees. The Ismar Freysinger School was a smaller but more religiously-oriented school for refugees. Those schools and other educational groups played a very important role in providing a basic education in Judaism during the War. Hebrew classes and traditional orientation to Jewish education stressed that Jews are a distinct national group, bound together by Judaism.

Zion was an integral part of Shanghai Jews' conception of Jewish identity. The Shanghai Zionist Association, the SZA, was founded in 1903 with Sir Elly Kadoorie as its first president. The SZA was one of the three earliest Zionist organizations in Asia and sent representatives to the Sixth Zionist Congress. The SZA also won the support and endorsement of the Chinese government to the Balfore Declaration. New streams of Zionism were introduced into Shanghai with the arrival of Russian Jews. In 1920s and 30s, Shanghai saw the emergence of all kinds of Zionist organizations, such as the Revisionist, the Mizrachi, the Poalei Zion, the Betar, and the Irgun. While the organizations were very active, conflicts among them were limited as they found common ground on major issues. In April, 1947, more than eight thousand Jews gathered to protest the hanging by the British authorities in Palestine of four Irgun activists. After the founding of the State of

Israel, the Shanghai Betar and Irgun sent two groups of young volunteers to Palestine in fall 1948 to join the War of Independence.

In September, 1932, following hostilities with the Japanese, a Jewish platoon, gathering together all Jewish members of the corps, became a respected unit of the Shanghai Volunteer Corps. It was commanded by Captain Noel S. Jacobs. The Platoon expanded on May 23, 1933, to become the all-Jewish Hebrew Company under Jacobs's command. The majority of its members were Russian Jews. The collar of their uniform sported a metal Shield of David with the letters SVC. One of their undeclared aims was to acquire military experience for eventual participation in the fight for Jewish independence in Palestine.

Cultural life was extremely rich in Jewish communities in Shanghai. From 1903 to 1945, more than fifty Jewish newspapers and magazines were published in English, Russian, German, French, Hebrew, Yiddish, and Polish. Among them, *Israel's Messenger, Our Life, The Jewish Call, Shanghai Jewish Chronicle* exerted a great impact on Jewish life in the city. Many books in Hebrew, Yiddish, and English on Judaism were printed. Pray-books and Jewish calendars were local products, as were Talmuds, Bibles, and books by Moses Maimonides.

Jews in Shanghai, especially the Sephardim and the Central European refugees, suffered a great deal during the Japanese occupation of the city. Their businesses were ruined as the economy declined. After the attack on Pearl Harbor, some Sephardic Jews who had British passports were interned as enemies of Japan. Under pressure from Nazi Germany, on February 18, 1943, Japanese authorities proclaimed the establishment of "the Designated Area for Stateless Refugees" in Shanghai, ordering Jewish refugees who had arrived from Europe since 1937 to move into the area within a month. The area became the well-known "Hongkou Ghetto." Those who continued to work outside of Hongkou needed special passes with the hour of their return clearly specified. Those who failed to return in time were often punished or had their passes confiscated. Confinement, poor diet and sanitation, in addition to restrictive methods of Japanese surveillance, put thousands of Jews in a difficult, unpredictable, and dangerous situation and to real suffering.

The Harbin Jewish Community: The Harbin Jewish community can be considered a large umbrella organization that covered an area of Northeast China and today's Inner Mongolia of China, where thousands of Jews settled from the end of the nineteenth to the mid-twentieth century.

Harbin as a Chinese city was founded in 1898 when Russian engineers chose it as the headquarters for the Chinese Eastern Railway Company. The railway to be built from Manchuria to Vladivostok was part of a 1896 treaty between China and Russia ensuring mutual assistance against any future Japanese aggression. To build the railway, Russia also obtained "extraterritorial rights" two and half miles on each side of the railway. Harbin soon became a thriving Russian town and Russian Jews gravitated to this part of China. Beginning with the construction of the Chinese Eastern Railway from Manchuli to Hailar, Jews from Russia began to settle in Northeast China and Inner Mongolia.

Jews were almost free from persecution because Tsar Nicholas II, at the end of the nineteenth century, was anxious to Russify and encouraged immigration of Russians, including Russian Jews, to this region in order to strengthen Russian influence. He declared that Jews willing to settle along the railway would be allowed freedom of religion, unrestricted business rights, and quota-free education. Besides, Russian authorities in Northeast China did not want to show the Chinese that any white man—even a Jew—could be treated as inferior to an Asian. Many Russian Jews fleeing pogroms in Odessa, Kishinev, and other towns, decided to move to Northeast China for permanent settlement.

The Jewish population in Harbin grew quickly. On February 16, 1903, the Jewish Minority Community was founded, numbering some five hundred people. After the Russian defeat in the 1904-1905 Russo-Japanese War, many demobilized Jewish soldiers in the Tsar's army settled in Harbin and were soon joined by their families. The Bolshevik Revolution of 1917 and subsequent Russian civil war brought a flood of refugees, both White Russians and Jewish, to Harbin. In the 1920s there were as many as fifteen thousand Jews in Harbin and nearby towns, making the Harbin Jewish community the largest (at the time) in the Far East as well as in China.

The Japanese occupation of Northeast China in 1931 and the establishment of the Japanese puppet state of Manchukuo in 1932 had a negative impact on the Harbin Jewish community. The Japanese economic domination and harsh treatment of Jews coupled with the general lawlessness and anti-Semitic attacks caused many Jews to leave for Tianjin and Shanghai. The Jewish population of Harbin was reduced from thirteen thousand in 1929 to less than five thousand in 1939.

Jews in Harbin were homogenous, consisting primarily of Russians and a small number of Poles. The Jewish Religious Community of Harbin as it was named at the time was a well-organized and supreme governing body. It stood for all Jews in the area and served all their needs. Its by-laws define the main functions as: tending to the religious needs of the Jewish immigrants; managing the funds of the synagogue and the rabbi; managing the Jewish traditional method of slaughter of livestock; managing the Jewish cemetery and organizing funeral services; registering births, deaths, marriages and divorces; dealing with the Chinese authorities, and acting according to the laws of China; supervising the Jewish school for the immigrants; organizing cultural and educational activities; handling of all kinds of charities to needy immigrants and etc.

The Harbin Jewish Cemetery was established in 1903 with a small synagogue of its own. The Central Synagogue was built in 1907. In 1921, the New Synagogue was built. Both were orthodox. The first rabbi of the community was Shevel Levin, who had previously served in Omsk and Chita in Siberia. Rabbi Aaron Kiselev served in Harbin from 1913 until his death in 1949. Dr. Abraham Kaufman, the community

leader since 1919, played a leading role. He chaired the Far Eastern Jewish Council and three times from 1937 to 1939 ran the Conference of Jewish Communities in the Far East. He was arrested by the Soviet Red Army in 1945 and taken back to the Soviet Union for ten years of hard labor.

The Harbin community was active and comprehensive. Besides synagogues, it ran a school, library, hospital, two banks, a home for the aged, and numerous charitable organizations. A Talmud Torah was established in 1919, providing a traditional education for children and young people. The community had many publications in Russian and in Yiddish. Among them, *Yevreskaya Zhizn* was published from 1920 to 1940. Cultural and social activities such as theatrical performances and musical offerings, enriched the community's life. Zionism also played an important role in communal life. All kinds of Zionist organizations existed, including Poalei Zion, Bund, Betar, Agudat Israel, and Revisionist Zionism in Harbin. Because of Zionist spirit and influence, quite a few individuals and families made Aliyah in the twenties and thirties.

In 1937, the community created the Far Eastern Jewish Council, which in turn held the Conference of Jewish Communities in the Far East three times from 1937-1939. Each conference was attended by several hundred Jewish representatives from Tianjin, Shanghai, other Chinese cities, and Kobe in Japan. A decision was reached at the 1937 conference that all Jewish communities in China would be combined into a single autonomous association covering all religious problems, educational, cultural, social, and economic activities, support orphanages and care for refugees from Central Europe, and register all Jews and all the Jewish organizations in the Far East.

The Harbin community suffered a heavy blow at the end of WWII, when the Russian Red Army declared war against Japan and entered the city. Dr. Kaufman and other Jewish leaders were arrested, charged with anti-Soviet activities, and forcibly taken to the Soviet Union. While the community survived, many who could started to leave.

Adjacent Jewish communities: Beside Harbin, there were a number of small Jewish communities established in various cities in the early twentieth century in Northeast China and Inner Mongolia, such as Hailar, Manchuli, Dalian, Mukden, etc. All of them were connected with the Harbin Jewish community either economically or socially.

The Jewish settlements from Russia concentrated in Hailar and Manchuli, two major cities of Inner Mongolia at the beginning of the twentieth century. Most of them were merchants of foreign trade and forestry. Places of worship were set up in Hailar in 1910 and in Manchuli in 1912. Manchuli Jews ran a private school, situated at the railroad station. Operating four days a week, it included four grades and counted eighty students and five teachers.

Jewish settlers from Russia came to Dalian in 1900. They were few in numbers, but Jews began to trickle to the city from Harbin after the Russo-Japanese War of 1904-1905. On December 8, 1929, the Dalian Jewish Society was inaugurated. It had fifty-eight members in 1929 and one hundred-eighty in 1940. Among the first Jews to arrive in Dalian was Joseph Trumpeldor, who had been captured in the Russo-Japanese War and was the first Jewish officer decorated by the Tsar for bravery.

The Tianjin Jewish Community: Jews might have settled in Tianjin as early as the 1860s, when the city became an open port for foreign trade. However, there was no Jewish organization until 1904, when the Tianjin Hebrew Association was founded. The community consisted mostly of Russian Jews. As a result, the Association was registered with the Russian Consulate in Tianjin and considered an organization of Russia. The population of the community grew rapidly after the October Revolution in Russia in 1917 and again after the Japanese occupation of Northeast China in 1931, when many Jews came from Harbin. In 1935, the Jewish population of Tianjin reached some twenty-five hundred, probably the highest figure in its history.

Most Jews in Tianjin engaged in commercial activities, especially the fur trade. There were more than a hundred fur firms owned by Jews. Furs were obtained in Northeast China but sorted and processed in Tianjin. Fur products were chiefly shipped to American and European markets. Other export business also involved Tianjin Jews. Though most Jews in the city were secular and business oriented, they fasted on Yom Kippur, held family seders, observed the specific diet of Passover, and attended services on the High Holidays. Every household celebrated the major freedom festivals of Hanukkah and Purim. They also marked Lag B'Omer.

The Tianjin community had a committee to take care of the needs of its members. A Jewish cemetery was created in 1904. Leo I. Gershevich, a fur merchant in Tianjin, served as the communal leader for many years. Under his leadership, in October, 1925, a school was established to teach Judaism and secular subjects. There were one hundred thirty-two students in 1934. In 1928, a Jewish club was founded and soon became the center of communal life. It housed a library with a few thousand volumes of books and reading rooms. A benevolent society and interest-free loan fund relieved the poor and helpless or set them on the road to self-support.

For the community's first three decades, worship was conducted in a small rented apartment. The community started fundraising for a synagogue in 1937, building a house of worship in 1939. Rabbi Levi was in charge. Today, the building remains standing and Star of David is clearly seen.

Zionist activities played an important role in the community, involving many young people. A few hundred refugees from Europe were taken in by the community during WWII. A grand gathering was held in front of the synagogue upon the news of the founding of the State of Israel in 1948. The community had strong ties with the Harbin Jewish community and participated in all three Conferences of the Jewish Communities in the Far East.

The Tianjin Jewish community also served Jews in nearby area such as Qingdao and Beijing. Though no Jewish organization was ever established in Beijing, a

Jewish association was founded in Qingdao. Most Jews in Qingdao were of Russian origin, though the first Jews were mainly German citizens who came as merchants, bank employees, or diplomats at the end of the nineteenth century. The population increased after the Russian October Revolution. In 1920, Jews formed a congregation for religious activities. They had a synagogue of their own. For many years F.M. Torabinskii, a Russian Jew, served as head of the congregation. In 1940, two hundred twenty-one Jews resided in Qingdao. After WWII, an American Navy warship was stationed in the city. Quite a few Jewish servicemen joined the community. In the 1950s, all Jews left.

Jews in Post-War China: The surrender of Japan brought some hope for Jews in China. For the European refugees, the first positive change was the complete resumption of communication with the outside world and the flow of much-needed money into the community. The arrival of American armed forces provided jobs and opportunities. Moreover, they were able to move including to go to a third country to join family or relatives. The majority started to plan to leave, not unexpected since they had wound up in China in the first place only because they had no other choice. Countries such as the United States, Canada, and Australia became the refugees destinations if visas could be obtained. However, the doors of most countries were still not widely open. The founding of the state of Israel created a different choice. In 1948, Israel opened an office in Shanghai. About ten thousand Jews made Aliyah.

For the Sephardim and Russians, China had been home for a generation or more, and many of them considered remaining. Some started to invest and others to rebuild their businesses. But their hopes were short-lived. In 1946, civil war broke out between the Nationalists and Communists, and the Sephardim and Russians also began to leave. Well-established Jewish families in the city, such as the Sassoons, the Kadoories, had transferred their business to elsewhere (the Sassoons in the Bahamas; the Kadoories made Hong Kong a residence and center of their enterprises). Thus, by the time the Communists took over in 1949, most Jews had already left China. Only a few thousands remained and lived in Chinese cities for another ten years before their final departure.

The 1950s marked the end of an era of Jewish life in China. Radical changes within Chinese society made it difficult for Jews to lead a meaningful life or to build up their businesses there. Jews who came to China at different times for various purposes believed that it was time for them to leave, and they left by thousands annually. By the mid-1950s the total number was less than one thousand. Because of the declining Jewish population, various organizations were either diminished or merged. When the American Joint Distribution Committee closed its Shanghai office in 1951, the Council of the Jewish Community, created in Shanghai in 1949 after the founding of the People's Republic of China, took over the responsibility of administrative work in connection with the repatriation and resettlement of China's Jews to all parts of the world. By July, 1956, the centralized management of the properties and the internal affairs of both the Ashkenazic and Sephardic Communal Associations, which had been handling their affairs separately for the prior fifty years, finally merged into the Council's office. The Council not only represented the Shanghai Jewish community but also the Jewish communities in Tianjin and Harbin. It was in charge of the general budget and migration affairs of those communities, and its annual reports include all the communities. It took over complete responsibility for the welfare of Jews remaining in Tianjin after the liquidation of the Tianjin Hebrew Association in 1958.

The economic and financial status of the majority of the remaining Jews steadily worsened during the 1950s because most of them were planning to leave. Their priority concern was no longer to establish their life and business in China but how and when to leave the country. The departure rate remained high, over 25% each year. For instance, from 1955 to June 1956, 283 Jews left China. Among them, 113 were from Shanghai, 139 from Harbin, fifteen from

Tianjin, seven from Dalian, and ten from Qingdao. Though destinations for them were various (thirteen countries plus Hong Kong), statistics showed that the number one destination was Israel (131 Jews), followed by the USSR (ninety Jews).

By June 30, 1956, the remaining Jewish population in China was 519 according to the Council of the Jewish Community in China. The distribution of those Jews was 171 in Shanghai; 233 in Harbin and Hailer; and 115 in Tianjin and the nearby area. Among them, the majority (409) originally came from Russia and were citizens of the USSR. Three years later, the population had declined by another almost 50%, to 251 (72 in Shanghai, 26 in Tianjin, and 153 in Harbin). Over 90% of them were of Russian origin; they remained because, since both the USSR and China were communist, leaving would make little difference in their circumstance. Additionally, Russian subjects holding Soviet passports needed clearance from the Soviet Citizens Association and the Soviet Consulate General. This clearance was more difficult to obtain in the north of China and particularly in Harbin. It often happened that, after the exit permit was granted, it would be canceled just before the migrant's intended departure. The individual, having liquidated his business and personal affairs, was left in limbo until his fate was decided some months later. Even so, mot of these Jews left after relations between the USSR and China became hostile in the early 1960s. This author does not have any official documents to tell the exact number of their departure.

With the shrinking community, religious and culture life was severely disrupted. Though religious life in general continued, it became difficult to maintain synagogues. The New Synagogue on Chao Yang Road, which was built in 1941, served as the only living synagogue in Shanghai for years. However, because the expense of maintaining the large premises in the face of dwindling attendance and growing financial need among the local Jewish population could no longer be justified, it was decided to dispose of the synagogue building. The transaction was concluded in July, 1956,

and the buyer was the House and Land Control Bureau of the Chinese People's Government. The reason to sell it to the Bureau was the Bureau offered high price. Several Torah Scrolls and a quantify of religious books owned by the local community were shipped to the Ministry for Religion of Israel as a gift.

Still, religious services continued on Sabbaths and holidays in the prayer hall at the Jewish Center. Matzoth were prepared and distributed free of charge to all needy Jews in Shanghai. They even sent Matzoth (by the hundreds of pounds) by train for remaining Jews in Tianjin. Jewish education was not neglected. For instance, a Hebrew class was inaugurated in 1956 to teach the fundamentals and beginnings of Hebrew.

In Harbin, the community continued to perform many charitable works in the 1950s, though it had a close relation with the Council of Jewish community in Shanghai. The Shelter House in Harbin housed inmates. Free meals were distributed to inmates and to dependents of the community. Low-priced meals were served to those in need in the Jewish dining room to people. Medical care was granted to the needy. Doctors were called to attend the sick. Indigent migrants irrespective of their destinations were provided before their departure with clothing and monetary assistance. The community also took care of the Jewish cemetery in Harbin.

The Jewish population in Harbin District was one hundred fifty-three by the end of June, 1959, the largest Jewish community in China then. The Harbin Jewish community was the only one which was able to keep its synagogue building by the end of 1950s. Daily services had continued to be held in the synagogue with large attendance for the Sabbath and holidays prayers by 1959. Children's parties on Purim and Hanukkah were still organized. The Jewish community of Harbin stopped functioning on November 20, 1965.

In Tianjin, there were one hundred and thirty Jews, including children, in 1955. Due to the shrinking population and difficult financial status, the Association decided to sell its synagogue building in

1955. The deal was closed in May, 1955. With the anticipated departure of all Jews from the Tianjin District, the liquidation of the Tianjin Hebrew Association was suggested early in 1957. On September 27, 1957, application to close down the Association was filed with the local authorities and a notice published in the Tianjin newspaper. The liquidation was completed in January, 1958. This brought to an end of the Association, which had existed for over half a century. Before the final closing of the Association, a Torah was sent to Israel, and useful archives were sent to the Council in Shanghai for future reference. The welfare of the remaining Jews was taken over by the Council.

Jewish culture activities, such as publishing newspapers and organizing performances, halted. The Shanghai Jewish Club, which was first established in the 1930s and served as one of the cultural centers for Shanghai Jewry, closed its doors on December 31, 1955. Over 30,000 selected books from the Club's library were shipped to the Ministry for Education and Culture in Israel as a gift. However, a reading and recreation room was created in the Shelter House, making newspapers, magazines and remaining books accessible to every Jew in Shanghai.

Thus the Jewish community in modern China, which had lasted for about a hundred years, faded away by the end of 1950s. By 1966, the start of China's Cultural Revolution, only a few elderly Jews remained and eventually died in China. The practice of Judaism in mainland China ceased completely.

Jews in Contemporary China: Despite these events of the 1950s and 1960s, the history of Jews and Judaism in China did not permanently end. Thanks to China's reform and "Open Door Policy" since 1979, the goals of which were to attract foreign investments and to establish ties with the rest of the world, especially with western countries, a Jewish presence in China was revived. Nowadays there are not a small number of Jews living in Chinese cities such as Beijing and Shanghai. With more and more Jews come to work, invest, study, and live in China, the practice of Judaism once again has become a part of life in Chinese society.

In 1980, twenty-five Jews who had come to Beijing from North America to pursue careers in business, journalism, diplomacy, or for academic study, held a Passover seder in Beijing. In the 1990s, the Beijing Jewish community took shape as more Jews live, work, or study there. In 1995, Friday night services began to be held weekly at the Capital Club of Beijing. Sabbath prayer books and a Torah were donated to the community, enabling celebration of all major holidays. On both the High Holy Days and Passover, the community can expect to have two hundred present. Other important landmarks for the community include its first *bar mitzah* in 1996 and its first *b'rit millah* in 1997. This community is headed by Roberta Lipson and Elyse Silverberg, two Jewish businesswomen, and affiliated with the Progressive movement of Judaism. In 2001, a new development occurred. Rabbi Shimon Freundlich from the Chabad-Lubavitch movement settled in Beijing and began working to build an Orthodox congregation there.

Jews began to return to Shanghai in the 1980s too. They were attracted by Chinese open-door policy. As Shanghai becomes more and more cosmopolitan, the Jewish presence in the city becomes more obvious. In the mid-1990s, they established the Shanghai Jewish Community. Rabbi Shalom Greenberg from Chabad-Lubavitch in New York arrived to serve this community in August, 1998. His commitment has infused new life into the growing Jewish community. Rabbi Arthur Schneier, President of the Appeal of Conscience Foundation from New York, donated a Torah to the community, which has reached two hundred-fifty members. Regular Sabbath services and kosher meals have been implemented. Jewish education also started in Shanghai, with child and adult education classes, bar and bat mitzvah training, and social brunches. On the first day of Rosh Hashanah, in September, 1999, a Jewish New Year service was held at the Ohel Rachel Synagogue, for the first time since 1952, when the synagogue was closed. It likely that the Ohel Rachel Synagogue will become a permanent house of worship in the near future.

In 2001, the community started to publish a monthly bulletin, *Update*, with information about holidays and other religious and social activities. Though Rabbi Greenberg is from the Chabad movement, he is determined to serve all Jews. In fact, Jews in different denominations have prayed together since 1998 in Shanghai.

The Jewish Community in Hong Kong: The community in Hong Kong is unique and needs to be addressed separately, because Hong Kong had been under the British rule since 1842 and reverted to Chinese sovereignty in 1997. The history of the Hong Kong Jewish community continues from its past to the present days.

The beginning of the Hong Kong Jewish community was more or less similar to that of the Shanghai Jewish community. It was founded by the same group of Jews who came to China after the Opium War to seek business opportunity and development. The leading members of the community, such as the Sassoon Family, the Kadoorie Brothers, lived and invested in both cities though with emphases on Shanghai before 1940s as Shanghai had more business at that time. However, the Jewish Diaspora in Hong Kong, unlike that in Shanghai, has its continuity and unbroken history of over one hundred and fifty years. The practice of Judaism also survives in Hong Kong without a break.

The first Jews arrived in Hong Kong in 1843 and 1844, the years immediately following the ceding of Hong Kong to the British under the Treaty of Nanjing, which brought unprecedented access to China for foreign merchants and the promise of security of business. A small community of Jewish merchants, by and large from Bombay and Calcutta with Sephardic origin, was taking the shape from as early as the 1860s. The number of Jews in Hong Kong reached seventy-one in 1881. Ashkenazim started to arrive in the 1880s and 1890s, when pogroms broke out in Eastern Europe. By 1900, there were about one hundred and fifty Sephardim living in Hong Kong.

The communal life started shortly after Jews settled in Hong Kong. The Jewish cemetery in Hong Kong was first established in 1857, the year of the first Jewish burial in Hong Kong. In 1870, the first synagogue was set up in a rental house on Hollywood Street. The community started to worship together. In 1881, a new synagogue in memory of Sir Jacob Sassoon's mother, Leah, replaced the older one. On Yom Kippur of 1896, sixty-seven attended the service.

The first ten years of the twentieth century was a period of consolidation of the community. Three things put it on a solid foundation. First, the Ohel Leah Synagogue was constructed in 1901 as a gift for the Hong Kong Jewish community from the Sassoon Family. It was consecrated in 1902. The synagogue is still in use today and is a landmark of the city. Second, the communal cemetery was enlarged in 1904 with assistance of Sir Matthew Nathan, the only Jewish Governor of Hong Kong. Third, a Jewish recreation club was created for all Jews with a donation from the Kadoorie family in 1905 and enlarged in 1909, symbolizing a community-focused spirit.

The community stopped growing as most Jewish merchants were attracted to Shanghai, which developed dramatically and proved to be a better place for business and investments from 1910 to 1936. The Japanese occupation of mainland China in late 1930s caused many Jews from Shanghai, Tianjin, and Harbin to escape to Hong Kong. But the condition for the Jewish community were doomed when Japan occupied Hong Kong in 1941. The following four years were the darkest page in the history of the Hong Kong Jewish community as community leaders were detained, placed in camps, and business suffered. However, the Hong Kong Jewish community recovered after WWII and remained steady in the following thirty years. The 1980s witnessed great development of the community as Hong Kong's economy grew rapidly. Based on a survey conducted in 1989, 64% of Jews in Hong Kong came in 1980s.

An openness to and acceptance of the diverse nature of Jews from many parts of the world characterized early Jewish life in Hong Kong. The community did not employ a rabbi until the 1960s, though it benefited from the services of visiting rabbis over the years. Observant members of the community, including Lady Muriel Kadoorie's father, David Gubbay, often conducted services. The first officially appointed rabbi arrived in 1961. In 1985, Rabbi Mordechai Avtzon from Chabad-Lubavitch was invited to serve the community for one year. However, he remained and created a center for the Chabad-Lubavitch movement in Asia in 1986. The establishment of the Chabad-Lubavitch center in Hong Kong is a noticeable trend. Its slogan is "Bringing Jews in the Far East closer." Two rabbis now in Shanghai and Beijing are sent by the Center.

In 1969, a Hebrew school was set up in Hong Kong to promote Jewish education. At first, classes were conducted on Sundays and weekday afternoon. By 1973, school attendance had grown to eighty children. In 1991, the Carmel Jewish Day School was established to give a full-time education option for the community's children. Now over a hundred pupils attend the school.

In recent years, Hong Kong's growing population has led to a diversification in the religious life of the community. Four congregations now have their own rabbis and places of worship. They are Orthodox Ohel Leah Congregation, the Chabad-Lubavitch Congregation, the Progressive United Jewish Congregation, and the Conservative Shuva Israel Congregation.

Religious links between Hong Kong and China have enjoyed a revival since the mid-1980s, following the revival of Jewish Diaspora in China. The Ohel Leah Synagogue was quick to support these activities by serving as a source for Pesach supplies and various educational materials. Also since the 1980s, the Hong Kong Jewish community has strengthened its ties with Israel. The community center is a home for Israeli representatives in Hong Kong.

In order to maintain its vibrancy in the Far East, express its confidence in the future of Hong Kong, and uphold its commitment to Jewish continuity in Hong Kong, the Jewish community redeveloped the site of the Jewish Recreation Club and turned it into a modern Jewish Community Center in the early 1990s. The project was completed in 1995 and serves the entire Jewish community of Hong Kong.

Hong Kong is recognized as a thriving commercial and financial center of increasing international importance that moves at an extraordinarily fast pace. When Hong Kong reverted to China on July 1, 1997, the Jewish community remained committed to the territory. According to the law, a good many Hong Kong Jews have become Chinese citizens or have long-term residence rights. There were 2,500 Jews living in Hong Kong according to the statistics of the Israeli embassy, as of February, 1998. It is now estimated that five thousand Jews live in Hong Kong. By any standard, the Hong Kong Jewish community is the largest, most prosperous, and best-organized Jewish community within Chinese territory.

The Jewish Community in Taiwan: The Jewish presence in Taiwan is also unique, as Taiwan remains out of control of the Communists and under a separate administration. Jews began to appear in Taiwan after the retreat of Chiang Kai-shek and his forces to Taiwan in 1949. The first Jews were those who served in the U.S. army stationed in Taiwan in the 1950s and Jewish businessmen. Jewish religious services were first organized and held in the military compound for Jewish personnel. High holidays were celebrated. In the 1970s, as the Taiwan economy boomed, more and more Jews came to Taiwan. Since Taipei, the capital of Taiwan, is where most Jews lived or worked, the Jewish community was established there in 1975. Yaacov Liberman, who was born in Harbin and went to Israel in 1948, was elected as the community leader. The Communal Center is in a rented villa in Tienmou, a residential suburb of Taipei where most Jews lived. In 1989, the resident Jewish population was one hundred forty-eight from a dozen countries, such as Australia, Canada, England, France, Germany, Israel, Panama, South Africa, Switzerland, and the United States. Among them, a few families are permanent residents; the majority are businessmen or employees of companies who conduct and supervise business in Taiwan.

Regular Sabbath services are held on Friday evenings at the synagogue at the

Community Center, conducted by its members or visiting rabbis. The community runs a Sunday school, offering Jewish traditional education for children of the community.

Besides Sabbath services at the Community Center, the community provides visitors and those who stay downtown regular Sabbath services at the President Hotel in downtown Taipei. Prayer books, prayer shawls, kosher wine, Havdalah candles, and spice boxes are kept in the hotel. A monthly bulletin is published with material on all holidays and other religious activities. The community is a member of the Asia Pacific Jewish Association.

Prospects for the future: China has been undergoing dramatic changes since 1979. Largely as a result of economic reform and progress, Jews as well as other foreigners have been attracted to its society. Their growing number is noticeable, and the Chinese government has begun to realize that it is necessary to create a cultural environment for foreigners if China wants to keep them and attract more to come. This kind of cultural environment includes the need for religion. That is why permission was given to Chabad-Lubavtich rabbis to practice Judaism in China.

Parallel with the open-door policy and more liberal life style for Chinese, intermarriage between Chinese and foreigners has been occurred. Reports say that quite a few are intermarriages between Jews and Chinese (in most cases between Chinese woman and Jewish man). This brings new meaning to the practice of Judaism in China, as those Chinese may be converted to Judaism sooner or later. In a long run, it will affect their life and the life of their children.

Issue of the Jewish Cemeteries: The issue of Jewish cemeteries is an integral part of the question of Judaism in China. There was a communal cemetery for Kaifeng Jewry before 1642. However, it was destroyed by the 1642's Yellow River flooding and replaced with family cemeteries. Three of these still exist in Kaifeng. They are the Jin's, Shi's, and the Li's. Only the Jin's family graveyard has a headstone.

The Jewish cemeteries in Shanghai, Tianjin, and Harbin have a different history. Over five thousand Jews who died in China were buried in those cemeteries in about a hundred years. Before the mid-1950s, all Jewish cemeteries in Shanghai, Tianjin, and Harbin were intact, with all graves and memorial stones constantly kept in good condition. However, the development of those cities necessitated the removal of the Jewish cemeteries to new sites.

Tianjin was the first city to make such a request. Agreement for transfer of the Jewish cemetery and re-burial of the remains was reached in June, 1956. The work started on July 25, 1956, and was completed on September 13, 1956. A new chapel was erected at government expanse and consecrated on November 25, 1956, in the presence of thirty-five members of the Tianjin community. The municipal government agency responsible for the realization of the scheme showed remarkable tact and consideration in providing a satisfactory new site, divided from adjacent plots by a strip three meters wide and in undertaking the transfer and re-burial of the remains strictly in accordance with Jewish religious laws (no work to be done on the Sabbath, for instance). The final re-erection of 559 monuments was completed in November, 1957. The address of the new cemetery site is at Chin Lin Chwang.

In Shanghai, the authorities first informed the council that no further burial should be effected in any of the Jewish cemeteries, which were all in the city district. A separate plot in a public cemetery was allotted for future burials. Then, in 1958, the Council was asked to transfer the four Jewish cemeteries in Shanghai to a new site some, 15 km. from the city limit. The Wei-ming Lu (ex Baikal Road) Cemetery, founded in 1917, the biggest Jewish cemetery in Shanghai, consisting of 1,692 graves, was moved first, beginning on September 26, 1958. The work was completed on November 10, 1958 and completed on December 3, 1958. Because of the colossal size of most of the monuments, the removal of the stones to the new cemetery took several months. By the end of June 1959, about five hundred monuments were re-erected.

The second to be removed was the Ting-hai-kong Lu (ex Point Road) Cemetery, founded in 1940 for the use of Central European refugees during World War II, consisting of 834 graves. This work was done from November 2, 1958, to November 20, 1958. The transfer of monuments took a little more than a month, from December 7, 1958, to January 11, 1959. Re-erection of monuments of all 834 graves was completed on April 12, 1959.

The removal of the other two cemeteries, the Hwang-pe Lu (ex Mohawh Road) Cemetery, founded in 1862, consisting of 304 graves, and the Fah-yuan Lu (ex Columbia Road) Cemetery, founded in 1941, consisting of 873 graves, had not commenced by June, 1959. Most likely they were removed in 1960s, after the council was liquidated.

The allotted land for the new Jewish cemetery is big enough to hold the graves from all the four Jewish cemeteries. After all the graves are centralized in the new cemetery and re-erection of monuments completed, a hedge will be make around the boundaries of the new cemetery, while trees will be planted along the main roads and cross-paths. This author has no idea if this plan was ever fulfilled. The address of the new site of the cemetery is Gi'an Public Cemetery, Wei-jia-jiao, Western outskirts of Shanghai. It does not now exist any more now. Most likely it was destroyed during the Chinese Culture Revolution from 1966-1976.

The Harbin Jewish community was asked to move its cemetery to a new site some 17 km. from the old one. Eight hundred fifty four graves were transferred and a small house was built in the new cemetery for religious requirements.

According to a report by Teddy Kaufman, President of the Israel-China Friendship Association and a son of the leader of the Harbin Jewish community Dr. Abraham Kaufman, the new cemetery is 46 km. away from the city. Six hundred monuments and gravestones were found in the new cemetery in 1994 when he visited. According to his account, there are 876 graves in the new Jewish cemetery now. Twenty-three of them appeared between 1958, the year of the transfer, and November 20, 1965. Among those who were buried there were Zalman ben Leib Hashkel, the first Harbin rabbi, and Rabbi Gaon Aharon Moshe ben Shmuel Kiselev, the Chief Rabbi of the Jewish communities of the Far East. In fall of 1996, the new fence and gate of the Harbin Jewish Cemetery was completed.

The Hong Kong Jewish cemetery is perhaps the only one that remains intact and in its original place since its founding on Chinese territory.

Chinese Policy towards Judaism: What, if there was any, has been official policy of China toward the Jews and their religious practice? While no documents related directly to this issue have ever been found, it appears that a liberal policy of "respecting their religion and changing not their customs and traditions" was followed by Chinese governments through history. The policy applies not only toward Jews and Judaism but also toward all foreign aliens and their faith. Accordingly, the dynasties or governments have instituted lenient policies toward the Jews, permitting them to live within the country, to practice religious activities, and to erect synagogues.

That policy was reflected in the case of Kaifeng Jews, whose stele records that the Song dynasty emperor gave permission for Jews to live in the then capital of China and to follow their own traditions.

The respect of the Chinese to Jews and Judaism is further shown by the grants of land by officials of different dynasties for the building or rebuilding of the synagogue. There is a presumption that in 1163 special permission was requested and granted to construct a unique building for the synagogue in Kaifeng. Presumably the same kind of permission was requested and granted each time the synagogue was destroyed, either by fire or by flood. The reconstruction of the synagogue in 1421 was under the direct sponsorship of the prince of Zhou, who was the younger brother of Ming emperor Chen Zu. The Imperial Cash Office subsidized the project. The 1489 inscription records confirm this. In 1461, a flood destroyed the synagogue completely except for its foundation. After the floodwaters subsided, the Jews of Kaifeng, headed by Ai Qin, petitioned the provincial commissioner, requesting a decree confirming the right of the community to rebuild the demolished synagogue on the original site of the ancient one. The permission was soon granted, and Kaifeng Jewry was able to reconstruct the house of worship; it was dedicated in 1489.

The best expression of that policy is perhaps a horizontal inscribed plaque granted by a Qing emperor, as well as vertical plaques and scrolls with couplets given them by local officials for the dedication of the newly completed synagogue that replaced the one destroyed in the Yellow River flood of 1642.

The local government once enacted a regulation that "strangers and carriers of pork cannot pass near the synagogue." This shows that the Jews of Kaifeng had absolutely full freedom of religion and that their customs are respected. There is no period in the entire history of the diaspora where the Jews enjoyed similar respect.

In the Republican period (1911-1949) the fact that a large number of Jewish refugees from Europe escaped to China suggests that Chinese authorities had a very positive policy toward Jews and their religion. They were given permissions to stay, to establish organizations, and to build synagogues. The Chinese government issued a number of statements to endorse Zionist movement. For instance, in 1920, Dr. Sun Yat-sen, the founding father for the Republic of China, wrote a letter to N.E.B. Ezra, secretary of the Shanghai Zionist Association, expressing support for the Jewish national cause. His letter says: "I have read your letter and copy of *Israel's Messenger* with much interest and wish to assure you of my sympathy for this movement which is one of the greatest movements of the present time. All lovers of democracy cannot help but support the movement to restore your wonderful and historic nation which has contributed so much to the civilization of the world and which rightly deserves an honorable place in the family of nations."

In 1947, Dr. Sun Fo, the son of Dr. Sun Yat-sen, and Chairman of the Chinese legislative body at the time, wrote to endorse once again the Zionist movement. His letter goes: "I wish to state that the Zionist

Movement is championing a worthy cause. I am glad that the late Dr. Sun Yat-Sen's sympathy for, and support of, the movement have produced results. As a lover of democracy, I fully endorse my late father's views."

The Chinese government during World War II was very sympathetic to Jewish refugees and acted to assist them by proposing to set up a settlement in Southwest China for those who were suffering in German occupied countries in Europe in 1939. According to the plan, the Chinese government would offer Jewish refugees the same rights of residence, work, and governmental protection as Chinese citizens. The plan was proposed after the annexation of Austria to the Reich in March, 1938, the fruitless Evian Conference on Jewish Refugees in July, 1938, and Kristalnacht, the massive persecution on German Jews after the attempt on the life of Secretary of the Legation vom Rath in Paris, which unleashed furies raged without bounds and restraint all over Germany and Austria with helpless Jews as their victims. The program unfortunately could not be implemented.

After the Communists took over, the Chinese government, especially local governments of cities where Jews lived, instituted a liberal policy toward the Jewish religion, permitting Jews to organize and carry on their regular activities. The Judaism was recognized as an approved religion. The Shanghai New Synagogue remained in operation until it was closed in 1956 because the severely decreased number of Jews. Special consideration and respect have been consistently shown to Jewish religious requirements by the authorities. In 1993, to mark the historic visit of Israeli President Chaim Herzog to China, the Shanghai government turned the original building of the Ohel Moses Synagogue into a museum. In 1998, the Shanghai government spent over $60,000 to restore the Ohel Rachel Synagogue as a historic site and open it to the public. The Harbin Jewish cemetery is now well taken care of by Chinese authorities. Though Judaism is not a religion recognized by the Chinese Government, two rabbis from Chabad-Lubavitch live in China to supervise religious practice and life in Beijing and Shanghai with the permission from Chinese government. All these can well be viewed as its respect for Judaism and Jewish people.

Bibliography

Kranzler, David, *Japanese, Nazis, and Jews. The Jewish Refugees Community of Shanghai, 1938–1945* (New York, 1976).
Leslie, Donald D., *The Survival of the Chinese Jews* (Leiden, 1975).
Leslie, Donald D., *The Chinese-Hebrew Memorial Book of the Jewish Community of Kaifeng* (Canberra, 1984).
Malek, Roman, ed., *From Kaifeng . . . to Shanghai. Jews in China, Monumenta Serica Monograph Series XLVI* (Sankt Augustin, 2000).
Pollak, Michael, *Mandarins, Jews and Missionaries* (Philadelphia, 1980).
White, William C., *Chinese Jews* (Toronto, 1942).

Xu Xin

CLONING: There is no gainsaying the fact that the world has witnessed quantum leaps in scientific and technological advances since the mid-nineteenth century or, according to Jewish reckoning, since 5600, i.e., the year six hundred in the sixth millennium. As foretold by the *Zohar, Bereshit* 117a, the benefits are not merely pragmatic; the explosion of human knowledge is categorized by the *Zohar* as the direct result of heavenly inspiration and serves to herald the advent of the eschatological era of the seventh millennium.

God revels himself in the processes of nature with the result that insightful understanding of the laws of nature is, in at least some minuscule way, tantamount to apprehension of the deity. Thus Maimonides, *Hilkhot Yesodei ha-Torah* 2:2, writes that love of God is acquired by reflection upon his wondrous created works in which his wisdom can be discerned and, in *Hilkhot Yesodei ha-Torah* 4:12, Maimonides declares that increased understanding of the nature of created entities carries with it enhanced love of God. Accordingly, the perfection of the universe of which the *Zohar* speaks in describing the burgeoning of knowledge as the harbinger of the eschatological era is at one and the same time both preparation in the physical sense, comparable to Sabbath preparations carried out on the preceding day, so that, with coming of the messiah, humanity may enjoy undisturbed leisure to engage in spiritual pursuits and perfection in the sense of intellectual preparation and development in the form of appreciation of the grandeur of creation, and hence of the Creator, so that humans will be equipped for a more profound understanding of the nature of God that will be attainable in the eschatological era.

There can be no doubt that unraveling the mysteries of procreation and the genesis of human life are integral to this process. Attempts to fathom those mysteries are entirely laudatory. Whether or not those endeavors yield any licit practical benefit is secondary; their major value, as well as that of all aspects of theoretical science, lies in qualitatively enhanced fulfillment of the commandment "And you shall love the Lord, your God" (Deut. 6:5). The legitimacy of acting upon such scientific information is another matter entirely. Surely every thinking person recognizes that not everything that can be done should be done; that which is possible is not for that reason moral.[1]

Not everything that *can* be done *should* be done. But it is a truism that, in the usual course of human events, that which *can* be done *will* be done.

Since the early 1970s, ethicists have grappled with the implications of human cloning.[2] What was then a vague specter now looms as an imminent reality. With the most recent breakthrough in the cloning of fetal mice in Hawaii, it is evident that "advances in science are coming faster than even the most confident scientists had imagined."[3] Dr. Lee Silver, a mouse geneticist and reproductive biologist at Princeton University, described the speed at which cloning has progressed as "breathtaking" and added, "Absolutely, we are going to have cloning of humans."[4] The protestation of scientists such as Dr. Ryuzo Yanagimachi, whose cloning experiments have electrified the scientific world, that "we should stick to reproduction the way that Mother Nature did for us"[5] notwithstanding, it is now conjectured that in vitro fertilization clinics will add human cloning to their repertoires within the next five to ten years.[6]

The new era of reproduction technology was ushered in with the birth of Dolly on July 5, 1996, at the Roslin Institute in Roslin, Scotland.[7] The birth of a cloned sheep was the culmination of research undertaken by Dr. Ian Wilmut on behalf of PPL Therapeutics Ltd., a small biotechnology company with headquarters in Edinburgh. The purpose was to use sheep to generate drugs for use in treating human diseases such as hemophilia and cystic fibrosis. Genetic engineering had already been employed to produce sheep whose milk contains a drug, alpha-1 antitrypsin, that is used in treatment of cystic fibrosis. The purpose of cloning sheep was to avoid the laborious and expensive process of genetically engineering large numbers of animals individually. With cloning, once an animal has been genetically adapted, the process need not be repeated; the animal can simply be cloned and, since all its clones will have identical genetic characteristics, the clones will produce the same drug.[8]

Research in cloning techniques has implications far beyond the goal of facilitating the manufacture of pharmaceutical products from genetically altered cells, which itself is potentially of far-reaching benefit in the treatment of numerous diseases and disorders. Cells of mature organs are capable of reproducing themselves but cannot be altered to form the cells of different organs. In effect, the DNA of differentiated cells is programmed to reproduce cells of one specialized type and of no other. Thus, for example, if a pancreas is destroyed, a new pancreas cannot be generated by other cells in the body. Successful cloning of adult cells demonstrates that, when inserted into an ovum, the program of a cell's DNA can be reversed thereby allowing the cell to reproduce and develop into cells of other bodily organs. When the process is more fully understood, it may become possible to create particular organs to replace ones that become diseased or destroyed.

As noted, with the successful cloning of Dolly, the prospect of human cloning became much more than a theoretical conjecture. The initial reaction of both ethicists and scientists was that human cloning is morally unacceptable. Then President Clinton, following the recommendation of the National Bioethics Advisory Commission, banned the use of federal money to conduct human cloning experiments and requested that privately funded enterprises adhere to a voluntary ban on human cloning. Nevertheless, at present, other than in California,[9] the cloning of a human being is perfectly legal in the United States, although it is prohibited by law in Britain, Spain, Denmark, Germany, and Australia.[10]

The climate of opinion has changed rapidly. Three decades ago, two fertility experts, Sophia J. Kleegman and Sherwin A. Kaufman, wrote that reproductive breakthroughs pass through several predictable stages. Reactions proceed from "horrified negation" to "negation without horror" to "slow and gradual curiosity, study, evaluation" and, finally, to "a very slow but steady acceptance."[11] The *volte face* that has occurred with regard to the prospect of human cloning is best expressed in a headline that appeared in the *New York Times*: "On Cloning Humans, 'Never' Turns Swiftly Into 'Why Not.'"[12] In that article Dr. Steen Willadsen, the cloning pioneer who developed the fundamental methods for cloning animals, is quoted as saying that it is just a matter of time before the first human is cloned. Earlier, John Paris, a Jesuit ethicist, remarked that he is certain that humans will be cloned: "I can't imagine a world in which someone won't try it. There are two things that drive man— power and money. And fame leads to fortune. Someone will try it."[13]

There is ample reason to assume that Jewish teaching would not frown upon cloning of either animals or humans simply because it is a form of asexual, and hence "unnatural," reproduction. B. San. 65b, relates that Hanina and Oshia met every Friday for the purpose of perusing *Sefer Yetzirah* in order to create a calf for their Sabbath meal. This anecdote is recounted by the Gemara without the slightest hint of censure. The text incontrovertibly yields two principles: (1) asexual husbandry, at least with regard to animal species, is morally innocuous; and (2) harnessing metaphysical forces, or "white magic," at least when practiced by masters of the Kabbalah, is acceptable. Although there is nothing in this narrative that may be cited as providing an explicit basis for extending such sanction to creation of a hybrid, interbreed, or genetically engineered animal, the report certainly reflects acceptance of the legitimacy of asexual, and hence homologous, reproduction of animals.

Although, from the vantage point of Jewish tradition, animal cloning presents no ideological or halakhic problem, the same cannot be said with regard to the cloning of a human being.

The ethical implications of fetal experimentation which, by its very nature, may result in the birth of a defective neonate were analyzed some time ago by the late Professor Paul Ramsey.[14] In the early days of *in vitro* fertilization, Professor Ramsey argued that such a procedure represented an immoral experiment upon a possible future life, since no researcher can exclude the possibility that he may do irreparable damage to the child-to-be. In the words of Professor Ramsey: "We ought not to choose for another the hazards he must bear, while choosing at the same time to give him life in which to bear them and to suffer our chosen experimentations."[15]

This argument is no less applicable to homologous reproduction than to artificial conception and is entirely consistent with the norms of Torah ethics. Jewish law does not sanction abortion motivated solely by a desire to eliminate a defective fetus, nor does it sanction sterile marriage as a means of preventing transmission of hereditary disorders. However, it does discourage marriages that would lead to the conception of such children. B. Yeb. 64b, states that a man should not marry into an epileptic or leprous family, i.e., a family in which three members have suffered from those diseases. This declaration represents a eugenic measure designed to prevent the birth of defective children. It follows, *a fortiori*, that overt intervention in natural processes that might cause defects in the fetus would be viewed with opporobrium by Judaism.

It has also been suggested in some quarters that cloning may be morally acceptable in situations in which the sole child of parents who have become infertile develops a terminal disease. By means of cloning, the parents could use a cell obtained from the child to create another child who would be an exact replica of the child they are about to lose. However, tragic as such cases may be, there is nothing in those circumstances halakhically to distinguish the situation from more usual situations of infertility.

Nevertheless, there are some very rare situations in which cloning, despite the attendant risks, may be regarded as moral and even laudatory. Despite the contrary view of some early-day authorities, the overwhelming consensus of Rabbinic opinion is that restrictions governing interpersonal relationships, including the prohibitions against theft and "wounding," are treated no differently from purely religious prohibitions and are suspended in face of danger to human life.

There have been unfortunate cases of children afflicted with leukemia whose only chance of survival is a bone marrow transplant. To be successful, a donor must be genetically compatible; otherwise the transplant will be rejected. When bone marrow of family members is incompatible, finding a suitable match is exceedingly difficult. There have been cases of the mother of such a child becoming pregnant in the hope that the newly-born child will be a suitable donor. However, the statistical probability that the child will be a compatible donor is only twenty-five percent. If cloning were available, parents, in such rare situations, could clone the ill child. The newly-born infant would be disease-free but would be genetically identical to its afflicted sibling. Medically, the child would be an ideal donor.

There may well be other forms of research requiring cloning designed to find a cure for disease that may benefit individuals who are in the category of a *holeh le-faneinu*, i.e., individuals for whom the danger and potential benefit is regarded as actual rather than merely hypothetical. Under such limited circumstances—and only in such circumstances—human cloning, when scientifically prudent and undertaken with appropriate safeguards, may be deemed appropriate and halakhically sound.

More significantly, cloning technology may prove to be extremely beneficial in cell and tissue therapy. Embryonic stem cells have the ability to differentiate into any cell type and, in theory, could be produced from human blastocysts. Perfection of cloning procedures would make it possible for a person to provide the nucleus of his own cell to replace the nucleus of a donor egg. Stem cells could then be taken from the developing blastocyst and induced to differentiate in culture.[16] Those cells would be genetically identical to those of the person from whom the nucleus was taken, with the result that cell and tissue replacement would be possible without the problems of rejection currently attendant upon transplantation. Rejection of transplants occurs because the body's immune system recognizes the transplanted tissue as foreign. Cloned tissue is genetically identical to the tissue from which it is cloned and hence will not be rejected. The goal of such technology would be the cloning of human tissues and organs rather than of human beings. Although the cloning of human beings is highly problematic, the cloning of tissues and organs for therapeutic purposes is entirely salutary.

Society certainly has reason to regard development of cloning technology with concern. Such concern is by no means limited to the exaggerated fear of the specter of mad scientists engaging in cloning for nefarious purposes (à la *The Boys from Brazil*). Quite apart from the earlier discussion regarding concern for potential defects in the clonee, society has reason to fear that untrammeled cloning may result in a disproportionate number of clones of one gender, that a multiplicity of persons identical to one another may spell confusion and give rise to an assortment of social problems, and that idiosyncratic preferences may create an imbalance in the distribution of physical attributes and human talents. These and other demographic concerns are quite real. Tampering with natural processes in a manner that would lead to social upheaval is not included in man's mandate "to fill the earth and conquer

it" (Gen. 1:28). Assuredly, society is justified in preventing such a situation from arising. Accordingly, society has both the right and the obligation to regulate experimental endeavors designed to perfect techniques necessary for successful cloning of humans. The goal of such regulation should be assurance that those skills be utilized only for purposes that are beneficial to society.

Notes

[1] Cf., the statement "...what is technically possible is not for that reason morally admissible," Congregation for the Doctrine of the Faith, *Instruction on Respect for Human Life in its Origin and on the Dignity of Procreation (Donum Vitae)* (February 22, 1987), introduction, sec. 3. Although that document is not an expression of Jewish teaching, the validity of the quoted axiom is self-evident.

[2] See Willard Gaylin, "The Frankenstein Myth Becomes a Reality: We Have the Awful Knowledge to Make Exact Copies of Human Beings," in *New York Times Magazine*, March 5, 1972, pp. 12-13, 41-49.

[3] *New York Times*, July 23, 1998, p. A1.

[4] Ibid., p. A20.

[5] *New York Times*, July 24, 1998, p. A12.

[6] *New York Times*, July 23, 1998, p. A20. In an editorial accompanying the report of the cloning of Dolly, the editors of *Nature* voiced the opinion that "Cloning humans from adults' tissues is likely to be achievable any time from one to ten years from now." See *Nature*, vol. 385, no. 6619 (February 27, 1997), p. 753.

[7] A full report of the methods employed in causing that event to occur was published by I. Wilmut, et al., "Viable Offspring Derived from Fetal and Adult Mammalian Cells," in *Nature*, vol. 385, no. 6619 (February 27, 1997), pp. 810-813.

[8] See Gina Kolata, *Clone: The Road to Dolly and the Path Ahead* (New York, 1998), p. 25.

[9] *New York Times*, December 2, 1997, p. A24.

[10] *Clone*, p. 32.

[11] Sophia J. Kleepman and Sherwin A. Kaufman, *Infertility in Women: Diagnosis and Treatment* (Philadelphia, 1966), p. 178.

[12] December 2, 1997, p. A1.

[13] *Clone*, p. 39.

[14] Paul Ramsey, "Shall We 'Reproduce'?" in *Journal of the American Medical Association*, vol. 220, no. 10 (June 5, 1972), pp. 1346-1350, and vol. 220, no. 11 (June 12, 1972), pp. 1480-1485; and idem, *The Ethics of Fetal Research* (New Haven, 1975).

[15] Paul Ramsey, *Journal of the American Medical Association*, vol. 220, no. 11, p. 135.

[16] The most frequent discussion of this issue in a medical context is in conjunction with post-mortem dissection of a corpse. For a discussion

of the propriety of destroying nascent human life generated in this manner and at this very early stage of development see this writer's *Contemporary Halakhic Problems*, IV (New York, 1995), p. 24, n. 10, and his *Bioethical Dilemmas: A Jewish Perspective* (Hoboken, 1998), pp. 209-211.

J. David Bleich

Codification of Jewish Law— Medieval: The sources of Jewish law are scattered widely. Ancient Jewish texts were not organized so as to discuss all the laws pertinent to a subject in single entries; rather, the laws are enumerated by the needs of larger discussions of legal principles. Thus the Talmud could discuss six legal topics in regards to one principle on one page and another ten in regards to another principle on another page. The subject matter of one topic might be continued hundreds of pages later in another discussion. Codifiers thus needed to integrate widely flung topics into single categories, even though the principles governing the particulars might be quite diverse. In the new organization, various insights emerged so that the code did not merely pass down a heritage but re-evaluated the heritage by framing new ways to see old materials. Thus codification not only summed up the achievements of the past but produced new territory for further discovery.

In light of this, study of legal traditions and their codification should stand at the helm of all Jewish studies. Z. Fraenkel's "Entwurf einer Geschichte der Literatur der nachtalmudischen Responsen," in *Jahresbericht des judische-theologische Seminars "Fraenckelscher Stiftung,"* (Breslau, 1865), and detailed articles by J. Lauterbach, L. Ginzberg, and moderns such as I. Ta-Shma begun this work. Still, not much has been done to investigate the history of Jewish law. Ch. Tchernowitz, *Toledot haHalachah* (New York, 1935-1950) *and Toledot haPoskim* (New York, 1946-1948) attempted descriptive analysis. More recently, E.E. Urbach, *haHalachah Mekorotehah veHitpat'chutah* (Givatayim, 1984) and Y.D. Gilat, *Perakim beHishtalshelutah haHalachah* (Bar-Ilan, Ramat-Gan, 1992) have made incisive contributions to this enterprise.

Other scholars are interested in historical data, economic facts, and social information but not the legal theories and principles of the sweeping collections of codes and *responsa* in their own right. Such studies are useful in setting the legal works in historical perspective. The texts form an entire universe and their internal dialogues and arguments run a centuries long course. Each major work reflects tension with the local customs of places different from those of its authors and even with the prevailing customs of the locale of the authors. Maintaining the authority of the authors often required later glosses, which harmonized these tensions. It thus could be argued that changes in law and practice resulted much more from dealing with fresh life situations than from raw legal dynamics. One should be wary of speaking about "development." The legal decisors had to be innovative to use the authoritative but fertile words of past sages in new ways to justify their innovative decisions. The works of certain decisors became authoritative due to their intellectual statures and pious reputations. The ancient rabbis thus accurately said that a legal scholar is greater than a prophet (B. B.B. 12a). The prophet merely forecasts the resurrection of the dead; the legal scholar resurrects the living—not only the living word of God, as they saw it, but the very life of the community. Theirs was God's work, holy and sacred. They sensed their responsibility was not merely entrusted to them by their communities but by God. The study of these works encompasses no less than the study of the heart of Jews until modern times.

The history of Jewish law during the First and Second Temple periods is veiled from historical enquiry. In the nineteenth century, scholars held that a single antique law had slowly given way to a newer talmudic halakhah. Abraham Geiger used various Greek biblical texts and psedepigrapha, Samaritan texts, Syriac Bibles, and the works of Josephus and Philo to show that many communities had laws different from those of the rabbis. He argued that certain rabbis espoused these earlier laws and that some versions of Targumim also preserved them. In the Rabbinic period, he claimed, these laws slowly changed to conform to new ideas that drove a wedge between the Pharisees and Sadducees. He also claimed that some parts of Rabbinic literature actually preserve the older law, which is buried within the formulations of newer laws. Since the Dead Sea Scrolls preserve older readings while the later Masada scrolls are closer to Rabbinic ones, a few scholar have reconsidered Geiger's thesis. They suggest that Hillel (or another rabbi/Pharisee) brought the Rabbinic biblical texts together with another version of halakhah from Babylonia. They suggest that this version of the written and oral law was of equal antiquity with the older Palestinian laws. At present there is no way to settle these issues.

Be this as it may, we can trace the foundations of medieval law from the period of the Mishnah, to the Talmud, to the Geonic works, and then into medieval codes. We can see how laws that applied in one circumstance were adjusted to take on different forms from those plainly stated in earlier texts. Still, it is not clear that changes in rulings always responded to cultural changes. The evidence, rather, often points to the decisor's legal endeavors' being separated from the issues of contemporary life. Thus, while historians have attempted to identify cultural reasons for differing approaches to Jewish law, they have not been able to contend with the extent to which authorities from widely devergent times and cultures often made identical legal choices, often repeating older traditions and neglecting the needs of their own cultures. Thus halakhists have served as walls against encroaching dominant cultures.

Jewish law preserved timeworn tradition in far-flung communities by orally circulating its culture for many hundreds of years within the foreign cultures that dominated Jews. Various groups taught these laws with considerable divergence but with remarkable similarity and unity as well. Only in the eighteenth century did the Ashkenazic legal tradition hit a barrier that prevented the entirety of Jewish law from forming the culture of the Jew. Prior to this, foreign influences were subtly absorbed and addressed but never became outright the framework of the Jew's life. When the Jew, even the most traditional, entered modern European society, as a pariah to be sure, the civil and judicial aspects of halakhah became more and more restricted until only the ritual and family aspects of the massive legacy continued to be addressed in any practical manner. After the Temple fell 70 C.E. it had been noted that God was confined now to the four ells of the halakhah (B. Ber. 8a). Of this legacy barely one ell survived in the life of the modern Jew. That one ell has had to expand to fill the space of the four ells.

If we examine the fertile ground of Spain, we find the codes of Alfasi (11 c., Morocco/Spain), Maimonides (12 c., Spain/Egypt), Jacob son of ROSH (14 c., Spain), and Joseph Caro (16 c., Spain/Portugal/Turkey/Palestine). The progression shows an interesting development in Sephardic Jewry. Alfasi decides law among the various options left by earlier decisors but follows the order of the Talmud, shows the talmudic arguments, and removes almost all homiletic material. Maimonides organizes topics into categories and subdivisions bringing all sources to bear but innovating little in the content of the decisions except to remove the talmudic dialectics and add homiletic material. Alfasi and Maimonides might be considered a single work since, by looking at Alfasi, one sees the material from which Maimonides composed his code. Jacob's TUR (presenting 13,350 practical laws) built on Maimonides (presenting 15,000 laws both practical and Temple oriented) organization and refined it. He amalgamated his father's French and German traditions. He cites arguments of decisors over controversial decisions and fixes the law. Joseph Caro's *Shulhan Arukh* keeps TUR's organization but drops almost all homiletic materials. He inclines to Maimonides' views, incorporates the views of some later decisors, and does not often present the arguments of past decisors or their rationales.

From Alfasi/Maimonides to TUR we see a lapse of two centuries, and from TUR to *Shulhan Arukh* we see another two centuries. In these interim centuries, more codes were produced in Ashkenazic lands. Following the publication of Maimonides' code, we find SMAG (Moses of Coucy) imitates

Maimonides' presentation of his *Sefer haMitzvot* and incorporates his rulings from his code with additions of German and French practices but generally follows the wording of the Talmud. ROSH (13 c.) imitates the style of *RIF* with additions of the French and German Tosafists. After *TUR* we find *SMAK* (Isaac of Corbeil) producing a new code for German and French communities. In the same period of the late thirteenth century, we have *Hagahot Maimunniyot*, which became incorporated as a commentary to Maimonides *Mishneh Torah*. He in fact incorporated the German and French practices. *Shulhan Arukh* was first printed in 1565, a full century after *TUR* (1475). Other works remained in manuscript for the most part.

In the period between Maimonides and Jacob *TUR*, we find German authors like the authors of *Mordecai* and *Sefer Mitzvot Ketanot* (SMAK) composing code-like treatises. But the widespread works that became normative were the Spanish ones, albeit with Ashkenazic commentaries. *TUR* is glossed by *BAH* (Joel Sirkes 1561-1640) and *Darkei Moshe* (Moses Isserles). *Shulhan Arukh* was glossed by *Rema* (Moses Isserles, 1527-1572), *Magen Avraham* (Abraham Gombiner, 1637-1683), *Sefer Meirat Eynaim* (or *SMA*, Joshua Falk 17 c.), *ShACH* (Rabbi Shabbtai ha-Kohen, 1621-1662), *TAZ* (David ben Shmuel ha-Levi, 1586-1667), *Bet Shmuel* (Shmuel ben Uri Shraga Phoebus, late 17 c., a commentary to) *Helqat Mehoqeq* (Moses Lima of Brisk early 17 c.).

In the wake of the shifting of communities from Muslim Babylonia to Muslim Spain and from Palestine to Germany and from both Muslim Spain and Christian Germany to Christian Spain, the unique patterns of community law and custom were disturbed. Only after a process of acculturation and accommodation leading to legal conciliation did the codes emerge to solidify matters. At times the latest authority held sway, at other times the majority opinion won out, and at other times the more prominent authority won the day. We need to observe that each code is produced in the long aftermath of political upheavals when Jewish communities had settled into their new situations. *RIF*/Maimonides' code

is produced as Islam establishes its culture in North Africa, Spain, and the East and Jews feel their culture overwhelmed by emerging Islamic fanaticism. Maimonides fled Spain to come to Egypt. *TUR*'s code is established as Christianity dominates Spain and Europe and wants to dominate the world. The author's father fled Germany to come to Spain. Caro's *Shulhan Arukh* becomes established as the refugees from Spain and Portugal find refuge in the Ottoman Empire and Jewish scholars recognize the need to find a single authoritative voice. Caro himself was such a refugee.

With the merging of communities in the wake of dislocations, the homogeneity of hundreds of years of life in a unified Kehilla ended. The new communities needed guidance to navigate their new heterogeneous society, in which Jews with different traditions lived in close proximity. The codes answered such needs. These particular works do not always illustrate high points in Jewish culture but rather points in which scholars want to demonstrate the vision that they are re-establishing the Torah for generations that survived mass conversions, expulsions, and martyrdoms. Maimonides attempted to replace the Talmud for the masses with his work, *TUR* wanted to produce a work that would become the accessible curriculum for all Jews, and Caro sought to establish a practical textbook for young scholars to become fluent in Jewish law. Apparently, none of them envisioned that their work would ever be replaced.

Codes were written at the end of periods of intense halakhic activity, when Jewish life looked chaotic and previous codes were applied variably or disregarded entirely. Now a code would attract re-interpretations commensurate with current opinion. The mingling of communities after political shifts created confusion, and new codes came to adjudicate the constant shifting of opinion that resulted. As earlier works ceased serving their purposes, scholars saw the practicality in producing a work not merely as an appendage to the tradition but to stand on its own without reference to earlier works. As the earlier codes were cluttered by commentaries, new ones attempted to redo them, incorporating the bend of the commentaries into a single work, only to attract new commentaries. Since the commentaries were not immediately printed on the page with the code, it became cumbersome for the student to use the code. The convergence of swelling of commentary and historical insecurity worked in favor of the production of new codes addressing new audiences. The *Shulhan Arukh* was the first to have commentaries attached to it within a century of its production and thus became a fixed text until the present. This is so even though new codes and commentaries appeared frequently.

The new works do not at all appear to indicate the degree of social and political change of Jews but, on the contrary, look fixed, authoritative, and beyond time or condition. They present a picture of communities that lived suspended in their own never-changing culture. It is true that commentaries do show the conservative nature of the code and attempt at times to show how the principles should work in present times. Different communities might follow different rules. The study of law and works of decisors gave the impression of a stable society with no social or political change. Indeed for the Jew there was little. As they were politically weak and socially outcast, their codes produced the sense of a territory with effective courts and power. Jews saw themselves living in a kingdom ruled by God with Rabbinic authorities adjudicating God's will throughout their small towns and larger cities. Jews understood themselves to have the superior culture, the one chosen by God in its every detail. If not for sin, God would surely redeem Israel immediately. With the growth of messianic longing, the codes brought stability to a world too ready to follow the next messiah who would pronounce that Jewish piety had served its purpose to mend the broken world.

The roots of the Jewish legal practices go back to the very roots of ancient Israel. Our very first indications of law in the Bible already indicate that God gave these laws to Moses. Yet the Bible is reticent about most of the ways in which the covenantal society ought to function and quiet about the details of how these ways were lived

and taught for centuries. Various theories of these details developed in post-biblical times. One particular view of these laws circulated above all others and, eventually, the laws according to this view were collected and set down in the Mishnah. The idea was that God had communicated all necessary details to Moses. However, the Mishnah was not pedagogically attuned. Its books could begin with the most obtuse materials. The Mishnah's topics reflected the unstated, theoretical principles that generated the various laws. This arrangement served as a magnet to develop legal theory beyond the pure statement of law. However, no one could study the materials without extensive training and tutoring. These laws continued to be passed down orally, to be debated and further discussed. Refinements of the Mishnah's laws were eventually redacted into the Talmuds. Yet the laws continued to be taught orally by the heads of the academies who maintained the tradition of the oral law. With the total dispersal of the Jews under the Muslims and Christians, the fluid text was set down in several rescensions. The Talmud proved to be an unwieldy work for the shifting communities. A need arose for scholars to sift through talmudic and midrashic materials to standardize practices and strengthen the scattered Jews with uniform decisions.

Many teachers and students had written notes on various topics. The very talented teacher, Ahai (mid 8th c.) organized legal and homiletic materials based on the discussions of the Talmud(s) and Midrashim around the weekly Torah readings. Typically, he began by exploring legal problems connected to the Torah reading ("May our masters instruct us"). To answer, he combined Scripture and talmudic materials in most creative narratives. Apparently in opposition to the Karaites, he stressed Rabbinic legislation and followed the Babylonian Talmud and Palestinian Midrashim quite literally in reading Rabbinic laws back into Scriptures. In a few instances he utilized the Talmud Yerushalmi. He completed his work in the land of Israel after leaving the Babylonian academy of Pumbeditha. His work had a lasting influence on his successors.

Yehudai Gaon and his students (8 c.) produced a noteworthy compilation of laws. The *Halachot Pesukot* (= *sefer re'u*), which has not reached us in prime condition, is a compendium of laws based on talmudic statements. It follows the order of the talmudic chapters but there has been some internal reorganization to keep subject matters together in orderly progression. The interesting facet of this work is that it is written in Hebrew and slavishly translates Aramaic talmudic phrases, which sound rather odd in Hebrew. These translations were popular with later scholars who cite talmudic passages sometimes in the Hebrew form of the *Halachot Pesukot*.

Following this work (some place it earlier), we find the popular *Halachot Gedolot* attributed to Shimon Kayyara, which organizes legal material according to the schema that there are 613 commandments. This is the first known work in which the author presents his purposes and methods in an introduction. The presentation is somewhat dry and lacks legal analysis. The bare law is given utilizing the talmudic and midrashic language of the source. The work utilizes language of *Halachot Pesukot* and even the *She'iltot*. Of interest is the emphasis of hanging rabbinic laws on biblical verses and considering them biblical. It seems this work is also aimed at undermining the claims of Karaites that Rabbinic Jews have deserted the plain sense of the Torah. Following this work, we find a spate of Geonic texts based on varying enumerations of the 613 biblical commandments. There are also works dedicated to listing at length the rules concerning single legal subjects. Saadia Gaon wrote both of these types. Yet the crowning achievement of deciding talmudic law belongs to Isaac Alfasi.

The *RIF* (Rabbi Yitzhak ben Ya'acov Alfasi, 1013-1103) copied out talmudic discussions in his massive *Sefer haHalachot*, omitting opinions he thought were to be rejected. Sometimes he gathered together laws on certain subjects and wrote exclusive works on them. His writings attracted a number of important commentaries and like works. The most important of the latter was penned by Moses Maimonides (*RAMBAM*,

1135-1204), whose work is loosely based on the practical decisions of the *RIF* but in presentation and analysis is entirely original. Maimonides mentions consulting ancient talmudic texts to clarify readings in some four places. He developed a style of Hebrew legal language that has held throughout the centuries. His code, the *Mishneh Torah* (or *Yad haHazakah*), in fourteen volumes followed neither the order of Scripture nor the order of the Talmud. Maimonides organized the entire legacy of Rabbinic Judaism into a comprehensive presentation of the logic and form of all laws in the tradition, practical or non-practical. He omitted all names of talmudic rabbis in order to give the impression of a single unified document that transcended time or geography. On the other hand, Rabbenu Asher ben Yehiel (1250-1327), known as *ROSH*, composed a reworking of the legal passages of the Talmud along the lines of the *RIF* but utilizing the methods of the French and German Tosafists. His son Jacob (fourteenth c.) wrote the second totally comprehensive code, the *Arba'a Turim*, based on his father's approach. It remained for Joseph Caro to couple the *TUR*'s precise form of organization with a comprehensive approach that harmonized Maimonides' rulings with the Tosafist's approach to Talmud.

Maimonides wrote his work in a succinct Hebrew style after the manner of the Mishnah and legal Midrashim but not without lapses into Arabic syntax and medieval Hebrew prosody. Although he adhered to Alfasi's legal decisions, his work is totally different in style and content. His organization, first and foremost, is dependent on commandments from the Bible, and he divides his chapters into units showing the logical and sometimes chronological development of laws. What he has done can be compared to a mechanic who goes to a hundred buildings to find screws and discrete parts, some hidden under carpets, and then constructs of them a handsome automobile. Maimonides (perhaps with a minor exception) does not reveal the reason he arranged his topics as he has, and the student must grapple with the logic of his plan over the fourteen volumes of his composition. Except when he found compelling reason to do otherwise, he kept the order of topics close to that of Scripture or the Mishnah. With astounding clarity and incredible ingenuity, he wove together sources from Scripture, Targumim, the Talmuds, the legal Midrashim, the aggadic midrashim, and sources no longer known to us.

The reader senses that no word is missing, nothing extraneous. For example, in the Laws of Hanukkah 3:1, Maimonides adds a few words to B. Shab. 21b. Whereas the Talmud leaves it that a miracle occurred so that a vial of undefiled oil sufficient for one day lasted a full eight, Maimonides adds that such time was needed to produce fresh, undefiled oil. The narrative reads so smoothly and so coherently that one does not sense that Maimonides interpolated into the familiar narrative his own clarifying material. What goes unstated in the Talmud, Maimonides says. His aim was to provide a clear insight into the finely honed systems of talmudic legal pronouncements. He seamlessly blended classical sources, his own exegesis, and terms and ideas of previous codifiers together. Close examination shows he said more than meets the eye, and many have tried to unravel his deceptively simple writing to show his profound achievements. Many great scholars have spent their lives contemplating his every word.

Maimondes' *Book of Commandments* (*Sefer haMitzvot*), written in Arabic, developed his fourteen principles for deciding the mechanisms of how the rabbis determined scriptural law. He followed this by a detailed listing and exposition of the positive and negative commandments in the Hebrew Bible. Besides considering this work and his work on the legal portions of the Yerushalmi, one can gain further insight into Maimonides' methods of talmudic study by examining his *Commentary to the Mishnah*, completed when he was thirty-three. Also his letters shed much light on the rulings in his codes. Only by considering the pertinent talmudic passages and cognate literatures can one appreciate Maimonides' labors. His approach was to prefer the plainest understanding of his sources without harmonizing conflicting passages, as was the method of the Tosafists. Maimonides therefore considered many talmudic arguments based on Scripture merely to be poetic articulations of Scripture's breadth but not really the intent of the Scriptural verse. The laws were binding within the Rabbinic system but not that of Scripture. It bears noting that Maimonides' desire to teach some elements of Aristotelian science created a stir in scholastic circles that lasted for centuries.

Maimonides philosophical insights into the nature of theodicy, providence, prophecy and other issues were reserved for his introduction to his commentary on Mishnah Avot, called *Eight Chapters*, and his *Guide for the Perplexed*. His legal code is a work of extreme diligence and is the only post-mishnaic work to cover the entire span of Jewish law, including the laws of kings, sacrifices, and purities. This work has stimulated more study of the Talmuds than any other legal work. He examined the finest and most ancient manuscripts of the Bible and the Talmuds, at times telling us about his collections. He tells us about a Talmud manuscript that dated to about 700 written on parchment. Maimonides' concern with sociological and psychological issues shines through his presentation. Note his listing of the sixth of the positive commandments in his *Book of the Commandments*.

> By this biblical injunction we are commanded to mix and associate with wise men. [We are instructed] to be constant in their gatherings. [We are to accomplish such association] through every possible manner: service, fellowship in food and drink, and business affairs. The purpose in our doing so is that we may succeed in emulating their actions and in acquiring true views from their words.

In "The Laws of Doctrines" (*Hilchot De'ot*) 6:2 he describes this commandment in greater detail, but here he reverses the task of the verses cited in his *Book of the Commandments*. An examination of the talmudic sources shows some slight conflation of sources and even personal additions in his code. At times Maimonides deletes explanatory additions in the talmudic texts in order to present the original forms more clearly; at other times he expands the classical sources. But there is next to nothing in his laws that cannot be found somewhere in the traditions, Babylonian and Palestinian, talmudic and midrashic, scriptural and targumic. Where there is, he tells us what his personal opinion would be.

An interesting example of the complexity of Maimonides rulings derives from Maimonides' belief that the Jews' supreme duty is to sanctify God, *kiddush ha-shem*. A central requirement of this duty is that, in particular circumstances, one must surrender one's life rather than reject God and God's laws. In his *Book of Commandments*, Maimonides registered the duty of sanctifying God's Name as the ninth positive commandment:

> The meaning of this commandment is that we are commanded to publicize the true faith in the world, and not to fear any consequences, so that, even if there come a tyrant who calls on us to deny him, the Exalted One, we are not to obey him. Rather, we must be prepared to give up our very lives, and not to have him think that we have denied him. We must do this [even though one might outwardly obey,] although in our hearts we would still believe in him, the Exalted One. . . . Every Jewish person is obligated to sanctify God's name . . . as was stated in the Sifra, "I am the Lord who has taken you out of Egypt to be your God"—this means, "in order that you shall sanctify my name in public."

Maimonides in "Laws of the Foundations of Torah" (*Hilchot Yesodei haTorah*) 5:1 states:

> All members of the Jewish people are commanded to sanctify the great Name of God as it is written: "And I will be sanctified among the people of Israel (Lev. 22:32)." They are admonished not to profane it, as it is written: "And thou shalt not profane my holy Name (Lev. 18:21)."

Maimonides, Laws of the Foundations of the Torah 5:2, 3, follows the ruling of Yohanan (B. San. 74b) that to fulfill the commandment of sacrificing one's life to sanctify God's name requires that ten Jews witness the act of martyrdom. Yohanan noted that the verse, "And I shall be sanctified among the people of Israel" (Lev. 22:32) had been interpreted to mean among at least ten Jews. On the other hand, there are three laws, idolatry, illicit

sexual relations, and murder, where the rabbis learned that one must forfeit one's life and not transgress even in private. The same would apply to any commandment a Jew was forced to abrogate in times of persecution, when Jews were being forced to apostatize. An abrogation of any commandment under duress is tantamount to apostasy.

In his *Letter on Apostasy* [*Igeret haShemad*], Maimonides writes that the performance of the commandment of the sanctification of God's name was the objective of the Exodus, and he summarizes what he said in his *Mishneh Torah* on the subject:

> Just as the profanation of God's Name is such a great sin, so also the sanctification of God's name is a great mitzvah. A very great reward is in store for him on its account. . . . The rigor of this commandment can be seen when it is compared to the other commandments in the Torah. Regular commandments (in normal times) must be abrogated to save one's life, but not that of "And I will be sanctified among the people of Israel." It is the only one that overshadows the saving of one's life. The principle of "And thou shalt live by them" which means "and not die for them" does not apply to the positive command to sanctify God's name.

A quick glance at the laws of Foundations of the Torah 5:4 shows us how serious the law of sanctifying God's name is:

> Anyone who disregards the obligation to live and martyrs himself when he should have lived will forfeit his soul. But one who martyrs himself under the proper circumstances sanctifies God's name . . . while if he did not he desecrates God's name. . . . Still he cannot be punished by any court for he acted under duress. . . . Yet, one who can escape from the evil tyrant and does not . . . is considered as one who willfully worshipped idols and will be chased out of the afterworld to the lowest level of hell.

Nimukei Yosef (Joseph Habiba, 14 c.), the acclaimed student of RAN (Rabbi Nissin Gererondi, 1310-1375), claimed that Maimonides himself would permit a well known pietist and saint to martyr himself where that act was certain to instill faith and resolve among the general Jewish population in trying times.

But Maimonides was silent on the question of how far one can go to avoid getting out of a situation that would call for martyrdom. It was common for the Jews in Germany and France to martyr themselves during the Crusades, especially that of 1096. Many Ashkenazic decisors permitted such acts of popular martyrdom where the letter of the law did not demand it if the Jewish faith was endangered. Among these were the Tosafists. But in *Letter on Apostasy* Maimonides took another path. He recommended that in times of persecution when Jews are killed if they do not convert to a non-Jewish faith, one is to hide in one's house and escape the country at the first opportunity. Yet, he did not strongly condemn those who were forced to submit, although they should have chosen to martyr themselves.

Would Maimonides have permitted one to pretend to be a non-Jew to escape persecution and martyrdom? *Radbaz* (David ibn Zimra, 16 c.) claims not. Nimukei Yosef does not cite what he thinks Maimonides would have said on the matter but claims it is clear that such behavior should be permitted as long as he does not profess with his mouth that he is a convert. Muslims used to claim that Maimonides himself had converted to Islam during the Almohades' persecutions, but there is no reason to accept their word when they have claimed the same about other important Jews. *Radbaz,* who has harsh words for anyone who would give into pressure or even pretend to be a Christian, lived during the martyrdoms and apostasies of the Spanish and Portuguese Inquisitions.

After 1215, the edict of the Fourth Lateran Council required Jews to dress differently from non-Jews and to pay taxes to the Church on properties that had been purchased from Christians. The effect was a series of wide ranging ordinances passed by local communities to require Jews to wear special clothing, usually a badge of shame, and to pay general taxes to Christian clergy. It appears that even prior to, this various communities had required Jews to pay such taxes.

Let us examine background materials that reflect on this problem. We begin with a startling connection of sources on the Ten Commandments as framed by (Shlomo) Ephraim son of Aaron of Lunshitz in his biblical commentary called *Kli Yakar, The Precious Vessel.* He noted that unlike the last eight commandments of the Decalogue, the first two are phrased as God speaking in direct address to Israel in the first person ("I am the Lord . . . thou shalt not have other gods before me") and not in reference to God in the third person. Why so?

> The final eight commandments of the Decalogue apply in the land and out of the land, whether the temple is standing or not standing. On the other hand, the first two commandments, Exod. 20:2, *viz,* "I am (the Lord thy God who took you out of the land of Egypt from the house of bondage)" and "Thou shalt not have (other gods before me)" can only apply when Israel dwells on their own soil and God communes with them directly and does not conceal himself. When we, his children, are banished from his table (divine presence in the Temple), then the words "I am the Lord thy God" have no viable reality to them. Our sages have noted that "One who dwells outside of the land is *as if* he has no God." Likewise the words "thou shalt not have *other gods*" have no viable reality to them in our exile. The bible stated that *there* (in the lands of the nations) you will worship *other gods* which RASHI explained to mean that payment of taxes to gentile clergy is considered by the Torah as if one did worship (other gods).

For *Kli Yakar,* RASHI and the sages have equal authority to give definitive meaning to the texts. For him, the first two commandments have no absolute possible applications while Jews live in foreign cultures and are thus cut off from the possibility of divine communication and cultural, economic integrity. Paying taxes to support gentile clergy is tantamount to idol worship; the implication remains that Jews are not to do anything further to worship idols, and thus Ephraim of Lunshitz drew the connection between other gods in the ten commandments, "other gods" in Deuteronomy, and RASHI's limitation of the limit a Jew can allow himself in social and political integration with foreign religious cultures.

Rabbi Asher ben Yehiel, ROSH (13 c.), a student of Meir of Rothenberg, developed an interesting mixture of code and commentary to the Talmud. By reviewing each phrase of the Talmud as the subject to applicable rulings, he rephrased the Talmud subtly to reflect the views of the Tosafists. Where Alfasi had been content to omit talmudic interpretations of the Mishnah that he saw as too wide of the intent of the Mishnah, ROSH included them. In tandem with acting as paraphrist of the Talmud to sharpen his own legal views, he revised the text of the Tosafists to reflect the clarity of his own views of them. He does not name those he rejects, but it is clear he does at times argue with Alfasi and Maimonides and others. ROSH (2:4) to Avodah Zarah (84) says that those who think the Talmud Yerushalmi permits one to pretend to be an idol-worshipper to save his life is mistaken. For in pretending to be a gentile, he in fact makes himself a gentile, since tyrants want Jews to act as gentiles and not as Jews. Such pretense is tantamount to conversion and renunciation of the Jewish faith. On the other hand, if there are persecutions against rabbis and a rabbi denies he is one, he has not renounced his faith, since there are many faithful Jews who are not rabbis.

ROSH, consistent in his outlook, states in Baba Qamma (ROSH 10:11) that it is forbidden for a Jew to pretend to be a non-Jew even if just to escape from paying tariffs to gentiles. It is tantamount to denying his religion. His interpretation of a talmudic passage (B. B.Q. 117a) is to oppose views such as the German student of RASHI who edited (and at times changed) RASHI's talmudic commentary (Baba Qamma ch. 10) and attached it to the RIF (under RASHI's name). This editor of RASHI's commentary to the Talmud understood the Talmud to mean that, in theory, one can pretend to be a gentile, by wearing forbidden mixtures, to evade taxes as long as there is no infringement of Jewish laws. In practice, one should not evade the tax laws, or any monetary laws, of countries in which one dwells. It is doubtful he would say this categorically where loss of life or limb was involved. On the other hand, like the ROSH, Radbaz tells us that it is clear no Jew can pretend to be a gentile even when no issue of ritual infringements are present. He says this in his commentary to Maimonides' Code, Laws of

Forbidden Mixtures 10:18. Further, in his responsa, Radbaz (s. 1137) gives us greater detail:

> Whether to save money or even life it is forbidden to claim to be a gentile. If one asks him who he is, he is to say, "I am a Jew" and trust in God. By saying he is a gentile, he has acknowledged he adheres to their faith even though it was to save his life . . . but many erred in the Inquisition of Portugal and thought because they were not baptized they could say they were gentiles to avoid martyrdom.

As we saw, there was some question in the mind of the student of RASHI if such was really the law. Along these lines, Nimuke Yosef thinks the Tosafists similarly would have permitted such pretext to save money and all the more so to save a life. Nevertheless, Nimuke Yosef agrees if there was a specific decree that Jews were to dress like gentiles or die, then the Jew would properly have to let himself be martyred and not pretend to be a gentile. On the other hand, if the decree was to force Jews to become apostates, then he should not let himself be martyred if he could escape by donning gentile garb.

> He should dress like a gentile to escape worshipping their gods so he can flee the country. . . . He has no intention of enjoying his predicament and what he is doing is permissible since he is required to save his life. . . . The Talmud (B. Ned. 62b) permitted a scholar to pretend to be a fire worshipper to escape levies. The Tosafists (not in our collections) think the Talmud permitted this case because God is compared in Scriptures to a burning fire (Deut. 4:24). So the scholar merely prevaricated—in his own mind he thought about worshipping the fiery God described in Scriptures although the Zoroastrians would have interpreted his words more literally. Other commentators have reasoned the Talmud means the scholar prevaricated because he understood his admission to mean he is a servant to real fire-worshippers (see RASHI's commentary to Deut. 4:28 and the Targum to it also) likely based on the notion that the Targum includes serving idolaters under the phrase worshipping foreign gods in a permitted way. According to the Talmud, it is permissible to mislead gentiles this way for monetary gain. It is logical one can certainly mislead them to save one's life. In the cases under discus-

sion the persecuted Jew makes absolutely no verbal profession but dresses like a gentile. Given the above scenarios, that kind of misdirection definitely should be permitted.

Apart from the cited Babylonian sources, he found Palestinian *midrashim* (Gen. R. 82 s. 8; s. 14) which reported that scholars changed their clothes to escape being noticed in times of persecution. However, when questioned, they admitted they were Jews and were martyred. *Nimukei Yosef* argues that merely dressing as a gentile (without verbal profession) to escape persecution should be completely lawful. *Nimukei Yosef* likely understood the ROSH would agree with his analysis. ROSH, in his commentary to B. Ned. 62b, notes that a scholar (who has disciplined limits not to bend the rule further) may lie and say he is an attendant to priests of an idol in order to escape certain taxes. One is reminded of the Targum and RASHI's claim (Deut. 4:28) that God had cursed Israel for their sins with going into exile and serving attendants of idol worshippers there. We will have opportunity to take another look at ROSH's position when we discuss the work of ROSH's son in this matter. *Nimukei Yosef* justifies his own position by citing relevant sources. Both *Rashba*, Shelomo ben Aderet (1235-1310) (*responsa*, 84), and *Tashbetz* (*responsa* 416, Shimshon bar Zadok, a student of Meir of Rothenberg whose decisions he recorded by dictation and a contemporary of ROSH) in their *responsa* were adamantly opposed to any pretense to be a gentile, even if just to dress as one. This likely represents the view of Meir of Rothenberg as well. The issue was not simple, but it did get resolved.

Rashba, a codifier of law in his own right, was recognized as an independent thinker who did not allow the weight of authority to weigh against clear thinking. *Rashba* pioneered the idea of twin works, one presenting a thorough discussion of opinions of decisors from the Talmud onwards, the other a short statement of law based on the conclusion of his historical survey of opinions. The method came to the forefront with the twin works *Beit Yosef* and *Shulhan Arukh* of Joseph Caro.

Throughout the medieval period, the German and French Jews produced many codes, some of limited and some of greater scope. Some, like that of Mordecai ben Hillel (1240-1298), dealt with the mechanics of deriving proper observance from talmudic sources. Others, like the *Sefer Mitzvot Gedolot* (SMAG) of Moshe ben Ya'acov of Coucy (1240-1300), listed the biblical commandments and discussed the pertinent Rabbinic debates. Collections of law abounded, and it fell to the son of Rabbi Asher (ROSH), known as *Jacob Ba'al haTURIM*, to organize the chaotic mass of literature. He knitted aggadic and legal theories to form a smooth fabric of legal traditions, easily accessible under specific topics. This work is a masterpiece of organization, with each law in its expected chronological order of daily, monthly, and festival ritual. The laws of marriage and divorce, of civil proceedings, and food laws are laid out in proper sequence. This work fully integrated talmudic legal and midrashic sources, specifying various differing views in the Talmud. He showed how Maimonides, ROSH, or others worked their way through the authoritative sources. He clarified the majority rulings and added ethical advice based on homiletic sources he integrated into the legal discussions. It is little wonder that the greatest legal minds of the fifteenth and sixteenth centuries attached their own works to this celebrated code.

In *Yoreh De'ah* 157, TUR writes:

> It is forbidden for one to say he is a gentile in order that he not be killed. Since he says he is a gentile, he acknowledges their faith and denies Judaism. However, if one has been sentenced to death by gentiles and can save himself by taking refuge in a gentile temple, my father, ROSH (*Responsa* 19), allowed him to flee there, for that does not constitute idol worship.

No differently than his father, TUR skirted the issue of the permissibility of dressing like a gentile to escape persecution. However he noted that simply walking into a temple is not forbidden if he does not participate in any worship. In this he follows both Nissim Gerondi (1310-1375, called RAN) and ROSH against the view of *Rashba*, who forbade giving any impression one is a gentile under any circumstances. The rabbis in Mishnaic times record an extreme view that mentions a rabbi who had forbidden taking refuge in a church to save one's life (B. Shab. 116a), but this seems to be a teaching only for the very pious who might opt to martyr themselves. *Rashba* took it as normative law.

Darkei Moshe, written by Moshe Isserles (the REMA, 1527-1572) lists the decisors (*poskim*) who allow prevarication in pretending to be a Christian. The German *Terumat haDeshen* (Israel Isserlein, 1390-1460), *responsa* 197, in a lengthy discussion, permits acting like a gentile to save one's life, including dressing like a gentile so long as one does not violate any ritual laws, even though he might give the impression he is breaking certain laws. This legal thinker composed a book of nearly six hundred issues in which he began with a question and provided practical solutions. Problems of religious persecution form a central interest. *Kol Bo* forbids any of this in time of religious persecution and requires martyrdom. Nothing is known of this author, not even his name, but his mastery of the sources makes his work of importance right into modern times. Joseph Caro, in his *Beit Yosef* commentary to the TUR, allows dressing like a gentile, as did Joseph ben Solomon (RIK, 1429-1480) (*responsa* 88), citing *Hagahot SMAK*, that one may do so under all circumstances and not just to save his life. BAH (Joel Sirkes, 17th c., Poland) emphasizes that some decisors permitted someone to disguise himself as a Christian only to save his life.

In his *Shulhan Arukh, Yoreh De'ah* 157, 2,3, Caro copied the wording of TUR but added one sentence: "*But* if for the purpose that he not be recognized as a Jew he may change his clothes; in times of persecution it is permitted since he does not say he is a gentile." The final word belongs to Moshe Isserles, whose extensive glosses on the *Shulhan Arukh* adopts the moderate attitude of *Nimukei Yosef*, who does not permit outright lying but who does permit more subtle subterfuges in times of severe threat:

> And it is permitted then even to wear forbidden mixtures. Although it is forbidden to outright say he is a gentile, he can use equivocal expressions. It is lawful even though the gentile is misled into thinking he is a non-Jew, since he himself is aware he means something else entirely. He can use any such means to mislead them into thinking he is a non-Jew . . . specifically in times of grave danger. Yet, if just for financial advantage he dons gentile clothing so he is not recognized as a Jew, whether to avoid custom duties or similar expenses, then it is forbidden.

The force of the moderate views prevailed over the lenient views permitting dressing as a gentile to evade taxes, on the one hand, and the stringent views (*Rashba, Tashbetz*) forbidding for any reason giving the impression one is a gentile, on the other hand. *Knesset haGedolah* wonders if there is a source that permits prevaricating by a scholar who knows where to draw the line (and if asked would admit to being a Jew). After all, that is the law of the Talmud, and it seems the RAN certainly understood matters that way. *Poskim* like the ROSH, *Nemukei Yosef, Maharshal* (Shelomo Luria, 1510-1573), and *Maharil* (Ya'acov ben Moshe ha-Levi Moellin, 1360-1427) saw that only in cases of imminent death could one prevaricate. Hayyim Benevisti, author of *Knesset HaGedolah*, a commentary on the TUR, wonders how anyone arrived at this conclusion. The case of the Talmud concerns scholars' avoiding taxes, not saving their lives. Various *poskim* have allowed prevarication even to save money if the tax collectors were thieves who wanted to exploit Jews against their own law. REMA and others, it appears, did not permit this. He answers that the *poskim* wrote the law for non-scholars and permitted everyone to prevaricate (including dressing like a gentile) only to save their lives. They understood the Talmud to mean that only scholars could escape taxes by prevaricating while others could save their lives in that manner. But no one could profess to be a Christian. On the other hand, *Sefer Hassidim*, whose pious rules at times went to radical extents, proclaimed that if one was mistaken for a Christian, he had to correct it and declare he was a Jew. *ShacH* realized that Jewish merchants and travelers in his area of Poland habitually dressed like Christians, and he justified their behavior within the received legal traditions.

Our study shows that the general trend of *halakhah* involves local communities' asking questions to local authorities on matters that had not been settled in earlier codes. Either the circumstances requiring innovative approaches had not yet surfaced or the method of the decisor did not allow him to introduce materials not discussed by the Talmud and Geonim. The fresh answers circulated in books of responsa and eventually found their way into commentaries on the codes. These commentaries became accepted as normative and enjoyed equal authority with the codes to which they were attached. The result is that the rulings entered into the next codes to be produced. Thus TUR used the phrasing of Maimonides or ROSH. *Shulhan Arukh* then incorporated these laws and interjected the rulings of the authoritative *responsa* into the codes. The normal complaint against the process is that the codes tend to have their own systematic progressions and the talmudic sources get left behind in the natural principles through which codifiers mediated the *responsa*. Later commentators had to justify the results of the codification process by going back to the talmudic sources and reinterpreting them to fit the common practice as codified. Codes tended to take on a life of their own. In modern times, the proliferation of codes in the nineteenth and twentieth centuries led to modern codes' losing their appeal so that the responsa literature has become the essential tool of the *posek*.

It remains for us to discuss the author of the *Shulhan Arukh* and his major glossator, Moses Isserles. Joseph Caro was born in Spain (or Portugal) but left before the ominous expulsions. At this time, Sephardic Jews spread into Ashkenazic lands. These people had been more integrated and assimilated into Spanish society than Ashkenazic Jews had been into French and German society. The refugees considered their culture superior and discounted the ancient customs of Ashkenazic society. Caro settled in Turkey and became a master of every facet of Jewish literature. Having little patience, his temperament was completely of a legal nature, and he had little sympathy for aggadic lore or ethical advice. He turned poetic insights into legal strictures and ethical recommendations into statutes.

Caro's *Beit Yosef* commentary to the TUR code is a masterpiece of research into the

legal opinions of all the major thinkers from the Talmud to his day, with detailed emphasis on the views of Alfasi and Maimonides. Nevertheless, his researches tended to ignore the French and German legal tradition and in some ways even erred in the Spanish, talmudic tradition. This tradition had reached its final development with the classic presentation of Maimonides. After that, the northern Spanish scholars, beginning with Nachmanides, adopted the methods of the French and German schools. By the nature of their study they could never reach any finality in deciding the sense of talmudic passages. TUR represents the attempt to bring that tradition to finality by incorporating both French and German methods with the Spanish ones. The *Beit Yosef* commentary to the TUR attempted to widen the scope of the TUR and focus Jewish law into the talmudic tradition of Maimonides.

Caro's mystical tendencies were part of his age. The suffering and dispersions had been so great that messianic hopes were afire everywhere, and *kabbalah* became the perfect vehicle to expand Jewish hopes. Caro received a special ordination given to him and three other judges allowing them to become part of a supreme court, should the messiah come, that could function as the Sanhedrin did in Temple times. His colleague who enjoyed the same ordination was his harshest critic, Moses ben Joseph of Trani—known as *Mabyt*. Joseph Caro (1488-1575), David ibn Zimra (1480-1573) and Moses ben Joseph of Trani (1500-1580) sat on the tribunal of Jerusalem. Caro's subconscious rose to conscious levels in an entity referred to as the Maggid, an alter-ego manifestation that counseled him, speaking through his throat.

Caro's code was originally divided into thirty sections with the hope that a scholar could review the entirety every thirty days. It was not really meant to compete with the TUR, which it soon did. However, many great scholars pointed out its shortcomings in that it had removed the reasons for the laws and presented just the dry bone of a decision. They complained that it was replacing talmudic study as the center of Judaism. Nevertheless, those who praised it wrote commentaries to fill in its lapses so that it could fully operate as a code. Eventually these commentaries were printed on the margins of the *Shulhan Arukh*, assuring it of being the total legacy of practical legal decisions. It was printed in an entirely new format rivaling those of Maimonides and the *TUR*. It was accepted as the work par excellence among the majority of Sephardic rabbis, a position it retains until the present. Caro's code became the standard reference work for *poskim* after the seventeenth century, and two centuries later further codes, modeled after *Shulhan Arukh*, abridged and updated his work for various communities that had customs not listed by *REMA*.

Isserles had begun by writing a commentary to the *TUR* to correct the lackings in the *Beit Yosef* commentary. This commentary, *Darkei Moshe*, showed the mastery and genius of the young Isserles and established him as the leading scholar of Poland. His commentary, the *Mapa* (*Table Cloth*), explained difficulties in the *Shulhan Arukh* (*Set Table*), corrected errors, argued against some of its rulings, and established Ashkenazic customs as binding for all time on Ashkenazic Jews. He widened the scope of the *Shulhan Arukh* by citing variant opinions. His work was incorporated into the very text of the *Shulhan Arukh* in smaller letters of a different font. With the new commentaries of *REMA*, *TAZ*, *Magen Avraham*, and *ShacH*, and *SMA*, *Shulhan Arukh* became a code that was functional and authoritative for establishing Jewish law in a more or less unified format. The labors of Maimonides and *TUR* had reached completion as legal codes, and whatever new codes might now be produced were destined to follow the decisions of Caro. We should point out that Mordecai Yaffe in his *Sefer HaLevushim* (10 volumes) had produced a code incorporating encyclopedic discussions like those of *Beit Yosef* and conclusions of law like those of *Shulhan Arukh* as a workable code, but that attempt was not widely followed, and until recently his work was not even reprinted. The scope was not universal enough. In the eighteenth century, Elijah of Vilna (*GRA*) attempted to find the source of all laws and customs in the *Shulhan Arukh* by recourse to the Talmud and Bible. His approach was ingenious for its clarity, brevity, and simplicity. But no one has managed to duplicate this approach.

The commentaries to the *Shulhan Arukh* allowed Caro's code to be workable providing that one re-adjusted the decisions of Caro in light of the later commentaries printed with it. Opposition to the code dwindled, and with the rise of Sabbateanism, Frankism, and Reform, all of which undermined the authority of local rabbis, the *Shulhan Arukh* became the symbol of traditional Jewish law. It has remained in this position and still attracts authoritative commentaries, who have updated it into the twentieth century.

Herbert W. Basser

CODIFICATION OF JEWISH LAW—MODERN:

In the nineteenth century, even as Jews were granted citizenship in European countries, political antisemitism increased, and, through programs of religious repression and secularization, many governments embarked on programs to sever Jews from their traditions and to assimilate them into general society. The Rabbinic leadership in Eastern Europe sensed that the mind-set that had sworn loyalty to the *Mishneh Torah*, the *Tur*, and the *Shulhan Arukh* was on the verge of disappearing. Poverty and hardship cut deeply into Jewish societies that, through faith and obedience to Rabbinic leadership, had weathered bad storms in the past. As the face of Europe changed and there did not seem to be a place for the Jew in modern society, Jewish responses varied. The growth of Hassidism was one response, the attempt to build a Jewish homeland, another. As always, absorption in the vision of self-power and the picture of an orderly society had strong appeal. So as many Jews looked for greener pastures by emigrating, assimilating, and modernizing, others sought the refuge of the well-regulated lifestyle that was a Jewish Kingdom on earth. Zionism had appeal for some, but for many the life of faith and tradition still held promise.

Jews had recovered from the repression of Islam and the collapse of the Gaonate in the twelfth century and recovered from the strength of Christendom's armies in the fourteenth. Again, they recovered from the collapse of Spanish Jewry in the fifteenth century. Each time, they produced a new legal code. Now in the nineteenth century, with the collapse of Rabbinic authority in the wake of new political and social structures, a new crisis loomed. As a result of economic factors, Jews left the well-governed Jewish life of the *shtetel* in search of a more open life in the city. In the urban setting, they found a variety of Jewish and non-Jewish life-styles, free from previous social pressures. Secularism, socialism, and communism were all temptations for the economically deprived Jew. In addition, the application of steam power to machinery meant that paper and printing became cheaper and broadly accessible.

The challenges of technology encroached into Eastern European Jewish life, but this same technology provided the means to meet the challenges. The response to the transitions once again was a renewed activity in collecting the laws of the past and re-presenting them anew. The new halakhic works, for the most part, did not seek innovative ways to pave the future. They demonstrated that mastery of Jewish law still could lead to the vision of God's halakhic dimension. If anyone was convinced that these laws were antiquated, they could see first hand that the most eminent authorities of the day still lived in the halakhic world. It was the authors of these works who affirmed the eternity of the lifestyle that defined them. More than such works served the needs of communities, they served the needs of the authors. This was their way of coping with adversity and threats from without and within.

Between 1810 and 1907, we find a fresh interest in Eastern Europe in writing popular codes. We note the works *Hayei Adam* (Vilna, 1810), by Rabbi Abraham Danzig (1748-1820); *Kitzur Shulhan Arukh* (1864), by Rabbi Ganzfried Solomon (1804-1886); *Arukh Hashulhan* (1884-1903), by Rabbi Yehiel Michal Epstein (1829-1908); and *Mishnah Berurah* (1894-1907), by Rabbi Israel Meir Kagan (1838-1933).

Each writer incorporated local customs and approaches to legal problems that suited their constituencies so the reader had no need to consult any further work. These authors preserved past legacy in simple form but still incorporate the spirit of the *Shulhan Arukh* of Joseph Caro. They increasingly wrote bare-boned codes in language that the average student might be expected to know—usually indicating their sources in brackets.

The *Hayei Adam*

Born in 1748 in Danzig Germany, Rabbi Abraham Danzig studied with Rabbis Joseph Lieberman and Ezekiel Landau (*Nodah Byehudah*). After his marriage, Rabbi Danzig relocated to the city of Vilna, the home of the famed Elijah (*Gra*). He served from 1794 to 1812 as *dayan* (rabbinical judge).

Though Rabbi Danzig published numerous works, his fame came from his *Hayei Adam*, which presents the essential teachings of legal decisors on the rules of *Shulhan Arukh, Orach Hayim*. On the cover page of the first edition of the *Hayei Adam*, which was published anonymously, Rabbi Danzig stated his intended readership and his purpose in writing this work as follows:

1) The first benefit is that even a boy of thirteen can now study and understand nearly all the laws of the *Shulhan Arukh* in a short period of time, whereas an experienced student [without having read this book] will take some years of effort to do so.

2) Heads of households, for whom the burden of earning a living is heavy, can read this book during their periods of rest. That is because the language is easy to understand and everything is clearly and completely explained, so that the person who wishes to delve in it will not have to compare subject to subject.

3) [This book is advantageous] even for those heads of households who study the Talmud and its major commentaries daily, because the *Shach* has written in *Yoreh De'ah* that they fulfill their requirement for Torah learning with it. [Such Jews] are obligated to study halakhic rulings but have no time to study the *Shulhan Arukh* and its commentaries as well in order to quench their thirst and to know all the laws in their true sense and reasoning like experienced Torah scholars.

4) [This book is advantageous] even for those who study the *Shulhan Arukh*. Since

it is well known that the rationale for a law is not given in the *Shulhan Arukh*, nor whether it constitutes a Torah or rabbinical law, [the *Shulhan Arukh*] is like a sealed book. It therefore requires extraordinary effort to study the words of the latter [halakhic authorities] which are also obscure. Thus when a person reads this book, he will properly understand the words of the *Shulhan Arukh*.

5) Those who study the commentary *Magen Avraham* know that his statements are very profound but also contain many typographical errors. In this book, [the reader] will find rest and satisfaction and will understand *Magen Avraham's* enlightening words.

6) Even seasoned Torah scholars and rabbis will find [in this book] novel legal interpretations, so that when a halakhic question arrives they will mostly be able to find [the answer] in this book. The author discusses [the issue] and shows the sources from which he derived the law. One who wishes to disagree with his conclusion may do so, but [even so] his analysis will have been rendered easier. The author has nearly exhaustively explored each doubtful area that may arise in any of the laws from any of the sections of the *Orach Hayim*.

7) It is known that the laws of the *Shulhan Arukh* are scattered in many places. On who is not fluent in all [sections of] the *Shulhan Arukh* and the latter [halakhic authorities] will not easily find the law. In this book, each and every law is found in its place. From each and every law a rule will be made for this matter. When [the reader] searches in the table of contents, he will easily find that which he seeks.

I hereby admonish anyone who has the ability to understand the *Shulhan Arukh* properly not to rely upon me for actual guidance until he also examines the *Shulhan Arukh*.

Another text he published, *Hochmat Adam* (Vilna, 1810), covers the laws in the section *Yoreh De'ah* of the *Shulhan Arukh*. He also prepared an addendum titled *Binat Adam*, which was an in-depth discussion of Danzig's adjudications. *Nishmat* and *Binat Adam* were for scholars who had the ability to analyze of Jewish law.

In addition, he penned a brief work called *Kuntris Matzevat Moshe* dealing with the laws of mourning. Rabbi Danzig prepared and named this section in memory of his son Moshe, who died in the winter of 1814 at the age of twenty. He also pub-

lished in memory of his son *Zichru Torat Moshe* (Vilna, 1817), a synopsis of the laws of the Sabbath much used to this day by young Orthodox Jews. This volume concludes with *Mitzvat Moshe*, a synopsis of biblical and Rabbinic laws. He also wrote a comprehensive introduction to all his works in this publication (*Zichru Torat Moshe*) and prepared *Toledot Adam* (Vilna, 1818), a commentary on the Passover Haggadah. Though *Beit Avraham* (Vilna, 1821) was intended primarily as a last will and testament to Rabbi Danzig's family, it was published posthumously as a general tome of proper Jewish conduct and, like all his books, was intended for the Jewish layman.

During his lifetime, Danzig published two editions of the *Hayei Adam* with introductions. Here he stressed that the study of law has priority over the theoretical, analytic, and pilpulistic study of the Talmud. Even the primary codes of Jewish law, such as Joseph Caro's *Beit Yosef* and Moses Isserles's *Darkei Moshe*, were too difficult and time-consuming for the layman to comprehend. *Hayei Adam* is intended to allow the less knowledgeable to fulfill the mitzvah of Torah study and to practice the laws properly. With proper discipline, he suggests, a student studying his *Hayei Adam* could reach a high level of knowledge of law at the end of one year. Joseph Caro had thought his *Shulhan Arukh* could do the same in thirty days. Danzig's claim seems more realistic.

He writes, "It was reported to me that great and able Torah scholars reviewed my work and stated that it served for them as a review of the *Shulhan Arukh*. . . . In addition, they found many new laws in my work." Danzig grouped the materials of his book according to what he termed *klallim* (principles). Rather than employing the divisions (chapters and paragraphs) found in the *Shulhan Arukh* he attempted to organize the subject matter more finely. If the issues discussed were thematically related, he arranged them in one *klal*. For instance he grouped together the laws of Sabbath and the weekday prayer, which Caro placed in two separate sections. Similarly, Caro spread out nineteen chapters (182–201) concerned with one theme, laws of *zimun* (an introductory formula to the "grace after the meal"), while in *klal* 48, Danzig arranged them all together. And while Caro has the laws of *mezuzah* and railings in *Shulhan Arukh Yoreh De'ah in* chapters 285-291, Danzig gathered them together into a single section (*klal* 15). Rabbi Danzig felt laws concerning daily life (*Hayei Adam*), such as mezuzah, Torah study, honoring one's parents and elderly persons, saying of the kaddish, etc., which Rabbi Caro had placed in another volume, *Yoreh De'ah*, all belonged together.

If the issues were not practical, relevant to his time, or required the educated decision of a Rabbinic authority, Danzig did not include them in *Hayei Adam*. Before his time, codes had analyzed the methods of using stoves on the Sabbath, such as ancient stoves (*kira*) or (*kupach*), but he excluded these issues, since they were not relevant to the nineteenth century. When he felt that a theme required special attention, he preferred to deal with them in a separate work. For example, while he discussed rules for scribes in the general laws relevant to every Jew, he prepared a separate volume on how to write phylacteries. In an addendum inserted in the text of the laws, he added in brackets alternate opinions concerning the specific law at hand.

Hayei Adam also included a separate work titled *Nishmat Adam*. This took the form of a codicil placed on the bottom of the same page of the law to which it was related and presented an in-depth discussion of that law. In discussing different Rabbinic positions as well as offering his own analysis, Rabbi Danzig assured his work a major place in the history of legal codes pioneered by Rashba in the fourteenth century. Twin codes and legal decisions had usually required two separate volumes. Rabbi Danzig incorporated both in one volume.

Unlike many of his generation, he did not hesitate to adjudicate legal disputes among leading rabbis and to state his reasons with rare insight. Where Rabbi Danzig introduced his own decisions, he would often include his process of thinking in the *Nishmat Adam* codicil. The author of the *Hayei Adam* put great importance on the *Mishneh Torah* of Maimonides and the classic commentaries of the *Shulhan Arukh*.

While Caro had omitted general ethical motivations of the laws, Rabbi Danzig create new sections for them not found in the *Shulhan Arukh*. For example, in section 142, he elaborates on the many moral and ethical aspects of repentance. He explained every word in the *vidui* ("confession") of the Yom Kippur prayer service, and even prepared a special introduction to the Yom Kippur prayer entitled *"tfilat zaka,"* which today is included in most Orthodox Jewish prayer books. Typical of his approach is section 68, where he discusses the proper mindset to observe the laws. In section 20, he wrote that the institutional prayers are divided into four sections to parallel the four spiritual worlds of Lurianic kabbalah. He introduced (reminiscent of *Tur*) his listings of the laws of the Sabbath with a discourse based upon *midrash* and *aggadah*. In section 2 (laws pertaining to washing hands in the morning), Danzig elaborated on the effects these rituals have on one's soul. His primary source for the ethical, moral, and spiritual themes is the *Sefer Yereim*, but there are also excerpts from such books as the Zohar, the writings of Isaac Luria, *Hovat HaLevavot*, and others. This approach seems to have intended to soften the reader to accept his stringent legal decisions.

Rabbi Danzig's *Hayei Adam* was widely accepted. The work has gone through numerous editions, and groups were organized throughout various Jewish communities to study his text. Such groups persist until today.

Kitzur Shulhan Arukh: Rabbi Danzig's *Hayei Adam* proved too taxing for many, and its subject matter did not embrace the totality of subjects discussed in Caro's *Shulhan Arukh*. Its rules suited Poland and Germany but omitted the legal traditions of Hungarian Jews. Solomon Ganzfried (1804-1886), prolific as a commentator of Talmud and author of many works, accordingly produced the *Kitzur Shulhan Arukh* (Abridged Code of Jewish Law, Ungavar, 1864). Omitting the detail and halakhic rationales for each law, he offered a concise decision in rather simplified legal language. For the final thirty-six years of his life, Ganzfried served in Ungavar as its chief Rabbinic judge. He died in 1886.

Ganzfried's writings include *Keset Sofer* (Ofter, 1835), which pertains to the laws of writing Torah scrolls and the Book of Esther. It also includes comments by Moses Sofer of Pressburg, a revered leader of Hungarian Jewry, known as the *Hatam Sofer*, as well as approbation by him. Ganzfried saw fourteen editions of *Keset Sofer* through the press in his lifetime. In a later edition he included an addendum entitled *Lishkat HaSofer*, concerning the letters of the Torah. He also penned a commentary to the prayer book *Derech HaHayim* of Rabbi Ya'acov of Lissa (Vienna, 1838); *Pnei Shlomo* (Zolklev, 1846), a commentary on many tractates in the Babylonian Talmud; *Torat Zevach* (Levov, 1848), concerning the laws of ritual slaughter; *Lechem V'Simlah* (Levov, 1861), on the laws of menstruation and the construction of ritual baths; and *Ohalei Shem* (Ungavar, 1878), discussing names of men and women (plus an addendum, *Shem Yosef*). His debates with students of the leading decisor of the time, Saul Nathanson, were recorded in his *Milchemet Hovah* (Werber, Jerusalem, 1882). Other works included *Michseh LeOhel*, *Edut BeShoshanin*, *Ofel VeBochen*, and *Shem Shlomo* (Varol, 1908), on diverse topics from the Babylonian Talmud.

But Ganzfried's best-known work remains the *Kitzur Shulhan Arukh*, which has been translated into many languages, including several times into English. Although there is no introduction, the author summarized his goal in a few short sentences. His goal in this handy digest of the *Shulhan Arukh: Orach Hayim, Yoreh De'ah, Even Ha'ezer*, and *Choshen Mishpat* was to offer a reference work that everyone could consult as the need arose. It also served as a book of instruction to introduce students to the subject matter of Jewish law. In the course of twelve years, the author published his work thirteen times. In the last edition during his lifetime he gathered all the revisions he had made over the years and produced a fully completed and revised edition. He wrote that he based his corrections not only upon his research but also from the comments he received from other scholars. The book was accepted and acclaimed by many leading authorities of its time. The focus was practical halakhah and omitted laws and customs, which were widely known and needed no further description. He depended upon the writings of Ya'acov of Lisa, Shneur Zalman Schneerson of Liady (author of an abridged code himself, *Shulhan Arukh Harav*), and Abraham Danzig author of the *Hayei Adam*.

Although Ganzfried's work is abridged, he frequently commences its sections with brief non-halakhic introductions. These are adapted from writings such as Maimonides, *Sefer Hayashar*, *Hayei Adam*, and other works on ethical behavior (*musar*). For example, in the "Laws of Hanukkah" (section 139), the text of Maimonides' *Mishneh Torah* is provides historical background. In the "Laws of the Scroll of Esther" (section 141), the text of the *Hayei Adam* (Klal 154, paragraph 3) is slightly reworded and employed.

The greater part of the *Kitzur Shulhan Arukh* is concerned with almost all the themes found in Caro's *Orach Hayim*. Yet we also find many topics from the other three sections of the *Shulhan Arukh*. For example, from *Yoreh De'ah* he included such laws as charity, baking, salting, gentile cooking, relationships with gentiles, witchcraft, circumcision, education, forbidden foods, vows, parental honor, menstruation, the ritual bath, mourning, and agricultural issues (*chadash*, *orlah*, and *kilayim*). From *Chosen Mishpat* he presented the laws of borrowing and lending, sabbatical loans (*shmitat kesafim*), thievery, damages—financial and bodily—borrowing and renting, lost and found item, cruelty to animals, and many other topics. From *Even HaEzer* he included the laws pertaining to marriage. But he selected only what was relevant to the lay Jew and omitted what was relevant only to Rabbinic judges.

The popularity of the *Kitzur Shulhan Arukh* encouraged scholars to write commentaries on it. Rabbi Hayim Yeshayah HaCohen published his comments in the monographs *Misgeret HaShulhan* (Lublin, 1889) and *Lechem HaPanim* (Lublin, 1888). After Rabbi Ganzfried's death, these were published together with the text of the *Kitzur Shulhan Arukh*. More recently, the rulings of *Mishnah Berurah* were published as an addendum to discuss the aspects of laws found in Ganzfried's code. *Sha'arim Metzuyanim BeHa-*

lakhah, published by Solomon Braun (New York, 1951), is still very popular as it records rulings from after Ganzfried's time. Shemuel Bornstein published two works based upon the *Kitzur Shulhan Arukh*, *Minchat Shabbat* (Warsaw, 1905) and *Madanei Shemuel* (Petrikov, 1904). Newer works have appeared using the *Kitzur Shulhan Arukh* as their model, but the original still thrives on its own merits.

Mishnah Berurah: Rabbi Israel Meir Hakohen Kagan-Poupko (1838-1939) achieved prominence for his saintly personality. His personality, teachings, and writings today more than ever guide the behavior of Ashkenazic observant Jews. He was born in Zhetel, Poland on February 6, 1838. At the age of seventeen, already a prominent Talmudic scholar, he married his stepfather's daughter, Frieda, and settled in the small town of Radun. There he created a yeshiva, later known as Yeshivat Hafetz Hayim. A warm and humble person, Rabbi Kagan sought out personal contacts with his fellow Jews. Although burdened with the responsibilities of the yeshiva and deeply involved in his writings, he attended numerous conferences and public gatherings that allowed for his involvement in various Jewish issues as well as for interaction with Jewish laymen. He was very involved in establishing educational institutions for Jewish boys and in later years for girls as well. Kagan was also active in the development of the *Agudat Israel* organization, the world organization of Orthodox Judaism. He died in Radun on September 15, 1933.

Rabbi Kagan wrote twenty-one works. The most widely known are *Hafets Hayim* (*He Who Desires Life*; Vilna, 1873), a code of the laws of slander, gossip, and tale-bearing; *Mahaneh Israel* (*Camp of Israel*; Vilna, 1881), dealing with matters pertaining to the Jewish Russian soldier and his life in the military; *Ahavath Chesed* (*Loving Kindness*; Warsaw, 1888), on all aspects of human relations; *Nidhei Israel* (*Dispersed of Israel*, Warsaw, 1893) and *Shem Olam* (*Everlasting Memorial*; Warsaw, 1893), intended to keep Jews who were emigrating to Russia, Palestine, and America loyal to the Jewish heritage; *Likutei Halakot* (*Anthology of Laws*;

Petersburg, 1900-1925), dealing with the Temple service when the messiah comes; *Homat Hadat* (*Fortress of Faith*; Petersburg, 1905), concerning the importance of Torah and Torah education; *Torat Habayit* (*Torah of the Home*; Petersburg, 1907), emphasizing the importance of Torah study in the home; *Taharat Yisrael* (*The Purity of Israel*; 1910), *Geder Olam* (*The Eternal Fence*; Warsaw, 1890), and *Beit Yisrael* (*The House of Israel*; Petersburg, 1928), all dealing with the laws of family purity, ritual baths, and hair coverings.

His greatest work, which remains the strongest influence on orthodox practice today and whose authority is final, is *Mishnah Berurah* (Lucid Learning; 1884-1907), in six volumes. This is not a code. Kagan recognized that Caro's *Shulhan Arukh* held the primary place for codes and should never be supplanted. The format of commentary was the proper and time-honored way to decide law, and so his work comments phrase by phrase on Caro's *Orach Hayim*. He reprinted the text of the *Shulhan Arukh* along with three of its classic commentaries, Moshe Rivkash's *Beyer Ha-Golah*, Yehudah Ashkenazi's *Beur Hetev*, and Margoliot's *Sha'arei Teshuvah*. Below these three texts Kagan positioned his own commentaries.

Alongside his *Mishnah Berurah* synopsis of the proper way to observe the law of the *Shulhan Arukh* he included two other works page by page. *Sha'ar Hatzion*, in a footnote style, cites the sources to many of the citations found in the *Mishnah Berurah*. *Beur Halakhah* (Explanation of Laws) offers an in-depth analysis and discourse on specific laws presented in the *Mishnah Berurah*. It is clear then that he follows the twin commentary notion wherein one can find a simple statement of the practical law as well as an involved legal discussion of the pertinent authorities and talmudic sources. Rashba had first promulgated this notion, and later Caro produced two separate works, while Danzig had entwined the two into a single work. Now Kagan placed the two types of works side by side and cross-referenced them. It should be pointed out that while Rabbi Kagan personally edited every word, he was helped in the massive undertaking by family members who were his research assistants, and he left certain matters as they saw fit, even though he held other views. As a result, there are slight contradictions here and there.

Kagan's purpose, like that of earlier codifiers, was to produce a work that could be studied daily so that Jews might know the proper procedures to follow minute by minute. Hence he wrote only on that section of *Shulhan Arukh* that contained the laws of morning, afternoon, and evening practices on weekdays, Sabbaths, and festivals. Caro's code in and of itself was insufficient without much knowledge of the Tur's code or Caro's massive *Beit Yosef* commentary. Kagan digested this material and presented it in a palatable form for his readers, together with the hundreds of other authoritative works that had appeared since Caro's time. He was able to offer a position of consensus emerging out of the myriad legal arguments that had gone on for centuries. He followed the later decisors where conflicting opinions had no resolution. In his introduction, he cites twenty-three later authorities used in his decision-making. The influence of the legal methodology of the Gaon of Vilna is apparent throughout him work. Simcha Fishbane summarizes Kagan's method as follows:

> a. *Commentary*: These passages are concerned with the *Mishnah Berurah's* interpretation, clarification, glosses, and textual corrections of the *Shulhan Arukh*.
> b. *Adjudication*: In cases of dispute between Caro and Isserles or other authorities who gloss the *Shulhan Arukh*, Kagan presents his rulings. Furthermore, he offers his halakhic decisions in instances not discussed by earlier adjudicators. Kagan deals with the situations related to the statements of the *Shulhan Arukh* but not explicitly dealt with by these authorities, as new halakhic concerns of his social milieu. These rulings stand in addition to Kagan's halakhic decisions based upon the adjudication of the *Shulhan Arukh* or latter authorities.
> c. *Ethics*: Kagan is widely identified as a man of ethics (*musar*). His large number of ethical publications stress the search for moral and religious perfection through a stringent observance of halakhah. Kagan integrates his ethical and moral beliefs into his halakhic approaches and decisions, thus encouraging stringent adjudication. While the majority of these cases are implicit, they

can also be found explicitly. For example, section 244 sub-paragraph 35 of the *Shulhan Arukh* concerns the accommodative maxim "in the case a loss of money is involved." After discussing the lenient possibilities related to this maxim, Kagan concludes with an ethical suggestion: "but fortunate is he who trusts in God and does not seek out various leniencies for Shabbat."

> d. *Contemporary issues*: Although the *Mishnah Berurah* was structured as a commentary to Caro's code, Kagan suggests in his introduction to Volumes One and Three that his concern is also with contemporary halakhic issues. He intends to offer the reader a guide to proper halakhic behavior. In his introduction to Volume Three he states this purpose: "From the works of the *Acharonim* (latter authorities) I have also collected many new ideas applicable to everyday life nowadays. My aspiration is that with the help of God, whoever will now study this [body of] law will come to know each law, together with the reason and underlying thesis [for it], in both theory and practice."

In addition to the fourfold taxonomy, the analysis of content in the *Mishnah Berurah* subsumes Talmudic and halakhic principles. For example, in sub-paragraph 32, cited above, Kagan discusses the Talmudic principle concerning a Torah prohibition and the halakhic principle of "permitted in the case of monetary loss." This in particular covers the analysis of the *Mishnah Berurah's* explicit and implicit accommodative and stringent views and rulings. The term accommodative (*kulah*) and stringent (*chumrah*) in the *Mishnah Berurah's* text are to be understood within the context of later authorities adjudications. Kagan's decisions are specifically dependent upon the analysis and rulings of the *Acharonim*. Therefore, when the *Mishnah Berurah's* adjudication chooses to be lenient or stringent, or when it refers to one of theses terms in its text, its intention reflects the lenient or stringent view of these *Acharonim*.

The following literary features are found in the *Mishnah Berurah*.

1) Use of traditional Rabbinic vocabulary constructed from Mishnaic and Talmudic Hebrew and Aramaic as well as expressions and phraseology related to the theme under discussion found in post-Talmudic jargon.
2) Verbatim duplication of latter Rabbinic authorities.

3) Interpolation of the author's interpretation within the quotes found in the text.
4) Interpretation of texts, concepts, and words.
5) Adjudication based upon the majority of most recent authoritative rulings cited.
6) The adaptation of accepted halakhic principles. For example, in the case of Torah law, one must rule stringently.
7) Former Rabbinic authorities (*Rishonim*) are used only when essential, as in a case in which their decision is required to render a solution to a problem not satisfactorily resolved by the *Acharonim*, or when cited by other commentators cited by the author.
8) Latter Rabbinical authorities are cited.
9) Dependence on a textual version of a later authority rather than the source, and siding with a primary *Acharon* rather than with the *Shulhan Arukh*.
10) The incorporation of non-halakhic materials, such as ethics.
11) Short decisive statements with minimum dialectics (*pilpul*).
12) Cross-referencing through the *Shulhan Arukh* and the commentaries.
13) The sources referred to in the text are predominately other adjudicators and *Shulhan Arukh* commentators, not responsa or talmudic commentaries.
14) Not citing the entire or exact source.

The *Mishnah Berurah* has become the contemporary halakhic work of halakhic standards. Study groups and classes on this work abound in Orthodox synagogues and yeshivot. Contemporary decisors refer to it as a matter of course.

Arukh HaShulhan: The *Arukh HaShulhan* was compiled and published by Yechiel Mechel Epstein (1829-1908). Before completing his studies, Epstein married Michla, the daughter of Rabbi Ya'acov Berlin, from the city of Mir, and who was the brother of Naftali Zvi Yehudah Berlin (popularly known as the Netziv). In 1862, Epstein received his first Rabbinic appointment in the town of Novosybkov. This town housed both Habad hasidim and non-hasidim, who lived peacefully side by side. Here he published his first book, *Or LeYesharim* (Light for the Upright). Later Epstein accepted a position in the small town of Lubitz, on the outskirts of Novogrudok, Lithuania, and then became rabbi of Novogrudok itself. During the forty-three years until his death in 1908,

he continued to establish himself as a leading authority. Seeking his adjudication, rabbis from all over Europe and America corresponded with him on halakhic issues. His major writings are *Or LaYesharim* (Zhitomir, 1869), a commentary on the *Sefer HaYashar* of Ya'acov Tam; *Leil Shemurim* (Warsaw, 1889), a commentary on the Passover *Haggadah*; *Mechel Mayim*, published posthumously, a two page commentary on the Jerusalem Talmud, was included in the 1928 edition in Vilna by the Romm publishers; and *Kol Ben Levi*, a book of Epstein's sermons. *Arukh HaShulhan He'atid* was published posthumously. It deals with themes relevant to messianic times and includes the laws of agriculture (1938-1946), *Sanhedrin, Mamrim, Melachim, Shekalim, Kiddush HaChodesh* (1962), and *Kodashim* (1969). All were published in Israel by Mosad Harav Kook. The work is based primarily on Maimonides' *Mishneh Torah*, the only code that addressed these issues.

Arukh HaShulhan is a nine volume code of Jewish law that consists of both novellae and halakhic rulings on the four parts of Rabbi Caro's *Shulhan Arukh*. In 1884 (Warsaw), Epstein published the first section, on *Hoshen Mishpat*. This was readily accepted in the Rabbinic community and achieved almost instant popularity, thus earning him an international reputation as a halakhic decisor. The section on *Yoreh De'ah* was published in 1894 (Warsaw), *Even Ha'ezer* in 1903 (St. Petersburg), and *Orach Hayim* in 1903 (St. Petersburg), and Volume 9, on sections of *Yoreh De'ah*, in 1991 (Hoboken). Although in its external organization the work follows the chapters found in Caro's *Shulhan Arukh*, in its internal arrangements it conforms to Maimonides' *Mishneh Torah*. Such conformity is found primarily in sections that do not deal with daily rituals. The discussions of *Orach Hayim* is far less dependent on Maimonides than are the other sections.

Epstein begins each law with a survey of the history of that particular halakhah. He analyzes the disputes among rabbis concerning the details of the ruling and offers his opinion on the proper form of the law. Besides serving its primary purpose as a functional code of practical law, the book is useful as a reference work, because it analyzes the major opinions of Caro's code and its subsequent commentaries. Although his library was not as extensive as that of Kagan, Epstein managed to uncover and record rulings of very early decisors. He was careful to cite his sources from previous legal works and both Talmuds.

Epstein cites rules that had fallen out of practice, giving them renewed force, and he derives new applications of law from older sources that he thought should be followed. His goal was to produce a systematic body of consistent law, even if not all the rulings were applicable in modern times. He followed Maimonides' decisions concerning court rulings that were only applicable in times when there was a Jewish monarchy, such as the laws governing cities of refuge and various high court procedures. Nevertheless, he noted dissenting opinions. When Epstein presented a dispute, it is only for the purpose of background clarification before he rendered the decision he considered binding. He sought to give the final halakhic summation of all halakhah existing up to his day. His decision is usually based on the rulings of the latest authority that he found cogent. Nevertheless, he readily employed such expressions as "in our time," "our custom is," and "in our country" to point out changes in customs and living conditions. These terms are frequently used as formularies at the conclusion of rulings concerned with current social realities.

Unlike Kagan's approach in the *Mishnah Berurah*, Epstein perceived halakhah as an ongoing process for living communities and frequently gave weight to lenient practices that had developed over the ages. He proposed his own legal justifications for these decisions. When analyzing a question, he at times proposed new explanations for the past rulings. As a result of these explanations, he determined that some statutes were only pertinent to past eras when conditions had varied widely from those of the modern age. He recognized that advances in technology presented new challenges to the applications of Jewish legal principles, and he noted that social norms had developed as well. In *Arukh HaShulhan, Orach Hayim* (65:21) he states, "There is a reality [today] that was not so in previous generations." His daring independence can be seen in the fact he did not publish a single approbation for his *Arukh HaShulhan*, an almost unheard-of practice even in today's world. Epstein's *Arukh HaShulhan* ranks next to the *Mishnah Berurah* as a guide for the daily life of the halakhically conscious Jew. It has been published many times and in many editions. No Rabbinic library is complete without it, and, in most cases, no Rabbinic student or adjudicator will endeavor to do research without consulting it.[1]

Bibliography
Fishbane, Simcha, *The Method and Meaning of the Mishnah Berurah* (Hoboken, 1991).

Note
[1] The authors thank Lynn Visson and Ira Robinson for their help in preparing this entry.

SIMCHA FISHBANE
HERBERT BASSER

***CONVEROS* IN MEDIEVAL SPAIN:** The phenomenon of mass Jewish conversion under threat of death or expulsion originated with the policy of persecution of the Jews in the Iberian peninsula, which began as far back as the end of the Roman times, continuing under the Catholic Visigoth kings, the fanatical Muslim rule, and, then, once more, under the rule of Catholicism.

In the *Carta-enciclica*, Bishop Severus relates of the conversion of the Jews of Mahon in Minorca, which probably occurred in 417 or 418: first came persecution; this was followed by the burning of the synagogue; and finally the Jews were baptized *en masse*. We can find additional details of these events in the *Altercatio Ecclesiae et Synagogae*, which is considered by several authors, including V. Segui and J. Hillgarth, to be a *commonitorium* by Bishop Severus.

The beginning of the Visigoth kings' oppression of the Jews coincided with the formers' conversion from Arianism to Catholicism (589). A great historian of the Jews in early medieval times, B. Blumenkranz, believes this date is actually the beginning of the tragic suffering of the Jews throughout the entire Middle Ages. The fact that the Visigoth kings became Catholics provided a disproportionately political dimension to the ratio between political and religious factors. This point is worth emphasizing, since the religious consideration was central in the zeal to achieve an absolute unification of the kingdom, and the anti-Judaism inherent in Catholicism became a factor that was to return when Ferdinand and Isabella ascended the throne.

The harsh edicts issued by the Visigoth kings against the Jews in the seventh century have been studied and described by various historians, from J. Juster and S. Katz to L. Garcia Iglesias and J.L. Lacave. We can state unequivocally that the seventh century was one of uncertainty, persecution, and suffering for the Jewish *conversos*, whose property had been taken away, families destroyed, sons removed from their parents to be brought up as good Catholics, and who, in addition, were rigorously forbidden to do anything that could be construed as having a connection with their previous faith. They survived these conditions until 711, when the Visigoths were defeated in the Moorish conquest.

The conversos' tragedy was doubled in Al-Andalus under the rule of the Moorish Almohades, a dynasty characterized by its extreme religious fundamentalism, which led to the forcible conversions of both Jews and Christians and, consequently, to the flight of many Jews including, in 1150, Maimonides and his family.

Both in the Middle Ages and in the preceding era, mass conversions were generally the result of the use of force, but what made the situation in the Iberian Peninsula in 1391 so different from anywhere else in Europe was not just the large number of conversions that resulted from the persecution and slaughter of the Jews; it was the fact that the conversions continued, reaching their peak in Spain in 1492, the year of their expulsion, and in Portugal in 1497, when a royal decree was issued ordering the Jews to convert *en masse*.

Entire communities were compelled to convert, renounce the religions of their forefathers, and, all at once, take their places as Christians in Spanish society. Neither the state nor the church were prepared for such a transformation; nor did they have the resources needed to cope with the difficulties resulting from an entire ethnic group's converting to a new and unknown religion, in a Christian country, among a different, autochthonous population. It was another matter altogether when an entire people or nation on the outer fringes of Christianity received the sacrament but continued to live in their own country, maintaining their traditional social structure. In the case in point we are talking of an entire community with a different faith who underwent conversion and were compelled to integrate in the Christian environment. *Conversos* were supposed to acquire equal status and be welcomed into purely Christian population, proud of their Christian faith. It may be demonstrated that just as new converts had absolutely no chance of assimilating, neither were the original Christians prepared to accept the social and national integration of people who had up to then been objects of contempt and loathing, people perceived as being to blame for the death of Christ.

These conversions were not, then, restricted to just the social upheavals of 1391, but also continued over the coming years, sometimes under official pressure, as when Jews were forced to live in ghettos and wear marks to identify them, sometimes by the use of incentives, as demonstrated by Ferdinand I of Aragón, who awarded high positions and even titles of nobility to any important Jews who were prepared to enter the bosom of the Church. In addition, hundreds of Jews were converted by the fiery oratory of fray Vicente Ferrer and many more, in the wake of the Tortosa Dispute (1413-1414), headed by the *converso* Jerónimo de Santa Fe (previously Rabbi Yehoshua Ha-Lorqui) and under the patronage of the anti-Pope Benedict XIII.

Throughout the endless debating in Tortosa, respected Jews volunteered to be baptized. Among these were the La Caballería family as well as their friends and acquaintances. A few weeks later some of these *conversos* turned up with Christian names, holding important administrative and political positions. We mention only a few examples. Fernando de la Caballería, formerly Bonafos, who had been serving the king of Aragón since December, 1412, was appointed the king's chamberlain and treasurer in December, 1414, these posts having previously been considered out of bounds for Jews. Another was Don Vidal de la Caballería, the son of the famous Don Benveniste Ben Labi, a Hebrew poet and one of the Jewish community's leaders at the beginning of the Tortosa Dispute. He took the Christian name Gonzalo and also began working in the state's financial administration. Incidentally, just as he had been an outstanding poet in Hebrew before his conversion to Christianity, so afterwards he turned his cultural/humanist talents to translating Cicero's works of philosophy from Latin to Castilian. His teacher and family friend, the venerable poet Rabbi Salomon de Piera, converted to Christianity with him.

Thus a new social class emerged in fifteenth century Christian Spain, a class of *Judeoconversos*, or New Christians; Jews who, for one reason or another, changed their faith to Christianity through baptism. In Castilian, the word *converso* is unambiguous in meaning, in contrast to Hebrew, which has two words, *anus* and *meshumad*; the former means someone who has been forced to convert, the latter is someone who has converted of his own free will, the implication being that he is a renegade.

Most *conversos*, despite their new status, did not move away from their original homes, but remained living alongside those who were still Jews. They remained there, either carrying on with their usual occupations or attempting to find new professions, preferably among their Christian neighbors. Although they were regarded as part of the Catholic congregation, *conversos* were actually a group apart; the Christians did not regard them as equal members of society. Neither the Church, the state, nor the local authorities managed to find a way to enable *conversos* to fully integrate into and be absorbed by Christian society. It took generations before those who wished to become fully part of Christian society could behave as though they were the equals of any other Catholic Spaniard. Throughout this period, the New Christians suffered from discrimination and isolation (officially, at least) from

their Jewish "brethren" and could not—even if they so wished—be assimilated by the Catholic congregation as members with full rights. We must, of course, recall that this applied to Jews who, having been compelled to accept baptism, were now trying desperately to return to their ancient faith, the millenary tradition of their forefathers. This is why the *conversos* seem to be a "transitional society," one that had abandoned Judaism but was not permitted to fully integrate into Christian society.

Conversion, which should per se have paved their way into Christian society, failed to do so. The *conversos* were unable to make Christians forget either their Jewish past or the Christians' hatred of this past. The Christians were afflicted with hatred for both Judaism and the Jews; "old" Christians were more distrustful of *conversos* than they were of Jews who had kept their old religion and people. As Spaniards would say, these latter had never "changed their spots;" they had not behaved treacherously, while the *conversos*, having renounced their faith and people, might well treat their new, adopted faith in the same way. Nevertheless, the *conversos*, who expected nothing from Christian society, did enjoy a powerful spiritual strength originating in their attachment to and nostalgia for all that Christians venerated, as we shall see later.

There were two basic reasons why the *converso* problem began to acquire the dimensions of a national problem in the period preceding Spain's unification: on the one hand, the Spaniards' reactions to the New Christians' attempts to integrate into Spanish society as equals and, on the other, the Spaniards' reactions to those *conversos* who decided to shun contacts with their Christian environment. In this latter sense, the old Christians' indifference as against the *conversos*' reluctance to assimilate into their society was more significant than their rejection of the other group, the baptized who did truly desire to integrate. In this context, it is my feeling that "majority versus majority" relations, as it were, are a more feasible assumption than a majority, on the one hand, and, on the other, a series of isolated individuals who wished to integrate. *Conversos* who were unwilling to integrate regarded their baptisms as the product of a moment of weakness and believed they were destined to return to their ancient faith and traditions. This being so, our question is, how did those Jews who persisted in maintaining their faith react to the *conversos*? The answer is simple, as we see from the Talmudic proverb: "A son of Israel, even if he has sinned, is still a son of Israel" (B. San. 44a). *Conversos* who wished to return to their ancient faith were taken back as brethren, as though nothing had happened: "*Conversos* and Jews were one people, united by bonds of religion and messianic hopes," according to Yitzhak Baer in his monumental *History of the Jews in Christian Spain.*

Without entering into a discussion of the degree of sincerity of those conversions and without denying that there were undoubtedly many that were spontaneous, one thing must be said: old Christian society absorbed the enormous numbers of New Christians through the use of force rather than by applying the tolerant Pauline doctrine of missionary activity designed to lead to conversion. This, of course, created many problems, of which the worst was the likelihood that this anomaly would become a focal point for the emergence of additional social and religious friction. What we are dealing with, then, is an authentic transition from the Jewish problem to the problem of the *conversos* (as defined by E. Benito Ruano in his study of the origins of this problem).

The *Judeoconversos*' Social Integration: This is not the place to discuss either the problem of the Judaizer *conversos*—those who feigned their loyalty to their new faith while inwardly remaining loyal to the religion of their forefathers—or that of those *conversos* who wavered, waiting for the chance to leave Spain and go back to being true Jews; we wish to look at the other side of the coin, that is, those *conversos* who had unhesitatingly and of their own free will converted to the religion that was being imposed on the Jews by force and sometimes even violence. We are not discussing Jewish martyrology but trying to emphasize a unique and complex aspect of the *converso* phenomenon. The contemporary authors and documents bear witness to the fact that the philosophical and intellectual education then customary for Jews of higher social status encouraged this conversion, while the lower classes and women remained more adherent to the faith of their fathers and so tended more towards crypto-Judaism.

Yitzhak Baer develops this concept, attributing the blame for the many defections from the Jewish camp to philosophical Averroism, with all its tendencies towards skepticism. Nevertheless, it seems that the large number of spontaneous conversions that occurred in rabbinical circles must be taken into account, as well as conversions by other groups that, in the same circumstances, had not come into contact with Averroism and many of whom converted without any connection with their social or educational standing. We believe that it was not necessarily the intellectual Jews of that time whose conversions were influenced by their attraction to Averroist ways of thinking.

As an example, let us look at the case of the renowned rabbi of Burgos, Salomon Halevi, who later, under the name of Pablo de Santa María, became the bishop of that town. We mention him not just because he is an example of the type of *converso* we wish to discuss but also because his conversion sparked an extensive literary controversy in Burgos' Jewish community. We learn a great deal from this controversy about the motives that led Jews like him and others on his level rapidly to alter their deep-rooted beliefs and lifestyles. An echo of the dispute can be found in the letter Halevi received after his conversion from one of his previous disciples, Yehoshua Ha-Lorqui, a rabbi and physician from Alcañiz. In this letter Ha-Lorqui not only expressed his astonishment at his mentor's conversion, he also confided that he, too, had religious doubts. In an attempt to define or identify the factors in his former teacher's conversion, Yehoshua Ha-Lorqui enumerated four factors that could have prompted it:

> Did you perchance lust after riches and honors? . . . Or did the study of philosophy cause you to change so radically and to regard the proofs of faith as vanity and delusion, so that you therefore turned to things

more apt to gratify the body and satisfy the intellect without fear and anxiety and apprehension? Or, when you beheld the doom of our homeland, the multitude of the afflictions that have recently befallen us, which ruined and destroyed us, the Lord having almost turned away his countenance from us and given us for food to the fowl of the air and the beasts of the field—did it then seem to you that the name of Israel would be remembered no more? Or perhaps the secrets of prophecy have been revealed to you and the principles of faith—matters not revealed to the great pillars of faith whom we had with us in all the ages of our Exile; and you saw that our fathers had inherited falsehood, that they had but little comprehension of the intent of the Torah and the Prophecy, and you chose what is true and established?

Pablo de Santa María answered him briefly, advising him to apply himself to a serious study of the Christian doctrine, advise Jerónimo de Santa Fe (as he was later to be known) undoubtedly took, since in his anti-Jewish treatise *Ad convincendum perfidiam judaeorum* (1412) he demonstrated a profound knowledge of Christianity. In addition, his contribution to the Dispute of Tortosa (1413-1414) proved that even before his conversion Jerónimo de Santa Fe had devoted himself to studying the Christian doctrine. We do not know whether Pablo de Santa María's reply answered the questions his former disciple had raised, since all that remains is the conclusion; the most interesting section, that in which we assume he gave Ha-Lorqui those answers appropriate to the latter's erudition in the Talmud and the Torah, is missing.

In Aragón, too, the conversions were producing despair, and there, too, we have a great deal of written evidence. One example is the poem by Salomón de Piera (who later was himself among the converts) which he sent to R. Moses aben Abez, as follows:

That day death's angels ransacked my
  home . . .
Around my house the foe encamped,
Built his ramparts and his ramp
And broke inside; there lustily
He sacked and pillaged pitilessly . . .
My sons sought the safety of the stony cliff,
  and fled
Without a blessing on their head.
—My fine young bucks, who in captivity

Now banished are by iniquity!
Hunted like fledglings, I know not where
They rest tonight; nor whether they are
Not somewhere sold or slaughtered; nor on
  what pyre
Their bodies' flesh is broiled by fire . . .
The earth is clean dissolved and broken
  down,
And down is come the town's foundation
  stone.

For many of these Spanish Jews, two factors, their scientific and humanist education and their desire to be received at court, contributed to an increase in defections from Judaism. Salomón Bonafed's poetry is redolent of the hesitations and uncertainties bedeviling those around him. He fired his arrows laden with irony at Jews who turned their coats with such ease. The physician and poet Astruc Rimoch de Fraga, who converted in 1414 together with his son, taking the name Magister Francesch de Sant Jordi, sent a contentious letter to Saltiel Bonafós, the son of the physician Isaac Bonafós Saltiel and son-in-law of Rabbi Isaac bar Séset, encouraging him to follow his example. Salomón Bonafed answered this letter. The devious, subtle, complex style of these letters is very different from the scholasticism of the classical controversies.

As an example, let us look at the names of Pablo de Santa María's family of *judeoconversos* (the Levis of Burgos) who played important roles in fifteenth and sixteenth century Spain. Some of them—Pablo de Cartagena, Gonzalo de Santa María, Alonso de Santa María, Juan Díaz de Coca—were successful heads of such churches as those of Cartagena, Burgos, Astorga, Plasencia, Sigüenza, Oviedo and Calahorra. Others, for example Pablo and Alonso de Santa María, the historian Alvar García, the nun Teresa de Cartagena, the Franciscan fray Iñigo de Mendoza, the poet Cartagena and the Maluenda family, enriched Spanish literature with works of uniquely creative genius.

Particularly outstanding in national politics were the brothers Pablo and Alvar García, Pedro de Cartagena, Alvar Sánchez de Santa María and the Bishops Gonzalo and Alonso, all the sons of Pablo de Cartagena, and others who were descended from Don Pedro de Cartagena. In the military sphere, great renown was won by, among others, that same Don Pedro de Cartagena, his sons and grandsons, among them Alonso de Cartagena and Alvar de Cartagena. In both ecclesiastical and lay diplomacy several of these families, from Pablo and Alvar to Gonzalo and Alonso de Cartagena, were prominent for their achievements. All in all, there was no aspect of lay or ecclesiastic life, literature, the army, politics, diplomacy, and economics in those centuries where one of this noble family from Burgos was not prominent.

As with the de Cartagenas, many other *conversos*' merits earned them entry into the cavalry orders and the nobility, and some attained senior positions in the court administration. We could enumerate many more names but shall restrict ourselves to only a few of the most prominent and unique. Some of the most outstanding examples of the documentation dealing with *converso* families and their connections to the upper classes in Spanish society, particularly the nobility, are *El Libro Verde de Aragón* and *El Tizón de la Nobleza de España*, with which we deal later.

Among the outstanding descendants of that same Bishop of Burgos we mentioned earlier, Pablo de Santa María, was his son Pedro de Cartagena, who was the king's champion and commander of the cavalry as well as being the conqueror of the town and fortress of Lara, where the kings of Castille had so often found themselves powerless.

Another example was Diego Arias Dávila, the lord of Puñonrostro and founder of the Davila dynasty, whose descendants became synonymous with the upper ranks of the Spanish aristocracy. Among them were Pedro, better known by the name of Pedrarias, lord of Torrejón de Velasco, Diego's eldest son, who also succeeded him as Lord High Chamberlain. When he was removed from office, Pedrarias joined some of the aristocratic opponents of Henrique IV, who dared not raise a finger against him since his wife was a Mendoza y Carillo from Toledo. Nor should we forget that Archbishop Primatus Alfonso Carillo, his wife's cousin, was the most powerful figure in fifteenth century

Spain and Pedrarias' brother Juan was the bishop of Segovia.

Juan Pacheco, Magister of Santiago in the reign of Henrique IV, was the founder of the Villena dynasty and betrothed to the Catholic Isabel when she was still a princess. His brother Pedro Girón was Magister of Alcantara under Henrique IV and founded the Osuna dynasty. Both their parents were of Jewish descent, originating in the Tavira family. Through their marriages, Juan's daughters introduced *converso* blood into the following aristocratic houses: Benavente, Villafranca, Aranda, Florencia, Castroleda, Infantado, Montesclaros, Tabora, de las Navas, Priego, Soria, Almuñecar, Albuquerque, Medellín, Ayamonte, Alcaudete, Oropesa, Maqueda, Fuensalida and Teba. Among the descendants of Pedro Girón, the aristocratic houses of Osuna, Palma and Arcos de Vélez are particularly noteworthy.

Also worth mentioning are Andrés Cabrera, the Alcaide of Segovia, who was a close confidant of the Marquis de Moya and, with his wife, maintained personal friendships with the Catholic kings, and Alonso de Burgos, the bishop of Cordoba, who was ennobled and became the count of Pernia. *Conversos* also appear in the family tree of the following families: de la Puebla, Alcalá, Castro, del Carpio, Valencia, Nájera, Buendía, Cerralbo, Andrade, Montemayor, Falces, Algaba, Medinaceli, Coruña and Cifuentes.

Moving on to Aragón, we find the names Santángel, Sánchez, Clemente and de la Caballería, all among the kingdom's greatest lords, whose blood runs in the veins of some of Spain's noblest families. Then there were the sons of Alonso de Aragón and the *conversa* María Coneso de Zaragoza; one was ennobled as Count of Ribagorza, another became bishop of Tortosa and later, archbishop of Tarragona, while the third was elevated to the position of prior of Cataluña and also appointed Commendador of San Juan. Also descended from Alonso de Aragón and María Coneso were Francisco de Aragón, the son of the first duke of Villahermosa, who married the *conversa* Leonor Zapata, heiress to a great fortune, and their grandson, Alonso of

Gurrea and Aragón, who became the second duke of Ribagorza and married Isabel, the daughter of the duke of Cardona.

The Bacas of Aragón were descendants of Nuño Cabeza de Vaca, the lord of Melgar and Melgarejo, and one of his Jewish vassals; they were granted the barony of Figueruela and had family connections with the Luna family, who were lords of Illueca and, on their sons' side, were connected with the Mendozas, lords of Sangarrén, and the Cerdáns, the lords of Castellar.

Reading the *Libro Verde*, the "Burke's Peerage" of the Aragonese aristocracy, we find many noble families whose blood was intermingled with that of notable *conversos*. Among these families some of the most prominent were the Moncada, the lords of Aytona; the Gurrea, the lords of Argavieso; the Mendoza, the lords of Garón; the Ixares, the counts of Belchite; the Moncayo, the lords of Rafales; the Torrella, the lords of Torrecilla; the Bardají, the lords of Estercuel; the Almazán, the lords of Maella; the Urreas, the lords of Aranda; the Liñán, the lords of Catina; the Cerdán, the lords of Castellar; the Pomar, the lords of Ligues and Ciprés, the Luna, the lords of Luna; the Francia, the lords of Bureta, and many others such as the Mur, the Artal, the Bolea, the Arellano, etc.

These few of the many examples we could give are sufficient to illustrate the phenomenon of *converso* blood running through the veins of the country's greatest lords, both temporal and ecclesiastical.

In the case of Castille, these *conversos* became almost a social and political bloc in the stormy times of the reign of Juan II of Castille and the governorship of Don Alvaro de Luna. In later years, this naturally led to a situation in which they were the objects of the "old" Christians' hatred and loathing, since their conversion to Christianity had brought them some of the highest positions and offices in the civil and ecclesiastical administration.

Many of the *conversos* continued to work in commerce and tax farming; others proved to be efficient and successful in the management of urban local authorities. *Conversos* were outstanding in both the literature and the politics of the time, and some (for example, the Santa María clan, along with those who had joined them, such as the Maluenda, the Cartagena and others) attained senior positions in the king's councils. The *conversos'* situation may be said, if not always, then at least in a majority of cases, to resemble that of the court Jews we encounter throughout the history of the Jews of Spain, with the one great difference that the *conversos* had changed their external garb, either because they were forced to or for motives that had nothing to do with religion.

On the other hand, the fragility of this appearance of social integration must be emphasized; even during the first half of the fifteenth century, as we know, there was a fiercely anti-*converso* movement that tried to prevent them from entering positions that had been barred to them when they were still Jews.

It took almost two generations for Christian society to become truly aware of the troubles produced by the mass conversion of the Jews. Opinions on this problem began to appear as early as in the 1440s, for instance, the "*Espejo de la Nobleza o Tratado de Fidalguía*" by Diego de Valera (Chapter IX). It was only in 1449, however, that the co-existence problem took a turn for the worse. Then Pedro Sarmiento, the mayor of the Toledo Court of Appeal and Main Repostero to King Juan II, rebelled and took control of the city. It is not known whether the outrages against the Toledan *conversos*, which first broke out on January 27 of that year, coincided with or followed the Sarmiento Rebellion. After a brief study of the links between the perpetrators of the outrages and Pedro Sarmiento, we can say that they were sufficiently close, and the hypothesis that the rebellion and pillaging were planned together and in agreement is not without grounds.

The rioting began after Don Alvaro de Luna asked Toledo for a loan as its contribution to the war between Castile and Aragon. Since the population declined to pay, he sent tax collectors to seize the money, with orders to use force if necessary. These tax collectors were *conversos*, and their methods aroused the Toledans' ire. Now the ancient hatred re-emerged, mounting to unprecedented heights. On January 27, all Toledo's church bells began to ring as a signal for "old Christians" to attack the *conversos*. The Toledo massacre was rightly considered not to be a purely local event, since the rioting spread out to beyond the city walls, spilling over into the neighboring Ciudad Real. An outburst of previously-restrained hatred had now flared up, a popular reaction to the *converso* problem, but the rabble's leaders also included priests and seglars. The massacre did not originate in quarrels among neighbors, but was an overt reaction to the *conversos'* entry into the Christian social institutions and their access to public positions they could never have attained as Jews. The request for a loan and the measures used to collect the money were only the spark that ignited these feelings.

Another symptom of this open war was Pedro Sarmiento's Verdict Statute (1449). Sarmiento explicitly demanded the *conversos'* dismissal from all the public offices in Toledo, citing the extension to the canonical law of the 4th Council of Toledo (633), "*judaei, et qui ex judaeis sunt*" (Canon 65), as well as other rulings. The extension contains two definitions in the single phrase. Although the word "*judaei*" poses no difficulties, there are questions about the sense of "*ex judaei sunt.*" It is in the essence of this phrase that the controversy between Sarmiento and his followers, on the one hand, and the *conversos'* defenders, on the other, may be found. On this paragraph Sarmiento based his accusation that the fourteen jurists who were on trial for holding public office in Toledo had committed a crime. His reasoning was simple: if the *conversos* are proved to be Jews, the full severity of the above laws may be brought to bear on them. From this it follows that what happened in Toledo was a typical Inquisition process, designed to prove that *conversos* were purely and simply Jews.

Immediately after the promulgation of the Verdict Statute, various contentious writings dealing with the question of the New Christians' right to participate in the public life of Castilian society began to appear. Taking sides in this literary war, which H. Beinart has called "the polemics of the writings," were, on the one hand, those who, for religious or racial reasons, were sworn enemies of Judaism and, on the other, those who advocated the unity of the Christian faith, emphasizing the evangelical precept of brotherhood and the awareness of the unity of humankind. As can be expected, for the most part the latter comprised recent *conversos*, some of whom were of high and renowned Hebrew lineage; they pleaded for unity and brotherhood among believers, both Old and New Christians, probably from the fear that the outbreak of social racism that was ultimately to give birth to the blood purity laws would harm them too.

Among the most prominent of the advocates of the "*causo conversa*" was Alonso de Cartagena, whom we have already mentioned, the bishop of Burgos and son of Pablo de Santa María, who had been baptized as a child and so could be called a first generation *converso*. In his book of apologetics *Defensorium unitatis christianae* (1449), he explained that in the abovementioned sentence of the Toledan Council, the term "*judaei*" should be taken as meaning original Jews who had never converted and who maintained the Mosaic Law, while "*qui ex judaeis sunt*" meant anyone who maintained that law, even if they had no Jewish origins, that is, those who were guilty of Judaizing. Nevertheless, in his attitude to the problem of the *conversos* of Jewish origin, he emphasized that he regarded Jewish origins as an advantage and welcomed the *conversos*, saying that through baptism they would acquire the traits of the Hasmoneans. Any Jews who made the decision to be baptized would be welcomed into the Catholic congregation. The Visigoth legislation was basically aimed at people who accepted baptism and then reverted to their former faith, in this case, Judaism.

Another writer who took an active part in this dispute was a Jewish *conversa*'s son, Juan de Torquemada, a Spanish cardinal in the curio of Pope Nicholas V and uncle of the Grand Inquisitor Tomas de Torquemada. In his concern for the purity of the Catholic faith he wrote the *Tractatus contra madianitas et ismaelitas adversarios et detractores filiorum qui de populo israelitico originem traxerunt* (1450) against those enemies of the *conversos* who dared to write "slanders in the name of a legal process" and to demonstrate to all the glory and nobility of the Hebrew race. In his introduction, he justified the use of the term "*madianitas et ismaelitas*" by saying it was his name for the enemies of the *conversos*: "They are the enemies of the Chosen People mentioned in the Bible," he thundered, calling them the emissaries of the Devil and foes of God.

Another noteworthy descendant of the *anusim* was Fernán Díaz de Toledo, speaker of the Royal Council and a confidant of Alvaro de Luna (whose Jewish name, according to García de Mora, was Moisés Hamomo). He wrote the "*Instruccion de Relator*," which is directed at Lope Barrientos, the bishop of Cuenca and formerly tutor to Enrique IV, and is a plea for protection for the persecuted class of Jewish *conversos*. In the "*Instruccion*" he rejected the use of the term *conversos* for former Jews, since in actuality they should not have been made to convert as though they were gentiles; they were at home, and the Christian doctrine was their own law, so no more should have been required of them than to undergo baptism and belief that our Lord was the King Messiah who had been promised by the prophets.

Fernan de Toledo was evidently speaking in general terms and lacked a factual basis for this opinion. It may be that as one of King Juan II's courtiers he was unable to go into every aspect of the *converso* problem; in this he resembled Torquemada, who did not even mention it. The only person to deal with the issue seriously and come up with a far-reaching project for integration was Alonso de Cartagena, who grasped the true dimensions of the drama of the *conversos*, who had abandoned their people and been rejected by the new community they wished to join. In his plan, Cartagena raised the idea of granting the *conversos* titles or a social status equivalent to those they had held when still Jews. Cartagena mentioned three types of high office: religious, legal, and civil. These divisions had also been maintained by the Jews when they

lived in their own country and enjoyed political independence. Cartagena says:

> . . . courage is to be found only among the aristocracy, not the masses. Jews are generally considered to be natural cowards. Once they are baptized, however, the former Jew loses all his weaknesses and can perform deeds of extreme bravery. Courage, intelligence, military skills—qualities they have inherited from their forefathers—re-emerge and reach a peak, all this thanks to their baptism. Through conversion Israel's golden age, that of the period prior to the advent of Jesus, is reborn . . . this is why conversion brings new qualities to Christianity to add to those already in existence among Spaniards of purely Christian origin . . . [Here we can undoubtedly find a reference to his brother, Don Pedro de Cartagena, the Captain General of Castille.] These qualities were not lost with the advent of Christ or following the Crucifixion; it is only those who persist in their blindness [that is, who continued to adhere to their Judaism] who must be denied every title and privilege . . . after they are baptized they will be worthy of any position. . . .

In addition to taking a progressive step by proposing a plan for total assimilation, Cartagena's stand was clear enough. Each *converso* would enter society to take up his previous, pre-conversion status ("the common folk will join their peers; merchants will be among merchants, soldiers with their like, clerics with their fellows . . . keeping *conversos* on the lowest rung of the social ladder could lead to them abandoning their new faith because of disappointment . . ."). What this meant was that the problem of the *conversos* could only be solved by understanding, goodwill, and integration into Christian society in accordance with their previous social standings, as well as being granted some of their former privileges and honorifics. This project reflects the concern of Cartagena and Christian society in general about how to cope with the problem of the *conversos*, individually and collectively. Cartagena confronted the issue in all its aspects when he realized that he was dealing not only with a religious problem of conversion but with something far more serious, that is, social integration. Without this it would be impossible to resolve the problem of the *conversos*; Christian Spanish society had to be willing to take the *conversos* to its heart. At the same time, as an essential condition for their assimilation, the *conversos* would have to eliminate all traces of their Jewish past. Once fully integrated into Christian society, they would be expected to give of their best, drawing on those qualities that had been renewed by virtue of their baptism.

Cartagena's plan, however, involved some difficulties, the major ones being the Spaniards' perception that *conversos* were innately different; in addition, some of the *conversos* probably found the plan unacceptable. It was, nevertheless, a landmark, conceived by a man with a unique view of the future when it came to a solution to the problem.

To these three writers of Jewish descent we may add Don Lope de Barrientos himself, the only "old Christian" to come out in defense of the *conversos* and in favor of their integration into Christian Spanish society, who wrote (c. 1450) his *Contra algunos cizañadores de la nacion de los convertidos del pueblo de Israel*. Some say that in this essay he used the ideas of Fernan Díaz de Toledo on the effectiveness of baptism in integrating the *conversos*, the danger of apostasy caused by discrimination, and the psychological and social difficulties of Jews considering conversion. The works by these four authors were the first to arouse public interest in the *converso* problem and were thus the first attempts by *converso*-Christians to discuss a solution to an apparently insoluble problem.

This argument continued into the 1460s and then, too, someone who was himself of *converso* origin, Fray Alonso de Oropesa, emerged to champion the *conversos*. He wrote *Lumen ad revelationem gentium et gloriam plebis Dei Israel de unitate fidei et de concordi et pacifica aequalitate fidelium* (1451-1465[!]). Oropesa may be described as having a relatively moderate ideology, unique in his time, and clinging to Paulist doctrine and the *"Philosophia Christi,"* as did the Erasmians later. It is of interest to add that, in an ironic twist of history, Oropesa's religious order, the Order of St. Jerome, was one of the first to apply the laws of purity of blood, in 1486-1495. There were, however, different circumstances surrounding each of the statutes.

In contrast to Oropesa, Alonso de Espina, who some attribute with being of *converso* origin, was prominent in his extreme opposition to the integration of *conversos* into Christian society. He regarded both *conversos* and Jews as heretics, but the Jews were at least overtly so, while the *conversos* made a pretence of being Christian. In his *Fortalitium fidei*, he raised the idea of expelling all the Jews from Spain. He thought this would result in the *conversos'* complete assimilation into Christian society. Espina reminded the authorities of the Jews' expulsions from England, France, and Germany. He claimed that, as these countries had succeeded in surviving without Jews, so, with the help of God, could Spain. Espina was also extreme in his solution to the *converso* problem. He proposed an intensive inquisition of all *conversos* and severe punishments for all heretics. He attacked the *conversos* as Jews in Christian garb who had succeeded in penetrating the Church:

> No one investigates the errors of the heretics; and those rapacious wolves have entered your flock, O Lord. This is because the true shepherds are few and the mercenaries are many, and because those who are mercenaries do not come to feed the flock but, rather, to shear its wool. The young ass is falling, and there is no one to raise her. The soul is being extinguished, and there is no one to help her. Nobody thinks about the perfidious Jews, who blaspheme against your name, nor [do they think about] the unfaithful, who secretly perform unheard-of cruelties, because their donations and their bribes have blinded the eyes of the judges and the prelates, of both the priests and the people. Among your preachers, [O Lord], there are few who seek the light, because they distance their ears from the truth and [then] once more hearken to non-truths.

Anti-Jewish Polemics: It is noteworthy that in the fifteenth century the *conversos'* social isolation and need for self-defense drove them to write not just Christian apologetics, through which they attempted to both justify Christianity's intellectual foundations and, at the same time, testify to the sincerity of their belief, but also to exploit their literary skills and inside knowledge to attack Judaism, possibly in the belief that by so doing they would lessen the popular hatred of the *conversos* and erase the stain of their origins.

One thing must be made clear: one way or another, the *conversos* had a hard time of it, spiritually speaking, even if they encountered no overt difficulties in Christian society. The *converso* always had to expect that there would be gossip around him, and the higher he rose in society, the more hatred and envy were to be anticipated. There were cases in which the *converso* brought disgrace upon his family, and he did not always find himself in a sympathetic environment; for the most part he had to enter an alien society, devoid of friends and relatives. There were many incidents of families' being torn apart when the wife and children did not follow the father. *Conversos* also lost their social positions and standing and there were incidents of *conversos'* having to toil in their new environment to arrive at a status similar to that they had enjoyed before this. Most tragic was that many of them also became impoverished, since they had left their property and assets behind in the Jewish community and if they had been money-lenders, as Christians, this was now out of bounds. Needless to say, their public baptism was a disgrace for relatives who remained Jewish, the saddest thing being that for many of them it was their pride alone that prevented them from returning to Judaism.

What emerges from this complex situation is that the *conversos* cannot be regarded as one monolithic group, as their reactions and behavior patterns varied greatly, going beyond the four classes of *conversos* discussed by Jose Faur in a fascinating typological study. At this point, I would like to stress that most of the works of Christian polemics were actually written by *conversos*, some of the most significant of whom were Rabbi Samuel from Morocco, who was baptized in Toledo in 1085 and wrote *De adventu Messiae praeterito liber*; Petrus Alphonsi, formerly Rabbi Moisés ha-Sefardí, who was baptized in Huesca in 1106 and wrote, first in Arabic and then in Latin, the renowned work *Disciplina clericalis* and, in the field of interfaith polemics,

Dialogus Petri cognomento Alphonsi, ex Iudaeo Christiani et Moysi Iudaei; Paulo Christiani, who in 1263 represented the Christian side against Nahmanides (Rabbi Moses ben Nahman) in the Barcelona debate held in the presence of James I of Aragón; Alfonso de Valladolid, formerly Rabbi Abner de Burgos, author and *Mostrador de justicia* (1270-1348); Jerónimo de Santa Fe, who presided over the Tortosa Dispute (1413-1414); and also Pablo de Santa María, whom we have mentioned before and whose work *Scrutinium Scripturarum*, written in 1443, was considered to be one of the best works of Christian apologetics written in Spain. There were also writings by *conversos* such as *Zelus Christi contra Judaeos, Saracenos et infideles* by Pedro de la Caballería, *Ensis Pauli* (also known as *de mysteriis findei*) by Pablo Heredia and the *Tractatus contra iudaeos* by Jaime Pérez de Valencia.

Two of these polemicists of Jewish origin, Petrus Alphonsi, who lived in the twelfth century, and Jerónimo de Santa Fe, are particularly noteworthy for the role they played in the greatest of the religious debates in Spain, that held in Tortosa in 1413-1414. In his *Dialogus*, Petrus Alphonsi remarks on the transition between the patristic period and that of the *reconquista*. In a lively dialogue he defends his conversion and presents the motives that led him to it in the form of an imaginary argument with himself, since the two figures in the *Dialogus*, the Jew and the Christian, are none other than Moysi, which was his name as a Jew, and Petri, the name he took when he converted. Although he also attacks the Muslim faith, almost the entire tract, which is divided into twelve chapters to make it easier to find the different subjects, addresses mainly the Jewish faith. It contains a great deal of the philosophical speculation typical of the time, but what is noteworthy here with regard to the originality of the work is the fact that it makes use of many texts from the Talmud, texts that were also used in the Tortosa Debate.

Petrus Alphonsi's attack on the Talmud, which is based on the, as it were, errors it contains, set a precedent for what was to happen towards the end of the Tortosa Debate when, in the same way, Jerónimo de Santa Fe also attacked the Talmud. His article on the "Errors of the Jews in the Talmud" contains a compilation of Rabbinic texts that were scrupulously selected and translated into Latin so as to achieve a tendentious presentation of the nature of the Talmud, based for the most part on quotations from the *Midrash* and the *Haggadah*, that is, using functionally homiletic literary texts and narrative, legendary material totally unconnected with the Talmud's binding texts. Right from the start the rabbis who appeared in the Tortosa Debate made it unambiguously clear that they were not committed to these quotations, thus continuing with a policy they had learned from Nahmanides in the Barcelona Debate of 1263. Their position on the Haggadah, from the beginning to the end of the arguments, remained consistent and united.

In the Tortosa Debate, Jerónimo went back to the use of quotations from the Talmud that were more or less indefensible because of their theological or moral subject matter. He also made use of implied slighting of Jesus or offensive Talmudic rulings on idolatry, Canaanites, the sons of Noah, and gentiles, all terms, according to the former rabbi from Alcañiz, that were euphemisms for Christians. After having presented his thesis on these various errors, Jerónimo concludes that the Talmud is an anti-Christian book, a conclusion easily reached when one deems any mention of alien peoples or idolatry to refer to Christians and Christianity.

Jerónimo exploited his great knowledge of the literature of the Talmud, Midrash, and biblical commentaries of a homiletic nature to develop a campaign of proselytism. Although he started out by trying to use talmudic material to convince the Jews of the advent of the messiah in the form of Jesus of Nazareth, he finally admitted that he had no belief at all in the Talmud, with the exception of those sections he could exploit and, even then, only if they served his purposes. His attitude towards the Talmud was extremely ambivalent and, when circumstances required, he had no hesitations about emasculating texts or taking them out of context to make them fit his thesis. Nevertheless, he did not deny the genuine value the Jews attached to certain sections of the Talmud, and in the minutes of the debate he admitted that the Jews regarded some of the talmudic quotations as being legendary rather than binding, so they were not committed to believing in them.

Jerónimo's accusations led to the promulgation in May, 1415, of Benedict XIII's papal bull *Etsi doctoris gentium.* Jerónimo himself read out sections of his anti-Talmud tract in the Tortosa Debate, and the arbiters, as the converted former rabbi had intended, condemned the Talmud, making it an offence not just to read it in Spain, but even to own a copy; this ban applied to the book that, 130 years earlier, Raimundo Martí had used to testify to the truth of the Christian doctrines and that King Alfonso X of Castille (1252-1284) had requested be translated into Castilian.

A comparison between the two great debates held in Spain, in Barcelona and Tortosa, leads to three conclusions. First, in these arguments, the *conversos,* who fulfilled the role of very special advocates of the Christian side, were of enormous importance. In addition to their demonstrative zeal in working to convince their former brethren to convert, they contributed their very extensive knowledge of Rabbinic literature and their crucial awareness of Judaism's strong and weak points. The second conclusion is that in both debates the anti-Jewish polemics took on a new appearance, different from that of the past, which had been based exclusively on biblical quotations. Now, with the aid of the *conversos,* the Christian argument was based on Rabbinic literature. The third conclusion is that both the Barcelona and Tortosa Debates constituted a frontal assault on the very essence of Judaism, its principles, its faith, and its literature. The confrontation was theological in nature but altogether missionarizing in its intentions. It was a robust attempt, using the Rabbinic literature, to convince the "superior" class of Jews of the truth of Christianity.

The *converso* phenomenon was reflected not only in theological-polemical works but also in chronicles, correspondence writings, poetry, satirical literature, etc., in all of which one can find data relating to the purity of blood and the problem of the *conversos*. The rioting of 1449 was the first, but not the only, violent anti-*converso* expression among Spanish society. Others occurred in various places: in the years 1452, 1467, 1473 and 1481, a National Inquisition began to take vigorous action against the *conversos*. Here it is worth quoting, as an example of the Spanish people's attitude to the New Christians, the cynical yet realistic words of the chronicler Fernando del Pulgar: "I believe, señor, that there are *some sinful* evildoers (*conversos*) but that the others, who are the *majority*, commit evil because they follow the *sinful minority* and these *would* follow the righteous *if there were any*. But if the earlier converted ones are such *bad Christians*, the new ones will be *very good Jews*."

Parallel with such prejudiced statements, some ideas had begun to emerge on how to distance the Jews from Christian and *converso* communities. These ideas led to practical restrictions on the Jews and even harsher measures: in 1483, expulsion from the diocese of Seville and Cordova; in the same year, an order forbidding the Jews to remain in Cuenca for more than three days consecutively; in 1486, expulsion from the diocese of Zaragoza and Albarracín; in 1490, an order forbidding Jews to remain overnight in Bilbao; and, of course, in 1492, the general Edict of Expulsion from Spain.

The propaganda of those who were opposed to the *conversos* and their integration was, as we have already indicated, based on Visigoth and Church legislation banning the Jews and their descendants from holding public positions with jurisdiction over Christians. Bat-Sheva Albert has conclusively demonstrated how our authors proved that by *ex illis* the canonists were referring to Christians of Jewish origin, without entering into the question of whether or not they behaved like Jews. In any case, those who were opposed to the *conversos* maintained they should be treated as Jews, not only because of their origins but also because of their religious behavior. This was the first expression of an idea that later became the ideological cornerstone of

the Inquisition, one which, as H. Beinart has aptly observed, was based directly on Alonso de Espina's theory.

The tendency of old Christian society to consider every *converso* a Jew at heart is, in my opinion, the principal motivation for the anxiety of the apologists which characterizes the group of writings dealing with the Verdict Statute. Their common, unarguable determination was that integration through the grace of baptism was evangelically perfect; they cited the unity, loving kindness, harmony, and equality among all believers as characteristic signs of the perfection that Christ designated for his Church.

This was not just a platonic, theoretical argument, but one with very practical consequences. Most of the writers were highly conscious of the crude way in which popular fables confirmed the constant danger represented by the *converso*, using the same ideas that were used in a negative sense to describe Jews, such as their falseness, their devotion to low-level occupations and usury, the danger to society posed by *converso* physicians, their infiltration into key positions (in the case of *conversos* in municipal councils and religious orders), etc. The forged correspondence between the Jewish community leader of Toledo, Chamorro, and the Jewish community leader of Constantinople, Yussuf (c. 1454), is an excellent illustration of this situation. The Constantinople community leader is alleged to have suggested that by adopting Catholicism, *conversos* would be able to destroy it from within:

> Dear Brothers in Moses. We have received your letter telling us of your troubles and misfortunes, which hurt us as much as they do you. The opinion of our rabbi and community leaders is as follows:
> Regarding what you say about the king of Spain's forcing you to become Christians: do it, because you have no choice!
> Regarding what you say about his order to take over your businesses: turn your sons into merchants so that, little by little, they will take over theirs.
> Regarding what you say about their taking over your synagogues: turn your sons into clerics and theologians, so that they will destroy their churches.
> And regarding what you say about their

oppressing you: try to turn your sons into lawyers, prosecutors, notaries, and counselors, so that they will always understand public dealings and in the fullness of time they will be able to overcome them and take vengeance on them.

Do not deviate from these instructions and, by your experience, you will see that you will go from being the suppressed to being the masters.

Yussuf, leader of the Jews of Constantinople

In the sacralized mentality of Spanish society, where intolerance was an undisputed principle, the specter that most terrified everyone was heresy, which was considered to be far more profoundly significant than the term itself may imply. Because of this, purity of blood [= purity of faith] became the prime goal and inevitable means for religious, social and political calm. Heresy's greatest danger did not come from the Jews alone but was also to be found among the *conversos*. Their Jewishness was biological, genetic, and, since it was hereditary, very difficult to eradicate, as B. Netanyahu has demonstrated in his *The Origins of the Spanish Inquisition in the Fifteenth Century*, and as was understood to be perceived even in the New Christians' physical characteristics.

The essence of this misconception stemmed from the mentality of this period. Most Christians believed that even baptism did not erase the original sin of being Jewish. In vain the *conversos*' defenders stressed the sincerity of the conversions. Even one hundred years after the events in Toledo (c. 1556), one of the greatest of the apologists, Fray Domingo de Baltanas, had to pile up historical arguments to prove the honesty of the baptized *conversos* and eliminate the unjustified prejudices against them. In his famous argument against discrimination and rejection, he named many *conversos* as personal examples of honesty and virtue.

This misconception, which was shared by both simple and aristocratic people, persisted well into the seventeenth century. Divine punishment against the descendants of the deicides became translated into external, physical characteristics: long nose, bad body odor, tail, round shoulders, and men-

struation even by males among those guilty of spilling Jesus' blood. Despite Isaac Cardoso's apology, *Las excelencias de los Hebreos*, which made use of varied and successful methods, both ironic and serious, to contradict these superstitions, anti-Jewish and anti-*converso* tracts were more popular, as Y.H. Yerushalmi has demonstrated. It was convenient to attribute to the *conversos* the image and accusations that had accompanied the Jews over the ages. Everything was bound up with religion, as was natural in society's sacralized mentality. The name *converso* was applied not only to the Jew who had himself converted to Christianity but also to his children, grandchildren, great-grandchildren, and so on. Suspicions aroused by their conversions and, consequently, the suspicion of heresy were directly tied up with their social, cultural, religious, and political conduct.

Since the controversy centered on the holding of public positions, some of the *conversos*' defenders found themselves concerned not only for their own political and economic futures but also for that of their families and relatives. This concern became more understandable with the exhaustive integration project that Alonso de Cartagena proposed in his *Defensorium* for the *conversos*' absorption into Christian society. He understood the true dimensions of the drama of the *conversos*, who had abandoned their people and been rejected by that new community they wished to enter. In his plan, Cartagena came up with the idea that keeping the *conversos* on the lowest rung of the social ladder might lead them, in their disappointment, to abandon their new religion; therefore they should be awarded honorifics or social status: "*Consequens est ut reverentiam suis individuis, regibus regiam, ducibus ducalem, comitibus comitalem, marchionibus marchionilem, baronibus baronilem, et sic per diversos gradus.*"

Cartagena's plan for social integration was nevertheless problematic. This was mainly because of the Spanish mentality, which regarded the *conversos* as being innately different, what Eloy Benito Ruano called "other Christians." In addition, Christian society probably did not have the means or positions available to implement this integration. It is also conceivable that some of the *conversos* were opposed to it. In any case, this project was unique among the other approaches to the problem. Alonso de Cartagena's theorems perceived the future differently from others, and thus his solution, too, was different and did not take the immovable mentality of rejection into account.

The whole polemic for and against the *conversos* proves the extreme confusion prevalent in Spanish society in the second and third generations after the mass conversions, at a time when the *conversos'* assimilation into Christian Spanish society was supposed to have been complete. The *conversos*, however, were not recognized officially by either the Church or the monarchy as an integral part of society, even when the Catholic King Ferdinand and Queen Isabella decided to resolve the problem. The *converso* poet Antön de Montoro, who was himself present at the riots in Córdoba and Carmona (1474), described the *conversos'* frustrations in a poem he dedicated to Queen Isabella:

> O tailor, bitter and sad,/Who does not feel his grief!/For seventy years you have lived,/And in all of them you always said:/I survived under oppression/And never betrayed the Creator./I said the Credo and worshipped,/Thick rashers of bacon/And rare meat I ate,/I heard the Mass and prayed/And crossed myself,/Yet never could erase the stain of being a confeso.

His poem of complaint is tragic, because the only way out he sees for the *converso* is to be burned at the stake.

To summarize, the early attacks on *conversos* in Toledo (1449) gave birth to the spirit of the National Inquisition. Even though the Holy See immediately condemned them, such attacks flourished under the rule of the Catholic monarchs. These early attacks indirectly led to the continuing debate in Spanish society over the Jewish-*converso* issue. Spain was compelled to choose between unity and division, consolidation and internal debility. The debate on the place of Jews and *conversos* in Spanish society did not reflect well on Spain's greatness; quite the contrary. It reflected its weakness, both civil and religious, in the second half of the fifteenth century.

Bibliography

Baer, Y., *A History of the Jews in Christian Spain*, 2 vols. (Philadelphia, 1966 and 1992).

Beinart, H., "The Converso Community in Fifteenth Century Spain," in Barnett, R.D., ed., *The Sephardic Heritage* (London, 1971), pp. 425-456.

Beinart, H., *Conversos on Trial* (Jerusalem, 1981).

Netanyahu, B., *The Origins of the Inquisition in Fifteenth Century Spain* (New York, 1995).

MOISÉS ORFALI

D

DIALECTICS IN JUDAISM: A dialectical argument is a give and take in which parties to the argument counter one another in a progression of exchanges (often, in what seems like an infinite progress to an indeterminate conclusion). The dialectical argument addresses not the problem and the solution alone but the problem and the various ways by which a solution may be reached. It is not a set-piece of two positions, with an analysis of each, such as formal dialogue exposes with elegance; it is, rather, an unfolding analytical argument, explaining why this, not that, then why not that but rather this; and onward to the other thing and the thing beyond that—a linear argument in constant forward motion. A dialectical argument is not static and merely expository, but dynamic and always contentious. It is not an endless argument, an argument for the sake of arguing, or evidence that important to the Talmud and other writings that use the dialectics as a principal mode of dynamic argument is process but not position. To the contrary, the passage is resolved with a decisive conclusion, not permitted to run on.

An example of a dialectical argument: This passage occurs at B. B.M. 5B-6A, concerning M. B.M. 1:1-2. Our interest is in the twists and turns of the argument, on which the comments focus. The Mishnah-passage is the text that is being analyzed. The Talmud is in two languages, Hebrew and Aramaic; Aramaic is in italics. That is where we find ourselves in the heart of the argument, at the dialectical center of things.

The Talmud deals with a case of two claimants to an object each claims to have found. M. B.M. 1:1 is as follows:

A. Two lay hold of a cloak—
B. this one says, "I found it!"—
C. and that one says, "I found it!"—
D. this one says, "It's all mine!"—
E. and that one says, "It's all mine!"—
F. this one takes an oath that he possesses no less a share of it than half,
G. and that one takes an oath that he possesses no less a share of it than half,
H. and they divide it up.

The problem recalls the two women fighting before Solomon about the disposition of an infant child, but the law of the Mishnah and the decision of Solomon scarcely intersect. The issue now is addressed by the Talmud. What we wish to notice is how the Talmud forms a script that permits us to join in the discussion; if we don't read it out loud, we miss the compelling power of the passage, especially its systematic resort to applied reason and practical logic. And, we must not forget, we want to see precisely how a dialectical argument is written down as a text but provokes us to talk, engage in dialogue, with the text B. B.M. 5b-6a):

IV.1. A. This one takes an oath that he possesses no less a share of it than half, [and that one takes an oath that he possesses no less a share of it than half, and they divide it up]:

The rule of the Mishnah, which is cited at the head of the sustained discussion, concerns the case of two persons who find a garment. We settle their conflicting claims by requiring each to take an oath that he or she owns title to no less than half of the garment, and then we split the garment between them.

Now how does the Talmud undertake its sustained analysis of this matter? Our first question is one of text-criticism: analysis of the Mishnah-paragraph's word choice. We say that the oath concerns the portion that the claimant alleges he possesses. But the oath really affects the portion that he does not have in hand at all:

B. *Is it concerning the portion that he claims he possesses that he takes the oath, or concerning the portion that he does not claim to possess?* [Daiches, *Baba Mesia* (London, 1948) ad loc.: "The implication is that the terms of the oath are ambiguous. By swearing that his share in it is not "less than half," the claimant might mean that it is not even a third or a fourth (which is 'less than half'), and the negative way of putting it would justify such an interpretation. He could therefore take this oath even if he knew that he had no share in the garment at all, while he would be swearing falsely if he really had a share in the garment that is less than half, however small that share might be].

C. *Said R. Huna, "It is that he says, 'By an oath! I possess in it a portion, and I possess in it a portion that is no more than half a share of it.'"* [The claimant swears that his share is at least half (Daiches, *Baba Mesia, ad loc.)].

Having asked and answered the question, we find ourselves in an extension of the argument; the principal trait of the dialectical argument is now before us in three keywords:

1) but!
2) maybe the contrary is the case, so—
3) what about?

The argument is conducted by the setting aside of a proposition in favor of its opposite. Here we come to the definitive trait of the dialectic argument: its insistence on challenging every proposal with the claim, "maybe it's the opposite?" This pestering question forces us back upon our sense of self-evidence; it makes us consider the contrary of each position we propose to set forth. It makes thought happen. True, the Talmud's voice's "but"—the whole of the dialectic in one word!—presents a formidable nuisance. But so does all criticism, and only the mature mind will welcome criticism. Dialectics is not for children, politicians, propagandists, or egoists. Genuine curiosity about the truth shown by rigorous logic forms the counterpart to musical virtuosity. So the objection proceeds:

> D. *Then let him say*, "By an oath! The whole of it is mine!"

Why claim half when the alleged finder may as well demand the whole cloak?

> E. *But are we going to give him the whole of it?* [Obviously not; there is another claimant, also taking an oath.]

The question contradicts the facts of the case: two parties claim the cloak, so the outcome can never be that one will get the whole thing.

> F. *Then let him say*, "By an oath! Half of it is mine!"

Then—by the same reasoning—why claim "no less than half," rather than simply, half.

> G. *That would damage his own claim* [which was that he owned the whole of the cloak, not only half of it].

The claimant does claim the whole cloak, so the proposed language does not serve to replicate his actual claim. That accounts for the language that is specified.

> H. *But here too is it not the fact that, in the oath he is taking, he impairs his own claim?* [After all, he here makes explicit the fact that he owns at least half of it. What happened to the other half?]

The solution merely compounds the problem.

> I. *[Not at all.] For he has said*, "The whole of it is mine!" [And, he further proceeds,] "And as to your contrary view, By an oath, I do have a share in it, and that share is no less than half!"

We solve the problem by positing a different solution from the one we suggested at the outset. Why not start where we have concluded? Because if we had done so, we should have ignored a variety of intervening considerations and so should have expounded less than the entire range of possibilities. The power of the dialectical argument now is clear: it forces us to address not the problem and the solution alone, but the problem and the various ways by which a solution may be reached; then, when we do come to a final solution, we have reviewed all of the possibilities. We have seen how everything flows together, nothing is left unattended.

What we have here is not a set-piece of two positions, with an analysis of each; it is, rather, an unfolding analytical argument, explaining why this, not that, then why not that but rather this; and onward to the other thing and the thing beyond that—a linear argument in constant forward motion. When we speak of a moving argument, this is what we mean: what is not static and merely expository, but what is dynamic and always contentious. It is not an endless argument, an argument for the sake of arguing, or evidence that important to the Talmud and other writings that use the dialectics as a principal mode of dynamic argument is process but not position. To the contrary, the passage is resolved with a decisive conclusion, not permitted to run on.

But the dialectical composition proceeds—continuous and coherent from point to point, even as it zigs and zags. That is because the key to everything is give and take. We proceed to the second cogent proposition in the analysis of the cited Mishnah-passage, which asks a fresh question: why an oath at all?

> **2.** A. [It is envisioned that each party is holding on to a corner of the cloak, so the question is raised:] Now, since this one is possessed of the cloak and standing right there, and that one is possessed of the cloak and is standing right there, why in the world do I require this oath?

Until now we have assumed as fact the premise of the Mishnah's rule, that an oath is to be taken. But why assume so? Surely each party now has what he is going to get. So what defines the point and effect of the oath?

> B. Said R. Yohanan, "This oath [to which the Mishnah refers] happens to be an ordinance imposed only by rabbis,
>
> C. "so that people should not go

around grabbing the cloaks of other people and saying, 'It's mine!' " [But, as a matter of fact, the oath that is imposed in our Mishnah-passage is not legitimate by the law of the Torah. It is an act taken by sages to maintain the social order.]

We do not administer oaths to liars; we do not impose an oath in a case in which one of the claimants would take an oath for something he knew to be untrue, since one party really does own the cloak, the other really has grabbed it. The proposition solves the problem, but hardly is going to settle the question. On the contrary, Yohanan raises more problems than he solves. So we ask how we can agree to an oath in this case at all?

> D. *But why then not advance the following argument: since such a one is suspect as to fraud in a property claim, he also should be suspect as to fraud in oath-taking?*

Yohanan places himself into the position of believing in respect to the oath what we will not believe in respect to the claim on the cloak, for, after all, one of the parties before us must be lying! Why sustain such a contradiction: gullible and suspicious at one and the same time?

> E. *In point of fact, we do not advance the argument: since such a one is suspect as to fraud in a property claim, he also should be suspect as to fraud in oath-taking, for if you do not concede that fact, then how is it possible that the All-Merciful has ruled,* "One who has conceded part of a claim against himself must take an oath as to the remainder of what is subject to claim"?

If someone claims that another party holds property belonging to him or her, and the one to whom the bailment has been handed over for safe-keeping, called the bailee, concedes part of the claim, the bailee must take an oath in respect to the rest of the claimed property, that is, the part that the bailee maintains does not belong to the claimant at all. So the law itself—the Torah, in fact—has sustained the same contradiction. That fine solution, of course, is going to be challenged:

> F. *Why not simply maintain, since such a one is suspect as to fraud in a property claim,*

> *he also should be suspect as to fraud in oath-taking?*
> G. *In that other case, [the reason for the denial of part of the claim and the admission of part is not the intent to commit fraud, but rather,] the defendant is just trying to put off the claim for a spell.*

We could stop at this point without losing a single important point of interest; everything is before us. One of the striking traits of the large-scale dialectical composition is its composite-character. Starting at the beginning, without any loss of meaning or sense, we may well stop at the end of any given paragraph of thought. But the dialectics insists on moving forward, exploring, pursuing, insisting; and were we to remove a paragraph in the middle of a dialectical composite, then all that follows would become incomprehensible. That is a mark of the dialectical argument: sustained, continuous, and coherent—yet perpetually in control and capable of resolving matters at any single point. For those of us who consume, but do not produce, arguments of such dynamism and complexity, the task is to discern the continuity, that is to say, not to lose sight of where we stand in the whole movement.

Now, having fully exposed the topic, its problem, and its principles, we take a tangent indicated by the character of the principle before us: when a person will or will not lie or take a false oath. We have a theory on the matter; what we now do is expound the theory, with special reference to the formulation of that theory in explicit terms by a named authority:

> H. This concurs with the position of Rabbah. [For Rabbah has said, "On what account has the Torah imposed the requirement of an oath on one who confesses to only part of a claim against him? It is by reason of the presumption that a person will not insolently deny the truth about the whole of a loan in the very presence of the creditor and so entirely deny the debt. He will admit to part of the debt and deny part of it. Hence we invoke an oath in a case in which one does so, to coax out the truth of the matter."]
> I. For you may know, [in support of the foregoing], that R. Idi bar Abin said R. Hisda [said]: "He who

[falsely] denies owing money on a loan nonetheless is suitable to give testimony, but he who denies that he holds a bailment for another party cannot give testimony."

The proposition is now fully exposed. A named authority is introduced who will concur in the proposed theoretical distinction. He sets forth an extra-logical consideration, which of course the law always will welcome: the rational goal of finding the truth overrides the technicalities of the law governing the oath.

Predictably, we cannot allow matters to stand without challenge, and the challenge comes at a fundamental level, with the predictable give-and-take to follow:

> J. But what about that which R. Ammi bar. Hama repeated on Tannaite authority: "[If they are to be subjected to an oath,] four sorts of bailees have to have denied part of the bailment and conceded part of the bailment, namely, the unpaid bailee, the borrower, the paid bailee, and the one who rents."
>
> K. *Why not simply maintain, since such a one is suspect as to fraud in a property claim, he also should be suspect as to fraud in oath-taking?*
>
> L. *In that case as well, [the reason for the denial of part of the claim and the admission of part is not the intent to commit fraud, but rather,] the defendant is just trying to put off the claim for a spell.*
>
> M. *He reasons as follows: "I'm going to find the thief and arrest him." Or: "I'll find [the beast] in the field and return it to the owner."*

Once more, "if that is the case" provokes yet another analysis; we introduce a different reading of the basic case before us, another reason that we should not impose an oath:

> N. *If that is the case, then why should one who denies holding a bailment ever be unsuitable to give testimony? Why don't we just maintain that the defendant is just trying to put off the claim for a spell. He reasons as follows: "I'm going to look for the thing and find it."*
>
> O. *When in point of fact we do rule, He who denies holding a bailment is unfit to give testimony, it is in a case in which witnesses come and give testimony against him that at that very moment, the bailment is located in the bailee's domain, and he*

fully is informed of that fact, or, alternatively, he has the object in his possession at that very moment.

The solution to the problem at hand also provides the starting point for yet another step in the unfolding exposition. But enough has passed before us to make the main point.

What we have accomplished on our wanderings is a survey of opinion on a theme, to be sure, but opinion that intersects at our particular problem as well. The moving argument serves to carry us hither and yon; its power is to demonstrate that all considerations are raised, all challenges met, all possibilities explored. This is not merely a set-piece argument, where we have proposition, evidence, analysis, conclusion; it is a different sort of thinking altogether, purposive and coherent, but also comprehensive and compelling for its admission of possibilities and attention to alternatives. What we shall see, time and again, is that the dialectical argument is the Talmud's medium of generalization from case to principle and extension from principle to new cases.

The Role of Dialectics in the Talmud: The Talmud translates Pentateuchal narratives and laws into a systematic account of Israel's entire social order. In its thirty-seven topical presentations of Mishnah-tractates, the Talmud portrays not so much how people are supposed to live—this the Mishnah does—as how they ought to think, the right way of analyzing circumstance and tradition alike. That is what makes encounter with the Bavli urgent for the contemporary situation. To a world such as ours, engaged as it is at the dawn of a new century by standard reckoning, in a massive enterprise of reconstruction after history's most destructive century, old systems having given way, new ones yet to show their merit and their mettle, the Talmud presents a considerable resource.

The Bavli shows not only a way of reform, but, more valuable still, a way of thinking and talking and rationally arguing about reform. When we follow not only what the sages of the Talmud say, but how they express themselves, their modes of critical thought and, above all, rigorous argument, we encounter a massive, concrete instance of the power of intellect to purify and refine. For the sages of the Talmud, alongside the great masters of Greek philosophy and their Christian and Muslim continuators, exercise the power of rational and systematic inquiry, tenacious criticism, the exchange of not only opinion but reason for opinion, argument, and evidence. They provide a model of how intellectuals take up the tasks of social criticism and pursue the disciplines of the mind in the service of the social order. And that, I think, is what has attracted the widespread interest in the Talmud as shown by repeated translations of, and introductions to, that protean document. Not an antiquarian interest in a long-ago society, nor an ethnic concern with heritage and tradition, but a vivid and contemporary search for plausible examples of the rational world order, animate the unprecedented interest of the world of culture in the character (and also the contents) of the Bavli.

The Talmud embodies applied reason and practical logic in quest of the holy society. That model of criticism and reason in the encounter with social reform of which I spoke is unique. The kind of writing that the Talmud represents has serviceable analogues but no known counterpart in the literature of world history and philosophy, theology, religion, and law. That is because the Talmud sets forth not only decisions and other wise and valuable information, but the choices that face reasonable persons and the bases for deciding matters in one way rather than in some other. And the Talmud records the argument, the constant, contentious, uncompromising argument, that endows with vitality the otherwise merely informative corpus of useful insight. "Let logic pierce the mountain"—that is what sages say.

Not many have attained the purity of intellect characteristic of this writing. With the back-and-forth argument, the Talmud enlightens and engages. How so? The Talmud sets forth not so much a record of what was said as a set of notes that permit the engaged reader to reconstruct thought and recapitulate reason and criticism.

Indeed, the Talmud treats coming generations the way composers treat unborn musicians: they provide the notes for the musicians to reconstruct the music. In the Talmudic framework, everything is in the moving, or dialectical argument, the give and take of unsparing rationality, which, through our own capacity to reason, we are expected to reconstitute the issues, the argument, the prevailing rationality. The Bavli makes enormous demands upon its future. It pays a massive compliment to its heirs.

In that aspect, the Talmud recalls the great philosophical dialogues of ancient and medieval times. Readers familiar with the dialogues of Socrates as set forth by Plato—those wonderful exchanges concerning abstractions such as truth and beauty, goodness and justice, will find familiar the notion of dialectical argument, with its unfolding, on-going give-and take. But, still, they will be puzzled by the chaos of the Talmudic dialectic, its meandering and open-ended character. And they will miss the formal elegance, the perfection of exposition, that characterize Plato's writings. So too, the Talmud's presentation of contrary positions and exposition of the strengths and weaknesses of each will hardly surprise jurisprudents. But the inclusion of the model of extensive exposition of debate surprises. Decisions ordinarily record the main points, but not the successive steps in argument and counter-argument, such as we find here. And, more to the point, we expect decisions, while much of the Talmud's discourse proves open-ended.

The very character and the style of the Talmud's presentation certainly demand a kind of reading not ordinarily required of us. But it is one that class room teachers undertake all the time: reconstructing thought from notes, turning a few words into a whole presentation. What we are given are notes, which we are expected to know how to use in the reconstruction of the issues under discussion, the arguments under exposition. That means we must make ourselves active partners in the thought-processes that the document. Not only is the argument open-ended, so too the bounds of participation know no limits.

Indeed, it is the very reticence of the Talmud to tell us everything we need to know, the remarkable confidence of its compilers that generations over time will join in the argument they precipitate, grasp the principles they embody in concrete cases, find compelling the issues they deem urgent—it is that remarkable faith in the human intellect of age succeeding age that lifts the document above time and circumstance and renders it immortal. In transcending circumstances of time and place and condition, the Talmud attains a place in the philosophical, not merely historical, curriculum of culture. That is why every generation of its heirs and continuators found itself a partner in the on-going reconstruction of reasoned thought, each adding its commentary to the ever-welcoming text. To a discussion of how we know the world through the discourse of the class room, the Talmud has a formidable contribution to make. It is a piece of writing that does more than define an entire civilization. Rather, it demonstrates how education, properly carried on, recapitulates the highest rationality of the civilization that sustains the school and is sustained by it.

JACOB NEUSNER

DISABILITIES, JUDAISM AND: Judaism defines disabilities as the inability to hear and speak, the inability to learn because of mental illness, mental disability, or immaturity and, to a lesser extent, the inability to see, and physical disabilities. Priests are considered disabled if they are physically blemished in some way or have impure bloodlines. Judaism does not define impure bloodlines and physical blemishes, such as an irregularly shaped head, as disabilities in regular Israelites.

The basic theory of disabilities depends, in the main, on an individual's ability to receive knowledge, communicate verbally, and act upon his intentions. In Rabbinic literature, these qualities are known as *da'at*. One who has *da'at* is not disabled. One who does not have *da'at* is disabled. The source for this theory lies in a general theology found in Rabbinic literature that imputes perfection to ritually pure, full-grown, healthy, fully-sensate, free, educated, morally-upright, visibly-male men (e.g., men with beards). However, each person, no matter how disabled, was seen as precious; created in God's image.

This group of persons who epitomizes disabilities is embodied in the category *cheresh, shoteh v'katan* (a deaf-mute person, a person with mental illness or mental disability, and a pre-verbal minor; e.g., M. Yeb. 18, M. B.Q. 4:4). Such persons were stigmatized, spoiling their social identity and discrediting them in society. One of the greatest aids we have in understanding the category *cheresh, shoteh v'katan* is another category, that of women, slaves, and minors. If the former category epitomizes stigmatization, then the latter embodies liminality. Women, slaves and minors clearly had *da'at*. They were, however, unable to act on that *da'at* because they were not male, free, or mature enough and were, therefore, unable to consistently actualize their intentions. This caused women, slaves, and minors to be consigned to a liminal position in the sages' society.

The minor who is like the *cheresh* and *shoteh* is an infant who, while having his own will, did not have *da'at* in the sages' understanding of that word. The minor who is like women and slaves was an older, verbal minor who could gradually become capable of acting as a full participant in Jewish life. The ideal Jewish participant in the sages' system—a grown, free male with functioning *da'at*—begins life as a stigmatized person, moves into a liminal position, and finally grows into a full participant. In this sense, everyone was deemed disabled at some point in his life.

Blindness and physical disabilities, such as lameness or a malformation of the hands, compromised participation only in certain, limited aspects of the sages' system. With regard to most activities, blind and physically disabled persons are not even considered to be liminal: they are visibly marred, but functionally satisfactory. They are fully credited participants in the sages' system, except in those limited areas where vision or mobility are absolutely necessary. For example, three times a year, Israelites were to come to the Temple and appear before God (this is the mitzvah named *r'ayon*; Deut. 16:16, Exod. 23:8). With regard to this commandment, blind and physically disabled persons were deemed disabled. Though women, slaves, and minors (and presumably others) came to Jerusalem during the festivals (Deut. 16:11, 14), only males were required to appear with an offering.

The festivals of Passover, Shavuot, and Tabernacles are intimately linked to the agricultural cycle of harvesting and planting. It is on these holidays that the Israelites must appear in the Temple with an offering. If, at these moments, God is "inspecting the troops," as it were, and determining if they are worthy of further support and agricultural bounty, it is logical that, at such a moment of transition, all Israelites who appeared at the Temple for "inspection" would be required to be as close to the ideal as possible.

> The makeup of the congregation at these moments had symbolic significance. Calendrical rites . . . almost always refer to large groups and quite often embrace whole societies. Often, too, they are performed at well-delineated points in the annual productive cycle and attest to the passage from scarcity to plenty (as at first fruits or harvest festivals) or from plenty to scarcity (as when the hardships of winter are anticipated and magically warded against). To these also one should add all rites de passage, which accompany any change of a collective sort from one state to another, as when a whole tribe goes to war, or a large local community performs a ritual to reverse the effects of famine, drought, or plague. Life-crisis rites and rituals of induction into office are almost always rites of status elevation; calendrical rites and rites of group crisis may sometimes be rites of status reversal. At such a moment, when the entire community goes through a liminal, i.e., intrastructural, phase, apparently only the best representatives of the group participate in the ritual which reinforces the society's structure.[1]

The list of those exempt from performing this commandment is extraordinary in its completeness. It effectively eliminates anyone who is not a blemishless, full-grown, free male with *da'at* (M. Hag. 1:1):

> All are obligated to appear [at the Temple on the festivals] except a *cheresh*, *shoteh*

v'katan, an hermaphrodite or an androgen or women and slaves who have not been freed or the lame [man] or the blind [man] or the sick [man] or the old [man] or the one who cannot go up [to the Temple Mount] on his feet. Who is [considered] a *katan*? Anyone who cannot ride upon his father's shoulders and go up from Jerusalem to the Temple Mount. This is the opinion of the House of Shammai. But the House of Hillel say, "Anyone who is unable to hold his father's hand and go up from Jerusalem to the Temple Mount, as it is written, "Three pilgrimages" (Exod. 23:14).

"Pilgrimages" in Hebrew is *regalim*, which also means "legs." The House of Hillel takes this to mean that one must appear on his own two legs. The Tosefta to M. Hag. 1:1 adds ritually impure persons to the list of those exempt from this *mitsvah*. In its discussion of the obligation to appear at the Temple on the festivals, Y. Hag. 1:1, 76a provides a rationale for the exclusion of selected groups of people:

> . . . the lame: Since it is written, "pilgrim-festival" [*r'galim*, "feet" and they cannot walk on theirs].
> The sick: Since it is written, "And you will rejoice" (Deut. 16:14).
> The old: Since it is written, "*r'galim*" [and the aged cannot come by foot].
> Said R. Yose: The intent of both exclusions is to impose a lenient ruling. If one can rejoice [being in good health] but he cannot walk, I cite in his regard the reference of Scripture to pilgrim festivals. If he can walk but cannot rejoice [being sick] I cite concerning him the reference of Scripture to rejoicing. [None of them need make the trip.]

This is an innovation. Until now, our sources have excluded groups of persons from the obligation to perform this commandment without an explicit rationale. Here, the Talmud labels its motivation as leniency: the journey is arduous and those who are lame, sick, or old need not make the trip.

At B. Hag. 2b-3a, the sages emphasized an emotional aspect associated with the festivals: the obligation to rejoice, which does not require physical perfection but only *da'at*.

> Likewise it is also taught: All are obligated to appear [at the Temple] and to rejoice

except a *cheresh* who can speak but not hear, [or] hear but not speak, who is exempt from appearing. But even though he is exempt from appearing he is obligated to rejoice. But [a *cheresh*] who can neither hear nor speak and the *shoteh v'katan* are exempt even from [the obligation of] rejoicing, since they are exempt from all the precepts stated in the Torah.

The Bavli divides the *r'ayon* into component parts: (1) appearing, which requires physical and mental perfection, and (2) rejoicing, which requires *da'at*.

Some of the most important discussions of disabilities are connected to the issue of separating the agricultural gift called heave-offering (*terumah*). The act of separating *terumah* is an excellent example of accomplishing something through intention, blessing, and action. The whole nature of the act of separating *terumah*, that is, differentiating one thing from another, is the epitome of having *da'at*: one has the intention to differentiate, can verbalize this intention, and has the wherewithal, physically and materially, to act upon it.

Terumah was produce separated from the harvest and given to the priests as a gift. The amount of *terumah* to be set aside was anywhere from 1/60th to 1/40th of the crop (M. Ter. 4:3). A blessing was said upon separating *terumah*, and, ideally, the person reciting the blessing should be able to hear himself say it. Once it was separated, *terumah* could only be consumed by priests and their families in a state of ritual purity, and this food could not revert to the status of *hullin*, i.e., food fit for consumption by ordinary folk or by priests in a state of ritual impurity.

Since the *cheresh, shoteh v'katan* were thought to lack *da'at*, they were excluded from this mitzvah (M. Ter. 1:1):

> Five [sorts of persons] may not separate *terumah*, and if they did separate *terumah*, that which they have separated is not in the status of *terumah*: (1) *hacheresh*, (2) *v'hashoteh* (3) *v'katan*, and (4) one who separates *terumah* from [crops] that are not his own, and (5) a non-Jew who separated *terumah* from [crops] of a Jew, even by permission—that which he has separated is not *terumah*.

Who, then, may separate *terumah*? First of all, they must have *da'at* as the first exclu-

sion of this passage makes clear. The *cheresh, shoteh v'katan* were thought not to have *da'at*, and, thus, their separation of *terumah* is not considered valid, even when this might seem illogical, e.g., when the physical act is performed correctly. This passage is followed by a definition of a *cheresh's* disability (M. Ter. 1:2):

> A *cheresh* who speaks but cannot hear may not separate *terumah*, but if he did separate, that which he has separated is valid *terumah*. The *cheresh* of whom the sages spoke in all cases is one who can neither hear nor speak.

There seem to be two meanings that can be attributed to the term *cheresh*. It can refer to one who cannot hear but can speak (e.g., one who has lost the ability to hear in old age) or to one who can neither speak nor hear. The general rule is that when the Mishnah speaks of a *cheresh*, it refers to the latter, not the former.

T. Ter. 1:1-4 fleshes out the definitions and historical conditions behind the Mishnah's ruling that the *cheresh, shoteh v'katan* do not validly separate *terumah*, even *ex post facto*.

> R. Isaac says in the name of R. Eleazar: "[That which has been separated as] *terumah* by a *cheresh* does not enter the status of *hullin* [even though it is not valid *terumah*] because it is a matter of doubt whether or not he has understanding.
>
> "What do they do for him? The court appoints for him administrators [and] he separates *terumah* and they validate it on his behalf. [If the *cheresh* has understanding, the sanctity of the *terumah* depends on him alone. If not, the action of the administrators is sufficient to make the *terumah* valid.]...."
>
> [One who] hears but does not speak—that is a mute. [One who] speaks but does not hear is a *cheresh*. And each of these is equivalent to a person of sound senses (*pikeiach*) in every respect.
>
> Who is a *shoteh*? One who goes out alone at night, and who sleeps in a graveyard, and who rips his clothing, and who loses what is given to him. [If he is] at times a *shoteh* [and] at times lucid, this is the general principle: Whenever he is a *shoteh*, behold, he is [considered] a *shoteh* in every respect; [but whenever he is] lucid, behold, he is [considered] a person of sound mind (*k'pikeiach*) in every respect.
>
> R. Judah says: "A *katan* whose father left

him in a [cucumber] field, separates [*terumah*] and his father says on his behalf: 'That which he has separated is [valid] *terumah*.'" They said to him: "It is not he [the *katan*] who separated *terumah* but his father [who] validates it after him."

The Tosefta expresses doubt whether the *cheresh* has *da'at* or not, and this throws the *cheresh's* separation of *terumah* into doubt, as well. Is it discredited or not? Because the Tosefta appears to be unable to decide one way or another, it is decreed that an executor validates the *cheresh's* separation. This is a "belt and suspenders" solution: if the *cheresh* has *da'at*, then his intention is not discredited, and his separation is valid; if he does not have *da'at*, the validation of the executors will make it valid *terumah*.

According to T. Ter. 1:3, a *shoteh* is, in short, one who behaves in an insane manner. The Tosefta recognizes that mentally ill persons may experience periods of rationality and that mentally disabled persons may exhibit adequate functioning in selected areas of behavior. The Tosefta validates actions taken by these persons during those periods and in those areas.

The *katan* who might separate *terumah* is old enough to help his father with the harvest. This is a child of perhaps five or six, certainly not one of two or three. Like the *cheresh*, this child's *terumah* is validated by a person with recognized, valid intention.

In the matter of separating *terumah*, blind persons are considered impaired, but not completely so (M. Ter. 1:6):

> Five [sorts of persons] may not separate *terumah*, but if they have separated it, that which they have separated is valid *terumah*: The mute person or the drunk person or the naked person or the blind person or the person who is in a state of ritual impurity because of a seminal emission may not separate *terumah*; but if they have separated it, that which they have separated is valid *terumah*.

Each of the listed persons is disqualified because he lacks a requisite skill or condition for the proper separation of *terumah*. The mute person cannot say the blessing. A drunk person would neither be able to say the blessing correctly nor set aside the best

of his crops. A naked person and one who is impure because of a seminal emission are prohibited from reciting the blessing. Blind persons were deemed unable to select the best of their crop. However, if such persons did separate *terumah*, that which they have separated is valid *terumah*. In other words, a blind person may not set aside the best produce, but since he is understood to be able to formulate the intention—*da'at*—required to carry out the act of separation, that which he has separated nonetheless is in the status of *terumah*; because they were performed with proper intention, his actions are valid. Again, the blind person does not occupy a liminal position, i.e., an intrastructural position, but merely a position within the sages' structure that is blemished. Once accomplished, the blind person's deeds are considered completely valid (as are the mute person's).

B. Shabbat 153a-b further analyzes the category *cheresh, shoteh v'katan*. (This passage is in Aramaic, except for the terms and the quotations from earlier sources.)

> *M. Shab. 24:1: If darkness falls [on the evening of the Sabbath] upon a person on a road, he entrusts his purse to a gentile, but if there is no gentile with him, he places it on an ass. . . .*
> *Gemara*: [If there is] an ass and a *cheresh, shoteh v'katan*, he [should] place it on the ass and not give it to the *cheresh, shoteh v'katan*. What is the reason? These [persons] are human beings, and this [ass] is not [human].
> [In the case of] a *cheresh* and a *shoteh*, [he should give it] to the *shoteh*. [In the case of] a *shoteh* and a *katan*, [he should give it] to the *shoteh*.
> The [sages] were asked: What [if the choice is between] a *cheresh* and a *katan*? According to R. Eliezer there is no question, for it was taught: R. Isaac said in R. Eliezer's name: "The *terumah* of a *cheresh* does not revert to an unconsecrated status, because there is doubt [whether the *cheresh* has *da'at* or not; T. Ter. 1:1]. The question concerns the anonymous sages' view. For we learned: *Five [sorts of persons] may not separate terumah, and if they did separate terumah, that which they have separated is not in the status of terumah: hacheresh, v'hashoteh v'katan . . .* (M. Ter. 1:1).
> What [should be done about our original question]? [Should] he give it to the *cheresh* since the *katan* will arrive at understanding (*da'at*)? Or perhaps he should give it to the *katan*, because a *cheresh* may be confused

with an adult of sound senses (*pikeiach*)? Some say: He [should] give it to the *cheresh*. Some [others] say: He [should] give it to the *katan*.

This passage responds to the Mishnah's categorization of a Jew, gentile, and ass. The Bavli fills in the intermediary categories, adding the logical justification it perceives necessary. It develops a continuum that spans a range from "more like an animal" to "more like a 'normal' human being." The entries in the continuum are in this order: ass, *shoteh*, *cheresh/katan*, sensate Jew.

The *shoteh*, *cheresh*, and *katan* are unambivalently stigmatized. Since they lack *da'at*, it is preferable for them to violate the law by carrying on the Sabbath than for a Jew who has *da'at* to do so. The issue is one of appearance for the sages. The sages here assume that a *shoteh*'s disability is visible and that a *cheresh*'s is not. If the *cheresh* carries the purse on the Sabbath, it appears that a person with *da'at* is violating the law, which would be demoralizing and shocking. Poised against this is the argument that the *katan* is developing *da'at*, and it would be harmful to start the child on a sinning path by having him carry on the Sabbath. The issue is left undecided.

The role of a blind person or a *katan* or a person in rags in a synagogue service reveals the specific nature of each one's disability (M. Meg. 4:6):

> A *katan* may read the Torah and translate [its text for the congregation], but he may not [spread a cloak over his head and recite the prayers preceding and following the] Shema, nor go before the ark, nor lift his hands [in the priestly blessing].
> One who has holes in his clothes [may spread a cloak over his head and recite the prayers preceding and following the] Shema and translate [the text of Torah for the congregation], but he may neither read the Torah nor go before the ark nor lift his hands [in the priestly blessing].
> A blind person may [spread a cloak and recite the prayers preceding and following the] Shema and translate [the text of the Torah for the congregation but he may not read from Torah, since he cannot see].

Someone inappropriately dressed, or one whom other members of the congregation feel is unqualified to recite a prayer, must be dealt with in a way that preserves the

honor of the congregation. Presumably, one could lead the Shema and translate Scripture from one's seat. The blind man and the one in rags are permitted to perform these functions since they do not require that these persons move from their places, which might be disruptive to the service.

The honor of the congregation and the solemnity of the service must not be impaired. However, if the inappropriately dressed or blind person can participate without offending the community's sensibilities, they are permitted to do so. The Torah, however, could not be read from one's seat, nor could the priestly blessing be offered except from the *bimah*; hence the person in rags and the blind person are not allowed to participate in these rituals. The *katan* here is certainly competent in many ways: he can read and could lead prayers; but permission is not granted to him to lead the Shema, since he is not yet subject to this commandment.

Sometimes, to achieve a predetermined outcome, the sages use disabilities to make rulings that go beyond the sphere of logic. For example, they mandate that parents of a stubborn and rebellious son (Deut. 21:18-21) may not testify against him if one of them has an amputated hand or foot. Ordinarily, such a condition would not prevent a person from testifying. But because the sages wanted to limit the application of the death penalty, especially in this case, they used any means possible to disqualify witnesses to it (M. San. 8:4, Sifre Deut. Piska 219).

The passage about absolving the community of guilt regarding an abandoned corpse (Deut. 21:1-9) is juxtaposed, in the Torah, with the one about the stubborn, rebellious son (Deut. 21:18-21). In fact, they are mirror images of each other. In one, a guilty party is taken outside the city and killed. In another, an innocent person is discovered, slain, outside the city. In one, the person is accused by parents, who are certainly authority figures. In the other, the collective "parents" of the town, the elders, communally proclaim their innocence of this blood. Y. San. 8:5, 26b, explicitly draws the parallel between the parents of the stubborn, rebellious son and the elders of the city:

Just as you expound about his father and mother, so you should expound about the elders of the court, as it is said,

"And they shall go out"—to exclude the lame.

"And they shall say"—to exclude the mute.

"Our hands have not spilled"—to exclude those with maimed hands.

"And our eyes have not seen"—to exclude the blind.

The Scripture tells [us] that just as the elders of the court must be whole in righteousness, thus they must be whole in their limbs.

What does wholeness of limbs have to do with complete righteousness? There is no obvious reason why a person who has a maimed hand could not be wholly righteous and function quite well as an elder. These requirements for physical wholeness involve a metaphor and its logical corollary:

physical perfection > perfect righteousness

physical imperfection > imperfect righteousness

The state of a person's body may serve as a metaphor for his inner state. Physical wholeness and blemishlessness metaphorically testify to a person's utter, moral wholeness. Conversely, any physical blemish or disability may attest to a person's intellectual or moral imperfection. That these extensions may be in error, i.e., that a beautiful, blemishless person may be utterly evil and that a person with disabilities may be completely righteous, is obvious. Nonetheless, these metaphors are validated by passages such as this one.

Priests are considered disabled if they are physically blemished in some way or have impure bloodlines. Lev. 21:16-24 explicates the details of priestly disability with a long list of imperfections that disqualify a priest from officiating in the cult:

And the Lord spoke to Moses, saying: Speak to Aaron, saying, A man of your lineage, for [all] their generations, who has a blemish shall not come near to offer the bread of his God. For any man who has a blemish shall not come near: [whether he] is a blind man or a lame man or [has] a flat nose or any extra [limb or growth] or a man who has a broken leg or a broken hand or a crooked back or [is] a dwarf or has obscured sight in [even one] eye, has

scurvy or scabs or has crushed testicles. Any man of Aaron's lineage who has a blemish shall not draw nigh to offer the fire [offerings] of God. He has a blemish; he shall not come near to offer the bread of his God. He shall eat the bread of his God, [both] of the most holy, and of the holy. But he may not go [in]to the veil [before the ark], nor come near to the altar, because he has a blemish. Let him not profane My holy [places]: for I the Lord [Myself] sanctify [these places]. And Moses spoke [these words] to Aaron and to his sons and to all the children of Israel.

A priest with any of the disabilities mentioned here would not be able to officiate in the Temple cult. The priest mediates between heaven and earth; between holy and profane. To survive in such a dangerous position, the priest had to be fit for the company of angels: blemishless, pure of lineage, and ritually pure. Priests with blemishes were barred from officiating in the cult, but they could still eat the priestly emoluments (e.g., *terumah*, Lev. 21:22). They also served in the Temple's Wood Chamber, sorting wood for the altar (M. Mid. 2:5). A priest could also blow the trumpet (a lame priest was observed doing so; T. Sot. 7:16) and bestow the priestly blessing from the Temple *ulam* if he had no visible defects on his face, hands or feet (T. Sot. 7:8). M. Bek. 7 elaborates on the Torah's descriptions of physical blemishes that disqualify priests from officiating in the cult.

Blemishes in one's bloodlines were just as disabling as physical defects to priests. When it was discovered that a priest's mother had been a divorcee, that priest dressed himself in black and left the Temple (M. Mid. 5:4). If a priest married a divorcee, he underwent the humiliating ritual of *k'tsatsah*. The members of his family would bring a barrel of fruit to the town square, break the barrel open, then announce that their brother had married inappropriately and that his seed would not be mingled with their seed (B. Ket. 28b).

One of the most salient passages for understanding the Torah's theology of disabilities arises when Moses protests to God that he cannot lead the Israelites from slavery to freedom because he has a speech impediment (Exod. 4:10-11):

And Moses said unto the Lord: My Lord, I am not a man of words, neither yesterday nor the day before nor ever since you have spoken to your servant, for I am slow of speech and slow of tongue. And God said to him, "Who puts a mouth in a person? And who makes him mute or deaf or seeing or blind? Is it not I, the Lord?

The first part of God's retort directly addresses Moses' concern. Just as God has made Moses "slow of speech," God can cure him, too. But the second part of God's reply does not bear directly on Moses' case and may be taken as a general statement that God is the provider of *all* the faculties.

Obviously, physical perfection was important to the priests. How could this concept be applied to lay Israelites? By requiring Israelites to respect and treasure all human bodies. Gratuitously inflicting bodily harm would incur severe penalties (Lev. 24:15-22, Exod. 21:22-27):

> And you shall speak to the children of Israel, saying: Whosoever curses his God shall bear his sin. And he that blasphemes the name of the Lord shall surely be put to death; all the congregation shall certainly stone him, likewise the stranger and the home-born [shall stone him] when he blasphemes the Name shall he be put to death. And whoever [fatally] smites any person shall surely be put to death. And whoever [fatally] smites a beast shall make it good: life for life. And whoever blemishes his neighbor; as he has done, so shall it be done to him: a break [in a limb] for a break [in a limb], an eye for an eye, a tooth for a tooth: as he has blemished a man, so shall he be blemished. And whoever kills an animal shall make it good and whoever kills a man shall be put to death. You shall have one manner of law, as well for the stranger, as for the homeborn for I am the Lord your God.

There are many similarities between the priestly attitude toward physical blemishes and the attitudes expressed here. First of all, the same word for blemish, *mum*, is used here as it was used in Lev. 21:17 and 22:20 to describe blemishes in priests and sacrificial animals. Here, too, animals and humans are paired, and the death of one is likened to the death of the other. The maiming of a person is paired, in this passage, with the cursing of God. The implication is clear: human bodies are not to be

harmed as God is not to be defied. Either transgression will yield separation from the community, up to and including being executed. Blaspheming God, denying God's existence and singularity, is the equivalent of killing God, and it merits death.

God is perceived to be responsible not only for the proper functioning of the body, but for those aspects that mark it as living and sensate (B. Nid. 31a, B. Qid. 30b):

> Our rabbis taught: There are three partners in a person, the Holy One, blessed be he, his father, and his mother. His father sows the white [substance, i.e., semen] out of which [come the child's] bones and sinews and nails and the brain in his head and the white in his eye. His mother sows the red [substance, i.e. blood] out of which [come the child's] skin and flesh and hair and blood and the black of the eye. And the Holy One, blessed be he, gives him spirit and breath and beauty of face and seeing eyes and hearing ears and walking legs and understanding and insight. When the time comes for him to depart from the world approaches, the Holy One, blessed be he, takes away his portion and leaves the portions of his father and mother with them.

God is an integral partner with man and woman in the genesis of a human being. What God contributes are the faculties—the ability to see, hear, speak, walk and understand—in other words, what makes a human being unique among God's creatures.

Disabled persons, or persons who simply have a distinctive appearance, are considered part of God's creation. Blessings were to be said on seeing persons with remarkable physical constitutions or persons who have become disabled or are afflicted with disease (T. Ber. 6:3):

> One who sees an Ethiopian, or an albino, or [a man] red-spotted in the face, or white spotted in the face, or a hunchback, or a dwarf says: Blessed [are you Lord our God, ruler of the universe, who creates such] varied creatures.
>
> [One who sees] an amputee, or a lame person, or a blind person, or a person afflicted with boils, says: Blessed [are you Lord our God, ruler of the universe] the true judge.

The implication is that all these persons are part of God's creation and that any feeling experienced upon seeing them should be consecrated with a blessing. One whose condition makes him or her physically distinctive is not considered judged by God. Such a person is one of the wide variety of creatures created by God. However, one who is visibly disabled or ill, i.e., one to whom the "true judge" blessing applies, *is* deemed adjudged by God.

Each person's body, regardless of its state of disability, is to be honored and protected. Cursing a person with hearing disabilities or putting a stumbling block before a person with impaired vision is forbidden (Lev. 19:14). Even if persons with hearing disabilities would never know they'd been cursed, and even if persons with seeing disabilities, presumably stumbling anyway, would not be more greatly harmed by a stumbling block, *God* knows, and such actions are offenses before the deity. This is even true when a person is seen as barely alive, as is the case for a person with hearing disabilities (Sifra, Kedoshim 3:13-14, B. Tem. 4a, B. Shev. 36a):

> "Do not curse a deaf person." I have here nothing but a deaf person. From whence [do I know] to augment [the verse to refer to] every person? Scripture says, "[Judges you shall not curse] nor a prince of your people shall you revile" (Exod. 22:27). If so, why is it said, "a deaf person"? A deaf person is distinctive in [that he is] alive. This [phrasing of the verse] excludes the dead person who is not alive [and there is no prohibition against insulting the dead].
>
> "And before a blind person do not place a stumbling block." Blind in a thing [i.e., a blind spot]. [If] a man came and said to you: The daughter of so and so, how is she [with regards to eligibility to marry into] the priesthood? Do not say to him: She is fit, and she is unfit. If he would take advice from you, do not give advice to him that is not fit for him. . . . This matter [of giving honest advice] is transmitted to the heart [i.e., only known to the heart], as it is said, "And you shall fear the Lord your God, I am the Lord" (Lev. 19:14). [Because only God knows whether you were sincere or not.]

The difference between the way a person with hearing disabilities and one with visual disabilities is viewed is dramatically displayed in this exposition. The person with hearing disabilities demonstrates that no living person should be cursed. From this, it is learned that a person with hearing disabili-

ties was especially mentioned because he is the lowest form of living humanity. He is living, but, otherwise, he is so far outside the realm of everyday life that he is closer to death than to life (Mekhilta Nezikin 5, on Exod. 21:17 and 22:27, B. San. 66a).

Persons with visual disabilities, on the other hand, are not even considered as a literal image! The concept "stumbling block before the blind" is immediately taken as a metaphor for vulnerability of any sort that impairs a person in a specific way (e.g., lack of good judgment). Persons with visual disabilities are a symbol for someone who functions with some impairment but who operates validly in society. (See B. A.Z. 6a-6b, B. B.M. 75b, B. Qid. 32a for more examples of "stumbling blocks before the blind.")

Israel is sometimes characterized as a person with a disability. Isaiah 42:18-20 chastises Israel for willfully disabling herself:

> Hear, deaf ones and look [in order] to see, blind ones! Who is blind but my servant? Or deaf, as my messenger whom I sent? Who is blind as the one I send, and blind as God's servant? Seeing much but observing nothing; [having] hearing hears but not attending.

Israel's deafness and blindness are not due to any lack of properly functioning organs. It is specifically stated: God's servants have eyes and ears which operate but they are too stubborn and willful to see and understand the truth of God's message with those organs. When they stop being recalcitrant, "blinding themselves" to the reality of God's presence, they will become a "light to the nations" who "open the eyes of the blind" (Is. 42:6-7). Here, the "blind eye" is clearly meant as a metaphor for bringing knowledge of God to those who lack it. Sight stands for insight.

In the powerful prophetic image of Isaiah's Suffering Servant (52:13-53:5) we find an explicit linking of sin, disabilities, suffering, and atonement. The Suffering Servant is clearly disabled and wounded. His wounds, like the sacrifices in the Temple, make an expiation for sin:

> Behold, my servant shall prosper, he shall be exalted and extolled, and be very high.

As many were astonished at you, saying, Surely his visage is too marred to be human, and his form, to be from humanity['s mold]: so shall he startle many nations; kings shall shut their mouths: for that which they had not been told them shall they see; and that which they had not heard they shall comprehend. Who [would have] believed our report? and to whom is God's arm revealed? For he grew up before him as a tender plant, and as a root out of a dry ground: he had no form nor comeliness, that we should look at him, and no countenance, that we should desire him. He was [the most] despised and rejected of men; a man of pains, and knowing sickness: and we hid (as it were) our faces from him; he was despised, and we considered him not. But he has borne our sicknesses and endured our pains; yet we considered him stricken, smitten of God, and afflicted. But he was wounded because of our transgressions, bruised because of our iniquities: his sufferings were that we might have peace, and by his injury we are healed.

If the Suffering Servant is a symbol of Israel, then Israel is depicted as a person with disabilities. The Servant's strengths come not from his physical perfection but from his intellectual and spiritual qualities.

Disabilities can atone for sin, embodying the principle "With the measure that a person measures shall they mete [out] to him" or, more colloquially, *midah k'neged midah*, simply, "measure for measure." This principal may be seen in our earliest sources. The life story of Jacob is shaped by disabilities in some of its characters. Jacob is able to steal his brother's birthright because his father Isaac's eyes have grown dim (Gen. 27:1). Poor eyes will then set Jacob up, almost immediately, for a fall. Jacob flees his angry brother Esau and goes to his uncle, Laban. Jacob, looking at Laban's daughters, disdains the elder daughter because of her poor eyes (Gen. 29:17). Jacob, who disregarded the rights of an elder sibling (his brother), now attempts to disregard them again, wanting to marry Rachel before her elder sister Leah. Laban, Leah, and Rachel collude to marry Jacob off to Leah. As Jacob tricked his father and sibling, exploiting the opportunity of his father's poor vision, so Jacob is tricked by a father and a sibling because of his distaste for Leah's poor eyes. Jacob's lust for the birthright and for Rachel made him "blind."

The Mishnah is well aware of this biblical principle of symmetry. Only two passages in the entire Mishnah speculate on the causes of disabilities, and they both utilize the idea of "measure for measure." Samson sins with his eyes (Jdgs. 16:1) and is therefore blinded (M. Sot. 1:8, Mekhilta, Shirata 2, on Exod. 15:1).

This principle of "measure for measure" is applied explicitly to disabilities in the other passage from the Mishnah that speaks of the causes for disabilities. This passage addresses the question, "Who is entitled to help themselves to *peah* (the corners of the fields that are to be left unharvested so that the poor might glean them" (Lev. 19:9-10, 23:22))? Persons with disabilities are allowed to avail themselves of this aid (M. Pe. 8:9, Mekhilta Kaspa 3 on Exod. 23:8, Sifre Deut. 144, B. Ket. 105a-b):

> And anyone who is not lame or blind or limping and makes himself [appear to be one of these] will not die of old age until he becomes like one of them, as it is said, ("And he who seeks evil, it shall come to him;" and it is [further] said,) "Justice, justice shall you pursue" (Deut. 16:20). And any judge who takes bribes and perverts justice will not die of old age before his eyes have grown dim, as it is said, "And a bribe you shall not take, for the bribe blinds the seeing" (Deut. 16:19).

The cause of disabilities, suggests this passage, can be found in the principle of *midah k'neged midah*. Trying to abscond with public charity through the ruse of pretending to have disabilities leads one eventually to develop such disabilities. Similarly, injustice, "turning a blind eye" to the truth, eventually leads one to become blind. The correspondence is clear.

Sexual impropriety was also seen as a source of disabilities; specifically, birth defects (B. Ned. 20a-b):

> R. Yohanan ben Dahavai said: "The Ministering Angels told me four things: 'People are born lame because [their parents] overturned their table [during intercourse]; mute because they kiss "that place; deaf, because they converse during intercourse; blind, because they look at "that place.'" . . .
> R. Yohanan said: These are the words of R. Yohanan ben Dahavai. But the sages said: The halakhah is not according to

R. Yohanan ben Dahavai. Rather, each person may do what he wishes with his wife [regarding intercourse]. It is like meat that comes from the butcher shop. If he wishes to eat it salted, he eats it; broiled, he eats it; cooked, he eats it; boiled, he eats it. And [it is just] so with fish that comes from the fish shop.

Some hold that sexual intercourse conducted without proper decorum results in disabled children. This is certainly as strong a sanction as one could imagine against a behavior considered to be undesirable. While the sages could not assure the most decorous behavior during sexual intercourse, they could encourage it by this most strenuous of means.

The Modern Period: Stigmatization of persons with disabilities continues in contemporary Judaism, though it is becoming less and less prevalent. Indeed, modern authorities seem intent on being as inclusive as possible where persons with disabilities are concerned. Isaac Herzog, chief rabbi of Israel until 1959, mandated a creative, inclusive stance toward persons with hearing disabilities:[2]

> Those [rabbis] who remain in the ivory tower and say the schools [for the deaf] are not good enough do not realize the techniques that have been developed in the schools. . . . You have got to do so and then remove all limitations that still exist surrounding the technically deaf-mute.

Indeed, new definitions of deafness and muteness have made the category of the *cheresh* all but irrelevant:[3]

> The ability to speak, no matter how acquired and even if the speech acquired is imperfect, is yet sufficient to establish full competence in all areas of Halakhah.

Inclusiveness toward persons with visual disabilities is also part of contemporary Jewish ethics, even when no explicit textual basis can be found for such a stance. For example, while blind persons are still not allowed to ritually read from Torah, they may participate in the central rite of the Bar or Bat Mitzvah ceremony: the recitation of the Haftarah selection from the prophets:[4]

> A blind child [is permitted] to read the Haftarah from memory or from a Braille text. . . . Reading from a printed text [the

practice almost all contemporary congregations follow] is in any event tantamount to reading without any text at all but, nevertheless, is permissible in the case of the Haftarah because of the reason cited in Gittin 60a: "At a time when it is necessary to work for the Lord, make void thy law."

The possibility of participating in Bar or Bat Mitzvah ceremonies is made available to almost all children today, regardless of their mental, visual, or auditory disabilities. Women and children still occupy liminal roles in some Jewish communities. However, in many Jewish movements (Conservative, Reform, Reconstructionist, and Renewal) women have become complete participants in Jewish life.

Bibliography

Bleich, J. David, "Survey of Recent Halakhic Periodical Literature: Status of the Deaf-Mute in Jewish Law" in *Tradition* 16:5 (1977), pp. 79-84.

Schein, Jerome D. and Lester J. Waldman, eds., *The Deaf Jew in the Modern World* (New York, 1986).

Notes

[1] Victor Turner, *The Ritual Process: Structure and Anti-Structure* (Ithaca, 1969), p. 168.

[2] Jerome D. Schein and Lester J. Waldman, eds., *The Deaf Jew in the Modern World* (New York, 1986), p. 17.

[3] J. David Bleich, "Survey of Recent Halakhic Periodical Literature: Status of the Deaf-Mute in Jewish Law" in *Tradition* 16:5 (1977), p. 80.

[4] J. David Bleich, *Contemporary Halakhic Problems, Volume II* (New York, 1983), pp. 32-33.

JUDITH Z. ABRAMS

DISEASES IN JEWISH SOURCES: There are many ways to approach the subject of biblical and talmudic medicine. One method is to study the Bible sequentially and identify medical passages and diseases. For example, in Genesis, the Bible relates that when Abraham came to Egypt he told Pharaoh that Sarah was his sister and not his wife. As a result, Pharaoh took her, and God afflicted Pharaoh and his family with a mysterious disease (Gen. 12:17). What was this sickness?

Later in the book of Genesis we are told that Sarah, at the age of ninety years, gave birth to Isaac. How was this possible? Did her menses return? Was this event purely a miracle? What were the medical circumstances surrounding the birth? Another incident concerns the Patriarch Abraham's nephew, Lot, who protected two angels in Sodom against physical harm at the hands of the inhabitants of that city. The angels afflicted the wicked people with blindness (Gen. 18:11). What kind of blindness was this? Was it trachoma? Was it physical, mental, or psychological blindness? Was it temporary or permanent?

Some illnesses are clearly stated. For example, when God came to visit Abraham following his surgery (Gen. 18:1), it is clear that the operation was a circumcision. Not so clear, however, is the meaning of the disease *tzara'at* to which large sections (chap. 13:1ff.) of the book of Leviticus are addressed. Although commonly translated as leprosy, there is serious doubt in the minds of many as to the validity of this interpretation. Some consider *tzara'at* to be elephantiasis; others syphilis, and yet others "a malignant disease of the skin." At least two biblical commentators consider *tzara'at* to be a social disease and not a medical condition at all. To fully examine such a subject requires an in-depth investigation of the medical, historical, and linguistic aspects of *tzara'at*, with a search of citations in the Bible, the writings of ancient and medieval Jewish and non-Jewish scholars, and perhaps even the paleontological evidence, if any.

A chronological methodology of the study of biblical and talmudic medicine represents only one approach. Another approach is to seek information in the Bible and Talmud concerning specific topics, subjects, or disease entities. For example, the ophthalmologist interested in Jewish medical history may ask himself: Where are eye illnesses discussed in the Bible and/or Talmud? Which eye illnesses are described? What is stated about them in terms of diagnosis, treatment, cause, prevention, etc.? Or, one can seek information about diabetes, gallstones, jaundice, anemia, arthritis, or a variety of specific disease entities or symptoms. What do the Bible and/or Talmud say about each of these?

Another approach is to seek material in the Bible and Talmud about individual body organs, such as the heart, the brain, the kidney, and others. A variety of broader subjects, such as air pollution, legal medicine, dietetics, anesthesia, general surgery, and many more can also be looked for in the Bible and Talmud. Finally, the Talmud contains sayings and teachings by sages who were physicians as well as talmudic scholars.

This essay presents a selection of medical conditions and diseases and briefly cites the pertinent biblical, talmudic and other classic sources. The conditions and diseases are presented in chronological order and do not reflect any sequence of importance. Since the subject of biblical and talmudic medicine is so vast, the author made arbitrary selections of topics. The interested reader is referred to more in depth presentations of these and many other diseases in several widely available books and monographs, listed in the bibliography.

A few general comments about illness in ancient Jewish sources will introduce the reader to the subject. Abraham introduced the world to old age, Isaac to suffering, and Jacob to illness (Gen. Rabbah 65:9 and 97:1). Until Jacob there was no illness (Gen. 48:1; B. B.M. 87a; B. San. 107b). Until Elisha, no sick person ever recovered (B. B.M. 87a). Elisha died of his third sickness (2 Kings 13:14; B. San. 107b). Six things help the sick to recover from illness: cabbage, beets, dry sisin herbs, tripe, womb, and liver. Some also say small fish (B. A.Z. 29a). Six things are a good prognostic sign for a sick person: sneezing, perspiration, open bowels, seminal emission, sleep, and a dream (B. Ber. 57b). Ten things cause exacerbation of illness: eating beef, fat roast meat, poultry, roast egg, pepperwort, cress, milk, or cheese; shaving; and bathing (ibid.). Some add nuts and large cucumbers (B. A.Z. 29a).

Eighty-three sicknesses depend on the gall, and all can be rendered ineffectual by eating one's morning bread with salt and drinking a jugful of water (B. B.M. 107b). Morning bread is an antidote against heat and cold, winds, demons, and the evil eye. The most common cause of illness and death is a cold, which may result from one's own negligence (ibid.). Some sages say that most people have themselves to blame for their illness and death (Lev. Rabbah 16:8; Y. Shab. 14:14). A change in one's diet or lifestyle is the beginning of sickness (B. B.B. 146a). One may become ill from eating onions (B. Erub. 29b). Garlands or plants cure illness (B. Shab. 66b). Hot blankets are used to relieve chills and cold compresses to relieve fever (B. Nid. 36b).

A sick person requires guarding (B. Ber. 54b). Visiting the sick is a meritorious act and a religious obligation. For a dangerously ill patient the Sabbath may be desecrated (B. Bes. 22a). If one is deathly ill, one recites the *viduy*, or confession prayer (B. Shab. 32a). A sick person recovers from illness when his sins are forgiven (B. Ned. 41a). If a person falls ill, he should not tell anyone the first day so that he does not have bad luck (B. Ber. 55b). One should not inform a sick person of the death of a close relative (B. M.Q. 26b).

A diagnostic test using a hard-boiled egg is described (B. Ned. 50b) and was used by the physician Mar Samuel on himself (B. Yeb. 116b). Divine healing of illness (Psalms 103:3) is desirable, but many illnesses have a fatal outcome. A person who recovers from illness recites a special blessing of thanksgiving (B. Ber. 54b).

Amputee: When the Jews received the Torah at Mount Sinai, all physical defects were healed and there were no amputees (Tanhuma, Exod. 19:8). Legend relates that the Jews exiled to Babylon after the destruction of the first Temple cut off their thumbs so that they would not have to sing songs of Zion and play musical instruments before Nebuchadnezzar (Midrash Psalms 137:4; Yalkut Shimoni, Psalms 137). Bar Kokhba had two hundred thousand soldiers, each of whom cut off one of his fingers to demonstrate his courage (Lam. Rabbah 2:5; Y. Ta. 4:8). The captured King Adoni-Bezek had this thumbs and toes cut off by Judah and Simeon just as he had done to his enemy kings (Judges 1:6-7). Amputation of limbs does not exist as a punishment in Jewish law. The biblical verses "And thou shalt cut off her hand" (Deut. 25:12) and "a hand for a hand" (Exod. 21:24 and Deut. 19:21) are interpreted to refer to monetary compensation (B. San. 29a and B. B.Q.

83b). The command of King David to amputate the hands and feet of the murderers of Ish-Boshet was after their deaths (2 Sam. 4:12).

The Talmud speaks of surgical amputations (B. Git. 56a), women amputees (B. Yeb. 105a), and amputation of the hand as a life-saving measure (Y. Naz. 9:58). Lepers used to bury their arms in small earthen mounds near cemeteries (B. Ket. 20b). An amputation that includes the knee joint is said to be fatal (B. Nid. 24a). Nahum Gamzu was a quadruple amputee, probably secondary to leprosy (B. Ta. 21a). A procedure is described for someone who needs a limb amputated on the eve of Passover and wishes that both he and the physician remain ritually clean by not handling the amputated limb, which is unclean (B. Ker. 15b).

In talmudic law, someone who cuts off the hand of his fellow man must pay a variety of penalties including pain, damages, medical treatment, enforced idleness, and humiliation (B. B.Q. 85a). Anesthesia or analgesia for amputations is also described (B. B.M. 83b). A handless person cannot function as a judge (Y. San. 8:26) nor can he offer testimony as a witness (B. San. 45b). If a man or woman is handless, the prescribed procedure for a suspected adulteress cannot be carried out (B. Sot. 27a). If one sees an amputee, one should say "Blessed be the true Judge" (B. Ber. 58b). A person missing some fingers cannot spin flax or silk (Song of Songs Rabbah 8:11), even if only one finger is missing (Midrash Psalms 8:2).

Askara: *Askara* (diphtheria) affects primarily children (B. Ta. 27b), but also adults (B. Sot. 35a; B. Yeb. 62b), causing death by asphyxiation (Lev. Rabbah 18:4), the hardest death of the 903 types that exist. The death throes are vividly portrayed in the Talmud (B. Ber. 8a and 40a) and may represent diphtheritic croup. The biblical *magepha* (Num. 14:36) is said to refer to *askara* or epidemic croup (B. Sot. 35a). During Temple times, the priestly divisions fasted every Wednesday so that the *askara* should not attack children (B. Ta. 27b). *Askara* is punishment for the sin of slander and therefore afflicts the mouth and throat

(B. Shab. 33a). Preventive measures include eating lentils, salting all foods, and diluting all beverages with water (B. Ber. 40a).

Baldness: Anterior baldness is called *gabe'ach*, and posterior baldness is called *ker'ach* (Lev. 13:40-41; T. Neg. 4:9; B. Neg. 10:10). A bald-headed man was the subject of ridicule in antiquity (B. Sot. 46b) as was the case with the prophet Elisha (2 Kings 2:23). Immorality of women may be punished by the divine infliction of baldness (Is. 3:17). Sorceresses are referred to as bald-headed (B. Pes. 110a). "Baldheaded buck" is an abusive term for a castrate (B. Shab. 152a). A curse is to wish baldness on someone (Y. Shab. 20:17). A bald-headed priest is disqualified from serving in the Temple (B. Bek. 7:2) because of his unsightly appearance (B. Bek. 43b). A bald man, on the other hand, does not have to worry about dust or sand flying into his hair (Gen. Rabbah 65:15). A treatment for baldness is discussed in the Midrash (Ecc. Rabbah 1:8). For men to pluck out their white hairs, as was practiced by some women, is forbidden (B. Shab. 94b), since it might eventually lead to baldness (B. B.Q. 60b). Female war captives shaved their heads as a sign of mourning for their relatives killed in the war (Deut. 21:12). The prophet Micah exhorts the people to shave their heads as a sign of mourning for their children taken into captivity (Micah 1:16).

Causes of baldness include illnesses such as leprosy (Lev. 13:42); an act of God; the use of a depilatory caustic substance (B. Neg. 19:10); severe emotional trauma such as fright upon seeing a snake (Exod. Rabbah 24:4); shearing off the scalp hair as a sign of mourning, an act prohibited to Jews (Deut. 14:1), especially priests (Lev. 21:5), as a heathen custom; or the forbidden plucking out of one's hair as a sign of mourning (Ezra 9:3).

Birth Defects: Cohabitation with a menstruating woman was thought to result in malformed or leprous infants (Lev. Rabbah 15:5). Babies born circumcised need to be carefully examined for true congenital absence of the foreskin (B. A.Z. 27a; B. Yeb. 71a). Half-human, half-goat-like newborns are cited in the Talmud (B. Nid. 23b), as well as newborns with facial dis-

figurements, anencephaly (ibid., 24a), webbed hands and feet (ibid.), absence of the lower half of the body, or fusion of the lower limbs (ibid.). A newborn child with wings or with very long hair (B. Nid. 24b; B. Erub. 100b), with two backs or spinal columns (B. Nid. 24b), or with a hunchback (B. Bek. 43b) or crooked spine (B. Nid. 24a) can survive into adulthood.

The Bible speaks of a giant with six fingers and six toes (2 Sam. 21:20). A thirty-day-old child with two heads is the subject of a talmudic legal discussion (B. Men. 37a). A *sandal* is a flat "squashed" fetus, or fetus papyraceus, that resembles a flat sole fish (B. Nid. 25b) and is delivered together with a normal newborn child (ibid., 26a). It was thought that superfetation, whereby a pregnant woman became pregnant again and the younger fetus was squashed by the earlier one (T. Nid. 2:6), is possible. To prevent this occurrence, a pregnant woman should use an absorbent tampon during cohabitation (B. Yeb. 12b).

Boils: The biblical *shechin* and *ababuot* (Exod. 9:8-11) may represent boils, blisters, or perhaps a form of eczema. The moist form is curable; the dry one is not (B. Bek. 41a). Other biblical skin afflictions (Deut. 28:27) may also refer to boils. Different types of boils, quick flesh, burning, and their like are described in the Talmud (B. Neg. 1:5ff.). A boil and a burning are obviously different (B. Hul. 8a).

Nahum was blind and his body was covered with boils because he once postponed giving food to a poor person and the latter died of hunger (B. Ta. 21a). A man was once healed of his boils and scabs by a "magical" formula (B. Qid. 39b). A levir was once afflicted with boils (B. Yeb. 4a). A man with boils may be forced to give his wife a divorce (B. Ket. 77a). A folk remedy for boils is described at B. Shab. 67a.

Childlessness: Infertility is a curse, and fertility is a blessing (Exod. 23:26; Deut. 7:14). A person without children is considered as if excommunicated by heaven (T. Pes. 113b). A barren woman might prefer death to childlessness (Gen. 30:1). A childless man is regarded as dead (B. Ned. 64b; B. A.Z. 5a; Gen. Rabbah 71:6; Exod. Rabbah 5:1). The key to childbirth is one of three keys that God himself administers and does not entrust to an emissary (B. Ta. 2a; B. San. 113a). A number of barren women are described in the Bible, all of whom eventually had children: Sarah (Gen. 11:30), Rebecca (Gen. 25:21), Rachel (Gen. 29:31), the wife of Manoach (Judges 13:2), Hannah (1 Sam. 1:2), the woman from Shunam (2 Kings 4:14), and Ruth (Ruth Rabbah 7:13). The sages say that these women were at first barren because God desires the prayers of the righteous (B. Yeb. 64a). A number of additional reasons for the matriarchs' barrenness are also cited (Song of Songs Rabbah 2:21). Male barrenness is also recognized (B. Ned. 91a).

Abraham used to pray for barren women and they conceived (Gen. Rabbah 39:11). God remembers barren women as he did for Sarah (Lev. Rabbah 27:14), Hannah (Num. Rabbah 14:1), and the woman from Shunam (Deut. Rabbah 10:3). God blesses the Jews (Deut. 7:14) by saying there shall be no male or female barren among them (Deut. Rabbah 3:6). The Lord also opens his good treasure (Deut. 28:12), which means he will keep the key to barrenness locked up (Deut. Rabbah 7:6). Just as God makes barren women fertile, so the righteous can make barren women fertile (Song of Songs Rabbah 1:4:2). The prophet sings about barrenness (Is. 54:1), although one weeps and mourns for a person who died childless (B. M.Q. 27b). Childless women are like prisoners in their houses because of the disgrace they feel to be so afflicted (Gen. Rabbah 71:1). Childless couples may have marital relations even in years of famine to help them overcome their childlessness (B. Ta. 11a). If a man lives with a wife for ten years and she bears him no children, he should take another wife (B. Yeb. 64a), although male infertility could be the cause; polygamy was then allowed. Manoach and Hannah disagreed among themselves as to who was the infertile partner in their childless marriage (Num. Rabbah 10:5). Some Rabbinic scholars became impotent because of long scholarly discourses (B. Yeb. 64b). The wife of a man who dies childless must be married by the deceased husband's brother in a levirate marriage to preserve the name of the deceased (Deut. 25:5-6).

Diarrhea: A person with diarrhea is ill in his intestines and needs to treat it before it worsens (B. Sot. 42b). Some patients also have fever and swollen abdomens (Avot de Rabbi Nathan 41:1). The disease may be very painful (B. Shab. 11a) and even bring one to tears (Lam. Rabbah 2:15; B. Shab. 151b). Because of the pain, patients with diarrhea are forgiven for their sins and do not see the face of Gehenna (B. Erub. 41b). Thus, diarrhea may be a good omen (B. Ket. 103b) in that righteous people die of diarrhea. Judah the Prince suffered from diarrhea (ibid., 104a), as did King Belshazzar (Song Rabbah 3:4). Yose wished diarrhea upon himself (B. Shab. 118b). The expression *gava* for "he died" refers to diarrhea (Gen. Rabbah 62:2). Such people die suddenly while fully conscious (B. Erub. 41b). King Jehoram is said to have suffered from severe dysentery so that his "bowels fell out" and he died (2 Chron. 21:14-18).

Priests in the Temple who walked barefoot on the marble floors and ate a lot of sacrificial meat suffered from diarrhea and had a special physician to care for them (B. Sheq. 5:2). Another cause of diarrhea is a change in one's lifestyle or eating habits (B. Ned. 37b). Eating rich foods may spoil one's festival joy because of diarrhea (B. San. 101a), which is called an evil affliction (Prov. 15:15). Eating without drinking can also lead to diarrhea (B. Shab. 42a). Thus, one should drink one cupful of water with each loaf of bread or other food (B. Ber. 40a). Also to prevent diarrhea one should eat bread immersed in vinegar or wine in both summer and winter (B. Git. 70a). Wheatbread, fish brine, and beer can cause diarrhea (B. Shab. 108a). So, too, coarse bread, fresh beer, and raw vegetables (B. Pes. 42a), as well as certain types of wine (B. B.B. 97b). White bread, fat meat, and old wine, however, do not cause diarrhea (B. Pes. 42a).

Remedies for diarrhea include the external rubbing of the abdomen with oil and wine (B. Shab. 134a) or the application of heat (ibid., 40b). An Egyptian concoction of barley, safflower, and salt is a binding potion (B. Shab. 110a; B. Pes. 42b). Also helpful is old apple wine (B. A.Z. 40b), old grape juice (B. Ned. 9:8), lemonade (Lev.

Rabbah 37:2), dates (B. Ket. 10b), and various compounded medications (B. Git. 69b).

Diarrhea is a favorable prognostic sign in sick patients provided it is not dysentery (B. Ber. 57b). Hydrops or leukophlegmesia is cured if the patient develops diarrhea (B. Yeb. 60b). One should not visit patients with diarrhea because of embarrassment or in order not to contract it (B. Ned. 41a). A perfume pan was placed near patients with diarrhea (B. M.Q. 27b).

Dislocations: Jacob dislocated the head of his femur when he wrestled with an angel (Gen. 32:26). Legend relates that when Noah emerged from the ark, a lion pushed him so that he limped (Lev. Rabbah 20:1). Job speaks about a dislocated shoulder (Job 31:22). Mephiboshet was lame in his feet (2 Sam. 4:4), perhaps because of dislocated vertebrae sustained in a fall. Belshazzar may have had a dislocated hip (Dan. 5:6). If a person's jaw is dislocated, "the ear should be raised to its proper position" (B. A.Z. 28b).

Dislocation of the jaw in an animal renders it unfit to be offered in the Temple (B. Bek. 6:10). If most of an animal's ribs are dislocated or fractured the animal's life is in danger (B. Hul. 57a). Not so for birds (ibid.).

Dropsy: Dropsy or *hydrakon* (hydrops) is a divine punishment for immoral sexual behavior (B. Yeb. 60b) and other sins, such as the golden calf (B. Yom. 66b). Dropsy also occurs as a result of withholding one's bowels (B. Ber. 62b; B. Tam. 27b); therefore, the maxim: "Much feces, much dropsy; much wine, much anemia" (B. Bek. 44b). Dropsy is said to be caused by an abnormal mixing of water and blood in the body (Lev. Rabbah 15:2). The sages describe three types of dropsy: the thick one is punishment for sin, the swollen one is caused by hunger (hypoproteinemia or nephrotic syndrome?), and the thin one is caused by magic (B. Shab. 33a). Several famous talmudic sages suffered from it (B. Shab. 33a), probably due to hunger. A person afflicted with dropsy may die suddenly (B. Erub. 41b). It is not clear whether the abdominal swelling of a suspected adulteress after she drank the bitter waters represents dropsy.

Dwarfism: Nebuchadnezzar, king of Babylon, is said to have been a midget or dwarf (Gen. Rabba*h* 16:4). A male dwarf should not marry a female one, lest their offspring be a dwarf of the smallest size (B. Bek. 45b). According to Ibn Ezra and Targum Jonathan, the biblical term *dak* (Lev. 21:20) refers to a midget or dwarf.

A dwarf is described in the Talmud in relation to violation of Sabbath laws (B. Shab. 5a). Bald-headed people, dwarfs, and the bleary-eyed are unfit for the priesthood because "they are not like the seed of Aaron" (B. Bek. 43b). The suggestion that Abba Saul was a dwarf is rejected in the Talmud (B. Nid. 24b).

A woman whose son was a dwarf saw him in her imagination as "tall and swift" (Gen. Rabbah 65:11) but everyone else saw him only as a puny dwarf (Song Rabbah 2:15:2).

Epilepsy: The biblical term "fallen down" probably refers to epilepsy. Hence, Balaam (Num. 24:16) and King Saul (1 Sam. 19:24) are said to have suffered from epilepsy (Maimonides' Mishnah Commentary, M. Git. 7:5). Body humors and gases play a role in the causation of epilepsy (Ibid., Git. 7:1). Demons may also play a role (B. Git. 70a; B. R.H. 28a; Lev. Rabbah 26:5). Hereditary factors were also recognized in that a person should not take a wife from a family of epileptics (B. Yeb. 64a). Immoral sexual behavior is strongly discouraged in Judaism and may be the basis for several talmudic statements about epilepsy: A woman who copulates in a mill will have epileptic children (B. Ket. 60b). He who copulates immediately after defecation (B. Git. 70a) or by the light of a lamp will have epileptic children (B. Pes. 112b). He who stands naked in front of a lamp or who cohabits in a bed in which a baby is sleeping will become epileptic (B. Pes. 112b). Cohabitation after bloodletting may also lead to the birth of epileptic children (Lev. Rabbah 16:1). Some post talmudic Rabbinic decisors consider epilepsy to be an infectious disease, but most agree with modern medical knowledge that it is not. The talmudic sages know that certain epileptics have seizures at specified times (B. Ket. 77a).

The diagnosis and treatment of epilepsy was carried out by competent physicians, not by priests or exorcists (Lev. Rabbah 26:5). Amulets were used both to prevent and to treat epilepsy (B. Shab. 61a; T. Shab. 4:9). One also recited incantations (B. Shab. 67a). The condition known as *kordiakos* (B. Git. 7:1) is interpreted to refer to withdrawal seizures in the course of delirium tremens secondary to alcoholic intoxication. Some rabbis rule that a single convulsive episode defines a person as an epileptic, whereas other rabbis require three episodes. Controversy exists as to whether or not epilepsy is life-threatening.

Legally, an epileptic is unfit to serve as a priest in the Temple even if he only had a single seizure (M. Bek. 7:5). An epileptic may serve as a cantor in the synagogue if his epilepsy is dormant or controlled (Responsa *Chatam Sofer*, *Yoreh Deah* #7). Similarly he may serve as a ritual slaughterer (ibid.). Undisclosed epilepsy may be grounds for divorce. An epileptic can testify in a legal proceeding while he is well, provided his mind is clear (B. Ket. 20a; Maimonides' *Mishneh Torah*, Edut 9:9).

Eye Diseases: The Rabbinic sages describe various stages of eye inflammation (B. Bes. 22a; B. A.Z. 28b; B. Bek. 44a). *Techila uchla* is the first sign of eye inflammation. *Rira* is a discharge of pus (conjunctivitis). *Ditza* refers to shooting or sharp pain in the eyes. *Dama* refers to bloodshot eyes. *Dimata* means excessive tearing. *Kadachta* means local inflammation. *Meridah* is said to be protrusion of the eye (Rashi, B. A.Z. 28b) or the flow of infectious pus from the eye (Rashi, B. Neg. 6:8). *Sof uchla* is the final stage of eye inflammation. When the infectious secretion dries on the eyebrows, it becomes like a membrane called *lifluf* (B. Miq. 9:2; B. Nid. 67a). *Zabalgan* (B. Meg. 26b) is one from whose eyes tears flow (Rashi, B. Meg. 24b).

The eyes of a man afflicted with a *raatan* (B. Ket. 77b) tear because of inflammation and his vision is defective as a result. Also beware of contagion from flies near him (ibid.). A *tziran* (B. Bek. 44a) is said to be a person with tearing eyes (Maimonides' *Mishneh Torah*, Biyat Mikdash 8:6) or with round eyes. Eyes that are *terutot* (B. Shab.

31a; B. Ta. 24a, B. Sot. 47a; B. San. 107b; B. Bek. 44a) are round (Rashi, B. Shab. 31a) and the eyelids are only partially open (Maimonides, *Biyat Mikdash* 8:5). *Simuka* (Y. Shab. 14:4) is a person with redness of the eyes as a sign of a dangerous eye ailment. *Pekiat ayin* (B. A.Z. 28b) refers to perforation of the eye as the final stage of a serious infection. *Barkit* or *barka* (B. Bek. 38b; B. B.M. 78b; B. Shab. 78a) is a white tissue that protrudes from the eye and is compatible with a corneal inflammation (keratitis). *Atzev* or *einav* (B. Bek. 38a) is a protrusion of part of the uveal layer secondary to corneal inflammation (Maimonides' *Mishnah Commentary*, M. Bek. 6:2). This condition may be the same as *barkit*.

Chavarvar (B. Bek. 38b) refers to sudden blindness from nerve weakness (Maimonides, M. Bek. 6:3), blindness (*Mishneh Torah*, Issurei Mizbeah 2:7), or cataract (*Aruch*, s.v. *eever*). Some authors consider it to refer to white spots on the eye and so to be a condition resembling *barkit*. The rabbis distinguish permanent from temporary or transient *chavarvar* by repetitive examinations of the eye during an eighty day period (B. Bek. 38b). Water in the eye (ibid.) refers either to constant tearing (*Rashi*, B. Bek. 38b) or the flow of water within the eye (Maimonides, M. Bek. 6:3), which, according to some authors, refers to the development of a cataract.

Causes of eye ailments and diseases are extensively discussed in the Talmud. A woman who eats cress has bleary-eyed children; if she eats small fish she has children with small or blinking eyes; if she eats eggs, her children have large eyes (B. Ket. 60b-61a). Drinking water from rivers or pools at night is dangerous and may lead to blindness (B. Pes. 112a). Drinking water in a pot is harmful and may cause *barkit* (B. Pes. 11b; B. Git. 89a). Living in a dark house causes one's eyes to blink (B. Ber. 59a). Prolonged weeping causes the eyelashes to fall out (Gen. 29:17; B. B.B. 123a). People who live in sandy places have eyes that are *terutot* (B. Shab. 31a).

Fever: *Kadachat* (Lev. 26:16), *daleket*, and *charchur* (Deut. 28:22) are all types of fever. A fever in the winter is severer than in the summer (B. Yom. 29a). A furuncle called *simta* sometimes causes fever (B. A.Z. 28b). For a bee sting or eye ailment associated with fever, bathing is dangerous (ibid.). One should visit a sick patient only after the fever subsides (B. Ned. 41a). Circumcision is postponed for a baby with fever (B. Yeb. 70a). Patients with fever often go for days without eating; hence the hypothesis that "fever nourishes" (B. San. 108b). If fever is not life threatening, it is salutary to the body, but one sage said: "I want neither the fever nor the theriac" (B. Ned. 41a).

Numerous folk remedies are discussed for fever (B. Shab. 67a; B. Git. 67b). Radishes are good for a patient with fever (B. A.Z. 28b). A fever present for two days is an indication for bloodletting (B. Git. 67b). The nail from the gallows of an executed person is efficacious against the febrile illness *ababita* (Y. Shab. 6:8). One sage with fever was cured by an incantation (Song Rabbah 2:16). When Rav died people took dirt from his grave as a remedy for quotidian fever (B. San. 47b). Assi died of pyemia with high fever (B. Ned. 36b). Burning fevers are considered life-threatening (B. A.Z. 28a). Fig juice was rubbed on one such patient (B. Pes. 25b). Another was treated with exorcism (B. Shab. 67a).

Gigantism: Giants existed in biblical times (Gen. 6:4; Gen. Rabbah 31:12). The spies whom Moses sent to explore the promised land claimed they saw giants (Num. 13:33). Og, king of Bashan, was the only giant remaining in his kingdom (Deut. 3:11). His bed was nine cubits long and four cubits wide, and his thigh bone was more than three parasangs long (B. Nid. 24b). Josephus describes giants in Hebron (*Antiquities*, Book 5, Chap. 2:3). The Philistine Goliath was a giant (1 Sam. 17:4), and his exploits are described in the Talmud (B. Sot. 42b). Whether or not any of these giants were acromegalics cannot be established with any degree of certainty.

The biblical term *sarua* (Lev. 21:18) is interpreted to refer to excessive growth and size of one limb, disqualifying such a priest from serving in the Temple (B. Bek. 3b). Ben Batiach is said to have had an unusually large hand or fist (B. Kel. 17:12). A certain R. Ishmael is also said to have had huge hands and was able to grasp four *kabs*

in one of them (B. Yom. 47a). Tall stature (gigantism?) was thought to be hereditary, in that the offspring of a tall man who marries a tall woman are tall children (B. Bek. 45b). The terms *kippuach* (T. Ber. 7:3; Y. Ber. 9:13) and *kippeach* (B. Bek. 7:6; B. Ber. 58b) refer to a very tall person or a giant (B. Bek. 45b). A series of very tall rabbis is enumerated in the Talmud (B. Nid. 24b).

Gonorrhea: A male with flux from his genitalia (Lev. 15:2ff.) is called a *zav* (Lev. 15:1-18), and a woman with intermenstrual flux is called a *zava* (Lev. 15:25-28). After the first emission, the man is called a *baal keri* and is ritually unclean for the day. After the second emission, he is unclean and has to count seven days, wash his garments, immerse in a ritual bath, and wait for sunset. After the third emission, he also has to bring sacrifices on the eighth day (B. Ned. 43b). If a woman observes a flux after her menses, she is unclean until evening. From then on, she is "on the wait" and, if there is a flux on the second day, she becomes unclean for seven days. A third day certifies her as gonorrheic, and she must then bring a sacrifice after ritual purification (B. Zab. 2:3).

Excessive eating and drinking was thought to be a cause of gonorrhea (B. Yom. 18a; B. Qid. 2b). A sufferer from gonorrhea who has a seminal emission requires ritual ablution (B. Ber. 26a). He or she may take the bath during the day (B. Yom. 6b), even in swiftly running waters (ibid., 78a), and even on Yom Kippur (ibid., 88a). A man with gonorrhea causes defilement by touching or carrying (B. B.Q. 25a). He cannot eat the paschal lamb (B. Bek. 33a). His spittle is the direct cause of levitical impurity (Lev. 15:18; B. Bek. 38a). He must examine himself to determine the number of emissions he has had (B. Nid. 13a). A woman can have gonorrhea before or after she gives birth (B. Ker. 9b).

When Israel stood at Mount Sinai, there were none among them with gonorrhea or leprosy (Lev. Rabbah 18:4). In the desert, however, people with gonorrhea were sent out of the camp (Num. 5:2). Gonorrheal flux and sperm emission differ in that the former resembles incubated egg whites and is pale, whereas sperm is "bound" and resembles the white of eggs (T. Zab. 2:4). Sperm issues from an erect penis whereas flux issues from a flaccid penis.

Gout: King Asa of Judah (915-875 B.C.E.) reigned for over forty years. In his old age he suffered from a disease in his feet considered to be gout (1 Kings 15:23). The Talmud (B. San. 48b, B. Sot. 10a) describes his illness as podagra, which feels "like a needle in the raw flesh." R. Nahman also suffered from it. Rashi (B. San. 48b) states that the name of this illness, podagra, "is the same even in our language," i.e., French, Rashi's native tongue. The expression "like a needle in the raw flesh" is used elsewhere in the Talmud (B. Ber. 18b, B. Shab. 13b, and 152a). Further mention of Asa's illness is found in 2 Chr. 16:12.

Another pertinent reference to gout is at M. Shab. 6:6, which describes a foot ailment called *tzinit*. The Jerusalem Talmud interprets this word to mean podagra or gout (Y. Shab. 6:8). The Babylonian Talmud, however, considers *tzinit* to refer to a corn or bunion (B. Shab. 65a).

Headache: The famous talmudic sage Rab said that he can tolerate any pain except headache (B. Shab. 11a). Another famous rabbi suffered from headaches for seven weeks following his drinking of the four prescribed cups of wine on the first night of Passover (Ecc. Rabbah 8:1; B. Ned. 49b). Yet another talmudic sage was unable to wear the head phylactery during the summer because his head was heavy from the heat (Y. Ber. 2:4). The final illness of Titus, in which a gnat flew into his nose, ascended into his head, and gave him incessant headaches, is vividly depicted in the Talmud (B. Git. 56b). An eminent rabbi cried out that the generation of the deluge brought headaches on humankind (Gen. Rabbah 34:11). A king once reminded his son about the place where the latter had a headache (Num. Rabbah 23:3).

One cause of headaches is the blowing away of the froth or foam of beverages such as beer or mead (B. Hul. 105b). Divinely induced headaches require repentance and the performance of good deeds (B. Shab. 32a). When Jabez prayed to the Lord to keep evil away from him (1 Chr. 4:10), he was referring to headache (B. Tem. 16a).

Another remedy for headache is to study Torah (B. Erub. 54a), because the words of Torah are an ornament of grace on one's head (Prov. 1:9). The standard medical therapy for headache was to rub the head with wine, vinegar, or oil (T. Shab. 12:11; Y. M.S. 2:53). A person with a headache should imagine that he is being put in irons (B. Shab. 32a).

Someone with a headache is exempt from living in a *sukkah* (booth) on the Festival of Sukkot (B. Suk. 26a). One should not visit patients with headache because speech is said to be harmful to them (B. Ned. 41a). Perhaps they prefer to lie quietly without speaking. The name of King Ahasuerus, associated with the holiday of Purim, is interpreted to mean headache inducer (Hebrew: *chash berosh*) (Esther Rabbah 1:3; B. Meg. 11a).

Plethora or an excess of blood is the cause of many illnesses (B. B.B. 58b) including migraine or hemicrania of the ancients. People or animals with congestion or plethora were placed in cold water to cool off (B. Shab. 53b). Once such an animal cools off, its flesh is not harmful for human consumption (T. Hul. 3:19). A variety of folk remedies are detailed in the Talmud to treat blood rushing to the head and migraine (B. Git. 68b). Animals with plethora were also treated with phlebotomies (T. Bek. 3:17). Leprosy is said to be caused by plethora (Lev. Rabbah 15:2; B. Bek. 44b).

Hemophilia: The sex-linked transmission of hemophilia was recognized by the talmudic sages (B. Yeb. 64b). Females carry the defective gene but are clinically healthy, and affected males suffer from this bleeding disorder. The key passage in the Talmud states (B. Yeb. 64b):

> For it was taught: "If she circumcised her first child and he died [as a result of bleeding from the operation], and a second one also died [similarly], she must not circumcise her third child." These are the words of Rabbi [Judah the Prince]. Rabban Simeon b. Gamaliel, however, said: "She may circumcise the third child but must not circumcise the fourth child."

Judah and Simeon do not differ on the question of the maternal transmission of the disease but on the number of repetitive events required to establish a pattern and to remove a subsequent similar event from the category of chance. This is a technical point of talmudic law. Although, in general, three repetitive events are necessary to establish a pattern, in matters of life and death, the view of Judah is upheld that two suffice. No other form of diagnosis was then available. The codifiers of Jewish law including Alfasi (loc. cit.), Maimonides (*Mishneh Torah, Milah* 1:18), Karo (*Shulhan Aruch, Yoreh Deah* 263:2, 3), and others all rule according to the opinion of Judah. Some Rabbinic authorities thought that males can also transmit this genetic bleeding disorder.

Hemorrhoids: The Lord smites his enemies with hemorrhoids (Ps. 78:66), as he did the Philistines (1 Sam. 5:6-12). Israelites would be similarly stricken if they sin (Deut. 28:27; B. Meg. 26b). The Talmud lists ten things that lead to hemorrhoids: eating the leaves of reeds or vines; eating unsalted animal palates, fish spines, or insufficiently cooked salted fish; drinking wine lees; or wiping one's anus with lime, clay, or pebbles previously used by others (B. Ber. 55a; B. Shab. 81a). Fresh grass should not be used to wipe oneself, because it may tear hemorrhoids (B. Shab. 82a). He who sits too long without walking (B. Ket. 11a) or who squats to defecate without sitting down may also develop hemorrhoids (B. Ber. 55a; B. Shab. 81a). Bleeding hemorrhoids may lead to collapse (B. Ned. 22a). Dates are helpful to treat hemorrhoids (B. Ket. 10b).

Melancholy: According to Josephus (*Antiquities*, vol. 10. Chap. 2:1), King Hezekiah was afflicted with a deep depression when he became ill because he was childless. The Talmud states that he voluntarily refrained from procreating because he foresaw that his children would be wicked (B. Ber. 10a). Both Nebuchadnezzar (Dan. 4:29-34) and Saul (1 Sam. 16:14) may have suffered from melancholy.

Dates are helpful for melancholy or bad thoughts (B. Ket. 10b). Heaviness of the heart (*yukra de libba*), for which remedies are prescribed (B. Shab. 140a; B. Git. 69b), may refer to depression or melancholy.

Mental Deficiency: Although deaf people may have normal intelligence, deaf-mutes are usually mentally deficient (B. Hag. 2b). They have weak understanding (B. Yeb. 113a) and cannot reflect well (B. Mak. 6:1). The term *shoteh* for fool or imbecile means "to roam about, " i.e., "absent-minded." Imbeciles are considered mentally deficient but not insane. They do not have full adult intellect and are legally equated with minors and deaf-mutes. Intermittent loss of intellect can occur in an intoxicated person suffering from *kordiakos* (B. Git. 7:1), who is temporarily confused. One's intellect weakens with advancing age (2 Sam. 19:36; B. Shab. 152b). One cannot cite proof from the action of imbeciles (B. Nid. 30b), as was once attempted in a case in which a child was found dead and the mother was suspected (B. Ket. 60b). A person can be sane at times and mad at other times (B. R.H. 28a).

Mental Illness: Mental illness or insanity (*shiga'on*) is divine punishment for wrongdoing (Deut. 28:28, 28:34; Zech. 12:4). A madman who claims he is a prophet is a false prophet (Jer. 29:26). King Nebuchadnezzar was mad in that he ate grass like oxen, and his nails grew long like bird's claws (Dan. 4:30). King Saul was terrified (1 Sam. 16:16), raved in his house (1 Sam. 18:10), stripped off his clothes, and lay naked (ibid., 19:23-24). Kind David feigned madness (ibid., 21:14).

The mentally ill go out at night alone, spend the night in the cemetery, and tear their garments and other things (B. Hag. 3b; B. San. 65b; B. Nid. 17a). A fool repeats his folly like a dog who returns to its vomit (Prov. 26:11; Lev. Rabbah 16:9). A person does not transgress unless a spirit of folly enters him (B. Sot. 3a). This includes immoral sexual behavior by wife or husband (B. Bek. 5b). A lunatic may have periods of clear or sound state of mind (B. Yeb. 31a). An intoxicated person behaves like a madman (B. Meg. 12b), because when wine enters the body, understanding leaves (Num. Rabbah 16:9). The Aramean army suffered from auditory hallucinations (2 Kings 7:6).

Mad people were put in prison (Jer. 29:26). The Talmud says that there are no medications for madmen (B. Git. 70b). A woman who killed a baby in order to remarry was said to be mad (B. Ket. 60a-b).

Paralysis: Breaking the neck of an animal causes paralysis (B. Hul. 113a). Alcimus became paralyzed before he died of apoplexy (1 Macc. 9:55). Philapator was also paralyzed and aphasic as a result of divine punishment (3 Macc. 2:22). Nabal became drunk at a feast, "became as a stone," and died (1 Sam. 25:38). The Talmud relates that he who feigns an illness such as lameness or paralysis will actually suffer from it (Y. Pe. 8:9; B. Bek. 45b).

Several instances of hand "paralysis" or incapacity include the cases of Eleazar (2 Sam. 23:10), Benjaminite soldiers (Judges 20:16), Ehud (Judges 3:15), and Jeroboam (1 Kings 13:4).

Puerperal Illness: Puerperal bleeding is considered part of normal birthing (B. Nid. 21b) and renders the parturient woman ritually unclean. Such a woman's limbs are disjointed and her natural strength does not return for two years (B. Nid. 9a). The puerperal illness known as *kuda* (B. A.Z. 29a) is, according to the commentaries, a cold that the woman caught on the birth stool. A herbal potion is prescribed for its treatment (ibid.). Death during childbirth is frequently mentioned in the Talmud, sometimes as punishment for not fulfilling religious precepts (B. Shab. 2:6). The death of a woman in confinement (B. Erub. 41b) may have been due to puerperal sepsis. Rachel (Gen. 35:18), the wife of Phinehas (1 Sam. 4:20), Michael, wife of King David (2 Sam. 6:23; B. San. 21a), and Queen Esther (B. Meg. 13a) all died during childbirth.

Rabies: Rabies (hydrophobia) is a disease of great antiquity, having been described in the pre-Mosaic Eshnuna Code of ancient Mesopotamia about four thousand years ago. Regarding bites of a rabid dog, M. Yom. 8:6 states: "If one was bitten by a mad dog, he may not be given the lobe of its liver to eat, but R. Matia b. Cheresh permits it."

The therapeutic use of parts of the rabid animal, particularly the liver, for individuals bitten by such an animal, was recommended by many ancient physicians. In the Talmud, only Matia b. Cheresh, who lived in Rome, advocates and permits this type of therapy, since he believed in its curative values, perhaps a forerunner of modern homeopathics). The other sages deny its curative value and hence prohibit its use, since it is derived from a non-kosher animal.

The Talmud describes the behavior of a mad dog and cautions against even only rubbing against it, lest one develop symptoms of hydrophobia. One talmudic sage recommends that one kill the rabid dog and avoid any direct contact with it (B. Yom. 83b). From these talmudic statements, it is obvious that the etiology of rabies was not understood, although the symptomatology was correctly recognized. Folk remedies for the treatment of someone bitten by a mad dog are presented in some detail (B. Yom. 84a).

The Y. Yom. 8:5 relates that Judah the Prince gave "liver" to his Germanic servant, who had been bitten by a mad dog, but in vain. The patient died, from which the Talmud concludes: "let no man tell you that he was bitten by a mad dog and lived." This statement is also found elsewhere in the Jerusalem Talmud (Y. Ber. 8:5).

A final statement dealing with the bite of a mad dog is found in B. Shab. 121b: R. Joshua b. Levi said: "All animals that cause injury [i.e., kill] may be killed [even] on the Sabbath." R. Joseph objected. "Five may be killed on the Sabbath, and these are they: the Egyptian fly, the hornet of Nineveh, the scorpion of Adiabene, the snake in the land of Israel, and a mad dog anywhere." This ruling is codified by Maimonides (*Mishneh Torah*, B. Shab. 11:4) and Karo (*Shulhan Aruch*, *Orach Chayim* 316:10). Other animal bites are mentioned in the Talmud (B. Yom. 49a, B. Hul. 7b, B. B.Q. 84a), but the wound inflicted was probably not associated with rabies.

Sciatica: The Patriarch Jacob wrestled with the angel of God and was wounded in his sciatic nerve and limped (Gen. 32:26ff.). Since then the consumption of this nerve is prohibited to Jews by divine decree (Gen. 32:33). The Talmud gives instructions about how to remove the sciatic nerve from freshly slaughtered animals (B. Hul. 89b). The removal of this nerve and its tributaries is quite difficult and requires considerable skill.

The talmudic term *shigrona* (B. Git. 69b) refers to sciatica. A ewe who dragged its hind legs was found at autopsy to be suffering from this malady (B. Hul. 51a, 59a). The treatment for this condition is to rub fish brine sixty times on each hip (B. Git. 69b). A person with pain in the loins was told to rub them with wine and vinegar or with oil, especially rose oil (B. Shab. 14:4).

Scurvy: A disease called *tzafdinah* is described in the Talmud in which gum bleeding is the major symptom. *Tzafdinah* in most Jewish sources, in both the classic German and English versions of the Talmud, as well as in modern Hebrew dictionaries is translated as scurvy. Yohanan suffered from *tzafdinah* and went to a Roman matron seeking a remedy (B. Yom. 84a). The symptoms of this disease are that if one puts anything between the teeth, the gums bleed. The story of Yohanan's scurvy and the remedy provided by the Roman matron is found elsewhere in the Talmud (B. A.Z. 28a) with minor variations.

Another talmudic passage states the following: R. Matia b. Cheresh said: "If one has pain in his throat, he may pour medicine into his mouth on the Sabbath, because there is a possibility of danger to human life, and every danger to human life suspends the laws of the Sabbath" (M. Yom. 8:6). Some talmudic commentators, notably Alfasi and Asheri, interpret this passage literally. Others, however, notably *Tur*, Bertinoro, and *Tosafot Yom Tov*, change the phrase "pain in the throat" to "pain in the teeth so that the gums begin to rot and the palate and throat become secondarily involved." Also supporting the latter viewpoint is Maimonides, who states in his commentary on the Mishnah, that "pain in the mouth means the gums, which are rotting, and if nothing is done, the palate will also rot." Whether Matia b. Cheresh described scurvy or another malady of the mouth, teeth, gums, and throat cannot be answered with certainty.

Another sage who suffered from presumed scurvy is Judah the Prince (B. B.M. 85a). He observed that Eleazar b. Simeon had submitted to much suffering for which he was divinely rewarded, in that his body

remained intact, defying decomposition and decay, for many years. Thereupon Judah the Prince undertook to suffer likewise for thirteen years, six through stones in the kidneys or bladder and seven through scurvy. The talmudic word for scurvy here is *tzipparna*, which is a variation of *tzafdinah*. Nathan b. Yechiel states that the manuscript versions of the Talmud in fact have the word *tzafdinah*. The English translation of the Talmud also renders *tzipparna* as scurvy.

That *tzafdinah* is an affliction of the teeth that is a potential hazard to life because it begins in the mouth but spreads to the intestines is also evident from the Jerusalem Talmud (Y. A.Z. 2:2, 10b). Whether *tzafdinah* represents true scurvy, as appears to be the opinion of most talmudic commentators and translators, or whether it is another ailment, such as pyorrhea, thrush, tooth abscess, or the like, as the medical description in the Talmud would appear to indicate, is a problem that may never be resolved.

Sterility: A hornet sting in the testicles (B. Sot. 36a), other serious injury to the testicles (B. Yeb. 75b), or severe brain injury can produce sterility (B. Hul. 45b). An oral potion used to treat jaundice may produce sterility (B. Shab. 109b-110b; 109b-110b; B. Yeb. 65b). A eunuch and an *aylonit* are obviously sterile. Famous barren women in the Bible are discussed elsewhere [see under Childlessness, above]. Men may be the infertile partner in some sterile marriages (Num. Rabbah 10:5). Isaac is said to have been infertile at first (B. Yeb. 64a). Some Torah scholars become impotent because of long talmudic discourses during which they hold back their micturition (B. Yeb. 64b). The sickness *raatan* (leprosy?) may interfere with potency (Lev. Rabbah 16:1). Illness in a man may lead to impotency (ibid.), as may psychic causes (Y. Ned. 11:42) and severe hunger (B. Ket. 10b). A man with hypospadias is sterile (B. Yeb. 76a) unless it is surgically corrected.

Sunstroke: Elisha the prophet promised the birth of a son to a barren woman from the town of Shunam who showed him hospitality. The prophecy was fulfilled but was followed by the tragic death of the boy from sunstroke (2 Kings 4:17-20). The child's revival by Elisha is then described (ibid., 34-35).

Some interpret this incident as of purely miraculous connotation. Radak, however, states that Elisha attempted to breathe on the child in order to provide warmth from the natural body heat that emanated from his mouth and eyes. Radak further states that most miracles are performed with direction and guidance from worldly and natural actions. *Metzudat David* states that Elisha tried to pour some of the life of his own body into the limbs of the child. Ralbag gives an identical interpretation but adds that "he [Elisha] did this after he prayed." Ralbag and Radak thus seem to consider a combination of natural and miraculous events as having contributed to the child's revival.

The type of illness that afflicted the child is clearly enunciated in the Jerusalem Talmud: "R. Manna stated that at harvest time accidents happen, because the sun only blazes on a person's head at harvest time, as it is written: 'And when the child was grown, it happened on a day, that he went out to his father to the reapers'" (Y. Yeb. 15:2).

The talmudic commentary *Korban Ha'-Edah* explains that at harvest time, a person may faint from the scorching sun and die. Another talmudic commentary, *Penei Moshe*, states that sickness or even death occurs at harvest time, because of the torrid sun, as in the case of the Shunammite boy. The same two commentaries interpret the phrase "who hast protected my head in the day of battle" (Ps. 140:8) to refer to sunstroke. The "day of battle" is thought to be the "day when winter kisses the summer;" thus, when summer ends and winter begins, one should cover one's head to avoid sunstroke in accordance with the aphorism, "The end of the summer is worse than the summer."

Another incident, nearly identical to that of Elisha and the Shunammite woman's child, is described in 1 Kings 17. Elijah, the predecessor of Elisha, warns King Ahab of Israel (reigned ca. 875-853 B.C.E.) of a drought that would last for several years. To escape the drought, Elijah traveled to Zarephath, where he received hospitality

from a widow who had an only son who fell sick and died because "there was no breath left in him" (I Kings 17:17-22). This phrase is interpreted by Josephus to mean that he appeared to be dead (*Antiquities* 8, 13, 3). Most biblical commentators, however, including Rashi, Ralbag, *Metzudat David*, and Radak, believe that the boy actually died.

Whether or not this boy also died of sunstroke is impossible to state, nor do the commentaries shed any light on the question. Although the precise clinical picture of heatstroke is not described in the Bible and Talmud, there seems little doubt that this medical entity was recognized at that time and was the cause of death in the case of the Shunammite boy.

Surgery: In talmudic times, the surgeon wore a leather apron (M. Kel. 26:5), strapped the patient to the table (T. Sheq 1:6), and used his knife (Exod. Rabbah 26:2) or other instruments that he kept in a special box (M. Kel. 16:8). Eleazar was given a sleeping potion (anesthetic?), taken into a marble chamber (operating room?), had his abdomen opened (laparotomy), and a lot of fat was removed (adiposectomy) (B. B.M. 83b-84a). An operation to "smooth" a fissured penis (hypospadias repair?) is described (B. Yeb. 75b). Operations to undo circumcision were performed in ancient times for social and personal reasons (epispasm). Surgical removal of the spleen was carried out without fatal results (B. San. 21b). Needles were used for extracting thorns (ibid., 84b). A surgeon who operates to save a person's life is not liable for the "wound" he inflicts (ibid.).

Wounds: Self-wounding (1 Kings 18:28) is biblically prohibited (Lev. 21:5, 19:28). Inflicting wounds on another (Lev. 24:19) or a pregnant woman (Exod., 21:22) is a punishable offense (B. Shab. 106a). A child is forbidden to wound a parent (B. San. 84b). Nevertheless, Abner pierced Asahel (2 Sam. 2:23), and Joab pierced Abner (ibid., 3:27). Spear wounds are often fatal (B. Yeb. 114b). Perforation of the aorta is a fatal wound (B. Hul. 45b). A hole in the trachea may not be fatal (B. Hul. 44a). Perforation or cutting of the esophagus is a life-threatening wound (B. Hul. 43a; B. Yeb. 120b). Heart wounds

(B. Hul. 45b) are discussed. Severed sinews or arteries usually result in death (B. Yeb. 16:3), although cauterization of the wound may prevent death (ibid., 120b). Defloration is considered to be a wound (B. Nid. 10:1). He who feigns a wound will eventually suffer from one (T. Pe. 4:14).

Wounds can sprout and granulate (Is. 1:6) or be flabby and atonic (Jer. 14:17, 15:18). The wound heals when flesh heaps up (ibid., 30:13) but does so differently in various people (B. B.Q. 84a) and more rapidly in children (B. Shab. 134b). Scraped cynodon root brings on flesh (B. A.Z. 28a). In biblical times, wounds were treated by pressing, bandaging, and oil fomenting (Is. 1:6). The balm of Gilead (wound balsam) was a famous wound healing salve (Jer. 8:22; B. San. 77b). Cotton or lint cloths and sponges, as well as garlic and onion peels, are bandaged and tied on the would (T. Shab. 5:3-4). The sponge acts as a wound protector (Lev. Rabbah 15:4). Rushes or reeds were also used and wrapped around an injured finger (B. Erub. 103b). Flocks of wool were also applied to the wound (B. Shab. 50a), with or without emollients or plasters (B. Yeb. 114b). The plasters were replaced when necessary (B. Erub. 102b). Chewed wheat kernels (B. Ket. 103a) and caraway (B. Shab. 19:2) are also healing in their effect. Wounds are anointed with oil and hot water even on the Sabbath (B. Shab. 128a), because they are considered dangerous if not promptly treated.

People also used manure from dung heaps as bandaging material (B. A.Z. 28a). Cauterization of arterial cuts (T. Yeb. 14:4), leprous lesions (B. Neg. 7P4), and compound bone fractures (T. Hul. 3:6) was also practiced in talmudic times. Cress in vinegar was used as a hemostatic (B. A.Z. 28a). Vinegar also heals wounds on the teeth or gums (B. Shab. 111a). Medicine was applied to the thigh wound of Abbahu (B. A.Z. 28a). Ashi sustained a wound when a donkey trod on his foot. He rubbed it with oil of roses (B. Shab. 109a).

An animal with a wound from rubbing against a wall or from a heavy saddle is treated with honey (B. Shab. 8:1; B. B.M. 38b) or squashed snails (B. Shab. 77b) applied to the wound. It is also given honey to eat (ibid., 154a). In humans, however, ingestion of honey and other sweets is harmful to wounds (B. B.Q. 85a).

Bibliography

Reichman, Edward, "Biblical and Talmudic Medicine: A Biobibliographical Essay," in *Encyclopedia of Medicine in the Bible and the Talmud*, pp. 1-9.

Rosner, Fred, *Encyclopedia of Medicine in the Bible and the Talmud* (Northvale, 1993).

Rosner, Fred, trans., *Julius Preuss' Biblical and Talmudic Medicine* (Northvale, 1993).

Rosner, Fred, *Medicine in the Bible and the Talmud, Selections from Classical Jewish Sources* (Hoboken, Augmented Edition, 1995).

FRED ROSNER

E

ECOLOGY IN ANCIENT JUDAISM: Ancient Israel is a well documented example of a sustained society. Archaeological records show that the Israelites were the first example in world history of a society that succeeded in managing a sustained management of their environment for about thousand and seven hundred years. After the beginning of Iron Age II (about the twelfth century B.C.E.), the oscillating pattern of settlement, recorded from the late Chalcolithic period throughout the Bronze Age,[1] was replaced by a continuous settlement at a high population density of the region until the seventh century C.E. that was, at least during the Talmudic time, twice as high as at the beginning of the twentieth century.[2] This success of a sustained settlement under semi-arid conditions for more than one millennium is unparalleled in world history.

Living conditions with limited resources: Since the much more fertile plains of Palestine were occupied by the technically far more advanced Philistines, the Israelites had to be content with the hilly lands of the Judean Hills. The geology of the land of Israel, especially the Judean Hills, is rather simple: the bedrock that can be found almost everywhere is calcareous.[3] That means the soils are extremely vulnerable, especially in the hilly regions. As long as good agricultural practice is employed the soils are fertile, but as soon as they are overused, they turn to karstlands. The climate in the region was also marginal and favored desertification.[4]

With regard to the ecological basis, the people who started to settle down on the Judean Hills some 3,400 years ago were actually living on the extreme edge of their possible existence. They settled in a region in which the climatic conditions changed over short distances and where desert-like conditions, such as extremely vulnerable soil, prevailed. Thus, the physical survival of a large population with a high standard of living depended on their ability to make the best use of their resources and to establish an advanced sustained yield form of agriculture. The colonization of the Judean Hills was possible only through conversion of the forests (cf., Josh. 17:14-18) and macchia to good fertile land by clearing the area and terracing the slopes.[5] They were then forced to develop a high standard of agriculture, since they had neither the fertile soils of the river oasis like the Egyptians and Babylonians nor the solutions to population problems that the Greeks and Romans had.

In contrast to other advanced cultures of the antique world, the Jews were forced to rely on intelligence, creativity, and experience to increase the productivity of the land without destroying its resources. From the beginning of the era of the Judean kings, the pressure under which the Israelites stood with their growing population was so great that, until the Babylonian exile, even the Negev was used for farming.[6] Someone who decides to start farming in the Negev must have very good reasons; otherwise that person would settle in a less hostile place nearby.

Metaphors used by the Israelites to describe the vulnerability of their land: The metaphor "milk and honey" is used several times in the Torah to refer to the promised land. The most indicative pericope is Deut. 11:8-15:

> and that you may live long in the land which the Lord swore to your fathers to give to them and to their descendants, a land flowing with milk and honey. For the land which you are entering to take possession of it is not like the land of Egypt, from which you have come, where you sowed your seed and watered it with your feet, like a garden of vegetables; but the land which you are going over to possess is a land of hills and valleys, which drinks water by the rain from heaven, a land which the Lord your God cares for; the eyes of the Lord your God are always upon it, from the beginning of the year to the end of the year. And if you will obey my commandments which I command you this day, to love the Lord your God, and to serve him with all your heart and with all your soul, he will give the rain for your land in its season, the early rain and the later rain, that you may gather in your grain and your wine and your oil. And he will give grass in your fields for your cattle, and you shall eat and be full.

In two ways, the authors of this pericope reveal the fragility of the land and the dependency of its fertility on the people's obedience to God's Torah. First, at the center is the statement about the quality of the land. Only if the Torah is obeyed, can there be fertility and well-being in the land of "milk and honey." Second, the land is compared to Egypt, from where the Israelites have come. The key expressions are "watering with the feet" and "garden of vegetables." Vegetable gardens are the most fertile ground in the world. They are tilled much more intensively and yield much higher harvests than normal agricultural fields. So this comparison is a good indicator of the fertility of Egyptian soil. Throughout in antiquity, Egypt was an agricultural paradise. Herodotus, who traveled all over the antique world, states that there was no region where "the fruits of the field were obtained with less trouble" (Historiae II. 14). Egypt was the granary of the Roman Empire, the country with the best soil and biggest harvests. "Watering with the feet" indicates furrow irrigation as a means of getting water into the fields. The fields of the Israelites in the Judean Hills were not vegetable gardens. Intensive high yield agriculture thus was not possible in the Judean Hills the way it was in the Nile Delta. In all, the land of "milk and honey" is not a paradise; it will be fertile only if the people carefully obey the Torah.

Unlike modern interpretations of the phrase, which more or less takes it to indicate conditions close to paradise, it meant that the lands available to the immigrants were far from being well suited for agriculture. "Milk" meant that these lands were visited regularly by nomads who let small cattle graze there. "Honey" indicated that bees found plenty of food there from wild flowers, whose honey could be collected by the people. Translated into modern plant sociology and knowledge of succession, this land was a macchia, a region of Mediterranean hard scrub, downgraded land with plenty of wildflowers that only careful management could convert to fertile, arable land.[7]

This interpretation of a land of "milk and honey" was absolutely clear to Isaiah, as shown by 7:14-16 and 21-25:

> Therefore the Lord himself will give you a sign. Behold, a young woman shall conceive and bear a son, and shall call his name Imman'u-el. He shall eat curds and honey when he knows how to refuse the evil and choose the good. For before the child knows how to refuse the evil and choose the good, the land before whose two kings you are in dread will be deserted.
> In that day a man will keep alive a young cow and two sheep; and because of the abundance of milk which they give, he will eat curds; for every one that is left in the land will eat curds and honey. In that day every place where there used to be a thousand vines, worth a thousand shekels of silver, will become briers and thorns. With bow and arrows men will come there, for all the land will be briers and thorns; and as for all the hills which used to be hoed with a hoe, you will not come there for fear of briers and thorns; but they will become a place where cattle are let loose and where sheep tread.

The first passage is extremely important to both Christianity and Judaism. It is one of the few prophecies in the Bible that deals with the messiah. Isaiah makes a clear statement about the conditions prevailing in the land when the messiah comes: downgraded and desertified, therefore, a land of "milk

(curd is a milk product) and honey." In the following passage, the conditions are further clarified: because of the sins of the people, i.e., the misuse of nature by the farmers, a macchia has been established.

The relationship between land degradation and the appearance of milk and honey, which was by no means a blessing for people that employed advanced agriculture, is blatantly evident in these prophecies. Isaiah declares what happens when people do not take care of the land. It will be turned back into a macchia, a land of "milk and honey." Even more important is that Isaiah connects the coming of the messiah with downgraded ecological conditions. Thus one can expect he will take care of this situation. In the first pericope, it says explicitly that the bad conditions of the land will prevail while the messiah is still young, before he can distinguish good from bad.

In any case, the prophecies of Isaiah make it clear that a "land of milk and honey" is not a paradise but a land that is principally suited for agriculture. Its conversion to fertile soil requires great care and good tillage. This land is unstable and vulnerable. If it is not properly cared for, or if it is overexploited, it will rapidly revert to the stage of milk and honey.

How unstable, vulnerable, and how utterly dependent on the blessing of the Lord agriculture was in this region becomes evident from a characterization of the land at Deut. 8:6-8:

> So you shall keep the commandments of the Lord your God, by walking in his ways and by fearing him. For the Lord your God is bringing you into a good land, a land of brooks of water, of fountains and springs, flowing forth in valleys and hills, a land of wheat and barley, of vines and fig trees and pomegranates, a land of olive trees and honey.

B. B.B. 147a explains:

> The northern wind is beneficial to wheat when it has reached a third of its ripening and is damaging to olive trees when they have blossomed. The southern wind is damaging to wheat when it has reached a third of its ripening and is beneficial to olives when they have blossomed. This was symbolized by the table in the north and the menorah in the south.

Two ecologically different groups of crop plants, both staples of human nutrition in ancient Israel, are listed to characterize the nature of the land: wheat and barley on the one side, the other five on the other (in the Bible, honey is not always the product of bees as we understand it today, but the term is also used for dates, a very important crop of that region).[8] For both groups, the weather between Passover and Pentecost (Shavuot), i.e., the period from roughly the end of March until the middle of May, determines the size of the harvest in that season. For wheat and barley, there must be at least some rainy days to allow the ears to ripen and to have full grains. Too much rain and cold weather, however, is detrimental to the five crops listed in the second group, which need warm weather while they are flowering. The rain is brought by the northern wind, the hot weather by the southern wind. To remind the people of this crucial fact for their survival as peasants, two items were always present on the altar in the Temple: showbreads and candles. The showbreads, which are made of grain, are placed on the northern part of the altar, and the candles, which stand for the second group of crops, on the southern part. These things symbolize the northern and southern winds, which are both necessary to achieve good and diverse harvests.

Thus the ancient Israelites developed a level of environmental sensitivity. They were aware of the fact that they had settled in an area with a fragile ecology. They knew that their land would be fertile only if it was managed with proper care. To them, this sense of vulnerability and dependency on nature was so important that, in the Talmud's much later understanding, they put symbols of their situation on the altar of the Temple.

Gen. 1:28: what does *dominatio terrae* really mean? Gen. 1:28 is the most misunderstood verse in the Hebrew Bible. In numerous incidents Western (i.e., Christian) civilization has apparently taken this passage to permit destruction of the environment. This has happened to such an extent that in 1970, at a conference on "Theology of Survival," a group of Protestant theologians went as far as to assert

"that any solution to the current environmental crisis would require major modifications of current religious values."[9] On the other hand, this is also the basis for a recently developing trend that ascribes the global crisis to "the Judeo-Christian tradition."[10]

Without regard for this one verse, the basis for a proper use of natural resources is laid down in the first chapter of Genesis. Examining this chapter, we realize that humanity's domination of the earth in fact is rather limited.

- The command "be fruitful and multiply" was also given to the animals, suggesting that people must populate the earth in the same manner as animals.
- Humans rule over the animals but do not feed on them. Plants are excluded from humanity's general dominion.
- The use of plants is restricted to the use of their fruits as food. This concession is the same that was given to the animals.

Translated into the language of ecology, this means that humanity has a special rank in the order of nature. People are allowed to use nature properly. This use, however, is restricted. They are not permitted to kill animals or touch plants in such a way that their basic existence is endangered.

Deeper insight is found in the pertinent commentaries, particularly Rashi. The most important point in Gen. 1:26-28 is the exact meaning of the words used to describe the relationship between humanity and the rest of creation, especially the two verbs: "have dominion" and "subdue." For Rashi, the first of these verbs cannot be as defined as it normally appears in English translation:

The expression *wredu* may imply dominion as well as declining—if he is worthy, he dominates the beasts and cattle; if he is not worthy, he will sink lower than them, and the beasts will rule over him.

This interpretation is breathtaking, and one wonders whether Rashi knew how revolutionary his analysis was. He states, in essence, that the same philosophy of conditional ruling applies here as in the Germanic concept of kingship. A king obtains his mandate, the Königsheil, from heaven on the condition that he is worthy. As long

the king has this mandate, his rule is sacro-
sanct. However, if it becomes evident that
he is not worthy, and so has lost his
Königsheil, a person who is able to prove
that the Königsheil has been transferred
to him may rise up and take over the kingship. In assuming that rules similar to these
are relevant to the relationship between
humanity and nature, Rashi reveals a very
modern concept of nature. Before the middle of the nineteenth century, the prevalent
view was of a static world system that was
basically unchanged since the beginning of
creation and that would not undergo any
basic changes in the future. Indeed, one of
the four pillars of the so-called Christian
Weltanschauung of that time, which made
Darwin's theory so difficult to accept, was
this very dogma.[11] Rashi, by contrast, envi-
sions a world that can change even to the
extent that the circumstance of control
might be completely reversed. The next
important word is *wekabsh(u)ha*, "subdue."
Rashi states:

> The word is written without the expected
> *waw* after the *shin*, so that it may be read as
> meaning: and subdue her (i.e., the woman),
> thereby teaching you that the male controls
> the female in order that she may not
> become a gad-about. . . .

For Rashi, it is self-evident that nature has
its own right to develop in harmony. This
is so basic for him that he states the relationship between humans and nature as a
model of the partnership between man and
woman in marriage. Since humanity must
permit nature to develop in harmony, a
husband has to treat his wife in such a
way that she does not develop into a gad-
about.

The last expression important in our considerations is the ending of the sixth day
(Gen. 1:31). Rashi states:

> The letter *he*, the numerical value of which
> is five, is added to the word *shishi* when the
> work of creation was complete to imply that
> he [God] made a stipulation with them that
> [creation] endures only upon the condition
> that Israel should accept the five books of
> the Torah. (B. Shab. 88a)

The part of the Talmud to which Rashi
refers is as follows:

> It is written: "And it was evening and it was
> morning, day the sixth." Why is the super-
> fluous *he* [= "the"] necessary? This teaches
> that the Holy, praised be he, made an
> agreement with his work of creation and
> said to him: If the Israelites accept the
> Torah, than you [the creation] will flourish,
> if not, I will turn you back into desert and
> emptiness.

The pericope, referred also at B. A.Z. 3a,
states that nature can only survive if
humankind keeps the Torah. So for the
Talmud, and of course for Rashi, the Torah
is not just a book of instructions on relationships between humans and between humans
and God. It also details how to treat creation. If this advice is not followed, God will
turn creation into desert and emptiness.

A second interpretation given by Rashi
for *yom hashishi* is:

> The whole creation (the universe) stood in
> a state of suspense (moral imperfection)
> until the sixth day—that is the sixth day of
> Sivan that was destined to be the day when
> the Torah would be given to Israel (B. A.Z.
> 3a).

According to this explanation, the words
"the sixth day" must be read together with
the opening words of the next verse (Gen.
2:1), so that the passage as a whole reads:
"On the sixth day of Sivan the heavens and
the earth were perfected." This reading is
actually present in the introductory verses
of the Jewish Friday-evening prayer at the
start of the Sabbath celebration.

Overall, Rashi's perspective on the
meaning of Gen. 1:28-31 is as follows:

> 1) Humanity has a mandate to dominate
>   the world, but this mandate is given on
>   the condition that people show them-
>   selves worthy of it.
> 2) From the verb "subdue," Rashi deduces
>   that a man must allow his wife to de-
>   velop into a full, mature person. His
>   freedom to dominate creation is again
>   limited.
> 3) Creation was only completed when the
>   Torah was given, and it can only survive
>   if Israel keeps the Torah.

Rashi makes a further important point that
deserves attention: The verbs "dominate"
and "subdue" describe a general ethical
attitude according to which nature has to
be dealt with benevolently. The general

rules implied by these verbs are made concrete in the Torah, which provides precise rules on how to treat nature.

The lists of forbidden animals occur in Leviticus and in Deuteronomy. Certain animals are clean and fit for human consumption, and others are unclean and not fit for consumption. To understand the full meaning of such a taboo, we have to keep in mind that these rules were imposed on a community that consisted mainly of peasants living in a densely populated area. In such an economy, there is always a shortage of dietary protein, and any available source of protein that humans could procure and that was allowed for consumption was used for food. We have ample evidence both from the Hebrew Bible (e.g., Prov. 6:5, 7:22) and the New Testament (Matt. 10:29) that even very small birds were caught and eaten.

In view of these considerations, the lists in Lev. 11 and Deut. 14 served two purposes. They laid down the rules for animal husbandry and were forerunners of today lists of species of wild animals that are allowed to be hunted in the wild.

Animals Allowed for Husbandry: Of all the mammalian species known by the Israelites, only ruminants were suitable for eating except for the camel and the hyrax. This means that only ruminants, i.e., those animals able to make the most efficient use of vegetation were allowed to be raised for human consumption.

To appreciate this ruling, one has to take a short look into the nutritional physiology of the animals that were domesticated and could be kept by farmers for different reasons: the horse, ass, and camel for transportation and work on the fields; the cow used both for work and for milk and meat; the sheep and goat for milk, wool, and meat; and, finally, the pig, which was raised for meat only. With regard to nutritional physiology, these animals can be divided into three classes. The first is represented by the horse, a grazing animal with no rumen: it therefore needs rather high quality food, mainly grass with a high proportion of cereals, such as oats. Horses were used for military purposes, transportation, and work. The pig falls into the second class, it is an omnivore that has almost the same dietary requirements as humans (note that the pig is quite frequently used as a scientific model for human nutrition today). In animal husbandry, pigs cannot be used only for production of meat. From the carbohydrates present in their food, horses and pigs, like humans, can digest in their stomach only those compounds that are either low molecular sugars or starch. Therefore, they need a high proportion of grain or other materials with starch in their fodder.

The ruling on animals forbidden for husbandry therefore forces farmers to make the best use of available resources and protects rich people from gluttony. Even people who had the resources to feed pigs with first-rate food, in order to produce much juicier meat than that of old goats or cows, were not allowed to do so.

Animals in the Water: Of all animals in the sea, rivers, lakes, and brooks, only those with fins and scales, i.e., fish, were considered fit for eating. This means that, excluded from consumption, frogs, toads, and newts were protected by the law. Once again, we have to bear in mind that froglegs and whole frogs and toads are part of the usual diet of many millions of humans today. But wherever they are harvested on a large scale, the ecosystem is deprived of the most important antagonist to mosquitoes, resulting in a higher rate of malaria infection. In several subtropical and tropical countries, the export of frogs is now prohibited for this reason. It can be assumed that the authors of Deuteronomy and Leviticus included this precept for exactly the same reason. There is no other good reason imaginable that would convince a protein-starved society to accept deprivation of an abundant and easily available source of protein, except care for the health of society as a whole.

The Lists of Forbidden Birds: Due to the close cultural contact with Egypt, Jews were familiar with the special treatment given to particular birds as part of Egyptian religious practice. Their approach, however, was very different from the Egyptian one and reveals a profound knowledge of ecological laws. This can be seen from the list of protected birds in the Torah.

1) The carrion eaters and "sanitation police" birds. Not only the conspicuous vultures are included in this list of birds that are very important for the health of cities, but, also, unlike all other similar practices in the East, ravens, crows, and magpies. This shows that the ancient Jews were excellent observers and had a thorough knowledge of the succession of birds that feed on carcasses. They protected not only the first very spectacular consumers of carrion, vultures, but also the less showy "secondary" consumers, the Corvidae, which take care of vultures' leftovers.

2) All birds of prey, including owls. It is a fact that birds of prey and owls are still traded as food at rural markets, for instance, in China. This stringent protection of all birds of prey as practiced in ancient Israel is unique to the ancient world. Once again, it reveals a detailed knowledge of the function of these birds in the maintenance of ecological balances.

3) All storks, ibises, and herons. We know from biblical evidence (e.g., Ps. 104:17) that at that time birds of this group were common in Palestine and even nested there frequently. Today we know that this group of birds fishes in ponds, thus keeping the numbers of diseased fish in check. In addition we know that they represent, together with the hoopoe and the bee-eater, the most efficient biological control of locusts,[12] which still are a menace in this part of the world. By protecting these birds, the Israelites established the best possible defense available at that time against an invasion of locusts. It was the most efficient protection available for their crops.

4) The bee-eater, the hoopoe, and all species of bats. Once again we can see a very precise logic behind the selection of birds and bats, which were put together with birds because they could fly so well, that were allowed to be eaten and those that were protected. There are several bird species in the same size class as bee-eaters and hoopoes, which are still very common in Israel today: the two big kingfishers, Smyrna kingfisher and grey kingfisher, the roller, the bulbuls, and Tristrams' grackle, to mention only the most common species. Of all these very conspicuous birds, the Israelites protected only the bee-eater and the hoopoe, knowing very well that these two species were extremely important in keeping down insect pests. These birds, in addition to bats, were the best antagonists to insects up to the size of locusts.

The only bird on this list that eats mainly grain and other parts of plants is the female ostrich, a very conspicuous bird, for which no purely "ecological" reason can be given. Overall, the list of birds forbidden to be eaten included by no means all birds inhabiting Palestine at that time. In general, birds were allowed to be touched and eaten. Only those species that were most valuable in maintaining the ecological equilibrium and that served as the most efficient biocontrol agent of insects, especially locusts, were carefully selected and protected from human predation.

Insects: These two passages illustrate the dire need people had for protein at that time. The agricultural society could not disregard any significant protein source, not even locusts and crickets. This is still true today in some regions of the world. I have seen hornet nests with the larvae and the developing imagines sold at markets in Yunnan, South China. These animals were offered as food in local restaurants, after they had been thrown into boiling fat.

Since large insects were obviously a desirable food and valuable protein source, some kind of answer had to be given in the Torah about their state of purity. The answer was very specific. All sizeable types of locusts were allowed to be eaten, all other insects were not. This regulation is ecologically wise. It permitted the collection of invading insects (locusts) and those obviously eating leaves and grass (crickets), thereby competing with the farm animals. All other insects, including their larvae, were protected. The message thus seems to be clear: people should harvest resources that cause ecological harm but otherwise leave nature as intact as possible.

Wild mammals, snakes, and lizards (Lev. 11:26-31): Here it is again stated that among all quadrupeds only ruminants are allowed for human consumption (with the exceptions stated above); all other animals are not allowed to be hunted or eaten.

Thus, groups of wild animals that provided very popular food in similar cultures of that time were excluded for human consumption. Cats and dogs, for instance, were and still are eaten all over rural Asia and are considered a delicacy. Bear meat was and is eaten by hunters all over the world. By forbidding the consumption of these animals of prey, the authors of the Torah acknowledged the important role of these animals in ecosystems. They take care of the natural equilibrium and prevent overpopulation of herbivores, which are a store of diseases of domesticated cattle.

We know from archeological evidence that during pre-Israelite times all kinds of snakes and lizards, even mice and rats, were eaten by people living in Palestine.[13] The Jews were forbidden to eat any of these animals, in spite of their abundance in the Holy Land. As in the case of birds, two lines of arguments can be advanced to explain the protection of these animals:

1) Sanitary reasons, which forbade the eating of mice, rats, and similar animals that transmit diseases; and

2) Ecological considerations, which protected all raptors because of their role in maintaining the biological equilibrium. In this group we also find lizards, which are biocontrol agents of insects, and snakes, which feed on mice and rats.

Interpretation of these Lists in Later Exegesis: Mishnah and Talmud: In the exegesis of the Hebrew Bible, there is a long-standing discussion about the criteria distinguishing clean and unclean animals. Already the sages of the Mishnah felt compelled to introduce additional criteria (M. Hul. 3:6):

A. The tokens [by which we know whether or not animals are deemed clean or fit] of cattle and wild beasts have been stated by the Torah. [Lev. 11:3].

B. And the tokens of fowl have not been so stated.

C. But sages have ruled: "Any fowl that seizes is unclean. Any [fowl] that has an extra talon [the hallux] and a craw, and the skin of the stomach of which [can] be stripped off is clean."

D. R. Eleazar b. Sadoq says "Any bird that parts its toes evenly [two in front and two in back] is unclean" [Lev. 11:3].

These new criteria for birds are of paramount interest, since they give a clear statement about the doubtful birds not directly mentioned in the list, specifying that raptors (which seize) are unclean and those that eat seeds (which have a craw and easily removable stomach skin) are clean. As outlined above, these criteria strongly support the ecological significance of these precepts. Especially in arid and semi-arid regions seeds are designed by plants for a long survival, and rotting is prevented by a very low moisture content of the seeds and a slow rate of water absorption. They are intended to germinate only after considerable wetting of the soil takes place in a long rain. This is why the desert starts to bloom only after sizeable rainstorms. Seeds are thus very dry food and not easily digested. Seed-eating birds have two means of coping with this situation. They have a craw in which the food is mixed with water and allowed to swell. In addition, they have very strong stomachs with a tough inner wall, wherein they even grind the seeds with small stones they have collected from the ground. So it is a clear indication that the bird is a seed eater and, therefore, clean for consumption, if a very strong inner skin can easily be peeled off from the stomach muscle beneath.[14]

Protection of Biotopes. The authors of the Hebrew Bible did not only protect animals and birds. They knew that protection was futile without the provision of niches and reserves in which birds and animals could live. This is evident in Is. 5:8-10:

Woe to you who add house to house and join field to field till no space is left and you live alone on the land. The Lord Almighty has declared in my hearing: "Surely the great houses will become desolate, the fine mansions left without occupants. A ten-yoke vineyard will produce only five gallons of wine, a *homer* of seed only an *epha* of grain."

If land is overused, no refuge is left for the birds and animals that control the many pests, and no place is left where they can build nests or hide under bushes or stones. In addition, fields on terraces that leave no space for bushes are much more prone to destruction by floods caused by heavy winter rainstorms. Hedges and bushes between the fields absorb the force of the water and protect the fields from erosion, and the seeds and seedlings from being washed away. For a certain time, there will be good harvests, and the owner will become rich because he has more land under cultivation. Therefore, he will be able to live in "great houses" and "fine mansions." In the long run, however, nature will fight back. In winter, the danger of erosion is much higher and in the case of any insect calamity that can be expected in this situation anyway, the lack of biocontrol agents will result in a destruction of his entire harvests.

Soil Care and Land Use. The "conquest" of the Judean hills by the Israelites in the early Iron Age is characterized by the change from an oscillating to a permanent pattern of settlement.[15] This was the start of a highly successful agriculture that was the economic foundation of the prosperous period of Iron Age II: the Israelite and Judean Kingdoms.[16] This change from an unstable to a sustained and high yield form of agriculture did not leave any marks that can be traced by archaeology. Terracing and other methods of land use thought to be the reason for this surprising success were already employed in the late Bronze Age.[17] Therefore it might be worthwhile to look for other reasons for this development. The hypothesis outlined here is that the high standard of Israelite biology and the development of rules that prevented overexploitation of the soils were the reasons for this success.

The Sabbatical Year. The precept of the sabbatical year appears at Exod. 23: 10-11 and Lev. 25:1-7. This concept was unique in the region. There are no records of similar laws either in Babylonia or in Egypt, the dominating civilizations east and west of Palestine. These laws are a counterbalance to humanity's tendency to abuse its power over the rest of creation.[18] The precept as outlined in Leviticus clearly shows that its main intention is to protect the soil, i.e., to give the soil a rest. The concomitant rest for the people is a minor matter and not the primary goal of the law. This can be seen from several facts. The law was valid only in the countryside; the cities had no sabbatical year. In addition, it was not only forbidden to practice agriculture but also to utilize any of the possible crops which might grow spontaneously. This means that the whole net production of organic matter, including the parts to be removed from the plot during harvest, seeds and fruits together with the leaves and stalks attached to them, remains in the fields and is subsequently incorporated into the terrestrial carbon cycle.

Such an increase in organic matter in the soil has two beneficial effects. The first is an activation of the soil microflora. This leads to an enhanced weathering of the soil, which results in an increase in available nutrients. Those parts of the litter that are not readily degraded and the moiety of stable organic matter that is formed during the action of the micro-organisms finally enter the humus fraction of the soil. This part of the soil plays a decisive role in water retention. Humus has a high water storage capacity. The water status of soils, i.e., the ability to absorb and retain the water and make it available for plants, mainly depends on its humus content. Thus the sabbatical year made important contributions to the fertility and water status of the soil. This was especially important in calcareous soils, which make up the majority of the Judean hillsides.

Such a special care of the soils was imperative for the maintenance of soil fertility in the Judean Hills. Israelite agriculture at that time was probably among the most advanced in the ancient world. This can be shown by the yields in grain which were achieved in ancient Israel (Table 1).

Table 1: Yields of wheat in Palestine (kg/ha)[19]

		Bad years	Good years
Israel	200 C.E.	500	1,000
Italy	100 C.E.	434	1,085
Jordan	1948-63	440	730
Egypt	100 C.E.	average: 1,750	
Palestine	1910		
Arabic Sector		538	761
Jewish Sector		546	2,750

Although the fields in Israel get only about half as much rain as they do in Italy and in spite of the fact that the stress caused by evapotranspiration is twice as high in Israel as compared to the conditions in the fertile ranges of Italy, the yields in ancient Israel were comparable to those obtained in ancient Italy. Such a high standard of agriculture in this region was not achieved again before the foundation of the State of Israel. The figures make it obvious that in spite of the fact that the Israelites settled in marginal lands, by no means comparable to the big river fed oases of Egypt and Babylonia, they were most successful farmers who achieved a very high yield.

Such an intensive use of arable land must have inevitably resulted in a deterioration of the soil, leading to a decrease in overall fertility within a few years. To prevent this degradation of the soil, the Israelite farmer had two major means: the sabbatical year and the continuous fertilization of the soil. The sabbatical year was similar to the three-fallow system developed in Central Europe fifteen hundred years later. The authors of the Bible observed the exhaustion of the soil after intensive use; they saw the need for a "rest" of the soil; consequently they treated it the same way as human beings, giving it a complete rest every seventh year.

The commandment of the sabbatical year is the only example in the Torah in which Israelites express severe doubts whether the law could be tenable (Lev. 25:20-22):

> And if you say, "What shall we eat in the seventh year, if we may not sow or gather in our crop?" I will command my blessing upon you in the sixth year, so that it will bring forth fruit for three years. When you sow in the eighth year, you will be eating old produce; until the ninth year, when its produce comes in, you shall eat the old.

The blessing that comes after the grand concept of soil care (and restoration of property, not dealt with here) more or less summarizes what was outlined above with regard to the favorable effect of the sabbatical year. It may not have always worked exactly as promised, but in principle it is absolutely clear that the extreme care the Israelites took to keep their soil fertile was the main basis for sustainable agriculture.

Without such extreme care, the soil would have quickly deteriorated. Therefore the overall yield of the soil indeed did justify this rather bold promise.

The Rule of Diverse Kinds: Deut. 22:9 states: "You shall not sow your vineyard with two kinds of seed, lest the whole yield be forfeited to the sanctuary, the crop which you have sown and the yield of the vineyard." The prohibition of sowing annual crops in stands with perennial crops such as wine, olives or fruit trees, is very important. It prevents the soil from being overexploited. The roots of grapevines or fruit trees are allowed to make full use of the soil in which they have been planted. The possible short time profit of growing wheat or other grain in addition to the trees or grapes is prohibited because this would destroy and degrade the soil in the long run. The Mishnah states very clearly that a distance of sixteen *amot* (about seven meters) must be kept between the vine or olive tree and the closest field of annual plants (M. Kil 4:1).

Orlah—The Restriction of Using the First Fruits of Trees: Lev. 19:23-25 states:

> When you come into the land and plant all kinds of trees for food, then you shall count their fruit as forbidden; three years it shall be forbidden to you, it must not be eaten. And in the fourth year all their fruit shall be holy, an offering of praise to the Lord. But in the fifth year you may eat of their fruit, that they may yield more richly for you: I am the Lord your God.

The prohibition of harvesting any fruits for three years means simply that the entire organic matter produced by a tree during this time returns to the carbon cycle of that very soil. Not only the leaves but also the fruits, which can amount to up to 40% of the net production of organic matter, are not removed from the plot of land where the tree grows. This is a significant contribution to the humus fraction of the soil and has a positive impact on several soil parameters, as outlined above. In view of this background, the blessing at the end of this pericope, which promises higher yields after the fifth year, is understandable. Due to an input of organic matter equivalent to three consecutive sabbatical years, the fruit trees had a much better start and were bound to grant a higher yield.

The Ban on Small Cattle M. B.Q. 7:7 prohibits raising small cattle in the land of Israel. This is an addition to Jewish law, implemented immediately after the destruction of the Temple, when the Sanhedrin had established itself as the supreme authority of Jewry.[20] As far as written records reveal, it is the first and only law ever given in the history of humankind that severely limits the rights of people to pursue the most attractive economic activity in order to save the ecology of a country from decline and disaster.

After the massive destruction of the country during the Jewish War and the confiscation of fertile land by the Romans,[21] the economic situation of the Jewish population was disastrous. Once again they were confined to the less fertile hilly lands that were not attractive for the Roman agricultural system. In such a situation, the best economic activity would have been to raise small cattle, sheep and goats, in a semi-nomadic way. This transition from sedentary farmers to semi-nomadic herdsmen is the almost inevitable first step from degraded formerly arable soils to deserts; the farmland again becomes a land of "milk and honey." At present this is happening almost everywhere on the edge of the huge desert belt that ranges from Mauretania across Arabia, Iraq, Iran, Afghanistan, to the Chinese deserts. This switch from farming to herding is the most decisive event in the desertification of this part of the world.[22] For the Jewish farmers after the Jewish War, it would have been, however, the most profitable activity possible. Even the Talmud states: "If you want to get rich, go into the small cattle business" (B. Hul. 58b; this appears in a list of behaviors and actions considered by the sages to be wrong.)

The only way to implement this law was to outlaw a transgressor. The Talmud gives a vivid example of how far this ostracism went. Not even a sick person who needed goat milk as a cure for his disease was allowed to keep small cattle (B. B.Q. 80a):

> The rabbis taught: A pious person suffered once from pain in the chest and the physi-

cians declared that there was no other way treatment than to suck every morning warm milk. A goat was fetched and tied to the pedestal of his bed, and he sucked from it every morning. One day, his colleagues visited him. When they saw the goat tied to the pedestal of his bed, they turned back, saying: "An armed robber is in his house, and we shall go to him?" They made an investigation about his way of living and did not find any sin, except the sin concerning this goat. On his deathbed he said: I know that I did not commit any other sin, except the one concerning the goat, because I did not follow the words of my colleagues.

The sages knew perfectly well the ecological background of this law (ibid.):

> R. Ishmael said: "My ancestors belonged to the householders of Upper Galilee, and the only reason why they were destroyed was because they let small cattle graze in their forests."

This ruling, which severely impeded the economic activities and the freedom of choice of their followers, was the basis for the country's ecological recovery. This became a flourishing region until the Arab conquest in 640.

This part of the Mishnah has become the subject of intense discussions among historians. There are convincing arguments at hand to show that the law was quite strictly adhered to by the vast majority of the Jews.[23] The intense discussion of the law in the Talmuds can rightly be taken to indicate that it was tough on the population but that, in spite of the hardship, it was implemented and never revoked. The small cattle ban in the Mishnah is flanked by additional rules in the Talmud that have the same goal, preservation of the land's fertility. If, for instance, an animal nipped off the growth of a young tree, the owner of the animal had to pay a high fine to the tree's owner (B. Ket. 105a, B. B.Q. 58b). As another example, a fruit tree had to be preserved after it reached a certain stage (M. Sheb. 4:10).

The move of the sages and the boldness of the Sanhedrin, which decided in favor of the most efficient way to save endangered nature, reveals the high standard of ecological knowledge and conscience in ancient Israel. Humankind has a long way to go until it again reaches this level of environmental consciousness and willingness to take necessary actions in order to protect natural resources.

Bibliography

Hüttermann, A., *The Ecological Message of the Torah: Knowledge, Concepts, and Laws which Made Survival in a Land of "Milk and Honey" Possible* (Atlanta, 1999).

Notes

[1] Finkelstein, I., "The Great Transformation: The 'Conquest' of the Highland Frontiers and the Rise of the Territorial States," in Th.E. Levy, ed., *The Archaeology of Society in the Holy Land* (London, 1988), pp. 349-365. This oscillation in population resembles the pattern that was observed in the South-West of the United States for the Anasazi, the Pueblo Indians, during the last millennium before the white settlers came (R. McGuire, et al., eds., *Hohokam and Patayan, Prehistory of Southwestern Arizona* (New York, 1982), p. 657. After all other hypotheses were ruled out as causes for the periodical decline of the settlements, the current view is that the Indians failed to establish sustained agriculture, leading them, from time to time, to move on to a new location. Such a practice would have been impossible for the Israelites. There simply was no other place to which they could have gone.

[2] A. Ben-David, *Talmudische Ökonomie* (Hildesheim, 1974), p. 46, considers a population of 1-1.5 million inhabitants in Israel in talmudic times realistic. Others suggest much higher numbers.

[3] F.N. Hepper, *Illustrated Encyclopedia of Bible Plants* (London, 1992).

[4] J.P. Palutikof, et al., "Climate and Climatic Change," in C.J. Brandt and J.B. Thornes, eds., *Mediterranean Desertification and Land Use* (Chichester, 1996), pp. 43-86.

[5] O. Borowski, *Agriculture in Iron Age Israel* (Winona Lake, 1987).

[6] M. Evenari, L. Shanan, N. Tadmor, *The Negev. The Challenge of a Desert* (Boston, 1971).

[7] N. Hareuveni, *Nature in Our Biblical Heritage* (Kyriat Ono, 1980), p. 11.

[8] Loc. cit.

[9] Quoted in the New York Times, May 1, 1970, from E.G. Freudenstein, "Ecology and the Jewish Tradition," in *Judaism* 19, 1970, pp. 408-414.

[10] The discussion started in the late 1960s in the United States. See L. White, "The Historical Roots of our Ecologic Crisis," in *Science* 155, 1967, pp. 1203-1207, and many others.

[11] E. Mayr, *One Long Argument: Charles Darwin and the Evolution of Modern Evolutionary Thought* (Boston, 1991).

[12] Mauersberger, loc. cit., p. 84.

[13] B. Bender, *Farming in Prehistory: From Hunter-Gatherer to Food-Producer* (London, 1977).

[14] This interpretation is in contrast to the view of Mary Douglas, who considers means of locomotion as the most crucial feature for distinguishing clean and unclean animals. See her *Purity and Danger: An Analysis of the Concepts of Pollution and Taboo* (London, 1966), p. 188, and *Implicit Meanings: Essays in Anthropology* (London, 1975), pp. 249-318.

[15] I. Finkelstein, "The Great Transformation: The 'Conquest' of the Highland Frontiers and the Rise of the Territorial States," in Th.E. Levy, ed., *The Archaeology of Society in the Holy Land* (London, 1998), pp. 349-365.

[16] J.S. Holladay, Jr., *The Kingdoms of Israel and Judah: Political and Economic Centralization in the Iron IIA-B (ca. 1,000-750 B.C.E.)*, in ibid., pp. 367-398.

[17] Finkelstein, loc. cit.

[18] D. Fink, "Shabbat and the Sabbatical Year," in E. Bernstein, ed., *Ecology and the Jewish Spirit: Where Nature and the Sacred Meet* (Woodstock, 1998), pp. 112-120.

[19] A. Ben-David, *Talmudische Ökonomie* (Hildesheim, 1974), p. 106.

[20] G. Alon, *The Jews in Their Land in the Talmudic Age* (Cambridge, 1989).

[21] Ibid.

[22] It is obvious to everybody familiar with or doing research in these areas that over-grazing is the most crucial factor in the deterioration of pasture land. See, among many others, K.M. Leisinger, and K. Schmitt, *Überleben im Sahel* (Basel, 1992), p. 38; W.D. Swearingen and A. Bencherifa, *The North African Environment at Risk* (Boulder, 1996), pp. 36, 77, 99, 100, 181, 188; L.P. Bharara, *Man in the Desert. Drought, Desertification and Indigenous Knowledge for Sustainable Development* (Jodphur, 1999), pp. 210-214; especially in the Eastern Mediterranean: A.J. Conacher and M. Sala, "The Causes of Land Degradation. 2. Vegetation Clearing and Agricultural Practices," in A.J. Conacher and M. Sala, eds., *Land Degradation in Mediterranean Environments of the World*, pp. 285-307.

[23] Alon, op. cit.

ALOYS HÜTTERMAN

ELECTION OF ISRAEL: Few can dispute the accuracy of Jon D. Levenson's statement: "There is probably nothing in Judaism that has attracted so much attention and generated so much controversy as the biblical idea that the Jews are the chosen people."[1] Praised and despised, reinterpreted and misunderstood—this doctrine remains central in the minds of both Jews and non-Jews. For many Jews it has been, and still is, the cornerstone of their identity. As Rabbi Arthur Hertzberg put it: "The essence of Judaism is the affirmation that the Jews are the chosen people; all else is commentary."[2] For anti-Semites it has been the ultimate evidence that the Jews are chauvinists who look down on all other peoples.[3] For many friends of the Jews and for many Jews themselves, it has been a source of embarrassment.

The Bible: In the biblical narrative, the idea of election is first expressed in the story of Abraham, who was elected and called by God to leave his people and settle in Canaan. And God promised to bless him and to make him a blessing (Gen. 12:2f.). The universalistic tendency is seen already here when it is said that "all peoples on earth will be blessed through you" (Gen. 12:3b).[4] God made a covenant with Abraham, promising him the land of Canaan as an everlasting possession and pledging to make a great people of his offspring (Gen. 15:5, 17:2-22; cf., Neh. 9:7f.). An interesting fact is that in the Bible, and especially in the Psalms, the election of Israel is more often connected with Jacob than with Abraham (see, e.g., Ps. 78:71, 105:6, 135:4).

After the exodus from Egypt, the idea of an elected people is an important feature in the covenant.[5] Israel is to be for God "a kingdom of priests and a holy nation" (Exod. 19:6). This idea is especially important in the Deuteronomistic tradition.[6] Israel is called "the people of his [the Lord's] inheritance" (Deut. 4:20; cf., 1 Kings 8:51), "his treasured possession" (Deut. 7:6, 14:2, 26:18), and "a people holy to the Lord your God" (Deut. 7:6, 14:2, 26:19). Israel is said to have been chosen "out of all the peoples on the face of the earth" (Deut. 7:6, 14:2), "above all the nations" (Deut. 10:15), and God is said to have declared that he will set Israel "in praise, fame and honor high above all the nations he has made" (Deut. 26:19; cf., 28:1).

But why was Israel elected? The Bible does not tell. The revelation to Abraham was sudden and unanticipated. But Deut. 7:7-8 is very explicit on what was not the reason of election:

> The Lord did not set his affection on you and choose you because you were more numerous than other peoples, for you were

the fewest of all peoples. But it was because the Lord loved you and kept the oath to your forefathers that he brought you out with a mighty hand and redeemed you from the land of slavery, from the power of Pharaoh king of Egypt.

In other parts of the Bible, the idea of the elected people is not a frequent theme. In the Psalms, God is praised for what he has done for his people, including the election. The psalmist says that "the Lord has chosen Jacob to be his own, Israel to be his treasured possession" (Ps. 135:4), "the people he chose for his inheritance" (Ps. 33:12, cf. 78:71). Another metaphor for the same claim calls Israel "the sheep of his [God's] pasture" (Ps. 100:3, cf., 79:13; 95:7). And about God's revelation of his word and his laws it is said: "He has done this for no other nation; they do not know his laws" (Ps. 147:20).

The only passage in the Prophets that uses the expression "my treasured possession" is futuristic (Mal. 3:17). The relation between election and responsibilities is clearly expressed in Amos 3:2: "You only have I chosen of all the families of the earth; therefore I will punish you for all your sins." Other passages mention the election (e.g., Jer. 7:23, 11:4; Ezek. 20:5), and some predict a new covenant when Israel again will be the people of God (e.g., Jer. 24:7; 31:33; 32:38, Ezek. 11:20; 36:28; cf., Is. 14:1). The only prophet for whom the concept of election is very important is Deutero-Isaiah (see, e.g., Is. 41:8f., 43:10, 20f., 44:1f., 45:4). In the latest biblical books there is no mention of the election of the people—except for the quotation of a psalm in 1 Chron. 16:13— only of the election of Jerusalem, a descendant of David, and the Levites.

A notable, and for twentieth century politics important, fact is that the concept of the election of the people is connected with the promise of the land. Abraham was promised that his offspring would inherit the land of Canaan, and the words declared after the exodus strongly reiterate the same sentiment (Deut. 4:37f.; cf., Ps. 473f., 105:43f., 135:10-12):

> Because he loved your forefathers and chose their descendants after them, he brought you out of Egypt by his Presence

and his great strength, to drive out before you nations greater and stronger than you and to bring you into their land to give it to you for your inheritance, as it is today.

The Rabbinic Literature: The idea of election is central in the Rabbinic period. "Over and over again in the Talmud stress is laid upon the intimate and unique relationship which exists between God and His people."[7] This is not unexpected. During this period the Jews experienced many difficulties—the Temple had been destroyed, the state had ceased to exist, and the people had been dispersed—so that the belief that God has a special relationship to the people must have been an important source of strength. The rabbis also emphasized the election with such strength because the political reality—the Jewish state had perished and the Jews were dispersed and weak—was totally contrary to such a belief. The unhappy state of the Jews became one of the main arguments in the anti-Jewish polemics in the Christian Church. It was considered to prove that God had turned away from the Jewish people.[8]

According to some rabbis, the election of Israel was predestined before the creation of the world (Gen. Rabbah 1:4). This idea made election absolute and independent of any circumstances. It meant that no failure of the Jewish people whatsoever could alter the fact that they were the chosen ones, the children of the one and only God for ever (Sifre to Deut. 32:5-6; B. Kid. 36a). Other rabbis, however, expressed a different opinion. They described the election of Israel as having happened not before creation but in history. Furthermore, it was conditional. ". . . if you are holy then you are mine" (Mek. to Exod. 22:30; cf., Sifre to Deut. 14:1-2, B. Kid. 36a). As Ephraim Urbach put it: "First Israel must sanctify themselves and only thereafter do they merit to be called a holy people."[9]

One popular thought in the Talmud and midrashim is that chosenness is a burden. "Because God loved Israel, he multiplied sufferings for him" (Exod. Rabbah 1:1).[10] Chosenness means responsibility, requiring one to guard, preserve, and obey the Torah. A tradition that now enters Judaism

is the notion that the Torah was offered to many people but that Israel alone accepted it (Num. Rabbah 14:10; Sifre to Deut. 33:2-6), or, to put it in other words, chose God and his Torah. Thus the chosen people becomes the choosing people.

The idea of belonging to a chosen people and the animosity and oppression from the surrounding world sometimes led to chauvinistic statements about other peoples. The harshest utterance is Simeon ben Yohai's "Kill the best of the gentiles! Crush the head of the best of snakes" (Mek. to Exod. 14:7).[11] He also states that gentiles are not classified as men (B. Yeb. 60b-61a). An exhortation to utter a curse when passing by a cemetery of gentiles appears at B. Ber. 58b. What must be remembered is that this nationalistic-chauvinistic tendency, which undeniably exists in the Rabbinic literature, is counterbalanced by a more universalistic one. One also has to distinguish between what can be read in a text and what the consequences of that statement have been. Thus, in the words of Bernard J. Bamberger, "there are, indeed, some brutal and bloody pages in our ancient texts; we would be happier if they did not exist. Yet such passages have had surprisingly little impact on Jewish theology or even on popular Jewish thought."[12]

The Rabbinic literature also expresses the idea that Israel was chosen and given the Torah because of its merit. Israel is as strong among the nations as the dog is among animals and the cock among birds (B. Bes. 25b). In Num. Rabbah 3:2, an interesting analogy is used: just as a person chooses the good figs from a basket, so God makes choices. But other passages state that the fact that the Israelites were persecuted was the reason for their election (Lev. Rabbah 27:5). Overall, however, the great majority of the rabbis say nothing about merits; instead they attribute the election of Israel to a mere act of grace on the part of God.

The idea that the election of Israel meant Israelites' moral superiority finds some support in the literature. In B. Shab. 145b-146a, the lust of gentiles is explained: "For when the snake had sexual relations with Eve, he dropped into her a filthy drop [of lust]. When the Israelites stood at Mount Sinai, their lust came to an end, but since the gentiles did not stand at Mount Sinai, their lust did not come to an end."[13] While human wickedness is hereditary, Israelites are liberated from it because of a miracle connected to the giving of the Torah. There is thus a clear difference between Jews' and gentiles' nature, a view that can be called essentialist, because it claims that there is some mystical or metaphysical essence that inheres in a Jew and makes him different from non-Jews.[14] Even the acts of charity and mercy of gentiles could be explained by the claim that they were made with wrong motives (e.g., B. B.B. 10b).

That the concept of the chosen people was not in general understood in any biological or otherwise hereditary way is shown by the fact that proselytes were accepted. Although it is possible to find criticism of proselytes—"Proselytes are as hard on Israel as a scab"[15] (Yeb. 109b; Qid. 70b; cf., Yeb. 47b)—the common opinion is one of total acceptance and equality with other Jews (see, e.g., Mek. to Exod. 22:20; B. Yeb. 47b, B. Ber. 28a).[16] B. Pes. 87b declares that God's intention with the diaspora was to increase the number of proselytes. A gentile who takes up the study of the Torah as his occupation is equaled to the high priest (Sifra to Lev. 18:5; B. A.Z. 3a; B. B.Q. 38b).[17] For the Torah is not the Torah of the priests, Levites, or Israelites, but the Torah of Man, *Torat ha-Adam* (Sifra to Lev. 18:5).

All gentiles were expected to follow a moral code, called the seven commandments of the sons of Noah. These commandments, in the later Jewish tradition connected with the biblical story of God's covenant with Noah after the flood, were considered God's first covenant made with the whole of mankind. While the covenant with Israel contains 613 commandments, this covenant contains only seven, concerning "setting up courts of justice, idolatry, blasphemy, [cursing the Name of God], fornication, bloodshed, thievery, and cutting a limb from a living beast"[18] (B. San. 56a).[19] Gentiles who follow these commandments will earn divine approval and will have a portion in the world to come (see T. San. 13:2, where different opinions on this issue

are expressed). The concept of the Noahide covenant is one reason Jews have been so uninterested in proselytizing. "Those who think outsiders can have a proper relationship with God as they are will feel less of an impulse to make them into insiders."[20]

In sum, the Rabbinic literature—true to its character as a multifaceted work—presents various and also contradictory statements concerning the nature of the election of Israel.[21] The universalistic tendency—most clearly expressed in the concept of the Noahides—does not change the fact that the election of Israel is viewed as something self-evident. Although the rabbis readily acknowledged the universality of God, that did not diminish in any way his particular loving relationship with his chosen people.[22]

Medieval Jewish Thought: When the Christian Church became a powerful force in Europe, the situation for the Jews changed dramatically. The Jewish self-understanding of being the people chosen by God and singled out among the nations was challenged by the majority religion. The Church claimed that the covenant with Israel had been replaced by the new covenant in Christ, that the Church was the new Israel, and that Christians were the chosen people.[23] Although medieval Judaism softened its attitude towards Christians, e.g., by stating that the Talmud did not include Christians, who worshiped the living God,[24] in the category of idolaters—it was absolute in its conviction that the election of Israel had not been cancelled and that the Jews were the chosen people. But the question is: what does that chosenness mean?

Two towering figures within medieval Jewish thought represent two different interpretations of the election of Israel. Judah Halevi (1075-1141) affirms an essentialist understanding of the election, whereas Maimonides (1135-1204) interprets the election in a different way.

In his famous work *Sefer ha-Kuzari*, Halevi based the pre-eminence of Israel on God's election. From Adam onwards, God only chose individuals until he chose the whole people of Israel. The election of Israel was not an arbitrary act, for God had prepared the people for a long time so that they "became worthy of having the divine light and providence made visible to them" (1:95; cf., 1:47).[25] The sons of Jacob are said to have been "distinguished from other people by Godly qualities, which made them, so to speak, an angelic caste" (1:103). For Judah Halevi, chosenness means privilege (5:20). There is in the world a clear hierarchy, a decisive difference between Jews and gentiles as well as between human beings and animals:

> The lowest plant occupies a higher rank than the noblest mineral, the lowest animal is higher than the noblest plant, and the lowest human being is higher than the noblest animal. Thus the lowest follower of the divine law occupies a higher place than the noblest heathen. For the divine law confers something of the nature of angels on the human mind, a thing which cannot be acquired otherwise. . . . A monotheist is, therefore, preferable to the pagan, because the divine law empowered him to lead an angelic life and to reach the degree of angels, though it has been sullied and defaced by his frowardness. Some traces will always remain, and the fire of his longing for it is not quite extinguished (5:20).

There is, thus, a higher quality also in those members of the chosen who are disobedient. They remain part of the elected "on account of their descent and nature" (1:95). God rested his divinity on *all* of them. It "even descended on their women." Judah Halevi even talks about Israel as a "perfect fruit" and about "the purity of their lineage" (ibid.).

We have here both the idea of merit as the basis for election and of election as an essentialistic notion of the nature of the Jews. Halevi explains the fact that the pre-eminence of the Jews is not apparent in the concrete world through reference to the diaspora. Dispersed among the nations, the Jews are scattered limbs, dry bones. But even in this state of degradation, they still possess spiritual life, contrary to the other nations who are bodies of marble and plaster, in which neither spirit nor life has ever dwelled (2:30). Therefore the Jewish accomplishments are of the highest standard within many fields: astronomy and music (2:64f.; cf., 4:29), science (2:66), and language (2:67-81).

Judah Halevi's essentialist view of the Jewish people naturally made him suspicious of proselytes. If election was based on heredity and blood, no conversion could make a non-Jew a real part of the chosen people. But he was not totally negative towards converts; "any gentile who joins us unconditionally shares our good fortune, without, however, being quite equal to us" (1:27). The status of different people is not based on creation but on the Torah and on God's revelation in history. And God led the people of Israel out of Egypt and gave the Torah to them, because "we are the pick of humankind" (ibid.). By converting, a gentile is drawn closer to God, but he is not equal to a Jew from birth, because he will never be able to reach the highest level of religious attainment, i.e., becoming a prophet (1:115).[26]

In his principal philosophical work, *The Guide of the Perplexed*,[27] Maimonides touches on the concept of chosenness in passing. When emphasizing the supremacy of the prophecy of Moses over other prophecies, he states that the understanding of Moses is different from what was discerned by those who came later in Israel, and further removed from the prophecy within other religious communities (2:35). With this statement, Maimonides not only declares the supremacy of the prophecy of Moses but also the absolute supremacy of the prophecy of Israel.[28] For him, the Jews are superior to non-Jews, a superiority that derives from possession of the Torah.

When Maimonides discusses the importance of proper language, he mentions the obscene language of the songs and stories of ignorant and sinful gentiles, "suitable for them but not for those to whom it has been said: And ye shall be unto Me a kingdom of priests, and a holy nation" (3:8). In the same context, Maimonides declares why Hebrew is called the Holy Language: it does not contain any words for the male and female genitals or for copulation. The words used to express these things are expressions deriving from other words. The interesting thing is not Maimonides' prudish attitude but his conviction that the people chosen by God is morally on a higher level than other peoples. He also quotes with emphasis the passage at B. Shab. 146a, about how lust was taken away from the Israelites but not from the nations (2:30).

We thus notice that Maimonides did not dwell on the idea of chosenness, but that he considered the Torah to be superior to all other laws, and that he expected a morally better behavior from Jews than from other peoples. Because he considered almost all non-Jews to be idolaters, he prescribed strict separation between Jews and gentiles and also urged discrimination against gentiles (see, e.g., *Mishneh Torah* I, iv, ix and x; XI, v, iv, 11).[29]

Although Judah Halevi and Maimonides agree on the superiority of the Jews, they differ concerning the foundation of this superiority. For Maimonides, it has nothing to do with descent, as his attitude towards converts shows. Potential converts should be informed of the "heavy weight of the yoke of the Torah" in order to induce them not to convert (*Mishneh Torah* V, i, xiii, 14). If they still want to convert "they should be accepted" (ibid.) and should be "regarded as Israelites in every respect" (*Mishneh Torah* V, i, xii, 17). Thus Maimonides in his famous letter to Obadiah the proselyte assured the confused convert that he could join even in prayers and blessings that talked about what the Lord has done for "us," because there "is no difference whatever between you and us."[30]

Maimonides was proud of Judaism and the Jewish people, but he did not consider their superiority to be innate. For him Jewish identity was a matter of religious commitment, not descent. He denied that the Jews were in character and nature essentially different from other people. Their superiority was founded entirely upon the Torah. By accepting the Torah, any person could become part of Israel, and in the messianic age this would happen with all human beings. In the meantime, God protects all the righteous according to their righteousness, non-Jews as well as Jews.[31]

If we compare these two great Jewish thinkers from the Iberian peninsula we can say, in the words of David Novak, that Halevi "sees the people of Israel as being a unique entity, having all the excellences of human nature plus excellences that could not have come from human nature," while Maimonides sees the difference between the Jewish people and the nations as "one of degree, not one of kind."[32] Or we can say, in the words of Baruch Frydman-Kohl, that Maimonides holds "that *Judaism* is a philosophical community with common beliefs that entails common practices and hence, open to all who wish to join, while Halevi will be seen to describe the *Jews* as a unique ethnic group which others may join, but in which converts are still distinct."[33]

The view of Maimonides represents the mainstream of Judaism, but there has been support also for the essentialist interpretation of Judah Halevi. The famous Judah Loew of Prague, known as Maharal (1512-1609), claimed that the difference between the Jewish people and other nations was not one of belief and practice but of inner nature. The people of Israel had by nature a unique predisposition to the Torah, and it was because of this that they accepted it. The election of Israel was collective (not individual); it was based on the principle of grace rather than merit, and it was metaphysical and not ethical, i.e., it was unconditional, not dependant on the behavior of Israel.[34] All persons and nations differ from each other. The people of Israel was, according to Maharal, of a superior religious and moral caliber. Contrary to other nations, Israel has an inclination for the absolute, a tendency towards the holy, and a disposition for prophetic inspiration.[35]

Jewish mysticism, Kabbalah, held an extremely essentialist view of the Jewish people, making a pronounced distinction between Jews and non-Jews, as can be seen from the kabbalistic classic *The Zohar*.[36] The nature of the immortal souls of Jews and gentiles was different, i.e., the soul of the Jew originated from the realm of holiness, while "the spirit which is found in the idolatrous nations issues from the realm of uncleanliness and is not, properly speaking, 'man;' therefore it is not covered by this name and has no portion (in the future world)" (Bereshit 20b; cf., Emor 104b, Jethro 86a). Novak has rightly commented that in "the kabbalistic literature the distinction between Israel and the nations was elevated to an ontological principle."[37]

This can also be seen in the kabbalistic view of proselytes. When a gentile converted to Judaism, it was believed that a new soul descended upon him from heaven, but it was not a soul of the same high spiritual caliber as the souls of those born as Jews. On the contrary, it was "a great humiliation for the holy soul to enter into a 'stranger,' namely, into a proselyte" (Mishpatim 95b). Therefore "you cannot compare one who comes from the holy root and the stock of truth to one who comes from an evil stock and from an abhorrent root" (Vayikra 14a-b).[38]

Modern Jewish Thought: In the nineteenth century, Judaism saw the birth of organized non-Orthodox Judaism, and since then there has been a growing heterogeneity. One can, therefore, find not only different but very divergent interpretations of the election of Israel.

The essentialist interpretation maintained by Judah Halevi and the mystical tradition has been preserved within Hasidism. The father of Hasidism, Israel Baal Shem Tov, known as the Besht (1700-60), subscribed to the same essentialist view of the Jew as in the Kabbalah and saw a spark of holiness in every Jew, even in the unfaithful. There is, thus, an innate holiness in the Jew that no wicked behavior can destroy. This view has been carefully developed and given mystical kabbalistic features in Habad Hasidism, as can be seen in the classic work of this branch of Hasidism, *Tanya*, by the father of Habad Hasidism, Schneur Zalman of Lyady (1745-1813).[39] Roman A. Foxbrunner summarizes Rabbi Schneur Zalman's view of Jews and gentiles thus: "Gentile souls are of a completely different and inferior order. They are totally evil, with no redeeming qualities whatsoever. . . . All Jews were innately good, all gentiles innately evil."[40] Present day Habad Hasidism follows in the footsteps of its founder and believes that each and every Jew has a Jewish soul of divine nature. Even if a Jew ignores God's will, his or her inner, objective Jewish identity is greater than the external, subjective will. "The inwardness of a Jew . . . remains intact in every Jew, regardless of his outward status and whatever the outward circumstances may be."[41]

Modern thought with its emphasis on reason and universalism does not accept essential differences between ethnic groups. Distinctions that exist are said to be the result of natural or social phenomena. In mainstream modern Jewish thought, however, one can find a more subtle form of essentialism. Especially in Reform Judaism, there was initially a more liberal version of the idea of the innate quality of the Jewish people. When the distinguishing quality of Judaism was no longer seen in a rigorous observance of mitzvot and in the following of Jewish tradition, it was seen in the "ethical monotheism" brought to the world through the religious genius of the Jews. Abraham Geiger (1810-1874) stated that, as the Greeks had a special talent for art and science, so the Jews had a religious genius, a gift of prophecy that made them the people of revelation.[42] This claim is an expression of the biological interpretation that there is a unique quality given to the Jewish people. This is not racism, but it is an example of the *Völkerpsychologie* so much in fashion in nineteenth century Germany.[43] The Reform rabbi Frederic A. Doppelt declared in the 1940s that "Israel chose God not as a matter of voluntary choice but as a matter of spiritual determinism. . . . It was not the result of trial and error . . . but of his native character and the natural bent of his spirit."[44]

The most common way of interpreting the concept of election is, however, to see it as a purely religious, not biological, fact, connected to the covenant between God and Israel. This election is not a privilege but imposes a greater burden of responsibility. This greater responsibility is shown by the essence of the two covenants, the one with the Jews and the one with all other nations. Every individual Jew has traditionally been obliged to follow 613 commandments. A non-Jew, on the other hand, is considered to be righteous—and thus to have a portion in the world to come—if he follows the seven commandments of the sons of Noah. The Sinai Covenant is, thus, a heavier burden to carry than the Noahide Covenant, although the faithful naturally do not experience it as a burden but as a blessing.

This has normally been the Jewish defense against the accusation of superiority. Contrary to traditional Christianity (*nulla salus extra ecclesiam*), Judaism has never taught that there is no salvation outside itself. Judaism is thus a more tolerant religion. The Jewish preference is one of greater responsibility. More is asked of a Jew than of a non-Jew. But this interpretation also claims a uniqueness for the Jews that, while not making them into a *Herrenvolk*, does place them on a higher level. In the words of Rabbi Bernard J. Bamberger:

> One who accepts a hard task, a heavy responsibility, an arduous office, can hardly be unaware that this is an honor and a distinction; to pretend that it is not would be both dishonest and silly.[45]

Modern non-Orthodox forms of Judaism do not emphasize the keeping of mitzvot as the crucial feature of Judaism. The early Reform movement, in particular, claimed that the unique Jewish contribution to world history was the faith of the prophets, often called "ethical monotheism." The election of the Jews was seen as a means of spreading this message. The fact that the Jews lived dispersed throughout the world facilitated the "mission of Israel" in the spread of ethical monotheism. Therefore, in the beginning, the Reform movement did not consider the diaspora a catastrophe, and vigorously rejected Zionism. To enhance the establishment of peace, justice, and righteousness among all people was seen as the right way to be faithful to the vocation to be a holy people. This is well expressed in the phrase: to be in the messianic vanguard. World events in the twentieth century decisively weakened hopes for an immediate fulfillment of the messianic dream, a universal brotherhood of humankind as a result of Jewish influence. Modern Reform Judaism has, therefore, returned to Jewish traditions and now increasingly combines religious observance and mending the world (*tiqqun olam*). As Rabbi Eric H. Yoffie, President of the Union of American Hebrew Congregations, has said:

> God has commanded us and needs us to study Torah, engage in prayer, and observe the rituals of our tradition. Most of all, the Eternal One needs us to resuscitate in the world the fundamental values of Torah—that human life is sacred, that justice is a supreme value, and that freedom is the touchstone of civilization—and to bring repair, wholeness, and sanctity to all of humankind.[46]

Whether the election of Israel is interpreted as a vocation to a Torah-true life or to the spreading of ethical monotheism or to both, the essence of the concept lies in the notion that God chose Israel for a special purpose and that, Israel therefore is unique, different from other nations.

In modern times, most Jewish concepts have been challenged, re-interpreted, and sometimes rejected. That is also the case with the notion of election. The interpretation of the doctrine of election is, naturally, connected to one's notion of God. A person who does not believe in a personal God, can self-evidently not believe in divine election, there being no God who chooses.[47] Today, many Jews are atheists or agnostics. Also many religious Jews have a view of God that differs substantially from traditional theism. As a consequence their view of election is also different. "It is we who proclaimed ourselves chosen, not God."[48]

Whether there is a God or not, and whether this God has chosen any people or not, are questions of belief. That the Jews have considered themselves chosen is, however, not a question of belief. It is an undisputable fact. The lowest common denominator concerning the election of Israel is the fact that this doctrine has been central for Judaism through the ages.

But if there is no God or if God did not choose Israel, this doctrine is false. But the fact that a doctrine is false does not mean that it is harmful or negative. On the contrary, most Jews who do not believe in divine election still appreciate the doctrine. It has kept the Jews together, it has given them strength and self-respect especially in difficult times, and it has challenged them to live in an exemplary way. But this is not enough for continuing to proclaim the doctrine. "While one can understand the psychological value of such belief during years of isolation and humiliation, one cannot on such pragmatic grounds justify its morality and truth."[49]

The modern rejection of the doctrine of election is connected with Mordecai M. Kaplan (1881-1983), founder of Reconstructionism, who, throughout his long career, fought all attempts to defend the traditional doctrine. According to Kaplan, the doctrine of chosenness had a value during the times of humiliation and oppression, but today it cannot be upheld because it is ethically dubious. It implies—despite all claims to the contrary—Jewish superiority. There are so many other ways of developing self-respect—ways that look to the future instead of to the past, to personal accomplishment rather than to collective pride—that there is no need of inviting the undesirable consequences of belief in the superiority of one's people, whichever people that be.[50]

Kaplan rejects all apologies for the traditional doctrine of election. The claim that the Jews are not better than other people but that they *ought* to be better he considers chauvinism. "We ought to be better than we are. But to say that we ought to be better than others implies that we regard ourselves as being inherently superior to them."[51]

The doctrine of election is not only immoral. For Kaplan it is impossible because God is not one who chooses. Kaplan's God was an impersonal force. Because people very much like to believe that there is something special about their nation or group, Kaplan introduced the term "vocation." Every nation and every individual has a vocation, a calling to fulfill some purpose, to contribute in its own way to the common good of mankind. Kaplan sees the Jewish vocation as to "promulgate, by its way of life, the truth of the universal presence of God in all religions, and the universal obligation of every man to use his traditional *sancta* for glorifying not merely his own people or church, but mankind as a whole."[52] This cannot be seen otherwise than as a modification of the doctrine of election and of a universal mission of Israel, cleared of all self-elevation (like thanking God "for not having made us like the other nations"). Arnold M. Eisen comments about this: "Chosenness, ushered unceremoniously out the front door, was in more modest dress smuggled in through the back."[53]

If the concept of divine election is reduced to the idea of vocation, it can easily be universalized. Like the Jews, every other nation can view its relation to God through a perspective of calling and vocation: God has chosen us to fulfill some specific purpose, and others for some other purpose. ". . . in affirming the chosenness of Israel, I am not denying that other peoples, nations, groups, and creeds have their vocation, their dignity, their worth," as Bamberger has stated.[54] A belief in a literal, divine election does not exclude this kind of universalism, but it preserves an important distinction between, on the one hand, the election of Israel, which is of divine origin or superior to all other divine callings, and, on the other hand, all other concepts of national uniqueness and vocation, which are human in origin or at least inferior to the election of Israel and the revelation connected to it.

Today it is not unusual to interpret the concept of election as a way for the Israelites to respond to God and to express their love for him and, similarly, to consider all nations and persons to be called to hear the divine address and to respond in love and learn that they also are chosen. Rabbi Dudley Weinberg writes:

> Every beloved knows himself to be chosen; nor does his awareness of election require that no other should be elected. Faithful love rejoices that others are also beloved. If this means that God 'makes covenants' with other peoples, then that is what it means. A doctrine of multiple covenants would in no way damage the uniqueness of the covenant with Israel. Every covenant, every relationship of mutual trust and love, is unique.[55]

But the tendency nowadays to universalize the concept of election, and to see all individuals and nations as potentially chosen, has one important condition, as expressed by Rabbi Max J. Routtenberg: "I would regard all nations with a formulated purpose as 'chosen,' provided the various national purposes are 'for the sake of Heaven' "[56]

The problem is that so many ideas of uniqueness and vocation are not "for the sake of Heaven" but are born out of nationalistic and egoistic aspirations. Some of these ideas have been disastrous for humankind. Because only a few Jews have interpreted the idea of the election of Israel in a chauvinistic manner, Judaism cannot be accused of having invented the concept of national superiority. But it is a fact that the Jewish concept sometimes has constituted a model or a prototype for perverted ideas of superiority. Rabbi Emmanuel Rackman has commented as follows:

> That various theories of national and racial superiority derive from a Jewish idea troubles me. But I cannot abandon a conviction because of its perversion by others, any more than I would outlaw sex because some men practice sodomy.[57]

It is to be noted that Judaism is not more self-centered or intolerant than any other monotheistic religion. On the contrary, Judaism is, as we have seen, more tolerant when it comes to the issue of salvation. And, as the legendary leader of German Reform Judaism, Leo Baeck (1873-1956), has pointed out, exclusivity is a logical consequence of any belief: professing one faith means holding another to be wrong, walking one way means rejecting the other ways.[58]

That a person believes that he or she is part of a group that is chosen, loved by God, and special is unproblematic as long as he or she does not consider that all other people have not been chosen, are not as much loved, and are therefore inferior. In the words of Rabbi Jacob B. Agus:

> We may call ourselves chosen, "set apart," "called," or what have you—providing always that we do not draw the negative inferences from this doctrine and apply them to the non-Jewish peoples, as if they were "un-chosen," "undistinguished," or "uncalled." Our affirmation of "chosenness" is our way of appreciating the peculiar gifts of our past and of our destiny. In other traditions there are other ways.[59]

Bibliography

Eisen, Arnold M., *The Chosen People in America. A Study in Jewish Religious Ideology* (Bloomington and Indianapolis, 1983).
Lundgren, Svante, *Particularism and Universalism in Modern Jewish Thought* (Binghamton, 2001).
Novak, David, *The Election of Israel. The Idea of the Chosen People* (Cambridge, 1995).

Notes

[1] Jon D. Levenson, "The Universal Horizon of Biblical Particularism," in Mark G. Brett, ed., *Ethnicity and the Bible* (Leiden, New York, Köln, 1996), p. 143.

[2] *The Condition of Jewish Belief. A Symposium Compiled by the Editors of* Commentary *Magazine* (New York, London, 1966), p. 90.

[3] In German, as in some other languages, it is possible to establish a connection between the Jewish concept of election and theories of racial superiority through a simple play on words: The *Volk des Herrns* becomes the *Herrenvolk*.

[4] Unless otherwise noted, biblical quotations are from *The New International Version (NIV)*. How the verb *nivreku* should be translated in this verse is not evident. *NIV*'s version "will be blessed" is one alternative, another is "shall bless themselves." See, e.g., E.A. Speiser, *Genesis. Introduction, Translation, and Notes* (Garden City, 1964), p. 85.

[5] According to Hans Wildberger, *Jahwes Eigentumsvolk. Eine Studie zur Traditionsgeschichte und Theologie des Erwählungsgedankens* (Zürich and Stuttgart, 1960), pp. 36f., the connection between the concept of election and the covenant is secondary.

[6] Th.Z. Vriezen, *Die Erwählung Israels nach dem Alten Testament* (Zürich, 1953), p. 47, calls the deuteronomistic theology a "Erwählungstheologie." Cf., Klaus Koch, "Zur Geschichte der Erwählungsvorstellung in Israel," in *Zeitschrift für die Alttestamentliche Wissenschaft* 67 (1955), pp. 214-217.

[7] A. Cohen, *Everyman's Talmud* (New York, 1975), p. 59. Solomon Schechter, *Aspects of Rabbinic Theology* (New York, 1961), pp. 46f., writes that "there is not a single endearing epithet in the language, such as brother, sister, bride, mother, lamb, or eye, which is not, according to the Rabbis, applied by the Scriptures to express this intimate relation between God and his people."

[8] The fact that the chosen people of God lived in a state of submission to the nations was difficult for many Jews to accept, as can be seen from the complaint in 4 Ezra 6:55-59.

[9] Ephraim Urbach, *The Sages. Their Concepts and Beliefs* (Jerusalem, 1975), p. 529. A lengthier discussion of who chose whom first—did God choose Jacob or did Jacob chose God—is found in Sifre to Deut. 32:7-9.

[10] This is how A. Cohen translates the statement (op. cit., p. 60). S.M. Lehrman, *Midrash Rabba Exodus* (London and New York, 1983), p. 3, translates: ". . . because of his love for Israel . . . doth he heap upon them chastisement" and gives the alternative reading, "He chastises them with suffering."

[11] This is how Cohen translates this statement (op. cit., p. 66). Jacob Z. Lauterbach, *Mekilta deRabbi Ishmael I* (Philadelphia, 1933), p. 201, translates: "The nicest among the idolaters—kill. The best of serpents—smash its brains." The word for gentiles is sometimes translated "idolaters" to stress that the bad thing with these people was not their being non-Jews but that they

worshiped idols. Cohen claims (op. cit., p. 66) that the reason for this harsh utterance was personal experiences of oppression that Simeon b. Yohai had, while Benjamin W. Helfgott, *The Doctrine of Election in Tannaitic Literature* (New York, 1954), pp. 97f., suggests that this statement was a battle-cry of the Bar Kokhba revolt, quite normal for times of war hysteria.

[12] Bernard J. Bamberger: "The Concept of Israel," in Bernard Martin, ed., *Contemporary Reform Jewish Thought* (Chicago, 1968), p. 126.

[13] J. Neusner's translation: *The Talmud of Babylonia II.E* (Atlanta, 1993), p. 94.

[14] That gentiles, despite their nature, could become proselytes is in the same passage explained by the fact that even though they were not at Mount Sinai "their stars were there."

[15] J. Neusner's translation: *The Talmud of Babylonia XIII.D* (Atlanta, 1992), p. 124. Maimonides interpreted this statement as condemning those who become proselytes for ulterior motives (*Mishneh Torah* V, i, xiii, 18).

[16] For a discussion of the relationship between conversion to Judaism and the original election by God, see David Novak, *The Election of Israel. The Idea of the Chosen People* (Cambridge, 1995), pp. 177-188.

[17] But, cf., B. San. 59a, which holds that a gentile who occupies himself with Torah deserves death. This opinion is most probably anti-Christian (Cohen, op. cit., p. 63).

[18] J. Neusner's translation: *The Talmud of Babylonia XXIII.B* (Chico, 1984), p. 154.

[19] The other passages containing the seven commandments of the sons of Noah—T. A.Z. 8:4; Gen. Rabbah 34:8; Seder Olam Rabbah 5—contain the same commandments with slightly different words. Other passages—Gen. Rabbah 16:6; Pesikta de-Rab Kahana 12; Song Rabbah 1:2; Deut. Rabbah 2:25—states that these universal commandments were given to Adam. Still another tradition talks about thirty commandments of the sons of Noah (e.g., Gen. Rabbah 98:9; B. Hul. 92a). For an analysis of the Rabbinic concept of the Noahide laws and its later interpretation, see David Novak, *The Image of the Non-Jew in Judaism. An Historical and Constructive Study of the Noahide Laws* (New York and Toronto, 1983).

[20] Levenson, op. cit., p. 148.

[21] "Both the Bible and Rabbinic literature say so many things about what it means to be 'a peculiar people' that almost any view will find its support in the sources." Dow Marmur, *Beyond Survival. Reflections on the Future of Judaism* (London, 1982), p. 176.

[22] Helfgott, op. cit., p. 2.

[23] This challenge arose with the birth of Christianity, but became more difficult when Christianity rose to power in Europe. A thorough study of the early rabbis' way of handling this challenge is B. Helfgott, op. cit. Jacob Neusner, *Judaism and Christianity in the Age of Constantine. History, Messiah, Israel, and the Initial Confrontation* (Chicago and London, 1987), deals with how Judaism responded to the challenge of Christianity with respect to Israel's history, the messiah, and the identification of Israel.

[24] Gustaf Marx, *Die Tötung Ungläubiger nach talmudisch-rabbinischem Recht. Quellenmässig dargestellt* (Leipzig 1885), pp. 33-47; Jacob Katz, *Exclusiveness and Tolerance. Studies in Jewish-Gentile Relations in Medieval and Modern Times* (Oxford, 1961), pp. 106-128. Maimonides explicitly stated that Christians were idolaters (*Mishneh Torah* I, iv, ix, 4). G. Marx, op. cit., p. 12, states that Maimonides without doubt was "ein Christenhasser." On Maimonides' view of Christianity, see David Novak, *Jewish-Christian Dialogue. A Jewish Justification* (New York and Oxford, 1989), pp. 57-72. The issue of the Jewish definition of the Christians as idolaters and other related issues were the objects of a heated discussion in Germany in the 1880s. A position between the anti-Semites and the Jewish apologists was that of Gustaf Marx, whose *Jüdisches Fremdenrecht, antisemitische Polemik und jüdische Apologetik. Kritische Blätter für Antisemiten und Juden* (Leipzig, 1886) is a good introduction to the discussion.

[25] This and other quotations are from Hartwig Hirschfeld's translation: Judah Halevi, *The Kuzari (Kitab al Khazari). An Argument for the Faith of Israel* (New York, 1964).

[26] See Daniel J. Lasker, "Proselyte Judaism, Christianity, and Islam in the Thought of Judah Halevi," in *Jewish Quarterly Review* 81 (1990), pp. 75-91. Jochanan H.A. Wijnhoven, "The Zohar and the Proselyte," in Michael A. Fishbane and Paul R. Flohr, eds., *Texts and Responses* (Leiden, 1975), p. 121, characterizes Judah Halevi's view as follows: "There is a metaphysical *super additum* in the Israelite, to whom the gift of prophecy alone belongs, which is lacking in the proselyte, and *a fortiori* in the gentile."

[27] I cite the English translation of Shlomo Pines, Moses Maimonides, *The Guide of the Perplexed* (Chicago and London, 1963).

[28] Maimonides considered it, if not theoretically, then at least in practice, impossible for non-Jews to reach the level of real prophecy. Not even Aristotle did that. See Menachem Kellner, *Maimonides on Human Perfection* (Atlanta, 1990), p. 30. Cf., Jakob Levinger, "Die Prophetie als gesamtmenschliche Erscheinung nach der Lehre des Moses Maimonides," in *Judaica* 42 (1986), pp. 80-88.

[29] For a description of Maimonides' view of gentiles in general and Christians in particular, see Marx, *Die Tötung Ungläubiger nach talmudisch-rabbinischem Recht*, pp. 16-32.

[30] Quoted from Isadore Twersky, ed., *A Maimonides Reader* (New York, 1972), p. 476.

[31] This non-chauvinistic view of Jewish superiority by Maimonides has been emphatically stressed by Menachem Kellner, concerning Maimonides' views of ethics, prophecy, immortality, the messianic age, proselytes, the defini-

tion of a Jew, and the nature of Torah in his book *Maimonides on Judaism and the Jewish People* (Albany, 1991), and concerning Maimonides' view of the Jewish people in his article "Chosenness, Not Chauvinism: Maimonides on the Chosen People," in Daniel H. Frank, ed., *A People Apart. Chosenness and Ritual in Jewish Philosophical Thought* (New York, 1993), pp. 51-75.

[32] Novak, *The Election of Israel*, p. 226.

[33] Baruch Frydman-Kohl, "Covenant, Conversion and Chosenness: Maimonides and Halevi on 'Who Is A Jew?'" in *Judaism* 41 (1992), p. 66.

[34] Benjamin Gross, *Le Messianisme juif. "L'eternité d'Israël" du Maharal de Prague (1512-1609)* (Paris, 1969), pp. 115-125; Ben Zion Bokser, *From the World of the Cabbalah. The Philosophy of Rabbi Judah Loew of Prague* (New York, 1954), pp. 165-167.

[35] Katz, op. cit., pp. 138-142; Gross, op. cit., pp. 103-106.

[36] I have used the translation of Harry Sperling, Maurice Simon, and Paul P. Levertoff: *The Zohar* (London, 1956).

[37] Novak, *The Image of the Non-Jew in Judaism*, p. 267.

[38] There are more passages, some not so negative, in the *Zohar* about proselytes, but the dominant attitude is very negative, well represented by these quotations. See Wijnhoven, op. cit., pp. 120-140.

[39] In the first two chapters of *Tanya*—and frequently repeated later on—it is explained how the souls of the Jews are derived from the divine whereas the souls of the nations are derived from the evil. Therefore, even the apparently good that non-Jews do is in fact not good: ". . . all the good that the nations do is done from selfish motives . . . all the charity and kindness done by the nations of the world is only for their own self-glorification." In chaps. 18 and 19 (cf., chaps. 25 and 41), it is emphasized that even in the lowest Jew there is a spark of the divine, which can be seen in the fact that he rather sacrifices his life than deny the Holy One. Quoted from Schneur Zalman, *Likutei Amarim—Tanya* (London, 1973).

[40] Roman A. Foxbrunner, *Habad. The Hasidism of R. Schneur Zalman of Lyady* (Northvale and London, 1993), pp. 108f.

[41] Menachem M. Schneerson, *Letters by the Lubavitscher Rebbe 1956-1980* (Brooklyn, 1981), p. 13.

[42] Abraham Geiger, *Das Judentum und seine Geschichte bis zur Zerstörung des zweiten Tempels* (Breslau, 1865), pp. 33-36. Similarly, e.g., Kaufmann Kohler, *Studies, Addresses, and Personal Papers* (Philadelphia, 1931), p. 178.

[43] One of the prominent figures of nineteenth century German *Völkerpsychologie* was the Jewish philosopher Moritz Lazarus (1824-1903), who co-operated with Geiger. Lazarus served, e.g., as the president and Geiger as the vice president of the synod in Leipzig in 1869, and Lazarus was the first head of the board of trustees of the

Hochschule für die Wissenschaft des Judentums, the Reform Seminary in Berlin, where Geiger was a teacher (Michael A. Meyer, *Response to Modernity. A History of the Reform Movement in Judaism* (New York and Oxford, 1988), pp. 189-191).

[44] Quoted from Arnold M. Eisen, *The Chosen People in America. A Study in Jewish Religious Ideology* (Bloomington and Indianapolis, 1983), p. 58. Similarly the Conservative rabbi Robert Gordis, *Conservative Judaism. An American Philosophy* (New York, 1945), p. 54, who claimed that although genius was rare, a spark of the prophetic spirit "dwells in nearly every Jewish heart, waiting to be fanned to a mighty flame."

[45] Bamberger, op. cit., p. 130.

[46] "What Do American Jews Believe?" in *Commentary* August, 1996, p. 93.

[47] It is to be remembered that a faith is not always logically consistent. Eisen has, thus, claimed that a generation of Conservative rabbis accepted a traditional concept of chosenness although they did not profess a God who could choose. "Reaffirming chosenness, they left the nature of the Chooser ill-defined" (Eisen, op. cit., p. 114).

[48] Arthur Green in "What Do American Jews Believe?" p. 43.

[49] Harold M. Schulweis in *The Condition of Jewish Belief*, p. 218.

[50] Mordecai M. Kaplan, *Judaism as a Civilization. Toward a Reconstruction of American-Jewish Life* (Philadelphia and New York, 1981), pp. 43f. After the Holocaust, Kaplan stated that those who interpret the doctrine of election as if the Jews possess hereditary traits that qualify them to be superior in the realms of the religious and the ethical assent "to the most pernicious theory of racial heredity yet advanced to justify racial inequality and the right of a master race to dominate all the rest of mankind" (*The Future of the American Jew* (New York, 1948), pp. 215f.)

[51] Kaplan, *Judaism as a Civilization*, p. 254. But, cf., what he wrote fourteen years later: "If we wish to foster Jewish group solidarity, we must live up to a higher ethical standard than the average. No other justification for our remaining an identifiable minority will avail" (*The Future of the American Jew*, p. 55, italics removed).

[52] Kaplan, *The Future of the American Jew*, p. 230; see pp. 228-230.

[53] Eisen, op. cit., p. 86. A similar criticism of Kaplan's view of vocation is found in Ze'ev Levy, "Judaism and Chosenness: On Some Controversial Aspects from Spinoza to Contemporary Jewish Thought," in Frank, ed., *A People Apart*, p. 103.

[54] Bamberger, op. cit., p. 130.

[55] *The Condition of Jewish Belief*, p. 249.

[56] *The Condition of Jewish Belief*, p. 188. Similarly Norman Solomon, *Judaism and World Religion* (London, 1991), pp. 166f.: ". . . any nation whose self-awareness involves a relationship with God is to the extent that it does so an

embodiment of the messianic idea—it is an 'Israel.'"

[57] *The Condition of Jewish Belief*, p. 182.

[58] Leo Baeck, *Das Wesen des Judentums* (Wiesbaden, 1983), p. 64.

[59] Jacob Agus, *Jewish Identity in an Age of Ideologies* (New York, 1978), p. 324.

SVANTE LUNDGREN

ETHIOPIA, JUDAISM IN: The history and practice of Judaism in Ethiopia presents a unique chapter in the history of Judaism throughout the world. The Beta Israel (Falasha), the vast majority of whom resided in Ethiopia until the early 1990s, preserved a form of non-Talmudic Judaism well into the second half of the twentieth century. Since their immigration to Israel, this religious system has undergone radical changes. The bulk of this article is devoted to the description and analysis of their religious life in Ethiopia. The changes that have taken place since their arrival in Israel are also discussed. However, no discussion of Judaism in Ethiopia can ignore the fact that the Ethiopian Orthodox Church has, more than any church in the world, remained faithful to the letter and spirit of the Old Testament, preserving a long list of biblical customs and traditions. As we shall see, the specific nature of Beta Israel Judaism can only be fully understood within the larger context of Ethiopian Judaism as represented by the Beta Israel themselves, the Church, and several smaller groups.

The Origins of Ethiopian Judaism: According to some Ethiopian traditions, half the population of the ancient Ethiopian kingdom of Aksum was Jewish prior to the introduction of Christianity in the third and fourth century. While there can be little doubt that this is a considerable exaggeration, the overwhelming impact of biblical and Hebraic patterns on traditional Ethiopian culture is undeniable. Indeed well into the twentieth century, much of Ethiopia remained embedded, as Ullendorff put it, in "attitudes, beliefs, and a general quality of life . . . forcefully reminiscent of the Old Testament world."

Numerous biblical customs have survived in the practice of Ethiopian Christians. Thus, for example, male children are circumcised on the eighth day after birth. The Saturday Sabbath long held sway in Ethiopia and figured prominently in the ritual, liturgy and theological literature. Traditional Ethiopian dietary laws conform closely to those of the Old Testament, including the prohibition of pork. The threefold division of churches in Ethiopia clearly replicates the architectural structure of the Temple in Jerusalem. On the literary level, the biblical ethos of Ethiopian Christian culture is epitomized in the country's national epic, Kebrä Nagast (The Glory of Kings), which depicts the rulers of Ethiopia as descendants of Menilek I, the putative son of King Solomon, and Makedda, the Queen of Sheba.

While some scholars have contended that these elements derive not from direct Jewish *influences* but primarily or even exclusively from the imitation of the Old Testament, this approach does not appear satisfactorily to explain all the available data. In particular, it does not account for the existence of numerous Jewish-Aramaic or Hebrew loanwords, such as *tabot* (ark), *'orit* (Torah), *haymanot* (faith) and *'arb* (eve, Friday) in the Ethiopic version of the Bible. It is generally agreed that these Aramaic words were not introduced by Syriac-speaking missionaries or other Christians. Rather, they belonged to a pre-Christian Jewish leaven in Ethiopian culture.

Scholars remain divided as to the provenance of these Jewish influences. Some, relying on Ethiopian legends, contend that Judaism was already brought to Ethiopia in the time of King Solomon, by either the Queen of Sheba or her son, Menilek. Others drawing on Rabbinic tradition, contend that it arrived via the Ten Lost Tribes, especially the Tribe of Dan. More firmly based, is the claim that Jews from Egypt, perhaps from the military garrison of Elephantine, brought a priestly hierarchy, temple worship, and sacrifices to Aksum. However, the bulk of the evidence would seem to support the idea that Jewish immigrants from South Arabia (around the area of modern Yemen), were the primary carriers of Judaism and Jewish influences to Ethiopia.

On the basis of the cultural elements and loanwords, it appears that the first carriers of Judaism reached Ethiopia between the rise of the ancient kingdom of Aksum at the beginning of the Common Era and its conversion to Christianity in the fourth century. They used Aramaic for religious purposes and probably brought texts in that language, and perhaps Hebrew, with them. Given the predominantly literary and linguistic (as opposed to archaeological) evidence for their presence, there appears to be no reason to assume that they were as numerous as Ethiopian legend suggests. Initially they settled in the Aksumite region of Eritrea and northern Ethiopia and mingled with their pagan and later Christian neighbors. Thus they had an important impact on Ethiopian culture in its formative period.

Until the 1970s, most scholars described the history of Christianity and Judaism in Ethiopia as a small scale recapitulation of the history of those two religions elsewhere in the world. According to this view, a small ancient Jewish population was supplanted by a later Christian community, leaving behind only a small residual Jewish population. The Beta Israel, it was claimed, were an archaic group, religious and cultural survivors from pre-Christian Aksum.

Since the mid-1970s, a new scholarly consensus has emerged, which, although conceding the existence of early Jewish influences on Ethiopian culture and civilization, questions the survival of a distinct Jewish group culturally and socially separate from the surrounding population. Rather, it suggests the existence of a spectrum of groups that differed with regard to the emphasis they put on Christian and Judaic elements. According to this perspective, the Beta Israel must be understood first and foremost as an Ethiopian ethnic group, and their ethnogenesis should be dated to the fourteenth to sixteenth centuries. During this period, a combination of political, economic, religious, and social factors led to the emergence of a group known to others as "Falasha" and calling themselves the Beta Israel or Isra'elawi.

Religious Life In Ethiopia:[1] As this brief historical discussion suggests, the Judaism of the Beta Israel consisted of a combination of beliefs and practices that drew upon biblical and pan-Ethiopian elements. Historically, scholars have been divided as to which of these are most important to an understanding of their tradition. While some scholars and the Beta Israel themselves contend that Beta Israel religion is essentially an archaic form of Judaism, others view it as primarily Ethiopian in its origins, form, and content. Although the first of these hypothesis cannot be totally excluded, the influence of the Ethiopian surroundings would appear to be predominant. Most of the "Jewish" elements in Beta Israel religion can be shown to be the product of Ethiopian Christian influence or the deliberate imitation of practices found in Old Testament and biblical texts. In particular, it is possible to demonstrate that numerous elements of Beta Israel religion, including its literature, liturgy, and clerical hierarchy, developed in Ethiopia during the course of the past five centuries.

Whichever of these views we choose to adopt, it must be stressed that with few exceptions sources on Beta Israel religion date from the middle of the nineteenth century onward. Accordingly, the historical depth of the reconstruction presented below should not be exaggerated. While much of the Beta Israel religious system certainly predates the nineteenth or perhaps even the fifteenth century, the antiquity of individual elements should not be assumed.

Finally, it must be noted that although the Beta Israel were literate and possessed a number of religious texts (see below), theirs was primarily an oral tradition. Not only did they not possess until comparatively recently written calendars, but more importantly their religious doctrines and practices were neither preserved nor transmitted in a written form. Ritual experience, word of mouth, and community consensus were all far more important than formal codification. Regional variations in religious practice were common and the norms of observance flexible. Accordingly, the synthesis presented below is far more systematic and rigid than anything that existed in Ethiopia, where the flow of events and the exigencies of history took priority over any written canon.

Belief System: In reconstructing the beliefs of the Beta Israel, it must be remembered that they do not possess any explicitly theological texts. Thus their doctrines must be reconstructed from scattered references in literature, prayers, and literary works as well as interviews with informants conducted in recent years. In this context, it must also be stressed that few if any Beta Israel were able to produce a systematic account of their belief system.

The belief system of the Beta Israel had at its core the belief in one God, the Lord of Israel, creator of heaven and earth. He is the God of the Biblical patriarchs, who spoke to Moses and revealed himself on Mount Sinai. He was usually referred to in their liturgy by the Ge'ez terms Egzi'abeher or Amlak. However, the Hebrew terms Adonay or Elohe as well the Agaw (Cushitic language) terms Adara and Heziga were also used. None of these terms are unique to the Beta Israel: the Ge'ez and Hebrew names are used by Ethiopian Christians, and the Kemant, a neighboring Ethiopian people, use those from Agaw. Some Beta Israel texts also include various "magical" names of God.

Although the Beta Israel did not accept such Christian ideas as the trinity or devotion to Mary and the saints, both angels and demons figured prominently in their cosmology. Gabriel, Mikael, Rafael, Rufel, and Fanuel are a few of the angels whose names appear in Beta Israel literature. Mikael was particularly important and was commemorated on the twelfth day of each month by a holiday in his honor.

The Beta Israel shared with both Christian and Muslim Ethiopians as well as other people of northeast Africa a belief in hostile spirits known as *zar*. The numerous zar spirits were believed to possess individuals, particularly women, adolescent girls, and other marginal figures. In some cases, attempts were made to exorcize the zar, but often the spirit would be appeased with gifts or other favors to it through the possessed individual. In Ethiopia, zar "doctors" would assist the possessed, usually in the context of a cult group comprised of other similar individuals. The zar cult flourished in Ethiopia and has continued in Israel as well.

Despite their belief in a very detailed and multi-leveled cosmology, the Beta Israel did not believe divine intervention to be a regular occurrence and situated it primarily in the distant past. In contrast, they believed that all people are judged after their death. Indeed, the judgment of souls forms one of the major themes in their literature (see below), and confession played a prominent role in their religious practice. The souls of those who have been faithful to God and obeyed his commandments are conducted to paradise by the angels. Sinners, idolaters, blasphemers, thieves, etc. are consigned to Sheol.

They also believed in a final judgment at the end of days. They shared with Christian Ethiopians a belief in a Davidic messiah named Tewodros. Indeed, it was this belief that led a large group of Beta Israel to embark on a failed journey back to the promised land during the reign of the Ethiopian Tewodros (1855-1868). Some Beta Israel texts also assign important precursor roles in the messianic drama to the prophet Elijah and the angel Mikael. The latter is said to be responsible for the resurrection of the dead.

Religious Hierarchy: The clerical structure of the Beta Israel like most aspects of their religious life in Ethiopia was markedly different from that of other Jewish communities. Rather than a Rabbinic hierarchy trained in the intricacies of a halakhic system, they possessed a priestly heritage that claimed to be modeled on a biblical pattern. In fact, its overall structure, which in the past included monks, priests, deacons, and clerics known as *debtarotch*, showed a marked resemblance to that of their Christian neighbors.

From the middle of the fifteenth until the end of the nineteenth century, monks (*manokse, malokse*) were the principal religious leaders of the Beta Israel. According to Beta Israel tradition, monasticism was introduced to the community by Abba Tsabra, a Christian monk who initially reached them as a missionary seeking to convert them. Instead he is said to have joined their community and assisted in the articulation of their unique religious identity. His most important disciple is believed to have been Tsaga Amlak, a son of the powerful emperor Zar'a Ya'eqob (1434-1468). Abba Sabra is credited not only with the introduction of monasticism, but also with the composition of the religious liturgy and certain religious texts. One of his disciples is believed to have introduced the Sa'atat (Horologium). Later monks are said to have led religious revivals in the nineteenth century.

Although some Beta Israel monks were hermits, most lived in monasteries. Horharwa, the largest monastery, is said to have held two hundred monks. Young boys from ten or twelve years of age were educated in monasteries. At around age eighteen or twenty, they would decide whether to remain as monks in the monastery or return to the world and raise a family. Individuals who left the monastery often became married priests (Kahenat, Qessotch). Celibacy, poverty, fasting, and other forms of mortification were characteristics of Beta Israel life. Despite its clear relationship to Christian monasticism, Beta Israel institutions clearly served not to assimilate them to their surroundings but to define their religious identity as a separate non-Christian community.

The decline and virtual disappearance of Beta Israel monasticism during the twentieth century appears to be related to a number of factors including a disastrous famine (1888-1892) and criticisms from both Christian missionaries and representatives of world Jewry, most notably Jacques (Ya'acov) Faitlovitch. Following the famine in which over a third of all Beta Israel perished, the community could no longer afford a celibate clerical elite. Moreover, external critics denigrated Beta Israel monasticism as being non-biblical and non-Jewish in both its form and content.

Among the Beta Israel, the priesthood was not hereditary, nor was it limited to a particular family or clan. In principle, any male born to a family with an unblemished history and possessing the necessary means could be educated for the position. However, since early education was usually the responsibility of the family, the priests

tended to be clustered in certain extended families. In contrast to the monastic clergy, the priest (Kahen, Qes) married, raised a family, and lived with his secular neighbors in a village. A widowed priest can remarry, but only to a virgin.

The Beta Israel priests fulfilled numerous tasks. They recited prayers during the week and on the Sabbath and holydays. They also performed sacrifices and officiated at rites of passage, such as circumcisions, naming ceremonies, funerals, and memorials for the dead. (However, purity laws prohibit them from having contact with a corpse or personally performing a circumcision.) In each region, the local priests were responsible for determining the precise day on which holidays were observed. Although they did not usually engage in healing through charms and amulets, they did recite prayers for the sick. Every Beta Israel had a priest who was his or her confessor. Confession was not performed at specific times, but most Beta Israel sought absolution at least once a year and performed a final act of contrition before dying. The priests were also important communal leaders, who along with the elders regulated communal behavior and mediated disputes. In each region, one priest was designated as the high priest. In the nineteenth century, there were four such high priests, but by the middle of the twentieth century this number had shrunk to two, in Gondar and Tegre. In exchange for these services, the priest received gifts of money, salt, grain, fruits, and livestock. Nevertheless, most priests supported themselves as farmers or craftsmen.

During his period of training, a candidate for the priesthood served as a deacon (diyaqon). In this position he assisted in the prayers, carried firewood and water, and cared for animals destined for sacrifice. He also learned to read and write, studied the Bible and other texts, and familiarized himself with the liturgy and ritual practice.

The term debtara (pl.: debtarotch) literally means a "tent" or "tabernacle." It is applied to unordained or defrocked clergy who assist the priest in conducting the liturgy. Often the debtara is a priest who has divorced, or an individual who is unfit for the priesthood. The *debtarotch* are often skilled in the performance of sacred music. They are, moreover, educated and often served as scribes. During the twentieth century, the *debtarotch*, like the monk, practically disappeared. Traditionally, they occupied an ambiguous position in society. Despite their role in the religious system, they were also associated with less socially acceptable activities, such as magic and healing. The *debtara* not only copied religious texts but also wrote amulets and charms.

Ritual and Liturgy: Beta Israel religious life was centered around the prayer house (*salota bet*), which is also called a *masgid* (from the root *sagada*: to bow) or *beta maqdas* (sanctuary). A prayer house was constructed in any village that had a priest and/or a significant Beta Israel population. Although the precise details of construction varied from case to case, there were certain common features. The prayer house was usually constructed at the highest place in the village. Moreover, like Ethiopian Orthodox churches, it had a tripartite structure that recalled the threefold division of the biblical Temple.

Sacred objects such as the Orit, priestly garments, books, and ritual vessels where kept in the holy of holies of the prayer house. Entry into it was strictly regimented. Not only were there separate entrances for priests, secular men, and (mainly older or celibate) women, but lepers, slaves, and those rendered impure through sexual intercourse, contact with a corpse, etc. were excluded.

The recitation of prayers was the central activity of Beta Israel practice. Prayers were recited on all holidays and at major stages in an individual's life cycle. Although on occasion recited in the open air, prayers were most commonly chanted in the prayer house. The performance of the prayers was often accompanied by the beating on a drum (nagarit) and the sounding of a gong (*qaccel*). In addition, the priests held staffs (*maqwamiya*), which supported them during long hours of standing in prayer. Prayers were at times accompanied by ritual dances in which priests moved in a circle, waving these staffs in the air. The music of the prayers was known as *zema*, and although

a theoretical distinction existed between the words of the liturgy and the melodies, in practice the two were practically inseparable.

Most Beta Israel prayers were in Ge'ez, although there were also some portions in Agaw, a Cushitic language. Neither of these languages has been spoken by the Beta Israel in recent times, and hence most prayers could not be understood by community members.

The Beta Israel classified their prayers in several ways. On the one hand, they were categorized according to the holiday on which they were recited. More broadly, passages that recurred in the liturgy of several annual festivals (see below) were designated as such: annual festival prayers. Prayers recited on fast days, for penance at funerals, and in commemoration of the deceased were known as absolution (*fethat*). Alongside these classifications, the Beta Israel also distinguished day and night prayers and divided these further with regard to the time of day they were recited.

Another major feature of Beta Israel religious practice was the performance of sacrifices (*Qwerban, Maswa't*). Until middle of the nineteenth century, sacrifices were offered by the Beta Israel on many holidays, during rites of passage, as well as at times of trouble or distress, such as illness or drought. During the twentieth century, however, there was a sharp decline in the frequency of sacrifice due to both economic distress and criticisms voiced by foreign representatives of Judaism and Christianity. Thus, with the exception of Passover (*Fasika*), New Years, and commemoration ceremonies, the institution all but disappeared.

Traditionally, sacrifices were offered in the open air on an altar or other site designated for the purpose. Sacrifices were not performed in the prayer house unless it was built of stone. Only whole unblemished animals could be offered as sacrifices. In addition to animal sacrifices, the Beta Israel brought offerings of bread and beer to the prayer house on Sabbaths and other festivals. There a member of the clergy accepted the offering and blessed them, turning to face Jerusalem.

The Liturgical Cycle: In their daily lives, the Beta Israel used the standard Ethiopian calendar, which consisted of twelve months of thirty days each and an additional month of five or six days. However, for the computation of feasts (*ba'al*) and fasts (*tsom*), they used a lunar calendar composed alternately of thirty or twenty-nine days. Every four years, an additional month was added. Although this calendar drew from written sources, including the Pentateuch, Enoch, Jubilees, and a computus of Egyptian origin known as Abushaker, there was no written calendar. The beginning of each month and the precise day for the commemoration of each festival was based on observation of the moon. Thus the date of the new moon was crucial for the correct calculation of other holidays. Since each priest determined the calendar in his village or villages, periodic meetings were necessary to correct any discrepancies that had emerged. In addition, the frequent observance of monthly festivals assisted in the proper computation of holidays each month and over the course of the year.

Among the most important Beta Israel holidays and fasts were:

Sanbat (Sabbath): Whether considered in the context of Rabbinic Sabbath observance or traditional Ethiopian Orthodox Christian respect for the Saturday Sabbath, Sabbath observance is one of the major themes of their literature (see below) and had a central place in their religious life. The Sabbath was perceived of as a semi-divine female figure who offers respite to the sinners in hell and intercedes on the behalf of those who honor her. Not surprisingly, the Beta Israel themselves at times compare their devotion to the Sabbath to Christian devotion to Mary.

Preparations for the Sabbath began on Friday with washing of clothes, bathing, and preparation of food. However, the beginning of the holiday was usually delayed until well after sunset. A special bread known as *Berkweta* or *Maswa't* was baked and eaten. Sabbath observance was particularly strict: no work was done, no fires were lit (including Sabbath candles), no food cooked, no journey undertaken. Sexual relations were forbidden. The Beta

Israel did not fast on the Sabbath unless it coincided with the Day of Atonement. Circumcisions were not performed on the Sabbath until after sunset.

The Beta Israel treated every seventh Sabbath with particular respect and viewed it as a day particularly suited for confession and the absolution of sins. The fourth week of the fifth month was the traditional date of a festival known as Yasanbat Sanbat (the Sabbath of Sabbaths) or Langato (seven). Selections from the liturgy for this day include selections from Arde'et (see below), the song of Moses (Deut. 32), and passages from Exodus.

In addition to the Sabbath, the Beta Israel observed every Monday and Thursday as fast days. On such days they ate no food from sunrise to sunset.

Monthly Celebrations: Traditionally the Beta Israel observed a number of monthly celebrations. The first day of each month was celebrated in keeping with biblical custom, marked by prayers and a communal meal of bread and beer. The tenth, twelfth and fifteenth of each month served as monthly reminders of annual holidays. The tenth of each month commemorated the day of Atonement (Astasreyo), celebrated on the tenth day of the seventh month; the twelfth of each month of marked Ma'rar, which fell on the twelfth day of the third month; this was also the day on which the angel Mikael was honored each month. The fifteenth of each month was commemorated as a reminder of Fasika (Passover) and Tabernacles, which fell of the fifteenth of the first month and the seventh month respectively. Finally, the twenty-ninth of each month served as a preparation for the new moon and commemorated Sigd, which fell on the twenty-ninth day of the eighth month. Over recent years, the observance of lunar holidays lapsed in Ethiopia.

Annual Holidays: Most of the annual holidays observed by the Beta Israel are based on biblical precedents and have parallels in the celebrations of other Jewish communities. However, prior to the twentieth century they did not observe festivals such as Shemini Aseret, Simhat Torah, Hanuukah, Purim, Lag Ba'omer, the fast of

Gedaliah, or Tu b'shevat. Moreover, they did observe one unique annual holiday, Sigd, which they attributed to biblical precedent from the time of the return from the first exile. Fast days usually involved abstinence from food throughout the day and from animal products during the evening as well.

The Beta Israel celebrated Fasika or Qwerban in commemoration of the exodus from Egypt from the fifteenth to twenty-second days of the first month. The day before the holiday was observed as a fast day (Tsoma Fasika). On the eve of Fasika, the Beta Israel sacrificed a sheep and recounted the story of the exodus. However, they did not have a Passover Seder or text of the Haggadah. The Beta Israel observed Fasika with tremendous strictness. New clay cooking vessels were prepared each year. All food was prepared daily to prevent leavening over night. The usual pancake-like Ethiopian bread known as *enjara*, which is made with fermented batter, is replaced by a flat cake known as *qitta*.

The fast of Tomos (Tsoma Tomos) is observed from the first to tenth days of the fourth month. The exact reason for this observance is not clear. Both rabbinical Jews (seventeenth day) and Karaites (ninth day) observe fasts during the (tenth) month, Tammuz, commemorating the breach of the walls of Jerusalem by the Romans. It is not clear if there is a connection between these customs and those of the Beta Israel or if this is connected to the biblical custom of a fast of the fourth month (Zech. 8:19).

The fast of Ab (Tsoma Ab) is observed from the first to the seventeenth day of the fifth month in commemoration of the destruction of the first Temple. In the past, the holiday ritual included the ascent of a mountain and prostration similar to that observed on Sigd. When questioned on the length of their fast, Beta Israel priests explained that in Ethiopia they were still mourning the exile.

The eighteenth day, Asartu wasamantu, of the sixth month commemorates the deaths of Abraham, Isaac, and Jacob.

Berhan Saraqa (The light appears) was celebrated on the first day of the seventh month and coincided with the New Year,

Rosh Hashanah. Like its pan-Jewish counterpart, it was associated with the patriarch Abraham. Indeed it was sometimes called Tazkara Abreham (the commemoration of Abraham), and the Testament of Abraham was read. The sacrifice of Isaac was also commemorated through the sounding of a ram's horn.

Astasreyo (to forgive) was celebrated on the tenth day of the seventh month. Like Yom Kippur, it was the most important fast of the year and the only one celebrated even if it coincided with the Sabbath. Before the observance began, community members requested forgiveness from each other for sins committed during the year. Many Beta Israel also confessed to their father-confessor on this day. Prayers for the forgiveness of sin were recited throughout the night of the ninth and all of the tenth.

One of the most interesting Beta Israel observances on Astasreyo was the ritual known as *emen*, in which millet was scattered on stones in an act of repentance. Yet another occurred during the afternoon prayers. Midway through the ritual, members of the community jumped up and down, ululating and hissing. Only after several minutes, when the dust raised made it hard to breathe, was the service resumed. The jumping is said to have purged people from sin.

Ba'ala Matsallat was celebrated from the fifteenth to the twenty-second of the seventh month, coinciding with Sukkot (Tabernacles). The Beta Israel did not build booths, nor did they make use of the four species (palm, myrtle, willow, citron). However, the holiday was associated with the wanderings in the desert. Fresh leaves were scattered on the floor of the prayer house. Although in the past the entire holiday may have been observed as a period of rest, more recently only the first and last days were so honored.

Sigd (from the Ge'ez term *sagada*, to bow) is a pilgrimage festival celebrated by the Beta Israel on the twenty-ninth day of the eighth month, on the fiftieth day after Astasreyo. There are several interpretations of its significance. Some associate the holiday with the renewal of the covenant during the period of Ezra and Nehemiah (Ezra

8-10), and passages from these texts were part of the holidays liturgy. However, the scriptural texts concerning the revelation at Sinai (Exod. 19-20) and the Decalogue were also read and associated with the holiday. In many aspects, Sigd recalled the pattern of supplication and confession that characterizes Christian observances known as Mehella (Supplication). Indeed, the holiday was sometimes referred to by this name.

Sigd was celebrated on the summit of a mountain that was not contaminated by tombs, non-Jews, or animal remains. On the day of the festival, the Beta Israel ascended the mountain carrying stones on their heads as a sign of submission. These stones were then used to create a circle within which the ritual was conducted. The clergy brought various ritual objects, including a copy of the Orit. In addition to the texts already mentioned, the liturgy included sections from the Astasreyo ritual as well as three repetitions of the *emen* ceremony. During the first part of the holiday people, fasted; however, when they descended the mountain in the afternoon, a festive meal was held.

Although the Beta Israel did not celebrate Purim with a reading of the megillah and other ceremonies, they did observe the fast of Esther (Tsoma Aster) in commemoration of the queen's fast, as recounted in the Esther 4:16. There appears to be some confusion regarding the precise day of this observance, because the name of the third Ethiopian month, Hedar, is similar to the Hebrew month of Adar. However, the fast has usually been observed between the eleventh to the thirteenth of the eleventh month.

The holiday of Ma'rar (Harvest), which corresponds to Pentecost (Shavuot), was celebrated on the twelfth day of the third month, seven weeks after the last day of Fasika (and not seven weeks after the second day, as in other Jewish communities). Grain or bread were brought to the prayer house, where they were blessed by the priest. This ceremony was followed by a communal meal. Some Beta Israel informants report that prayers regarding the giving of the law at Sinai were recited.

Another Ma'rar was celebrated on the twelfth day of the ninth month, seven weeks after the festival of Sukkot (Ba'ala Matsallat). This date was chosen to better coincide with the actual harvest in the Ethiopian agricultural cycle.

Ritual Purity and Rites of Passage: Ritual purity played a central role in Beta Israel, both in the regulation of internal communal relations and defining their differences from their mainly Christian neighbors.

The Beta Israel were particularly devoted to the laws that governed female purity during menstruation and after giving birth. Even when the observance of other purity laws began to decline, these rituals were maintained with a special tenacity. Unlike Rabbinic laws of *niddah* as interpreted today, these rules applied not only to married women but to single women, widows, and even servants residing with the Beta Israel. According to Beta Israel practice, a menstruating woman left her house and entered a menstrual hut known as a *yamargam gojo* (the hut of the curse) or *yadam gojo* (the hut of blood), where she remained for seven days. This hut was located at the edge of her village and demarcated by a border of stones. Only her children and other women, who brought her food, were allowed to enter. At the completion of seven days, the woman immersed herself and washed her clothes before returning home.

Often a pregnant woman, especially in the case of a first child, traveled to her mother's village to give birth. When she went into labor, she entered the menstrual hut along with two midwives. (They were rendered impure through their contact with her and had to purify themselves before returning to the community.) When the child was born, the woman of the village emitted twelve cries if it was a boy and nine if a girl.

For Beta Israel boys, circumcision (*gezrat*) took place on the eighth day after birth, unless this fell on the Sabbath, in which case the ceremony was delayed until after sunset. Prayers were recited by a priest, but either a man or a woman could perform the circumcision. In either case, the circumciser had to be purified before returning to the community. After circumcision, the mother and infant entered the *yaras goj o* (birth hut), where they remained thirty-nine days.

Female circumcision was practiced by the Beta Israel in Ethiopia. The custom appears to have been in decline throughout the twentieth century. Unlike male circumcision this ritual had no fixed day and minimal religious content. Female circumcision was only performed by women. Two weeks after the birth of a girl, the mother and child entered the birth hut where they remained for sixty-six days.

Forty days after the birth of a boy and eighty days after the birth of a girl, the mother and child ended their isolation. A priest gave the baby its name and immersed it in water. Despite the obvious similarities to Christian baptism, which also takes place on the fortieth or eightieth day, the Beta Israel prefer to emphasize the biblical mandate for the separation and purification of the mother. The Ethiopic text known as the book of the disciples (Arde'et) was read as part of this ceremony.

The Beta Israel believed it to be of the utmost importance that the dead receive a proper burial and be properly commemorated. A person who felt death approaching, would offer a final confession to his or her spiritual guardian. If possible, a person was buried on the day of death or the following day. However, funerals were not performed on the Sabbath or Day of Atonement. Cemeteries were located at the outskirts of villages and divided into sections for priests, elders, wives of priests and elders, ordinary people, and children. Suicides were not buried in the cemetery.

Priests recited psalms, prayers of absolution (*Fethat*) at the funeral. For seven days after the funeral, close kin of the deceased abstained from work. One the seventh day, a sheep or goat was sacrificed, and a feast was prepared. The *tazkar* is observed annually on the anniversary of the death.

Throughout history the number of people who converted in order to join the Beta Israel community was probably small. The major exceptions to this rule were servants and slaves, who had to be converted, or at least ritually purified, in order to live with the Beta Israel. Beta Israel conversions to Christianity and in some cases Islam were much more common. Converts or those rejoining the Beta Israel after having joined other religious communities were (re)integrated in similar ceremonies. The candidate brought a bar of salt to the priest and was given chickpeas and water to sustain him during a seven day period of exclusion. During this period, he or she was taught the main points of the faith, particularly the Ten Commandments. This was naturally much more intensive for a new convert than for those rejoining the community. After seven days, candidates washed themselves and their clothes, had their head shaved, and then rejoined the community. A brief ceremony was performed during which the candidate prostrated before the priest and was given bread to eat.

Literature: Any consideration of Beta Israel literature must begin with the Bible. Their version of the Old Testament, known as the *Orit*, is identical to that of the Ethiopian Orthodox Church. Not only was it translated primarily, perhaps exclusively, from the Septuagint, but it also included such apocryphal and pseudepigraphical works as Tobit, Judith, Ben Sira, and most importantly Enoch and Jubilees. The last of these is especially important to the Beta Israel and appears to have had an important influence on their religious life and calendric system. Owing to the expense of preparing handwritten parchment manuscripts in Ethiopia, copies of the *Orit* were comparatively rare in Ethiopia. Often the Beta Israel acquired a manuscript that had been written by Christian scribes. In Ethiopia, copies of the *Orit* existed in book (codex) rather than scroll form. The Beta Israel are not familiar with the Talmud or later Rabbinic literature. There is, moreover, no evidence that the Beta Israel were ever familiar with Hebrew or possessed any Hebrew literature.

In addition to the aforementioned biblical works, the Beta Israel possessed a number of non-canonical works. Almost without exception, the literature of the Beta Israel did not originate within their community, nor did it reach them directly through

Jewish channels. Rather, the majority of Ethiopian "Jewish" texts reached the Beta Israel through the mediation of Ethiopian Christian sources. With one or two exceptions, the Beta Israel appear to have chosen works whose Christian versions already displayed a clear biblical-Jewish tone. Thus the Christian versions could be adapted for Beta Israel use without the necessity of major rewriting.

Mota Muse (The Death of Moses), Mota Aron (The Death of Aron), and the Gadlat (Testaments) of Abraham, Isaac, and Jacob all relate the deaths of biblical figures. Arde'et (The Disciples) contains Moses' secret teachings to his disciples (the leaders of the twelve tribes). This book, which is recited at the purification ceremony of a woman after she gives birth, also exists in a Christian version, in which Jesus teaches his disciples. Nagara Muse (The Conversation of Moses) contains a dialogue between Moses and God, in which the divine essence and the punishment of the dead are explained.

The importance of the Sabbath forms the focus of works such as Te'ezaza Sanbat (The Commandments of the Sabbath), Nagara Sanbat (The Teachings of the Sabbath) and, to a large extent, the homiletic work Abba Elijah.

The fate of the soul after deal is yet another central theme of Beta Israel literature. In addition to Nagara Muse, it is discussed in several other works. Matshafa Mal'ekt (The Book of Angels) describes a struggle between the angel of light and the angel of darkness over the souls of the deceased. In the Apocalypse of Baruch, the angel Sutu'el shows Baruch the heavenly Jerusalem and the different levels of Hell as well as a vision of the end of times. In Matshafa Gorgoryos, the angel Mikael shows the prophet Gorgoryos the glories of paradise and the punishments of Hell.

Other Beta Israel works include Baqadami Gabraigzi'abeher (In the Beginning God Created), Weddase Tebab (The Praise of Wisdom), Gadla Sosna (The History of Susanna), and numerous prayers.

At least seven of the Beta Israel texts were translated into Ge'ez from Arabic sources. Since such translations did not begin until the later thirteenth or early four-teenth century, none of these works can predate this period. Indeed, it appears likely that most of these texts reached the Beta Israel in the fourteenth or fifteenth century. However, one of them, Nagara Muse, dates to the eighteenth century. Given the ritual-cultic importance of books such as the Arde'et, Mota Muse, and Gadla Abreham, which are read respectively at purification ceremonies, funerals, and on the New Year, this dating has a significance beyond the realm of literature, since it confirms a comparatively late dating for these elements of the religious system.

As noted above in the discussion of ritual and liturgy, the recitation of prayers played a major role in Beta Israel religious life. Although many such prayers have been preserved in manuscript form, there is no complete written text of the liturgy. Many prayers appear to have never been committed to writing and were passed from generation to generation in oral form. Similarly, the musical performance was transmitted orally. Most prayers are recited in Ge'ez, but there are some passages in Agaw. From a textual point of view, the texts draw heavily on the Bible, particularly the Orit and the Psalm of David (Mazmura Dawit). Certain texts such as Deut. 6:5 or Isa. 6:3 recur in many points in the liturgy.

Although most scholars have focused on the written literature of the Beta Israel, in recent years, their oral traditions have received long overdue attention. This corpus includes historical traditions, ritual practices, and interpretations of and commentaries on written texts. While most Beta Israel have only a passing familiarity with this material, clergy and other elders often serve as vital repositories of communal memories. More broadly, though somewhat removed from religion in the narrow sense, the Beta Israel also preserve a body of proverbs, folktales, and popular songs. Most of these are secular in character and reflect the folk wisdom that accumulated over generations. Some, however, concern or reflect the Beta Israel's special circumstances as Jews living as a minority among a powerful, largely Christian population.

External Influences and Recent Changes: Although Beta Israel religious practice developed and evolved throughout its history, changes became particularly obvious during the past hundred years as a result of contact with representatives of World Jewry.

As noted above, both linguistic and cultural evidence support the idea that there were early Jewish influences on Ethiopian civilization. However, there is no comparable evidence for Jewish influences in later periods. Despite the proximity to Egypt and Yemen, the Jewish populations of those countries do not appear to have had any direct cultural influence on Ethiopia following the rise of Islam. Thus it was only in the second half of the nineteenth century that the Beta Israel came into contact with other Jewish populations. In the wake of the efforts by European missionaries to convert the Beta Israel to Protestant Christianity, Jewish groups in Europe decided to investigate this distant and threatened Jewish community. In 1867, Joseph Halévy became the first practicing Jew to visit the Beta Israel in Ethiopia. His travel reports are one of our earliest detailed descriptions of their society and religious life. Halévy was not pleased by much of what he saw in Beta Israel religious life, and he made no effort to hide his displeasure. However, he spent only a few months in their presence, and his impact on their daily life was very limited.

The arrival in Ethiopia in 1904 of Halévy's student, Jacques (Ya'acov) Faitlovitch, marks a turning point in the relationship between the Beta Israel and the outside Jewish world. The "normalization" of Beta Israel religious life was an important part of Faitlovitch's agenda. Like the Christian missionaries who preceded him, he was very critical of such features as animal sacrifice, monasticism, and ritual purity. Although he was not as successful as he hoped in reforming the Beta Israel, and his impact varied tremendously from region to region, his introduction of external Jewish elements began a process that has continued to this day. At the same time, general social changes and patterns of modernization, including modern education and in a few cases urbanization, also altered some aspects of traditional Beta Israel life.

Faitlovitch's activities were cut short by the Italian Fascist invasion of Ethiopia. In his absence, the Italian scholar Carlo Alberto Viterbo retained contact, but was less intrusive in his attitude towards Ethiopian Judaism. Following the restoration of Imperial rule in Ethiopia, Jewish contacts resumed and pressures for change renewed. Purim was first celebrated in some Ethiopian villages in 1953, the same year that Hebrew prayer books (Nusach Ashkenaz) were distributed and a Jewish Agency school was opened in Asmara. In the 1950s, two small groups of Ethiopian youths were taken to Israel and educated by Youth Aliyah. Upon their return they began to introduce such elements as Hebrew prayers, Hanukah, and the lighting of candles on Sabbath eve. In 1959, Rosh Hashanah (two days), Yom Kippur, and Sukkot were observed in their standard Jewish form for the first time in Ambober, the Beta Israel village most exposed to outside influences. In 1961, 1,500 copies of an Amharic booklet on holiday and Sabbath observance were distributed by the Jewish Agency. Elements of "normative" Jewish practice, such as the use of Torah scrolls, began to be introduced in the celebration of *Sigd*.

Perhaps the clearest testimony to the impact of outside influences was found in the prayer house in the village of Ambober, as observed in the 1970s, just prior to the beginning of emigration to Israel. A stone building built in a square shape, it had a tin roof with a Star of David. In additional to parchments of the Orit, it also had a small donated Hebrew Torah scroll. Hebrew prayer books and prayer shawls were found side by side with such traditional Ethiopian objects as umbrellas, drums, and gongs.

Changes in Israel: Beginning in the 1970s, hundreds of Beta Israel began to arrive in Israel. By the end of 1985 and the completion of two airlifts from the Sudan ("Operation Moses" and "Operation Sheba"), over fourteen thousand Ethiopian immigrants had come on *aliyah*. By the completion of Operation Solomon in May, 1991, this number had risen to over forty thousand. A decade later, over fifty thousand Ethiopian immigrants had reached

Israel. When these are coupled with the children of Ethiopian descent born in Israel, their total number is close to eighty thousand. Although contacts with representatives of world Jewry had brought about certain changes in Beta Israel belief and ritual in Ethiopia, these pale in comparison to what occurred in Israel.

Although the Beta Israel was recognized as a Jewish community by Israel's religious and secular authorities, serious questions existed regarding the personal status of individual community members. While most Beta Israel immigrants were recognized as Jews under Israel's Law of Return, Rabbinic authorities were concerned that non-halakhic conversions and divorces performed in Ethiopia had resulted in a large number of Ethiopians who were not halakhically Jewish or should be designated *mamzerim* (of impaired status). In the early 1980s, all Ethiopians entering the country were required to undergo a conversion or "reunification" ceremony that included ritual immersion, acceptance of the *mitzvot*, and (in the case of men) symbolic recircumcision (*hatafat dam brit*). Later the demand for circumcision was dropped, and, following a protest in 1985, only couples wishing to marry were expected to undergo the other rituals. Demands for such ceremonies have declined in recent years. However, the arrival in Israel of large numbers of "Falas Mura," descendants of Beta Israel who had converted to Christianity, has meant that many immigrants who arrived after 1991 have had to undergo a complete or partial conversion to Judaism.

Given the monopoly that Orthodox religious groups enjoy over religious services in Israel, it is not surprising that Beta Israel clergy were not allowed to retain their clerical status. Under Israeli law, they are not recognized as clergy and do not have the right to perform rituals such as weddings, circumcisions, or funerals. Moreover, the dissolution of communal life in the course of *aliyah* and the resettlement of immigrants with no regard for prior village associations inevitably resulted in a disruption of ties between priests and their followers. Most priests (*qessim*, as they are known in Israel) have continued to perform some religious

duties and to participate in ritual gatherings. Moreover, some attempts have been made to recognize the existence of the priests as a corporate group. A council of priests, for example, advises the Israeli rabbinate on the status of Ethiopian couples wishing to marry.

A small number of younger priests have undertaken studies that enable them, at least in theory, to exercise some formal religious functions, and some priests are among the Ethiopians who have been trained as rabbis. However, the number of Ethiopian rabbis remains small, and not even all of these actually serve as rabbis. Ethiopian synagogues have been established in a small number of communities, but, unlike other Israeli immigrant populations, these are the exception rather than the rule.

Not surprisingly, the move to Israel has produced a clear generational division among the Ethiopian population with regard to observance. As a rule, elders have tended to be more faithful to traditional Ethiopian practice. Youngsters, who are much more exposed to both secular and religious Israeli lifestyles, usually favor one of these options at the expense of their parents' form of Judaism. Nowhere is this clearer than in the case of marriages, in which the traditional Ethiopian prohibition against intermarriage within seven generations has tended to be replaced by five generations or even less for young people marrying today.

In Ethiopia, the different religious communities (Jews, Muslims, Christians) were distinguished not only by doctrines and ritual but also by strict rules of social separation. Members of one community did not consume meat slaughtered by and for members of the other communities. It is significant therefore to note that in Israel many elderly Ethiopians do no consume meat prepared by the state approved ritual slaughterers. Rather, they prefer to purchase an animal and have it slaughtered and prepared for consumption by their own officials, ideally a priest.

Ethiopian traditions of ritual purity have also weakened seriously since their arrival in Israel. Israeli authorities made a conscious decision not to facilitate the observance of menstrual separation. Separate rooms or buildings were not provided for immigrant women while they resided in absorption centers or other forms of public housing. Moreover, Rabbinic demands for ritual immersion as part of a conversion ceremony discouraged Beta Israel women from going to the *mikveh*, lest this be interpreted as submission to this dictate. The comparatively late age of marriage of Beta Israel women in Israel, as well as their unprecedented presence in the educational system and workforce, are yet other factors that discourage traditional menstrual observances.

Although it is still possible for women to observe the days of separation after the birth of children, this custom has also changed dramatically. Most Ethiopians visit a woman after she gives birth, and some will kiss and touch a post-partum woman and her baby. Others will enter her room, but refrain from contact, and the most traditional will not even enter the room. Whatever the form of observance, purification and naming ceremonies, forty or eighty days after birth, remain popular and, in the case of male children, are often celebrated with more fervor than the circumcision.

Funerals continue to be among the largest and most important gatherings of the Ethiopian community. Although the burial itself is controlled by the official Israeli rabbinate's *hevra kadisha* (burial society), the mourning rituals with their pubic laments and *tazkar* commemoration ceremonies remain largely unchanged.

Most Beta Israel holidays that parallel pan-Jewish observances have been assimilated to their non-Ethiopian equivalents. In a few cases, some distinctive Ethiopian practices remain. Thus, some families still sacrifice or slaughter a sheep on Passover. Sabbath observance often begins well after sunset. Astasreyo observances remain far less somber than the equivalent Yom Kippur observances. Lunar celebrations and other monthly celebrations that had already declined in Ethiopia have all but disappeared except among some elders. At the same time, many families, particularly those with children in the Israeli school system, have begun to celebrate Purim, Hanu-

kah, Simhat Torah, and other festivals unfamiliar to them in Ethiopia.

The Ethiopian's unique pilgrimage-covenant holiday, Sigd, continues to be celebrated in Israel with a central national ceremony conducted in Jerusalem. Israeli dignitaries, politicians, and religious officials join with the pilgrims, who usually number several thousand. In the spring of every year, on Jerusalem day, which celebrates the reunification of the city in 1967, the Ethiopian community holds a ceremony in memory of those who perished in an attempt to reach Israel.

Epilogue: During the twentieth century, Beta Israel Judaism ceased to exist in its customary form. Initially, contact with representatives of world Jewry led to changes in Ethiopia of an indigenous tradition that had existed for hundreds of years. However, in the last decades of the century, the move to Israel of virtually all practicing Beta Israel put an end to Jewish communal life in Ethiopia. Moreover, the pressures on Ethiopian immigrants to adopt lifestyles similar to those of either their religious or secular Israeli neighbors have led to a large-scale abandonment of Ethiopian customs and practices. At the dawn of a new millennium it appears unlikely that much more than remnants and scattered elements of Ethiopian Judaism will survive beyond the next few decades.

Bibliography
Kaplan, Steven, *Les Falashas* (Turnhout, 1990).
Kaplan, Steven, *The Beta Israel (Falasha) in Ethiopia* (New York, 1992).
Leslau, Wolf, *Coutumes et croyances des Falachas*, Travaux et memoires de Institut d'Ethnologie 61 (1957).
Salamon, Hagar, *The Hyena People: Ethiopian Jews in Christian Ethiopia* (Los Angeles, 1999).
Schwarz, Tanya, *Ethiopian Jewish Immigrants: The Homeland Postponed* (London, 2001).
Shelemay, Kay K., *Music, Ritual and Falasha History* (East Lansing, 1989).

Note
[1] With the emigration of virtually the entire Beta Israel population to Israel by 1991, their religious system ceased to be a functioning reality. Accordingly, all discussions of religion in Ethiopia have been worded in the past tense.

STEVEN KAPLAN

G

GENETIC ENGINEERING: Genetic engineering has made it possible to manipulate the DNA of microorganisms, animals, and plants in order to satisfy human needs. Science has developed bacteria that ingest petroleum in order to alleviate the environmentally devastating effects of oil spills, sheep whose milk contains a drug used in treatment of cystic fibrosis, and a host of genetically modified foods. One third of the harvest of corn, soybeans, and canola in the United States is genetically modified to make the crops resistant to insects. At least in the laboratory, it is possible to remove DNA from a salmon that keeps the fish from freezing and to introduce it into strawberries in order to produce a freeze-proof strawberry. It is also possible to introduce animal genes into plants. A small company in Syracuse has contracted with a scientist at the University of Connecticut to develop a genetically engineered cat that will not cause allergies, an effort that may prove to be highly profitable, since it could allow countless numbers of people who cannot now do so to keep cats as pets. Scientists at the University of Florida have patented a method of implanting a silkworm gene into grapevines to make the vines resistant to Pierce's disease, a blight currently menacing vineyards in California. The silkworm gene kills the bacterium responsible for the blight.

There is, of course, reason to be concerned with regard to possible deleterious effects of genetically modified foods upon humans. There is evidence that corn that has been genetically modified to produce a toxin that kills a caterpillar called the European corn borer may also kill monarch butterflies. Genetically modified crops may produce unfamiliar proteins that might prove to be allergenic, toxic or carcinogenic. These concerns are appropriately addressed both by the scientific community and by government regulatory agencies.

The theological and religious question is whether we have the right to intervene in the natural order by mixing and mingling the genetic material of diverse species.

There is no reflection in Jewish tradition of a doctrine that establishes a global prohibition forbidding humans to tamper with known or presumed *teloi* of creation. There are indeed individual thinkers who have explained the rationale underlying particular *mitzvot* in a manner echoing such a concept. Biblical commandments prohibiting interbreeding of species and the mingling of diverse agricultural species certainly lend themselves to such an interpretation. Although Rashi, in his commentary to Lev. 19:19, regards those restrictions as *hukkim*, i.e., arational statutes not subject to human inquiry, Nahmanides, in his commentary on the same verse, takes sharp issue with Rashi and opines that interbreeding and prohibited mingling of species are forbidden as constituting illicit tampering with creation. Nahmanides states that every creature and every plant is endowed by God with cosmically arranged distinctive features and qualities and is designed to reproduce itself as long as the universe endures. Interbreeding and cross-fertilization produce a reconfiguration of those distinctive qualities and also compromise reproductive potential. By engaging in such activities, we usurp the divine prerogative in producing a new species or entity with its own novel set of attributes and, presumably, a species less than optimally suited to fulfill the divinely ordained *telos* associated with the original species.

Ibn Ezra has been understood as presenting the matter in a somewhat different light in declaring that the Torah prohibits crossbreeding of species because the act thwarts propagation of the species and hence represents an injustice to the animals who are prevented from fulfilling the divine purpose of propagating their respective species.[1] Accordingly, ibn Ezra explains the prohibitions against the mixture of agricultural species as well as the combination of linen and wool in the cloth of a garment as violative of the natural order decreed by the Creator.[2] Rabbi Samson Raphael Hirsch had no difficulty explaining the prohibition regarding *sha'atnez* (the mixing of linen and wool) in similar terms. Indeed, Rabbi Hirsch understood all *hukkim* as reflecting the principle that humanity should not interfere with the order and harmony—and hence the *telos*—of creation.[3] According to Rabbi Hirsch, such laws are distinguished from *mishpatim*, or so-called rational commandments, only because our duties toward our fellow humans are more intelligible to us by virtue of our recognition of our own needs and aspirations. That particular purposes are similarly assigned to animals and even to inanimate objects is not immediately grasped by the human intellect and hence *hukkim* are depicted as arational. It is noteworthy that, although Rabbi Hirsch regards these commandments as designed to prevent interference with divinely ordained *teloi*, unlike natural law theologians, he regards the *teloi* themselves as not being readily apparent to human reason. That understanding of the nature of *hukkim* is certainly confirmed by the fact that no natural law philosopher has ever asserted that the manufacture of linsey-woolsey or even agricultural hybridization is intuitively perceived as interfering with the divine plan for creation.

Were it to be assumed that tampering with the ostensive or presumed nature of animal species is always forbidden, most forms of genetic engineering would be illicit. No bacterium is designed by nature to clean up oil spills by metabolizing petroleum or to excrete human insulin for use by diabetics. In the absence of evidence in Rabbinic sources to the contrary, it must be assumed that, even accepting Nahmanides' explanation of the prohibition against interbreeding or Rabbi Hirsch's broader analysis of the rationale underlying *hukkim* in general, biblical strictures must be understood as limited to those matters explicitly prohibited.[4]

Indeed, there is a perceptible tension between the concepts enunciated by Nahmanides and Rabbi Samson Raphael Hirsch and the many midrashic sources indicating that man is an active partner in the process of creation and, as such, is charged with bringing creative processes to completion. Indeed, the biblical charge to Adam exhorting him to "fill the earth and conquer it" (Gen. 1:28) seems to give Adam *carte blanche* to engage in any form of conduct that is not specifically proscribed. The problem is readily resolved if it is understood that, in general, the functions and *teloi* of the products of creation are not immutable; that the Creator did not intend to bar man from applying his ingenuity in finding new uses and purposes for the objects of creation;[5] and that there is no injustice to animal species or inanimate objects in doing so. Immutability of function and *telos* is the exception, not the rule. Thus, for example, it has never been suggested that manufacture and use of synthetic fibers in the making of clothes is in any way a contravention of either the letter or the spirit of the law.[6] The exceptions were announced by the Creator as formal prohibitions. It is precisely because human reason cannot intuit, or even comprehend, when and under what circumstances contravention of the natural order is inappropriate that these commandments are in the nature of *hukkim*.

More generally, humanity's creative power, at least to the extent that it does not involve creation of novel species, is extolled in Rabbinic sources. The divine appellation "*Shaddai*" is understood in Rabbinic exegesis as an acronym "*she-amarti le-olami 'dai*'—Who said to My universe, 'Enough!'" Thus the verse, "I, the Lord Shaddai" (Gen. 17:1) is rendered by *Midrash Rabbah* 46:2, "I am the Lord who said to the universe 'Enough!'" Rabbi Jonathan Eibeschutz, *Tiferet Yonatan, ad locum*, followed by Rabbi Joseph Ber Soloveitchik, *Bet ha-Levi, ad locum*, explains that, in his creation of various artifacts, God arrested their development before completion. Man plants a seed, the seed germinates, a stalk grows, and kernels of wheat develop. The Creator could well have made it possible for the kernels to crumble into flour, for the flour to absorb rain or moisture from the atmosphere, for the wind to churn the water-drenched flour so that dough be formed, and for the heat of the sun to bake the mixture in order to yield a product that might literally be termed a "breadfruit." Instead, the Creator arrested the process long before its completion and ordained that grinding the wheat, mixing the flour with water, kneading the dough, and baking the bread be performed by man. Similarly, the flax plant could have been endowed with properties causing strands of flax to separate and intertwine themselves in a cloth that might grow in the shape of a cloak. Instead, the process is arrested and brought to completion by man. Indeed, B. Shab 30b declares that in the eschatological era the land of Israel will yield "cakes" and "linen garments." *Bet ha-Levi* explains that the import of that statement is simply that, in the end of days, God will allow the processes of creation to reach their destined end by modifying the natural order in a manner that will permit the creative process to become complete and thus spare man any travail. In the interim, however, God has declared, "Enough!," i.e., He has precipitously interrupted the process of creation and co-opted man, who must complete the process, as a collaborator in fashioning the universe.

It is abundantly clear that human intervention in the natural order is normatively interdicted only to the extent that there are explicit prohibitions limiting such intervention. Moreover, there is no evidence either from Scripture or from Rabbinic writings that forms of intervention or manipulation not expressly banned are antithetical to the spirit of the law. Quite to the contrary, Jewish tradition, although it certainly recognizes divine proprietorship of the universe, nevertheless, gratefully acknowledges that while "The heavens are the heavens of God" yet "the earth has he given to the sons of man" (Ps. 115:6). In bestowing that gift upon mankind, the Creator has granted man dominion over the world in which he lives and over the living species that are co-inhabitants of that world. Man has been given license to apply his intellect, ingenuity, and physical prowess in developing the world in which he has been placed subject only to limitations imposed by the laws of the Torah, including the general admonition not to do harm to others, as well as by the constraints imposed by good sense and considerations of prudence.

The tension between the role of man as the agent of completing the work of creation and biblical prohibitions against certain forms of interference in the natural order is

elucidated by Rabbi Judah Loew, popularly known as Marahal of Prague, in his *Be'er ha-Golah*, chap. 2:3, *s.v. Masekhet Pesahim*. B. Pes. 54a states that the creation of a number of entities was planned by God before the first Sabbath, but they were not actually created until the conclusion of the Sabbath. Upon the conclusion of the Sabbath "the Holy One, blessed by he, bestowed understanding upon Adam and he took two stones, rubbed them one upon the other and fire emerged; [Adam] brought two animals, mated one with the other and from them emerged a mule." Clearly, this statement reflects the notion that the potential for both fire and interspecies is the product of divine creation and that the potential became actualized through the intermediary of human intelligence that is itself a divine gift.

Maharal notes that, although interbreeding of diverse animal species was clearly interdicted by the Torah, the Sages certainly regarded the breeding of mules by Adam as a fulfillment of the divine plan. Maharal boldly declares that the fact that God has prohibited a certain act does not necessarily mean that God has renounced the effect of that act. Thus crossbreeding of animal species was prohibited to Israel at Sinai but was not forbidden to Adam because the breeding of mules was incorporated in the divine blueprint for creation. A distinction must be drawn between act and effect. And, if disdain for the effect is not the rationale underlying the prohibition of the act, there exists no basis for expanding the prohibition to encompass any act that is not formally within its ambit.

Man's role is "completion" (*hashlamah*) of the process of creation. Insofar as "completion" of creation is concerned, it is the divine plan that such development take place. Maharal asserts that it is the divine will that even interspecies such as the mule come into being, although not in circumstances that involve violation of Torah law. Thus crossbreeding was permitted to Adam because emergence of interspecies is integral to "completion" of the universe. According to Maharal, crossbreeding by a person who is not commanded otherwise (or in situations in which the prohibition

Detail of painting on the western wall of the Dura Europos Synagogue, Syria, 245 C.E. Reconstruction, 1:2 (Photo courtesy Beth Hatefutsoth Photo Archive, Tel Aviv, Israel)

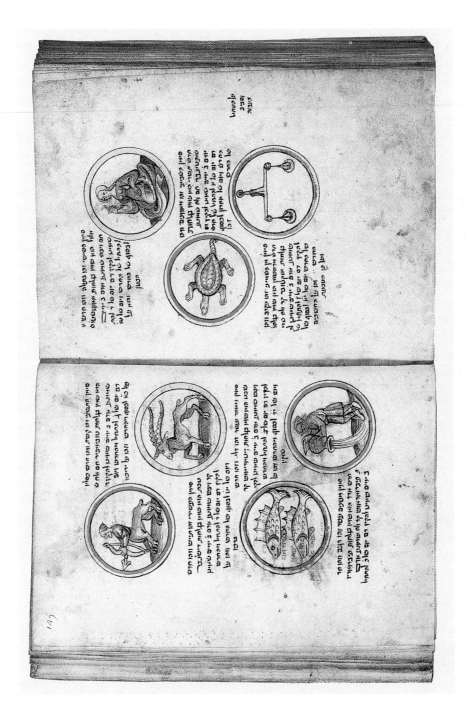

Astrology and Medicine, a collection of medical treatises. Southern Germany 1480-1500. (Photo courtesy Beth Hatefutsoth
Photo Archive, Tel Aviv, Israel)

Biology and Judaism. House-keeping class for Jewish women, sponsored by the Women's Aid Organization, Vilna 1938. The two signs in Ivrit distinguish between meat (r) and dairy (l). (Photo courtesy YIVO Institute for Jewish Research, New York, USA)

Statue of Rabbi Moshe ben Maimon (Maimonides) by Amadeo Ruiz Olmos (1964).
Tiberias Square, Cordoba, Spain, 1982. (Photo courtesy Beth Hatefutsoth Photo Archive,
Tel Aviv, Israel)

Chao Ching-Cheng of the Jewish community of Kaifeng, brother of Chao Wen-K'uei. (Photo courtesy Beth Hatefutsoth Photo Archive, Tel Aviv, Israel)

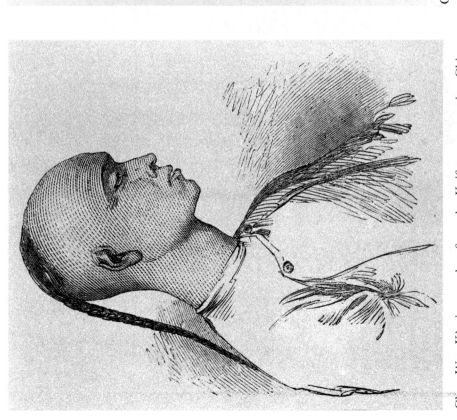
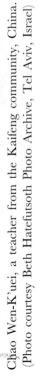

Chao Wen-K'uei, a teacher from the Kaifeng community, China. (Photo courtesy Beth Hatefutsoth Photo Archive, Tel Aviv, Israel)

Judaism in China. The synagogue in Kaifeng Fu. (Photo courtesy YIVO Institute for Jewish Research, New York, USA)

Group of Kaifeng Jews, with the initiators of the convention for the re-establishment of the Kaifeng community, held in Kaifeng, China, in May 1919. (Photo courtesy Beth Hatefutsoth Photo Archive, Tel Aviv, Israel)

Mishne Torah, by Moses Maimonides. Hebrew manuscript, from Italy, 1180. National and University Library, Jerusalem. (Photo courtesy Giraudon/Art Resource, New York, USA)

רבינו אליהו מווילנא (הגר"א)

Codification of the Law: HaGra, the Vilna Gaon.

The Habit of a RELAPSE or IMPENITENT going to be burnt.

The place and manner of EXECUTIONS

Conversos in Spain : illustrations from *A History of the Marranos* by Cecil Roth (1975, Ayer Co. Pub.).

Seder plate (German, 1790), on which the symbolic foods are arranged during the Seder dinner. It shows scenes from the Haggadah, the story of the Exodus read during the home celebration. Hechal Shalom Wolfson Museum, Jerusalem. (Photo by Erich Lessing, New York, USA)

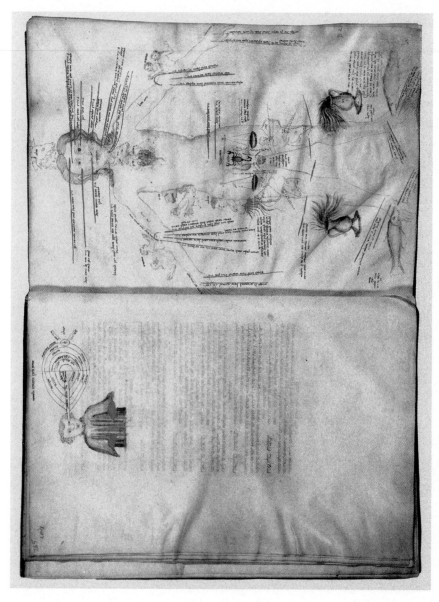

Bloodletting man. Manuscript, Provence, France c.1400. The manuscript contains several medical texts, mostly translated fragments of the Medical Treatise of Jean of Damascus (Photo courtesy Beth Hatefutsoth Photo Archive, Tel Aviv, Israel)

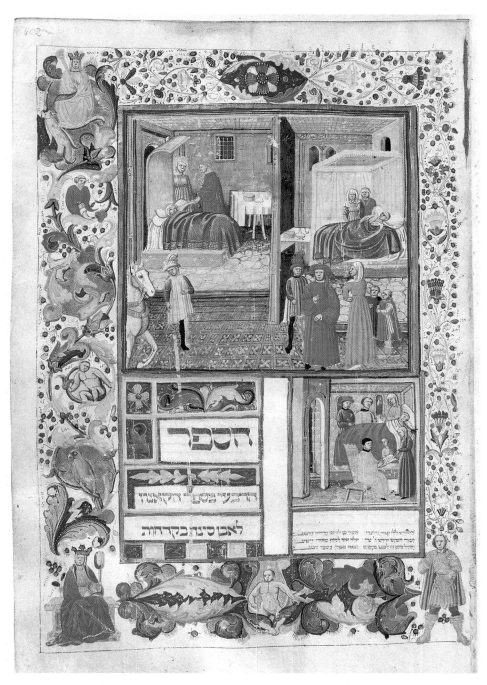

Caring for the sick - Page from *The Canon of Avicenna*. Manuscript of the Hebrew translation of Ibn Sinna's medical treatise. Ibn Sinna was the 11th century physician and philosopher. Ferrara, 15th century. (Photo courtesy Beth Hatefutsoth Photo Archive, Tel Aviv, Israel)

Moses and the Ten Commandments (c. 1900). Oil on canvas misrach (prayer panel) in the form of a neo-Gothic altar. Judaica Collection Max Berger, Vienna, Austria. (Photo by Erich Lessing, New York, USA)

Dance around the golden calf (second half 15th century). Regensburg, Regensburger Dom, western façade, northern tower. (Photo courtesy Bildarchiv, Marburg, Germany)

Hebrew class at the school in Addis Ababa, Ethiopia, 1924. First on the right is Taamarat Emanuel. (Photo courtesy Beth Hatefutsoth Photo Archive, Tel Aviv, Israel)

Falasha (or Beta Israel) village. Gondar province, Ethiopia. (Photo by Ivo Romein, Gouda, The Netherlands)

Falasha (or Beta Israel) woman baking bread in the traditional way. Gondar province, Ethiopia. (Photo by Ivo Romein, Gouda, The Netherlands)

Sacrifice of Isaac by J.W. Schirmer, Berlin, Germany. (Photo courtesy Bildarchiv, Marburg, Germany)

Judaism in Greece. A group of Jewish survivors in post-war Saloniki, assembled to say 'Kaddish' for the dead.

Torah Study in Congregation B'nai Israel, a Reform synagogue in Albany, Georgia, USA. (Photo by Dana Kaplan, Albany, Georgia, USA)

Karaite marriage contract (Jerusalem, 1870), concerning the marriage between Karaite community leader Japheth ha-Levi ben Moses ha-Levi and his bride Sultana bat Isaac Tzaddik. (Photo courtesy Library of the Jewish Theological Seminary of America, New York, USA)

Karaimes. From *Description ethnographique des peuples de la Russie* by Theodore de Pauly (1862). Drawn by C. Huhn. Lithographed by J.B. Kuhn. (Photo courtesy Library of the Jewish Theological Seminary of America, New York, USA)

Joseph, Jewish king of the Khazars, dictating a letter for Hisdai Ibn Shaprut, The Jewish statesman in Cordoba, Muslim Spain, 10th century. (Photo courtesy Beth Hatefutsoth Photo Archive, Tel Aviv, Israel)

At the grave of R. Raphael Encaoua, Sale, Morocco, 1995. R. Raphael Encaoua (1848-1935), head of the Supreme Rabbinical Tribunal in Rabat for many years, is buried in the Jewish cemetery in Sale. His grave is a focal point for pilgrims on Lag ba'Omer (Photo courtesy Beth Hatefutsoth Photo Archive, Tel Aviv, Israel)

Mourning women at a Jewish cemetery in Tetuan, Morocco. (Photo courtesy Beth Hatefutsoth Photo Archive, Tel Aviv, Israel)

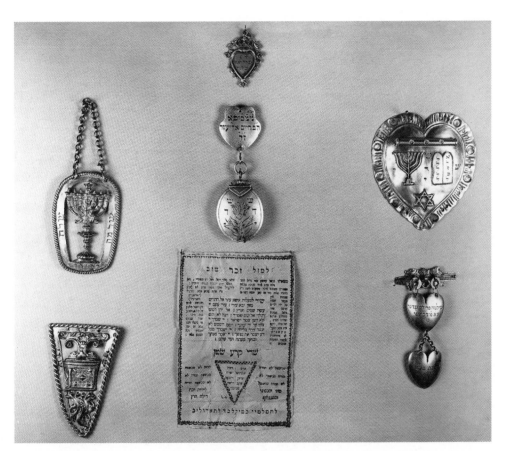

Group of amulets (with menorah — heart-shaped with crown — heart-shaped with menorah, tablets and mogen David — two hearts joined by rings — with flower hanging on plaque 'shaddai' — with flaming altar). Jewish Museum, New York. (Photo courtesy Jewish Museum/Art Resource, New York, USA)

Protective childbirth amulet. Silver, Persia 18th-19th centuries. (Photo courtesy Beth Hatefutsoth Photo Archive, Tel Aviv, Israel)

Second title page for *Seder Berachot*, a collection of prayers and blessings of the Spanish Jews. Amsterdam, Holland, 1687. The illustrations include: blowing the Shofar, circumcision, take the meal, blessing of new moon, Havdalah and sowing.

(Photo courtesy Beth Hatefutsoth Photo Archive, Tel Aviv, Israel)

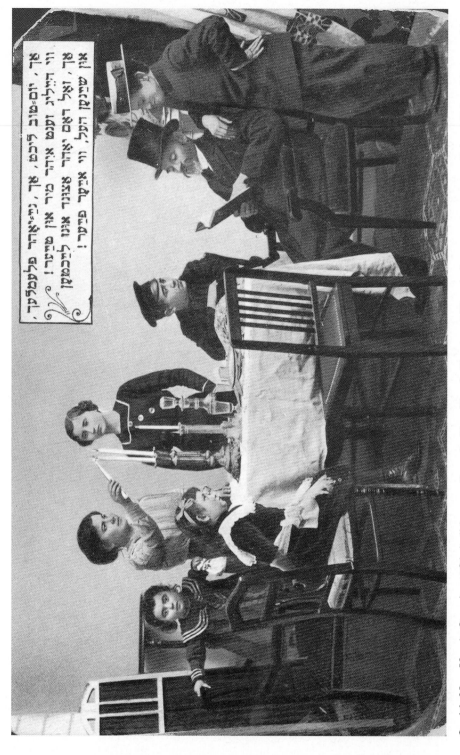

Jewish New Year's Greeting: 'Oh holiday candles, oh, New Year's Flames, / How holy are you to me and dear!/May this year shine on us now / and shine on us brightly, as does your fire!' (Photo courtesy YIVO Institute for Jewish Research, New York, USA)

Jewish New Year's greeting card; Two women blessing candles (Photo courtesy YIVO Institute for Jewish Research, New York, USA)

Bat Mitzvah at the Synagogue of the Reform Community in Arnhem, Holland, 1976. (Photo courtesy Beth Hatefutsoth Photo Archive, Tel Aviv, Israel)

does not apply) does not constitute a violation of the divine will or of the divinely ordained *telos* because "the way of Torah is one thing and the way of completion is another matter entirely."

Genetic manipulation involving even the introduction of a gene of one species into the genotype of an alien species does not constitute a violation of the prohibition against crossbreeding. *Hazon Ish, Kila'im* 2:6, notes that violation of the commandment occurs only in directly causing copulation between two living animals. *Hazon Ish* declares that artificial insemination designed to produce an interspecies is not forbidden just as an intervivos organ transferred from one species to another is not forbidden. It is thus quite obvious that genetic manipulation, since it does not entail a sexual act involving partners who are members of different species, cannot be regarded as forbidden.

A similar principle applies to genetic manipulation of agricultural species. Rabbi Shlomo Zalman Auerbach, *Minhat Shlomoh*, II, no. 97, sec. 27, declares that pollination of one species with pollen of another species does not result in a fruit that would be halakhically classified as a hybrid. Thus, although Rabbi Auerbach affirms that the fruit of an *etrog* tree produced as the result of grafting of a lemon branch may not be used on *Sukkot* for purposes of fulfilling the *mitzvah* of the four species, nevertheless he regards pollination as an entirely different matter. Accordingly, rules Rabbi Auerbach, if an *etrog* is pollinated with the pollen of a lemon tree, the resultant fruit is an *etrog* and may be used for fulfilling the *mitzvah*. Rabbi Auerbach declares that the prohibition against hybridization of species applies only to the planting or grafting of vegetative material that might independently yield fruit or a seed that might germinate independently. Pollen can never grow into fruit; hence, for purposes of Halakhah, introduction of foreign pollen does not affect a species' identity. Again, it is quite obvious that such pollination conducted artificially by humans is not prohibited. Similarly, it follows that introduction of a gene of a foreign species is not forbidden as a form of hybridization since an iso-

lated gene can never develop into a tree or into a plant.

Notes
[1] See Abraham ibn Ezra, *Commentary on the Bible*, Lev. 19:19 and Rabbi Judah Leib Krinsky, *Karnei Or, loc. cit.* See also Rabbi Abraham Chill, *The Mitzvot: The Commandments and their Rationale* (Jerusalem, 1974), p. 236.
[2] See the supercommentary to ibn Ezra of Rabbi Shlomoh Zalman Netter, Lev. 19:19, published in the Horeb edition of the Pentateuch (Jerusalem, London, New York, 5711). A similar interpretation was earlier advanced by *Ohel Yosef* and *Mekor Hayyim* in their respective works on ibn Ezra published in *Margaliyot Torah* (Stanislaw, 5687).
Mekor Hayyim understands ibn Ezra's comments regarding interbreeding of animal species in a like manner. However, these scholars' understanding of the passage in question is less than compelling. Cf., Rabbi Abraham Chill, *The Mitzvot*, p. 236.
[3] See Rabbi Samson Raphael Hirsch, *The Nineteen Letters of Ben Uziel*, Eleventh Letter: *idem, Horeb*, sec. 327.
[4] Rambam, *Guide for the Perplexed*, Book III, chap. 37, regards the *hukkim* as prohibitions designed to deter idolatrous conduct. The actions in question, he asserts, were cultic practices associated with pagan worship and sacrifice. According to Rambam's understanding of these commandments, there is no hint of a negative attitude with regard to intervention by humans in the natural order.
[5] Cf., Rabbi Joseph B. Soloveichik, "Confrontation," in *Tradition*, vol. VI, no. 2 (Spring-Summer, 1964), p. 20.
[6] It is indeed the case that one finds occasional comments in Rabbinic writings representing those prohibitions in phraseology that is general and unqualified. See, for example, the sources cited *supra*, note 2. Nevertheless, it seems to this writer that those comments must be understood in the manner herein indicated.

J. DAVID BLEICH

GOD, IMAGE OF: Gen. 1:26, 1:27, and 9:6 all state that humankind was made or created *beselem 'elohim*,[1] usually translated "in the image of God." Gen. 5:1 additionally asserts that humankind was made *bidmut 'elohim*, "in the likeness of God." The four texts as rendered in the so-called Authorized Version or King James Version (hereinafter KJV) of the Bible read as follows:

1) And God said: Let us make man in our image, after our likeness, and let them have dominion over the fish of the sea. . . . (Gen. 1:26)

2) So God created man in his own image, in the image of God created he him; male and female created he them. (Gen. 1:27)

3) This is the book of the generations of Adam. In the day that God created man, in the likeness of God made he him. (Gen. 5:1)

4) Whoso sheddeth man's blood, by man shall his blood be shed: for in the image of God made he man. (Gen. 9:6)

Since the time of Philo Judaeus of Alexandria in Egypt in the first century C.E., it has been widely held that only the human intellect is "in the image of God." Other Judaic voices, unafraid of anthropomorphism—ascribing human features to God—suggested that it is precisely the physical form of humans that might be compared to God. For example, a passage that appears twice in Gen. Rabbah responds to the obvious question of how it is possible that humans could be "in the image of God" when, in fact, people look so much like monkeys: "Four matters were changed in the time of Enosh: The mountains became rocks. The dead began to feel [worms]. People's faces became like those of apes. People became vulnerable to demons."[2]

Gen. 4:26b, "At that time it was begun [huhal] to call upon the name of the Lord," can also be interpreted, "At that time calling upon the divine name was profaned." The latter understanding of the text is utilized in Rabbinic literature to account for the origin of polytheism. Replacing human beings' original God-like faces with ape-like faces would be the appropriate punishment for humans' having treated animate and inanimate objects of God's creation as though they were gods. Nevertheless, the dominant view in both Gen. 1-9 and in Rabbinic literature[3] is that humankind continues to be "in the image/likeness of God." This idea is emphasized by Gen. 5:1-3, here quoted in the New Revised Standard Version [hereinafter NRSV]:

This is the list of the descendants of Adam. When God created humankind, he made them in the likeness of God. Male and female he created them, and he blessed them and named them "Humankind" when they were created. When Adam had lived one hundred thirty years, he became the father of a son in his likeness, according to his image and named him Seth.

The clear and obvious meaning of the latter text is that whatever is implied by the assertion in Gen. 1:27 that humankind had been created "in the image of God," the feature of humanity thus referred to was not lost with the expulsion from paradise but passed on by Adam to Seth.[4] Moreover, Gen. 9:6 asserts that this very same characteristic of humankind was inherited by the descendants of Noah.

It is commonly acknowledged that the basic meaning of both of the Hebrew nouns *selem* and *demut* is "statue," whether of a person, god, or any other entity.[5] This fact is highlighted by the ninth century B.C.E. bilingual inscription in Aramaic and Akkadian on the statue of Hadad-Ishi from Tell Fekheriyeh.[6] Line 1 of the inscription reads: "The statue, which represents Hadad-Ishi, which he [Hadad-Ishi] placed before the deity Hadad who belongs to Sikan [place name]." This line reflects the idea that in the same way that a statue of a god is able to represent that god, the statue of a person can take the place of that person. Therefore, a ruler who is unable to make a personal visit to the temple of a particular god or goddess can place a statue of himself or herself in that temple.[7] This practice can, of course, be compared to the modern Jewish custom according to which a mourner, unable to attend synagogue daily to recite the *kaddish* for a departed relative, may send a representative to recite the prayer in her or his stead for the prescribed period of time, be it eleven months for a parent or thirty days for a sibling, child, or spouse.

Just as the Aramaic word *demuta*, "likeness," appears in line 1 of the Tell Fekheriyeh inscription in the meaning "statue," so does the word *salma* "image" appears in line 22 with the same meaning. There we read, "The statue, which represents Hadad-Ishi, King of Guzana and of Sikan and of Zaran." Line 26 of the inscription again employs the word *demuta* to mean statue when it states, "He [Hadad-Ishi] made this statue better than (the statue) that preceded this (one)." In line 27 of the Aramaic text, *salmeh sam* means, "He [Hadad-Ishi] placed a statue of himself." The synonymity of the two Aramaic terms *salma* and *demuta* is further demonstrated by the Akkadian version of the inscription on the front of the statue. This Akkadian version employs the single noun *salmu* meaning "statue" as the counterpart of both the Aramaic words *salma* and *demuta* without distinction. Consequently, the inscription intimates that it is foolish to seek a distinction between Heb./Aram. *selem*, "image," and Heb./Aram. *demut*, "likeness" in Gen. 1-9.[8] The inscription makes it very likely that the literal meaning of *selem* and *demut* in chaps. 1 and 9 of Genesis is "statue." Moreover, the inscription strongly suggests that "in the likeness of God made he him" (Gen. 5:1) and "in the image of God made he man" (Gen. 9:6) are synonymous.

Jeffrey H. Tigay already called attention to some of the reflections in Rabbinic literature of an awareness that the phrases *selem 'elohim* and *demut 'elohim* in Gen. 1-9 refer to God's having a physical form and that the physical form of humans resembles that of God.[9] Among the most famous of these texts is the following narrative found in Lev. Rabbah 34:3:

> When Hillel the Elder would take leave of his disciples, he would walk along. His disciples said to him, "Master, where are you going?" He would say to them, "To carry out a religious duty." They said to him, "And what is the religious duty that Hillel is going to do?" He said to them, "To take a bath in the bathhouse." They said to him, "And is this a religious duty?" He said to them, "Yes. Now if as to the king's statues, which they set up in their theatres and circuses, someone is appointed to scour and wash [the icons], and people pay him a wage on that account, and not only so, but he is exalted with the great men of the realm, we, who are created in the image, in the likeness, as it is written, 'For in the image of God he made man [Gen. 9:6], all the more so [is it a religious duty to wash ourselves]!'"[10]

The non-metaphoric understanding of "image of God" in Gen. 1-9 is likewise reflected in the following narrative contained in Gen. Rabbah 8:10:1:

> Said R. Hoshayya, "When the Holy One blessed be he, came to create the first man, the ministering angels mistook him [for God, since man was in God's image] and wanted to say before him, 'Holy [holy, holy is the Lord of hosts]' (Isa. 6:3). To what may the matter be compared? To the case of a king and a governor who were set in a chariot, and the provincials wanted to greet the king, 'Sovereign!' But they did not know which one of them was which. What did the king do? He turned the governor out and put him away from the chariot, so that people would know who was king. So too when the Holy One, blessed be he, created the first man, the angels mistook him [for God]. What did the Holy One, blessed be he, do? He put him to sleep, so everyone knew that he was a mere man. That is in line with the following verse of Scripture: 'Cease you from man, in whose nostrils is a breath, for how little is he to be accounted'" (Isa. 2:22).[11]

Neusner concludes, "Man—Adam—is in God's image, interpreted in a physical way, so the angels did not know man from God. Only the fact that man sleeps distinguishes him from God."[12]

Tigay, on the other hand, immediately moves on from his observation that indeed the non-metaphoric interpretation of "image/likeness of God" in Genesis is reflected in Rabbinic literature to his admirable attempt to prove that in the Akkadian usage of the expression *salmu* there is a firm philological basis for the contention of medieval Jewish philosophers and modern biblical exegetes that biblical Heb. *selem 'elohim*, "image of God," is a metaphor for "intellect."[13]

The following are five of the Akkadian texts Tigay quotes in order to demonstrate that, in fact, the interpretation of the expression "image of God" in Gen. 1-9 as a metaphor is not necessarily eisegetical, since such a usage is amply attested in texts from ancient Mesopotamia:

> The father of my lord the king is the image of Bel.[14]
> My lord the king is the image of Bel.[15]
> The king, lord of the lands is the image of the god Shamash.[16]
> The exorcist is the image of the god Marduk.[17]
> He [King Tikulti-Ninurta] is the image of the eternal Enlil, who hears what people say (which is) the counsel of the world.[18]

The tendency to prefer the metaphorical interpretation of "image of God" in the

Book of Genesis stems from the fact that, for nearly one millennium, Jews have accepted the Aristotelian philosophy that held that any entity that has a body is less perfect than that which has only form.[19] For both Aristotle and Maimonides, the "form" means the "abstract idea," which may or may be not embodied in matter. Materiality or form is a source of vulnerability and imperfection.[20] Ultimately, this philosophical theory means that if the deity is devoid of matter, it is impossible to influence God, even psychologically. Indeed, Aristotle's philosophy holds that God is the "unmoved mover." On the other hand, as Abraham Joshua Heschel demonstrated, the God of Israel described in the Bible and in Rabbinic literature is not the "unmoved mover" but rather the "most moved mover."[21] It follows that whoever wishes to understand the Bible's theological messages would do well to put aside Aristotle's basic ideas about God and instead to look seriously and closely at the text of Genesis as regards the first human who was fashioned "in the image/likeness of God." We have no reason whatsoever to believe that Scripture employs a metaphor unless Scripture employs the standard syntactical indicators of metaphor.

Close examination of the Assyrian texts that Tigay cites to support his claim that in the ancient Near East the phrase "image of god/God" served as a metaphor for wisdom reveals an essential difference between the syntax of those Assyrian texts and that of the five texts from Gen. 1-9 cited above. In an Assyrian or biblical Hebrew metaphor, either (1) the object of comparison is the subject of a nominal sentence, while the object to which it is compared is the predicate of that same nominal sentence; or (2) the object of comparison is the predicate of the nominal sentence, while the object to which it is compared is the subject. Typical biblical examples of the first structure, in which the object of comparison is the subject of a nominal sentence, are the following:

> Your eyes are doves [NRSV] (Song of Songs 1:15)
> I am the rose of Sharon, and the lily of the valleys [KJV] (Song of Songs 2:1)

Typical biblical examples of the second structure, in which the object of comparison is the predicate of the nominal sentence, are the following texts:

> A bundle of myrrh is my wellbeloved unto me [KJV] (Song of Songs 1:13)
> A cluster of henna blossoms is my beloved to me [cf., NRSV] (Song of Songs 1:14)
> A garden locked is my sister [NRSV] (Song of Songs 4:12).

In each of these five quotations and wherever Hebrew Scripture employs a metaphor there is, of course, no prepositional phrase including a comparative particle, which would qualify the comparison as a *simile*, but only a nominal sentence. In contrast to this syntactical structure characterizing both the biblical Song of Songs and the Assyrian texts cited by Tigay, in which various persons are compared to the image of one or another deity, there is not one metaphorical structure in our quotations from Gen. 1-9. In none of the latter passages is there a nominal sentence that states that the human is *selem/demut 'elohim*, "image or likeness of God." Instead, in three places, Genesis states that the first human has been fashioned *beselem 'elohim*, and in one place it states that the first human was created *bidmut 'elohim*.

Since, as we saw, the fundamental meaning of the word *selem* is "statue." it follows that *selem 'elohim* means "statue of God." However, such a "statue" of God simply does not exist in the various ancient Israelite religions reflected in 1) biblical law (Exod. 20-24; Lev. 18-27; Deut. 11-26); 2), the rules for temple building and sacrificial worship (Exod. 25-32; 35-40; Lev. 1-17; Num. 28-29); 3) biblical Wisdom Literature (Prov.; Job; Ecclesiastes); or even 4) biblical narrative, with the obvious exceptions of those stories describing the actions of those "who do not do what is proper in the eyes of the Lord." Such narratives include the story of the golden calf in Exod. 32; the account of the divine image fashioned by Micah (Judg. 17); the story of the Danites in Judg. 18; or the account of the sons of Jacob being ordered to "put away" the "foreign gods" found in their possession (Gen. 35:1-2).

It is explicitly stated in Gen. 1:26 that

God planned to make the first person *kid-mutenu*, meaning "like a statue of God."[22] Such being the case, when we read in each of the four passages quoted above from Genesis that the original human was made, or should have been made, *in the selem* or *in the demut* of God, the question remains as to the meaning of the prefixed preposition, *be*. Obviously, in the verses under consideration here, the preposition *be* does not appear in its primary meaning, which is "in" or "within."[23] The less well attested meaning "despite" will not fit here either.[24] It is most reasonable to suggest that in the only four instances in the entire Hebrew Bible in which the text treats favorably a statue of God, employing *selem 'elohim* or *demut 'elohim* to designate "a statue of the God of Israel," the prefixed preposition *be* must represent the so-called *beth pretii*, which denotes "in place of."[25] The message was quite clear, but Aristotle's philosophy managed to cast into the shadow the statement in Gen. 1-9, according to which the first human being and all that creature's descendants—both female and male—were the replacement or the substitute for an image/statue of God. What is stated in the creation narrative in Gen. 1:1-2:4a and, again, in the flood narrative is that the original "Adam"—both male and female—was the substitute for the sacred statue that represents a myriad of other gods in the various religions of the ancient Near East and elsewhere. The message is that each and every human being, by virtue of being a person, is a sacred object, an entity any deliberate physical or psychological damage to whom represents sacrilege. Gen. 9:5-6 forbids human beings to shed each other's blood because humans have been created *beselem 'elohim*, i.e., as substitutes for a statue of God placed in a temple. In other words, each and every human being is, according to Gen. 1-9, the most sacred ritual object in the religion of Israel. It follows that injury to a person is an offense far more serious than the desecration of a Torah scroll or a temple. The Torah scroll contains the written names of God, while the Temple is God's palace. Human beings, on the other hand, are veritable physical representations of God Himself/Herself. They are, in fact, God's physical representatives on earth.

Tragically, many of the religions that consider the Bible—and with it Genesis, and most especially the so-called Priestly creation narrative in Gen. 1:1-2:4a—one of their highest sources of religious inspiration did their very best to ignore the literal reading of the text. Significantly, one of the questions that is often asked in all branches of modern Judaism is, "What possible value is there in philological/historical exegesis of Hebrew Scripture for Judaism the religion as against idle curiosity?" A direct answer to this question is to be found with respect to Gen. 1-9. We have seen that the narrative of Gen. 1-9 in its most direct and literal meaning teaches the sublime idea that the human being is a sacred entity. Humans must respect themselves and everyone else who shares the divine image without regard to differences in gender, race, national or religious origin, age, academic degree, socio-economic status or any other distinguishing factors.

It is vital to note that the application of the most basic rules of biblical philology—attention to the lexicon, the grammar and syntax of Biblical Hebrew and Aramaic, and the cultural context of ancient Israel—makes possible the recovery of the original and widely unknown meaning of one of the most frequently quoted texts in Hebrew Scripture. It is equally worth noting that the original philological meaning of Gen. 1:27 and its theological implications are clearly spelled out in Rabbinic midrash, a deep well of philologically sound ancient exegetical traditions, which, mostly because of outmoded theological biases, is not sufficiently and properly tapped in contemporary biblical exegesis.

Bibliography

Hurowitz, Victor (Avigdor), "Did King Solomon Violate the Second Commandment?" in *Bible Review* 10 (1994), pp. 24-33, 57.

Kadushin, Max, *The Rabbinic Mind* (3d ed., New York, 1972).

Luttikhuizen, Gerard P., ed., *The Creation of Man and Woman: Interpretations of the Biblical Narratives in Jewish and Christian Traditions* (Leiden, 2000), pp. 62-75.

Notes

[1] The initial consonant of the Hebrew word *selem* and its cognates in Aramaic and Akkadian corresponds to the letter *sade* (or *tsade*) in the word *masa*, "unleavened bread," pronounced *ts* in modern Hebrew. In biblical and ancient Near Eastern studies, this consonant is commonly represented by s with a sublinear dot. For simplicity, this consonant is represented throughout this entry by s.

[2] Gen. Rabbah 23:6. The translation is taken from Jacob Neusner, *Genesis Rabbah: The Judaic Commentary to the Book of Genesis* (Atlanta, 1985), vol. 1, pp. 259-260; the text appears verbatim also in Gen. Rabbah 24:6.

[3] See Jacob Neusner, *The Theology of the Oral Torah* (Montreal and Kingston, 1999), pp. 365-366.

[4] Contrast Jeffrey H. Tigay, "'He Begot a Son in His Likeness after His Image' (Genesis 5:3)," in Mordecai Cogan, Barry L. Eichler, and Jeffrey H. Tigay, eds., *Tehillah Le-Moshe: Biblical and Other Studies in Honor of Moshe Greenberg* (Winona Lake, 1997), pp. 139-147.

[5] For the Hebrew word *slm*, see Francis Brown, S.R. Driver, and Charles A. Briggs, *A Hebrew and English Lexicon of the Old Testament* (Oxford, 1952) [hereinafter *BDB*], pp. 853-854; as for the Aramaic word *slm* see *BDB*, p. 1109; for Akkadian *salmu*, see A.L. Oppenheim, ed., *The Assyrian Dictionary of the University of Chicago* [hereinafter *CAD*], vol. 16 (Chicago and Glückstadt, 1962), pp. 78-85. For the Hebrew word *demut*, see *BDB*, p. 198a. See also Jeffrey H. Tigay, "The Image of God and the Flood: Some New Developments," in Alexander M. Shapiro and Burton I. Cohen, eds., *Studies in Jewish Education and Judaica in Honor of Louis Newman* (New York, 1984), pp. 170 and 178, n. 2.

[6] Tigay, "The Image," p. 170; regarding the inscription, see Ali Abu-Assaf, Pierre Bordreuil, and Alan R. Millard, *La Statue de Tell Fekherye et son Inscription bilingue assyro-araméenne* (Paris, 1982); Jonas Greenfield and Aaron Shaffer, "Notes on the Akkadian-Aramaic Bilingual Statue from Tell Fekheryeh," in *Iraq* 45 (1983), pp. 109-116; Frank Moore Cross, Jr., "Paleography and the Date of the Tell Fahariyeh Bilingual Inscription," in Z. Zevit, S. Gitin and M. Sokoloff, eds., *Solving Riddles and Untying Knots: Biblical, Epigraphic and Semitic Studies in Honor of Jonas C. Greenfield* (Winona Lake, 1995), pp. 393-409.

[7] *CAD*, vol. 16, p. 81; W. von Soden, *The Ancient Orient*, translated by D.G. Schley (Grand Rapids, 1994), pp. 189-190.

[8] Contrast W. Randall Garr, "'Image' and 'Likeness' in the Inscription from Tell Fakharieyh," in *Israel Exploration Journal* 50 (2000), pp. 227-234.

[9] See Tigay, "The Image," p. 170, and the studies referred to there, p. 178, n. 5.

[10] The translation is taken from Jacob Neusner, *Judaism and Scripture: The Evidence of Leviticus Rabbah* (Chicago and London, 1986), p. 558.

[11] The translation is taken from Neusner, *Theology of the Oral Torah*, p. 366.

[12] Ibid., p. 366.

[13] Tigay, "The Image," pp. 171-174; similarly, E.M. Curtis "Image of God," in *Anchor Bible Dictionary* (New York, 1992), vol. 3, pp. 389-391; Paul E. Dion, "Resemblance et image de Dieu," in H. Cazelles and A. Feuillet, eds., *Dictionnaire de la Bible, Suppl.* tome 10, fasc. 55 (Paris, 1981), pp. 365-403; G.J. Wenham, *Genesis 1-15*, Word Biblical Commentary, Vol. 1 (Waco, 1987), pp. 29-32; C. Westermann, *Genesis 1-11: A Continental Commentary*, translated by John J. Scullion (Minneapolis, 1984), pp. 142-160.

[14] Robert Francis Harper, *Assyrian and Babylonian Letters* (14 vols.; Chicago, 1892-1914) #6, line 18; for the latest edition, see now Simo Parpola, *Letters from Assyrian and Babylonian Scholars*, State Archives of Assyria, vol. X (Helsinki, 1993), #228.

[15] Harper #6, line 19.

[16] Harper #5, r. 4-5; see now Parpola #196.

[17] G. Meier, "Die zweite Tafel der Serie bit meseri," in *Archiv für Orientforschung* 14 (1941-1944), p. 150, line 226; see Tigay, "The Image," pp. 172, 179, n. 10.

[18] W.G. Lambert, "Three Unpublished Fragments of the Tukulti-Ninurta Epic," in *Archiv für Orientforschung* 18 (1957-58), p. 50, line 18; see Peter Machinist, "Literature as Politics; The Tukulti-Ninurta Epic and the Bible," in *Catholic Biblical Quarterly* 38 (1976), p. 466.

[19] See Abraham Joshua Heschel, *The Prophets* (New York, 1971), vol. 2, pp. 27-47; and also Aristotle, *De Generatione*, 335b, 29-30; 324b, 18; Maimonides, *Guide to the Perplexed*, Part I, chapters 29; 54-59.

[20] Heschel, *The Prophets*, vol. 2, pp. 27-58.

[21] See Aristotle, Metaphysics, Book XII; cf., Heschel, *The Prophets*, vol. 2, pp. 14, 40-42.

[22] Gen. 1:26. This is the only instance among the four biblical passages that employs a simile. As regards Gen. 5:3, there are some Hebrew versions that read *wayoled bidmuto kesalmo*, "He begat in his own likeness like an image of himself," while other versions read *wayoled kidmuto besalmo*, "He begat like his likeness in an image of himself."

[23] The most common meaning of the prefixed preposition *bet* is "within;" see *BDB*, pp. 88-89.

[24] See *BDB*, p. 90; and Deut. 1:32; Isa. 47:9; Ps. 27:3.

[25] On this meaning of the prefixed preposition *be* in biblical Hebrew, see *BDB*, p. 90; Gen. 23:9; 30:16; Josh. 6:26; 1 Kgs. 2:23.

MAYER I. GRUBER

GREECE, PRACTICE OF JUDAISM IN:
This article is divided chronologically into
the Hellenistic, Byzantine, Ottoman, and
modern periods. In the ancient and medieval
periods, the *oekumene* of the Hellenes was an
expanding concept that included those areas
where Greek was the predominant language.
That defining principle continues to be the
basis for the nationalism of the modern
Greek state since its inception in the 1830s.
Hence, any discussion of the Jewish communities in "Greece" and their religious
practices should follow the expanding and
contracting boundary between the world of
the Hellenophones and the world of the
Barbarians. For the purposes of the present
inquiry, however, we shall focus our attention on the less studied lands surrounding
the Aegean, particularly mainland and insu-
lar Greece. The paucity of evidence neces-
sitates a caveat regarding any generalization.
Therefore the following entry is organized
around the scattered extant evidence.

While the Bible knows of Greece (most
likely Anatolian Ionia = Yavan) and its inhabitants as early as Genesis, it only acknowledges Jews living in the "islands of the sea"
in the latter prophets. These islands and
other settlements are identified in the Greek
translation of Ezekiel (second century B.C.E.).
We have no data (excluding the handful of
slave manumissions) on the origins, identity, or practices of these Jews, save for the
testimony of Josephus Flavius (who married
a Cretan Jew) that the early Seleucid kings
settled military colonies of Jews in Anatolia.
One may speculate that the divine name
IAO SABAOTH may have some connection with such origins, although the process
of the latter's syncretistic development
throughout the eastern Mediterranean is not
recoverable to date.

Hellenistic Period: It is from the Helle-
nized milieu that Greek-speaking Jews drew
their outward identity. One of the major
principles of the diaspora (a Greek term reflecting normal dispersion and colonization,
as opposed to the Hebrew "galut," meaning
exile) is the dominating influence of the
majority population on the Jews in its midst.
The tension between accommodation to
local culture and rejection or adjustment of
that which is forbidden by Jewish sources

is the central question of the study of Judaism in its diaspora as well as in its homeland.
Polytheistic cultures, originally divided by
linguistic differences, more easily melded in
a syncretism that is evident already from
the mid-fifth century B.C.E. The town of
Selinous in southwest Sicily, for example,
was subject to Carthage, and a newly discovered Greek lead tablet shows an easy
integration of Punic and Hellenic religious
practice and nomenclature, e.g., Zeus Meili-
chios.[1] Judaism in the period of the monarchy was monotheistic, however complex its
manifestation among Israelites and Judeans,
and so its accommodation had religious and
cultural limits.[2]

This tension, shifting in its emphases according to the changing patterns and vicissitudes of historical development, is constant
in the struggle of Jews to maintain their
own identity, whether in the "sweet servi-
tude" of tolerating empires or the harsh
realities of competing ideologies or nationalistic cultures. So, for example, the Tannaim
prohibited the mixing of meat and milk at
the same meal and of course discovered the
apt biblical proof text (e.g., Exod. 23:19;
B. Hul. 115b; Mekhilta d'Rabbi Ishmael,
Kaspa, 5). Yet such a prohibition is clearly
later than the biblical text—whatever the
meaning of the proof text for its own time—
and can only be understood by the ubiquity
of the mixed meat/milk dishes prevalent in
Greek society. Against the influence of such
social intercourse, the Tannaim literally forbade the possibility of Jews and Greeks eating together. One wonders to what extent
the pre-Tannaitic Aegean Jews were affected
by such a ruling, since a contrary menu is
supported by Abraham's hospitality (Gen.
18:8) to the messengers heralding Sarah's
miraculous pregnancy. Philo, who would
have been read by Greek-speaking Jews
(although evidence to that effect in Greece
is lacking), argues the literal meaning of the
text and so would allow the cooking of a
kid in any other animal's milk.[3]

The well-known passage by Philo (*Legatio ad
Gaium*, 281-2) about the extent of the Aegean
diaspora, primarily in southern Greece, only
suggests well-integrated communities thor-
oughly at home in a Greek-speaking milieu.[4]
We learn more about the accommodation

of Aegean Jews from another first-century source: the letters of Saul/Paul of Tarsus and the record of his travels in the Acts of the Apostles. If Paul indeed came from the southern Anatolian Tarsus, then he was familiar with the Greek tradition of a dieing and resurrecting god (Dionysios) and the great mother goddess of grain (Ceres). When he developed the former along with his rejection of the ritual law (cf., Deut. 30:6; 1 Cor. 10:25), he found sympathetic ears among some Jews and among others within the orbit of Jewish ethical influence (so called God-Fearers). His radical challenge to the table laws of Moses and traditions of ritual purity engendered a hostile response in the synagogues he visited in western Anatolia and Greece (i.e., Thrace, Macedonia, Attika, Peloponnesos), if we can accept as accurate the reports in Acts and Paul's letters. Those in Corinth, whom he baptized, presumably Jews, bore Greek and Latin names, a hint at the accommodation in the Greek-speaking diaspora and the laxity that developed from it.

Archaeological evidence: We are on safer ground when we look at the archaeological remains of Aegean synagogues for evidence of religious practices.[5] The siting of synagogues near water has been traditionally explained as necessitated by the tradition of the mikvah and its need for "living water." A later source, the Italian Tosaphist Isaiah of Trani (end twelfth century) notes that Greek Jews (i.e., Romaniotes from their still valid Roman citizenship), both male and female, used the sea for ritual bathing and complains that the women substituted the bathhouse for the mikvah (Teshuvot HaRID, #62). Isaiah also emphasizes in connection with other customs that they still followed Palestinian customs. Yet it was inconvenient for the synagogue Jews of Athens and cities further inland to use the sea, and so some sort of accommodation had to be made. The Greek baths were an easy alternative. The discovery of a first-century synagogue in Salonika at the northern edge of Plateia Eleutheria—some fifty meters from the present sea—supports the earlier theory, yet the impressive Samaritan synagogue (fifth century?) in the Roman agora was certainly dependent on the sophisticated water pipes that permeate that public area. On the other

hand, the early synagogues (late second or early first century B.C.E.) on the island of Delos contain cisterns that may have been used as a mikvah.

A fragment from the synagogue in the Athens agora attests to a ritual iconography that includes the lulav and menorah (lacking base). A stone plinth from Corinth dated to the third century C.E. is decorated with three menorahs (open rectangular base), two lulavs, and an ethrog on one side. A late tenth/eleventh-century gravestone from Corinth depicts an early representation of the Temple menorah with its more accurate tripod base.[6] The synagogue on Delos has extant an elaborate seat or throne called by scholars the "Throne of Moses" and was possibly used by the teacher, preacher, or head of the community or for some particular rituals (compare the "Seat of Elijah," below). Such iconography, though sparse, is a clear emphasis on the ritual practices celebrating the Torah Judaism that commemorates the Jerusalem Temples and characterizes the Jewish experience.

On the other hand, Greek Jewry was Greek-speaking, and its Torah was in Greek, as was nearly all of the extant Jewish literature (preserved by the Greek Church) imported from Egypt, the center of a creative project to translate a Hebrew based Jewish culture into a Greek based Jewish culture. Philo is the most important witness to this successful attempt to recast biblical Judaism in a Middle Platonic mold. But there were others, such as the poet Ezechielos with his Passover play and the spate of Jewish historians—whether they are read as apologists or polemicists vis-à-vis their Hellenistic environment (as preserved in Eusebius, *Praeparatio Evangelica*, early fourth century). The lack of Jewish writing from the Aegean world is conspicuous in its silence save for the career of Paul of Tarsus and John of Patmos. On Delos and its neighboring island of Reneia, where the graveyard was sited, several important inscriptions were found. Two from the second century B.C.E. invoke "The God of the spirits and of all flesh" to avenge the murder of two maidens, Heraklea and Martina, on the day "when all are engaged in fast and supplication." Such inscriptions attest to the antiquity of the Jewish custom of reciting memorial prayers for the dead in Greece. Other inscriptions identify the Jewish god as "Theos Hypsistos," the "Highest God" or just "Hypsistos," which translate the ubiquitous biblical and Rabbinic "El Elyon." The use of IAO as a Greek transliteration of YHO, already a biblical theophoric prefix or suffix that appeared throughout the Hellenic world, soon became part of the syncretistic world of magic among the polytheists along with its cognates IAO SABAOTH, etc. It is reflective of the Greek inability to aspirate and, thus, to this day, Greek Jews cannot articulate the "heh" or "ḥet." In talmudic times, Greek Jews in Palestina were prohibited from public reading of the Torah due to this defect. One might wonder how Aegean Jews read 1 and 2 Maccabees, especially the distinction between Hellenism (*hellenismos*) and Judaism (*ioudaismos*), the two neologisms introduced by the author of 1 Maccabees to contrast Torah Jews to syncretizing Sadducees. It must have seemed strange to the accommodating Hellenophones of the Aegean to read that Hellenists were Jews so assimilated to Greek society as to constitute a mortal danger to Jews true to the Torah of Moses. This tension between Hellenophones and Hebraiophones would resurface periodically in the Balkans and occasionally result in government intervention.

The lack of identifiable texts to describe Jewish practices in Greece forces us to rely—and cautiously—upon the complexity of a handful of archaeological remains. These show a variety of Judaisms in Greece during the late antique period, ranging from syncretistic magical cults to Jewish Christians, to highly sophisticated Samaritan communities with branches in Salonika and Athens and a presence on Delos. Nor should this variety ignore the strong Jewish identity that permeated the synagogues that rejected Paul's radical reinterpretation of the covenant. A Samaritan synagogue inscription perhaps from fifth century Salonika attests to a wealthy and well-established community.[7] Samaritan sophists also taught in Athens. In Corinth, the Cave of Lamps has given up several inscriptions with references to angels, while a number of lead magic seals with Judaized references (e.g., IAO) have

survived from a number of cities, e.g., Beroea (Veria) in Macedonia, Amphipolis in Thrace, Phthiotis in Thessaly. In Corinth, where Paul founded a gentile church, a marble fragment reading (restored) "synagogue of the Hebrews" raises questions about the community that worshipped in that building. The inscription is rather unsophisticated (contrary to the monumental inscriptions of public buildings) and may possibly have served either a poor segment of the Jewish community or a synagogue for their slaves (rather unlikely). Another possibility is that it may represent a working class Judeo-Christian synagogue whose members called themselves Hebrew rather than (the modern expected designation) Judaeans. A general rule we might follow is to assume a nascent Christian community in proximity to an existing Jewish community during the first four (possibly six) centuries century C.E. in Greece. The necessity to safeguard the physical body and the property inheritance of converts to Christianity in Christian Roman law codes supports such a working assumption.

Byzantine Period: The law codes of Theodosius II (401-450) and Justinian I (483-565) give us precious insight into the tensions within Jewish communities over the competition between a Torah based practice (in the Rabbinic sense) and the developing theology of faith in the messiahship and divinity of Jesus of Nazareth, whom Greek gentiles made the object of a new mystery religion.[8] Paul's followers from the fourth century on continued to find occasional recruits within the synagogue, and families were split over the conversion of a child to Christianity. One solution was to disinherit the convert. A series of Roman laws legislated that the convert should not suffer from the decision to join the majority culture that later became the official religion of the empire. The Codex Theodosius (CTh) forbade practicing Jews (primarily males) to marry Christians, to convert their slaves to Judaism, or to have social intercourse with Christians, e.g., go to public baths. Jews were also barred from participation in the political, legal, or military service of the empire, save for the burdensome decurionate that necessitated contributions to local treasuries. This increasing isolation was perhaps a determining factor in the demographic decline of the Jewish population throughout the empire in succeeding centuries (and worldwide until the late seventeenth-eighteenth centuries, which reversed the process).

The Empire, now Christianized, was hard put to destroy the growing interstice between Judaism and Orthodox (Nicaean) Christianity, which rapidly filled with heresies of varying degree (see list and description in Appendix to CTh, ed. Clyde Pharr). Jews did not want to extend to all Judaizers the protection of their status as a *religio licita*, while Christianity eschewed any other interpretation than the mystery of the Nicaean creed and a non-Judaizing practice of it. Dozens of heresies abounded, particularly in calendar matters: what was the proper date to celebrate Easter. Easter is the single most important holy day to Christians—(*He Heorte*—The Holiday) celebrating as it does the miracle of the resurrection of a crucified Jewish teacher identified as both messiah and a manifestation of God and so defining the Truth of Christianity. While the problem of the date of Easter was an internal and integral Christian problem, nevertheless it was intimately tied to the Jewish Passover, during which the crucifixion and resurrection occurred. Justinian tried to bypass the issue by ordering the Jews (i.e., the legally recognized community) to delay their celebration of Passover until after the Orthodox Easter, whose date however had to be calculated according to the Jewish calendar. Such a travesty of religious practice did not last long and was soon abandoned. Ultimately the western church and eastern churches calculated their own formulae for the holiday that even today bracket the traditional date in the Jewish calendar.

More informative is Justinian's edict (Novella 146 (553)) banning the teaching of the *deuterosis*, which should be understood to be the oral tradition in addition to the Mishnah. That ban stemmed from an internal Jewish quarrel over the language to use in the reading of the Torah. (Most likely Greek Jewry followed the Palestinian trienniel cycle of Torah portions with extensive midrashic exposition.) Apparently there had been a migration of Hebrew literate scholars to Constantinople who demanded that the

Torah be read publicly in Hebrew. (This incident, by the way, is the first mention of the Hebrew language in Greece.) The Romaniotes refused to change their practice (as we derive from later sources) of reading the first few verses in Hebrew and the remainder in Greek. That is to say that among Aegean Jewry, Greek replaced Aramaic as the language of interpretation of the Torah. Which particular version in Greek was used however (Septuagint, Aquila, or some other) is unknown and probably varied among communities; Origen's Hexateuch allows for a variety of known and unknown alternatives. The Romaniotes turned to the Emperor Justinian in his capacity as Pontifex Maximus (i.e., Most High Priest) to help them retain their Hellenism. Justinian ordered that they could read the Torah in any vernacular they chose, although he advocated the Septuagint now encoded with Christian interpretation. Justinian further identified as blasphemy any attempt to deny the resurrection or the last judgment or the existence of angels, the latter prevalent in the popular Judaism and Christianity of the empire.

Jews responded to this interference in their religion (the emperor ominously called it a "*superstitio*"—a prelude to possible outlawing as he did in the case of the rebellious Samaritans) by increasing the composition and use of the piyyut (from the Greek *poesis*) to versify the oral law. In this way they introduced the essentials of their Judaism into the still legal synagogue. The tradition of composing piyyutim continued in Greece through the nineteenth century. How this ban on *deuterosis* affected Jewish scholarship in Greece is unclear. The tradition of Jewish scholars migrating from Byzantium to Khazaria during the persecutions and forced baptisms of Basil I (ninth century; recorded for southern Italy in *Meggilat Ahimaaz*) and Romanos Lekapenos (tenth century) indicates that Judaism survived such attacks.[9] The revival of Hebrew and Jewish scholarship in southern Italy during the ninth-eleventh centuries does not however prove a similar phenomenon in Greece proper. Nevertheless Greek students are recorded in the Babylonian academies and in the West. A Hebrew epitaph in rhymed prose from

Corinth (late tenth or mid-eleventh century) coupled with a bilingual text listing technical terms from the talmudic tractate Kilayim suggest an indigenous survival of scholarship in Greece. Kilayim is important for the manufacture and trade of textiles that the Jews had to control in order to conform with biblical rules for kashrut. Zidkiyahu HaRofe (thirteenth century) alludes to an interesting local accommodation that harks back to a Thracian custom recorded by Herodotos, namely that Romaniote Jews permitted the mixing of wool and flax. Other Mediterranean Jewries considered such a practice a violation of the biblical prohibition of mixing animal and vegetable material in the same garment.

Romaniotes and Karaites: A unique book from the end of the eleventh century indicates the depth of scholarship preserved by Greek Jewry. The *Midrash Lekah Tob* of Tobias b. Eliezer of Kastoria is a commentary on the Torah that bears comparison with its contemporary, the *Perush* of Rashi. The rich compendium of sources cited by its modern editor, Solomon Buber, as well as its influence among successive generations of scholars until the modern period identify its value as a contribution to Jewish knowledge. Tobias uses Tannaitic and Amoraic sources as well as sixth-century Byzantine midrashic sources. In Genesis, he has extensive excursuses on the rules of circumcision (sub Isaac) and the *shofar*, which leads him to an explication of the ten days of repentance following the New Year. His citation of his father (*floruit*, mid-eleventh century), whose generation corresponded to the period of destruction of the scholarly communities of Bari and others in Southern Italy, attests longstanding Byzantine tradition. The appearance of two major contemporary commentaries on the Torah (*Lekah Tob* and *Perush Rashi*) similar in methodology attests to the legacy of south Italian (still Byzantine) Jewry and its perpetuation of Palestinian Jewish traditions (customs, scholarship, ideology, the piyyut, synagogue and ritual art, etc.). That legacy would continue to influence Jews in Germanic and Slavic lands for the next millennium.[10]

Later centuries show a continuity of Romaniote scholarship. Benjamin of Tudela throws open a window to the widespread and well-established communities in Greece. Judah al-Harizi praises the scholars and the wines of Thebes, center of the silk industry in Central Greece, already noted by Benjamin in the 1160s. In the fourteenth century Shemarya Ikriti (1275-1355) was a well-known philosopher (*Ha-Mora* and *Amatzyahu*) and commentator on the Bible and the works of Abraham ibn Ezra. He is the first known Greek scholar to translate ancient Greek philosophers from the original; his grandson continued the tradition at the beginning of the fifteenth century in Patras. Shemarya's student Judah ibn Moskoni recorded his visits to a number of scholarly libraries throughout the Aegean region in search of super-commentaries on Abraham ibn Ezra and fragments of *Sefer Yosippon*. He edited an edition of the latter, which was to serve as the basic text for the sixteenth-century printed version.[11]

Paralleling Tobias ben Eliezer is the appearance of Byzantine Karaite scholarship (e.g., Tobias ben Moses of Constantinople), reflecting the transference of Karaite learning (in Arabic) of the Jerusalem academy to a Greek-speaking milieu. Tobias engaged in a serious polemic throughout his *Lekah Tob* against Karaism, an indication of the spread and challenge of the movement in Byzantium. The Byzantine Rabbanite-Karaite polemic would continue through the fifteenth century and only begin to be resolved under the aegis of the adjustment of Greek-speaking Jews to the new Ottoman environment when Rabbanite teachers took Karaite students. East European Karaites continue to the present day to rely on the texts produced in Byzantium: Yehudah Hadassi's polemic against the Rabbanites *Eshkol ha-Kofer*, Aaron ben Yosef ha-Rofe's biblical commentary *Sefer ha-Mivhar*, Aaron ben Elijah's biblical commentary *Keter Torah*, his compendium of Karaite philosophy *'Etz Hayyim* and his code of Karaite law *Gan Eden*; and the fifteenth-century authoritative code of Elijah Bashyachi of Adrianople, *Addereth Eliahu*.[12]

The Karaites of Byzantium abandoned the rabbinical designation of the seventh month (Tishre = September) for the New Year and reverted to the biblical month of

Nisan (March). By following the sighting of the moon, their calendar produced different holiday dates than the Rabbanites; only later would they adjust to an oral tradition as their settlements distanced from Israel. Their ritual for slaughtering was more strict, and their definition of kashrut more complicated. They also eschewed candles on Sabbath eve until the reforms of the Bashyatchi family in the fifteenth century split the Karaite community into two camps over the issue. Practice demanded that every male be prepared each Sabbath to read publicly from the Torah. Byzantine Karaites inserted numerous piyyutim of the golden-voiced Rabbanite poets of Spain into their liturgy. Their philosophical treatises utilized ancient Greek sources, and they continued to castigate Saadia Gaon, their greatest and most effective critic, through the fifteenth century. Their biblical commentaries openly used Rabbinic sources, in particular the Mishnah, which they claimed preceded the Rabbanite heresy. The different calendar occasionally led to public rows between Karaites and Rabbanites over the desecrating of holy days (so Benjamin of Tudela's description of the fence dividing the two groups in the Jewish Quarter of the capital located in Pera).

Byzantine Rabbanite practice followed Palestinian customs, used Palestinian tannaitic sources, developed the Palestinian piyyut, was influenced by contemporary Byzantine magic and superstition—*Meggilat Ahima'az*, albeit from southern Italy, parallels Byzantine hagiography—and followed Mishnaic guidelines in its textile industry with local adjustments. Arranged child marriages also appear in thirteenth-century sources. Theodore Gastor has collected a number of ancient and medieval Greek customs and beliefs that invaded Greek Judaism, and some that became more widespread, e.g., "*sandak*" from the Greek *syntechnos*.[13] The *sandak*, who is the "godfather" at the Ashkenazic *brit milah*, sits in the Seat of Elijah; the latter custom too has been claimed as a Romaniote tradition. Beginning with the Crusades messianic movements manifested themselves in Greece, while from the thirteenth century on messianic and kabbalistic manuscripts proliferated, incorporating

new intellectual developments as quickly as they appeared in Egypt (Rambam) and Spain (Abraham ibn Ezra and *Zohar*). In sum, we have to acknowledge that the cultural dominance of a Greek-speaking Orthodox civilization coupled with the influence of Palestinian traditions produced the seed that flourished in Greece and southern Italy and matured in the Rhineland where it established the basis for later Ashkenazic Judaism. At the same time, Greek Judaism flourished in its ancestral accommodation to the Greek (now Christian) environment and remained au courant with contemporary Jewish life.

The Romaniote rite (*mahzor*), one of the three Balkan area synagogue cycles, is characterized by an ongoing creative tradition of hymnography in Greek and Hebrew. The other two, known as Mahzor Korfu and Mahzor Kaffa (Crimea), are attested from the late Byzantine period. There is little doubt however, that these reflect traditions older than that of the *Seder Amram Gaon*, the earliest extant rite (ninth century) and reflect a combination of Palestinian Pharisaic traditions influenced by the reforms imposed by Emperor Justinian in the sixth century. The model for the synagogue service (and for the Church as well) is based on the Temple cult and is relatively standardized. Local differences however characterize the autonomy of the synagogue, and even within the Greek orbit there were variations dependent on time and place. Jews in the Greek orbit followed the customs of the land of Judah according to Isaiah of Trani, that is to say that the Greek-speaking Jews maintained the ritual traditions of the Palestinian-oriented diaspora.

Ottoman Period: Immigrants to Greece from all periods brought their own practices, and so the multiplicity and variety of synagogue rites proliferated in Greece even before the arrival of the Sephardim in the sixteenth century. The latter maintained into the twentieth century their identity through proliferation of their ancestral synagogue traditions. This immigrant phenomenon, which characterized Ottoman Jewish life, was a continuation of the Byzantine precedent, which reflected ultimately the complexity and autonomy of the Roman Jewish

diaspora. The Balkan rites are characterized by the addition of numerous piyyutim
by local composers.[14] The Karaites added
Sephardic piyyutim already before the expulsions from Spain. After the sixteenth century, the latter begin to appear within the
Romaniote service. The presence of piyyutim in Greek characterizes the Greek diaspora prayer service, e.g., for the New Moon,
as well as readings of biblical passages—
Jonah and Torah portions wherein the
beginning verses are in Hebrew and the
remainder in Greek. The Greek tradition
flourished in the Greek-speaking areas of
the Ottoman Caliphate and survived into
the twentieth century until the Holocaust.[15]

A query posed to Moses Kapsali, the
chief rabbi of Constantinople after the
Ottoman conquest in 1453 and a Romaniote, asked if a certain custom was allowed
the Jews according to halakhah. Kapsali
replied that it was the responsibility of the
questioner to search the entire tradition back
to the Bible in order to find a justification
or prooftext for the custom. Thus Kapsali
responded to the multi-cultural Jewish traditions of late Byzantine Jewry and prepared
the way for subsequent Ottoman Jewry to
adjust to the flood of Sephardim who began
to arrive at the beginning of the sixteenth
century. The latter found on their arrival
that the majority of Greek-speaking Rabbanites and Karaites had been transferred
to the new capital of the Ottomans, where
most were legally defined as *sügrün* (forcibly
resettled). This status restricted individual
Jews in their various synagogue communities (named for their provenance in Greece
and Anatolia) from the freedom to resettle
elsewhere.

Iberian Influx: We see that Greece,
since the late Byzantine period, was characterized by a multi-congregationalism that
parallels the post nineteenth-century *lands-
mannschaft* character of contemporary Jewish
communities. The Sephardim arrived in
great number after the beginning of the sixteenth century and settled in those areas
from which the Romaniotes had been removed. The Sephardim predominated in
northern Greece (along the Via Egnatia
from Durazzo to Constantinople, now called
Istanbul from the Greek *'eis ten Polin* (to the

City) as the locals had referred to the capital when it was Greek). This established
their predominance in Macedonia and
Thrace, which lasted until the Holocaust of
the twentieth century. The Sephardim were
defined as *kendi gelen* (voluntary immigrants),
which allowed them relative freedom of
resettlement. They brought with them a
multiplicity of customs and practices as well
as a fully developed intellectual tradition
based primarily on Babylonian and other
Islamic Jewish and post-Maimonidean scholarship, and a halakhic mix of Ashkenazic
and Sephardic learning based on Jacob b.
Asher's *Arb'aa Turim* law code. They eschewed a centralized authority, especially a
Romaniote one, and through their religious
leaders and their court Jews ended the institution of chief rabbi filled by the Romaniote, Elijah Mizrahi, the successor to Moses
Kapsali, in 1526. (The office went into limbo
until its revival in the nineteenth century
as the *haham basilik* (office of the chief rabbi).)
The victory effectively ended Romaniote
influence in Istanbul, even as it had been
superseded in Greece proper where Salonika
had emerged as the major intellectual and
economic center for Balkan Jews. Yeshivot
and *kehillot* proliferated with local practices
reflecting the variety of pre-expulsion Spanish
traditions, many of which lasted to the twentieth century.[16]

The newcomers organized their *kehillot*
around synagogues that bore the names of
their cities of origin, and each preserved
local customs until the twentieth century.
Successive generations broke off from parent synagogues and formed new ones. Their
majority imposed the Sephardic *mahzor* in
most areas of Greece, save for Epiros, where
the Romaniote tradition predominated, and
Corfu and Crete, where the Italian rite competed with the Romaniote. The pattern of
multi-congregational organization lent an
autonomy to each synagogue—recognized
officially by the Ottomans even after the
establishment of the *haham basilik* in the nineteenth century—that contributed greatly to
the variegated forms of Judaism practiced
throughout the Ottoman Caliphate. Each
major town in Greece had numerous synagogues, each reflecting different customs,
traditions, and even language with autoch-

thonous Romaniote and immigrant groups from Spain, Italy, North Africa, and occasionally Ashkenazic.[17]

Salonika: Scholarship flourished in Salonika during the sixteenth-seventeenth centuries and left a legacy that continues to influence the Jewish world. The Sabbath service is even today ushered in with the "Lekhah Dodi" of Shlomo Alkabez, which he composed in Safed. Sephardic scholarship represents the heritage of the Iberian intellectual experience that was supported by three elements. First was the transfer of scholars and their libraries via Italy, where they absorbed and integrated the Italian Renaissance intellectual revolution. Second was the economic creativity of Sephardim in the great urban centers of the Ottoman realm, in particular Salonika, where the Sephardim outnumbered the Christian and Muslim populations combined. The Responsa of RaSHDaM (R. Shmuel di Medina), the leading halakhist in Salonika in the sixteenth century, are a goldmine of information on the legal status and the economic activities of Jews in the region. Third was the printing press that allowed the printing of Spanish Rabbinic classics and the prodigious literary output of the first and second generations of the Sephardic migration. All three of these elements would decline during the seventeenth century and contribute to the intellectual and religious shift of leadership to the Ashkenazic Jews of Eastern Europe. Even so the influence of this sixteenth-century creativity provided an important stimulus in the areas of halakhah and mysticism to the northern Ashkenazim.

Important scholars of Salonika included: Isaac Adarbi, author of *Divrei Rivot* and *Divrei Shalom*; Moses Almosnino (c. 1515-c. 1580), successful preacher and author of commentaries on Psalms (*Yedei Moshe*), Pirkei Avot, and the Pentateuch and prayer book (*Tefillah le-Moshe*) and others; Hayyim Shabtai (Maharhash, before 1555-1647) chief rabbi of Salonika in the seventeenth century and a leading and prolific halakhist of the period; and his students Aaron ben Hayyim Abraham ha-Kohen (1627?-1697), author of responsa *Parah Mattei Aharon*, and Hasdai b. Samuel ha-Kohen (1605?-1678), author of responsa *Torat Hesed*; Joseph b. Isaac Almosnino (1642-

1689) wrote important responsa, published in *Edut bi-Yhosef*; Hayyim Yehudah b. Hayyim (late seventeenth century) served as rabbi of Ioannina and a number of his responsa appear in other collections.

Elsewhere in Greece, scholarship flourished in both Hebrew and Ladino (the religious dialect of Judeo-Spanish from *ladinar*, to translate the Bible into Latin, i.e., Spanish) during the sixteenth and seventeenth centuries. In the west: Solomon Cohen (Mahar-SHaKh) of Zante; Benjamin ben Mattathias, author of important responsa *Binyamin Ze'ev*, and his son-in-law Samuel b. Moses Kalai, author of *Mishpetei Shmu'el*, both of Arta; Moses Alashkar who founded a short-lived yeshivah in Patras at the beginning of the sixteenth century during his peregrinations from Spain to Egypt; Isaac Obadiah of Patras, author of *Iggereth Dofi ha-Zeman*. In the north: Isaac Frances of Kastoria, author of *Pnei Yitzhak*. And on the islands of Rhodes: Ezra Malki, author of *Malki ba-kodesh*, and Yedidiah Tatikah, author of *Ben Yadid*; and Crete, which was famous for its scholarship, including the Kapsali and Delmedigo families. The best known among the latter was Joseph Solomon Delmedigo (YaSHaR of Candia), the prolific polymath and widely traveled physician on whose gravestone in Prague is written: "He practiced what he preached—he was just to everyone—the glorified rabbi, scholar, divine philosopher, and mighty one among physicians." Even more scholars are listed in David Conforte's (of Salonika) bio-bibliographical dictionary *Kore ha-Doroth*, most important for his notices of Mediterranean scholars of the sixteenth-seventeenth centuries.

Judeo-Greek continued as a spoken and written language throughout the Jewish settlement in Greece until the post WWII period. A number of piyyutim and translations of the Torah, Jonah, Job, and several of the Prophets (Kings and Ezekiel) have survived in manuscript and in print. After WWII a translation of Psalms, written in rhymed couplets with a fifteen syllable line (ancient style of *dekapenta*) was published by Asher Moisses, who also translated the prayer book and the Passover Haggadah into modern Greek. Byzantine Karaites too preserved Judeo-Greek into the twentieth century.

Judeo-Spanish literature proliferated during these productive centuries, aided by the spread of printing presses. The poetic style called *coplas* is extremely popular for both religious and secular themes, while Spanish *romanceros* of the medieval period continue to constitute the repertoire of Sephardic women throughout their diaspora. In the sixteenth-seventeenth centuries, translations of Sephardic Rabbinic classics appeared in Judeo-Spanish, e.g., Bahya ibn Pakuda's, *Hovot ha-Levavot*, Isaac Aboab's *Menorath ha-Ma'or*, Joseph Caro's *Shulhan Arukh*, and Elijah b. Benjamin ha-Levi's *Shevet Musar*. The ethical treatise of Moses Almosnino, *Regimiento de la Vida*, appeared in Salonika in 1564. The Ladino Torah appeared in 1547, less prominently sited than the Greek translation, which occupied the column next to the binding. The most influential and popular religious work is the *Me'am Lo'ez* of Jacob Culi, begun in 1730, who published only the first volume on Genesis before he died. A lively secular press and translations from European belles-lettres and original works characterized the advent of modernity in Salonika in the late nineteenth century.

Within a generation after the expulsion from Spain, the intercultural relations between Jews of differing halakhic tradition—Romaniote, Sephardi, Ashkenazic, Mustarib'a—brought Ottoman Jewry to the brink of chaos. One early example may suffice: if a woman engaged but not married were to die, what was the fate of the bridal gifts? The Sephardim followed the thirteenth-century *takkanah* of Tolitola that differed from the Romaniote custom. In the Talmud, the husband becomes the sole heir upon engagement, a practice that the Romaniotes continued to follow, while the *takkanah* allowed half of the estate to the woman's family. It was in recognition of these difficulties, resulting from regional halakhic tradition and congregational variation, that Joseph Caro compiled his two major works: *Beth Yoseph* and its handbook *Shulhan Arukh*. The Ottoman legal distinction between the Sephardic and Romaniote Jews imposed economic and social restrictions on the latter that contributed to their mutual separation. Intellectually, too, the Sephardim looked down upon the Romaniotes as "*gregos*," and both groups disparaged the Ashkenazim as "garlic eaters." The former role of the Romaniotes as translators of ancient Greek texts for the Arabic- and Spanish-speaking Sephardim was long forgotten. The rapid and permanent spread of Sephardic influence was assisted by the printing presses in Venice and Istanbul and soon in Salonika and Safed.

Economic Practices: In Salonika, a huge and successful textile industry had developed after the arrival of the Sephardim. The economic and halakhic aspects of this industry occupied many of the responsa that emanated from Salonika, in particular the collection of RaSHDaM (Shmuel di Medina). The Sephardim renewed an older Jewish textile industry that had disappeared as the Byzantine economy declined and its Jewish population moved to the neighboring Ottoman capital in Edirne (1361-1453). In Thrace to the north of Greece, the later introduction of tobacco as a cash crop was to have important ramifications for the development of a poor but skilled modern Jewish working class. By the eighteenth century the silk industry in which Jews had predominated was expanded from the Morea (southern Greece) to Thrace, where its markets were in the twin centers of the Caliphate: Salonika and Istanbul. Many of the responsa from the Balkans mention these industries and their halakhic problems. Earlier in fourteenth-fifteenth century Venetian controlled Crete, we learn of Jewish control of wine and cheese making for the kosher market in Byzantine Constantinople. Indeed the petty merchants of Greece engaged in the cloth trade (*iphasmata*) from import and export to local trade and manufacture throughout the Jewish experience in Greece.

An interesting chapter in Jewish halakhah and economics that had repercussions throughout the Central and East European Ashkenazi world occurred in western Greece during the eighteenth and nineteenth centuries. The phenomenon has not been integrated into the history of the period; indeed the intricacies of the story have only recently been elucidated.[18] About the mid-eighteenth century the citrons of western Greece began to dominate the *ethrog* market (the second-century Mishnah already knows of the Greek citrons; hence the trade may be quite old).

The desirability of this fruit for the fulfillment of the commandment of Sukkot brought great wealth to the Jews of Corfu, who were the intermediaries for the citrons grown in western Greece and shipped from Parga to Corfu. Soon it captured the market via Italy for the Askenazim of the north, who had to import the Mediterranean fruit. (Needless to say, currents from Zante were also imported, but there was no halakhic problem with currents.) The problem emerged when the charge was raised that the tree that produced the citron was grafted, which made the citron improper for ritual use. Italian rabbis followed by scholars in the north debated the definition of grafted and the means to identify its signs and then the merits of the Greek *ethrogim* vs. the Genoa ones. Behind the scholarly discussion that permeates the responsa of the period lay several economic factors. First was the near monopoly that the Greek *ethrogim* had captured; second was the non-Jewish ownership of the orchards and the frequent charges that non-kosher *ethrogim* were shipped for ritual use.

Anusim: Two burning and interrelated problems confronted the Jews of Greece during the sixteenth century, both of them emanating from the events of the 1490s in Spain and Portugal. The first was the immediate and continuing problem of the *anusim* (forced converts in Rabbinic designation; *conversos* or *neos christianos* in contemporary Spanish; *marrano*—perhaps derived from Spanish pig—in slang), who arrived from Spain and Portugal and their overseas possessions during the sixteenth and seventeenth centuries. The second was the question posed by the faithful populace and their intellectual leaders: how could the God of Abraham, Isaac, and Jacob allow the destruction of the greatest Jewry of the diaspora and the persecution of its survivors throughout the civilized world? These two problems would generate new and creative intellectual responses that would shape Jewish life and thought in Greece into the twentieth century. The first question occupied the great halakhists of the Ottoman world on the day-to-day level. Joseph Caro and Jacob Berab attempted to reconstitute *semikha* (Rabbinic ordination) in Safed based on

an older teaching of Rambam who remarked that only a Sanhedrin could impose thirty-nine stripes and only legally ordained scholars could reconstitute the Sanhedrin. Such a punishment would be considered sufficient for public as well as psychological penance by *anusim*. The *semikha* affair was a failure and the halakhists struggled on. At the same time, the *anusim* and their descendents continued to probe for an explanation of the disasters. Ultimately, they found it in the mystical/kabblistic teachings of Isaac Ashkenazi Luria in Safed. Luria's cosmology, though based on older Jewish sources, was a creative realignment of the relationship between creation and exile. God had sent Iberian Jewry into exile to remind the Jews that God was in a self-imposed exile since creation. And it was the duty of the Jew to redeem creation through fulfillment of the commandments (as detailed in Caro's *Shulhan Arukh*).

Luria's teachings are the antecedent for the messianic movement of Shabbetai Tsvi in the seventeenth century. Luria's treatment of the ten stages of creative emanations that devolved to our worldly reality solved two problems for his disciples. The "breaking of the vessels" (*shevirath ha-kelim*) provided an explanation to the chaotic complexity of the changing contemporary world; more so it provided a solution to the perennial problem of the existence of the evil that permeated the world. To Luria, evil was a by-product of the creative process that could be overcome by good intention (*kavanah*) in fulfilling the mitzvot. Evil then was not a malignant (intelligent) force, but rather an impediment planned by God and programmed into the creative process as part of his experiment to see whether creatures with free will would choose to do good when faced with the opportunity to do evil. The printing of the Zohar in mid-century (Italy, 1558) made available to a wider public this bible of the kabbalists and its sophisticated neo-platonic cosmology. Salonika soon became the center—due to its concentration of Jews, its intellectual depth, and its economic resources—of a widespread kabbalistic explosion that followed upon the decline of Safed in the last third of the sixteenth century.

The phenomenon of messianism in its Safed incarnation was fueled by a number of Sephardim from Salonika (and Edirne/Adrianople). The teachings of the Egyptian Isaac Ashkenzi Luria spread slowly through the Balkans and Italy into Eastern Europe and prepared the way for the messianic explosion centered in the figure of Shabbetai Tzvi of Izmir, whose family had originated in Patras. In the latter thirteenth-century Patras had hosted Abraham Abulafia, whose wife came from that city, on a number of occasions; Abulafia is known to have left in Greece both writings and students of his unique messianic and mystical teachings, and his kabbalah, based on an inner mysticism (*ma'ase merkavah*), continued to exist alongside the more prevalent interest in cosmology among his Spanish contemporaries (*ma'ase bereshit*). His various teachings interestingly parallel those of Gregory Palamas (fourteenth century), the founder of the Greek Orthodox mystical movement known as hesychasm. The influence of Abulafia's texts would be manifest among those who sought a mystical union with God, or at least had prophetic, if not messianic pretensions. Interest in mystical and messianic texts characterized Romaniote Jewry throughout the Byzantine period, and a rich corpus of texts remains in manuscript awaiting their student, e.g., *Eben Saphir* of Elkanan b. Moses Kalkes (fourteenth century). Two texts written in Greece by the Sephardic scribe Shem Tob b. Jacob ibn Polia during the first third of the fifteenth century, *Sefer ha-Peli'ah* and *Sefer ha-Kanah*, influenced Shabbetai Tzvi and continue to influence East European Ashkenazic mysticism.

Despite the continuing interest in mysticism among Romaniote Jews, it was the messianic movement of Shabbetai Tzvi that was to sweep up in its fervor the Jews of Greece, and in the wake of its debacle spawn a number of sects that flourished on the margins of Greek Jewry. During the mid 1650s, Shabbetai Tzvi visited a number of cities in Greece from Patras to Salonika and into Thrace (Adrianople), where he gained supporters. Even after his apostasy, his reservoir of strength was to remain in Salonika until the twentieth century. His prophet, Nathan of Gaza, later took up residence in Kastoria, where he taught and penned a number of his later tracts. A year before his death in 1680, his disciple Isaac Ḥazzan of Kastoria penned a series of homilies on a number of Psalms that developed the sectarian doctrine. The "messiah's" banishment to Dulcigno (Ulinj) in Albania in 1673 kept alive his influence in a number of circles, primarily in Salonika and elsewhere in neighboring Greece, where the Doenme added a nuanced interpretation of Judaism and Ottomanism that anticipates the more modern accommodation of Judaism to secularism. The Doenme movement fragmented even as it flourished in Salonika until the twentieth century and sprouted branches in Jewish centers surrounding the Aegean Sea. It reached Poland via the career of Jacob Frank, who visited the Salonikan center a number of times before he led his followers into the Polish Catholic Church in 1759. Contact however was maintained between the two groups into the twentieth century.

Doenme: The Doenme were followers of Shabbetai Tzvi who converted to Islam yet continued to practice a messianic form of Judaism even after their leader's death in 1676. An inner circle of "*ma'aminim*" (believers) provided a guide to a larger circle of pseudo-Sabbatians for generations. The former sanctified "Eighteen Commandments," among which the prohibition on fornication was muted according to the tenets of the sect. Shabbetai's widow (Johebed/Aisha) of two years, daughter of the prominent rabbi Joseph Filosof, returned to Salonika and proclaimed her brother Jacob Querido as the new "mystical vessel" wherein Shabbetai's messianic soul had reincarnated as the prophet of the movement. In 1683, some two-three hundred families in Salonika converted to Islam, where the center of the movement remained until 1924. Beginning with Shabbetai Tzvi, the Doenme ("converts" in Turkish) most likely maintained ties with the Bektashi dervishes. Many of the Sephardic *niggunim* preserved in Salonika were indebted to the Bektashi school of music that had been founded in Adrianople/Edirne. How these tunes reached the normative Jewish community is unknown; however, the porous lines between the Doenme and the other Jews who constituted a majority of the population of Salonika until the 1920s would have facilitated the adoption of the Muslim music by any interested synagogue *ḥazzan*. The Shi'ite Muslim doctrine of dissimulation (*takīye*) continues to be practiced by descendents of the Doenme to the present day. Gershom Scholem notes in his seminal study of the Doenme (1971) that the most radical sect of the Doenme buried its dead, including its leader, Baruchya Russo/Osman Baba, close by the Bektashi monastery in Salonika. Baruchya Russo, ca. 1700, had been proclaimed to be the reincarnation of Shabbetai Tzvi, and his followers split off from a splinter group of "believers" that had rejected the leadership of Jacob Querido soon after he was proclaimed by his sister. Baruchya was considered by his followers to be divine, and his grave was so honored by his followers from 1720 until 1924. As late as the twentieth century, a Doenme would appear at the western gate of Salonika to greet a reincarnated Shabbetai Tzvi, although to which of the three sects of Doenme he belonged is unknown.

Outwardly the Doenme appeared as Muslim Turks, and estimates suggest that they constituted about half of the total "Turkish" population of Salonika in the last seventy-five years of Ottoman domination of that city; their descendents transferred to Turkey in 1924, during the exchange of population between Turkey and Greece. The sects of Doenme possessed secret synagogues in the center of their respective neighborhoods that abutted the main Jewish quarters. There they practiced their secret rites, which differed considerably from the Islam they openly practiced in their own mosques, where they spoke Turkish. In private they spoke Judeo-Spanish and continued to study Hebrew until it was lost to a transcribed caricature of the original. A prayerbook, published by Scholem in 1942, shows the continuity with the traditional Sephardic rite, despite the alterations to acknowledge the messiahship of Shabbetai Tzvi and kabbalistic terminology. The most salient aspect of the Doenme was their sexual promiscuity, which followed upon Shabbetai Tzvi's and Baruchya's abolition of incest prohibitions in the Torah. The latter was sanctified by later theologically nihilistic and antinomian formulae that advocated total freedom from any restrictions in the world, e.g., "Freedom is the secret of the spiritual Torah." The Sabbatian movement and its Doenme aberration enriched the variety of Judaisms practiced in Salonika and facilitated the inroads of Ottoman Muslim influences among the community at large. In turn, according to Scholem, Salonikan Doenme were influential in the Young Turk Movement and the Committee of Union and Progress that brought Turkey into the modern world.[19]

Modern Period: The Ottoman Caliphate in the Balkans began to disintegrate in the first quarter of the nineteenth century; the process was completed on the eve of WWI, save for the small enclave in eastern Thrace containing its first European capitol Edirne/Adrianople. The Greek state that won its independence welcomed its surviving Jewish communities, many of which had been decimated or destroyed during the ten-year war, and immigrants from other areas of Ottoman Greece and Turkey. More and more of the small provincial Jewish communities were incorporated into the state as it expanded during the nineteenth century until the Balkan Wars, which brought under Greek control the largest and most complex Jewish community in the Balkans, Salonika, Ottoman Selanik, now renamed Thessaloniki. Greek Jewry of the north had little time to adjust to modernity before the Nazi invasion that destroyed all but one thousand scions of its 55,000 pre-war community and ravaged its cultural and literary treasures. Little remains of its pre-war traditions, save for the income from ancestral properties that the community distributes among the remnants of the surrounding Sephardi and Ashkenazi communities as far afield as the Ukraine and Israel.

Greek Nationalist Challenges: Throughout the nineteenth and twentieth centuries, Greek Jewry faced two new challenges from the modern Greek state that later allowed the survivors of WWII to forge a new practice of Judaism whose future survival is uncertain. These challenges derive from two powerful Greek traditions that vie for control of society. One is the ideology of its nationalist revolution that harkens back to the pre-Hellenistic traditions of Athenian democracy. This tradition emphasizes a secular tolerance for diversity and a passion for learning in Greek and is expressed by a chaotic form of democracy that compares with that of ancient Athens. Jews, for the most part, have eschewed participation in the power struggles that characterize modern Greek politics. They have embraced the intellectual and political freedoms that make Greece a model of secular modernity that on the popular level echoes the ribald paganism of its ancestor. The other tradition is that of the Orthodox Church still mired in its ancient mystical and demonic traditions, but one that has adopted the secular tolerance for the Jews and officially maintains cordial relations with the handful of Jewish communities still surviving in Greece. There are today about five thousand Greek Jews within a population of some seven to eight million Christians, among whom the Orthodox predominate with a minority of Catholics and Protestants representing various social classes.

The Jews of modern Greece have one watershed at WWI and another at WWII. Until WWI, the number of Jews in Greece was small, yet the integration of the Jews into the new social and economic structure of the secularizing state was rapid, even unabashed for the immigrants from Central Europe and for the urban elite of Athens. The traditional synagogue changed its language to modern Greek, save in Corfu, where it remained Italian. Later, Rhodes would shift to Italian, while maintaining Judeo-Spanish as a mother tongue after the conquest of that island and others of the Dodekanisi by Italy. The Jews remained small merchants in the provinces and kept a relatively low profile as they and the Orthodox population attempted to deal with the inroads of modernity. A last ditch attempt against modernity by a combination of conservative French diplomats and tradition-minded Catholic clergy in the eastern Mediterranean initiated a series of Blood Libels that spread west from Damascus (1840) to Corfu at the end of the century. In credit to Greek intellectuals assisted by the Church—and contrary to Rome and its minions—these charges were denounced.

The Greek Jews, of whatever persuasion, have shown the ability to adjust to new circumstances. The displacement of the Greek dominance by the Ottoman conquest allowed the Sephardim to preserve their Spanish customs with but minor adjustment to the Turkish Muslim rulers. The Doenme, on the other hand, show a much more receptive attitude to Turkish Muslim influence, and shortly after WWI they transferred to Turkey as part of the Greek-Turkish exchange of populations. The rehellenization (primarily acquisition of language) of Greek Jews after the emergence of the modern Greek state proceeded rapidly; even the powerful autonomy of Salonika's political tradition was unable to protect its youth from the "graecization" of the 1920s and 1930s. During WWI, the dearth of special foods during the holidays allowed the rabbis to make substitutions of a doubtful halakhic nature, which provided a precedent for the heroic attempts to celebrate Passover in the besieged community during WWII. Prior to the war, the chief rabbi, Zvi Koretz, tried to alleviate the burden of importing matzot by negotiating for the purchase of baking ovens from Germany.

After WWI and the integration of Salonika, with its huge and complex Jewish community, the population remained Turkish- and Judeo-Spanish-speaking and continued its traditional ways. By 1922, Jews were no longer exempt from military service, which facilitated modernization and Hellenization among the young, the latter fostered by the Greek government, which imposed Greek studies in the autonomous Jewish school network. The community in general had to juggle its traditional formal autonomy with the new responsibilities imposed by the state. After the influx of huge numbers of Anatolian Greeks in the wake of the 1924 exchange of populations, the government changed the market day from Sunday to Saturday, which necessitated an adjustment by the Sephardic and Romaniote Jews throughout Greece. Shops were closed for Saturday morning in order to honor the Sabbath, and were opened until late Saturday to compensate for the loss of Sunday business. The great fire of 1917 crippled the Salonika Jewish community, which was supported by government subsidy and American Joint Distribution aid until the deportations of WWII. The wealthy continued their emigration, and this flight of wealth coupled with the mass emigration of youth to Palestine in the early 1930s left a poverty-stricken, conservative, and aging population continually under pressure to Hellenize to face the Nazi onslaught. Yet the yeshivot flourished and produced the religious leadership for the various communities in the neighboring Balkans and even as far as Jerusalem and also preserved the diversity of traditions with the city.

Modernity: Zionism was welcomed by the Jewish communities in Greece, although the public response was subdued until after the Salonika-based Young Turk Revolution of 1908. David Ben-Gurion spent nearly a year in Ottoman Salonika to learn Turkish in preparation for his study of Ottoman law, with the goal of running for Parliament. His experience of a "big city" nearly controlled by Jews strongly influenced, as he averred, his concept of what a modern Jewish state should look like. After the Balkan Wars, chapters were established throughout the country with the Mizrahi, or religious, Party becoming prominent among the wealthier leadership. Greek government officials supported the Balfour Declaration and its implied statehood for the Jews, most out of sympathy while others out of a desire to rid Greece, particularly newly acquired Salonika, of its "alien" population. Ze'ev Jabotinsky was a frequent and eloquent visitor to the city. Later in the 1930s, his Revisionists emerged as a force in Salonika and directed a large-scale immigration to Palestine in the wake of the Kambel riots that reflected the competition between the Anatolian refugees and the local Jews, stimulated by an anti-Semitic party called the Triple Epsilon, the latter supported by Nazi Germany since 1932.

Secularism and modernity made inroads among the Jews. The youth, beginning in 1936 with the dictatorship of John Metaxas that promoted an ancient Greek ethos, increased their grasp of the Greek language, which allowed many of them to survive the Nazi roundup of Spanish-accented Sephardim and escape to participate in the Resistance movement of the war. Salonika as a major port whose dockworkers were exclusively Jewish—such that the port was closed on the Sabbath—experienced the vicissitudes of the worldwide depression of the 1920s and 1930s. Narcotics and Rembetika (Balkan jazz) proliferated among the poor, and Jews contributed to each in parallel to the experiences of New York Jews during the same period. There was considerable emigration during the inter-war years: the rich to France, the poor to Palestine, and the middle class to the United States, where the oldest Romaniote synagogue was founded in New York City in 1908 and Sephardi communities appeared inter alia in Seattle and New York City. The competition between the Greek pressure to Hellenize and the educational opportunities of the French (AIU), German, Italian, British, and American schools drew from the community controlled schools many youth who were eager to integrate into the new opportunities of the open societies whose gateway was the university. The situation parallels similar trends in the United States, including the emptying of the provincial towns of their most aggressive and talented youth.

The Holocaust was particularly tragic in Greece.[20] Nearly all of the Jews of Thrace were deported to Treblinka where they were murdered upon arrival; only 1200 Jews out of some 45,000 deported in Spring, 1943, returned to Salonika; and most of the Jews of the former Italian zone of Occupation were deported in spring-summer, 1944. Greek Jewry was decimated, and, following the emigration of survivors to Israel, the United States, South America, and elsewhere in the post-war years, only some five thousand Jews remain out of a pre-war population that numbered between seventy and eighty thousand. Their camp experiences have been recorded by many Greek and non-Greek survivors and memorialized in *coplas* and other forms of poetry, in particular their solidarity, their musical skills, and their religiosity. Only a handful of pre-war religious traditions remained: a few survivors preserved the *niggunim* of Corfu, Ioannina, and Salonika. The Nazis confiscated most of the libraries and ancestral manuscripts that had survived the fire of 1917. Today only a handful of rabbis, some Greek, trained in Israel, others imported, function in Greece. Still there are Jewish schools primarily in Larissa, a strong and reciprocal connection with Israel (where over thirty thousand descendents of Greek, primarily Salonikan, Jews reside), an influential philanthropic base in Salonika that disposes of the income from the mass of properties returned by the Greek government to the community, old age homes, several Jewish museums, and a cadre of younger scholars who are trying to integrate the Jewish experience into the traditional histories of Greece.

Contemporary Jewish religious practice in Greece reflects an accommodation to modernity. The Sephardic *mahzor* is used in Greek translation. Recently the re-edited 1941 prayer book has been reissued in Salonika; a modern Greek version was published in Athens in 1974. Youth are, for the most, secularized, and those who remain in Greece are apt to intermarry. The laws of kashrut are generally ignored when eating out in Greek restaurants, and it is not uncommon for the non-Jewish caterers at Jewish functions to decorate a table with a pig's head. Still *brit milah*, *bar mitzvah* (for boys, a group ceremony at Shavuot—Pentecost—or some appropriate holiday for the girls), Jewish wedding, and funerals are regular occurrences, as well as a daily *minyan* in a number of synagogues. Holidays, given the demographic dearth, tend to be celebrated communally where the elder generation is able to pass along its pre-war heritage. There is a strong interest among the secularized youth for Jewish history in Greece, and the new museums in Athens and Salonika cater to them and the general Christian public, also curious about their ancestral presence in the region. The future of a Greek Jewry whose demographic base is slowly shrinking has been doubted by many observers. It is, however, premature to write the epitaph for the oldest diaspora in Europe that has much to teach us about accommodation and survival.

Bibliography

Ankori, Zvi, *Karaites in Byzantium: The Formative Years, 970-1100* (New York and Jerusalem, 1959).

Bowman, Steven, *Jews in Byzantium, 1204-1453* (reprint: New York, 2000).

Molho, Michael, and Joseph Nehama, *In Memo-*
riam. Hommage aux victimes des Nazis en Grèce. (Thessalonique, 1973).

Nehama, Joseph, *Histoire des Israelites de Salonique.* (I-IV: Salonique, 1935-36; V: Salonique, 1959; VI-VII: Thessalonique, 1978).

Starr, Joshua, *The Jews in the Byzantine Empire, 641-1204* (Athens, 1939).

Stavroulakis, Nicholas P., and Timothy J. DeVinney, *Jewish Sites and Synagogues of Greece* (Athens, 1992).

Notes

[1] Michael H. Jameson, David R. Jordan, Roy D. Kotansky, *A Lex Sacra from Selinous* (Durham, 1993).

[2] Zeev Meshel, *Kuntillet 'Ajrud. A Religious Centre from the Time of the Judaean Monarchy on the Border of Sinai*; Catalogue no. 175 (The Israel Museum, Jerusalem, Spring, 1978).

[3] *De virtutibus*, 142-44; *De charitate*, 601; see Joanna Weinberg, ed. and tr., *Azariah De'Rossi. The Light of the Eyes* (New Haven, 2001), pp. 142f.

[4] P. Jean-Baptiste Frey's 2 volume *Corpus of Jewish Inscriptions* (Rome, 1936; reprint of vol. I with updated material by Baruch Lifshitz, New York, 1975) is a valuable supplement to Juster's survey of the Jewish diaspora (below note 8).

[5] Conveniently collected by Nicholas P. Stavroulakis and Timothy J. DeVinney, *Jewish Sites and Synagogues of Greece* (Athens, 1992). See now Lee I. Levine, *The Ancient Synagogue. The First Thousand Years* (New Haven and London, 2000).

[6] Joshua Starr, "The Epitaph of a Dyer in Corinth," in *Byzantinisch-neugriechischer Jahrbuch* XII (1936), pp. 42-49.

[7] The elaborate stones from its complex, immured in the walls and gates of a Byzantine reconstruction of the fourteenth century, i.e., the Heptapyrgos of Anna Palaeologina, and the threshhold of the southeast gate exiting from the Rotonda to present day Aristotle University of Thessaloniki, are still unpublished.

[8] The classic study is Jules Juster, *Les Juifs dans l'Empire romain*, 2 vols. (Paris, 1914). The basic texts have been edited and translated by Amnon Lindner in two collections: *The Jews in Roman Imperial Legislation* (Detroit and Jerusalem, 1987) and *The Jews in the Legal Sources of the Early Middle Ages* (Detroit and Jerusalem, 1997).

[9] Joshua Starr, *The Jews in the Byzantine Empire, 641-1204* (Athens, 1939), chapter 1.

[10] In addition to the piyyut tradition in the *Megillat Ahima'az* of Southern Italy, there was a prolific continuation of the creativity throughout the later Byzantine and Ottoman periods. See Leon Weinberger, *Anthology of Hebrew Poetry in Greece, Anatolia and the Balkans* (Cincinnati, 1975); *Romaniote Penitential Poetry* (New York, 1980); *Bulgaria's Synagogue Poets: The Kastoreans* (Cincinnati, 1983); *Early Synagogue Poets in the Balkans* (Cincinnati, 1988). And for the later period, Benjamin Schwartz and Apostolos N. Athanassakis, "The Greek-Jewish Songs of Yannina: A Unique Collection of Jewish Religious Poetry," in *Modern*

Greek Studies Yearbook 3(1987), pp. 177-240.

[11] Steven Bowman, *Jews in Byzantium, 1204-1453* (reprint: New York, 2000), chapter 4.

[12] Zvi Ankori, *Karaites in Byzantium: The Formative Years, 970-1100* (New York and Jerusalem, 1959).

[13] Theodore Gastor, *The Holy and the Profane* (New York, 1955).

[14] Cf., Leon Weinberger, 1975, 1980, 1983.

[15] Daniel Goldschmidt, "'Al mahzor romania veminhago," in *Sephunoth* 8 (1964), pp. 205-236; Elias Messinas, *The Synagogues of Salonika and Veroia* (Athens, 1997).

[16] As recorded by Michael Molho, *Usos Y Costumbres De Los Sefardies De Salonica* (Madrid, 1950) in his wartime memoir (written in the mountains of Greece, 1943). A study of the Spanish sermon and its continuation in Salonika can be found in Marc Saperstein, *Jewish Preaching 1200-1800. An Anthology* (New Haven, 1989).

[17] See, for example, Leah Bornstein-Makovetski, "On the Power Struggle in the Jewish Community of Patras in the Sixteenth Century," in *Michael* VII (Tel Aviv, 1981), pp. 9-41 (Hebrew); Meir Benayahu, "The Sermons of R. Yosef b. Meir Garson as a Source for the History of the Expulsion from Spain and Sephardi Diaspora," in idem., pp. 42-205 (Hebrew).

[18] Yosef Salomon, "Pulmus Ethroge Korfu verik'o hahistori," in *AJS Review* XXV (2000/2001), pp. 1-24 (Hebrew).

[19] Gershom Scholem, *The Messianic Idea in Judaism* (New York, 1971), pp. 78-141.

[20] The seminal text, though outdated, is Michael Molho and Joseph Nehama, *In Memoriam. Hommage aux victimes des Nazis en Grèce* (Thessalonique, 1973). Further bibliography in Robert Attal, *Les Juifs de Grèce de l'expulsion d'espagne à nos jours. Bibliographie* (Jerusalem, 1984) and *Supplement*, and the comprehensive *Bulletin of Judeo-Greek Studies*. Articles on religious life in Greece during the last generations before the Holocaust are in the two memorial volumes (in Hebrew) on Salonika edited by Michael Molho, *Salonique. Ville-Mère en Israel* (Jerusalem and Tel Aviv, 1967) and David Rekanati, *Zikhron Saloniki. Grandeza i Destruycion de Yeruchalayim del Balkan*, I (1972)-II (1986) (Tel Aviv, 5732-5746).

STEVEN BOWMAN

J

JOSEPHUS, BIBLICAL FIGURES IN: At the very beginning of his *magnum opus*, the *Jewish Antiquities*, containing the history from creation to the outbreak in 66 C.E. of the Jewish revolution against Rome, Josephus solemnly assures his readers that he has set forth the precise details of the Scriptures, neither adding nor omitting anything (Ant. 1.17).[1] Actually, Josephus added numerous details and even whole episodes, notably the account of Moses' campaign in Ethiopia and his marriage to the Ethiopian princess (2.238-53), while omitting such passages as certain incriminating details in connection with Jacob's deception of his father in order to obtain his blessing (Gen. 27:18-29), the cunning of Jacob in connection with Jacob's flock (Gen. 30:37-38), the Judah-Tamar episode (Gen. 38), Moses' slaying of the Egyptian (Exod. 2:12), the building of the golden calf (Exod. 32), the grumbling and doubting before the second miraculous feast of quails (Num. 11:11-23), Miriam's leprosy (Num. 12:10), the story of Moses' striking the rock to bring forth water, which speaks of Moses' disgrace (Num. 20:10-12), the story of the brazen serpent (Num. 21:4-9), whereby Moses cured those who had been bitten by the fiery serpents, the account of Gideon's smashing of the Baal altar (Judg. 6:25-32), the story of Micah and his idolatry (Judg. 17-18), several passages (1 Sam. 20:6, 21:4-7, 26:19) that seem to cast a shadow upon David's reputation for piety, the identification of Elijah as a zealot (1 Kings 19:9, 14), which would have aroused the antagonism of the Romans in view of the role of the Zealots in the great uprising of 66-70 C.E., Elisha's cursing of the little boys who had jeered him in referring to his baldness (2 Kings 2:23-24) as well as his cursing of his disciple Gehazi for accepting gifts from Naaman (2 Kings 5:27), Jehu's conversion of the Temple of Baal into an outhouse (2 Kings 10:27), which would have aroused charges of intolerance, Jonah's extreme anger with God because he had forgiven the Ninevites after they had repented (Jonah 4:1), Hezekiah's ingratitude to God (2 Chron. 32:25) when he became sick, the charge (Neh. 2:19-20, 6:6) made by the neighbors of the Jews that the Jews were rebelling against the Persian king, the statement (Neh. 8:14, 17) that the Jews had failed to observe the commandment to dwell in *sukkot* since the days of Joshua, the infighting among the Jews in the days of Nehemiah (Neh. 5:6-7, 12; 13:4-11), and the gathering of the virgins in the Esther narrative (Esth. 2:19).

Apologetic concerns would seem to be behind these omissions.[2] A number of them may be explained as Josephus' attempt to refute the views of the Samaritans; thus he omits mention of a sanctuary at Shechem, the sacred city of the Samaritans, nor does he indicate that any religious ceremony took place there (5.115-16; cf., Josh. 24:1, 26).[3] The omission of the names of the kings whom the Israelites defeated when they entered the land of Israel (Josh. 12) and of the details of the division of the land among the various tribes (Josh. 13-17) is perhaps understandable because such information would probably be boring to the average reader, certainly the average non-Jewish reader. Likewise, we may understand the omission of the Song of Deborah (Judg. 5) and the prayer of Hannah (1 Sam. 2), since such poetical material would perhaps be inappropriate in a historical work. In one case, Josephus actually justifies his latitude, namely where he explicitly declares that he will not reproduce the Ten Commandments literally, since he claims that it is not permitted to do so, but that he will rather indicate their general import (3.90).[4]

A number of suggestions have been made to resolve the apparent failure of Josephus to live up to his promise not to modify the import of the biblical text: (1) Josephus may be presenting merely a novel reading; (2) since he asserts that Moses was the author of the biblical narrative (1.37) and since he suggests that the author is a human being, this gives him latitude to interpret the Bible; (3) Josephus is not telling the truth or is careless or relies on the ignorance of his readers, knowing how difficult it was to look up a particular passage without an index; (4) the phrase "neither adding nor omitting anything" is a stock formula, such as we find in Dionysius of Halicarnassus (*De Thucydide* 5 and 8), for merely affirming one's accuracy; (5) perhaps Josephus understood the

phrase as referring to the prohibition of adding to or subtracting from the commandments, whereas his changes are primarily in the realm of aggadic material; (6) perhaps he understood it to prohibit adding to the content of the Bible but to permit modifying the actual consonantal text; (7) perhaps by the Scriptures he meant not only the written Bible but also the Jewish tradition generally, including the much broader oral tradition later embodied in the midrashim; (8) perhaps he adopted an attitude similar to that of the Greek tragedians, who took great liberties with the traditional Greek myths, sacred though those myths were; (9) perhaps he had a broader understanding of the word "translation."

Abraham: Josephus' portrait of Abraham displays unity and coherence. Abraham emerges as a typical national hero. His character is built up through the aggrandizement of his adopted son Lot (1.175, 200-1), his natural son Isaac, his descendants by Keturah (1.240-41), and his wife Sarah (1.187). Josephus adds to Abraham's stature by emphasizing his antiquity (1.170, 186), his nobility of birth (1.148, 252-53), and his wealth (1.243, 250). He is depicted as possessing the four cardinal virtues—wisdom, courage, temperance, and justice, together with the spiritual quality of piety.

Because the Jews had been accused (Apollonius Molon, *ap.* Josephus, *Against Apion* 2.148) of being the most witless of barbarians, Josephus takes special care to emphasize Abraham's intelligence, which the latter displays in arriving at more lofty conceptions of virtue and theology than other men hold. The most prominent example of Abraham's power of logical deduction is his original and highly sophisticated proof of monotheism, which he bases on the irregularities of celestial phenomena (1.156). Far from being narrow-minded and selfish with his knowledge, Abraham, like a typical Hellenistic philosopher attending an international congress in going down to Egypt, declares his willingness to adopt the Egyptian priests' doctrines if he finds them superior to his own or, if he should win the debate, to convert them to his beliefs (1.161). Josephus presents Abraham as the one who taught the Egyptians the very sciences, notably mathematics and astronomy, for which they later became so famous (1.158).

Because the Jews had been reproached with cowardice (Apollonius Molon, *ap. Against Apion* 2.148), Josephus emphasizes Abraham's ingenuity and bravery as a general (1.172). This tradition is said to be continued in his sons by Keturah who joined the famous hero Heracles in his African campaign (1.240-41). Abraham's temperance stands in contrast with the frenzy of Pharaoh (1.162), Abimelech (1.207), and the Sodomites (1.200). His justice is seen in his truthfulness; Josephus carefully omits the instances of apparent dissimulation (Gen. 20:9). Because the Jews had been accused of hating non-Jews, Josephus emphasizes Abraham's hospitality and compassion, particularly toward the Sodomites and Abimelech (1.200, 259).

Josephus places great stress upon Abraham's piety. Passages in the Bible that seem to cast some doubt on this reputation, such as Abraham's asking God for a sign that he will inherit Palestine (Gen. 15:8) or his laughing in disbelief that at his advanced age he will have a child (Gen. 17:17), are carefully omitted.

Josephus avoids anthropomorphisms, especially, as in the scene of Abraham's bargaining with God with regard to the fate of Sodom (Gen. 18:16-33), when these reflect on God's lofty and just character. In general, he diminishes the role of God and tones down miracles. He is careful to justify God's decision to test Abraham by ordering him to sacrifice his son Isaac (1.224).

Because he was so sensitive about Jewish nationalism, especially after the quashed revolution against Rome in 66-74 and his own ignominious role in it, Josephus carefully avoids divine statements promising Abraham that his descendants will inherit a great nation (Gen. 17:8). In Josephus' view, the land of Palestine is not a gift from God but rather will be won—and presumably lost—on the field of battle (1.185). Significantly, the purpose of circumcision is not to serve as a seal of the promise of the land by God to Abraham's descendants but rather as a means to prevent assimilation (1.192).

Isaac: Unlike Philo and the rabbis, who aggrandize the figure of Isaac, Josephus, in order not to diminish the importance of Abraham, who was far better known to his gentile readers, gives much less attention to Isaac. Nevertheless, as with his other biblical heroes, he does develop the themes of Isaac's noble birth (1.229) and his reverence for his father (1.232). He avoids making Isaac a mere carbon copy of Abraham by omitting those instances, such as the barrenness of Rebecca (Gen. 25:21), the deception of Abimelech (Gen. 26:7), and the digging of the same wells (Gen. 26:180, where the biblical Isaac recapitulates his father's experiences.

Isaac, as a model for Josephus' contemporary Jews, is a man of peace who achieves security through reasonable calculation (1.261). He displays courage and calm determination in his successful dealings with the herdsmen who molest him (1.260-61). He shows self-control in his silence both when Esau marries foreign women (1.266) and when Esau returns from the hunt only to discover that Isaac had already given the blessing to Jacob (1.274). As for justice, Isaac at the Aqedah, when Abraham is about to offer him upon an altar as a sacrifice, declares that it would be unjust for him to disobey his father (1.232). He shows gratefulness, which is an integral part of justice, in his dealings with Abimelech (1.264). He exhibits sympathy for the oppressed in that he is moved by the tears of Esau (1.275). He manifests his regard for truth, which is so fundamental to justice, in his omission of the biblical Isaac's duplicity toward Abimelech, to whom he misrepresented his wife as his sister (Gen. 26:6). Isaac's supreme virtue is piety, which he shows in particular at the Aqedah (1.222).

Because Josephus was eager not to offend his Roman patrons, he avoids mention of God's promise to Abraham and Isaac and their descendants of a politically independent state in Palestine (1.234). Moreover, to counteract the charge of illiberalism, he declares that Isaac is to be the ancestor not only of the Jewish nation but of many others as well (1.235). In place of a divine covenant granting Palestine to Isaac's descendants, we are told that they are to conquer the land (1.185).

Josephus found himself in a quandary as to how to deal with Isaac's attitude towards the intermarriages of Esau because, while these were contrary to the Torah, voicing disapproval of them would give credence to the frequent charge that the Jews hate non-Jews. Josephus' solution is to make clear that Isaac was not consulted by Esau regarding the marriages but that once they took place, Isaac held his peace (1.266).

Jacob: In his portrait of Jacob, Josephus was confronted with his greatest challenge in his paraphrase of the Bible. On the one hand, Jacob, whose very name was changed to Israel, was, through his twelve sons, the direct ancestor of the twelve tribes of Israel; and hence, in a work that was manifestly apologetic and largely directed to gentiles, Josephus attempts to answer anti-Jewish charges by seeking to aggrandize Jacob's qualities of character in terms that would appeal to this audience—his genealogy (1.288-90), beauty (2.98), wealth (2.7), and the four cardinal virtues—wisdom (2.15, 17), courage (1.273, 282), temperance (1.305), and justice (11.169) (including generosity [1.329], and honesty [2.149]), as well as the fifth quality of piety (2.196). There are likewise apparent defects in his character that had to be explained or glossed over, notably his deceit in his dealings with his twin brother Esau and with his father-in-law Laban.

For Josephus, this posed a real dilemma, which he resolved in a threefold way—by diminishing or omitting the alleged defects in Jacob's character, by diminishing or omitting those of Esau, and by diminishing or omitting the conflict between the two brothers. Thus, in accordance with the first method, he omits the etymology of Jacob as "supplanter" (Gen. 25:26), which would have imputed to him an undesirably aggressive character. In the scene in which Jacob deceives his father into giving him the blessing, he omits Jacob's incriminating statement, an absolute falsehood, "I am Esau, thy first-born" (Gen. 27:19), and transfers the blame for the deception entirely to Rebecca, Jacob's mother (1.269). Josephus disposes of Jacob's treachery with the animals of Laban by omitting the account and, indeed, by shifting the charge of deceit to Laban himself (1.301). He is likewise careful to avoid antagonizing his gentile readers and hence stresses that Simeon and Levi acted without their father Jacob's permission in massacring the Shechemites (1.340).

A number of touches indicate that in this pericope Josephus, by deft handling of the figure of Esau, mostly involving omissions, is seeking to avoid antagonizing the Romans, who, it appears, were already in Josephus' time regarded as the descendants of Esau,[5] and to diminish the alleged conflict between the Jews and the Romans. Thus Josephus omits the struggle of the twins, Esau and Jacob, within their mother's womb (Gen. 25:22). Moreover, the oracle predicting that Esau would serve Jacob is changed to indicate that Jacob would "excel" Esau (1.257). He omits Esau's redness (Gen. 25:25), which was associated in antiquity with slaves' hair.[6] In the account of the sale of the birthright, more sympathy is evoked for Esau, since he is described as still a lad (2.2). Esau is more sympathetically portrayed, too, in his tremendous devotion to his father (1.269). The bloodthirstiness of Esau is omitted from Isaac's blessing (Gen. 27:40), and instead we are told that he will be renowned for strength in arms and labor (1.275). Again, the scene in which Jacob and Esau are reconciled becomes central in Josephus (1.325-36).

Joseph: Josephus shows extraordinary interest in the character of Joseph, partly because he bore his own name but, also, more particularly, because of what he saw as striking parallels with his own life, since both were child prodigies (2.9, *Life* 8), both were envied (2.10, *Life* 423), both showed extraordinary skill in interpreting dreams (2.63-90, *Life* 208-10), both were cast out by fellow Jews (2.17-33, *Life* 416), and both were exiled to a foreign land (2.39, *Life* 422). In the case of Joseph, this interest is shown particularly in the tremendous expansion of three pericopes—Joseph's dreams and subsequent enslavement (2.11-39), the episode of Potiphar's wife (2.41-59), and the final test of Joseph's brothers (2.95-166). Josephus' consistently positive approach to Joseph is in direct contrast to Philo's ambivalent attitude. His portrayal is, in large part, intended to answer the enemies of the Jews, who had charged them with being unpatriotic and with not producing leaders distinguished for wisdom. This rebuttal was particularly necessary and effective because Joseph was active in the very country, Egypt, that was the hotbed of anti-Jewish propaganda. In particular, Josephus' stress that Joseph opened his granaries to all because he held all men to constitute a single family (2.94) was intended to refute the canard that Jews hated non-Jews, as well as the claim that Jews were aggressive missionaries.

Joseph emerges as a model statesman, exemplifying Plato's portrayal of the philosopher-king and Thucydides' portrayal of his favorite leader, Pericles. Where the biblical narrative suggests shortcomings on Joseph's part, as, for example, his immaturity in his youth (Gen. 37:2), Josephus carefully and systematically omits such details.

In particular, Josephus, in his extra-biblical additions, emphasizes Joseph's good birth (2.9) and handsomeness (2.9), qualities so important to Josephus' intended non-Jewish intellectual audience. He stresses, going beyond the biblical text, Joseph's possession of the four cardinal virtues—wisdom (2.9, 46, 87) (including, especially, the ability to interpret dreams [2.65, 72, 80, 86]), courage (specifically, endurance in distress [2.43, 2.60]), temperance (including, particularly, modesty and the ability to resist sexual temptations [2.42]), and justice (above all, the qualities of humanity [2.94] and generosity [2.142], 2.191-93])—together with the virtue of piety (2.60, 122, 145), which is closely associated with these. In the case of this last virtue, Josephus treads a thin line between, on the one hand, emphasizing the centrality of God in all events concerning Joseph and, on the other hand, deemphasizing the role of God in Joseph's actual achievements (Gen. 39:3 vs. 2.39).

Moses: Because Moses was the one figure in the Jewish tradition who was well known to the pagan world and also because he had been reviled by several anti-Jewish writers, Josephus may be assumed to have felt a special need to paint a favorable picture of him. Several events in Moses' life presented a particular problem for Josephus, notably his murder of an Egyptian overseer (Exod. 2:12), his marriage to a non-Jewish woman Zipporah (Exod. 2:21), his lowly occupation of shepherd (Exod. 3:1), his timidity when he is selected by God at the burning bush to be the leader of the Israelites (Exod. 3:11), the leprousness of his hand at

one point (Exod. 4:6), his speech defect (Exod. 4:10) and his need to have his brother Aaron as his spokesman, his failure to circumcise his son (Ex. 4:24), his permission to the Israelites to "borrow" jewelry and clothing from the Egyptians (Exod. 12:35), his abandonment of his wife Zipporah (Exod. 18:2), his need to turn to his father-in-law Jethro for advice (Exod. 18:13-27), his anger in smashing the first set of tablets of the law (Exod. 32:19-20), his skepticism when God promises to supply the Israelites with meat (Num. 11:21), his marriage to an Ethiopian woman (Num. 12:1), his disobedience toward God in striking rather than speaking to the rock (Num. 20:11), and his inability to answer the complaints of Zelophehad's daughters (Num. 27:1-11). In almost all of the above cases, Josephus simply omits the embarrassing episode. On the other hand, Josephus is careful to avoid the undue aggrandizement and near deification of Moses such as is found in the Samaritan tradition and, to a lesser degree, in the Rabbinic writings. Likewise, because his sophisticated audience would undoubtedly have found the biblical miracles hardly credible, he tends to downgrade or rationalize them; or, as in the case of the miraculous crossing of the Sea of Reeds, he makes a point of noting the parallel of Alexander the Great's crossing the Pamphylian Sea (2.348).

Because the *Antiquities* is an apologetic work directed primarily to non-Jews, Josephus portrays Moses as embodying the external qualities of good birth (2.210) and handsome stature (2.224, 232), precociousness in his youth (2.230), along with the four cardinal virtues of wisdom (4.328), courage (2.238-253, 4.329), temperance (4.328-29), and justice (3.66-67), supplemented by piety (2.270-71, 3.302, 4.47). Moses' appeal to this audience is particularly effective, especially in his meeting the test of sedition and in coping with the unruly mob (4.12-36). Josephus' presentation on this point is highly reminiscent of Thucydides' portrait of Pericles, of Plato's description of the philosopher-king, of Virgil's portrayal of Aeneas, and of the traditional Stoic sage; while concurrently the role of Aaron as his spokesman is considerably downgraded. It is particularly as educator, legislator, and poet, and, above all, as general and prophet that Moses excels. In stressing these achievements Josephus shifts the focus from God to Moses.

Josephus' modifications of the biblical narrative of Moses are occasioned by his apologetic concern to defend the Jews against the charges of their opponents, particularly cowardice, provincialism, and intolerance.

Joshua: Josephus' portrait of Joshua emphasizes the importance of his leadership for the proper functioning of the common weal. Josephus' extra-biblical additions emphasize Joshua's possession of the four cardinal virtues—wisdom (5.118), courage (5.1, 45), temperance (5.103), and justice (which includes, in particular, honesty [5.75-76], fairness [5.78], generosity [5.48], and gratitude [5.30] and where the concern is to answer Jew-baiters)—as well as the fifth cardinal virtue, piety (5.116). In addition, Josephus adds to the biblical portrait by terming Joshua a prophet (4.165, 311); and inasmuch as, for Josephus, the prophet is charged not only with predicting the future but also with recording the past, Joshua is thus associated with Josephus' own profession, that of the historian. Josephus is especially careful to justify Moses' choice of Joshua as his successor (4.165). In view of Josephus' great admiration of and indebtedness to Thucydides, it is not surprising that Joshua emerges as the Jewish version of Thucydides' portrait of Pericles, with emphasis on his intelligence, ability to persuade and check crowds (3.308), and pragmatism.

Josephus employs his account of Joshua to answer the charges of Jew-baiters. Thus, in answer to the claim that Jews were harsh or even bloodthirsty in their conquest of Canaan, Josephus abbreviates and tones down or, in some cases, omits biblical descriptions of Joshua's treatment of the native Canaanites (Josh. 10:28-36, 11:11; 5.61-62, 67).

Whereas the rabbis portray Joshua as a student of Torah (Gen. Rabbah 6.9), the emphasis in Josephus is on his pragmatic leadership, particularly in war. In particular, Josephus is careful to tone down or rationalize miracles (5.16, 23-27). If, occasionally, Josephus does exaggerate, he is careful to do so in such a way as to add drama to the situation without stretching the credulity

of his readers (5.60). Moreover, he takes pains not to stress unduly God's role in Joshua's exploits in order not to detract from Joshua's own achievements (5.22). Moreover, Josephus, like Ibn Ezra, omits those passages that raise serious questions of authorship and date of composition of the book, which Rabbinic tradition attributes to Joshua.

In distinct allusion to his own times, when civil strife had torn the Jewish people apart during the war against the Romans, Josephus is careful to emphasize Joshua's ability in avoiding civil war and anarchy (5.114). Finally, in order not to antagonize his Roman hosts, Josephus omits references to the divine order to take possession of the land of Israel (Josh. 1:10-11 vs. 5.1).

Samson: Whereas the rabbis, in their portrayal of Samson, are concerned with word play, with the divine and the miraculous, and with the deflation of the heroic stature of Samson, and whereas Pseudo-Philo, in his Biblical Antiquities, exaggerates his exploits while comparing him unfavorably with Joseph, Josephus' portrait is strongly influenced by his concern to defend the Jews against the charges of their opponents.

Josephus emphasizes the nobility of Samson's ancestry on his father's side (5.276). He emphasizes Samson's sagacity, noting that he would have been able to outwit the Philistines were it not for a woman's treachery (5.290). He stresses Samson's bravery and, above all, his sheer strength and violence (5.277), but without resorting to undue exaggeration or the grotesque and without indicating that this strength was divine in origin. Samson's heroic stature is enhanced by reducing the role of his parents (5.287). In stressing Samson's tempestuous nature, Josephus depicts him as an Israelite Achilles or Heracles.

Josephus' Samson exhibits the virtue of moderation in his diet (5.285). Josephus protects Samson against the charge of injustice by denying that Samson plundered innocent by-standers (5.294) and tones down Delilah's charge that Samson had been untruthful to her (5.312). He omits as degrading the biblical description of Samson's being forced to engage in the menial labor of working at a mill (Judg. 16:21).

Josephus presents the Samson story as a Greek tragedy. Samson's downfall is due more to fate than to his own failings. Josephus enhances the romantic aspect of Samson's relationship with the Timnite woman by having him go to her alone and constantly and by having him perform his first great exploit, the strangling of a lion, in the course of one of these visits (5.286-87). Josephus heightens the dramatic suspense by focusing attention on the Timnite woman and her impending punishment by the Philistines if she fails to learn the answer to Samson's riddle.

The Delilah episode becomes more romantic in that she is depicted as a courtesan (5.306). Josephus builds up the romantic element and the suspense by having Delilah continually importune Samson to reveal his secret (5.310). The account, moreover, is more romantic in that Josephus omits the payment of money to Delilah by the Philistines (Judg. 16:18).

Josephus presents Samson as a human hero and omits completely biblical references to the fact that he was able to achieve his exploits through his being moved by the spirit of the Lord (Judg. 13:25). He likewise diminishes the divine element by omitting Samson's prayer to God prior to his grandest achievement, bringing the temple down upon the thousands of Philistines (Judg. 16:28). Finally, Josephus addresses his contemporary Jews in stressing the moral of the story, namely that one must not debase one's rule of life by imitating foreign ways, though, aware of the charge of misanthropy made against the Jews, he tones down the severe objections of Samson's parents to his intermarriage (Judg. 5.286).

Samuel: It is particularly striking that whereas the Bible refers to Samuel as a prophet only once, Josephus calls him a prophet or mentions his prophesying on forty-five occasions. Apparently, Samuel for Josephus did not have the drawbacks of Elijah, whose zealotry was embarrassing to Josephus, or of Daniel, whose prophecy of the overthrow of the Roman Empire must have made Josephus, the protégé of the Romans, rather squeamish. Hence, it is not surprising that he has a much longer encomium for Samuel (6.292-94) than for either

Elijah or Daniel. Josephus has dramatized, to a greater degree than the Bible, the annunciation of the birth of Samuel (5.345), but he is careful to avoid presenting him as a messiah-like figure, as does his presumed contemporary, Pseudo-Philo in his Biblical Antiquities.

Josephus also emphasizes Samuel's quality of leadership in searching for Saul when the latter disappears after being chosen as king (6.64). In Josephus' version, Samuel is not a mere mouthpiece or tool of God, nor is he subordinated to Eli the high priest. As a true leader, he is concerned for the masses (6.102).

In line with Josephus' portrayal of other biblical heroes, Samuel is presented as possessing the four cardinal virtues of wisdom (6.22), courage (6.28), temperance (6.34), and justice (6.32, 48), together with the fifth virtue of piety (5.349). His wisdom is seen particularly in his power of persuasion (6.19, 22), a quality that was a key to the success of Pericles, the leader whom Thucydides, Josephus' model as a historian, admired so much. Samuel's ability and courage as a general, as well as his power to encourage the Israelite army (6.24), are much more conspicuous in Josephus than in the Bible.

Josephus also stresses Samuel's moderate character and especially his temperance as compared with his sons' lack of this quality in their diets (6.34). Josephus emphasizes that Samuel administered perfect justice, again in contrast with the perversion of justice by his sons (6.34). He stresses his incorruptibility (6.48), another quality that Thucydides emphasized in his portrayal of Pericles. The one case in which God seems to advise Samuel to be less than honest (1 Sam. 16:2), namely when Samuel is going to anoint David as king in place of Saul, is kept vague in Josephus (6.157), thus saving the reputation of both God and Samuel. Connected with justice is the quality of kindness, which Samuel shows in trying unceasingly to influence God to forgive Saul for his disobedience of the divine command to exterminate the Amalekites (6.143-45). As for piety, Samuel affirms his complete and undivided loyalty to God (5.349).

Josephus uses the narrative of Samuel to present his political philosophy, particularly as to the best form of government, which he equates with theocracy (*Against Apion* 2.165). Again, like Plato, Samuel shows contempt for the masses (6.34).

Saul: The fact that Josephus devotes more space, as compared with his biblical source, to his account of Saul than to almost any other biblical personality and, above all, the fact that his encomium of Saul (6.343-50) is longer than that for any other biblical figure, Moses included, alerts us to Saul's importance and fascination for Josephus.

In his portrayal of Saul, Josephus occupies a mean position between that of the talmudic rabbis, who exaggerate his virtues, and Pseudo-Philo in his Biblical Antiquities, who denigrates him. Whereas in the Bible, Saul emerges as a mere puppet of the prophet Samuel, in Josephus he is portrayed as being on a par with Samuel, in whose sacrifices he joins.

In depicting the qualities of Saul, Josephus emphasizes his good birth (6.45), while taking care to indicate that, nevertheless, he did not show disdain for those of lesser birth. He stresses Saul's physical beauty (6.45). He portrays him as a sage-like figure presiding over a Sanhedrin-like group of seventy (6.52). Above all, he aggrandizes the courage of Saul in his military leadership and exploits, stressing the military difficulties that he had to overcome (6.67), exaggerating the ferocity of the enemy, and highlighting the skill that he displayed as a strategist (6.79), in contrast both to the Rabbinic portrait, which emphasizes the supernatural aspect of his military achievements, and to Pseudo-Philo, who depicts him as a coward. In particular, Josephus magnifies Saul's ability and magnetism as a psychologist in arousing his troops against his greatest military challenge, the Philistines (6.98). Moreover, in an extra-biblical touch, Saul shows sympathy for his people in their suffering. Above all, Josephus aggrandizes the heroism of Saul in going into his final battle, knowing full well, through the prophecy of Samuel, that he was destined to perish in it.

Josephus develops, even beyond the Bible, Saul's quality of moderation, which he identifies with modesty (6.63), though he is careful to avoid ascribing to him extreme modesty, since he realized that such a quality would be regarded negatively by his pagan readers.

Josephus explains away inconsistencies in the Bible's picture of Saul's piety. In particular, he takes care to present a defense of Saul's slaughter of the Amalekite women and children (6.136), while at the same time offering an aesthetic motive for his sparing the Amalekite king, Agag (6.137), though he is careful not to whitewash Saul's action completely. In the case of the murder of Abimelech and the priests of Nob, however, Josephus, himself a priest, exaggerates Saul's responsibility (6.268). Nevertheless, Josephus, by stressing Saul's feeling of remorse (6.290), increases readers' sympathy for him. He protects Saul's reputation by saying not a word about the sinfulness of Saul's suicide; indeed, he does not even raise the question whether his death was a suicide. Moreover, Josephus stresses Saul's *pietas* towards members of his family and towards his kinsmen generally (6.57).

Josephus rationalizes Saul's madness, explaining this clinically as a medical disorder (6.166). And Josephus takes measures to diminish Saul's jealousy of David, notably by omitting the scene in which Saul seeks to kill David while the latter is playing his harp (1 Sam. 18:10-11). Josephus likewise emphasizes that Saul, in his pursuit of David, was not really aware of what he was doing (6.250).

David: Josephus stresses David's wealth, presumably because the Jews were accused by such satirists as Martial (12.57.13) and Juvenal (3.10-16, 296; 6.542-47) of being a nation of beggars. In particular, he emphasizes David's courage (6.179-80). Josephus also stresses his hospitality (6.326), unselfishness (7.322-23), magnanimity (6.317), generosity (6.323), gratefulness (7.272), humanity (7.391), kindness (7.184), and mercifulness (6.290, 6.312), because the Jews had been charged with hatred of the human race by such calumniators as Apollonius Molon (*ap. Against Apion* 2.258) and Lysimachus (*ap. Against Apion* 1.309). Moreover, he notes the stress placed by David on the avoidance of political dissension, which had cost the Jews so heavily in the war against the Romans (7.372-73). Furthermore, there is, in order to make the narrative more appealing to his readers, an increased romantic element, especially in Josephus' amplification of the love of David and Michal (6.196, 199-200, 216) and of the friendship of Jonathan and David (6.208, 210).

Josephus has diminished the importance of David as king in the length of his final encomium (7.390-91), especially as compared with King Saul (6.343-50). We may suggest the following explanations for his doing so: (1) Josephus himself was descended from the Hasmonean kings rather than from the line of David. (2) David was extremely important for Christianity as the ancestor of the messiah; and while it is true that Jesus himself appears to assert that the messiah is not descended from David (cf., Matt. 22:41-45, Mark 13:35-51, Luke 20:41-44), and some of his contemporaries (John 7:41-42) are said to be unaware of a connection of Jesus with the House of David, nonetheless, by the time of Paul, Christians already believed that Jesus was descended from the family of David (Rom. 1:3), so that the Gospels (Matt. 1:1-7, Luke 3:23-38) have genealogies, differing to be sure in details, but agreeing in deriving Jesus' descent from David. Hence, to counteract the importance of David for the Christians, Josephus may have diminished his significance, just as, we may guess, he may have reacted against the claims of Christianity in his original version of the Testimonium Flavianum (18:63-64),[7] and even possibly in his version of the Flood story, in which he omits any reference to a covenant between God and man, so important for Christianity.[8] The diminished emphasis on miracles in David's career may likewise perhaps be seen as a reply to Christians, who emphasized Jesus' miracles, and may be in line with the point of view expressed in the story of R. Eliezer, who appealed to miracles but yet was overruled and even excommunicated (B. B.M. 59b). (3) He has omitted all reference to David as ancestor of the messiah, despite the fact that such a tradition was apparently widespread in his era, because he wished to stress for those of his Hellenistic Jewish readers his own repugnance to an independent Jewish state. To the extent that his Roman patrons would have been aware of the beliefs

of Jewish messianism, they would have objected to such a political figure who would seek to re-establish an independent Jewish state, precisely the goal of the revolutionaries against Rome in Josephus' own day, whom he attacks so bitterly. The fact that David is spoken of as "tawny" (6.164) might remind the reader of Esau, whose pottage is similarly described by Josephus; and hence this might associate David with the Romans, the very descendants of Esau, according to Rabbinic tradition. (4) Josephus' downplaying of David, to some degree, may reflect a more general stance, as seen in Pseudo-Philo's Biblical Antiquities[9] and in some of Rabbinic literature.[10] We may note, in particular, the stories of Josephus' contemporaries, Yohanan b. Zakkai (B. Git. 56a-b) and Joshua b. Hananiah (Gen. Rabbah 64.10), who sought a *modus vivendi* with the Romans and hence were eager not to antagonize them with talk of a messianic king. Such downgrading may also be seen in Josephus' use of the term "lad" in referring to David at the time of his being anointed king (6.164). Josephus' portrait of David is thus an important and typical reflection of contemporary considerations—political, religious, and cultural—that influenced his entire approach to historiography.

Solomon: King Solomon is a major figure in Josephus' attempt, in his rewriting of the Bible in his *Jewish Antiquities*, to answer the anti-Jewish charge that the Jews had failed to produce men of eminence. One indication of the importance of Solomon for Josephus may be seen from the fact that he cites more external evidence to support his account of Solomon than he does for any other biblical personality (8.55-56, 144-49).

Josephus, as in his portrayal of other biblical personalities, stresses Solomon's precociousness (8.2, 211) and wealth (8.40, 129) and qualities of leadership, notably his concern for his people (8.124). Solomon, like Josephus' other biblical heroes, emerges as possessing the four cardinal virtues—wisdom (7.381, 8.23), courage (8.24), temperance (7.361), and justice (7.356, 384), as well as the virtue of piety (7.338, 356, 374). Above all, Josephus stresses Solomon's wisdom. Unlike his portrayal in Rabbinic literature, where he emerges as the prototype of the

Talmudic sage and where many miraculous and supernatural elements are attributed to him, Josephus' Solomon is a rational king and judge. There are several indications that in his portrait of Solomon's adjudicating the case of the two mothers (8.26-34), Josephus has in mind the portrayal of Oedipus, the solver of the riddle of the Sphinx, by Sophocles, of whose works there is considerable evidence that he was fond.[11] We see this parallel notably in Josephus' additions to the biblical text—that others had attempted and failed to determine who the real mother was (8.30), that these others are spoken of as mentally blinded (8.30), that to solve the question required the use of intelligence (8.26), and that the case is compared to a riddle (8.30). Solomon is likewise presented as a kind of Oedipus in the cleverness and speed that he shows in solving the riddles and problems, whose difficulty is stressed, that are presented to him by Hiram the King of Tyre (8.143) and by the Queen of Sheba (8.166-67). Josephus, like Sophocles, emphasizes that it was the force of the hero's human reason, rather than divine inspiration, that enabled him to solve these problems.

Solomon is presented by Josephus as having studied the forms of nature philosophically (8.44). In addition, because of the popularity of magic in his day, Josephus develops a picture of Solomon as possessing skill in the art of exorcising demons (8.45-49).

In answer to the charge that the Jews are not masters of an empire, Josephus stresses that Solomon had subdued many nations (*Against Apion* 2.132). Josephus emphasizes his achievement in building up the defenses of his kingdom and in administering his state most skillfully in perfect peace (8.21), free from the civil dissension that Josephus so decried in his own day. He also embellishes the portrayal of Solomon's economic power (8.38, 163).

Solomon shows exemplary moderation, coupled with firmness, in his treatment of his brother Adonijah, who had attempted to seize the royal power during David's lifetime (7.362). Associated with this moderation is the quality of modesty, which Solomon, in an extraordinary extra-biblical addition, exemplifies in his admission that he had

actually been outwitted by a young Tyrian lad named Abdemon, who always succeeded in solving the problems submitted to him by Solomon and who, in turn, submitted others that Solomon was unable to solve (8.146).

The chief use of Solomon's palace, in Josephus' eyes, was for the administration of justice (8.133). Solomon's handling of the case of Shimei enhances his reputation for fairness (8.20). Solomon likewise exhibits the qualities of magnanimity (8.52), gratefulness (8.111-12), and generosity (8.141), which are closely connected with justice.

An indication of the emphasis Josephus places on Solomon's piety may be seen in the fact that twenty-three per cent of the occurrences of the words for "piety" and "pious" are found in his Solomon pericope, which comprises only seven per cent of Josephus' rewritten Bible.[12] Solomon, in Josephus' portrait, shows exemplary piety toward his father and his mother (7.392, 8.8)—a quality that would have been especially appreciated by Josephus' Roman audience, for whom one of Aeneas' major virtues was his *pietas* toward his parents. Moreover, Josephus adds a great number of details in his description of the beauty and wealth of the Temple, which Solomon built and which was his greatest act of piety (8.63-64, 88, 97). In particular, he stresses that Solomon applied much more energy to the building of the Temple than to his own palace (8.30, 131).

Josephus presents a rationalized version of the miracle that occurred at the dedication of the Temple (8.106). Moreover, whereas God in the Bible appears directly to Solomon, Josephus says a dream revealed to Solomon that God had heard his prayer (8.125, 196).

The friendship between Solomon and Hiram was important to Josephus in refuting the charge that Jews hate non-Jews. This may be seen from the fact that Josephus devotes a goodly portion of his apologetic treatise *Against Apion* (1.100-27) to reproducing evidence from the Phoenician archives and from the works of Dius and Manetho of Ephesus to illustrate the excellent relations between Solomon and Hiram. Above all, Josephus, in depicting Solomon as praying that God should grant all the requests of non-Jews when they come to the Temple, shows thereby that Jews are not guilty of hating non-Jews (8.116-17).

Josephus realizes that opposition to intermarriage might be regarded as evidence that in principle Jews hate non-Jews. He therefore is careful to base his opposition to Solomon's intermarriages on the wrongfulness of Solomon's yielding to passion (8.190)—a point of view that Stoics in his audience would surely have appreciated—and on the ground that intermarriage violated the law of his country (8.194).

Daniel: To understand Josephus' interpretation of the character of Daniel we must realize that he is addressing an audience of both Jews and non-Jews.[13] For the latter he emphasizes, going beyond his biblical source, Daniel's genealogy (10.186, 188), handsome appearance (10.186), and possession of the cardinal virtues of wisdom (10.186-89) (seen especially in his interpretation of dreams [10.194]), courage (10.255-56), temperance (10.187, 190-92) (which he identifies with modesty [10.203]), and justice (10.246) (which is coupled with humanity and unselfishness [10.241]), plus the fifth virtue of piety (10.255, 263). In addition, his Daniel shows the qualities of leadership (10.202, 251) so prized by Thucydides and Plato, whom Josephus and his audience so admired. Daniel is also referred to, as he is not in the Bible, as a prophet (10.246, 249, 269), a role Josephus also ascribed to himself (*War* 3.400-2).

Because Jews had reached positions of the highest importance during the Hellenistic and Roman periods and thereby aroused jealousy as well as charges of double loyalty, Josephus uses this story to show the broadmindedness of Jews toward non-Jews. In particular, he seeks to cast the kings—Nebuchadnezzar, Belshazzar, and Darius—with whom Daniel was closely associated in a more favorable light.[14]

And, yet, Josephus felt that he had to cater to a Jewish readership also. Though he might easily have omitted, as strictly speaking not relevant to his history, the reference in Nebuchadnezzar's dream to the stone that destroyed the kingdom of iron (Dan. 2:44-45), he nevertheless mentions it, albeit with the evasive remark that if anyone wishes to obtain more information about the matter he should read the Book of Daniel (10.210). Surely Josephus realized that only Jews were likely to follow this suggestion, just as it is they who would probably be aware of the interpretation of this passage as referring to the Messiah's triumph over the Roman Empire (Tanhuma B 2.91-92 and Tanhuma Terumah 7).

By emphasizing the honors accorded Daniel, Josephus also uses this material to answer the charge that the Jews are the most untalented of all barbarians (Apollonius Molon, *ap. Against Apion* 2.148). Moreover, in explaining Daniel's abstention from the king's food and wine as due to health considerations, Josephus answers the charge that the Jews have a way of life that is hostile to foreigners (10.190).

There is a relative de-emphasis on God and greater importance attached to the human role in history in Josephus' Daniel pericope (10.200). In dealing with the miracles of the book of Daniel, Josephus either rationalizes or says that Daniel was saved by divine providence (10.214), employing a term that was a favorite of the Stoics. Realizing the problem presented by angels both for Jews and non-Jews, he avoids mentioning them as effecting the miraculous rescue of Daniel from the lions' den (10.259). The fact that he closes his account of Daniel, and, indeed, the first half of the *Antiquities*, with an excursus on how mistaken the Epicureans are in asserting that the world runs by its own movement (10.277-81) is once again an appeal to the numerous Stoics in his audience.

Additional Portraits: To appreciate Josephus' rewriting of the Bible, it may be useful to compare his work with other efforts in antiquity to rewrite sacred material. Whether it is Greek playwrights rewriting plots from Homer and other sources of Greek mythology, or Dionysius of Halicarnassus' retelling of Roman legends, or midrashic or quasi-midrashic works, such as the Genesis Apocryphon, Jubilees, Pseudo-Philo's Biblical Antiquities, or Rabbinic Targumim or midrashic reworking of the Jewish Scriptures, we note that their authors feel no hesitation in taking liberties—and often very considerable liberties—with their sacred texts.

Within each of the works listed above, one notes tremendous variation in highlighting certain episodes, sharply abbreviating or omitting others, and adding totally new episodes. Thus, for example, Pseudo-Philo, on the basis of the Bible's mere mention of the name of Kenaz (Judges 3:9, 11) as the father of the judge Othniel inserts a lengthy pericope (*Bib. Ant.* 25-28) about his achievements; on the other hand, Josephus (5.182-84), has a much briefer account, and the Rabbinic literature (or at least that which is extant) has nothing at all about this figure. Josephus, on the basis of a mere mention in the Bible (Num. 12:1) of the fact that Moses married a Cushite woman, presents a lengthy episode of Moses' achievements as a general in a campaign against the Ethiopians and his marriage with the Ethiopian princess (2.239-53).[15] The historian Artapanus, who apparently lived in the second century B.C.E. and whom most regard as a Jew, has a briefer account that omits the romantic episode (*ap.* Eusebius, *Praeparatio Evangelica* 9.27.7-10); Philo, despite the length of his life of Moses, has nothing to say about this matter, and it is not until the Middle Ages that we find references to it in Rabbinic literature (Jerusalem Targum, Num. 12:1).[16]

Certain episodes are vastly expanded by Josephus, notably portions of the Joseph story (his dreams and subsequent enslavement [2.9-38], the episode of Potiphar's wife [2.41-59], and the final test of Joseph's brothers [2.124-59]), the rebellion of Korah (4.11-56), the episode of the Israelite men and the Midianite women (4.129-40), and the reign of Zedekiah (10.102-50, 154). Certain personalities, notably Jethro (2.258-64, 277; 3.63-74), Balaam (4.102-58), Ehud (5.185-97), Saul (6.45-7.6), David (6.157-7.394), Joab (7.11-19, 122-26, 135-41, 181-87, 191-93, 236-42, 245-47, 253-57, 281-92, 318-20; 8.13-16), Solomon (7.335-42, 348-62, 370-88; 8.2-211), and Jeroboam (8.205-45, 265-87), are given much more attention than others. Extraordinarily little attention is given to others, notably Aaron (3.205-11; 4.26-34, 54-58, 64-66, 83-85), Deborah (5.200-10), Jonah (9.207-14), and Nehemiah (11.159-83). The case of Zedekiah (10.102-50) is striking in that in the Bible (2 Kings 24:19) he is said to have done what was evil in the sight of the Lord, whereas Josephus (10.103), while admitting that Zedekiah was contemptuous of justice, places the blame for this upon his impious advisers and upon the masses. Similarly, Josephus presents a more balanced portrait of Ahab (8.316-92, 398-420), shifting more of the blame for his misdeeds to Ahab's role-model Jeroboam and to his wife Jezebel.

Most remarkable of all is Josephus' treatment of Kings Jehoash (9.177-78, 184-86, 196-202) and Jehoiachin (10.97-102): in the former case the Bible (2 Kings 13:11) uses its familiar formula that "he did what was evil in the sight of the Lord," whereas Josephus (9.178) says that he was a good man. In the latter case, whereas the Bible (2 Kings 24:9, 2 Chron. 36:9) states that Jehoiachin did evil in the sight of the Lord, Josephus (10.100) describes him as kind and just, epithets he elsewhere applies to such worthies as Samuel (6.194), Hezekiah (9.260), Jehoiada (9.166), Zedekiah (10.120), and Nehemiah (11.183). It is striking that some of these radical departures from the biblical text are paralleled in Rabbinic literature.

Likewise, very notable is the extraordinary variation in the length of the eulogies which Josephus appends to his pericopes on the various biblical figures: most extraordinary in this connection is his encomium for Saul (6.343-50), which is, amazingly enough, three times the length of the one for Moses (4.328-31), more than three times the length of David's (7.390-91), and seventeen times the length of Solomon's (8.211). These are important clues regarding Josephus' priorities in his rewriting of the Bible.

The main factor explaining Josephus' modifications of the Bible is apologetics, i.e., answering anti-Jewish charges. In this respect, the *Antiquities* is, in effect, a preliminary version of his essay *Against Apion*. In particular, Josephus takes great pains to defend the Jews against the canard that they hate non-Jews. Particularly significant is that Josephus in a number of instances avoids mentioning incidents in which Israelites, such as Gideon (Judg. 6:25-32), Asa (2 Chron. 15:8), Jehoshaphat (2 Chron. 17:6), and Josiah (2 Kings 23:7-19), desecrate altars, statues, and temples pertaining to non-Jewish cults. Especially noteworthy is Josephus' omission of the biblical statement (2 Kings 10:27) that King Jehu's men broke down the pillars of Baal and made it a latrine "to this day." Again, instead of mentioning the introduction of pagan idolatry by Manasseh, as does the Bible, he focuses upon the sins of the Jews themselves (10.39).

An effective method employed by Josephus to defend Jews against the accusation of misanthropy is to have non-Jews, such as Jethro and Balaam, praise Jews. Josephus' elevation of Balaam[17] and especially of Jethro[18] is in direct contrast to the treatment of Philo, who had denigrated these figures. Another method of response employed by Josephus is to present non-Jewish personalities, such as Balaam, Belshazzar, Nebuchadnezzar, Darius, and Ahasuerus, and even the Pharaohs of Abraham's, Joseph's, and Moses' day, in a more human and more sympathetic light.[19] In the case of Balaam, the contrast between Josephus' relatively unbiased portrait, stressing historical, military, and political concerns, and the negative portrayal by Philo, the New Testament, and the rabbis is particularly striking. In his portrayal of Balaam, as elsewhere, Josephus emphasizes that the Israelites do not interfere in the affairs of other countries. The fact that he does not blame Eglon for subjugating the Israelites but rather castigates the Israelites themselves for their anarchy (5.185) shows how eager Josephus is to avoid unnecessarily attacking non-Jewish leaders.[20]

One of the most serious Roman charges against the Jews asserted their dual loyalty. Consequently, Josephus makes every effort to dwell on the fidelity of Jews to their rulers, as seen particularly in the case of Joseph. He systematically avoids divine statements promising Abraham and his descendants that they will inherit a great nation (Gen. 12:7, 13:14-17, 15:18, 17:19-21), since this would clearly imply the overthrow of Roman rule. Thus, very significantly, the purpose of circumcision, in Josephus' view, is not to seal God's promise of the land to Abraham but rather, non-politically, to prevent assimilation (1.192).

Josephus is especially wary of messiah-like figures or ancestors of messiahs. Even though Elijah was apparently more popular among the people than Elisha, Josephus favors Elisha, since Elijah was regarded as a zealot and as the forerunner of the messiah.[21]

Josephus is careful to praise those who are properly submissive to the ruling powers; hence, his very positive portrayal of Jehoiachin,[22] Gedaliah,[23] Daniel,[24] and Ezra.[25] Over and over again he reiterates that not to accept the authoritative governance of the ruler of the state is to thwart the divine plan itself. Nationhood is not, he stresses, a *sine qua non* for Judaism; rather, subservience to the superpower would bring peace and prosperity.

One of the most troublesome problems confronting Josephus was how to deal with the issue of intermarriage and assimilation in the Bible. He realized that if he opposed these practices too strongly he might be accused of being illiberal. On the other hand, if he did not oppose them at all he would be charged by Jews among his readers—and there is evidence, especially in his sharp denunciation of the Israelites who had sinned with the Midianite women (4.131-55) and of Samson (5.286-88, 292-94, 306-13), and Solomon (8.190-94) for their liaisons with non-Jewish women, that Josephus was also trying to reach a Jewish audience, especially in the diaspora—with being a traitor to Jewish values. Josephus' solution, notably in his version of Ezra's initiative against mixed marriages (11.152), is to condemn these not so much in themselves but rather because of the yielding to passion, a point of view that would surely have impressed Stoics in his reading audience. Josephus' opposition to intermarriage is based on the need for a state to maintain its homogeneous character—again a point of view that those acquainted with the attitude of the Athenians under Pericles would have appreciated. Another solution to the dilemma of how to deal with the issue of intermarriage may be seen in Josephus' treatment of Nehemiah's severe handling of the issue, namely, he simply disregards Nehemiah's effort at verifying genealogies (Neh. 7:5). In the specific case of Aaron's and Miriam's criticism of Moses for marrying an Ethiopian woman (Num. 12:1), which would surely have subjected them to the charge of prejudice, especially since the Ethiopians were so highly respected in antiquity, Josephus once again resolves the problem by omitting the criticism altogether.

Another very delicate issue was that of proselytism by Jews, which was a very successful movement before, during, and after the time of Josephus.[26] The Romans looked upon this as undermining their state, since proselytes gave money and owed their loyalty to a Jewish state. Hence, Josephus is careful to omit the passage in which Jethro acknowledges God (Exod. 18:8-12), as this would seem to be an indication of conversion to Judaism. Again, though the Rabbinic tradition makes much of Ruth as the ideal proselyte (Ruth Rabbah 2.24), Josephus avoids all mention of this theme in his Ruth pericope. Whereas in the biblical book of Jonah (1:5) we find the non-Jewish sailors shifting from their own pagan gods to worship of the Hebrew God, in Josephus there is no indication as to whether the sailors were or were not Jews or which were the divinities to whom they prayed.

While it is true that Josephus emphasizes, in the preface to the *Antiquities* (1.14), that the main lesson to be learned from his work is that God rewards those who obey him and punishes those who do not, in point of fact, Josephus thereafter generally downgrades the role of God in order to emphasize the virtues and achievements of his biblical heroes. The most striking examples are his accounts of Samson[27] and Jonah.[28] In the case of Ruth, whereas there are twenty-two mentions of God in the biblical account, there is only one such reference in Josephus' version, at the very end (5.337). The case of Deborah is likewise exceptional because Josephus, in his misogyny, sought to downgrade Deborah's role, doing so by exalting God's.[29] Hezekiah also is a special case, since Josephus desired, perhaps because of Hezekiah's lack of subservience to the superpower of his day, not to build him up as a person and hence preferred to highlight his dependence on God.[30] Again, whereas the name of God is not mentioned at all in the Hebrew Book of Esther, Josephus, following the additions to the Book of Esther in the Septuagint, includes a limited number of references to God for dramatic reasons, namely in noting God's ironic laughter at Haman's prosperity and when moralizing about his downfall.[31]

Josephus shows his true colors in his treatment of miracles. Although these were less of a problem because the Stoics, the prevalent philosophical movement in Josephus' time, did allow for divine intervention in the world, Josephus on a number of occasions suggests that it is up to the reader to decide what to make of the biblical miracles he relates (1.108; 2.348; 3.81, 268, 322; 4.158; 8.262; 10.281). In any case, he frequently rationalizes miracles, such as those performed by or in connection with Moses (3.5-9, 13-32, 33-38), Samson (5.310-11), Elijah (8.319, 342) Elisha (War 4.462-64), Jonah (9.213), and Daniel (10.214). The extraordinary circumstances of the deaths of Moses (4.326) and Elijah (9.28) are rationalized in a manner highly reminiscent of the disappearance of Oedipus in Sophocles' *Oedipus at Colonus*. His inclusion of the miracle of Balaam's speaking ass (4.108-11) is perhaps because readers would think of the parallel of Achilles' speaking horse (Homer, *Iliad* 19.408-17). In any case, he takes various steps to make it more plausible and finally ends with the phrase that the reader is free to think as he pleases about it (4.158). Likewise, because angels presented a problem since they seemed hardly different from the pagan demi-gods, he avoids mentioning them or rationalizes their appearance in connection with Jacob (1.279), Gideon (5.213), Samson (5.277), Elijah (8.349), and Daniel (10.259), or he has God take their place.

Another charge, as we see from the essay *Against Apion*, made against the Jews was that their Scriptures lacked historical reliability. To answer this claim, Josephus cites an array of non-Jewish writers, notably Berossus (1.158), Hieronymus the Egyptian (1.94), Mnaseas of Patera (1.94), Menander of Ephesus (8.324), and Nicolaus of Damascus (1.159-160), to support the historicity of the Flood and of episodes in the lives of Abraham (1.160), Solomon (8.144-49), and Elijah (8.324). It is particularly effective that Josephus avoids the Septuagint's word for Noah's ark but rather uses the same word found in Apollodorus (1.7.2), Lucian (*De Dea Syria* 12), and Plutarch (13.968F) with regard to the ark of Deucalion, thus equating the Flood with the flood associated with that pagan figure.

As to difficult and embarrassing biblical

passages, such as the longevity of the patri-archs (1.108) or David's sin with Bathsheba (7.130-53), Josephus either rationalizes them or tries to explain them otherwise. On the other hand, of the six passages later cited by Ibn Ezra in his commentary on Deut. 1:1 that raise serious questions about the authorship and date of composition of var-ious books of the Bible, Josephus very sig-nificantly omits all of them. Nevertheless, apparently aware that some of his readers would be Jews who might well be acquainted with his biblical source, he does not totally omit but rather leaves ambiguous such passages as Balaam's (4.125) and Daniel's (10.210) apparent predictions of the over-throw of the Roman Empire. He resolves chronological difficulties and generally omits anthropomorphisms.

In order to appeal to his Greek readers, Josephus draws on, for both style and con-tent, major Greek authors, notably Homer, Hesiod, Aeschylus, Sophocles, Euripides, Herodotus, Thucydides, Plato, and Aristotle. The influence of Homer, notably in Jose-phus' implicit equating of Abraham and Priam, is particularly notable in his account of the binding of Isaac,[32] while that of Hesiod may be seen in his version of the original bliss of mankind.[33] There are striking par-allels between the binding of Isaac and Euripides' account of the sacrifice of Iphi-genia.[34] Josephus' development of the concept of *hubris* and of its consequences is clearly influenced by the Greek tragedians.[35] Like the tragedians, Josephus, particularly in his accounts of Samson (5.312), Ahab (8.409, 412, 419), and Josiah (10.76), dwells on the degree to which the reversal of one's fortunes is due to fate rather than to one's own fail-ings. The increase in suspense, as in his accounts of Joseph (e.g., 2.133), Samuel's choice of Saul as king (6.37-40), and Esther (e.g., 11.261), and the heightening of irony, notably in his version of the 'Aqedah (1.222-36), Absalom's death (7.173), Ahab and the Naboth episode (8.358), Daniel (10.260), and Esther (e.g., 11.253), are likewise influenced by his reading of the tragedians. The influ-ence of the Stoic philosophers shows itself in Josephus' depiction of the *apatheia* (free-dom from concerns) in his characterization of the original bliss of mankind[36] and in the constant stress on Providence, a concept so central in Stoic thought.

One might say that though Josephus is ostensibly merely paraphrasing the Bible, he is actually, like Thucydides, the histo-rian he admired and imitated so much, stressing the degree to which the present repeats the past and the degree to which, therefore, one can and should learn from past history. One might say, too, that though he is ostensibly writing about events that occurred hundreds of years earlier, he is, in fact, writing a second edition of his work about the Jewish War against the Romans. In particular, in his biblical portraits one sees parallels between the Jews' struggles against the Assyrians and Babylonians lead-ing to the destruction of the First Temple and their resistance to the Romans ending in the destruction of the Second Temple. Thus, very significantly, in the *Jewish War* (6.103-5), where Josephus refers to the period preceding the destruction of the First Tem-ple, he cites the example of Jehoiachin as a laudable precedent in putting country and Temple ahead of oneself.

Much of Josephus' rewriting is a thinly veiled denunciation of the civil strife that had cost the Jews so heavily in the recent war against the Romans. This explains his highlighting of the rebellions of Korah (4.11-56) and Absalom (7.194-244) and his vehe-ment attack on Jeroboam (8.205-45, 265-87), who, because he broke the unity of the Jew-ish people, is portrayed as an even greater rogue than Ahab and Manasseh. Particularly striking is the similarity in language used by Josephus for Jeroboam's sedition and that of Josephus' great rival, John of Gischala.[37] On the other hand, Josephus accentuates Joshua's and Gideon's ability to avoid civil war and anarchy (5.114, 231). There are contemporary overtones in his fierce attack on the ignorant and fickle mob in the Moses pericope and on demagogues in the Absa-lom and Jeroboam episodes (7.196, 8.212). To the Romans, who had suffered through a century of civil strife from the time of the Gracchi (133 B.C.E.) to the final triumph of Octavian (31 B.C.E.) and who were so proud of their respect for the legal tradition, such features would surely strike a respon-sive chord.

Josephus' tremendous concern with Korah (4.11-56) was doubtless influenced by the fact that Korah was a Levite who had attempted to usurp the privileges of the priests, an issue that was very much alive in Josephus' own day and, of course, of special concern to Josephus the priest. Likewise, Josephus' tremendous pride in his belonging to the first of the twenty-four courses of priests (*Life* 2) will help to explain his omission of Aaron's role in the building of the Golden Calf, as well as his fierce attack on Jeroboam for naming his own priests instead of recognizing those who were priests by birth (8.228). We may surmise as well that a major reason Josephus gives so little attention to Nehemiah is that he wishes rather to build up Ezra, who was a priest, whereas Nehemiah was a mere layman.

Our examination has led us to stress Josephus' own creative contribution.[38] He has carefully chosen from his many sources, motivated largely by apologetic and literary concerns. Consistent patterns emerge that explain his additions, deletions, and modifications. There is likewise consistency in language and style. Josephus emerges as a historian in the grand manner, deserving of the tribute paid to him by Jerome (*Epistula ad Eustochium* 22.35) as a second Livy, combining the best of the two great schools of historiography, the Isocratean, with its stress on moralizing, psychologizing, and dramatizing, and the Aristotelian, with its emphasis on scientific, empirical investigation.

Bibliography

Attridge, H.W., *The Interpretation of Biblical History in the Antiquitates Judaicae of Flavius Josephus* (Missoula, 1976).

Feldman, L.H., *Josephus's Interpretation of the Bible* (Berkeley, 1998).

Feldman, L.H., *Studies in Josephus' Rewritten Bible* (Leiden, 1998).

Feldman, L.H., trans. and commentary, *Judean Antiquities 1-4* (Leiden, 2000).

Spilsbury, P., *The Image of the Jew in Flavius Josephus' Paraphrase of the Bible* (Tübingen, 1998).

Notes

[1] All references to Josephus are to the *Antiquities* unless otherwise noted.

[2] The fact is that the rabbis themselves sanctioned the omission of the translation of certain biblical passages when they read the Bible in the synagogue (B. Meg. 25a-b), presumably because of the embarrassment involved. The list does not, however, completely coincide with Josephus.

[3] R.L. Coggins, "The Samaritans in Josephus," in L.H. Feldman and G. Hata, eds., *Josephus, Judaism, and Christianity* (Detroit, 1987), p. 270, argues that Josephus' omission of details about the Samaritans does not indicate that he intended this as a deliberate anti-Samaritan polemic, since this implies a great degree of subtlety both in Josephus and in his readers. T. Thornton, "Anti-Samaritan Exegesis Reflected in Josephus' Retelling of Deuteronomy, Joshua, and Judges," in *Journal of Theological Studies* 47 (1996), p. 129, n. 13, however, in reply, argues that Josephus may be relying on an anti-Samaritan source. We would add that in view of the generally systematic pattern in Josephus' omissions, not only in connection with the Samaritans but in many other matters that we have noted, such omissions should be taken seriously.

[4] As H.St.J. Thackeray, ed., *Josephus* (London, 1930), vol. 4, p. 360, n. a, remarks, Rabbinic literature offers no parallel for such a scruple. The third-century R. Samuel states that the rabbis prohibited the recitation of the Ten Commandments before the Shema in the daily service due to the insinuations of the heretics (*minim*) (B. Ber. 12a), presumably, we may suggest, because it would give these commandments undue prominence and might lead heretics to limit the obligatory requirements to the Ten Commandments alone. That such a prohibition was of long standing is indicated by the second-century R. Nathan (ibid.).

[5] See L.H. Feldman, "Josephus' Portrait of Jacob," in *Jewish Quarterly Review* 79 (1988-89), pp. 130-133.

[6] Feldman, "Josephus' Portrait of Jacob" (above, n. 5), pp. 123-124.

[7] See L.H. Feldman, ed., *Josephus* (London, 1965), vol. 9, pp. 48-51 on *Ant.* 18.63-64; and idem, "The *Testimonium Flavianum*: The State of the Question," in R.F. Berkey and S.A. Edwards, eds., *Christological Perspectives* (New York, 1982), pp. 179-199, 288-293.

[8] So A. Paul, "Flavius Josephus' 'Antiquities of the Jews:' An Anti-Christian Manifesto," in *New Testament Studies* 31 (1985), pp. 473-480.

[9] See, however, D. Mendels, "Pseudo-Philo's *Biblical Antiquities*, the 'Fourth Philosophy' and the Political Messianism of the First Century C.E.," in J.H. Charlesworth, ed., *The Messiah: Developments in Earliest Judaism and Christianity* (Leiden, 1992), pp. 261-275, who notes that although Pseudo-Philo, like most of the Jews of his time, has messianic hopes, he seems to be against a messiah in the present. Mendels argues that even the Gospels (e.g., Matt. 16:13-20, Mark 8:23-26, 9:2-13, 10:47-52), which are full of messianic allusions, nevertheless tone down messianism. There can be little doubt, nevertheless, that by the time of Josephus, there was vigorous expectation of a Davidic messiah, at least in certain circles, as we can see in a number of documents—the Qumran scrolls, the Testaments of the Twelve Patriarchs, and the Psalms of Solomon. See J.J. Collins, "Mes-

sianism in the Maccabean Period," in J. Neusner, et al., eds., *Judaisms and Their Messiahs at the Turn of the Christian Era* (Cambridge, 1987), pp. 104-105.

[10] Neusner, op. cit., pp. 265-282, concludes that the messianic idea has no place of consequence in the Mishnah, though he admits that it later became a driving force in Rabbinic circles. Cf., L.H. Schiffman, "The Concept of the Messiah in Second Temple and Rabbinic Literature," in *Review and Expositor* 84 (1987), pp. 235-246, especially p. 242, who comments on the lack of emphasis on messianism in Tannaitic materials and suggests that "the experience of the destruction of the nation and its cult center in the first revolt [66-74], and the prohibition of even visiting the ruins of Jerusalem in the second, must have led the sages to seek other means for the immediate redemption of Israel."

[11] See L.H. Feldman, "Josephus' Portrait of Solomon," in *Hebrew Union College Annual* 66 (1995), pp. 114-119.

[12] See ibid., pp. 129-130.

[13] On Josephus' audience, see L.H. Feldman, *Josephus's Interpretation of the Bible* (Berkeley, 1998), pp. 46-50.

[14] See L.H. Feldman, "Josephus' Portraits of the Pharaohs," in *Syllecta Classica* 4 (1993), pp. 52-54.

[15] For a discussion of this passage, its sources, and Josephus' possible reasons for inserting it, see L.H. Feldman, *Judean Antiquities* 1-4 (Leiden, 2000), pp. 200-202, nn. 663-664.

[16] See S. Rappaport, *Agada und Exegese bei Flavius Josephus* (Wien, 1930), p. 117, n. 143, for other medieval Jewish parallels.

[17] L.H. Feldman, "Josephus' Portrait of Balaam," in *Studia Philonica Annual* 5 (1993), pp. 48-83.

[18] L.H. Feldman, "Josephus' Portrait of Jethro," in C.A. Evans and S. Talmon, eds., *The Quest for Context and Meaning: Studies in Biblical Intertexuality in Honor of James A. Sanders* (Leiden, 1997), pp. 481-502.

[19] See Feldman (above, n. 14), pp. 49-63.

[20] See L.H. Feldman, "Josephus' Portrait of Ehud," in J.C. Reeves and J. Kampen, eds., *Pursuing the Text: Studies in Honor of Ben Zion Wacholder on the Occasion of His Seventieth Birthday* (Sheffield, 1994), pp. 189-193.

[21] See L.H. Feldman, "Josephus' Portrait of Elijah," in *Scandinavian Journal of the Old Testament* 8 (1994), pp. 61-86; "Josephus' Portrait of Elisha," in *Novum Testamentum* 36 (1994), pp. 1-28.

[22] See L.H. Feldman, "Josephus' Portrait of Jehoiachin," in *Proceedings of the American Philosophical Society* 139.1 (1995), pp. 11-31.

[23] L.H. Feldman, "Josephus' Portrait of Gedaliah," in *Shofar* 12 (1993), pp. 1-10.

[24] L.H. Feldman, "Josephus' Portrait of Daniel," in *Henoch* 14 (1992), pp. 37-96.

[25] L.H. Feldman, "Josephus' Portrait of Ezra," in *Vetus Testamentum* 43 (1993), pp. 190-214.

[26] See L.H. Feldman, *Jew and Gentile in the Ancient World: Attitudes and Interactions from Alexander to Justinian* (Princeton, 1993), pp. 288-341.

[27] See L.H. Feldman, "Josephus' Version of Samson," in *Journal for the Study of Judaism* 19 (1988), pp. 204-210.

[28] L.H. Feldman, "Josephus' Interpretation of Jonah," in *Association for Jewish Studies Review* 17 (1992), pp. 8-11.

[29] L.H. Feldman, "Josephus' Portrait of Deborah," in A. Caquot, M. Hadas-Lebel, and J. Riaud, eds., *Hellenica et Judaica: Hommage à Valentin Nikipowetzky* (Leuven-Paris, 1986), pp. 123-124.

[30] See L.H. Feldman, "Josephus' Portrait of Hezekiah," in *Journal of Biblical Literature* 111 (1992), p. 608.

[31] L.H. Feldman, "Hellenizations in Josephus' Version of Esther," in *Transactions of the American Philological Association* 101 (1970), pp. 168-170.

[32] L.H. Feldman, "Josephus as a Biblical Interpreter: The "*Aqedah*," in *Jewish Quarterly Review* 75 (1984-85), pp. 215-217.

[33] L.H. Feldman, "Hellenizations in Josephus' Portrayal of Man's Decline," in J. Neusner, ed., *Religions in Antiquity: Essays in Memory of Erwin Ramsdell Goodenough* (Leiden, 1968), pp. 340-342.

[34] Feldman, "Josephus as a Biblical Interpreter," pp. 219-222, 235-236, 242-246.

[35] See L.H. Feldman, "The Influence of the Greek Tragedians on Josephus," in Asher Ovadiah, ed., *The Howard Gilman International Conferences, 1: Hellenic and Jewish Arts: Interaction, Tradition and Renewal* (Tel Aviv, 1998), pp. 51-80.

[36] Feldman, "Hellenizations in Josephus' Portrayal of Man's Decline," p. 344.

[37] L.H. Feldman, "Josephus' Portrait of Jeroboam," in *Andrews University Seminary Studies* 31 (1993), pp. 43-46.

[38] So also P. Bilde, *Flavius Josephus between Jerusalem and Rome: His Life, His Works, and Their Importance* (Sheffield, 1988), pp. 141-150.

LOUIS H. FELDMAN

JUDAISM, THE SECOND HALF OF THE TWENTIETH CENTURY:

Jacob Neusner writes that "Judaism in America is different from Judaism as it has ever been known, and as it is practiced everywhere else in the world today."[1] The study of American Judaism is therefore a fascinating if complex phenomenon. The practice of Judaism in the United States in the second half of the twentieth century has been influenced by a number of factors. While this fifty-year period saw the development of the four major American Jewish denominations (Reform, Conservative, Orthodox, and Reconstructionist), American Jews were divided into those who observed Halakhah and those who only practiced selected elements of the Jewish legal system. Sociologists Marshall Sklare and Joseph Greenblum explained that for most American Jews, religious practices were acceptable if they could be redefined in modern terms, did not require social isolation, were responsive to and in relative harmony with what they perceived to be the dominant ethos of American religious culture, were child-centered, and required only periodic observance.[2] Even Orthodox Jews, for the most part committed to the observance of the full spectrum of Jewish religious practices, showed signs of selectivity in their degree of punctiliousness in their practice of different commandments. The difference in attitude and approach to practice between these two groups became more pronounced over the course of the second half of the twentieth century.

Traditional Judaism holds that all of the commandments of the Torah must be practiced in their entirety. In contrast, the American non-orthodox movements have consciously and deliberately set out to reinterpret traditional religious concepts and have made changes in how the Jewish religion is practiced. One accordingly must distinguish between American Jews who are committed to observing Judaism as a religion and those who wish primarily to retain an ethnic identity. Jacob Neusner has called this first group "Judaists" to distinguish them from those who see their Jewish identities as social or cultural rather than religious. The problem of distinguishing between "ethnic" and "religious" Jews is complex. Much religious behavior can be understood as expressions of ethnicity, and much ethnic identification may mask religious yearnings.

Much of the practice of American Judaism in the second half of the twentieth century took place in the synagogue. Jack Wertheimer summarizes a generally accepted view when he writes that "the American synagogue attracts more members and affords greater opportunities for participation than any other voluntary institutions established by Jews in the United States."[3] While Judaism had popularly been regarded as based on home practice, the synagogue attempted to fill the void left by steadily declining home-based ritual observance. This attempt was more successful in some cases than others. Some congregations grew into large, vibrant, lively places, while others developed reputations as "bar mitzvah factories." Many American Jews are willing to experiment with different types of religious ceremonies. They are searching for a vague sense of meaning, which frequently is described by the word "spirituality." The assumption is now prevalent that it does not really matter what you believe. What is important is to participate in the experience. This participation hopefully will create a spark of spiritual holiness that will enrich one's life by transforming one's soul. God may or may not play a central role in this process, but one does not have to believe in traditional notions of God in order to practice Judaism.

The practice of Judaism in the second half of the twentieth century has been deeply influenced by the impact of individualism on American society. Since the 1960s, Americans have come to regard religion more and more as a matter of personal choice rather than an inherited obligation. This choice includes being able to choose one's perspective within one's denomination, but it also includes the ability to choose from among different religious denominational alternatives. It even means having the choice of choosing whether to affiliate with any religious tradition or to remain completely removed from religious activity of any type. This individualistic approach has produced a religious marketplace in which faiths and denominations openly compete for believers from outside their congregational spheres to supplement their existing memberships.

Within Judaism, the Reform movement has been the most aggressive in participating in this religious marketplace, developing a series of programs to introduce non-Jews to Judaism. Sizable numbers have converted to Judaism, including many non-Jews married to Jewish partners. "Jews by choice" bring a different perspective with them into the synagogue. Some observers have noted that converts to Judaism see Judaism in more purely religious terms, whereas many Jews by birth see it in more ethnic terms. But this observation is only partially true and has to be supplemented by other ways of looking at the impact of converts on Jewish belief and practice. The 1990 National Jewish Population Survey indicates that there were approximately 185,000 converts to Judaism in the United States at that time. These individuals appeared to observe as many or more rituals as born Jews, an indication that many if not most converts take their new religion very seriously. In homes in which a spouse had converted to Judaism, rituals such as lighting Sabbath candles were more likely to be observed than in homes in which both partners were born Jews.

One of the problems in describing Judaism in the second half of the twentieth century is that the dominant American Jewish identity focused on what has been termed "civil Judaism." As Jonathan S. Woocher has explained, this Judaism affirms the unity of the Jewish people, their mutual responsibility, the need to work for the survival of the Jewish people in a threatening world, the centrality of the State of Israel, a nostalgic appreciation for the value of Jewish tradition, a stress on doing good deeds and promoting philanthropy, and seeing their Jewishness and Americanness as compatible and indeed complimentary forms of overlapping identity.[4] As a consequence, most American Jews did not see direct association between Jewish identity and actual religious practices. Instead, they focused on "feeling" Jewish, a subjective state that has become harder and harder clearly to identify and that is too amorphous easily to be transmitted from parent to child. As a consequence, many children and grandchildren of such Jews, even ones highly involved in the Jewish community, have drifted away from that community.

Distinctions within Orthodoxy: For the Orthodox and a small number of non-Orthodox traditional Jews, Judaism is defined through the halakhah, which dictates all aspects of daily life, ritual as much as ethical. Increasingly, however, sociologists have identified subgroups within Orthodoxy, defined by their adherents' level of ritual practice: "traditionalists" (also called ultra Orthodox or Haredi), "centrists" (until the 1980s frequently referred to as modern Orthodox), and "nominals" (also called non-observant Orthodox). Samuel Heilman and Steven Cohen categorized these three groups on the basis of indicative observances, beginning with the fact that Orthodox men show higher rates of ritual observance than Orthodox women, who are not understood to be obligated to perform many rituals, including prayer and donning phylacteries. Asking questions about fasting also proved a useful tool for distinguishing between the three subgroups, as only within the traditional Orthodox group did 100% of the men fast on all fast days.

Strictness of observance of the dietary laws also distinguished the three groups, as did observance of Sabbath law, with the traditional Orthodox being the most punctilious in both regards. Notably, while in the 1950s there were many non-observant Orthodox, whose use of electricity on the Sabbath, for instance, distinguished them from the traditional Orthodox, their numbers have dropped, as has their percentage of the Orthodox population in the United States. This makes sense because in the period surrounding World War II, many American Jewish immigrants and children of immigrants, while not strictly observant themselves, had grown up in Orthodox homes and had absorbed the belief that any other form of Judaism was inauthentic. But such non-observant Orthodoxy was a phenomenon of a specific generation. The following generation was far more Americanized and had far less emotional affinity with Orthodoxy. Some joined Conservative or Reform congregations, and a substantial number left religious life entirely.

Others were influenced by their Orthodox upbringing and embraced traditional Judaism as Baalei Teshuvah (singular, Baal Teshuvah), literally, people who repent. In the 1970s, the Baal Teshuvah phenomenon was widely reported in the Jewish and general press. Particularly influential was a long article written by Ellen Willis in *Rolling Stone Magazine* on her brother Chaim, who studied at Aish HaTorah Yeshivah and became an Orthodox rabbi. While Willis herself had no intention of becoming Orthodox, her description of the Baal Teshuvah world was generally sympathetic, and the article was repeatedly reprinted by Orthodox organizations. Many others noticed the phenomena and commented on it, in part because it went against what most observers expected would be the momentum towards greater acculturation and higher levels of assimilation. Despite the fact that this movement attracted a great deal of attention, the numbers involved were relatively small and within a few years a percentage of Baalei Teshuvah reverted to their original levels of observance.

Another distinction between the traditional and modern Orthodox concerned dating and sexuality. The traditional Orthodox followed the practice of arranging a small number of dates leading rapidly to a decision to marry. In some Hassidic communities, parents made the decision, and the marriage ceremony might occur after the couple had only met a few times. In contrast, the modern Orthodox have adopted many of the broader societies' attitudes. Even otherwise highly observant individuals may ignore prohibitions on pre-marital sexual contact. While the halakhah prohibits any physical contact whatsoever between unmarried men and women many modern Orthodox rabbis freely shake hands with women and even kiss them on the cheek.

In the 1950s and even later, there was little difference in practice between many Orthodox and Conservative congregations. Both groups used the term "congregation" rather than "temple," the common designation within Reform, to refer themselves. Worship was conducted almost entirely in Hebrew and few, if any, deletions were permitted. Male worshippers wore head coverings (*kippot*) and prayer shawls (*tallitot*), and traditional practices, such as the priests' blessing of the congregation (*Birchat Cohanim*) continued to be performed even in Conservative settings. The major difference was the fact that most Conservative synagogues allowed men and women to sit together, a practice countenanced in few Orthodox synagogues.[5] As the second half of the twentieth century wore on, the central Orthodox congregational organizations put a tremendous amount of pressure even on those few Orthodox congregations to eliminate the practice. They also pressured all congregations to erect a physical barrier between the men's and women's sections (*mehitzah*). Orthodox rabbis became more traditional and were unlikely to consider a post at a congregation that allowed such practices. In the 1950s, many young men from a Orthodox backgrounds attended Yeshiva College and the Orthodox Rabbi Isaac Elchanan Theological Seminary (RIETS) but then took a Conservative pulpit. By the end of the century, this was extremely rare.

The Conservative Movement: Marshall Sklare has argued that the Conservative movement was in large part a second generation phenomenon. In the post-World War II period, the attraction of the movement to this generation meant that hundreds of new Conservative synagogues were built throughout the country, particularly in suburbia. American Jews saw Conservatism as a happy middle-point between the Orthodoxy of their youth (or that their parents had left as to constraining) and the Reform temple that was seen as too "church-like." This appeal meant that practice in the Conservative movement varied tremendously. Nevertheless, by the 1950s, a Conservative style of religious observance was developed that was distinct from Orthodoxy on the one hand and Reform on the other. The Conservative movement emphasized observance of the Sabbath and the dietary law but allowed the use of electricity under certain circumstances and even permitted driving to Sabbath and holiday worship. Technology thus could foster ritual Jewish practice. Unfortunately, the distinctive Conservative approach to observance was never followed by the vast majority of the membership, which rejected strict norms of Sabbath and dietary observance.

In the ground-breaking decision allowing driving to worship services on the Sabbath or a holiday, the Conservative movement took into account the fact that most Conservative Jews did not make decisions regarding, for instance, where to live based primarily on the strictures of traditional Jewish ritual law. There was, however, a minority that held to strict observance of Jewish law and ritual. Daniel Elazar and Rela Mintz Geffen write that the distinction between elite and mass thus is "more characteristic of Conservative Judaism than of any other branches."[6] The distinction between the elite and masses made it possible for the more traditional elements in the individual congregations to exercise a high degree of control over all officially expected ritual practices. While the majority in most congregations observed few of the more demanding ritual behaviors, the elite ensured that the synagogue would insist in the public arena of a maximalist approach to religious practice.

This approach may have alienated numbers of nominally Conservative Jews. People unwilling to adopt the forms set forth by their congregations distanced themselves from religious practice in general. Still, by the 1980s, many members of Conservative congregations felt a renewed need to explore religious practices in the same way that Reform and Reconstructionist Jews were being encouraged to do. These experimental approaches included everything from New Moon (*Rosh Hodesh*) groups for women to meditative spiritual retreats. In the earlier decades, these experimental approaches at times were discouraged or even repressed by the elite because they ignored or violated halakhic ordinances.

By the mid-1980s, the senior Talmudists at the Conservative movement's Jewish Theological Seminary (JTS), who had been influential enough to stop many attempts at religious innovation had passed away or retired. Once JTS decided to ordain women in its Rabbinical school, most of the remaining traditionalists left the movement. They formed the Union for Traditional Conservative Judaism (UTCJ), later changing the name to the Union for Traditional Judaism (UTJ), an acknowledgement that they no longer shared core beliefs or practices with the Conservative movement. The UTJ stood for a rigorous halakhic approach to Judaism, which differed little from centrist or modern Orthodoxy. Led by David Weiss Halivni, the UTJ allowed for a self-conscious acceptance of critical scholarship. Weiss Halivni had taught Talmud at JTS before taking the Lucius N. Littauer Professorship of Classical Jewish Civilization at Columbia University. Weiss Halivni was determined to synthesize modern critical biblical scholarship with halakhic commitment. In his *Revelation Restored* and other works, he argued that it was possible to acknowledge the historical development of the biblical texts and at the same time to remain committed to the tradition of revelation.[7] But even the most liberal of the modern Orthodox refused to consider any sort of conglomeration or merger with Halivni's traditionalist movement. Its ideological origins and overt acceptance of critical scholarship meant that association with it would mark any associated group as definitively separate from Orthodoxy. We thus see the extent to which the Orthodox and non-Orthodox are divided by more than differences in levels of ritual observance.

Tradition within Contemporary Judaism: For many American Jews, religious practice is a way to express a connection to "the tradition," a distinctive concept in modern or postmodern society, quite different from what existed in the pre-modern world, when members of society followed traditional ways at least in part because they could not conceive of any other way of living. This is a fundamentally different situation from that of the American Jew who consciously and deliberately chooses to observe all or selected elements of the tradition. As Samuel Heilman puts it,

> To maintain tradition when all about you others do not, to define a world of sacred order when the profane is the order of the day, to assert that change need not occur when all around you everything has undeniably changed, is a fundamental transformation of the meaning of tradition, the sacred, and the past.[8]

American Jews have a choice whether to accept the tradition in whole or in part. They also have a choice how they will put those beliefs into practice. The Orthodox may choose to practice the tradition in its entirety in their belief that this is what God commands them to do. But most American Jews who choose to practice traditional rituals do so because those rituals speak to them. They understand that they are free to choose what practices to observe, to ignore, or even to transform into new forms. But how should these observances be understood? Charles Liebman distinguishes between "ritual" and "ceremony." The terms are used interchangeably in casual conversation, and they frequently are used in a general sense, even by specialists. But Liebman argues that "ritual" should be understood as stylized repetitious behavior that is explicitly religious. It involves intentional bodily engagement believed to be efficacious and connects the participant to the transcendent presence of God by allowing him or her to do exactly what God commanded. The worshipper believes that ritual sways God to perform or not perform a given act, but that this can only occur if the ritual is correctly performed.

Ceremony, on the other hand, is done in large part to affirm that the individual is a member of a social and cosmological order. It is a voluntary action intended to give meaning to the individual's life and so is not necessarily regarded as being commanded by God. The ceremony, accordingly, does not need to be performed in a precise manner. Rather, there is a large measure of flexibility which allows the participants to mold the ceremony to fit their needs and desires. The ceremony gives a concrete representation of the social order of the group and therefore is viewed as a serious and sometimes solemn event. But this can change over the course of time, depending on the ethos of the particular group. Since the ceremony is not believed to be preordained, it is appropriate to place certain individuals in charge of the preparation and performance. This may be the rabbi or cantor, or it may be a small number of congregational members. Either way, they are expected to prepare a ceremony that is both appropriate and suitable.

Orthodox Jews observe the mitzvot because they believe God commanded them to do so. Such observance thus qualifies as ritual. Non-Orthodox Jews, on the other hand, are unlikely to perform "rituals," because they do not believe that the precise manner in which a religious act is performed matters to God. Rather, increasing numbers of Jews perform "ceremonial" acts. When a woman lights candles in the synagogue even though the sun has already set, the congregation sees her act as symbolically ushering in the Sabbath. From a ritual point of view, lighting the candles after dark is prohibited. But from a ceremonial point of view, her act is meaningful and beautiful. Liebman provides other examples. Many Reform congregations conduct a ceremony in which three or even four generations of a family pass a Torah scroll from arms to arms, ending up with the Bar or Bat Mitzvah child's holding the scroll. This makes no sense from a ritual point of view, because the only ritual purpose for taking the scroll out of the ark is to read the weekly lection. But from a ceremonial point of view,

the congregation is celebrating the ties between grandparents, parents, and child in the symbolic context of the temple. The Torah passing ceremony emphasizes generational continuity and affirms each family member's participation in this transmission of Judaism in a world that seems to dismiss such ties.[9]

Another example is the increasing popularity of *havdalah*, a series of blessings that marks the distinction between the Sabbath and the secular week. In this short service, blessings over wine, spices, and light fulfill specific ritual obligations. But Liebman cites the use of *havdalah* within communal Jewish life as an example of the increasing importance of ceremonial behavior among non-Orthodox Jews. The ceremonies are far more elaborate than in traditional contexts and often conclude with all of the participants' holding hands in a circle and singing. Many find this inspiring and spiritually uplifting but are open about the fact that they have no intention of conducting this ritual in their homes the following week. At home, they do not observe even those ceremonies they very much enjoyed in the communal setting of a conference or other Jewish gathering.

Non-Orthodox Jews have such a sense of synagogue rites precisely because they see them as ceremony rather than ritual. Synagogue services are a series of symbolic representations that allow the worshipper to derive a variety or religious and spiritual meanings from what transpires. If those present are left largely untouched, they feel free to criticize the performance of the ceremony. This is a particular problem in the Conservative movement, where the majority of congregants see worship as ceremonial, while many of their rabbis view it as ritual. Reform benefits from the fact that clergy and laity alike recognize a symbolic purpose to religious activities. Virtually all Reform Jews hold that intention is what matters most and that the precise manner in which a religious act is performed is inconsequential. They thus confirm the importance of ethics over ritual.[10] Reform rabbis thus frequently recall the tale of the ignorant eastern European boy who whistles in the synagogue on Yom Kippur because he does not know any better. In response to the congregants' anger, the Baal Shem Tov declared that the boy had sent the most efficacious prayer to God: he did what he felt was right rather than simply what was demanded by the ritual.

The Reform movement's new interest in ceremony has attracted enormous attention. Many congregations observe two days of Rosh Hashshanah whereas earlier virtually all observed only one. Most congregations have increased the amount of Hebrew used in worship, and a series of new prayer books has appeared to meet this need. The latest ones include extensive transliterations, reflecting the reality that most congregants cannot read Hebrew sufficiently to keep up with the new trend. Even ceremonies such as *Tashlich*, an ancient folk custom in which, at the New Year, bread crumbs are thrown into flowing water symbolically to represent the casting away of sins, have been recovered. This has occurred despite the fact that once many Jews viewed this ceremony as smacking of superstition, so as to be exactly the type of custom modern Jews should avoid. But, clearly, times have changed, and Jews now inhabit a world in which it has become clear that logic and science cannot answer all questions. They intuitively understand that they need to seek out an emotional response to what they see around them that may not be explainable in purely rational terms. They are therefore much more open to at least trying new types of ceremonies. If the original meaning does not suit them, they work to fine new understandings. This approach has become particularly popular in Reform congregations, part of a dramatic reorientation in that movement.

Reform Jews once emphasized the "religious" aspect of their identity and minimized or even denied the ethnic component. The movement stressed that Judaism was an ethical system based on a pure form of monotheism. Traditional ritual was held to distract the worshiper from what is central in the Judaic message. Reform congregants thus came to expect a Sabbath experience comparable to the formal Protestant services their Christian neighbors attended. But over the course of the last generation, the Reform movement has moved dramatically towards embracing many of the traditional practices that had been jettisoned at the end of the nineteenth century.

Classical Reform Judaism developed a rigid and ossified form of practice that created its own orthodoxy. Neo-traditionalists comment that Classical Reformers are just as determined to prevent the performance of certain rituals as Orthodox Jews are determined to ensure that those rituals are done. In some cases, fervent opposition can develop over the reintroduction of rituals simply because of aesthetic concerns. For example, the marching of the Torah around the congregation was not done in Classical Reform congregations because such movement could not be carefully choreographed and because many found the traditional kissing of a prayer shawl or prayer book that had touched the scroll to be unseemly. While there was never any theological opposition to the practice, its reintroduction could create serious and ongoing conflict.

Increasing Reliance on Halakhic Codes: A number of scholars have observed that in pre-modern Jewish society, Jews knew what observances were expected or demanded. Living in a closed environment that remained constant over many generations made it natural to conduct oneself in a certain manner. But modernity undermined the stability. The sense of continuity was damaged, if not destroyed. It became harder instinctually to know how to practice Judaism. The Orthodox reacted by relying heavily on halakhic codes. Indeed, some believe this has contributed to the increasingly stringent decisions being made by Orthodox decisors, and thus Haym Soloveitchik has argued that the nature of contemporary Orthodox spirituality has been transformed, with religious texts now playing a controlling role in communal life far beyond what had been the norm in earlier generations. This was a new kind of religiosity, rooted in texts and transmitted in schools. The Orthodox home supplemented what was being taught in the yeshivah rather than the other way around. "Having lost the touch of His presence, they seek now solace in the pressure of His yolk."[11] Despite Soloveitchik's criticism, many Orthodox Jews in the yeshivah world are pleased with the increasing attention to halakhic texts and the higher degree of ritual conformity. Many non-Orthodox Jews likewise felt the absence of an all-encompassing Jewish society they could draw on culturally and religiously. But being neither willing nor able to commit themselves to an Orthodox lifestyle, some took whatever inspirations were available and improvised. This led to the creation of new observances and the re-casting of pre-existing ones to meet new spiritual needs.

The social implications of halakhic observance have changed, partly as a consequence of the increasing acceptance accorded to Jews and Judaism in the United States. As late as the 1950s, keeping kosher meant bringing lunch to work, that eating out was almost impossible, and that going away to a hotel for vacation, except in a few locations, was out of the question. By the 1980s, every major city and quite a few moderate sized ones had kosher restaurants, numerous hotels and resorts maintained kosher kitchens and some kashered their entire kitchens for Passover, and Rabbinic organizations scrambled to certify thousands of grocery-store products as kosher.

This wide-spread acceptance of observance made it much easier to be a traditional Jew and also seemed to be a tremendous victory for the modern Orthodox, who had long argued that it was possible to be both modern and Orthodox. But it also initiated a trend away from moderate Orthodoxy, such that, by the 1980s, the modern Orthodox were on the defensive. The traditional Orthodox accused them of compromising religious observance to the point where they were virtually indistinguishable from many non-Orthodox Jews. The problem was exacerbated by the fact that many of the teachers in modern Orthodox schools were quite traditionally observant. Thus the children in these schools in many cases were taught a perspective dramatically at odds with the ethos and practices of their parents. Moreover, even moderately observant parents felt that the ultra-Orthodox had a religious authenticity that they, who had compromised with American cultural mores, lacked. Eager to reinforce their Orthodox credentials, the modern Orthodox began to refer to themselves as "centrist" rather than "modern." Concurrently, the community adopted more and more stringencies. For example, whereas in the 1950s modern Orthodox women did not cover their heads after marriage, by the 1980s, this was a frequent practice. Virtually every aspect of halakhic behavior came under scrutiny.

As the twentieth century progressed, American Jews were observing fewer and fewer rituals. The pattern was for the grandparents, who may have come from Europe, to observe more, their children to observe fewer, and their grandchildren to observe little or nothing. The number of Jewish rituals performed was seen as indicating the individual's degree of assimilation, and the decreasing levels of observance thus were cited as proof that assimilation was increasing. But in recent years, sociologists have come to believe that the studies had overemphasized the simple question of whether a ritual, such as the lighting Hanukah candles, was performed. Rather, this information had to be supplemented with an understanding of why individuals were or were not practicing a given ritual. Further, there had to be sensitivity to the possibility that Jewish religious sentiment was being transformed in ways that were not picked up by the traditional questions. By the 1990s, a split seemed to emerge. Increasing numbers of Jews of all ages were rediscovering their Jewish heritage. Many were experimenting with various types of observances, including innovative approaches. At the same time, a large population was alienated from Jewish practice and seemed content to remain secular.

The emergence of a Jewish "civil faith" led many American Jews to work long hours as volunteers for the Jewish federation and other local and national Jewish organizations. Their Jewishness was expressed publicly. They defended Israel on T.V. and spoke about anti-Semitism at local churches. No one could accuse them of hiding their Jewish identities or of stressing private ritual observances over communal needs. But by the 1980s, many felt that this civic Judaism lacked spiritual content precisely because it was so public. Many Jewish institutional leaders observed little ceremony in their family lives. One rabbi told journalist Charles Silberman that "These federation leaders may be Jews in public, but they're goyim at home."[12] By the end of the century, this began to change, particularly among the younger generation of federation volunteers. This trend was encouraged by the federations themselves, which organized seminars and weekend retreats to expose volunteers to Jewish religion. Whereas once the federation maintained a strict neutrality—religion being divisive in a community split into distinct religious movements—over the past two decades it has emerged as a proponent of voluntaristic ceremonialism. Concern with the future of Judaism has been one of the major reasons.

Many of the older Jewish leaders have become increasingly concerned that the younger generation may not follow in their footsteps. And, indeed, many younger people are alienated from Judaism in any of its forms. But others are increasingly active. The Jewish practices of many younger people developed in response to exposure at summer camp or youth group rather than from what they observed at home or in their synagogue. These informal Jewish experiences are very important because they enable young people to see Judaism practiced in a vibrant environment, which is frequently in dramatic contrast to what they observe in their local communities, where Jewish practice might be uninspired and uninspiring.

Judaism has always been a religion in which holy texts and commentaries are central. And yet, it is clear that one cannot rely on the text to explain religious practice in the United States. Even among the Orthodox, religious practice can be idiosyncratic, depending on social and cultural factors in addition to halakhic ones. In the non-Orthodox denominations, religious practice is determined almost completely by subjective factors. The experiential element of religion is becoming more important, and practices that emphasize spirituality have gained in popularity as a result. In previous generations, religiosity was intrinsically connected to a comprehensive belief system. Jews of all denominations were also much more likely to accept the authority

not only of local rabbis but of denominational leaders. Tradition, however that concept was understood, also weighed heavily on the individual and congregation. By contrast, at the end of the twentieth century, individually centered spirituality is the criteria by which religious meaning is gauged. Synagogues that have been able to market themselves as emphasizing the experiential element of Judaism have generally gained membership, while those that have focused on intellectual discourse, social justice, or doctrinal rigidity have lost members. Many congregations have found that religious practices formerly held privately in the home can now be offered as communal activities that attract significant numbers. An example is the Sabbath dinner, once a home activity separate from the synagogue worship that might precede or follow it, but today frequently part of an encompassing Friday evening synagogue program, appreciated for its convenience and sociability.

Most American Jews have become comfortable with the personal picking and choosing of what frequently is referred to as "salad bar religion." Of course, most American Jews had picked from among the various traditional practices from their earliest days in the country. But it was regarded as a problematic reality that needed to be overcome or swept under the rug, depending on one's perspective. But by the 1980s, the American consumerist mentality had so influenced American attitudes to religion that a pick-and-choose approach to religion was no longer seen as problematic. Rather, American Jews were consciously and deliberately evaluating various Jewish practices to find a good "fit." Many wished to combine Jewish institutional affiliation with spiritual elements from Eastern practices, including Buddhism, Hinduism, Taoism, and Sufism. Particularly influential in the 1970s was Transcendental Meditation, a formal program of meditative practices taught in centers devoted to this spiritual approach.

Jewish religious leaders face the challenge of encouraging sincere spiritual seekers while at the same time preventing the emergence of syncretistic practices that might be incompatible with Judaism. Many Jews were, without a doubt, interested in combining practices from in and outside of their religion. While there were initially widespread concerns that this would destroy authentic Jewish practice, most congregations have been able to incorporate elements from outside without undermining Jewish religious authenticity. Many rabbis were concerned that congregants' religious practice was superficial. Further, some seemed to drop out entirely after their children completed Bar or Bat Mitzvah training. On the other hand, Southern Florida has emerged as a center of Jewish religious activities for the golden-agers. For example, seventy-six percent of South Palm Beach county's Jewish population and sixty-seven percent of North Palm Beach county's Jewish population was aged sixty or older at the end of the 1990s. Such senior citizens increase their level of Jewish practices and frequently become very active in their congregations. Many, particularly in places like South Florida, Arizona, or other retirement locations, join "condo congregations," located in or near a condominium.[13] Retirees tend to practice Judaism in different ways from younger singles or families, due in part to their different lifestyle.

Some Jewish practices have been lifted entirely out of the Jewish religious framework and pushed as spiritual practices that can be used by all. The primary example of this is the commercialization of Kabbalistic practices, esoteric mystical doctrines that have been transformed into bite-size psychological insights combined with quick spiritual exercises. Pop Kabbalah got a lot of publicity from the steady stream of Hollywood celebrities who spoke about how Jewish mysticism helped them beat depression or addiction or enrich their lives and bring them closer to their loved ones. Many American Jews expected their religious practice to help them solve personal or family problems. Whereas traditional Judaism placed ritual in the theological realm, American Jews place in the therapeutic. Spiritual practices are expected to connect people with the sacred, but also to help them make their lives easier, better, or fuller. Many American Jews believe or at least hope their practice would be psychologically and even medically beneficial. Even when no explicit promises are made, congregations often try to mold Jewish prac-

tice into the style of a health club workout. Synagogues have begun to market "spiritual workouts." For example, Temple Beth Sholom of Miami Beach, Florida, offered what they refer to as the "twenty-nine minute workout." The newsletter advises congregants to "wake-up early, drop the kids off, slip out of work, and join us for your morning spiritual exercise." This included ten minutes of Jewish "word or prayer or holiday of the week," followed by a ten-minute Hebrew lesson, and then ten minutes of learning and singing Jewish music.[14]

New Understandings of the Concept of Mitzvah: Arnold Eisen argues that scholars have wrongly associated the word mitzvah solely with Orthodoxy. These scholars suggest that a mitzvah is a commandment performed according to the halakhah. To perform a mitzvah, a Jew has to believe he or she is performing an act in direct response to the will of God. Practice cannot count as a mitzvah, according to this line of thinking, unless it enacts a religious belief. Eisen argues that "the restriction of 'commandment' to behavior that is directly ascribed to divine decree probably misses and misrepresents the vast majority of action performed by *premodern* Jews, let alone their modern descendants."[15] Eisen follows Franz Rosenzweig, who believed that Jews had observed the commandments over the course of hundreds of years because social reality compelled and made sense of those observances. This practice added richness and meaning to the lives of people who may have lived in poverty or suffered from religious persecution. Thus, the word mitzvah has a much wider denotation. As Eisen puts it, "if we ignore this wider denotation of Mitzvah, we miss a great deal of reflection and activity undertaken in response to complicated sets of imperatives arising out of the distinctive Jewish identity that such Jews recognized and wished to maintain."[16]

All of the American Jewish religious movements see themselves as advocates for the performance of mitzvot. The Conservative movement was the most influential in modern American Jewish attempts to redefine the word mitzvah in the context of halakhic practice. The Conservative movement was dominated by JTS for most of the twentieth century. After Cyrus Adler died in 1940,

Talmud professor Louis Finkelstein became the undisputed leader of the seminary and therefore the most influential man in the movement. By March, 1949, the Conservative movement had 365 affiliated congregations. That number was to rapidly grow. By 1954, it had 492 congregations. This growth was due primarily to new suburban congregations being founded at a rapid rate. But suburban life created new challenges the Conservative movement was not wholly prepared to face. There was always a struggle being waged within the seminary, the congregational body, and the Rabbinical association for influence in the movement. Until the end of the 1970s, JTS remained very traditional, with the exception of the Reconstructionist Mordecai Kaplan. Kaplan represented a minority within the Conservative movement that believed that Judaism was in a post-halakhic period. What was important was not law but standards. Eventually, the left-wingers would push Kaplan into allowing them to create their own movement, which became Reconstructionism.

Rector Saul Lieberman wielded enormous influence because of his vast talmudic scholarship and authoritarian determination to impose halakhic standards on the movement. But Albert I. Gordon, the leader of the United Synagogue, the Conservative movement's synagogue arm, believed that congregational leaders should play an important role in formulating Conservative ideology (and, by implication, policies on religious practices). This led to a series of confrontations with Louis Finkelstein and eventually resulted in Gordon's resignation.[17] Another power struggle developed when the Rabbinical Assembly, the movement's Rabbinical union, began to advocate an approach to the Agunah problem—which prevents from remarrying Jewish women who cannot obtain a divorce—that the JTS Talmud professors felt was unacceptable. Finkelstein successfully lobbied to create a Joint Law Conference that effectively ensured that the Talmud professors would control the process and could thus prevent the institutionalization of any policy they opposed. The conference was dissolved in 1968, which allowed the Rabbinical organization to proceed with a variation of its original plan.

The Conservative movement remained split into leftist, centrist, and rightist factions. While many of those on the left held radical theological views, the determining issue remained very much one's position on Jewish law rather than Jewish belief. At the same time, suburban congregations were developing their own culture, which respected traditional practice even as it abrogated halakhic commitment. By the time Gerson D. Cohen became chancellor in 1972, the movement was ready for change. Cohen was much more willing to consider change than his predecessor, and attention soon focused on the role of women in the ritual life of the Conservative synagogue.

Religious practice in general has been strongly influenced by the feminist movement. Women came to play a larger and larger role in contemporary Jewish practice. Egalitarianism has been accepted as obligatory in all Reform and Reconstructionist congregations and is the dominant form of practice in most Conservative ones. Women have become prominent not only as lay leaders but as rabbis and cantors in all but the Orthodox. The feminist revolution had a dramatic impact on Jewish practice in American Judaism. Particularly noticeable is the impact of feminism on the liturgy and liturgical practice. Prayer books are being re-edited to reflect gender sensitivity, or even gender neutrality. Many congregations that use older prayer books verbally change what is written in order to reflect this need. Foremothers as well as forefathers are now referred to in the Amidah as elsewhere in the liturgy.

In a broader sense, there has been a conscious effort to incorporate women's spirituality into liturgical experiences. This influence has been felt in the Conservative movement. In 1955, the Rabbinical Assembly issued a ruling allowing women to participate in the Torah service. In 1973, the Rabbinical Assembly law committee issued a ruling allowing women to be counted in a prayer quorum, the minyan. That same year, the United Synagogue adopted a resolution urging JTS to admit women to its Rabbinical school. This obviously was not a binding resolution, since the United Synagogue could hardly order JTS to make such a radical change. But it did make it clear to all that the lay leadership wanted change. In 1977, the Rabbinical Assembly adopted a resolution asking Chancellor Cohen to appoint a special committee to study the possibility of training women rabbis. He enthusiastically followed this suggestion, establishing the Commission for the Study of the Ordination of Women as Rabbis. In 1979, the commission issued a report that argued there was no halakhic barrier to the ordination of women. The committee's vote, eleven to three, indicated that there was wide support for such a decision. Cohen then attempted to bring the question to a vote among the JTS faculty. Many partisans on both sides of the issue saw the question as holding tremendous symbolic importance. Traditionalists saw it as the last stand for a Halakhic Conservative movement. Liberals saw it as an essential step in giving religious rights to all females. The debate, which went on for four years, became quite bitter. Some traditionalists felt it was inappropriate to allow all faculty to have an equal vote. They question how a professor of modern Hebrew literature or homiletics could evaluate the issue with the same legal depth of a Talmud professor. But a closed approach to decision-making was no longer acceptable in the Conservative movement. In October, 1983, the JTS faculty voted thirty-four to eight to accept women into the Rabbinical program. In May, 1985, Amy Eilberg graduated as the first woman ordained a rabbi by the Conservative movement.

Private Judaism and the Increasing Focus on Personal Spirituality: Due to the voluntaristic nature of Jewish life in the United States, levels of observance could be puzzling to someone expecting religious consistency. Some practices attracted a large enthusiastic following, while others were observed mainly by the most devout (or, more precisely, the most observant). Steven Cohen explains that many Jews are interested in observances that reflect their "affection for Jewish family, food, and festivals."[18] Cohen distinguished between those who had a "commitment to content" versus those who had a "commitment to continuity." For the many American Jews who were more interested in maintaining some sort of ethnic identity than expressing their theology through consistent ritual practice, holidays that connected them with family-related memories, experiences, and aspirations were most likely to be observed. They wanted to recall their positive childhood memories of certain Jewish holidays and to pass on their family legacy to their children by recreating similar scenes in their own homes. Furthermore, these holidays could evoke a higher spiritual importance by connecting members of the family with a sense of historical continuity and a transcendent religious message.

Many Jews crammed into packed synagogues for Rosh Hashshanah and Yom Kippur but then disappeared for most of the rest of the year. The two exceptions were Passover and Hanukkah, primarily observed in the home rather than the synagogue. Both parallel Christian holidays observed not only by Christians but celebrated in a secular manner by society as a whole. Hanukkah, in particular, has assumed an importance all out of proportion to its significance in the Jewish calendar, at least in part because of its proximity to December 25. The holiday's primary observance is the lighting of candles over the course of eight days. It also provides an opportunity for gift-giving, joyous songs, and special foods, all engaging within the family setting and, especially, to children, frequently the main focus of American religion. Sociologists and theologians have attempted to explain Hanukkah's huge popularity in terms of what it signifies religiously for American Jews. For example, Jacob Neusner notes that "it bears the message of defiance—the few against the many, the holy against the profane—and victory over oppression that Jews find congenial."[19] Numerous other explanations are certainly possible.

Passover similarly is primarily observed in the home. Despite the fact that it is one of the three pilgrimage festivals that are supposed to be celebrated with special prayer services in the synagogue, the holiday is primarily observed by holding family seder (ritual meals) on the festival's first or first and second nights. The seder comprises an extensive home ritual, printed in a special work called a haggadah. For decades, the most popular haggadah in America was the Maxwell House Haggadah, available free in supermarkets. But in the 1980s and 90s, virtually every Jewish group edited and published its own haggadah, each reflecting the groups specific theology and ideology. *Tikkun* magazine, a leftist publication, published yearly inserts that could be used as supplements to the traditional text. Other groups produced feminist haggadot, gay and lesbian haggadot, Zionist haggadot, university student haggadot, and so forth. Some focused on a particular social or political perspective, while others were more concerned with meeting the needs of a specific sociological target group.

Samuel Heilman points out that a polarization took place in the late 1960s and 70s, producing two distinct types of American Jew. The division occurred because there was a choice over how individuals would choose to express their Jewish identity in concrete behavioral terms. The more common type subordinated Jewish involvement to American identity. Heilman refers to these people as "Jewish-Americans" and explains that their Jewish attachments were similar to those of other hyphenated Americans, such as Italian-Americans or Irish-Americans. Such hyphenated Americans absorbed American values and American cultural patterns. They adapted their behavioral patterns to those most accepted and expected in the United States, leaving behind any behaviors associated with "the old country." What was left was lighting Hanukkah candles, a Passover Seder, which might or might not include an extensive ritual element, attendance at a synagogue for the High Holy Days, and the celebration of life cycle events with a rabbi and/or in a synagogue.

The second, smaller group was deeply committed to perpetuating Jewishness not only as an ethnicity but also as a religion. While not necessarily Orthodox, individuals within this group were likely to be highly observant. Even Reform Jews in this category were surprisingly observant in a manner consistent with Reform theology and practice. For many Jews in this category, Jewish identity became more and more all-consuming. Their daily and weekly activities were substantially filled up by Jewish activities

of one sort or another. Many attended synagogue regularly and studied in adult education classes one or more nights a week. Most sent their children to Jewish day schools, which obligated them to attend a wide variety of school-related functions. Most found that not only their religious lives but also their social lives revolved around Jews and Judaism. In between these two groups was a large middle that was not nearly as committed as the second group but not as assimilated as the first. But in the 1960s and 70s, the middle group eroded substantially. As Heilman writes, ". . . one either took Jewish life and Judaism more seriously and actively engaged it . . ." or ". . . one let meaningless rituals and old traditions fade . . ."[20]

But by the 1990s, sociologists began to identify a new middle group that deserves attention. Steven Cohen and Arnold Eisen refer to this segment of the Jewish community as "moderately affiliated American Jews."[21] Cohen divides American Jews into the moderately affiliated, the involved, and the peripheral. The moderately affiliated are still practicing certain rituals in relatively high percentages. For example, eighty-five percent attend a Seder. This is in contrast to ninety-six percent of the involved that do, and fifty-nine percent of the peripheral. Eighty-six percent of the moderately affiliated light Hanukkah candles as opposed to ninety-five percent of the involved and sixty-seven percent of the peripheral. But only fifty-two percent of the moderately affiliated are synagogue members, as opposed to seventy-eight percent of the involved, and sixteen percent of the peripheral.[22]

Charles Liebman presents two models to explain how the individual Jew has related to Judaism in the modern period. One model is that of public Judaism, in which the individual is seen as part of the collective entity. The individual has responsibility and obligations to fulfill toward this entity and does not have the right to pursue selfish interests to the exclusion of the collective needs of the Jewish people as a whole. Private Judaism refers to the individual meaning each person finds in the religion. For those privatized Jewish commitments, what matters is the spiritual benefit that the individual Jew derives from the beliefs and practices of the religion.[23] The 1980s and 90s were a time in which private Judaism became more and more popular, and public Judaism became less and less. Much of this was a reflection of the increasing focus on personal spirituality. In addition, many of the challenges that seem to require a corporate response had been solved. The Jewish people seemed more secure than they had at anytime in recent memory. While not at peace, the state of Israel was no longer facing a short-term threat to its survival. Soviet Jewry was no longer being refused permission to emigrate. Jewish communities in countries such as Syria that had been kept captive had been permitted to emigrate. Ethiopian Jews who had faced civil war and starvation had been airlifted to Israel. While isolated problems remained in such places as Iran, the general situation of world Jewry was good. American Jews thus felt free to turn their attention inward.

Notes

[1] Jacob Neusner, *Fortress Introduction to American Judaism: What the Books Say, What the People Do* (Minneapolis, 1984), p. 5.

[2] Marshal Sklare and Joseph Greenblum, *Jewish Identity on the Suburban Frontier* (Chicago, 1979), pp. 57-59.

[3] Jack Wertheimer, ed., *Jews in the Center: Conservative Synagogues and their Members* (New Brunswick, New Jersey, and London, 2000), p. 1.

[4] Jonathan S. Woocher, *Sacred Survival: The Civil Religion of American Jews* (Bloomington and Indianapolis, 1986), pp. 67-68.

[5] Jonathan Sarna, "The Debate over Mixed Seating in the American Synagogue," in Jack Wertheimer, ed., *The American Synagogue: A Sanctuary Transformed* (Cambridge, 1987), pp. 363-394.

[6] Daniel J. Elazar and Rela Mintz Geffen, *The Conservative Movement in Judaism: Dilemmas and Opportunities* (Albany, 2000), p. 71.

[7] David Weiss Halivni, *Revelation Restored: Divine Writ and Critical Responses* (Boulder, 1997).

[8] Samuel Heilman, *Defenders of the Faith: Inside Ultra-Orthodox Jewry* (New York, 1992), p. 13.

[9] Charles S. Liebman, "Ritual, Ceremony, and the Reconstruction of Judaism in the United States," in Roberta Rosenberg Farber and Chaim I. Waxman, eds., *Jews in America: A Contemporary Reader* (Hanover and London, 1999), pp. 307-308.

[10] Mary Douglas, *Natural Symbol: Explorations in Cosmology* (New York, 1996), p. 41.

[11] Haym Soleveitchik, "Rupture and Reconstruction: The Transformation of Contemporary Orthodoxy," in Rosenberg and Waxman, op. cit., p. 351. The article was originally printed in *Tradition* 28:4 (1994), pp. 64-130.

[12] Charles E. Silberman, *A Certain People: American Jews and Their Lives Today* (New York, 1985), p. 211.

[13] Joel L. Levine, "Why People in the Sunbelt Join a Synagogue," in Dana Kaplan, ed., *Contemporary Debates in American Reform Judaism* (New York and London, 2001), p. 57.

[14] *A World of Jewish Opportunities, Temple Beth Sholom*, vol. LX, no. 1-14 October, 2001.

[15] Arnold M. Eisen, *Rethinking Modern Judaism: Ritual, Commandment, Community* (Chicago and London, 1998), p. 11.

[16] Ibid.

[17] Abraham J. Karp, *Jewish Continuity in America: Creative Survival in a Free Society* (Tuscaloosa and London, 1998), p. 247.

[18] Steven Cohen, *Content or Continuity? Alternative Bases for Commitment* (New York, 1991), p. 4.

[19] Neusner, op. cit., pp. 75-76.

[20] Samuel C. Heilman, *Portrait of American Jews: The Last Half of the Twentieth Century* (Seattle and London, 1995), p. 72.

[21] Steven M. Cohen and Arnold M. Eisen, *The Jew Within: Self, Family, and Community in America* (Bloomington and Indianapolis, 2000).

[22] Steven M. Cohen, "Jewish Continuity over Judaic Content: The Moderately Affiliated American Jew," in Robert M. Seltzer and Norman J. Cohen, eds., *The Americanization of the Jews* (New York and London, 1995), p. 411.

[23] Charles S. Liebman, "Jewish Survival, Anti-semitism, and Negotiation with the Tradition," in ibid., pp. 442-443.

DANA EVAN KAPLAN

K

KARAITE JUDAISM: Karaite Judaism is characterized by its denial of the authority of the Oral Law of the rabbis as represented in the Talmud and Rabbinic codes. The denial of Rabbinic authority led Karaites (literally: scripturalists, but there are other suggested etymologies of the term) to develop their own fully formed alternative to Rabbanism (the common term for Rabbinic Judaism in the context of discussions of

Karaism), including religious practices, a legal system, biblical exegesis, and historiography. Karaites also wrote works of philosophy, theology, and philology comparable with similar treatises in Rabbinic Judaism. Karaism, which can be identified as a separate version of Judaism at least from the ninth century c.e., had its "Golden Age" in the tenth and eleventh centuries, with its principal center in the land of Israel. Thereafter, Karaism was characterized by a gradual rapprochement with Rabbanism in the many lands of Karaite dispersion. Although there are still Karaites communities today, most notably in the state of Israel, their impact on contemporary Judaism is well-nigh insignificant.

Karaite Origins (Eighth-Ninth Centuries): The Rabbanite version of Karaite origins is simple: a disgruntled office seeker was forced to invent his own form of Judaism in order to escape the death penalty, subsequently gathering around himself other malcontents and breaking away totally from normative Judaism. According to this account, which is first recorded in a twelfth-century source, the eighth-century Anan ben David was a candidate to be exilarch, the political leader of the Jewish community of Babylonia (Iraq), thought to be descended from King David. Since the rabbis had doubts about his worthiness and doctrinal loyalty, he was passed over in favor of his younger brother, Hananiah. Not letting the slight go unanswered, Anan declared himself the true exilarch, thereby incurring the wrath of the Muslim caliph who had confirmed Hananiah's appointment. In jail facing the death penalty for his challenge to the caliph, Anan was befriended by a Muslim prisoner who advised him to tell the caliph (after arranging an audience by the use of bribes) that he, Anan, was actually the exilarch of a religion different from that of his brother, a religion that had more in common with Islam than did Rabbinic Judaism. The stratagem worked, and after having been released by the caliph, Anan gathered around himself some remnants of the Second Temple sects that had also denied Rabbinic authority, thus creating a new religion, Karaism.

Whatever the historical value of this narrative, Anan himself was actually the founder of a group called Ananites, which competed with the Karaites until around the tenth century, when they seem to have coalesced together as Karaites. Anan, thus, was not the founder of Karaism, even though almost all discussions of Karaism begin with him. Perhaps this is the case since even the Karaites of later generations saw him as a pivotal figure in the development of their religion, relying on his supposed Davidic ancestry to impart greater authenticity to their movement. The story of Anan's separatism is convenient for Rabbanite historiography, since it affirms the assumption that any threat to Rabbinic Judaism result from personal ambition or other unworthy motives.

The Karaites, at least those who identify as part of the Jewish people, have a wholly different view of their origins. Since they believe that their form of Judaism is the original one given by God to Moses on Sinai, they ask when the Rabbanites invented a different kind of Judaism. Although Karaite historiography has changed through the centuries, they have always considered Karaism as original Judaism and Rabbanism the dissident sector. The divergent Karaite histories disagreed only on when schism entered Judaism, whether during the First or Second Temple period.

The contemporary Karaite explanation of the schism, based on a narrative originating approximately five hundred years ago, is predicated on a Talmudic account (B. Qid. 66a) of a massacre of sages under the first-century b.c.e. Hasmonean king Alexander Yannai. Into the vacuum caused by this massacre came Simeon b. Shetah, the brother of the queen, who escaped the persecution, went to Egypt, created a new religion based on the idea of an Oral Torah's having been revealed at Sinai, and then returned to the land of Israel, where he was able to impose the new religion because of royal patronage. Although many Second Temple Jews turned to Simeon's Pharisaism (the forerunner of Rabbanism), and others were followers of the equally unpalatable Sadduceism, the loyalists of the true Judaism were a group called the Zaddiqim, the righteous. The most noted representatives of this group, according to recent Karaite historiography, were the authors of the Dead Sea Scrolls (discovered in 1947). Indeed, there are some similarities between the Scrolls and medieval Karaite writings, and a prominent Scroll, the Damascus Document, was found in a medieval copy in the Cairo Geniza (discovered in 1896), indicating that at least one Second Temple literary work was available to the medieval Karaites. The proto-Karaites remained a small, marginal group until reinvigorated by Anan ben David, the exilarch, and they subsequently emerged as the Karaites as we know them today.

Neither account is fully plausible to contemporary historians. Although the Rabbanite story of Anan's revolt, despite its late provenance, is often cited in the literature, especially in works of a more general nature, its veracity is subject to debate. If, indeed, Anan was denied the exilarchate because of suspicions concerning his heterodoxy, then whatever schismatic tendencies he had existed before his putative imprisonment. Furthermore, what Muslim would advise a Jew to escape execution by telling the caliph that he was the head of an alternate Jewish religion rather than advising him to convert outright to Islam? As noted, Anan was the founder not of Karaism, but of Ananism. Alternatively, the Karaite narrative, based on Rabbinic sources, is suspect. Whatever similarities might exist between the Dead Sea Scrolls and Karaite literature are usually dismissed as a result of a fortuitous discovery of some of the Scrolls in the early ninth century. There is no indication, literary or other, of an ongoing non-Rabbinic form of Judaism between the destruction of the Second Temple in the first century C.E. and the emergence of Anan in the eighth century. Even if there were Second Temple precedents for a non-Rabbinic Judaism, the medieval emergence of Karaism should be seen in the context of Jewish life under Islam.

In looking for the true explanation of Karaite origins, a number of historians have posited that some Jewish communities, especially those distant from the Babylonian academies, such as in Persia, had their own local customs unrelated to Rabbinic exegesis of the Torah. The Talmud itself, edited perhaps by 600 C.E., although written from the viewpoint of the rabbis, contains hints that the Rabbinic form of Judaism was not followed by all Jews. When, however, in the eighth and ninth centuries, the Rabbinic academies, backed up by the Abbasid caliphate of Baghdad, attempted to spread Babylonian hegemony, both in terms of practice and institutional loyalty, the local communities resisted. The example of Islamic sectarianism may also have influenced the resistance to the imposition of Rabbanism on these Jewish populations. Rallied by early sectarian leaders, such as Anan and the ninth-century Benjamin of Nahawendi (in Persia), these dissident and peripheral groups eventually coalesced into an anti-Rabbanite coalition that called itself Karaism.

Some historians have considered socio-economic factors as contributing to the revolt against Rabbinic authority. The Babylonian academies are thought to represent the social and financial elite of the Jewish people, and, therefore, the less economically fortunate sectors of the community revolted against them. The problem is that there is little evidence that the Karaites were, indeed, mainly from one particular economic class. Others have pointed out incipient messianic movements of the seventh and eighth centuries as precursors of Karaism. No matter what explanation is offered, there is no scholarly unanimity concerning why, by the tenth century, there were two clearly recognizable competing versions of Judaism in the Middle East, whereas only a few centuries before we know only of Rabbinic Judaism.

The Golden Age of Karaism (Tenth-Eleventh Centuries): The founder of the Karaite community in the land of Israel was the late ninth-century Daniel al-Qumisi, originally from Persia. Al-Qumisi called upon diaspora Karaites to come to the land of Israel to worship God. He even suggested a practical program in which each diaspora Jewish community would finance the emigration of five representatives. Many Karaites must have harkened to his call, since, by the mid-tenth century, there was a major Karaite community in Jerusalem, mostly made up of members of the Mourners of Zion, who thought the messiah could be brought by ascetic practices devoted to mourning the destruction of the Temples.

During the early period of their sectarian

development, the Karaites found themselves the target of the polemical attacks of Saadia Gaon (882-942), the head of the academy in Babylonia and the most outstanding Rabbanite personality of the day. These pioneers also had to struggle with religious uncertainty, since Karaism was still in flux, with many different versions of Karaite practice (as attested by Saadia's Babylonian contemporary, Jacob al-Qirqisani, who said that no two Karaites agreed on anything and that the situation got worse daily). "Personal striving," in which individuals would come to their own conclusions as to the correct interpretation of the Bible, was an acceptable method of developing Karaite law, but it led to anarchy among the believers. The Karaite communities persevered, answering the dual challenges of external attack and internal disorder. Those in the land of Israel especially produced a fully formed rival version of Judaism and a literature to propagate it.

Saadia's anti-Karaite polemics were answered in the tenth century by Sahl ben Mazliah and Salmon ben Yeruhim, both of whom wrote missionary works and apparently engaged in personal missionary activity. Tenth-century Karaite biblical exegetes, such as Salmon, Yefet ben Eli and Joseph ibn Nuh, responded to Saadia's biblical scholarship and established specifically Karaite interpretations of Scriptures. Expertise in grammar was represented by David Alfasi and Joseph ibn Nuh, and the early eleventh-century Abu-l-Faraj Harun; a specifically Karaite form of Kalamic theology was propagated by the most dominant figure of the period, the late tenth-century Joseph al-Basir, and his eleventh-century student Yeshua ben Judah, who also was an expert in law and exegesis. Most important of all, Karaite law books, written by al-Basir, Yefet ben Levi, and others, and which contained a halakhah more or less acceptable to the major Karaite communities, were now available. Whereas reliance upon personal striving and consequent halakhic pluralism were characteristics of early Karaism, by the end of the Golden Age, the gates of "personal striving" were closed. The Jerusalem Karaite community, which was destroyed by the Crusader con-

quest in 1099, had succeeded in unifying Karaism and setting the pattern for further Karaite development.

Karaites in Byzantium (Eleventh-Sixteenth Centuries): Even before the breakdown of the Karaite community in the land of Israel, many Karaites found themselves exploring new areas of settlement. Some settled in North Africa, while others continued on to the Iberian peninsula. Almost all of our information about the latter comes from Rabbanite works, since Iberian Karaism left no literary remains. Given the prominence of the Iberian Rabbanite antagonists to Karaism, it appears that the sectarian community was quite influential. The Karaites were attacked by such Iberian Rabbanite worthies as Judah Halevi (d. 1141), Abraham ibn Ezra (d. 1167), Abraham ibn Daud (d. 1180), Maimonides (d. 1204), and Judah Al-Harizi (d. 1235). Although there is no definite evidence, Iberian Karaite communities may have survived until the expulsion from Spain (1492).

We know much more about the Karaite community established in the Byzantine empire. From the documents they left behind, we know that when these Karaites arrived, they faced the challenge of supplanting the land of Israel centered Karaism of the Golden Age with a form of Karaism that could meet the challenges of exile from the Holy Land. The first important Karaite systematically to tackle this difficulty was Tobias ben Moses the Translator, who had gone from Byzantium to the land of Israel for studies at the beginning of the eleventh century and who returned to lead his original community. Tobias instituted a literary project that translated the classics of land of Israel Karaism, originally written in Arabic, into a Greek-laden Hebrew. Eleventh-century Byzantine Karaites also initiated legal innovations that allowed them to adapt Karaite law to their own needs (such as a method of calendation that was not dependent upon observations of natural phenomena in the land of Israel).

Byzantine Karaism flourished, producing many important literary figures over the years, including Judah Hadassi (mid-twelfth century), whose compendium of law and lore is a virtual summary of all of Karaism before his time; Aaron ben Joseph, the Doctor (Aaron the Elder, late thirteenth century), whose biblical commentaries marked a break from classical Karaism in favor of Rabbanite thought (such as that of Maimonides); Aaron ben Elijah (Aaron the Younger, d. 1369), author of a philosophical treatise, a legal code, and a commentary on the Pentateuch; and Elijah Bashyazi (d. 1490), the final decisor of Karaite law. By Bashyazi's day, Rabbanism had made further inroads into Karaism, and it was the Bashyazi family that instituted legal reforms, such as the permission for Karaites to light Sabbath lamps before the advent of the Sabbath, so that there might be illumination in their houses on Friday nights (a Rabbanite practice eschewed by earlier Karaites in favor of total darkness on the Sabbath). In the early sixteenth century, there were still some creative followers of the Bashyazi family, such as Elijah's brother-in-law Caleb Afendopolo and Judah Gibbor, but the center of Karaite life had by now turned northward. Succeeding centuries were witness to the decline of this community, such that in Istanbul today, there are only around one hundred Karaites.

Eastern European and Crimean Karaism (Fifteenth-Twentieth Centuries): Karaites reached the Crimean peninsula at least by the thirteenth century and then made their way to Volhynia (especially the city of Lutzk) and Lithuania (especially the city of Troki/Trakai). Karaites in these areas developed their own Turkic language, written in Hebrew letters, and they slowly formed their own communities with little in common with Yiddish speaking Rabbanite Jews. Cultural and intellectual contacts between the groups continued, however, with some of the Karaites taking an interest in trends in Rabbanite thought, such as Kabbalah, and being in touch with Rabbanite leaders, such as Joseph Solomon Delmedigo (Yashar of Candia, 1591-1655).

Eastern European and Crimean Karaism produced a number of important leaders, who were courted by Christian Hebraists, who saw them as carriers of the authentic, pre-Rabbinic Judaism that flourished in the times of Jesus. Important Karaite authors were Isaac ben Abraham of Troki (late six-

teenth century), author of the widely used anti-Christian polemic *Ḥizzuq Emunah* ("Faith Strengthened"); his student Joseph ben Mordecai Malinowski of Troki (early seventeenth century), who completed his teacher's work; Mordecai ben Nissan Kokizow (late seventeenth century), author of the popular historiographical work *Dod Mordecai* ("The Beloved of Mordecai"); Solomon ben Aaron of Troki (late seventeenth, early eighteenth centuries) who composed the apologetic and historiographical work, *Apiryon Asah Lo* ("He Made himself a Palanquin;" cf., Song 3:9); and Simhah Isaac Lutzki (d. 1766), author of multiple treatises, bibliophile, historiographer, and proponent of Karaite Kabbalah. Perhaps the most prominent Karaite produced by the Eastern European and Crimean communities was Abraham Firkovich (nineteenth century). Firkovich, born in Volhynia but active mostly in the Crimea, oversaw the printing press in Eupatoria (Gozlow), which printed many of the Karaite classics for the first time. He also traveled the world amassing manuscripts, Karaite, Rabbanite, and Samaritan, which now comprise the Firkovich collections in the Russian National Library in St. Petersburg. The renewed access to these collections with the collapse of the Soviet Union has revolutionized Karaite studies in the last decade and will be a vital source for future Karaite scholarship.

Despite Karaite feelings of affinity with Rabbanite Jews, when Czarist Russia annexed areas of Jewish settlement in the late eighteenth century (Lithuania, Poland, and Crimea) and imposed harsh disabilities on the Jewish communities there, Karaites were ready to declare their separation from Judaism in order to avoid the new measures. Under the leadership of Simḥah Babovich, the Karaites petitioned the Czars to be recognized as a separate religious and national group. Whether or not the Karaites themselves actually believed that they were not Jews, they convinced the Czars, and later the Nazis, that this was the case. During World War II, both Rabbanites and Karaites were asked by the Nazis whether or not Karaites are Jews, and both groups answered in the negative. Karaites were not, therefore, specifically targeted for mass murder, although there were instances of Karaites' being murdered as Jews. Nonetheless, they paid a price for the denial of their Jewish identity. By moving farther and farther away from the rest of Jewry, Karaites eventually lost contact with even their own classics (written in Hebrew), and today Karaites in these areas retain little connection to their past and almost no association with Judaism. The transition to their being simply another ethnic group in the former Soviet Union has been complete, and their dwindling numbers (less than three hundred in Lithuania; perhaps around the same number in the Crimea; considerably fewer in Poland) do not bode well for future survival.

Contemporary Karaism: One community previously unmentioned is that of Egypt, which was at least a thousand years old when it virtually disbanded as a result of the wars between Egypt and Israel. This community was economically and socially prominent in the Middle Ages, maintaining close relations with the Muslim rulers. The most important Karaite Egyptians were the Tustaris, a family that originated in Persia and moved to Egypt in the early eleventh century, engaging in commerce and providing services to the Fatimid court. The Egyptian Karaite community also produced a number of scholars, whose works written in Arabic were generally inaccessible to the majority of Karaites in other areas of the world. The Egyptian community did, however, keep in contact with other Karaites, and in the modern period, some of the leaders of the Egyptian Karaite communities were imported from Turkey and the Crimea. The last ḥakham (sage) of the Egyptian community was the Crimean born Tobiah Babovich. Through the centuries, Egyptian Rabbanites and Karaites were generally amicable, and quite a number of cases of intermarriage are known from documents from the Geniza. An Egyptian Karaite, Moses Marzuk, was hung as an Israeli agent in 1955 as a result of the abortive Lavon affair. The Suez Campaign (1956) and the Six Day War (1967) were followed by mass Karaite emigration from Egypt, with only a handful of Karaites remaining.

When Egyptian Karaites were forced to leave their homes, most of them came to Israel, where there are now approximately 20-25,000 Karaites organized as "Universal Karaite Judaism." Karaite headquarters are in Ramle, which has a large Karaite population (and which was a center of Karaite life during the Golden Age). Other concentrations of Karaites are found in Ashdod, Ofakim, Beer Sheva, and the Karaite agricultural settlements of Mazliah and Ranen. They have their own communities (which include some Karaites from the Al-Hit region of Iraq), synagogues, religious leaders (since the thirteenth-century Karaites have referred to their leaders as rabbis, despite the association with Rabbanism), and institutions. The present Chief Karaite Rabbi is Elijah Marzuk, who succeeded Hayyim Levi, one of the more prolific contemporary Karaite writers. Another very active Karaite figure is Joseph Al-Gamil who has produced a number of original books as well as edited Karaite literary works, some of which had never previously been published. Contemporary Israeli Karaite literature is noted for its dedication to presenting a specifically Karaite point of view, not for its historical and doctrinal objectivity.

While not fully recognized *de jure* by the laws of the state of Israel, Israeli Karaites generally have autonomy in their own internal religious affairs. The community has suffered from the same secularization that has affected other Jewish groups from Islamic countries upon immigration to Israel. Furthermore, Karaites have had difficulties maintaining their sectarian identity in a Jewish country that is not overly sympathetic to the specifically Karaite form of Judaism (for instance, the national cycle of holidays follows the Rabbanite and not the Karaite calendar; and the dietary laws observed in public institutions are the Rabbanite ones). In the last few years, as their communities have become more economically viable, Israeli Karaites have devoted more attention to their spiritual and religious needs, producing a large number of books intended for the community's edification. Israeli Karaites are not well known among the general Israeli Jewish population and have little impact on religious, social, cultural, or economic life in the country.

Other Egyptian Karaites have made their

way to France and Switzerland (where tiny communities exist), but the greatest concentration of Egyptian Karaites outside of Israel is in the United States (mostly in the Bay Area in California). These Karaites have been characterized by assimilation and acculturation (both to Americanism and to Rabbanite forms of American Judaism), but recent efforts have been made to revitalize American Karaism. They maintain a synagogue in Daly City, California.

Karaite Practices: The most important distinguishing feature of Karaism is its unique interpretation of Jewish law (halakhah). Not having accepted the legal pronouncements of the Talmud and Rabbinic codes, Karaites generally had to work out their own interpretations of Scriptures and define the parameters of their religion. Influenced by Islamic legal thought, Karaism recognized four principles methods of establishing the correct law: biblical text, logical analogy, consensus, and transmission. Although many practices prescribed by Karaite halakhah mirror those of Rabbanism, still, the differences are significant and remain to this day.

Although Anan was not the founder of Karaism, it is instructive to look at aspects of his legal system that have certain common features with later Karaism. Anan forbade the use of fire on the Sabbath, either for illumination or for heating, as well as sexual relations and leaving the house on the Sabbath, except to go to the synagogue. The date of Passover was determined by the condition of the barley crop, and unleavened bread could be made only from barley. There was no prohibition of the eating of milk and meat or milk and foul together (while chicken was forbidden, and only pigeons were allowed), and no use of *tefillin* (phylacteries). The laws of incest were extended so that a husband's and wife's relatives became related, and, thus, forbidden, to each other; furthermore, uncle-niece marriages, allowed by Rabbinic Judaism, were as forbidden as the biblically proscribed auntnephew relations. Anan initiated a seventy-day fast (during daylight hours) and declared that circumcision was to be done only with scissors and not a knife (and not on the Sabbath).

Karaite halakhah included some, but not all, of Anan's practices. For instance, the seventy-day fast, the prohibition of leaving one's house on the Sabbath, and the method of circumcision were never adopted. The stringent incest restrictions were modified in the eleventh century, because it was difficult to find marriage partners in a small community when so many people were considered to be related to each other. The Sabbath prohibitions on fire and sexual relations were accepted, but in the fifteenth century Karaites began allowing use of fire kindled before the Sabbath. Other than these reforms and other examples of accommodation to reality and rapprochement with Rabbanite practices, the unified Karaite halakhah that emerged by the end of the tenth century has remained more of less constant since then. A summary of present day Karaite law demonstrates the major differences between Karaite and Rabbanite practices (remembering that many contemporary Karaites are negligent in observing the Karaite laws as prescribed in their sources):

Dietary Laws: Karaites refrain from eating milk and meat from the same species at the same meal to avoid any possibility of "seething a kid in its mother's milk" (Exod. 23:19, et al.). They do not, however, have a full separation of meat, or foul, and milk, and do not use different dishes for these two categories. Animals are slaughtered ritually at the neck as in Rabbanism, but a different blessing is said at the slaughter and different signs of the animal's health and suitability for ingestion are checked. Karaites prohibit parts of the animal allowed by Rabbanites (such as the fat tail). Karaites also reject the Rabbinic concept of *shi'urim*, a minimum amount of ingestion of forbidden foods before one is legally liable. Because of all these differences, observant Rabbanites and Karaites do not eat meat prepared in accordance with the other group's dietary laws and can engage in table fellowship only with difficulty.

Calendar: The Karaite calendar originally was determined by observation, both of the monthly new moon and of the new barley crop to determine leap years (adding an additional month before the month of Passover if the first barley plants, the biblical *aviv*, had not yet ripened). Over the years, such a system was recognized as unwieldy, especially in communities distant from the land of Israel, where the observations (at least of the barley crop) were supposed to take place. Eventually, Karaites adopted a system of intercalating their leap years according to the same procedure as in the Rabbanite calendar (seven out of nineteen years). The Rabbanite calculation of New Moons, based on the average conjunction of the sun, moon, and earth for the month of Tishrei only, with other months following upon that conjunction, was, however, not accepted. Instead, the beginning of each new month was calculated by determining when the moon would most likely be visible, a system that has produced controversy over the centuries, even in the past few years. Because of the divergence in methods of determining the New Moon, the Karaite date is often a day or two behind the Rabbanite one. The Karaite calendar in the land of Israel is also not in full coordination with the Karaite calendar in the Bay Area, where the ten hour time difference often means that the new moon can be sighted there on the day before its sighting in Israel. The annual calendar published by the Israeli Karaites lists the days of the holidays both for Israel and for San Francisco.

There are other differences between the two calendrical systems. Karaites do not observe two days of the New Moon as do the Rabbanites when the first day of the new month is on the thirty-first day after the first day of the previous month. Rabbanites use a system of "postponements" to guarantee that certain holidays do not fall on certain days of the week (causing legal and personal inconveniences). Karaites reject these postponements and, hence, any holiday can fall on any day of the week, depending on lunar calculation, except for Shavuot, which can come only on a Sunday (understanding with other sectarian groups that the counting of the Omer begins on "the morrow of the Sabbath," Leviticus 23:15-16, namely on a Sunday, not on the morrow of the first day of Passover). Karaites also eschew the Rabbinically ordained second day of the holidays in the diaspora and observe even Rosh Hashshanah (generally

called Yom Teruah) for only one day, both in and outside the land of Israel. They do not blow the ram's horn on Rosh Hashshanah, interpreting Yom Teruah as a day of calling out in prayer, not a day of sounding the horn. The ten days between Rosh Hashshanah and Yom Kippur are the Ten Days of Mercy, not Repentance.

Although Karaites and Rabbanites both follow the biblical cycle of holidays, there are other divergences between them. The four species (palm, citron, myrtle, and willow) are not waved as a part of the Sukkot ritual. Hanukkah, as a post-biblical holiday, does not appear in the Karaite calendar (although contemporary Israeli Karaites might celebrate it as an Israeli national holiday). In a leap year, Purim and Shushan Purim are celebrated in the first Adar; on Purim, the Book of Esther is read from a book, not a scroll. Some fast days are observed on different days than the Rabbanite equivalents: the Twenty-Fourth of Tishrei and not the Third (and called the Fast of the Seventh Month and not the Fast of Gedalya); the Seventh of Tammuz and not the Seventeenth; the Seventh and Tenth of Av instead of the Ninth.

Prayer and Synagogues: Originally, Karaites used only biblical passages, most notably from the Psalms, as their prayers. Gradually, some post-biblical compositions were allowed into the liturgy, some borrowed from Rabbanite practice. Karaites also began producing their own liturgical poetry for use both in the synagogue and for other observances. Nevertheless, the overwhelming majority of Karaite prayers are based on biblical texts. Thus, the Karaite prayerbook looks totally different from the Rabbanite one, and the central Rabbanite prayer of Eighteen Benedictions (*Shemoneh Esreh, amidah*) has no place in the Karaite liturgy. There are two mandatory Karaite prayers a day, morning and evening, with an additional service added on Sabbaths and holidays. A fringed garment (*talit*) is worn for morning prayer, its knots tied in a different manner than in a Rabbanite *talit*, and *tefillin* are not used at all (on the door post of Karaite homes is usually a small version of the Ten Commandments, not a mezuzah on parchment with biblical passages).

Karaite synagogues do not have chairs, and prayer is recited either standing, sitting on the floor, or in full prostration. Shoes are not permitted, and floors are covered by carpets. Although Karaite prayer practices recall Islamic patterns, Karaites insist that they actually reflect pre-Islamic models that go back to the Second Temple (where, indeed, there was full prostration and shoes were forbidden). Since the fifteenth century, the cycle of Torah readings is generally the same as in Rabbanite practice, beginning and ending on Shemini Atzeret (which has also been adopted by Karaites as Simhat Torah, another Rabbanizing innovation).

Sabbath: Since the fifteenth century, most Karaites have accepted the permission of lighting candles in advance of the Sabbath (without a blessing) in order to provide illumination once the Sabbath has begun. Fire is still prohibited for heating homes or warming food, and similar prohibitions control the use of electricity. Sexual relations are not permitted on the Sabbath (and holidays) in contrast to the Rabbanite advocacy of such relations on the Sabbath. The Rabbanite practice of erecting an *eruv* to allow carrying from one property to another is not accepted, but the prohibitions upon carrying are less stringent than among the Rabbanites. While, in the past, some Karaites may have questioned the propriety of violating the Sabbath in the case of a doubtful threat to life (such as for childbirth), today Karaites agree with Rabbanites that saving life takes precedence over Sabbath observance.

Purity and Impurity: Karaites claim that the Rabbanite dietary laws with the prohibition of eating milk and meat together have replaced the biblical laws of purity and impurity. Indeed, after the destruction of the Temple, most issues of impurity became mute in Rabbinic Judaism and are not part of everyday Rabbanite practice. Karaites, however, consider one to be impure after contact with a corpse, some animals, certain body fluids, and other items mentioned in the Torah as causing ritual impurity. The state of impurity is removed, after an appropriate waiting period, by washing one's body, not by immersing oneself in the Rabbinically ordained ritual bath (*miqveh*).

A woman's menstrual impurity, also removed by simple washing and not by immersion in a ritual bath, generally lasts the biblically prescribed seven days, without the necessity of waiting a full seven days after the completion of the menstrual flow (unless the flow itself lasts longer than seven days). During this period, a woman is prohibited from entering a synagogue.

Personal Status: Karaites do not consider a minor child to have fewer legal obligations than an adult; thus, even little children are expected not to eat on fast days. Traditionally, there has been no concept of bar mitzvah (let alone bat mitzvah for girls). Nevertheless, contemporary Karaite communities have introduced this idea, undoubtedly under the influence of Rabbanite practice and social pressure.

Karaites have different laws of incest (prohibition of uncle-niece marriage, for instance) and do not have either levirate marriage (*yibbum*) or its release (*halitzah*). Therefore, some Rabbanite marriages would be considered incestuous for the Karaites, and the products of these marriages would be unmarriageable (*mamzerim*). Rabbanites have a problem with Karaite marriageability, since, although Karaites have similar marriage and divorce regulations as do the Rabbanites, the exact forms of the wedding contract and ceremony, as well as the divorce writ, are different. Generally, Rabbanites accepted Karaite marriages as legally binding, necessitating a writ of divorce, but the Karaite divorces were not seen as legitimate. This is a result not only of the divergent Karaite divorce document but also of the Karaite regulation (at least in the modern period) that the court can issue a divorce to a woman even against the will of her husband. Thus, if a Karaite woman remarried after a Karaite divorce, the second marriage would be considered by the Rabbanites as adulterous and the children as *mamzerim*. As a result, many Rabbanite authorities prohibited marriages with Karaites because of the possibility that the Karaite partner was the descendant of an illegitimate second marriage some time in the past. It should be noted that the presumption of the Karaite status of unmarriageability is based on the acceptance of Karaites as Jews for all purposes. If they were not Jews, they could convert to Judaism and not have a problem of marriage.

Not all Rabbanites were of the opinion that it is forbidden to intermarry with Karaites. Thus, the sixteenth-century David ben Solomon ibn Abi Zimra (Radbaz) ruled that since Karaites and Rabbanites were not at all friendly, it was unlikely that two reliable Rabbanite witnesses would be at a Karaite wedding (the requirement for the marriage to have legal effect). Thus, the Karaite couple were not married as far as the Rabbanites were concerned, and the Karaite wife would not need a valid Rabbanite divorce before remarrying in order to maintain her future children's marriageable status in the eyes of the Rabbanites. Some Israeli rabbis follow this ruling and allow a marriage between Karaites and Rabbanites, with the proviso that the Karaite partner accept Rabbanite Judaism. Generally, though, both Karaites and Rabbanites frown upon intermarriage, the former more for reasons of Karaite continuity.

Civil Law: We have no indication that Karaite religious courts were ever able to enforce civil laws, and, therefore, Karaite legal discussions in this area were undoubtedly theoretical. Nevertheless, Karaites tended to a more literal interpretation of biblical civil law, such as understanding *lex talionis* as requiring actual corporal harm rather than monetary compensation as is the Rabbanite view.

Karaite Theology: In his code of Karaite Jewish law, the fifteenth-century Elijah Bashyazi recorded ten principles of Judaism: (1) The physical world was created. (2) It was created by a creator who did not create himself, but is eternal. (3) The creator has no likeness and is unique in all respects. (4) God sent the prophet Moses. (5) God sent, along with Moses, his perfect Torah. (6) It is the duty of the believer to understand the original language of the Torah. (7) God inspired the other prophets. (8) God will resurrect humans on the day of judgment. (9) God requites all individuals according to their ways and the fruits of their deeds. (10) God will send the messiah, the descendant of David. Anyone familiar with Rabbanite Jewish dogmatism, such as Mai-

monides' list of thirteen principles, notices immediately the similarity between the two religious systems. In fact, there is little to distinguish between classical Rabbanite and Karaite theologies, and some Karaite authorities have even preferred Maimonides' thirteen-fold division to Bashyazi's of ten principles. Although some of the more rationalistic thinkers of each group were skeptical of supernatural aspects of traditional theology, generally both Rabbanite and Karaite Judaism posit the existence of a singular, incorporeal God who created the world and who gave the Torah to Moses and inspired the other prophets. There is reward and punishment in this world and the next, and the promised future includes the coming of the messiah and resurrection of the dead. Karaite belief in afterworldly recompense distinguishes them from the Second Temple Sadducees, with whom they are often compared, a comparison much resented because of what they consider to be Sadducean heresy.

Karaite concepts of God were originally influenced by the Kalam theology of Islam. God is totally incorporeal and whatever attributes God has do not diminish God's absolute unity. Biblical anthropomorphisms are to be interpreted metaphorically, but Rabbinic statements about God that seem to indicate that God has a body, such as those found in some mystical works, like *Shiur Qoma*, are to be rejected out of hand. Despite their objection to mystical speculation about God, some early Karaites believed, as did some Rabbinic mystics, that the angels have permanent existence as God's divine glory. The best proof of the existence of God is through the demonstration that the world was created, a conclusion that can be attained by using cosmological arguments borrowed from the Kalam. God's justice is absolute, and all of God's actions are good.

Where Karaism and Rabbanism had their most fundamental disagreement was over the nature of Mosaic revelation. Rabbinic Judaism teaches that in addition to the Five Books of Moses (the Torah or Pentateuch), which were written down at Mt. Sinai, an Oral Torah was also revealed at Sinai and transmitted orally for many generations. The Oral Torah includes authoritative interpretations of the Written Torah, and Jewish law must follow its dictates rather than what might appear to be the literal meaning of the Bible. Eventually, the Oral Torah was written down in the Mishnah and Talmud, and later law codes, such as Maimonides' *Mishneh Torah* or Joseph Caro's sixteenth-century *Shulhan Arukh*, are based upon them. Thus, the Rabbinic interpretation of the Torah, even if it apparently contradicts the written word, is considered to be divine in origin.

Karaites rejected this Rabbanite doctrine. They considered the talmudic traditions to be one possible interpretation of biblical law, often to be rejected in favor of a more literal understanding. Rabbanite interpretations of Jewish law are certainly not of divine origin, and to the extent that they contradict the Torah, they are to be repudiated. With the later Karaite rapprochement with Rabbanism, there has been a greater willingness to accept Rabbanite exegesis when it is not in direct contradiction to Karaite practice. Nevertheless, Rabbanite legal traditions have never been accepted as divine in origin (and neither have Karaite traditions).

Because of the need to refer specifically to the text of the Torah in order to derive practical guidance, a number of Karaite dogmatists have emphasized the need to know Hebrew and to study the biblical text closely (the sixth principle on Bashyazi's list). This idea may go back to the credo attributed to Anan ben David, "Search well in the Scriptures and do not rely upon my opinion." Though there are good reasons to doubt this saying's attribution to Anan, it does represent an ethos of personal interpretation that was strong in the formative period of Karaism.

Despite the emphasis on biblical interpretation and its eschewal of Rabbinic tradition, it would be a mistake to assume that Karaism is a literalist biblical religion. Karaites also used canons of interpretation (such as logical analogy) to determine the law. Karaism developed its own traditions that are the basis of its practice. Karaites claim, however, that these traditions are not Sinaitic and that they do not contradict the written Torah.

Karaite attitudes towards other religions are similar to those of Rabbanism. It is true that the seventh century messianic pretender Abu Isa Ovadia al-Isfahani, who is considered by some to have been a precursor of Karaism, was willing to accept Jesus and Muhammad as authentic prophets to their own communities, but not to Jews, and a similar view is sometimes attributed to Anan. Generally, however, Karaites were not sympathetic to either Christianity or Islam, although influenced by both. Some of the fiercest anti-Islamic polemics produced by Jews (who generally eschewed attacking Islam) were written by Karaites, such as Jacob al-Qirqisani and Joseph al-Baṣir. Karaites in Islamic countries also engaged in anti-Christian polemics, as did their Rabbanite colleagues, usually in the context of discussions of divine unity. Such polemics are found, for instance, in the works of Qirqisani and Yefet ben Eli. Furthermore, among certain early Karaites there was a particular antagonism to non-Jews, with stringent enactments to regulate social contacts between the groups.

Although European Karaites were courted by Christian Hebraists, and some undoubtedly enjoyed the attention they received from the scholars with whom they corresponded concerning Karaite origins and practices, they were still not enamored of the Christian religion. Isaac of Troki's *Ḥizzuq Emunah* is an encyclopedic attack on Christianity, both a defense of Jewish interpretations of the Hebrew Bible and a critical reading of the New Testament, firmly in the tradition of the medieval controversial literature. This work was widely accepted among Rabbanite Jews, despite its Karaite authorship and its lack of defense of Rabbinic literature, a standard feature of Rabbanite anti-Christian polemical treatises. It was also well known among anti-Jewish Christian writers, a number of whom felt it was necessary to respond specifically to it. What makes Isaac's work particularly noteworthy is its knowledge of trends in the Lithuanian Reformation and his use of internal Christian controversies as an argument against the truth of the majority religion.

Karaite Intellectual Achievements: Throughout its history, especially in the earlier, formative periods, Karaism produced a body of literature that offers almost a full alternative to Rabbanite intellectual achievements. Although some genres of Rabbanite creativity, such as the responsa literature or science and medicine, are generally missing from the Karaite repertoire, most other fields of endeavor are well covered. Many of the Karaite works, again usually from the formative period, had an impact on their Rabbanite equivalents and are cited in Rabbinic treatises.

Halakhah: The first major work of sectarian law is Anan ben David's *Sefer Ha-Mitzvot* ("Book of Precepts"), which was not a Karaite work but which influenced later Karaism. This book, which has not survived in toto, was written in Aramaic and is reminiscent of Rabbanite legal works produced by the Babylonian academies. Benjamin al-Nahawendi also produced a short code written in Hebrew. The first major compendium of Karaite law was Jacob al-Qirqisani's massive *Kitab al-Anwar wa'l-Maraqib* ("The Book of Lights and Watchtowers"), which is an important source not only of law but also of heresiology, theology and polemics (against Rabbanites, Christians, Muslims, other Jewish sectarians and other Karaites). Qirqisani's intellectualistic and diasporan variety of Karaism gave way to the land of Israel centered Karaism of his Mourners of Zion contemporaries, but his code remained a classic of formative Karaism and a major accomplishment in its own right.

Karaite law was standardized by authorities in the land of Israel, most notably Levi ben Yefet (Yefet ben Eli's son) and Joseph al-Başir. These codes, written in Arabic, eventually gave way to works written in Hebrew, most notably Judah Hadassi's *Eshkol ha-Kofer* ("The Cluster of Henna;" cf., Song 1:14). This book was written in an extremely peculiar style (as a rhymed poem with each stanza an acrostic, each one alphabetically forward or reverse, with the same rhyme occurring throughout the book), but it fully encapsulated previous Karaite legal endeavors. It was also the last work of classical Karaism, and its author was still dedicated to the ethos of Mourning for Zion, even though he realized that this was not an option for most of his Byzantine co-religionists.

The last two great compendia of Karaite law were Aaron ben Elijah's *Gan Eden* ("Garden of Eden") and Elijah Bashyazi's *Aderet Eliyyahu* ("The Cloak of Elijah"). These two works demonstrate well the internal tensions in Karaite law, with Aaron's conservative approach to Karaite practice and Bashyazi's reforming tendencies (such as the permission to use Sabbath lamps). Eventually, Bashyazi's approach won out, and he is considered the final decisor of Karaite law. Nonetheless, there have been periodic challenges to his rulings and attempts to return to a more conservative practice. Some later Karaites objected also to the rationalist theology found in his code. Subsequent authors produced shorter treatises on particular subjects (such as calendar, ritual slaughter and personal status), but *Gan Eden* and *Aderet Eliyyahu* remained the authoritative legal codices.

Mention should be made of a major Egyptian Karaite codex, Samuel ha-Ma'aravi's *Kitab al-Murshid* ("The Guide"), written in Arabic in the fourteenth century, and translated into Hebrew in the seventeenth. Samuel's approach to Karaite law reflects the oriental traditions that were not as strong in Byzantium and eastern Europe, and his legal rulings had little impact on the majority of Karaites. Present day Egyptian Karaites follow the rulings of Elijah Bashyazi, rather than those of Samuel (although the Hebrew translation of his code has just recently been published for the first time in Israel).

Exegesis: The most outstanding Karaite biblical interpreter was Yefet ben Eli, who wrote Judaeo-Arabic commentaries on all the books of the Bible (with the possible exception of Lamentations). Composed during the latter half of the tenth century, after Saadia, his commentaries contain detailed refutations of Saadia's attacks on Karaite exegesis. Like Saadia, Yefet provided both translations into Arabic and running commentaries on the biblical books. Although some of the commentaries are literal, Yefet often looked for opportunities to interpret contemporary events in light of biblical passages, such as in his commentaries on the Prophets, Psalms, and Daniel. He also included digressions on theology in the commentaries. Yefet became known to the Rabbanite world by means of Abraham ibn Ezra's citations of his opinions.

Although Yefet was the chief biblical exegete and translator of the Golden Age of Karaism, he was preceded by Daniel al-Qumisi, Jacob al-Qirqisani, Salmon ben Yeruḥim, and David ben Boaz, who laid the groundwork for specifically Karaite interpretations of the Bible and was succeeded by Yeshua ben Judah (also occasionally cited by Abraham Ibn Ezra). Yefet's commentaries had long lasting influence on non-Arabic speaking Karaites by means of translations/ paraphrases found in the Byzantine compendium *Sefer Ha-ʾOsher* ("The Book of Richness") of Jacob ben Reuben, and in Tobias ben Moses' commentary on Leviticus, *Otzar Nehmad* ("The Desirable Treasure;" cf., Prov. 21:20).

Two major Byzantine figures produced original Hebrew biblical commentaries. Aaron ben Joseph wrote commentaries on the Pentateuch, *Sefer ha-Mivhar* ("The Choice Book") as well as on Former Prophets, Isaiah, Psalms, and Job (the latter is not extant), in which he incorporated many Rabbanite interpretations. He wrote that his turn away from classical Karaite exegesis was a result both of what he considered superior Rabbanite views and his inability to understand the peculiar Hebrew translations of the classics, which were the product of Tobias ben Moses' literary project. Aaron ben Elijah, whose entire literary oeuvre is marked by moderate conservatism, returned to some of the earlier Karaite exegesis in his *Keter Torah* ("Crown of the Torah"), a commentary on the Pentateuch. Later Karaites produced very little new in the line of biblical exegesis, although Judah Gibbor's *Minhat Yehudah* ("The Offering of Judah"), an epic poem summarizing the entire Pentateuch, should be mentioned.

Philosophy and Theology: We do not know much about Anan's theology, but Benjamin al-Nahawendi is well known for having posited the existence of a creating angel to whom the Bible refers when attributing physical qualities to God. In reaction to this theory, Daniel al-Qumisi denied the existence of angels. Al-Qumisi is also known for his objection to the use of reason for religious purposes, even though some of his works show a passing familiarity with, and employment of, Kalamic arguments.

The first two great Karaite theologians were Jacob al-Qirqisani and Yefet ben Eli, neither of whom wrote a specifically theological work, but both of whom injected much theological content into their other writings. Jacob and Yefet were well aware of Kalamic arguments and used them frequently in their works. Neither, however, was a full-fledged philosopher in the manner of Joseph al-Baṣir. Al-Baṣir was influenced directly by the Basrian school of Kalam whose chief representative was Abd al-Jabbar b. Aḥmad (d. 1025). Al-Baṣir wrote two major treatises of philosophy, *Kitab al-Muḥtawi* ("The Comprehensive Book) and *Kitab al-Tamyiz* or *Kitab al-Mansuri* ("The Book of Distinction" or "The Book Dedicated to Mansur"). Following strictly Kalamic patterns, al-Baṣir's began his book with epistemological considerations, following this with cosmological proofs for the creation of the world. Once it is established that the world was created, one knows that God exists. This God is one and incorporeal, described with essential attributes that do not impinge on absolute divine unity. Turning from the existence of God to discussions of theodicy, again along the Kalamic pattern, al-Baṣir argued for absolute divine justice that is a function of God's total self-sufficiency. Any manifestations of evil can be explained as mandated by God's wisdom, for the benefit of the suffering person, and, thus, not truly evil. Even animals receive compensation for unwarranted suffering, a doctrine shared with the Rabbanite geonim but rejected by Rabbanite Aristotelians and later Karaites.

Al-Baṣir's Karaite Kalam set the pattern of Karaite thought for two hundred years, during which time Rabbanite Jews turned away from the Kalam and pursued both neo-Platonism and, especially, Aristotelianism. Kalamic treatises were written by al-Baṣir's student, Yeshua ben Judah, in Arabic, and the Byzantine community both translated al-Baṣir's and Yeshua's works into Hebrew and composed its own original Kalamic treatises in Hebrew. The last major representative of Kalamic thinking was Judah Hadassi, even though he did not follow the classical Karaite Kalam in all its aspects. Hadassi was also the first Karaite to propose a system of Karaite beliefs, outlining ten principles similar to, but not identical with, Bashyazi's list.

Eventually Karaites also became captivated by Aristotelianism, especially as propagated by Maimonides. Aaron ben Joseph showed Maimonidean influence in his biblical commentaries, rejecting, for instance, Yefet's classification of prophecy in favor of a system based on Maimonides' teachings. Aaron ben Elijah wrote his philosophical opus, *Etz Hayyim* ("The Tree of Life"), as an attempt to synthesize Karaite Kalam and Maimonidean Aristotelianism. There are differences of opinion as to what were Aaron's own views, but the impact of Maimonides' *Guide of the Perplexed* on his thought and on his philosophical treatise are without doubt. As in the *Guide*, long sections of *Etz Hayyim* are dedicated to philosophical exegesis of the Bible, and the major issues of the *Guide*, namely, divine attributes, creation, prophecy, providence, and reasons for the commandments are all dealt with at length. In most cases, Aaron adopted opinions close to those of Maimonides, even as he defended the intellectual integrity of his Karaite predecessors with whom he disagreed. Aaron's synthesis of the Rabbanite and Karaite philosophical traditions did not last long, and in the fifteenth and sixteenth centuries, Byzantine Karaite thinkers (Elijah Bashyazi, Caleb Afendopolo, and Judah Gibbor) adopted the Maimonidean approach. Nevertheless, traces of classical Karaite Kalam remained in later Karaite treatises and can even be discerned in present day Karaite doctrinal works.

Karaites generally eschewed mysticism in its various forms. The rapprochement with Rabbanism, however, opened up Kabbalistic vistas for some Karaite thinkers. The major Karaite kabbalist was Simhah Isaac Lutzki, who wrote six Kabbalistic treatises and propagated the study of Kabbalah among Karaites, arguing that it represents true wisdom revealed to Moses on Sinai. Lutzki's Kabbalah was divorced from Karaite praxis and tradition, lacking the intimate relation that existed between Rabbanite Kabbalah and praxis, and it never caught on.

Philology and Language: Karaites were particularly interested in Hebrew, since only a thorough command of it allowed them to interpret the Bible in as literal and authoritative a manner as possible. Some even postulate that the great ninth-century Tiberian Massoretes (the Ben Ashers and Ben Naftalis) were Karaites, but this assumption has not won universal acceptance. Karaites were, however, pioneers of Hebrew grammar. The tenth- and eleventh-century David ben Abraham Alfasi, Joseph ibn Nuh and Abu al-Faraj Harun were the chief Karaite language experts, producing grammars and biblical glossaries. Later Rabbanite grammarians depended upon these works in their own language studies. Subsequent Karaites showed less interest in technical language studies, and no other Karaite linguistic works are as significant as the ones produced in the Golden Age.

Karaites can be credited with two other important linguistic accomplishments. When they began the eleventh-century literary project in Byzantium, they produced the first translations of Arabic works into Hebrew, predating the Tibbonide translations of the twelfth and thirteenth centuries. These translations are noteworthy for their opaque Hebrew and Greek glosses, making them practically impossible to understand without the original Arabic texts. Nonetheless, they represent an early attempt to find an appropriate Hebrew terminology to convey the meaning of Arabic technical terms. Although later Karaite writers adopted the Hebrew of the Rabbanite translations, a number of terms and phrases remain in Karaite Hebrew to this day.

Crimean Karaites also innovated their own language, Karaimic, which was the everyday language of Karaites in both Crimea and Eastern Europe. With the breakdown of the Karaite communities in those locations, the language has almost disappeared, despite some recent efforts to revive it. Still, much of Karaite non-sacral literature is written in this language, and a knowledge of it is necessary for research into Russian Karaism.

Karaism as an Alternative Form of Judaism: Over the course of its history, Karaism has provided Rabbinic Judaism with an alter-ego. Both forms of Judaism begin with many of the same premises, existence of God, revelation of the Torah to Moses, divine providence, and reward and punishment; yet they arrived at much different conclusions as to religious practices. Karaism has always represented a threat to Rabbanism, not because of great numbers or the possibility that the majority of Jews might turn to it, but because it undermines the very foundational myth of Rabbinic Judaism, that the legal interpretations of the rabbis are of divine origin, known already to Moses at Sinai. Thus, Karaites oftentimes have served as the ultimate Jewish "other," providing a foil for discussions of the authenticity of Rabbinic Judaism. Karaites, with no hope of achieving majority status, worried primarily about their own survival as a discrete movement. When survival seemed to mandate denial of their Jewish identity (as in Czarist Russia and under Nazi occupation), Karaites were willing to separate themselves entirely from other Jews.

The survival of Karaism throughout the centuries teaches us something about the nature of Jewish pluralism. As long as Karaites maintained their affiliation with the Jewish people, even when they abided by a different calendar, ate different food, and prayed in a different manner, they were accepted by the rest of the Jewish people as Jews. Intermarriage, though not encouraged because of technical problems relating to a possible non-marriageable status, did occur (and the two partners usually worked out in advance whose religious practices would be followed in their daily life). Occasionally, one side would persecute the other (especially the Rabbanites, who were the majority, persecuted the Karaites), and they might each turn to non-Jewish authorities for support in their internecine controversies. Still, both sides realized that their antagonism was a family affair between competing brothers. The final schism between Rabbanites and Karaites came only in those areas of the Russian empire in which Karaites denied their Jewish identity. Doctrinal and legal differences could be overcome; separation from the Jewish people caused an irreparable break.

There are a number of reasons Karaism did not usurp Rabbanism as the majority form of Judaism. Most notably, Rabbinic Judaism had developed over many years during which its halakhah adjusted itself to reality. Karaite law had a much shorter incubation period, and often the untenability of its precepts (such as the laws of incest or the prohibition of lights on the Sabbath) caused embarrassing ruptures until authoritative reforms could be put in place. Early Karaite law tended to be more inflexible than Rabbanite law, appealing to an intellectualist asceticism that was not conducive to a mass movement. Furthermore, to the extent that ninth- and tenth-century Karaism revived controversies that had been settled in the first century (such as whether Shavuot was always to be on a Sunday), it had little chance of overthrowing centuries of tradition.

Despite its failure to gain majority status, and the constant encroachments on its traditions by the tendency towards rapprochement with Rabbanism, Karaism has proven to be a tenacious antagonist to Rabbinic Judaism. It has survived under the most adverse conditions for over a millennium, at the least. Whether contemporary Karaites can meet the challenges of modernity in democratic societies, especially in Israel, which, though a Jewish country, is not sympathetic to Karaite needs, remains to be seen. History has taught, however, that all attempts at writing Karaism's obituary have so far been entirely premature.

Bibliography
Birnbaum, Philip, ed., *Karaite Studies* (New York, 1971).
Mann, Jacob, *Texts and Studies in Jewish History and Literature, Vol. II, Karaitica* (Philadelphia, 1935).
Nemoy, Leon, *Karaite Anthology* (New Haven, 1952).
Polliack, Meira, ed., *Karaite Judaism, An Introduction to the History and Literary Sources of Medieval and Modern Karaism* (Leiden, 2002).

DANIEL J. LASKER

KHAZARS AND JUDAISM: The Khazars (called *Kuzarim* in Hebrew and *Kazarn* in Yiddish) were a civilized, semi-nomadic Turkic-speaking people who founded an independent kingdom in about the year 652 in southern Russia near the Caspian Sea.

Before the establishment of Khazaria, the Khazars appear to have lived in the Terek and Sulak river valleys of the northern Caucasus for several centuries, but their earliest history is still obscure. Their closest relatives appear to have been the Turkic Bulgars and Sabirs. Writers such as Theophanes, Judah ben Barzillai al-Barsaloni, Martinus Oppaviensis, and the authors of the *Georgian Chronicle* and the Chinese chronicle *T'ang-shu* explicitly referred to the Khazars as Turks. However, according to the *Schechter Letter*, compiled in the 940s by an unknown Khazarian author, Khazarian women intermarried with Jewish men migrating northward from Armenia, and Jewish legends claimed that the Khazars were descended from the Hebrew tribe of Simeon. In an unusual section in the letter of the Spanish Jewish diplomat Hasdai ibn Shaprut to King Yosef, Hasdai referred to a claim he had heard that the Khazars were originally from Mount Seir, a place in the Middle East where the Edomites dwelled. The seventh-century Armenian historian Bishop Sebeos and the Arab geographer Dimashqi alleged that the Khazars were of Armenian descent. But the predominant Turkic ancestry of the Khazars is generally acknowledged among modern scholars.

The Khazar state employed many thousands of paid soldiers on a permanent basis at a time when, according to al-Masudi, no other standing armies existed in eastern Europe. Their military might was well-known to their neighbors, such as the Armenians and Georgians. The Khazarian army affected the future course of European history by holding back the Arabs from invading eastern Europe during the seventh and eighth centuries. In that respect, their vigorous defense of their kingdom's independence was similar to the way in which the Franks defended the West from the Arab conquests.

It is now known that the Khazars had an indigenous manufacturing industry that created many products for export, including jewelry, pottery, and other crafts. The Khazars were also agriculturalists and harvested such crops as barley, wheat, rice, melons, and cucumbers. Khazaria hosted traders from all over Europe and Asia who had arrived via the west-east Silk Road and the north-south Silver Route. The principal cities and towns of Khazaria included Atil, Samkarsh al-Yahud, Kerch (Bospor), Samandar, Sarkel, and Kiev. Atil, situated at the mouth of the Volga, was settled by Jews, Christians, Muslims, and pagans and had many shops, baths, and mosques as well as the kagan's palace. Samkarsh al-Yahud ("Samkarsh of the Jews"), on the Taman peninsula, was given its name due to its large Jewish population, which caught the attention of the Byzantine chronicler Theophanes. Kerch, ruled by an *archon*, was the Khazar center of the Crimea. Samandar, ruled by a Jewish governor, was settled by Jews, Christians, Muslims, and pagans and also contained shops, gardens, vineyards, and mosques. Sarkel, a city near the River Don, was the site of a large fortress built with limestone bricks. Part of Kiev was founded by the Khazars under the name "Sambata," and a Khazarian section called "Kozare" existed in the commercial district of Kiev, Podol.

The Khazar kingdom was organized as a dual-monarchy, with power split between two kings called the *kagan* and the *bek*. These kings collected tribute from many of the East Slavic tribes as well as from traders traversing their country. Khazaria also had a supreme court consisting of representatives of multiple religions (paganism, Islam, Judaism, and Christianity). The emperors of Byzantium regarded Khazaria as a formidable military and diplomatic power, which explains Emperor Constantine Porphyrogenitus' statement that correspondence he sent to the Khazars was marked with a gold seal worth three *solidi*—a greater value than the two *solidi* that accompanied letters to the Pope of Rome, the Prince of the Rus, and the Prince of the Hungarians.

Khazar religious practices prior to conversion: Prior to their adoption of monotheistic faiths, the Khazars professed the cults of Tengrism and Shamanism. The supreme god was named Tengri, ruler over all of the Earth. According to other sources, other Turkic deities included the fertility goddess Umay ("Placenta"), the divine twins Yir and Sub who speak in unison, and the military god Ärklig. Some facts are also known about the regular religious practices of the early Khazars. The *Life of Constantine* quoted from Khazar ambassadors who revealed that they bow eastward to Tengri. The Khazars manufactured amulets with shamanistic motifs, sacrificed animals as offerings to the gods, and ritually murdered their kings according to ancient Turkic custom. Additional statements may or may not be accurate. The Arab historian al-Tabari wrote that the early Khazars learned rain-making rituals and prayers. The anonymous twelfth-century Persian history *Mughmal at-tawârîh* stated that the Khazars practiced cremation. Under an entry for the year 730/731, the Syriac chronicle of Pseudo-Dionysus of Tell-Mahrê said that the Khazars lack a single God and are Magians (Zoroastrians), and then repeated the claim that the Khazars "do not agree that there is a God in Heaven" under a separate entry dated 731/732. The claim that the Khazars were Zoroastrians is rather dubious, even though there were a number of Zoroastrians who were relocated to the northern Caucasus by the Persians in the sixth century. It is likely that Pseudo-Dionysus actually meant "heathen" rather than "Zoroastrian" when he claimed that the Khazars were Magians. There is, similarly, no evidence that the Khazars ever professed Buddhism, even though their seventh-century Western Turkish overlord, Tong Yabghu, was a devout Buddhist.

There is considerable historical and archaeological evidence that Christianity became widespread among the "Huns" of the Khazar town Balanjar. There were, for example, churches in Balanjar. *History of the Caucasian Albanians* by the Armenian writer Movses Dasxuranc'i described the successful attempt of the Albanian Christian bishop Israyel in the 680s to reform the "Huns" by destroying their previous belief system. After winning support for Christianity among top Hunnic rulers, Israyel destroyed altars to Tengri and cut down a large oak tree that had been venerated by all the Huns and used it to construct a Christian cross, and the "Hunnic" kagan Alp required the Tengri priests to give up their "magic cubes," i.e., amulets that represented supernatural power. In the second half of the eighth and ninth centuries, Christian churches that served Khazars and members of other tribes were built in Khazaria's major towns on the Crimean peninsula, including Kerch, Tepsen, and Kordon-Oba.

There was also an Islamic phase in Khazar life, lasting from 737 until the 850s. This is evidenced by the fact that the king of the Khazars was forced to adopt Islam in 737, and also by the presence of commoner Muslim Khazars during this period as well as afterward. Even after the Khazars adopted Judaism, there were still some Muslim members of the royal family. Al-Istakhri related a story that a young bread-seller whom many Khazars thought was worthy of becoming the next kagan was ineligible because of his Islamic religion.

The Khazar conversion to Judaism: The vast dominion of the Khazars came under the rule of Judaism by the ninth century. The Khazars' adoption of Judaism, once evidenced only by assorted references in the medieval writings of chroniclers, travelers, and commentators and by a few Hebrew documents authored by the Khazars themselves, is now gaining archaeological confirmation.

Though it is widely believed that the Khazar leaders converted to Judaism to preserve Khazaria's independence against its Muslim and Christian neighbors, the pre-existing Jewish communities doubtless played a role in influencing their decision. The *Life of Constantine*, for instance, related how the Khazars were being urged by Jews and Arabs to adopt another religion around the year 860. Dimashqi similarly alleged that Jewish immigrants fleeing from the Byzantine Empire "offered them their religion." However, legend has it that the Khazars did not fully adopt Judaism immediately. Instead, we are told that they held a debate between representatives of the major monotheistic religions and that the Khazar kings, after inquiring into the beliefs and origins of these competing faiths, deliberately and decisively chose Judaism. The famous debate held in the Khazar court, though not preserved in documents contemporary to the event, was independently referenced by later Christian (the *Life of Constantine*), Muslim (al-Bakri), and Jewish (King Yosef, the *Schechter Letter*, and Judah Halevi) sources, each of which added various angles and biases to the story.

Al-Bakri's eleventh-century *Book of Kingdoms*

and Roads claimed that the Khazar king had initially been a pagan then experimented with Christianity, until finally coming to realize that his religious beliefs were false. He conferred with a high Khazar official, who told him that there were three groups that possessed "sacred scriptures." The official convinced the king to summon a Christian bishop and a Muslim scholar. The king had become acquainted with a Jew who was "skilled in argument," and this Jew asked the bishop what he thought of the prophet Moses and the Torah. The bishop responded by acknowledging the truth of Judaism's holy books. The king was curious about the bishop's own belief system, so he asked what Christianity entailed. When the bishop said "... Jesus the Messiah, son of Mary, is the Word and has revealed the mysteries in the name of God," the Jew advised the Khazar king that the bishop expounded a doctrine foreign to Judaism while accepting the core of Judaism. Unable to produce evidence in favor of Christianity, the bishop was dismissed, and a Muslim scholar was summoned. But al-Bakri alleged that the Jew hired someone to poison the Muslim during his journey to the king. Thus did the Jew succeed in convincing the king to embrace Judaism. It is clear that al-Bakri's account is an embellishment of the actual circumstances. No other source, for instance, spoke of the killing of the Muslim participant in the debate.

Parts of the *Life of Constantine* told the story of Saint Cyril's mission to the Khazars in 860-861. Saint Cyril was sent to the Khazar kingdom by the Byzantine emperor Michael III. It had long been the hope of the Patriarch of Constantinople, Photius (once called by the epithet "Khazar-face"), like religious and political leaders before him, to convert Judeans, Khazars, and other non-Christians to Christianity. Saint Cyril's mission represented a real opportunity to convince the Khazar king of the merits of Christianity. However, we are told that the mission was a failure. By the time Cyril arrived in the Khazar king's palace, the Khazar leaders had already learned that Judaism was a major religion worth consideration and that they could consult the Jews on religious matters, especially since

these Jews possessed Torah scrolls. Cyril's arguments in favor of Christianity were not fully accepted, even though the *Life* quotes alleged complimentary remarks the king made to Cyril with regard to certain beliefs the latter held. Before embarking on other missionary ventures, Cyril succeeded in converting only two hundred Khazars to his religion. The king of the Khazars, we are told, was not among the baptized.

The Jewish sources on the debate episode differ in certain respects both from the Islamic and Christian accounts as well as from each other. King Yosef's letter to Hasdai ibn Shaprut related the story of a predecessor of his, King Bulan, a wise and just ruler. Yosef said that an angel of the Lord ap-peared to Bulan in a dream, asking him to follow the commandments and laws of the Jewish God. Then the highest official of Khazaria also met the angel in a dream. "The Khazar king then gathered all of his officers and servants, along with the entire nation ... [and] the people accepted the religion ... and entered under the Wings of the Divine Presence." The neighbors of the newly-Judaized nation heard of Bulan's great reputation and invited him to convert to Islam or Christianity. But the king was not easily persuaded by their promise to give him precious metals and other gifts. He arranged to hold a debate between a Christian priest and a Muslim judge. Already familiar with many of the tenets of his new Jewish faith, yet still willing to consider alternatives, Bulan asked the Christian for his view of Judaism: "Which is better—the religion of Israel or the religion of Ishmael?" The Christian admitted the truth of Judaism by stating, among other things, that God had taken the Jews out of Egyptian slavery, provided the Jews with manna and water during their wanderings, and given them the Torah and the land of Israel. By contrast, the Christian had nothing but harsh words for the perceived beliefs and way of life of the Muslims. Next, the judge of the Muslim king was asked "The Christian or the Jewish religion—which one is better in your eyes?" The Muslim judge replied that Judaism encompasses God's Torah and righteous statutes and commandments, whereas the Christians eat pig meat and other impurities and are idolaters. King Yosef quoted King Bulan's concluding remarks: "If so, then you have admitted with your own mouths that Judaism is honorable. I have thus chosen Judaism, the religion of Abraham. . . ."

The *Schechter Letter*, whose author is unknown except that he was a Khazarian Jew who lived during the time of his master King Yosef, indicated that a king of the Khazars had some Jewish ancestry and began to gain interest in the Jewish religion. His new devotion to Judaism concerned the rulers of the Byzantines and Arabs, who questioned his decision. After hearing of these complaints from his officers, the king decided to send for Jewish, Christian, and Muslim sages to describe their respective religions. Each debated the merits of his own faith, but when the Jewish sages described the Torah's account of the six-day creation of the world, God's saving of the Jews from slavery, and the settlement of ancient Israel, the Greek and Arab sages confirmed that what they said was right. However, some issues were still not resolved, so the Khazar officials asked for the Torah scrolls that were kept in a cave in the plain of Tizul, somewhere north of the Caucasus. After the Jewish sages explained these books, the Khazars fully embraced Judaism, and their king adopted the Jewish name Sabriel. Once again, the Jewish representatives appeared to gain the upper hand by virtue of the shared Jewish root of the three competing faiths.

Judah Halevi, considered one of the most important Jewish philosophers and poets of all time, was a prolific writer in twelfth-century Spain. His most famous work, *Kuzari: The Book of Proof and Argument in Defense of the Despised Faith*, was composed in Arabic towards the end of his life to communicate his belief in the superiority of Judaism over other faiths. An unnamed Khazar king's conversion to Judaism serves as the core of the storyline, but the bulk of the work consists of imaginary conversations between the king and a rabbi relating almost entirely to religious matters outside of the context of Khazaria. However, the beginning of chapters one and two of *Kuzari* demonstrate that Halevi was familiar with at least the basics

of Khazarian history, and it is not improbable that he had access to rare Hebrew documents about the Khazars.

The author began by claiming that a king of the Khazars converted to Judaism "about four hundred years ago." This rather inaccurate estimate places the conversion at circa 740. Judaism among the Khazar Turks at this early date is not attested by any other source. The next part of the first chapter is equally fictional (but probably based upon King Yosef's description of the angel), relating how an angel spoke to the king while he dreamed. The angel warned the king that God did not approve of his actions. Yet, at first, the king did not heed the angel's call. After a repeat visit by the angel, the king felt the need to inquire into other philosophies. Eventually he asked a Christian scholar and a Muslim mullah about their respective faiths.

At first he had no inclination to ask a Jew, but after the Christian claimed that Christianity is an extension of the Torah and the mullah told him that the Bible is "full of the stories of Moses and the children of Israel," he became convinced that a conversation with a Jewish sage would be beneficial. A wise rabbi thus began to converse at length with the king. At the beginning of the second chapter, Halevi inserted an interesting summary of the Khazars' conversion to Judaism, supposedly taken from "the Khazar history books." These books, Halevi wrote, related how the king notified his chief officer about his recurring dream involving the angel of God. The officer then accompanied the king to a cave in the Warsan Mountains in the North Caucasus, the same cave referenced in the *Schechter Letter*. The king and his officer converted to Judaism and were circumcised there. After some time, the masses of Khazars converted to Judaism, learned the Torah from imported sages, and built a tabernacle modeled after that of Moses. The king continued to investigate Judaism through his discussions with the rabbi for many months or years, but eventually the rabbi decided to depart for the land of Israel.

Interestingly, the cave motif of *Kuzari* and the *Schechter Letter* was also recounted by Hasdai ibn Shaprut. Hasdai wrote that a "man of Israel" (= Sabriel/Bulan?) was eager to learn why some of his fellow countrymen used to pray in a particular cave, since the reason had been forgotten—that there were books of Torah there. The "man of Israel" found the sacred scriptures and brought them out, and the Khazars decided to study the law. Even more incredibly, Hasdai related that the Khazarian story of the cave was already known to his fellow Spanish Jews for a long time prior to his writing. It is not known precisely how, apart from the visit of a mysterious man named Eldad the Danite in the 880s, Spanish Jews prior to the tenth century would have received information about the Khazars, legendary or otherwise.

The conversion of the Khazar king and some of his subjects was also recorded by many other independent sources. Judaism was almost always noted in the medieval sources as having been the most important religion in the Khazar kingdom. It was often the only religion cited when referring to the Khazars. Christian of Stavelot wrote the following in *Expositio in Matthaeum Evangelistam*, composed circa 864:

> . . . And of the king Alexander we read that he turned to God and begged that the peoples of Gog and Magog—those who are now called the Khazars, who were once Hunnic peoples—be shut in, since he was unable to crush them through warfare. God heard him and shut them in their mountain, so that they came to stay behind with their people; and he placed copper gates in front of this mountain. . . . We know of no nation under the heavens where Christians do not live. For [Christians are even found] in the lands of Gog and Magog—who are a Hunnic race and are called Khazars, [and are] now a people that is stronger than those whom Alexander conducted, circumcized and observing all [the laws of] Judaism. The Bulgars, however, who are of the same seven tribes [as the Khazars], are now becoming baptized [into Christianity].

Denkart, a Persian work, contains the following attack upon non-Zoroastrian religions: "Thus, it is clear that the false doctrine of Jesus in Rome, that of Moses among the Khazars, [and] that of Mani in [Uyghur-ruled] Turkistan removed the strength and bravery that they [the Romans, Khazars, and Turks] formerly possessed. . . ."

The Establishment of Proofs for the Prophethood of Our Master Muhammad by Abd al-Jabbar ibn Muhammad al-Hamdani, composed in the early eleventh century, contains a fascinating section that purports to detail the conversion episode (translation: Shlomo Pines):

> One of the Jews undertook the conversion of the Khazars, [who] are [composed of] many peoples, and they were converted by him and joined his religion. [This happened] recently in the days of the Abbasids. . . . For this was a man who came single-handedly to a king of great rank and to a very spirited people, and they were converted by him without [any recourse to] violence and the sword. And they took upon themselves the difficult obligations enjoined by the law of the Torah, such as circumcision, the ritual ablutions, washing after a discharge of the semen, the prohibition of work on the Sabbath and during the feasts, the prohibition of [eating the flesh of] animals [that are forbidden] according to this religion, and so on. Perhaps the Jews do claim that this missionary worked wonders and miracles, for some of them think it is possible that the righteous among them have this power. This is more deserving of attention than the claims of the Christians.

Ahmad ibn Muhammad ibn al-Faqih al-Hamadhani, a tenth-century Arabic writer who lived in Baghdad, stated the following in his geographical work *Kitab al-Buldan*: "All of the Khazars are Jews. But they have been Judaized recently."

Several Karaite writers spoke of the Khazars' religion without claiming that the Khazars had adopted their sectarian form of Judaism. In the tenth century *Book of Gardens and Parks*, Jacob al-Qirqisani of Iraq wrote simply: ". . . the Khazars . . . accepted Judaism." In *Sefer ha-'Osher*, also from the tenth century, Jacob ben Reuven of Byzantium wrote that the Khazars were "a single nation who do not bear the yoke of the exile, but are great warriors paying no tribute to the gentiles."

Two Middle Eastern references to the literacy of the Khazars attest to their Jewish orientation. One is *Kitab al-Fihrist* by Muhammad ibn Ishaq an-Nadim of Baghdad, from the late tenth century, which stated: "The Khazars write Hebrew [letters]." The other is *Ta'rikh-i Fakhr ad-Din Mubarak Shah*, a Persian work composed in 1206, which stated: "The Khazars have a script related to the script of the Russians [Rus]. . . . The greater part of these Khazars who use this script are Jews."

Khazaria was regarded as the "country of the Jews" (*Zemlya Zhidovskaya*) in Russian folk literature (*byliny*). And the *Schechter Letter* informs us that some of the Alan people (neighbors of the Khazars to the south) also adopted Judaism.

In the time of the Islamic writers from whom chronicler Ibn Rustah copied, Judaism was of a limited nature in the Khazar realm, and the majority of the Khazars professed a religion like that of the Turks. (A later work, the anonymous twelfth-century *Risalat fi'l-Aqalim*, also used old sources to claim: "Their supreme king professes Judaism. . . . Most of them practice Islam.") But by the tenth century, Khazarian Jewish communities extended as far west as Kiev—many hundreds of miles from Atil. One document providing evidence of this is the *Kievan Letter*, which was discovered by Norman Golb in 1962. A page of parchment measuring 22.5 by 14.4 centimeters, it was written by the Khazarian Jews in Kiev in the early tenth century as a letter of recommendation on behalf of one of the members of their community, Jacob bar Hanukkah. Most of the letter was written in Hebrew, and it contains references to God, but it contains one word of Turkic that was added after these Jews signed their names to the document. The discoverer of the letter and his colleague, Omeljan Pritsak, argued that the six non-Jewish names on the *Kievan Letter* (KYBR, SWRTH, GWSTT', MNS, MNR, and QWPYN) are of Turkic Khazarian etymological origin and belonged to Khazar Turks who had converted to Judaism. Golb and Pritsak even claimed that the Cohens and Levites in the letter were Turks who had artificially adopted these ancient Hebrew priestly titles. Avraham Torpusman, on the other hand, countered that some of the names (notably Gostyata, which was used by the early Slavs of Rus) are Slavic in origin and probably belonged to early Slavic-speaking Jews of non-Khazar origin rather than Jews of Turkic origin.

In favor of Torpusman's view is the fact that Israelites scattered throughout the world often adopted local names and languages from their neighbors, even though they were not themselves of non-Jewish origin, and also the fact that the titles Cohen and Levite almost always meant patrilineal descent from priests and assistant priests of the ancient Judean Temple, and there is no actual evidence that the Khazar shamanist priests adopted these titles after their conversion. Accordingly, a Byzantine origin for some of these Kievan Jews cannot be ruled out. An argument has been made by Vladimir Orel that the element SWRTH in the name "Judah called SWRTH" derived from the Slavic term "*sirota*" (orphan), in the Jewish context of a proselyte whose new "parents" include Abraham, Isaac, and Sarah. But Marcel Erdal contended that the nickname SWRTH may derive from the Gothic word "*swarta*" (black). A Turkic origin for three of the other names—KYBR, MNS, and MNR—has not yet been successfully challenged. Most likely, the Kievan community was of mixed Hebrew-Slavic-Turkic origins.

Which holidays did the Khazars (and other Jews in the Khazar realm) practice? Some clues derive from personal names the Khazarians gave to their children. Hanukkah was the name of (1) a Khazar king, (2) the *Kievan Letter* signatory Hanukkah bar Moses, and (3) the father of the Kievan Jew Jacob bar Hanukkah. Pesach was the name of a tenth-century Jewish military general whose actions are described in the *Schechter Letter*. As additional evidence, King Yosef described how some of the Khazars returned from the fields to their homes in Atil during Hanukkah time. This doubtless means that they celebrated the Hanukkah festival upon their return.

It appears that the corpus of medieval written works relating to the Khazar conversion will not grow in the future. This increases the value of archaeological evidence in providing information about the specific elements of Judaism followed in the Khazar Empire. The archaeological materials are open to various interpretations, however.

A burial site in medieval Hungary, at Chelarevo in modern Serbia, contains a large number of graves with Jewish motifs engraved upon brick fragments, including menorahs, shofars, lulavs, etrogs, candle-snuffers, and ash-collectors. A small six-pointed Star of David appears on one of the fragments. The Hebrew inscriptions "Jerusalem," "Israel," and "Yehuda, oh!" were found on a few fragments. Many scholars have conjectured that this burial ground belonged to the splinter Khazarian Kabar group that joined the Hungarians in the ninth century. This is complicated, however, by the fact that the Jewish graves contained Mongolian skeletons and the surrounding non-Jewish graves held Avar materials. Mongolian anthropological elements do not appear to have been predominant in the Khazar Empire. Thus, it cannot be expressed with certainty that this was a Khazarian burial ground. The name of the Khazar kingdom does not appear on any of the artifacts at Chelarevo. However, the Avars tended to intermarry with a variety of other groups, including Slavs, and relations between late Avars and Khazars cannot be ruled out.

A badly worn image of a six-pointed Star of David was also found on a mirror from Khazaria. It is not known whether the symbol was given a Jewish significance by its creator. Less ambiguous, if authentic, is the alleged finding of a Khazar vessel from the Don river valley of Russia, upon which the word "Israel" was engraved in Hebrew characters four times. On the Crimean and Taman peninsulas, Khazarian and Hebraic imagery can often be found on the same artifact, including Turkic tribe symbols, suggesting a combination of Turkic ethnic origin and Jewish religion.

The burial practices of the Khazars were transformed sometime in the ninth century. For instance, shamanistic sun-amulets disappeared from Khazar graves after the 830s. The British historian Jonathan Shepard wrote that Khazar graves used to be filled with many riches, often more than those of other groups residing in Khazaria. But the Khazar graves lack objects that can be dated to the tenth century. Shepard drew the reasonable conclusion that this was due to the Khazar conversion to Judaism—a religion that does not permit the burial of weaponry, riding-gear, and jewelry with the deceased, nor the creation of trenches filled with animal sacrifices. Most of the written sources do speak of a full-scale switch from paganism to Judaism. The situation is, however, complicated by a gravesite in Sudak on the Crimea, where a Khazar nobleman was buried according to Jewish ritual, yet beside him was lain a man who had an ax-blow delivered to his head, presumably as a ritual of human sacrifice. This may be an isolated case of mixed Jewish-Shamanistic beliefs.

It is unlikely that the Khazar practice of Judaism resembled that of the Karaite sect. The *Kievan Letter* bears resemblance to typical rabbinical documents of the medieval period. Furthermore, King Yosef indicated that the Khazars studied the Talmud and Mishnah. Thus, from what we know from available evidence, the Judaism of the Khazars consisted, in part, of the following elements:

1) Circumcision;
2) Observance of Hanukkah;
3) Observance of Passover;
4) Observance of the Sabbath;
5) Study of Torah, Talmud, and Mishnah;
6) Prayer according to the proper order established by the Khazzans;
7) Refraining from foods banned by the Torah;
8) Washing rituals and ritual ablutions;
9) Simple burials;
10) Refraining from idol-worship;
11) Adherence to all the other guidelines of halakhah in addition to those listed;
12) Giving newborn children Hebrew names;
13) Constructing synagogues;
14) Using the Hebrew character set for writing;
15) Using the Hebrew language (for both literary and religious purposes);
16) Building a tabernacle in the shape of that built by Moses;
17) An open invitation to Jews from the rest of the world to settle in the Khazar country.

The influence of immigrant Jews and Jewish ideas in the Khazar kingdom substantially affected the future course of Khazarian history. Khazar Judaism bolstered the population's overall level of literacy, modified the Khazarian people's daily way of life (including burial and prayer customs), damaged Byzantine-Khazar relations, and brought the kingdom into contact with other Jewish communities.

The introduction of large numbers of Jews into the Khazar kingdom appears to have brought about an increase in literacy.

The Khazars were already familiar with the runic letters of their Turkic ancestors, and some of them used the Orkhon alphabet from Mongolia. Many Turkic inscriptions from the Khazars and Bulgars have been discovered in eastern Europe. But by the tenth century, as noted above, Hebrew parchment documents also began to be produced.

Beyond the hard facts of what is known to have changed under Khazar Judaism (such as the appearance of Hebrew names and Hebrew letters among the Khazars), there are several assumptions that may be made with high certainty. One of these is that the Khazars would have ceased praying eastward, since Jews are accustomed to praying in the direction of Jerusalem. Secondly, it may also be assumed that cremation never again occurred among those Khazars who adopted Judaism. Thirdly, old practices of the Khazar army, such as the sacrificing of the horses of enemies (practiced by them in the 630s against a defeated Persian army's horses), must have been abandoned. On the other hand, the Khazar system of justice apparently did not adopt a clean slate of Judaic principles, because it seems that some legal decisions were still decided in contradiction of Jewish law.

Khazar Judaism also affected international politics. Whereas the Khazar princess Chichek had married into the Byzantine royal family in the early 730s, leading to the adoption of the Khazarian *tzitzakia* as a popular garment in Constantinople, and the Byzantines and Khazars had cooperated in the construction of Sarkel in the 830s, Byzantine-Khazar relations began to deteriorate noticeably after the Khazar conversion of the ninth century. This is demonstrably due in part to the Khazars' Judaism and the Byzantines' long-standing anti-Jewish attitudes. Echoing his predecessor Patriarch Photius' anti-Jewish sentiments, the Patriarch of Constantinople in the late 920s, Nicholas I Mystikos, called the Khazars "a deluded nation, so nearly ravished from the bosom of piety by the evil demon" in a letter to the archbishop of Cherson. The author of the *Schechter Letter* called the Byzantine emperor Romanus I, a persecutor of Jews, "the evil one" around the 940s. The Byzantine at-tempts in prior centuries to establish permanent Christian bishoprics in Atil and north of the Black Sea had failed to attract most of the Khazars' religious devotion over the passage of time. Thus, Nicholas spoke of the need for "their fellowship with Christ our God and their salvation" to "finally be re-established." However, Nicholas had learned that some people in Khazaria had requested presbyters, so the archbishop of Cherson was sent to assist them. The *Schechter Letter* recounted that the Byzantine emperor had incited the Alans against the Khazars during the reign of the Khazar king Aharon. Indeed, the Byzantine emperor Constantine Porphyrogenitus wrote, around roughly the same time, that the Alan king could make war against the Khazars with the possibilities of considerable success as well as an alliance with the Byzantines. In short, despite the Byzantines' unrelenting desire to convert the Khazars away from their Judaism, the Khazars on the whole remained followers of Judaism, much to the dismay of their Christian and Muslim neighbors, who had been questioning their decision ever since the 860s. This led to a loss of respect and increase in hostility by the Byzantine rulers for their Khazar neighbors. Meanwhile, religious bonds grew between the Byzantines and the Alans.

The final years of the Khazars: While Khazaria was engaged in a series of serious struggles with Arab armies until the very end of the eighth century, the ninth century ushered in a period of relative calm in the steppes, known as the "Pax Khazarica." During this time, the Khazars maintained the ability to hold back warlike tribes such as the Turkic Pechenegs. This is often regarded as a reason the East Slavs were able extensively to colonize during that period. An internal dissention arose within Khazaria, however, as recorded by Emperor Constantine Porphyrogenitus. Constantine wrote of various tribes from Khazaria (collectively known as Kabars and probably consisting of both Turks and Iranians as well as Muslims and Jews, but said by the emperor to be "of the Khazars' own race") who left their homeland after a rebellion in which the Khazar government prevailed. One result was that the Hungarians and the Kabars learned each others' languages. Constantine added that the Kabars were more efficient warriors than their new Hungarian friends.

With the passage of time, external threats to the Khazar kingdom gained strength. These included the Rus, the Pechenegs, and the Byzantines. Adding to the troubles was the fact that Khazaria was a diverse country with a multitude of peoples from varying religious and ethnic backgrounds. It is historically not unusual for Turkic confederations and empires to collapse suddenly, only to regroup under a different name. The Khazars unfortunately headed for the same fate. Due to a paucity of sources relating to the fall and destruction of the Khazar state, it is difficult to know for certain what triggered its end. The common argument that Khazaria was economically dependent on its neighbors and that this caused a lack of self-sufficiency that led to a collapse is no longer viable, due to archaeological discoveries showing a strong industrial base in the country. The argument that Khazaria disintegrated in part due to its extreme heterogeneity, however, is still worth consideration.

In the late tenth century Prince Svyatoslav led the Rus to conquer Sarkel. Khazaria's woes were compounded by ever more intense incursions of the Turkic Pechenegs and Oghuzes. By the end of the 960s, the Khazarian city of Atil had been conquered and Sarkel was being transformed into a Slav-ruled city called *Byelaya Vyezha* ("White Fortress"). It is not clear how many of the Khazars were forced to adopt Islam and Christianity after 965, but there are indications that a number of them were forced to abandon their Jewish beliefs. The diminished Khazar state lost control of the Don-Volga trade route. The Rus and the Volga Bulgars, rather than the Khazars, gained the upper hand in trading activity, which had previously been largely under Khazarian control. In sharp contrast to the relative calm in the steppes during the peak of Khazaria's power in the ninth century, after the Khazars lost their empire, the wild Turkic tribes of the north that had been neutralized began to wreak havoc on the Rus state. By the second decade of the eleventh century, the Khazars were so weak

that their last ruler, Georgius Tzul, was conquered by the Rus and the Byzantines, and the Khazar state apparently ceased to exist as an independent entity. The oft-repeated claim that the Khazar state lasted beyond the year 1016 remains to be demonstrated. The fact that the Crimea retained the name *Gazaria* for several more centuries is not an indication that ethnic Khazars still resided there in great numbers. The references to "Khazaria" within the travelogues of Benjamin of Tudela and Rabbi Petakhia likely refer to non-Jewish, non-Khazar inhabitants of the Crimean and Taman peninsulas.

There are only a few unambiguous references to the Khazars' existence after the eleventh century. The Russian Chronicle recorded that a Khazar named Ivanko Zakharyich Kozarina (the Slavicized version of Ivan ben Zekharia) served in the Rus military at the start of the twelfth century. Abraham ibn Daud of Spain wrote in 1161 that he had personally become acquainted with Khazarian Jewish scholars studying in Toledo during his lifetime. It is logical to assume that those Khazars who settled in Hungary and Kiev left many generations of descendants. Scholars have sought Khazar descendants among a very wide range of peoples, including Szekely Huns of Transylvania, the Cossacks of Russia, Muslim North Caucasian Turks, Hungarians, East European Jews, Crimean Tatars, Crimean and Lithuanian Karaites, Krimchak Jews of the Crimea, Mountain Jews of the Caucasus, Azerbaijani Turks, Kazakh Turks, and others, though these investigations have not yielded many definitive answers. In particular the argument that the European Karaites are Khazars is refuted by a variety of evidence, including the non-karaitic orientation of the Khazars, the significant Middle Eastern vocabulary in the Karaites' Turkic dialect, and the discovery that the twentieth-century Karaites invented "Khazar cakes," "Khazar poems," and other cultural elements in an artificial attempt to recreate a past that did not belong to them.

The influence of the Khazars among the Hungarians and Rus: The Khazars had a significant influence upon their neighbors, including the Hungarians and the Rus. For instance, when Arpad was initiated as

Hungary's new king in the ninth century—thereby starting a new dynasty that would last until the beginning of the fourteenth century—he was elevated on a shield according to Khazarian custom. The Hungarian language contains hundreds of Turkic words, many of which may have come from Khazar-Hungarian contacts. The dual-kingship system of the Khazars was copied by both the Hungarians and the Rus. The early Rus princes of Novgorod and Kiev adopted the Khazar title *kagan*. However, aside from the word *kagan*, it is not certain whether any of the other Old Rus words of Turkic origin were derived from the Khazarian language. Several modern scholars—including Omeljan Pritsak, Jonathan Shepard, Simon Franklin, and Robin Milner-Gulland—assert that the trident symbol that adorns the official coat of arms of Ukraine was borrowed by the Kievan Rus' princes from the Khazars.

The Russian Chronicle includes a possibly legendary conversation held in Kiev between Khazar missionaries and the pagan Rus prince that supposedly occurred during the year 986:

> The Khazar Jews came [to the court of Prince Vladimir] and said: "We have heard that Bulgars (Muslims) and Christians came to teach you their religion. . . . We, however, believe in the one God of Abraham, Isaac, and Jacob." Vladimir asked them: "What kind of law do you have?" They answered: "We are required to be circumcized, we may not eat pork or hare meat, and we must observe the Sabbath." And he asked: "Where is your land?" They answered: "In Jerusalem." And again he asked: "It is really there?" They answered: "God got angry with our fathers and therefore scattered us all over the world and gave our land to the Christians." Vladimir asked: "How is it that you can teach people Jewish law even while God rejected you and scattered you! If God had loved you and your law, you would not be scattered throughout foreign lands. Or do you wish us [Rus] to suffer the same fate?"

Next, Prince Vladimir sent a group of men to the Byzantine Empire to witness the religious ceremonies in Constantinople. They reported back to him that the Byzantine ceremonies were greater than the others they knew. Afterwards, Vladimir conquered the Greek city of Kherson on the Crimean peninsula and decided to adopt Christianity and establish an alliance between Kievan Rus and the Byzantine Empire. This decision to adopt Christianity may have been a political one, and it is known that Vladimir married the Byzantine princess Anna soon afterwards. When Prince Vladimir rejected Judaism and chose instead to be baptized into the Orthodox Christian religion, he charted the future course of Russia's history. It is because of Prince Vladimir that the religious practices of the Greeks became widespread among the Eastern Slavs.

The Khazars remained an important part of the oral epic folklore (*byliny*) of the eastern Slavs for several additional centuries. The *bylina* "Ilya Muromets and the Warrior Jew" told how a mighty giant named Zhidovin (named for the Khazars' Judaism) waged war against Russian heroes. The *bylina* "Mikhailo Kozarin" related the story of a Khazarian hero of Kiev named Mikhailo.

In conclusion, although the surrounding nations modeled their systems of government and some of their customs after the Khazars, and may have even taken some words from the Khazarian language, the Khazars' Judaism was not chosen as their state religion.

The Khazar influence on medieval Jewry: The vizier and physician Hasdai ibn Shaprut (c. 915-c. 990), who lived at the start of the Golden Age of Sephardic Jewry and played a major role in advancing Jewish causes throughout the world in his day, drew inspiration from confirmation of the Khazar kingdom's existence. Hasdai began his letter by praising the greatness of the recipient, the king of Khazaria. A description of the land of Andalusia followed, accompanied by the enigmatic statement, not corroborated elsewhere, that the Spanish Jews Rabbi Judah bar Meir bar Nathan and Rabbi Joseph ha-Garis had once visited Khazaria. While extolling the many virtues of Spain's natural resources and kings, his letter also expressed the sorrow of the Jews for having lost their ancient homeland. Hearing of a Jewish kingdom's existence far to the East caused Hasdai and other Spanish Jews to rejoice (translation: N. Daniel Korobkin):

> We live in the diaspora and there is no power in our hands. They say to us everyday,

"Every nation has a kingdom, but you have no memory of such in all the land." But when we heard about my master the [Khazar] King, the might of his monarchy, and his mighty army, we were amazed. We lifted our heads, our spirits returned, our hands were strengthened, and my master's kingdom was our response in defense. Were it that this news would gain added strength, for through it we will be elevated further.

A great humanitarian, Hasdai also wrote to Empress Helena of Byzantium, mentioning the "land of Khazaria" in his correspondence, to try to secure religious freedom for the Byzantine Jews.

Hasdai's writings and interventions subsequently led to the knowledge of the Khazars being spread among other Spanish Jews. Judah Halevi's masterful book *Kuzari*—today considered to be the second most important Jewish philosophical work after Maimonides' *Guide to the Perplexed*—drew upon the story of the Khazars. Echoes of the Hasdai-Yosef correspondence appear in *Kuzari*. In turn, rabbis in later years learned about the Khazars from Halevi and expanded upon *Kuzari*'s storyline in their commentaries. Several, such as Shem Tov ibn Shem Tov (*ob.* 1430) and Gedaliah (about 1587), wrote that the converter of the Khazar king was a rabbi named Isaac ha-Sangari, and they claimed that his writings were preserved through the centuries and that Halevi drew upon them when writing *Kuzari*. This, however, is highly unlikely, even though Halevi had written within *Kuzari*: "As I found among the arguments

of the rabbi many which appealed to me and were in harmony with my own opinions, I resolved to write them down exactly as they had been spoken" (translation: N. Daniel Korobkin). Even more fanciful was Simon Akiva Baer ben Yosef's Yiddish tale *Ma'aseh ha-Shem*, which told how Abraham ibn Ezra, a friend of Judah Halevi, supposedly married one of Judah's daughters in the land of the Khazars.

As noted above, persecuted Jewish communities fleeing from Greece, Armenia, Mesopotamia, and Persia found refuge in Khazaria, where they could practice their religion freely. Whether these Jews outnumbered the Jewish Khazars is an open question. In any event, Khazaria may be seen as simultaneously a Jewish and a Turkic kingdom, where elements of Jewishness merged with steppe culture.

A relationship between the Khazarian Jews and the later Jewish populations of eastern and central Europe is still undetermined.

Bibliography

Brook, Kevin A., *The Jews of Khazaria* (Northvale, 1999).
Golb, Norman, and Omeljan Pritsak, *Khazarian Hebrew Documents of the Tenth Century* (Ithaca, 1982).
Golden, Peter B., "Khazaria and Judaism," in *Archivum Eurasiae Medii Aevi* 3 (1983), pp. 127-156.
Mason, Richard A.E., "The Religious Beliefs of the Khazars," in *The Ukrainian Quarterly* 51:4 (Winter 1995), pp. 383-415.

KEVIN ALAN BROOK

M

MISHNAH, ANALOGICAL-CONTRASTIVE REASONING IN: The paramount mode of reasoning in the halakhic process, represented by the Mishnah, can be referred to as "analogical-contrastive." The logic may be expressed very simply. All persons, things, or actions that fall within a single species of a given genus in a uniform system of classification follow a single rule. All persons, things, or actions that fall within a different species

of that same given genus in a uniform system of classification follow precisely the opposite rule. Stated in gross terms, something is either like or unlike something else within a single genus that validates comparison and contrast. If it is like that other thing, it follows its rule. If it is not like that other thing, it follows the opposite of its rule. That reasoning by analogy and contrast dominates in the formation of the

Mishnah's rules, and it is, therefore, its generative mode of thought. We can, accordingly, work our way back from conclusions that the Mishnah's authorship presents through the stages of reasoning that have led to reaching those conclusions.

To explain how this logic works, we first present the principal mode of discourse of the Mishnah, which is to set forth rules by means of lists of like or unlike persons, actions, or things. A common rule applies to the like, and the opposite rule to the unlike. On the surface, the Mishnah's philosophy is an exercise in *Listenwissenschaft*, and, beneath the surface, the Mishnah's philosophy carries forward the logic of comparison and contrast, expressed through the results conveyed by lists and the rules governing their items. This analogical-contrastive logic then validates the making of lists. So let us turn to the Mishnah's *Listenwissenschaft* as the first in the two stages of the exposition of the philosophical modes of thought of the document.

The Mishnah's logic of cogent discourse establishes propositions that rest upon philosophical bases, e.g., through the proposal of a thesis and the composition of a list of facts that (e.g., through shared traits of a taxonomic order) prove the thesis. The Mishnah presents rules and treats stories (inclusive of history) as incidental and of merely taxonomic interest. Its logic is propositional, and its intellect does its work through a vast labor of classification, comparison and contrast generating governing rules and generalizations. A simple contrasting case shows us that the stakes are very high. For that purpose, let us turn to a document our authorship knew well, namely, the written Torah.

The Pentateuch appeals to a different logic of cogent discourse from the Mishnah's. It is the cogency imparted by teleology, that is, a logic that provides an account of how things were in order to explain how things are and set forth how they should be, with the tabernacle in the wilderness the model for (and modeled after) the Temple in the Jerusalem abuilding. The Mishnah speaks in a continuing present tense, saying only how things are, indifferent to the were and the will-be. The Pentateuch focuses upon

self-conscious "Israel," saying who they were and what they must become to overcome how they now are. The Mishnah understands by "Israel" as much the individual as the nation and identifies as its principal actors, the heroes of its narrative, not the family become a nation, but the priest and the householder, the woman and the slave, the adult and the child, and other castes and categories of person within an inward-looking, established, fully landed community. Given the Mishnah's authorship's interest in classifications and categories, therefore in systematic hierarchization of an orderly world, one can hardly find odd that (re)definition of the subject-matter and problematic of the systemic social entity.

We may briefly dwell on this matter of difference in the prevailing logic, because the contrast allows us to see how one document will appeal to one logic, another to a different logic. While the Pentateuch appeals to the logic of teleology to draw together and make sense of facts, so making connections by appeal to the end and drawing conclusions concerning the purpose of things, the Mishnah's authorship knows only the philosophical logic of syllogism, the rule-making logic of lists. The Pentateuchal logic reached concrete expression in narrative, which served to point to the direction and goal of matters, hence, in the nature of things, of history. Accordingly, those authors, when putting together diverse materials, so shaped everything as to form of it all as continuous a narrative as they could construct, and through that "history" that they made up, they delivered their message and also portrayed that message as cogent and compelling. If the Pentateuchal writers were theologians of history, the Mishnah's aimed at composing a natural philosophy for supernatural, holy Israel. Like good Aristotelians, they would uncover the components of the rules by comparison and contrast, showing the rule for one thing by finding out how it compared with like things and contrasted with the unlike. Then, in their view, the unknown would become known, conforming to the rule of the like thing, also to the opposite of the rule governing the unlike thing.

That purpose is accomplished, in particular, though list-making, which places on display the data of the like and the unlike and implicitly (ordinarily, not explicitly) then conveys the rule. It is this resort to list-making that accounts for the rhetorical stress on groups of examples of a common principle, three or five for instance. Once a series is established, the authorship assumes, the governing rule will be perceived. That explains why, in exposing the interior logic of its authorship's intellect, the Mishnah had to be a book of lists, with the implicit order, the nomothetic traits of a monothetic order, dictating the ordinarily unstated general and encompassing rule.

And all this why? It is in order to make a single statement, endless times over, and to repeat in a mass of tangled detail precisely the same fundamental judgment. The Mishnah in its way is as blatantly repetitious in its fundamental statement as is the Pentateuch. But the power of the Pentateuchal authorship, denied to that of the Mishnah, lies in its capacity always to be heard, to create sound by resonance of the surfaces of things. The Pentateuch is a fundamentally popular and accessible piece of writing. By contrast, the Mishnah's writers spoke into the depths, anticipating a more acute hearing than they ever would receive. So the repetitions of Scripture reinforce the message, while the endlessly repeated paradigm of the Mishnah sits too deep in the structure of the system to gain hearing from the ear that lacks acuity or to attain visibility to the untutored eye. So much for the logic. What of the systemic message? Given the subtlety of intellect of the Mishnah's authorship, we cannot find surprising that the message speaks not only in what is said, but in what is omitted.

The framers of the Mishnah appeal solely to the traits of things. The logical basis of coherent speech and discourse in the Mishnah then derives from Listenwissenschaft. That mode of thought defines way of proving propositions through classification, so establishing a set of shared traits that form a rule which compels us to reach a given conclusion. Probative facts derive from the classification of data, all of which point in one direction and not in another. A catalogue of facts, for example, may be so composed that, through the regularities

and indicative traits of the entries, the catalogue yields a proposition. A list of parallel items all together point to a simple conclusion; the conclusion may or may not be given at the end of the catalogue, but the catalogue—by definition—is pointed. All of the catalogued facts are taken to bear self-evident connections to one another, established by those pertinent shared traits implicit in the composition of the list, therefore also bearing meaning and pointing through the weight of evidence to an inescapable conclusion. The discrete facts then join together because of some trait common to them all. This is a mode of classification of facts to lead to an identification of what the facts have in common and—it goes without saying, an explanation of their meaning.

The diverse topical program of the Mishnah, time and again making the same points on the centrality of order, works itself out in a single logic of cogent discourse, one that seeks the rule that governs diverse cases. And that logic states within its interior structure the fundamental point of the document as a whole. The correspondence of logic to system here, as in the Pentateuch viewed overall, hardly presents surprises. Seeing how the logic does its work within the document therefore need not detain us for very long. Two pericopes of the Mishnah show us the logic that joins fact to fact, sentence to sentence, in a cogent proposition, that is, in our terms, a paragraph that makes a statement. To see how this intellect does its work we return to familiar materials, those in which we have already discerned formalization of speech. We come first to Mishnah Berakhot Chapter Eight, to see list-making in its simplest form, and then to Mishnah Sanhedrin Chapter Two, to see the more subtle way in which list-making yields a powerfully-argued philosophical theorem. In the first of our two abstracts we have a list, carefully formulated, in which the announcement at the outset tells us what is catalogued, and in which careful mnemonic devices so arrange matters that we may readily remember the conflicting opinions. So in formal terms, we have a list that means to facilitate memorization. But in substantive terms, the purpose of the list and its message(s) are not set forth, and only ample exegesis will succeed in spelling out what is at stake. Here is an instance of a Mishnah-passage which demands an exegesis not supplied by the Mishnah's authorship.

MISHNAH BERAKHOT CHAPTER EIGHT

8:1.A. These are the things which are between the House of Shammai and the House of Hillel in [regard to] the meal:

[1] B. The House of Shammai say, "One blesses over the day, and afterward one blesses over the wine."
And the House of Hillel say, "One blesses over the wine, and afterward one blesses over the day."

[2] 8.2.A. The House of Shammai say, "They wash the hands and afterward mix the cup."
And the House of Hillel say, "They mix the cup and afterward wash the hands."

[3] 8:3.A. The House of Shammai say, "He dries his hands on the cloth and lays it on the table."
And the House of Hillel say, "On the pillow."

[4] 8:4.A. The House of Shammai say, "They clean the house, and afterward they wash the hands." And the House of Hillel say, "They wash the hands, and afterward they clean the house."

[5] 8:5.A. The House of Shammai say, "Light, and food, and spices, and Havdalah."
And the House of Hillel say, "'Light, and spices, and food, and Havdalah.'"

[6] B. The House of Shammai say, "'Who created the light of the fire.'"
And the House of Hillel say, "'Who creates the lights of the fire.'"

The mnemonic serving the list works by the simple reversal of items. If authority A has the order 1, 2, then authority B will give 2, 1. Only entry [3] breaks that pattern. What is at stake in the making of the list is hardly transparent, and why day/wine vs. wine/day, with a parallel, e.g., clean/wash vs. wash/clean, yields a general principle the authorship does not indicate. All we know at this point, therefore, is that we deal with list-makers. But how lists work to communicate principles awaits exemplification.

Through its mode of making connections and drawing conclusions, the next abstract allows us much more explicitly to identify the propositional and essentially philosophical mind that animates the Mishnah. In the following passage, drawn from Mishnah Sanhedrin Chapter Two, the authorship wishes to say that Israel has two heads, one of state, the other of cult, the king and the high priest, respectively, and that these two offices are nearly wholly congruent with one another, with a few differences based on the particular traits of each. Broadly speaking, therefore, our exercise is one of setting forth the genus and the species. The genus is head of holy Israel. The species are king and high priest. Here are the traits in common and those not shared, and the exercise is fully exposed for what it is, an inquiry into the rules that govern, the points of regularity and order, in this minor matter, of political structure. My outline makes the point important in this setting:

1. THE RULES OF THE HIGH PRIEST: SUBJECT TO THE LAW, MARITAL RITES, CONDUCT IN BEREAVEMENT

Mishnah Sanhedrin 2:1-5

2:1 A. A high priest judges, and [others] judge him;

B. gives testimony, and [others] give testimony about him;

C. performs the rite of removing the shoe [Deut. 25:7-9], and [others] perform the rite of removing the shoe with his wife.

D. [Others] enter levirate marriage with his wife, but he does not enter into levirate marriage,

E. because he is prohibited to marry a widow.

F. [If] he suffers a death [in his family], he does not follow the bier.

G. "But when [the bearers of the bier] are not visible, he is visible; when they are visible, he is not.

H. "And he goes with them to the city gate," the words of R. Meir.

I. R. Judah says, "He never leaves the sanctuary,

J. "since it says, 'Nor shall he go out of the sanctuary' (Lev. 21:12)."

K. And when he gives comfort to others

L. the accepted practice is for all the people to pass one after another, and the appointed [prefect of the priests] stands between him and the people.

M. And when he receives consolation from others,

N. all the people say to him, "Let us be your atonement."

O. And he says to them, "May you be blessed by Heaven."

P. And when they provide him with the funeral meal,

Q. all the people sit on the ground, while he sits on a stool.

2. THE RULES OF THE KING: NOT SUBJECT TO THE LAW, MARITAL RITES, CONDUCT IN BEREAVEMENT

2:2 A. The king does not judge, and [others] do not judge him;

B. does not give testimony, and [others] do not give testimony about him;

C. does not perform the rite of removing the shoe, and others do not perform the rite of removing the shoe with his wife;

D. does not enter into levirate marriage, nor [do his brother] enter levirate marriage with his wife.

E. R. Judah says, "If he wanted to perform the rite of removing the shoe or to enter into levirate marriage, his memory is a blessing."

F. They said to him, "They pay no attention to him [if he expressed the wish to do so]."

G. [Others] do not marry his widow.

H. R. Judah says, "A king may marry the widow of a king.

I. "For so we find in the case of David, that he married the widow of Saul,

J. "For it is said, 'And I gave you your master's house and your master's wives into your embrace' (II Sam. 12:8)."

2:3 A. [If] [the king] suffers a death in his family, he does not leave the gate of his palace.

B. R. Judah says, "If he wants to go out after the bier, he goes out,

C. "for thus we find in the case of David, that he went out after the bier of Abner,

D. "since it is said, 'And King David followed the bier' (2 Sam. 3:31)."

E. They said to him, "This action was only to appease the people."

F. And when they provide him with the funeral meal, all the people sit on the ground, while he sits on a couch.

3. SPECIAL RULES PERTINENT TO THE KING BECAUSE OF HIS CALLING

2:4 A. [The king] calls out [the army to wage] a war fought by choice on the instructions of a court of seventy-one.

B. He [may exercise the right to] open a road for himself, and [others] may not stop him.

C. The royal road has no required measure.

D. All the people plunder and lay before him [what they have grabbed], and he takes the first portion.

E. "He should not multiply wives to himself" (Deut. 17:17)—only eighteen.

F. R Judah says, "He may have as many as he wants, so long as they do not entice him [to abandon the Lord (Deut. 7:4)]."

G. R. Simeon says, "Even if there is only one who entices him [to abandon the Lord]—lo, this one should not marry her."

H. If so, why is it said, "He should not multiply wives to himself"?

I. Even though they should be like Abigail [1 Sam. 25:3].

J. "He should not multiply horses to himself" (Deut. 17:16)—only enough for his chariot.

K. "Neither shall he greatly multiply to himself silver and gold" (Deut. 17:16)—only enough to pay his army.

L. "And he writes out a scroll of the Torah for himself" (Deut. 17:17)

M. When he goes to war, he takes it out with him; when he comes back, he brings it back with him; when he is in session in court, it is with him; when he is reclining, it is before him,

N. as it is said, "And it shall be with him, and he shall read in it all the days of his life" (Deut. 17:19).

2:5 A. [Others may] not ride on his horse, sit on his throne, handle his scepter.

B. And [others may] not watch him while he is getting a haircut, or while he is nude, or in the bathhouse,

C. since it is said, "You shall surely set him as king over you" (Deut. 17:15)—that reverence for him will be upon you.

The subordination of Scripture to the classification-scheme is self-evident. Scripture supplies facts. The traits of things—kings, high priests—dictate classification-categories on their own, without Scripture's dictate.

The philosophical cast of mind is amply revealed in this essay, which in concrete terms effects a taxonomy, a study of the genus, national leader, and its two species, [1] king, [2] high priest: how are they alike, how are they not alike, and what accounts for the differences. The premise is that national leaders are alike and follow the same rule, except where they differ and follow the opposite rule from one another. But that premise also is subject to the proof effected by the survey of the data consisting of concrete rules, those systemically inert facts that here come to life for the purposes of establishing a proposition. By itself, the fact that, e.g., others may not ride on his horse, bears the burden of no systemic proposition. In the context of an argument constructed for nomothetic, taxonomic purposes, the same fact is active and weighty. The whole depends upon three premises: (1) the importance of comparison and contrast, with the supposition that (2) like follows the like, and the unlike follows the opposite, rule; and (3) when we classify, we also hierarchize, which yields the argument from hierarchical classification: if this, which is the lesser, follows rule X, then that, which is the greater, surely should follow rule X. And that is the whole sum and substance of the logic of Listenwissenschaft as the Mishnah applies that logic in a practical way.

If I had to specify a single mode of thought that established connections between one fact and another, it is in the search for points in common and therefore also points of contrast. We seek connection between fact and fact, sentence and sentence, in the subtle and balanced rhetoric of the Mishnah, by comparing and contrasting two things that are like and not alike. At the logical level, too, the Mishnah falls into the category of familiar philosophical thought. Once we seek regularities, we propose rules. What is like another thing falls under its rule, and what is not like the other falls under the opposite rule. Accordingly, as to the species of the genus, so far as they are alike, they share the same rule. So far as they are not alike, each follows a rule contrary to that governing the other. So the work of analysis is what produces connection, and therefore the drawing of conclusions derives from comparison and contrast: the and, the equal. The proposition then that forms the conclusion concerns the essential likeness of the two offices, except where they are different, but the subterranean premise is that we can

explain both likeness and difference by appeal to a principle of fundamental order and unity. To make these observations concrete, we turn to the case at hand. The important contrast comes at the outset. The high priest and king fall into a single genus, but speciation, based on traits particular to the king, then distinguishes the one from the other. All of this exercise is conducted essentially independently of Scripture; the classifications derive from the system, are viewed as autonomous constructs; traits of things define classifications and dictate what is like and what is unlike.

Now that we have seen how the Mishnah's fundamental mode of setting forth propositions appealed to the logic and structure deriving from Listenwissenschaft, specifically, the logic of analogy and contrast, we undertake a more difficult exercise. It is to prove that analogical-contrastive logic not only accounts for the document's formal traits but also explains how the document's authorship reached the conclusions that it presents to us. For that purpose, I demonstrate that it is through appeal to analogical-contrastive logic that the Mishnah's authorship reached conclusions, deriving from Scripture, upon which it built an entire tractate. For that purpose I turn to the conception of maddaf-uncleanness, which is paramount in Mishnah Zabim. I shall show that that generative conception emerged in a process of analogy and contrast, through four successive steps, from a proposition set forth in Scripture. Accordingly, what we shall see in acute detail is precisely how the Mishnah's analogical-contrastive reasoning actually worked.

The exercise in analogical-contrast exegesis turns to the concept of maddaf-uncleanness, which is stated at M. Zab. 5:2 as follows:

> Whatever is carried above the Zab is unclean. And whatever the Zab is carried upon is clean, except for something which is suitable for sitting and lying, and except for man.

This rule is illustrated with cases in which the finger of a Zab is underneath stones and a clean person is above them. The clean person is made unclean so that he imparts uncleanness at two removes and unfitness at one still further remove. If food and drink, a bed or a chair, and a maddaf-article not used for sitting and lying—are located above the stones with the Zab below, they impart uncleanness at one remove and unfitness at one remove. If the bed and chair are below, and the Zab above, they impart uncleanness at two removes and unfitness at one. If food, drink, and maddaf-objects are below and the Zab is above, they remain clean. Now this rule is treated as beyond dispute, and its details are taken for ranted. The Tosefta's version (T. Zab. 5:1A) concurs that food, drink, and maddaf-objects above a Zab are subject to a more stringent rule than food, drink, and maddaf-objects underneath a Zab, while a bed or chair underneath a Zab are subject to a more strict rule than a bed or chair located above a Zab.

In asking about the origins of this rather complex notion, we find no assistance whatever either in attribution, for all parties agree on the matter, or in attestations, for there is nor reference to the matter in the whole of the Mishnaic Division of Purities in which the principle of maddaf is at issue. The important point, then, is the distinction between what is carried above the Zab and what is carried below. If something not used for lying or sitting, inclusive of food and drink, is located above a Zab, it is clean. Only a bed or chair located below a Zab will be unclean, only because of bearing his weight even without directly touching him.

When we find a conception clearly present in the foundations or originating at the earliest strata of Mishnaic thought, we have to ask whether or not said conception may originate in Scripture. In the present case, by a very brief series of logical steps, the conception of maddaf-uncleanness, with its distinction between a chair or a bed below, and objects not used for sitting or lying below a Zab, and a chair or a bed above, and objects not used for sitting or lying above, a Zab, indeed emerges from Scripture itself. The process by which this rather complex conception emerges, moreover, is not through formal exegesis but through the hypothetical-logical reconstruction of the analogical-contrastive mode of exegesis.

Let us now proceed to the relevant Scrip-

tural passage and its layers of meaning. At the outset, I cite the verse and restate what it says in simple language. The secondary meaning of each verse is attained by generalizing upon the plain and unadorned statement in the Scriptural verse itself. There is then the tertiary meaning, the point at which I introduce conceptions drawn from our tractate. I believe that, in the main, principles at a second level of exegesis from Scripture, that is, tertiary meanings, represent little more than a further generalization of what Scripture says, on the one hand, and the (now surely eisegetical) introduction of a few simple and obvious distinctions necessitated or invited by that generalization, on the other. In some instances there is yet a fourth level of meaning, and this invariably is drawn by me from Mishnah-Tosefta.

The exercise is meant to demonstrate that each and every proposition of Mishnah-Tosefta derives either directly or indirectly, through processes of close reasoning, generalization, and secondary logical exegesis, from Scripture itself. At each point at which our abstract exercise produces a principle found in the Mishnah, the appropriate pericope is designated. The relationship of the Mishnah's unattributed pericopae to Scripture is then spelled out in detail in the following section. The net result is hypothetically to demonstrate in close detail that this aspect of the law of Zabim is little more than a logical expansion of Scripture, and that each such ex-pansion stands in close logical expansion of Scripture, and that each such expansion stands in close logical relationship to the foregoing, so that the result, at the end, is a very tight sequence of logical-exegetical steps. (All Mishnah references are to Mishnah Zabim.)

Scriptural Verse

> Lev. 15:4: Every bed on which he who has the discharge lies shall be unclean. And everything on which he sits shall be unclean.

Clear Implication (Plain meaning)

> The Zab imparts uncleanness by lying on a bed or by sitting on a chair.

Secondary Meaning

> 1. The Zab imparts uncleanness to objects which can be used for lying or sitting.

2. The Zab imparts uncleanness to objects used for lying or sitting by exerting the pressure of his weight on said objects.

Tertiary Meaning

A. The uncleanness of the Zab is transmitted by pressure.
B. Pressure is exerted through lying and sitting.
C. Other modes of exerting pressure, standing, leaning, being suspended, by analogy to lying and sitting, likewise transfer the uncleanness of the Zab to another object.
D. Pressure exerted by a lean person upon an object made unclean by a Zab will in like manner transfer the uncleanness from the object or the Zab to the clean person.

Mishnah
C:: expressed in Mishnah Zabim 2:4 (3:1-3, 4:1-7).
D:: expressed in Mishnah Zabim 3:1-3, 4:1, 5, 5:1-5.

Lev. 15:5: And any one who touches his bed shall wash his clothes and bathe himself in water and be unclean until the evening.

Touching the Zab makes a person unclean. His clothes are unclean.

Secondary Meaning

3. The Zab's uncleanness is transferred by contact,
    a. either a clean person's touching the Zab
    b. or the Zab's touching a clean person.
4. One who is made unclean by the Zab imparts uncleanness to his clothing.

Tertiary Meaning

E. One made unclean by the Zab makes utensils unclean.
F. Said utensils are cleaned by immersion.
G. Since Scripture specifies that touching the bed or the Zab (Lev. 15:7) effects the transfer of uncleanness, and since Scripture specifies that sitting or lying also effects the transfer of uncleanness, and therefore touching without exerting pressure of exerting pressure without touching imparts uncleanness.

Mishnah

E:: expressed in Mishnah Zabim 2:4
G:: expressed in Mishnah Zabim 5:1-9

Lev. 15:6: And whoever sits on anything on which he who has the discharge has sat shall wash his clothes and bathe himself in water and be unclean until the evening.

Sitting on the bed or chair made unclean by the Zab makes a person unclean. His clothes are unclean.

Secondary Meaning

5. The object used for sitting or lying to which the Zab has imparted uncleanness is unclean in exactly the same measure as the Zab himself.

Tertiary Meaning

H. Since said object is unclean exactly as the Zab, is unclean, it therefore transfers uncleanness as does the Zab, that is, if one exerts pressure on it (the plain meaning) or if one touches it, or if it touches the clean person or exerts pressure on the clean person.
I. One made unclean by the unclean bed of the Zab makes utensils unclean. Said utensils are cleaned by immersion.

Mishnah
5: M. 2:4C-D.
H: M. 2:4C-D (3:1-3, 4:1-7).
I: M. 2:4C-D.

Lev. 15:7: And whoever touches the body of him who has the discharge shall wash his clothes and bathe himself in water and be unclean until the evening.

Touching the person of the Zab imparts uncleanness. The clothes are unclean.

Secondary Meaning

6. There is no difference between touching the bed of the Zab (Lev. 15:5) and touching the person of the Zab (Lev. 15:7). The consequences are the same in all regards.

Mishnah

6. : expressed in M. Zab. 5:1

Lev. 15:8: And if he who has the discharge spits on one who is clean, then he shall wash his clothes and bathe himself in water and be unclean until the evening.

The spit of the Zab is unclean exactly as is the Zab or his bed. The clothing of the person spat upon by the Zab is made unclean.

Secondary Meaning

7. Fluids that exude from the Zab are unclean exactly as is his body or the bed he sits upon, etc.

Tertiary Meaning

> J. The ways in which the Zab and the bed made unclean by the Zab transfer uncleanness apply also tot he body fluids, so far as these modes of transfer are relevant: 1. touching, 2. carrying (below, Lev. 15:10b).

Mishnah

> 7:: expressed in Mishnah Zabim 5:6, 5:7

Lev. 15:9: And any saddle on which he who has the discharge rides shall be unclean. The saddle ridden upon by the Zab is unclean.

Secondary Meaning

> 8. Since the saddle is dealt with apart from the bed and chair, it is subject to a distinctive set of rules.

Mishnah

> 8:: expressed in Mishnah Zabim 5:8

Lev. 15:10a: And whoever touches anything that was under him shall be unclean until the evening.

An object located underneath a Zab is unclean.

Secondary Meaning

> 9. I take it that the simple meaning is derived by treating Lev. 15:10a as a continuation of Lev. 15:9, which is to say, "A saddle on which a Zab has ridden is unclean, and whoever touches anything on which a Zab rides (or: has ridden) is unclean."
> (But if we read the verse disjunctively, then it bears a different meaning. Mere location of an object beneath a Zab—even if he is not touching it, and even if he is not riding on it—imparts uncleanness to the object. Accordingly, we take account of the spatial relationships of objects to a Zab.)
> 10. And this yields the clearly required notion (L) that an object used for sitting, lying, or riding which is located beneath a Zab is unclean, even though the Zab has not sat, lain, or ridden on said object.

Tertiary Meaning

> K. Touching or carrying the saddle produces uncleanness, as specified.
> L. Touching an object located underneath a Zab, even though said object

is not touched by the Zab and even though said object is not directly sat, lain, or ridden upon by the Zab but merely bears the weight of his body, imparts uncleanness so that the formerly clean person is made unclean and furthermore makes his clothing unclean, and, by extension, imparts uncleanness to utensils in general.

Fourth Level of Meaning

> i. An object used for sitting and lying which is located underneath the Zab is subject to the uncleanness imparted by the Zab to objects upon which he has sat or lain, etc. It follows that the same sort of object located above the Zab is not subject to the uncleanness imparted by the Zab to objects used for sitting and lying.
> ii. An object not used for sitting and lying located beneath the Zab (but not touched by him or subjected to the pressure of his body-weight) is not unclean.
> iii. And, it follows in the rule of opposites, an object not used for sitting and lying which is located above the Zab will be unclean in some way or degree, not specified.

Mishnah

> 9-10:: expressed in Mishnah Zabim 5:1-3.
> K:: expressed in Mishnah Zabim 5:8.
> L:: expressed in Mishnah Zabim 5:1-3.
> i:: expressed in Mishnah Zabim 5:1-2.
> ii:: expressed in Mishnah Zabim 5:1.
> iii:: expressed in Mishnah Zabim 5:1-2.

Lev. 15:10b: And whoever carries such a thing shall wash his clothes and bathe himself in water and be unclean until the evening.

Carrying an object used for riding, sitting, or lying, and made unclean by the Zab makes the clean person who carries said object unclean. He makes his clothing unclean.

Secondary Meaning

> 11. The uncleanness of the Zab is conveyed through carriage. Specifically, if one carries an object, such as a bed or chair, made unclean by the Zab, one is made unclean as if he touched the Zab or as if he was subjected to the weight or pressure of the Zab or of an object made unclean by the Zab. This seems to me to follow naturally from the concept of pressure, since it is not possible to carry something without bearing its weight.

Tertiary Meaning

M. A person or an object which a Zab carries is made unclean. That is, just as there is no difference between touching the Zab or being touched by him, placing pressure upon the Zab or having the Zab's pressure applied to a clean person, so there is no difference between carrying the Zab and being carried by him.

N. The person made unclean in this way imparts uncleanness to his clothing, therefore to utensils.

Fourth Level of Meaning

iv. The person made unclean in these several ways makes his clothing unclean. Clearly, that is the case when the uncleanness of the Zab is transmitted to the person. It will follow, therefore, that when the Zab touches or exerts pressure on a clean person, the person is made unclean, and the clothing on the person is made unclean. Accordingly, it is when the clean person is subject to the uncleanness of the Zab, etc., that his clothing is made unclean: "he renders utensils unclean." When the person is no longer subject to the uncleanness of the Zab, he (of course) remains unclean. But he no longer will make his clothing unclean.

Mishnah

As above, Lev. 15:10a.
iv: M. 5:1, Joshua.

Lev. 15:11: Any one whom he that has the discharge touches without having rinsed his hands shall wash his clothes and bathe himself in water and be unclean until the evening.

The unclean person imparts uncleanness through touching. The person made unclean thereby transmits uncleanness to clothing.

Secondary Meaning

I see nothing in this verse that is both relevant to Zabim and new.

Lev. 15:12: And the earthen vessel which he who has the discharge touches shall be broken. And every vessel of wood shall be rinsed in water.

Earthen, or clay, utensils cannot be cleaned by rinsing, but only by breaking. Wooden utensils can be cleaned by immersion.

Secondary Meaning

12. Wooden vessels are subject to a different rule from earthen ones. That rule, moreover, will be the same as affects any other utensil which is cleaned through immersion.

Now to the Mishnah proper the entries that follow relate to, and I think are generated by, the primary allegation of Scripture or its logical developments, as specified.

1. M. 2:4: The Zab imparts uncleanness to the bed in five ways so that the bed imparts uncleanness to man and garments: standing, and sitting, lying, suspended, and leaning. The bed imparts uncleanness to man in seven ways so that he makes clothing unclean: standing, sitting, lying, suspended, leaning, contact, and carrying.

(Compare M. Kel. 1:3.)

1. The rule is specific, that the Zab imparts uncleanness to the bed in the specified five ways. The second component is distinct. How does the bed transmit uncleanness to the clean man? Omitted from consideration: How does the Zab impart uncleanness to the clean man? In point of fact, the Zab transmits uncleanness through touching and through being carried (= exerting pressure).

Sifra Mesora Zabim 3:1-3: Pressure exerted by Zab, even if he sits on top of a heavy stone, imparts uncleanness.

Sifra Mesora Zabim 2:7: If Zab lay down on chair, sat on bed, stands or is suspended, they are unclean = M. 2:4.

2. Sifra Mesora Zabim 11:1-2: Man who touches bed imparts uncleanness to clothing, but bed which touches bed does not impart uncleanness to clothing. Bed imparts uncleanness when under the Zab to impart uncleanness to man and clothing, but man under the Zab does not impart uncleanness to man and clothing.

2. The Zab imparts uncleanness when he touches a bed. The bed touching a bed does not impart uncleanness to clothing. The bed under the Zab imparts uncleanness as a bed, man does not.

Perhaps the several contrasts are based solely upon those established in Scripture, specifically, objects used for lying and sitting located underneath the Zab impart uncleanness to clothing, Lev. 15:10a. Man is not used for sitting and lying, therefore when located under the Zab, he does not. Along these same lines, Scriptures is clear, Lev. 15:5, that man who touches the bed washes his clothes—therefore imparts uncleanness to clothing (= utensils). Scripture is silent on the affect upon clothing of a bed which touches a bed made unclean by a Zab. It will have followed that what is stated explicitly at Lev. 15:5 then deliberately means to exclude what is omitted, which is the status of the bed which touches the bed. This is, of course, rather acute, since Scripture speaks of common occurrences, and it is difficult for a bed to reach out and touch another bed; Scripture's use of touching naturally is in the context of animate creatures.

3. M. 5:2: Whatever is carried above the Zab is unclean. Whatever the Zab is carried upon, but which is not touched by him, is clean, except for something used for sitting and lying (Lev. 15:10a) and except for man who carries the Zab (Lev. 15:10b).

+ T. 5:1.

Sifra Mesora Zabim III:3-7. Food, drink, utensils not used for sitting and lying which are above the Zab are made unclean on that account, proved by Simeon.

3. The important point here is the distinction between what is carried above the Zab and what is carried below him, without touching him. In the former case, there is uncleanness, and this applies, specifically, to food, drink and objects not used for lying and sitting (maddaf). If these are carried below the Zab, they are clean. Only man and bed and chair below the Zab are made unclean because of their serving to carry his weight even without directly touching him.

The illustration, M. 5: 2L-M, further indicates that what is unclean above the Zab—food, drink, maddaf (an object not used for lying and sitting)—is unclean in the first remove.

The principle is dual: (1) What is carried underneath the Zab is unclean, except for lying and sitting. (2) What is carried above the Zab is unclean. The relationship to Scripture is not self-evident. On the one side, we may readily account for the first principle. That an object used for lying and

sitting which was under the Zab is unclean is specified at Lev. 15:10a. But the rule excludes objects not used for lying and sitting. Perhaps the distinction begins at Lev. 15:9. The saddle on which the Zab rides is unclean. Lev. 15:10a, continuing this point, then specifies that whoever touches anything that was under him—thus, that has served him for sitting—is unclean. And, by exclusion therefrom, whoever touches something which has been located under the Zab but which the Zab has not used for sitting is not unclean. Accordingly, the object itself, if not used for sitting, does not become unclean if the Zab is located above it.

But whence the notion of maddaf? That is, how do we know that an object not used for lying and sitting and located above the Zab is unclean? At first glance, it appears that we come to the fourth level of meaning imputed to Lev. 15:10a (i, iii). (1) What is unclean beneath the Zab is not unclean above him. (2) Then: What is not unclean beneath the Zab is unclean above him. Objects not used for sitting and lying food and drink (2) are unclean above, because they (1) are clean below, the Zab. Thus: Objects used for sitting and lying are clean above, because they are unclean below, the Zab.

But the problem of maddaf is not so readily settled. We have to ascertain the meaning associated with the word in the earliest assigned pericopae. With the help of Kasovsky,[1] let us rapidly review the several meanings assigned to the word maddaf. The word is familiar as the name of an object— the bird trap at M. Kel. 23:5; the smoker of the bees (M. Kel. 16:7), required by context in both cases. This tractate, by contrast, knows that word to mean "an object, not used for lying or sitting, located above the Zab," and we need not review the passages in which the word appears in that meaning (M. Zab. 4:6, 5:2). The third meaning is "a status as to uncleanness," a definition to be made more precise when we return to M. Par. 10:1-2, and M. Toh. 8:2. The former requires the meaning, "A status as to uncleanness related to midras but of lower degree of uncleanness than midras." Thus M. Par. 10:1, assigned to Yavneans, on what can be made unclean with corpse-uncleanness and whether that sort of object likewise is unclean with maddaf-uncleanness)

Accordingly, in the context of M. Par. 10:1-2, maddaf can only mean, "a status of uncleanness," which, we know, is uncleanness in the first remove, effecting uncleanness for food and liquid. This same meaning is absolutely required at M. Toh. 8:2: If someone deposits with an ʿam haʾares a box full of clothing, Yose says, "When it is tightly packed, it is unclean with midras-uncleanness, and it is is not tightly packed, it is unclean with maddaf-uncleanness." Accordingly, once more, midras-uncleanness is set into contrast with maddaf-uncleanness. In this instance the point is that the ʿam haʾares is unclean as a Zab. If a Zab shifts an object not used for sitting or lying, we know, the object suffers maddaf-uncleanness and renders food and drink unclean. M. Ed. 6:2 further has a dispute of Joshua and Nehunya b. Elinathan with Eliezer, in which it is taken for granted, tangentially and within the structure of argument: "The un-cleanness of living beings is greater than the uncleanness of corpses, for a living being imparts uncleanness, by lying and sitting, to what is underneath him, so that it conveys uncleanness to man and utensils, and also conveys maddaf-uncleanness to what is above him, so that is conveys uncleanness to food and liquid, a mode of transferring uncleanness which a corpse does not convey." The same authorities—Joshua and Eliezer—are at M. Par. 10:1-2, and moreover, Yose continues the matter, at M. Toh. 8:2, taking the rule for granted, just as do Joshua and Eliezer. We need not review in detail Tosefta's usages of the same word, since all occur in the context of the correlative Mishnaic pericopae (T. Par. 10:2, 3, T. Toh. 9:4, T. Zab. 3:3, 5:1).

The two senses in which the word is used of course are complementary. M. Par. and M. Toh. know maddaf as a status as to uncleanness contrasted to midras, and M. Zab. uses the word to refer to objects which can enter that very same status as to uncleanness. Our translation in the present tractate has been required by its context. But the meaning in point of fact is complementary to that necessitated by the context of M. Par. and M. Toh.: What can become unclean with maddaf-uncleanness—

an object not used for lying and sitting and hence not susceptible to midras-uncleanness (a point familiar throughout our order e.g., Kelim Chapter Twenty-Four)—here is called maddaf. And M. Par. and M. Toh. know maddaf as that uncleanness imparted to something from something (used for lying and sitting) susceptible to midras. Our tractate, moreover, hastens to add: The status of maddaf-uncleanness is attained when an object not used for lying or sitting (also food or drink, explicitly included as well) is located above a Zab. Maddaf as the opposite of midras, of course, is contained in the pericopae of M. Toh. in particular, but also, with slight eisegesis, at M. Par.

The contrast between midras and maddaf, strikingly, is precisely the same the contrast as I have hypothetically imputed to the exegetes of Lev. 15:10A at i, iii. Indeed, midras and maddaf express exactly the same idea as is spelled out in the circumlocutions above. Our invocation, at that point, of the rule of opposites therefore is justified by the result of the present analysis of the consistent contrast, drawn in M., between midras and maddaf. The concept of maddaf, in its two, complementary senses, most certainly is attested by Joshua and Eliezer at M. Ed. and M. Par. Because of the givenness of the idea of M. Par., at both pericopae assigned to Eliezer and Joshua, I am inclined to suppose that the concept of maddaf-uncleanness and of objects susceptible no to midras, because they are not used for lying and sitting, but, under the specified circumstance, to maddaf-uncleanness, hence maddaf-objects, originates before 70.

4. M. 5:6: He who touches the Zab, Zabah, menstruating woman, woman after childbirth, mesora, or a bed or chair on which any of these have lain or sat. Touching and shifting, carrying and being carried, are equivalent.

+ T. 5:3: utensils are in the first remove.

4. The pericope so far as it deals with modes of transfer makes two points.

First, while one is touching these sources, he is able to impart uncleanness at two removes, unfitness at one. That is to say, just as at M. 5:1, he is like a Father of uncleanness, so far as food for heave-offering is concerned.

Second, touching is deemed equivalent

to shifting, carrying, and being carried.

That the uncleanness of the Zab is transferred to one who touches the Zab (etc.) is stated explicitly at Lev. 15:5. That one who carries such a thing is made unclean is stated at Lev. 15:10b.

The sole new point has to do with the inclusion of shifting as a mode of transfer of uncleanness. This is probably generated by the analogy to bearing the weight of the Zab, that is, carrying. the inclusion of shifting as a mode of transfer of uncleanness derives simply from the extension of Scripture's stated modes. One can hardly carry without shifting the object. The sole open question is whether we include even derivatives of the pressure of the Zab or of pressure upon the Zab, that is, vibration, movement which takes place indirectly and not directly. We do not, as the Ushans state.

5. M. 5:7: He who touches the flux of the Zab, his spit, his semen, his urine, and the blood of the menstruating woman (imparts uncleanness at two remove, etc.) All the same is touching and moving. Eliezer: Also carrying.

> 5.1. The specified excretions are unclean just as the Zab is unclean.
> 2. They transfer uncleanness just as the Zab transfers uncleanness, that is, through contact.
> 3. Shifting is equivalent to contact.

Touching the spit of the Zab effects the transfer of the Zab's uncleanness, so Lev. 15:8. The secondary point is the inclusion of other substances. The issue of carrying as equivalent to contact of course is not of equivalent antiquity.

6. T. 5:2B: Phlegm, mucous, saliva, and snot of Zab are like his spit. Tear, blood of wound, milk of woman, blood of mouth and penis are unclean only in the first remove. Flux, spit, urine are unclean as Fathers. Semen of Zab: Eliezer—does not impart uncleanness when carried; and sages—imparts uncleanness when carried, because urine is contained therein.

Sifra Mesora-Zabim 1:7-8: Zab imparts uncleanness through white flux, not through red flow (blood from penis).

Sifra Mesora-Zabim 1:9-13: Flux itself is unclean. Blood which exudes form the penis is not unclean as flux. His urine is unclean.

Sweat, rancid moisture, excrement are not unclean. Nine liquids apply to Zab: secretion, putrid sweat, excrement are clean in all respect; tear, blood, milk impart susceptibility to uncleanness as liquids; flux, spit, urine are unclean as flux.

Sifra Mesora-Zabim 3:8: Phlegm, slaver, and snot are equivalent to spit. Sifra Mesora-Zabim 1:3: Flux derives solely from the genitals, not from the nose or mouth.

There are two issues in the present set, first of all, the notion that the transfer of the Zab's uncleanness takes place not solely through touching the Zab, but also through touching other substances which exude from him. Second, other modes of transfer besides direct contact are of the same effect as direct contact. The matter of touching the Zab's spit is explicit at Lev. 15:8. Accordingly, not only the flux, but also spit is unclean. Then spit supplies an analogy for other such substances which are like it. Flux is like semen; urine derives from the same location. Phlegm, mucus, saliva, snot, all are treated as analogous to spit. The second issues is the analogy between touching and moving, on which all parties agree. Eliezer wishes to treat carrying as equivalent mode of transfer of uncleanness. His basis, surely, will be the diverse rulings which treat touching, shifting, and carrying as equivalent. At T. 5:2B, an Eliezer wishes to exclude semen of the Zab. If this is the same Eliezer, then M. 5:7 should contain the equivalent qualification, that is, adding carrying as a mode of transfer of uncleanness, and detaching semen from the opening list. We do not know which Eliezer is before us, one of the Yavneans or one of the Ushans. That is why we cannot adduce the present set as evidence that discussion of the interrelationships of the diverse modes of transfer uncleanness was carried forward at Yavneh, with the secondary notion that the issues were still live at that time. This is suggested by the pointed claim, intruded at M. 5:6, 7, etc., that the diverse modes do produce equivalent effects, or are the same as one another, which suggests that in the background are efforts seriously to distinguish among them. But the main point in Mishnah is that there are diverse modes, and that point derives from the obvious sense of

Scripture, which specifies touching or contact, carrying, lying or sitting, generalized into exerting pressure.

7. M. 5:8: He who carries saddle, is carried on it, and moves it, etc.

7. Carrying, being carried on, and moving, the saddle imparts uncleanness as if one were made a Father of uncleanness.

Carrying carrion, purification water sufficient for sprinkling.

+ T. 5:5A.

Here, too, the man is as if he were a Father of uncleanness.

M. 5:9: He who eats carrion of clean bird, while it is in his gullet, etc.

+ T. 5:10-12

This item is not relevant to Zabim.

Sifra Mesora-Zabim 4:2-3: Bed and chair impart uncleanness when they are carried.

Sifra Mesora-Zabim 4:1: Whoever touches saddle is unclean, but whoever touches what is under the saddle is not unclean on that account.

Carrying the saddle or being carried on it make a person unclean, so Lev. 15:10 states explicitly. That the bed and chair which are carried impart uncleanness is also at Lev. 15:10b. Touching the saddle produces uncleanness, so Lev. 15:10a. Lev. 15:10b then specifies that whoever carries something which has been underneath a Zab is unclean, which then is exclusive of merely touching the saddle. Nothing in this set brings us significantly outside the boundaries of Scriptural meaning, so far as I can see. (We omit reference to the matter of carrion, which is not within the thematic limits of our tractate.)

8. M. 5:10: He who touches a dead creeping thing, semen, one made unclean by corpse-uncleanness, mesora during period of counting clean days, purification water insufficient for sprinkling, carrion, and saddle . . . This is the general rule: Whatever touches any of all the Fathers of uncleanness listed in the Torah imparts uncleanness at one remove and renders unfit at one. Man in contact with a Father of uncleanness, imparts uncleanness at two removes, unfitness at one. Or: except for man, who, as a corpse, makes that which touches it into a Father of uncleanness and so that which is in contact with a corpse imparts uncleanness at two removes and unfitness at one more.

8. In all these cases, the one who touches the source of uncleanness is unclean only in the first remove, not functioning as if he were a Father of uncleanness.

Any object, other then man, in contact with a Father of uncleanness, is in the first remove of uncleanness.

M. 5:11: He who has a seminal emission is like one who has touched a dead creeping thing. He who has sexual relations with a menstruating woman is like one who is unclean by reason of corpse-uncleanness to bed and chair so that they render food and drink unclean, which the former does not accomplish.

M. 5:12: Ten items which are in the second remove of uncleanness and therefore render heave-offering unfit. Sifra Mesora-Zabim 2:8-13: Seminal emission does not cause uncleanness. Person unclean through mega, corpse, does not impart uncleanness to bed and chair.

The last units, M. 5:10-12, complete the construction of M. 5:6-9 by specifying sources of uncleanness, touching which leaves a person unclean only in the first remove, then in the second. The set contains no attestations, but in fact goes over the specifications of Scripture. What is pointed is the distinction between "whatever touches any of the Fathers of uncleanness" and "man who touches a Father of uncleanness," which is to say, the important point of M. 5:1, 6-9, upon which Joshua's further observation, about the difference between one's state while touching such a Father and after one has ceased to touch the Father, is based. It is, of course, the specification at Lev. 15:5, for the Zab, Lev. 15:21, for the menstruating woman, Lev. 15:27, for the Zab, and the comparison of the woman after childbirth to the menstruating woman, Lev. 12:2, 5, that the person who touches things on which the aforenamed have lain or sat washes his clothes, which leads to the stated conclusion.

Let us now, as I promised, relate the foregoing to M. Zab. 5:2.

M. Zab. 5:2: Whatever is carried above the Zab is unclean. Whatever the Zab is carried upon, but which is not touched by him, is clean, except for something used for sitting and lying (Lev. 15:10a) and except for man who carries the Zab (Lev. 15:10b).

The important point here is the distinction between what is carried above the Zab and what is carried below him, without touching him. In the former case, there is uncleanness, and this applies, specifically, to food, drink and objects not used for lying and sitting (maddaf). If these are carried below the Zab, they are clean. Only man and bed and chair below the Zab are made unclean because of their serving to carry his weight even without directly touching him. The illustration, M. Zab. 5:2L-M, further indicates that what is unclean above the Zab—food, drink, maddaf (an object not used for lying and sitting)—is unclean in the first remove.

Now to repeat, this is how analogical-contrastive reasoning works:

The principle is dual:

1) What is carried underneath the Zab is clean, except for an object used for lying and sitting.

2) What is carried above the Zab is unclean. The relationship to Scripture is not self-evident. On the one side, we may readily account for the first principle. That an object used for lying and sitting which was under the Zab is unclean is specified at Lev. 15:10a. But the rule excludes objects not used for lying and sitting. To review what has been suggested: The distinction begins at Lev. 15:9.

The saddle on which the Zab rides is unclean.

Lev. 15:10a, continuing this point, then specifies that whoever touches anything that was under him—thus, that has served him for sitting—is unclean.

And, by exclusion therefrom, whoever touches something which has been located under the Zab but which the Zab has not used for sitting is not unclean.

Accordingly, the object itself, if not used for sitting, does not become unclean if the Zab is located above it.

But, whence the notion of maddaf? That is, how do we know that an object not used for lying and sitting and located above the Zab is unclean?

We come to the fourth level of meaning imputed to Lev. 15:10a.

1) What is unclean beneath the Zab is not unclean above him.

2) Then: What is not unclean beneath the Zab is unclean above him. Objects not used for sitting and lying, food and drink (2) are unclean above, because they (1) are clean below, the Zab.

Thus: Objects used for sitting and lying are clean above, because they are unclean below, the Zab.

This exercise can readily be repeated for the principles and generative rules of three tractates, Negaim, Niddah, and the remainder of Zabim, all of which to begin with draw out and spell out Scripture's rules and principle for the mesora', the menstruating woman, Zabah, woman after childbirth, and finally, for the Zab, respectively. All deal with sources of uncleanness. Here the Oral Torah is contented to restate and develop through logical exegesis (not merely through formal exegesis, such as at Sifra, which is post facto) what is said in the Priestly Code. The reason is that at the outset the people among whom the Oral Torah, that is, the Mishnah, originates have no intention whatsoever to augment and enrich the laws of the sources of uncleanness and even those of the transfer of the uncleanness of those sources of uncleanness to men and utensils, food and drink, objects purified by immersion and objects purified by breaking, food which is unconsecrated, which is heave-offering, and which is Holy Tings.

Their original and fresh proposition concerns the locus of uncleanness, which is the world as well as the cult, and the means of removing uncleanness, in the world as well as in the cult. Accordingly, tractates on these matters begin in conception wholly autonomous of, and alien to, the Written Torah, because the Priestly Code, in its ultimate redaction, claims that cleanness and uncleanness are categories of the cultic metaphysic, not of the world outside the cult. The ultimate redactors who make such a claim in behalf of the Temple of course obscure the worldly locus of the laws of uncleanness, e.g., the corpse which lies in the tent imparts uncleanness to the utensils which are in the tent, and this without regard to the use of said utensils in the cult. Menstrual impurity has primary implications for the home, not only for the cult, despite the ultimate redactional claim stated in connection with the pericope of the Zab, the menstruating woman, and the Zabah at Lev. 15:31: Thus you shall keep the people of Israel separate from their uncleanness, lest they die in their uncleanness by defiling my tabernacle that is in their midst (see Jacob Neusner, *Purities* XVI, pp. 208-211).

It would be an error, however, to conclude that the Oral Torah represented by the Mishnah bears and essentially dual relationship to the Written one, that is, partly exegetical, partly autonomous. Even though tractates Kelim, Ohalot, Parah-Yadayim, Tohorot-Uqsin, Miqvaot-Tebul Yom, and Makhshirin begin in conceptions essentially autonomous of Scripture, while Negaim. Niddah, and Zabim (merely) spell out and develop rules laid down in scripture, all the tractates, whatever the character of their fundamental presuppositions in detail, share an approach which is distinctive to Mishnah in its very origins. All of them take an intense interest in details of cleanness. This fact is what marks them all, whatever their relationship to Scripture, as particular and Pharisaic. Even though everyone in the Land of Israel concurred that the Zab was unclean, not everyone developed the layers of exegesis, the secondary and tertiary conception, producing a tractate such as Zabim. So far as our extant sources tell us, whether or not others, e.g., in the Essene community at Qumran, observed the purity-laws, no on else took equivalent interest in developing the laws of Leviticus Chapters Twelve through Fifteen.

The detailed principles of tractates Negaim, Niddah, and Zabim in no way express conceptions definitive of and distinctive to Pharisaism, such as we observe at tractates Kelim, Parah, Tohorot, Miqvaot, and Makhshirin, and (possibly) at the shank of Ohalot (M. Oh. 3:6-16:2) as well. Authorities before 70, whom we assume are Pharisees, devote time and attention to the elucidation and extension of Scripture's rules. Extant evidence does not suggest that others did so. What is distinctive to the "Oral Torah" which we assume characterizes Pharisaism is detailed attention to matters of uncleanness. Others either took for granted and observed them or took for granted and ignored them. Accordingly, there are tow aspects to the analysis of the relationship of Zabim to Scripture, exegetical and eisegetical. Exegesis of a straight-forward, and (hypothetically) highly logical, sequential character produces Zabim. Not exegesis, but eisegesis imparts to Lev. 15:1-15 such importance that the exegetical enterprise to begin with is undertaken.

Note
[1] Chayim Yehoshua Kasovsky, *Thesaurus Mishnae* (Jerusalem, 1958), vol. IV, p. 353a.

JACOB NEUSNER

MOROCCO, PRACTICE OF JUDAISM IN: The settlement of Jews in Morocco dates back to Greco-Roman and even Phoenician times. The Jewish presence during the Greco-Roman period (beginning in 150 B.C.E.) is attested by archaeological remains, Jewish tombstones with both Hebrew and Latin inscriptions, and slabs from ancient synagogues. There are various interesting theories as to the origins of this community, some of a purely legendary nature, others more historical.

However, it is with the beginning of the Islamic period that Moroccan Jewry achieves cultural prominence. Soon after the establishment of Fez in the ninth century, that city became a great center of Jewish learning, attracting to its yeshivot students from Qayrawan, Baghdad, Andalusia, and other parts of the Jewish world. But Fez was not the only center of Jewish life and learning; there were others equally as important: Dar'a, Sijilmasa and Marrakesh in the south, and, later on, Sale, Sefrou, Meknes, and Tetouan in central and northern Morocco. Great yeshivot and centers of kabbalah were to flourish in all these cities.

Responsa from the Babylonian yeshivot to the Jewish communities of Fez and Sijilmasa, address them with the utmost reverence. Indeed, during the early medieval period, Moroccan Jewry served as a cultural bridge between the great Babylonian centers of Jewish learning and the newly emerging Jewish community in Spain. They were in a very good position to do so. Not only were their rabbis scholars in their own right, but they were also in constant contact with both communities and commanded the respect of both. Morocco even provided the young Jewish community in Spain with its first teachers in Hebrew poetry, philology, and Rabbinic learning. From Morocco in the tenth century came the first Hebrew grammarians, linguists, and poets (Judah ibn Hayyuj and Dunash ibn Labrat among others), and the first great talmudist and halakhist, Isaac Al-Fasi, known also as the *Rab Alfes* or the *Rif*. Ibn Hayyuj's philological discoveries revolutionized the scientific study of Hebrew grammar and lexicography; Ibn Labrat was the first to adapt features and conventions of Arabic prosody to Hebrew, thereby providing future Hebrew poets in Spain with an important tool and models for their poetry; while Al-Fasi established the first yeshivah in Lucena. These three individuals are rightly regarded as the founders of the Spanish school of Jewish learning and science that was to culminate in the Golden Age of Jewish culture and creativity in Spain. Throughout the Golden Age in Spain, Moroccan Jews continued to maintain close cultural and intellectual ties with Spanish Jewry.

Beginning with the middle of the twelfth century, however, a curtain of darkness descended on all the Jews of North Africa, especially on those of Morocco. The Almohad persecutions that lasted from 1148 to 1276 decimated most Jewish communities in North Africa. These persecutions, which swept like wildfire across Andalusia and North Africa, left the Moroccan Jewish community spiritually and numerically exhausted. But following the expulsion of the Jews from Spain in 1492, the community in Morocco was infused with new blood. Jewish exiles from Spain, known as *megorashim*, brought with them their rich cultural and spiritual heritage, thereby quickening and reinvigorating Moroccan Jewish life and culture. Immediately after their arrival, these exiles began enacting ordinances, known as *Tekkanot Hakhme Castilya*, to ensure that their communal and religious life in Morocco would continue to be conducted as it had been in Spain. One example of the early *takkanot* is the one requiring a husband to include in the marriage contract (*ketubbah*) a clause barring him from marrying a second wife without the explicit and voluntary permission of the first wife. This ordinance virtually eliminated the practice of bigamy. It achieved for the Sephardim essentially the same result that Rabbenu Gershom's *herem* (ban) on bigamy (which is not binding on Sephardim) had for the Ashkenazim.

Initially, the *megorashim* met with some resistance on the part of the indigenous community, known as the *toshavim*, especially in matters of rituals and some religious practices, but eventually the *megorashim* and their customs and practices (*minhagim*) prevailed throughout Morocco. Moroccan rabbis continued to enact *takkanot* as needed through the centuries, down to the 1950s. These ordinances helped to protect the rights of women and children and promote the stability of the Jewish family as well as respond to contemporary economic and social needs.

The Sephardic Legacy among Moroccan Jews: When the Spanish exiles arrived in Morocco in 1492, they found themselves among people whose culture they considered to be inferior to the one they had left in Spain. For Arab culture in Morocco, as elsewhere in the Arab world, was then in decline. Finding no new or fresh intellectual challenges, the exiles bent their intellectual energies and talents to conserving and preserving the cultural legacy they brought with them from Spain. They not only preserved and cultivated this heritage zealously but also did their utmost to amplify it. They continued to develop their own Jewish culture very much in the spirit and within the literary framework and context of the Sephardic tradition.

The attachment of Moroccan Jews to the Sephardic legacy found expression in many ways and on many levels. These include the liberal sprinkling of Spanish words and phrases in their Judeo-Arabic dialect, their personal and family names, their liturgy for the High Holidays and other special religious occasions, their love of Andalusian music, and their many customs and rituals.

Above all, this legacy is manifested in Moroccan scholarship and creativity in the fields of halakhic literature, religious poetry in Hebrew and Arabic, critical biblical exegesis, kabbalah, philology, and even historiography. Indeed, the output of Moroccan Jewry in these fields is most impressive. Every city and every period produced its rabbis, poets, and Jewish scholars of great renown. These rabbis and poets wrote a voluminous quantity of works in all branches of Jewish and Rabbinic literature. Because of the high scholarly quality of these works and the general Jewish interest of their contents, these works were to gain widespread acceptance throughout the Jewish world. Such were, for example, the biblical commentary of Hayim ben 'Attar, known especially among the Hasidim as the saintly *Or ha-Hayim* or *Or haHayim ha-Kadosh* (Leghorn, 1739); the responsa of Jacob Aben-Tzur (Alexandria, 1894), Reph'ael Berdugo (Krakow, 1891), Isaac Bengwalid (Leghorn, 1855), and Repha'el ben Simeon (Alexandria, 1912); the *piyyutim* (religious poems) of David ben Hassin (Amsterdam, 1807/Casablanca, 1931/Israel, 1973, 1999), Jacob Aben-Tzur (Alexandria, 1898), Repha'el Moshe Elbaz (Jerusalem, 1935), and Jacob Berdugo (London, 1855); the numerous historical works on Moroccan Jewry by Abner Tzarfati (Jerusalem, 1979), Jacob Moshe Toledano (Jerusalem, 1911, 1975), Joseph ben Naim (Jerusalem, 1930), and Joseph Messas (Jerusalem, 1969-1975); and finally the philosophical and theological works of Judah ben Nissim ibn Malka (Paris, 1954), and A. Eliyahu Benamozeg (Jerusalem, 1967). These are only some of the better known ones; there are many more.

It should be emphasized in this connection that Moroccan Rabbinic creativity was unique and came closest to the ideal established by the Spanish masters of the Golden Age in that this creativity was multidimensional. Moroccan rabbis wrote works on biblical and talmudic exegesis, halakhah, poetry, history, and theology.

This multidimensional aspect of Moroccan Rabbinic creativity is perhaps best illustrated by Moroccan *piyyutim*. Of all the manifestation of the Sephardic legacy noted above, it was in poetry that the two functions of preservation and creative amplification are most apparent. Of all the major literary genres, none was more jealously preserved and zealously cultivated than was poetry. Moroccan poets preserved and enriched the poetic legacy of Andalusian Jewry. They faithfully guarded both the form and the substance of the *piyyut* in terms of the traditional themes and techniques of composition.

Most Moroccan rabbis considered the composition of *piyyutim* and *melitzah* (rhymed prose) to be a desirable achievement of a *talmid hakham* (Rabbinic scholar). Thus, almost all great (and not so great) rabbis in Morocco composed *piyyutim* for various occasions, some more than others, but all did. It is no accident that all the great religious poets in Morocco, in most cases, were also the pillars of Rabbinic scholarship and the halakhic authorities of their time. For example, Jacob Aben-Tzur (1673-1753), one of the greatest halakhic authorities of his time, was equally famous for his *Mishpat u-Tzedakah be-Ya'akov*, a two volume collection of responsa and *takkanot* and his *'Et le-Khol Hefetz*, a collection of his *piyyutim* and *kinot* (lamentations). The same was true of all Moroccan religious poets; they were all renowned Rabbinic scholars.

By far the most illustrious of Moroccan poets was David ben Hassin who died in Meknes in 1792. His collection of *piyyutim* and *kinot*, entitled *Tehilah le-David* was first published in Amsterdam in 1807 shortly after his death; it was republished in Casablanca, Morocco, in 1931, and again in Israel in 1873. Most recently, Ephrayim Hazan of Bar Ilan University published a scholarly and annotated edition of this work (Lod, Israel, 1999).

The Moroccan *piyyut* was strongly religious; it was inspired by ardent faith, permeated with devotion, and distinguished by a deep attachment to the values of Judaism and a great love for the land of Israel. Noteworthy also is its popular character. Moroccan rabbis and laymen composed *piyyutim* for every occasion in a very lucid and simple Hebrew and in the local Arabic dialect. Moreover, these *piyyutim* were sung both in the synagogue and in the homes on holidays and at family celebrations to classical and contemporary Andalusian and Arabic music, a fact that made them and their melodies very popular. All this means that these *piyyutim* were not intended exclusively for the intellectual and scholarly elite; they were sung and enjoyed by everyone on all possible occasions. It is this popular aspect more than the literary one that accounts for their centrality in Moroccan Jewish life. There was no festive occasion, whether in the synagogue or in the home, that was not marked by the singing of appropriate *piyyutim*.

Religious, Judicial, Cultural and Educational Institutions: One of the most fundamental facts to be noted about Moroccan Jewry is that it was not fragmented into various denominations as was the case with European Jewry and is still the case in the United States. Some Jews were more observant than others; but they were all united under the leadership of their rabbis, *dayyanim*, and communal leaders. In keeping with the spirit of this communal and spiritual unity, Moroccan Jews created within the walls of the *mellah* (Jewish quarter) an entire infrastructure of communal, judicial, educational, religious, and social institutions. These include:

1) A fully autonomous Rabbinic judicial system with its local and national courts, scribes, and archives or *pinkasim*.
2) A whole galaxy of social and philanthropic organizations among which *bikkur holim, moshav zekenim, ezrat dalim, hakhnasat 'orhim, hakhnasat kallot, hevra kadisha*, etc., all designed to come to the assistance of the poor, the elderly, the widows and the orphans.
3) A full communal taxation system levied on all kosher products the revenues from which were earmarked for helping the needy and defraying other communal expenses.
4) A complete religious educational system starting with elementary education in the *Talmud Torah* or the *Em ha-Banim* and culminating in the great yeshivot where Moroccan rabbis, teachers, *dayyanim* (Rabbinic judges), *shohatim* (ritual slaughterers), *shelihe tzibbur* (cantors), and other religious functionaries were trained.
5) In the same *mellahs*, Moroccan Jews developed their own Jewish cuisine, their own Jewish music, and their own Jewish art. This was magnificently demonstrated by the exhibit, on "Moroccan Jewish Life" mounted at the Jerusalem Museum in the summer of 1973.

Some of these institutions warrant further discussions.

The Rabbinic Judicial System: As in other Muslim lands, Jews in Morocco enjoyed absolute judicial autonomy. As a result, the Rabbinic courts were recognized by the civil authorities, and their decisions were enforceable by these authorities. Every city had a *bet din* of three judges. In addition, there was a high court of appeals (*Bet din le-'ir'urim*) in Rabat.

The *dayyanim* (judges) were the most respected members of the community. The position of *dayyan* was a very prestigious and a lucrative one as well. It was the only paid Rabbinic position. Beginning in 1925 when the French authorities introduced administrative reforms in the Rabbinic court system, *dayyanim* were paid by the civil government on par with other civil judges. This arrangement remained in force after Morocco gained its independence in 1956. However, since there were to be only three judges in any city, the competition for such positions was understandably fierce.

Attached to every *bet din* were official scribes (*sofere bet din*) who were in charge of drafting all legal documents such as contracts, wills, marriage contract (*ketubbot*), and the like. They retained copies of every legal instrument that they issued in their *pinkasim* (registers or records). Every *bet din* also had an official translator (*greffier*) whose function was to translate into French (and later into Arabic) every one of the court's decisions. Each *bet din* kept full records of all its decisions. These *pinkasim* and court records constitute an invaluable source for the study of the legal, economic, and social history of Moroccan Jewry.

Rabbinic courts in Morocco adjudicated in all matters of Jewish law including matrimonial, civil, and commercial transactions. This resulted in a most productive period in halakhic literature. Speaking of Moroccan *dayyanim* and their work, Menahem Elon, the pre-eminent historian of Jewish jurisprudence, observed that "theirs was a unique case of 450 years of continued jurisprudence covering all aspects of Jewish law including family, civil, and commercial law." In short, they dealt with all parts of the *Shulhan Arukh*. In the process, they produced a most impressive corpus of halakhic works, including responsa, takkanot, and legal commentaries.

In their halakhic decisions, Moroccan rabbis and *dayyanim*, like other Sephardic *poskim*, tended to be lenient, flexible, and sensitive to the needs of the times. Commenting on this aspect of Moroccan halakhah, Elon observed further, "Moroccan decisors show great sensitivity to changing circumstances and the new exigencies of modern times; they show a readiness to deal with the issues head-on; and when the situation demands bold initiatives, they do not hesitate to enact *takkanot*."

Synagogues and the Rabbinate: With but a few exceptions, most synagogues in Morocco were small, private, family synagogues, usually attached to the owner's home. They were usually built by rabbis as a source of income, or by wealthy individuals in memory of a loved one. The exceptions were the magnificent *Nahor* and *Suiri* synagogues in Tangier and the *Sadoun* synagogue in Fez.

There was no paid position of synagogue rabbi. If the owner were not himself a rabbi, he would invite a rabbi (usually a prominent one) to be an honorary member of the synagogue. Some synagogues simply did not have a rabbi at all. The most important position in the synagogue, and the only paid one, was that of the *shaliah tzibbur* or *Hazan* (cantor); at times however, even this position was voluntary. Other important positions in the synagogue were the *shammash* (sexton) and the *paytan*. The *shammash* saw to the physical maintenance of the synagogue, collected synagogue membership dues and offerings, and awakened congregants in time for prayer. The *paytan* was a master of the entire repertoire of Moroccan *piyyutim* and of the traditional Moroccan-Andalusian music. He led the congregation in the singing of appropriate *piyyutim* on all festive occasions. Neither the *shammash* nor the *paytan* drew a salary; both depended on the congregants' generosity. A person who was called to the Torah on a festive occasion would usually make offerings to the rabbi, the *shammash* and *paytan*, to one or more charitable organizations, and for the maintenance of the synagogue.

The financial needs of most synagogues in Morocco were rather modest. Essentially, they consisted of the expenses for the maintenance of the synagogue and some income for the rabbi, if he was the owner of the synagogue and in need of such income. This relatively modest budget was met by minimal biannual membership fees supplemented by offerings made by congregants upon their being called to the Torah.

Synagogues in Morocco were not the center of Jewish life (as is the case in the United States). People went to the synagogue for prayers and some learning. There were no communal meals, no *kiddushim*, no food or drinks at any time. Therefore, synagogues in Morocco did not have kitchens, social halls, or even a *sukkah* on the festival of Tabernacles. Naturally, since synagogues were small and therefore intimate, members felt as one family. Following services, people usually visited with each other, and on occasion invited each other for lavish buffets in their homes. Generally speaking, Jewish life was lived in the home and in the streets of the *mellah*.

On regular Shabbats, services were usually brief. There was no repetition of the *musaf amidah*; there were no elaborate cantorial renditions of any prayer, no sermons, and no announcements. Services would begin at 7:30 A.M. and conclude at 10 A.M. or shortly thereafter. Rabbis usually held a *derasha* (discourse or homily) before the *minhah* service for those who cared to attend. During the week, most synagogues held services only in the morning, but not in the afternoon or evening; other synagogues met that need. For example, in Meknes a synagogue in the old *mellah* (known as R. Shema'ya's synagogue) held continuous *minhah* and *'arvit* services through the afternoon and the evening, thus accommodating the different schedules of all members of the community.

Jewish Education: Jewish education in Morocco was gradual and progressive and was provided by three distinct educational institutions: the *Talmud Torah*, the yeshivah, and various study groups known as *hevrot*. Until the beginning of the twentieth century, elementary education was provided by an independent *heder* system in which individual rabbis taught children in private synagogues without any central supervision or common curriculum. Beginning with the 1910s and 1920s, this chaotic system was replaced by a relatively modern centralized *Talmud Torah* or *Em ha-Banim* controlled and financed by the Jewish community. It should be pointed out at the outset that, traditionally, Jewish girls did not attend the *Talmud Torah*; however, they received their elementary education, both secular and religious, in the schools of the *Alliance Israelite Universelle*, which were established all over Morocco in the late nineteenth and early twentieth centuries.

Jewish boys received the first stage of their education in the *Talmud Torah* where, in addition to the basic skills of reading and writing, they learned the *parashah* and *haftarah* of the week, as well as certain books of the Bible, such as the Five Scrolls, Proverbs, Psalms, and Job. The Five Scrolls were usually studied before the appropriate holiday on which they were read in the synagogue. The Books of Proverbs, Psalms, and Job were studied throughout the summer months, especially between Passover and *Tish'ah be-Av*. The studies at this elementary stage involved translating the biblical text into spoken Arabic and learning the respective traditional Moroccan melodies for these texts. Following the establishment of the State of Israel, modern Hebrew replaced Arabic as the language of instruction, and the learning of modern Hebrew became an important part of the curriculum.

By the time a student arrived at the yeshivah, he had already been initiated in the study of the Mishnah, Gemara, and *Dinim* (practical laws) for the holidays, Shabbat, prayers, and other daily matters. This was usually achieved through private instruction or in the *Talmud Torah*, where students in the higher grades studied selected easy talmudic passages, *Pirke Avot* (*The Sayings of the Fathers*), as well as the Pentateuch with the commentary of Rashi.

Initiation in the study of the Mishnah and Talmud thus took place even before one entered the yeshivah. In fact, not everyone went to yeshivah; many Jews never did. Whatever Rabbinic learning they had was acquired in evening classes, in Saturday afternoon *derashot* or homilies, or in various study groups known as *hevrot*. These *hevrot* gathered regularly every Saturday night in private homes to hear and learn aggadah, laws, or *musar* (ethical teachings) from well-known teachers.

The yeshivah training *per se*, however, was reserved for those wishing to prepare themselves for careers as rabbis, *dayyanim*, or Rabbinic scholars (*talmide hakhamim*), and those who simply loved the study of Torah. Generally speaking, the yeshivot in Morocco were less institutionalized in their organization than their East European counterparts. Nor did they attract students from other countries, as did the celebrated Babylonian and Spanish yeshivot in medieval times. They were essentially local phenomena. They evolved around individual masters who were recognized as inspired teachers, religious and spiritual models, and men of renowned scholarly reputation. The individual masters who headed these yeshivot were either appointed by the local community, chosen by one or more benefactors who founded the yeshivah specifically for them, or were simply sought out by students who were attracted to them because of their personal, religious, and scholarly qualities. Interestingly enough, most of these yeshivot did not even have names. They were known simply by the masters who headed them and by the illustrious students they produced. But there were exceptions, and some were known by specific names.

The number of students at these yeshivot was rather small, not exceeding twenty or thirty who sat around their teacher. This resulted in an atmosphere of informality and in an intense relationship between the teacher and disciples. On the other hand, there was more than one yeshivah and more than one renowned teacher at any of the Torah centers of Morocco at any given period. The students were mostly local, for, as a general rule, every major city produced its own rabbis and judges who had been trained in its own yeshivot. Certain cities such as Meknes and Marrakesh, however, acquired a widespread reputation as great centers of Rabbinic learning and attracted students from all over the country.

The expenses required for maintaining these yeshivot were minimal. There was no physical plant to speak of, as instruction took place in one of the local synagogues (often the teacher's own) at no special cost. There were no dormitories, no large faculty, and above all no administrative overhead.

Students paid no tuition. The main expenses involved a modest salary for the teacher and some minimal aid to needy students, especially those coming from elsewhere.

The study of the Talmud in Moroccan yeshivot, as in most Sephardic ones, was halakhically oriented. It was studied with the ultimate aim of arriving at halakhic decisions (*le-ʿasoke shemaʾteta ʿalibba de-hilkheta*), and not merely as a intellectual exercise. This halakhic orientation was reflected in the program of studies that was always divided equally between Talmud and halakhah. The particular tractate studied at any given period was frequently chosen for the purpose of providing the talmudic background for whatever laws were being studied at the time. The study of halakhah involved a review of all Rabbinic literature relating to any given issue in Jewish law. This was achieved through the systematic study of the *Tur*, the *Bet Yoseph* and the *Shulhan Arukh* with its commentaries.

In addition to the study of Talmud and halakhah, the Rabbinic curriculum in Moroccan yeshivot included biblical exegesis and some aspect of Jewish thought. For the study of the Bible, the favored commentaries were Rashi, Radak (David Kimhi), and Abraham ibn Ezra. For Jewish thought, the medieval philosophical and theological treatises *Hovat ha-Levavot* (*The Duties of The Heart*) of Bahya ibn Pakuda, the *Kuzari* of Judah Halevi, and the *Shemonah Perakim le-Harambam* (Maimonides' *Eight Chapters*) were among the most popular texts.

All these subjects were studied in an informal setting. One did not have to register for specific courses. Advanced students sat together with novices, and each learned from the wisdom or mistakes of the other. There were no special examinations at the end of a year or semester, no accumulation of credits, and no special degree awarded. Ordination, or *semikhat rabbanut* was usually conferred in an assembly of rabbis and notables by the ordaining rabbi placing his hands on the head of the candidate and blessing him.

Customs, Rituals, and Religious Practices: Essentially, the *minhagim* (customs) of Moroccan Jews are similar to those of all Sephardim, for all Sephardim cherish a common cultural and religious heritage that goes back to the Golden Age in Spain. This is certainly true in matters of halakhah and liturgy. Thus, for example, all Sephardim regard Caro's *Shulhan Arukh* as the supreme halakhic authority, rulings of which are binding on all of them. Nonetheless, Sephardim from various parts of the world differ from each other in the precise way in which they express and practice this tradition. This is especially true with respect to food, music, and folklore, which inevitably reflect local influences. The colorful local customs lend to certain holidays and festive occasions an element of charm and local fragrance that give these celebrations their unique character. Such are, for example, the celebrations of *Mimouna* and *Hillula* as well as the institution of *Bakkashot* (discussed below), all of which are quintessentially Moroccan.

It is to be noted, however, that in Morocco as in other Sephardic communities (especially those in Islamic lands), all of life was essentially lived within a religious framework. Even folklore revolved around religious institutions. The following description of the Moroccan practice will focus on both uniquely Moroccan customs as well as those shared with other Sephardim.

Daily and Shabbat Services: Before the evening service of *ʿarvit*, Moroccan Jews recite *Le-David hashem ʿori ve-yishʾi* ... (Ps. 27) and other verses from the Psalms. Before *Rosh Hodesh*, they recite *Barekhi nafshi* ... (Ps. 104) as well, and during the holiday of Hanukkah, they recite *Mizmor shir hanukat* ... (Ps. 30). In some communities (such as in Meknes), the repetition of the Amidah by the cantor in the weekly *shaharit* and *minhah* services as well as the *musaf* and *minhah* of the Sabbath was not only discouraged but virtually eliminated. This was done in accordance with the strong recommendations of prominent Moroccan halakhic authorities.

On weekdays, a number of individuals would remain in the synagogue following the *shaharit* service to read the *Hok le-Yisraʾel*. This is a fixed daily program of study consisting of readings from the *parashah* and the *haftarah* of the week as well as from the biblical Writings, the Mishnah, Gemara, *Zohar*, and other legal and ethical works. This is a well-established tradition among most

Sephardim. It is based no doubt on Caro's recommendation in the *Shulhan Arukh* that, "After one leaves the synagogue, he should go to the house of study and set a fixed time for Torah study; a time that must never be skipped even if it means foregoing financial gain" (*Orah Hayim*, section 155:1).

Likewise, following the Saturday morning service, a number of individuals would remain in the synagogue in order to read together the *parashah* of the week "*shenayim mikra ve-ʿehad targum*." This involves the reading of every verse twice in Hebrew and once in Aramaic. Again, this is a tradition shared by most Sephardim. The origin of this practice goes back to the Talmud. B. Ber. 8a states: "Rav Huna says in the name of R. Ammi: A man should always complete his *parashah* together with the congregation, [reading] twice the Hebrew text and once the Aramaic *targum*, and even [verses that contain only names such as the verse] Atarot and Dibon…" Moroccan Jews continued to follow this tradition tenaciously even after their massive emigration to Israel.

On Friday evening, before the *Kabbalat Shabbat* service, like most Sephardim, Moroccans read (or rather chant) The Song of Songs. No doubt, this practice has kabbalistic origins.

Bakkashot: One of the most popular Moroccan cultural institutions is the *Bakkashot*. It may be described in popular terms as a concert or "sing-in" that took place around 3 A.M. every Friday night between Tabernacles and Passover, a season of long winter nights. This service was held by a number of *hevrot* or groups bearing the names of one of the biblical prophets, such as *hevrat Yehizkel Ha-Navi*, *hevrat Eliyahu ha-Navi*, etc. The *bakkashot* gatherings provided lovers of music and *piyyutim* an opportunity to get together and entertain themselves by singing *piyyutim*. This is reminiscent of the poetic tradition in medieval Spain, when Arab and Hebrew poets would entertain themselves by reciting and discussing poetry at nocturnal wine parties, testing each other's poetic mettle. Other members of the community, including rabbis and *dayyanim*, attended these gatherings as well and enjoyed the experience as much.

The *bakkashot* service would begin with the singing of the Song of Songs followed by *Tikkun Hatzot* (special midnight liturgy that included the chanting of many psalms, especially Ps. 51, the Psalm of Repentance). Following these preliminaries, the *Paytan*—and every such group had its own *paytan*—introduced the musical theme of the night. He led the participants in singing the appropriate *piyyutim*, selected for their thematic connection to the weekly portion of the Torah and for their melodic adaptability to the particular mode of Andalusian music chosen for the night. All participants, especially those with pleasant voices and a rudimentary knowledge of *piyyutim*, took turns, each singing a stanza. Towards morning, young boys joined in the singing of popular *piyyutim* and even modern Israeli songs. Throughout the service, participants were served refreshments. In short, this was a very festive religio-social gathering enjoyed by all, and reflecting Moroccan Jews' love for Andalusian music and *piyyutim*. Religiously speaking, it was perhaps inspired by the words of the Psalmist: "I arise at midnight to praise You for Your just rules" (Ps. 119:62).

The institution of *bakkashot* encouraged the composition of *piyyutim*, the training of *paytanim*, and the publication of anthologies of *piyyutim*. While every city had its *hevrot* of *bakkashot*, the city of Mogador was particularly renowned for its many expert *paytanim* and for its own anthology of *piyyutim*, entitled *Shir Yedidot*. Towering head and shoulder over all Moroccan *paytanim*, was Rabbi David Bouzaglo of Mogador, a Rabbinic scholar, a superb Hebraist and grammarian, a prolific poet, and above all *neʾim zemirot yisraʾel*, 'the sweet singer of Moroccan Jewry, whose many disciples are still active as *hazanim* and *paytanim* in Israel, France, Canada, and other diasporic Moroccan Jewish communities.

Passover, Lag ba-Omer, and Shavuot: The *Shulhan Arukh* introduces the laws of Passover with the statement, "We begin to inquire about the laws of Passover thirty days before Passover" (*Orah Hayim*, section 429:1). In Morocco, preparations for Passover began immediately after Purim. With the exception of matzot and kosher wine, all other foods including sweet preserves, condiments, and spices were prepared at home. Because all food for Passover had to be prepared in a kosher for Passover environment, cleaning for the holiday had to start fairly early in the process. The Community Council (*va'ad ha-kehilah*) had control over the distribution of matzot and kosher wine. Both of these items were taxed by the Council, and the proceeds of these taxes were earmarked for Passover provisions for all the needy in the community.

In matters pertaining to Jewish law and liturgy, Moroccan Jews follow common Sephardic practices. Like other Sephardim, they eat legumes (*kitniyot*) and rice on Passover. They also eat *matzah 'ashirah* ("rich matzah"), made with freshly squeezed orange juice, home made sweet wine (undiluted with water), eggs, and flour prepared specially for Passover. This is in accordance with Caro's rulings that permit both practices. Also, like other Sephardim, they begin the evening services of every holiday, major or minor, with the reading of a psalm thematically relevant to the day. In the case of Passover, it is *Hodu lashem ki tov . . . Yomeru ge'ule hashem . . .* (Ps. 107), the central theme of which is redemption.

Yet, apart from these and other halakhic and liturgical matters, Moroccan Jews, unlike other Sephardim, have a tradition rich in unusual and unique customs for Passover, some of which are still practiced by Moroccan Jews around the world. Following are some illustrative examples.

On the Shabbat before Passover, Moroccan Jews sing the *piyyut "Be-hag zeh ne'esah mofet va-nes,"* a rhymed didactic poem enumerating all the laws of *bedikat hametz* (the search for leavened bread). On the day before Passover, leftover *hametz* was burned in the street in small earthenware stoves, as children jumped around singing (in Arabic) *hametz 'ashir u-baba 'ashir, hametza 'ashira wima 'ashira* ("may Daddy and Mommy be rich"). *Lulavim* that had been kept from the last holiday of Sukkot for this occasion were burnt with the *hametz*.

The Sephardic recipe for the *haroset* is rich and spicy. Its ingredients include nuts, figs, dates, raisins, pomegranates, and many spices (cinnamon, ginger, and cloves). Some of the items on the Seder plate are also different from the ones used by Ashkenazim. For *karpas*, Moroccan Jews use celery, which in Arabic is called *krafs* corresponding to the Hebrew *karpas*. The outer leaves of romaine lettuce, which in Morocco are somewhat bitter, are used for bitter herbs (*maror*), while its inner leaves are used for *hazeret*.

Upon breaking the middle matzah (*yahatz*), the head of the family recites in Arabic, "Thus has God split the sea in twelve paths when our ancestors left Egypt led by our master Moshe ben Amram." The *afikoman* is not hidden but hung around the neck in a dramatization of the biblical verse, "their kneading bowls wrapped in their cloaks upon their shoulder" (Exod. 12:35). In some parts of Morocco, the scene was more dramatic. The men would tie a bundle containing the *afikoman* to a stick and hurry out of the house singing "in haste did we depart from Egypt, their kneading bowls wrapped in their cloaks upon their shoulder." In Meknes the *afikoman* was tied around the neck of the youngest child. The Seder plate is then lifted by the head of the family and passed over the head of everyone at the table while everyone sings "In haste (*bi-vhilu*) did we depart from Egypt; yesterday we were slaves and today we are free men; may we be next year in Jerusalem."

The *bi-vhilu* ceremony is followed by the chanting of the Haggadah as each member of the family takes his or her turn in chanting one paragraph in Hebrew and then translating it into Arabic. The entire Haggadah including the lively song *dayyenu* is translated into Arabic for the benefit of women and children. In general, Moroccan Jews are fond of Arabic translations. They also translate into Arabic the Book of Ruth on Shavuot, the hymn *Ein ke-Lohenu* as well as many *kinot* for *Tish'ah be-Av*. Surprisingly, in Morocco as well as in many other Sephardic communities, the *Mah nishtanah* (the "Four Questions") is chanted in unison by all or by any member of the family, not necessarily by the youngest child. Children take their turn with the rest of the family. Hence no special preparation is required on the part of anyone.

Dramatization is the order of the night. An interesting custom associated with the Seder is to set a small table with all sorts of greens and flowers as well as fruits and vegetables. This table is then covered or hidden under the dinner table. Just before reading the paragraph "'And numerous,' as it is said: 'I have caused thee to multiply like the growth of the field,'" it is brought out and uncovered as a visual demonstration of what is being read.

Some customs seem to defy explanations. One is the practice by Moroccan Jews of carrying with them a piece of the *afikoman* as a *segulah* (protection) throughout the year. Another related custom is connected with the *Omer*. On the second night of Passover, just before the counting of the *Omer*, the *shammash* distributes to all congregants a piece of new hard salt. This is kept throughout the year as a *segulah* against the "evil eye." Both these practices have been reported by many travelers, yet no one has been able to offer a plausible explanation for either.

Finally, the most spectacular Moroccan celebration associated with Passover is the *Mimouna* (or *Maymouna*) celebration on the night ending the holiday. It is a very festive and joyous celebration, and, in terms of its popularity, it is perhaps the most joyous occasion of the year among Moroccan Jews. In the home, festive tables were decorated with green stalks of new wheat and barley as well as flowers brought by Arab friends and well-wishers. The tables were laden with plates of honey, dry fruits, nuts, and other sweets. At the center of the table were a bowl of buttermilk and one of flour topped by a fresh fish and/or green beans.

The celebration began in the synagogue with a particularly festive evening service marked by the singing of appropriate *piyyutim*. At the conclusion of the service, the entire congregation would accompany the rabbi or *hazan* to his home singing along the way the traditional *piyyutim* for the occasion. At the rabbi's home, following a festive *havdalah* ceremony, traditional refreshments were served. The rabbi would then bless the entire congregation with the Priestly Blessing. Upon leaving the rabbi's home, each guest was blessed by the rabbi who managed to slip him or her several dates, a symbol of sweetness for the year to come.

Following this formal part of the celebration, people would visit other members of their families, and friends. On *Mimouna* night, every house was an open house, and guests were expected to partake of the traditional refreshments. In some communities, *muflita* (thin crepes) dipped in butter and honey was de rigueur. Prominent rabbis and *kohanim* (members of priestly families) held an open house all night long for all members of the community who sought their blessing. Indeed, many would begin their visits at the homes of most of the eminent rabbis. The streets of the *mellah* teemed with people making their way from one visit to another. Women dressed in their finest embroidered caftans. Bridegrooms would visit their fiancées bearing precious gifts (usually jewelry). Arab friends mingled easily with the crowd and were welcome everywhere. On the following day, *Mimouna* day, Jews relaxed leisurely in the park, at the seashore or a spring or any place near water. Some suggest that this has to do with the fact that the last day of Passover was actually the day of the splitting of the Red Sea.

No one knows for sure the origin of this celebration or even the meaning of the name *Mimouna*. A number of explanations have been suggested by various Moroccan rabbis (Joseph ben Naim, Joseph Messas, and Jacob Moshe Toledano, among others) at different times. Of all these explanations, the most popular among Moroccan Jews is that the word *Mimouna* derives from (or is the Arabic mispronunciation) of the Hebrew word *'emunah*, faith, that is, faith in the coming of the messiah. The source of this explanation, its proponents suggest, goes back to the talmudic statement, "In the month of Nisan the Jews were redeemed, and in the month of Nisan they will be redeemed again." Since, by the end of Passover, Nisan is almost gone, and the promised redemption has not yet taken place, Moroccan Jews reaffirm their faith in the messiah's ultimate coming, in the spirit of the dictum "even if he should tarry, still wait for him." Another popular explanation sees the connection of *Mimouna-Maymouna* with the name Maymoun. According to this explanation, Rabbi Maymoun, the father of Maimonides, died in Fez precisely on the last day of Passover. The Mimouna celebration is in lieu of a *hillula* celebrating his memory.

However, many contemporary scholars suggest that the reason for the celebration is more seasonal and agricultural than religious. These scholars associate the *mimouna* celebration with wishes for success and prosperity in the approaching harvest season. Indeed, the word *mimouna* in Arabic means "wealth and good fortune." Likewise, the popular greeting with which Moroccan Jews greet each other on both the night and day of the *mimouna*, *trebhu utsa'du* ("may you succeed and prosper") points in this direction. Finally, all items of food and greenery displayed on the *Mimouna* table on this night are symbols of good luck and plenty.

Lag ba-Omer—Hillula. The celebration of *Lag ba-Omer* is known in Morocco as the *Hillula* of Simeon bar Yohai. It is marked by much fanfare and great festivities that take place principally in the synagogue and in the local cemetery. At the synagogue on *Lag ba-Omer*'s eve, a festive evening service is followed by the reading of passages from the *Zohar* (usually, the last chapter of the *Idera Zuta*), the singing of the popular song *Bar Yohai*, as well as other appropriate Moroccan *piyyutim*. At the local cemetery, people pray, light candles, and sing *piyyutim* at the gravesites of local saintly rabbis (*tzaddikim*), very much in the spirit of the festivities held at the gravesite of Simeon bar Yohai at Meron in Israel. In many (but not all) communities, candles are sold in the synagogue or at the cemetery in memory of Simeon bar Yohai, Meir Baal ha-Nes, and other talmudic sages as well as renowned local *tzaddikim*. In some communities, the entire celebration including the evening service takes place in the local cemetery at the gravesite of the local *tzaddik*.

While every Moroccan city had its local saint(s), the most popular site for the celebration of the *Hillula* for Moroccan Jews was the gravesite of Rabbi Amram ben Diwan. He was an emissary from Hebron who visited Morocco in 1773 and, after a successful fund-raising tour of Morocco, died suddenly in 1782 in the northern town of Ouezzane. Ever since then, his gravesite has become a place of pilgrimage for the Jews of Morocco and the rest of North Africa. On *Lag ba-Omer*, Moroccan Jews would flock from all over to celebrate the *Hillula* in Ouezzane, where the festivities assumed the character of a national holiday. The celebration at Ouezzane was attended not only by notables of the Jewish community but by local French and Moroccan dignitaries as well. To this day, Moroccan Jews living in Israel, France, Canada, and the United States continue to return to Morocco periodically to participate in the *Hillula* celebration.

A number of general and local factors account for the prominence accorded by Moroccan Jews to the *Hillula*. First and foremost is the centrality of Simeon bar Yohai and the *Zohar* in their religious life. Throughout Morocco, one encounters study groups or *hevrot* for the study or recitation of the *Zohar*. In his *Between East and West: A History of the Jews of North Africa*, Andre Chouraqui notes that wherever ones goes in North Africa and especially in Morocco, one is likely to find groups of Jews, old and young, reading the *Zohar*. He notes further that even when they do not understand it, they read it, or rather chant it, with great fervor and concentration. This centrality of the *Zohar* has been institutionalized as a part of the *tikkun* (liturgical program) for the first night of Shavuot, *Hosha'anah rabbah*, and other occasions in the life cycle and the yearly cycle of Moroccan Jews. Likewise, the personality of bar Yohai, believed by most traditional Jews to have been the author of the *Zohar*, looms large among Moroccan Jews, surpassed only by that of Moses. Typical decorations in traditional Moroccan Jewish homes include pictorial representations of both Moses and bar Yohai.

Second, Morocco is famous for its cult of the tombs of saints among Jews and Muslims alike. In his monumental study of the subject, *Saint Veneration among the Jews of Morocco*, Issakhar Ben-Ami observes that some saints are respected and venerated by both Jews and Arabs.

Third, the general notion of pilgrimage to the gravesites of ancestors and *tzadikim* is attested in Rabbinic literature and reported in the travelogues of pilgrims to the land of Israel, who always prayed at the tombs of the patriarchs, the matriarch Rachel, King David, Meir Baal ha-Nes, and others. Finally, the notion of *zekhut avot* ("the merit of the Fathers") is given great weight by Sephardim. All these factors help explain the popularity of the *Hillula* of Simeon bar Yohai, and why it is celebrated with so much enthusiasm by many Moroccan Jews.

Shavuot. On each Sabbath between Passover and Shavuot, Moroccan Jews read one chapter of *Pirke Avot* (*The Saying of the Fathers*) as well as several chapters from Proverbs. In Meknes, the practice was that on Sabbath before the afternoon service, boys would line up in the synagogue near the ark and take turns chanting a paragraph of that week's chapter in Hebrew and then translating it into Arabic. The chapters from Proverbs, preceded the chapter from *Pirke Avot*; they were chanted by the entire congregation, also in Hebrew and Arabic.

The festival of Shavuot is a solemn holiday and most aspects of its celebration revolve around its special liturgy. Nonetheless, some uniquely Moroccan practices are associated with it. Following dinner on the first night of the holiday, people gathered in private homes for the prescribed *Tikkun lel Shavuot*, the special program of study (or readings) for the night. This program includes the reading of representative passages from each book of the Bible, the Mishnah, and the *Zohar* (the *Idera Rabba* and/or the *Idera Zuta*). The *Tikkun* concludes with the singing of the popular song "Bar Yohai." Refreshments were served throughout the night.

During the morning service on both days of Shavuot, before the Torah is taken from the ark, Moroccan Jews recite the *kettubah*. On the first day, they recite the *ketubbah* written by Israel Najara (a sixteenth century Syrian rabbi and poet), and on the second day they read the one written by Habib Toledano of Sale, Morocco. Both *ketubbot* are beautiful and charming poems written in the style and with all the details of a marriage contract, describing the symbolic marriage between God and the people of Israel. The *ketubbah* is read responsively by the *Hazan* and the congregation in the traditional melody in which an actual *ketubbah* is read at weddings. After the Torah is taken from the ark, Moroccan Jews dance with it as they do on *Simhat Torah*, while singing typical *piyyutim* for the occasion.

At the conclusion of the morning service, the *Azharot* (poetic enumeration of the 613 commandments) by Solomon ibn Gabirol are recited. On the first day the positive commandments are read, and on the second day, the negative ones. This is a practice shared by all Sephardim, although some recite ibn Gabirol's *Azharot* before the afternoon service. Before the afternoon service, Moroccans read the Book of Ruth, chanting each verse in Hebrew and then in Arabic translation. The first half of Ruth is read on the first day and the remaining half on the second day. Following afternoon worship, they also recite the *Azharot* written by Isaac b. Reuben al-Bargeloni, again the positive commandments on the first day and the negative ones on the second. Both the poetic structure of al-Bargeloni's *Azharot* and their melody are rather complex and require expertise on the part of those who chose to participate. Participants take turns, each chanting a stanza. Any mistake on the part of a reader evokes the immediate correction from the rest of the participants, who shout in Arabic in the same melody in which the *Azharot* are being chanted, "repeat, repeat—you do not know. . . ." This is done in an atmosphere of joviality and fun.

In the afternoon of both days of Shavuot, following the festive meal, Moroccan Jews engage in one of the strangest custom for the holiday. The men throw water at each other in their homes and in the street. Everyone and anyone is a likely target. As may be expected, children and young boys enjoy these water games most. One of the explanations offered by the late Rabbi Maymoun, in his *Hagim u-Mo'adim*, is that when the people of Israel heard the voice of God speaking to them directly on Mount Sinai, they were so overwhelmed by the experience that they fainted and nearly passed away. To revive them, God sent down heavy dew from heaven, whereupon the people said to Moses: "You speak to us and we will obey, but let not God speak to us, lest we die" (Exod. 20:16). In this explanation, the water games on Shavuot commemorate this happening.

Rosh Hashanah, Yom Kippur, and Sukkot: The Moroccan ceremonies, liturgy, music, and unique customs associated with the High Holidays and Sukkot provide ample illustration of customs shared by all Sephardim and of those unique to Morocco. Following are examples of both.

The liturgy for the *selihot* service is identical among all Sephardim. They recite this service every night or every day throughout the month of Elul and during the days between Rosh Hashanah and Yom Kippur. Syrians recite the service every morning immediately before the morning service; Moroccans recite the *selihot* in the morning before sunrise, while other Sephardim recite them at other times of the day. But all Sephardim, regardless of their origin, recite the *selihot* every day beginning with *Rosh Hodesh* Elul through Yom Kippur's eve.

Next to the prayer book for the High Holidays, *Tehilim*, the Book of Psalms seems to be the most important and popular book among most Sephardim. It is central in the devotional services during this period. Moroccans, like other Sephardim, read the entire Book of Psalms on each of the two days of Rosh Hashanah between lunch and the *minhah* (afternoon) service. With few exceptions, Sephardim also recite the full Book of Psalms on Yom Kippur between *musaf* and *minhah*. Among Syrians and Moroccans, a few individuals spend Yom Kippur night in the synagogue reciting the Psalms and readings from various Rabbinic texts.

Following *selihot* or the morning service, on the eve of either Rosh Hashanah or Yom Kippur, Sephardim conduct a *Hatarat Nedarim* or *Hatarat Kelalot* service. It is a semi-legal, semi-religious ceremony intended to annul all oaths, vows (*nedarim*) and curses (*kelalot*) uttered during the past year. Usually, the congregation divides into two groups which stand facing each other. Each group is represented by a reader who acts as its spokesman. One group requests the other to act as an earthly tribunal and declare all oaths, vows, promises, or curses uttered by members of the group as null and void, and the group acting as the court obliges by doing so. Then the roles of the groups are reversed, and the entire procedure is repeated, thus absolving the entire congregation of all obligations that may have been incurred by such vows and oaths.

Unlike the Ashkenazim, the Sephardim have no *yizkor* (memorial) service during the major festivals of Passover, Shavuot, and Sukkot. The only time any special prayer resembling *yizkor* is read is during the evening service of Yom Kippur immediately following *Kol Nidre*. This is known as the *hashkabah* or *hashkabot*, which simply means "prayer for the dead." Usually, a *hashkabah* is recited for all the past leaders of the congregation, the leaders of the community, and later for the deceased relatives of the congregants.

Special Foods and Ceremonies: Sephardic cuisine is generally known for its generous use of spices. Not so during the High Holidays season when spices are avoided and sweet dishes preferred. One interesting ceremony that is uniquely Sephardic is the *Yehi Ratzon* ceremony held on the two nights of Rosh Hashanah, a ceremony that may be described as a mini-seder. In addition to dipping apples in honey and praying for a sweet year, Sephardim eat an assortment of fruits and vegetables: dates, leeks, squash, spinach, Swiss chard, pomegranates, and sesame seeds. The ceremonial eating of these food items is explicitly recommended in the Talmud (B. Ker. 6a) and in the *Shulhan Arukh* (*Orah Hayim*, 683:1). Each item is used as a symbol to express prayers for freedom from evil and oppression and for being inscribed for a good year. In each instance, the eating of the fruit or vegetable is preceded by a prayer, *yehi ratzon*, "may it be the will of God," which plays on a word similar to the Hebrew or Aramaic name of the food item. For example, the *yehi ratzon* for *karti*, leek or onion, playing on the Hebrew root *krt*, "to cut off," asks: *she-yikaretu oyevenu*, "that our enemies be cut off." Likewise, the *yehi ratzon* for *silka*, spinach or Swiss chard, playing on the Aramaic root *slk*, "to be removed or disappear," asks: *she-yistaleku oyevenu u-mevakeshe ra'atenu*, "that our enemies and ill-wishers disappear." The *yehi ratzon* for pomegranates asks: *she-yirbu zakhuyotenu ka-rimon*, "that our good deeds be as numerous as pomegranates seeds." There is an appropriate *yehi ratzon* for every food item in this beautiful and appetizing ceremony.

Special Liturgy and Melodies. Both Ashkenazim and Sephardim have special melodies for the High Holiday prayers, and these are fairly standard. Naturally, the melodies associated by the Sephardim with the High Holidays derive from Andalusian, Greek, and Near Eastern music and therefore bear no resemblance whatsoever to those of the Ashkenazim. What is perhaps more important is that the special liturgy for Rosh Hashanah and Yom Kippur that has developed through the centuries is also radically different. The special liturgical poems, called *pizmonim, piyyutim, bakkashot,* or *tehinnot* that are sung by the Sephardim are all masterpieces of medieval religious poetry composed by such illustrious poets as Judah Halevi, Solomon ibn Gabirol, Moses and Abraham ibn Ezra, and others. Such popular gems of Sephardic cantorial music for the High Holidays as *Ahot Ketanah, Et Sha'are Ratzon, Elohay al tedineni,* and *El Nora Alila* are totally unknown to the Ashkenazim, just as the most popular pieces of Ashkenazic cantorial music for the season, such as *Untane Tokef, Hineni he'ani mi-Ma'as,* or *Hine Kahomer be-Yad ha-Yotzer,* are equally unknown to the Sephardim. All the Sephardic *pizmonim* or *selihot* are usually chanted loudly by the entire congregation to very beautiful, lively, and popular melodies that are surprisingly the same among all Sephardim.

Sukkot and Simhat Torah. When it comes to the holiday of Sukkot, decorations are the order of the day. All Jews, Sephardim and Ashkenazim, decorate the booth (sukkah) in one way or another. Moroccans, however, outdo themselves. They decorate not only the sukkah, but also the *lulavim* (palm branches) with shiny threads of lively and gay colors. This practice seems to be inspired by the following talmudic statements: (a) "The men of Jerusalem used to bind up the *lulav* with threads of Gold" (B. Suk. 36b); (b) "This is my God and I will adore him: [that is], adorn yourself before him in [the fulfillment of] precepts. Make a beautiful sukkah for him, a beautiful *lulav,* and a beautiful shofar" (B. Shab. 133b). For *Simhat Torah,* the synagogues were decorated with oriental tapestries, multicolored lights, palm branches, and flowers and greenery of all types, creating in the synagogue an aura of an oriental palace. On the morning of *Simhat Torah,* each child carried a tallcandle to the synagogue. All these were set next to each other around the *tebah* or *bimah.* The lit candles of various colors and designs added to the ambiance and festive atmosphere in the synagogue, while the traditional sweet melodies of the Moroccan liturgy blended harmoniously with the colorful and artistic décor. On the same morning, every boy who could read Hebrew would be called individually to the Torah. He was expected to read his own Torah portion, which he had prepared for the occasion in the *Talmud Torah.*

As everywhere in the Jewish world, the *hakkafot* of *Simhat Torah,* marching with the Torah, are marked with gaiety and excitement among all Sephardim. However, the procedure of the *hakkafot* varies among some. The Moroccans, for example, did not march carrying the Torah; rather, they marched around the Torah carrying their young children in their arms. At the conclusion of the *hakkafot,* the honors of returning the Torah scrolls to the ark were auctioned off among the women, who came dressed in their finest caftans for the unique chance to carry the Torah back to the ark. Following the synagogue service, the entire *hakkafot* ceremony was repeated in each home. A chair would be placed in the middle of the sukkah, and the adults would carry the young children, marching with them around the chair while singing the traditional *piyyutim* for the *hakkafot.* Similarly, a bridegroom and his family were expected to visit the bride-to-be on the night of *Simhat Torah* bearing all sorts of gifts. Once at her home, the entire *hakkafot* ceremony was repeated with the bride-to-be seated in the middle of the sukkah and everybody else marching and singing around her. As far as I know, these home *hakkafot* are unique to Moroccan Sephardim.

Minor Holidays and Fast Days—Hanukkah: Generally speaking, the celebration of Hanukkah in Morocco is a very subdued affair. It is limited to the recitation of special prayers in the synagogue, the lighting of the menorah in both the home and the synagogue, and eating *sfenj* or *beigners* (Moroccan doughnuts or fritters) freshly fried in oil, in commemoration of the miracle of the oil associated with Hanukkah. During the morning services throughout Hanukkah, in addition to the recitation of *hallel,* Moroccan Jews recite eight biblical verses containing the words *ner* (lamp) or *'or* (light), beginning with the verse *ner le-ragli devarekha...* ("Your word is a lamp to my feet...," Ps. 119:105). These verses are recited as the Torah is being taken from the ark. Among Moroccan Jews as among other Sephardim, only the head of the family lights the menorah for the entire family.

The notion of "Hanukkah Gelt (money)" popular among Ashkenazic children was unknown in Morocco. Nor were there any gifts or feasts associated with Hanukkah. The simple reason is that Jewish tradition does not mandate any feasts or gift giving for Hanukkah, and in Muslim lands Hanukkah did not have to compete with Christmas. On the other hand, Moroccan children received "Purim money" from parents, relatives, and friends of the family. This is in the spirit of *mishloah manot 'ish le-re'ehu u-matanot la-'evyonim* ("sending gifts to one another and presents to the poor," Est. 9:22).

But in Morocco, Jewish children expected to receive not only "Purim money" but "*Tish'a be-Av* money" as well. The reason offered by some Moroccan rabbis for this seemingly unusual custom is that children were given money on *Tish'a be-av* in the expectation that they would use it to buy toys. It was also assumed that children being what they are would break the toys and cry, and thus they would be crying for the destruction of the Temple. This is an amazing example of a *minhag* that was instituted specifically in order to instill in the tender soul of the Jewish child love for the land of Israel.

Tu Bishvat. On *Tu Bishvat*, Moroccan Jews conduct a ceremony described in detail in a book entitled *Sefer Peri Etz Hadar*. The ceremony includes appropriate readings from the Bible and *Zohar*, and eating the *shiv'ah minim*, the seven grains and fruits (wheat, barley, grapes, figs, pomegranates, olives, and dates) associated with the land of Israel, with the appropriate blessings. Usually, a number of wealthy individuals would host such celebrations to which they would invite the rabbis and notables of the community.

Purim. On the Sabbath before Purim, Shabbat *Zakhor*, Moroccan Jews like all Sephardim, chant *Mi Kamokha*, an epic poem by Judah Halevi that tells the story of Esther in rhyme. Adults as well as children played cards on Purim. This was done in commemoration of the lot (*pur*) cast by Haman, the word from which the holiday takes its

name. Children had great fun playing with their "Purim money," but many adults lost considerable sums. Rabbis protested vigorously against the practice, but to no avail.

Sephardim do not recite the *she-heheyanu* blessing before the reading of the *Megillah* during the day. During the reading of the *Megillah*, whenever Haman's name is read, children and adults alike make great noise with all sorts of noisemakers and stamp on the floor with their feet. Before the reading of the Torah during the morning service, money would be collected from all congregants (each according to his means) for "presents to the poor." This money would then be distributed to Jewish and non-Jewish poor who made the rounds of all synagogues to collect the money that was earmarked for them.

The exchange of gifts with one another (*mishloah manot*) was limited to family members. Parents would send gifts to their married children, older brothers to their married sisters, and bridegrooms to their brides-to-be. Items used for this exchange of gifts were not merely symbolic. People would actually send full roasted chickens, special Purim omelets, and an assortment of baked goods. An interesting feature of *mishloah manot* in Morocco was that the sender would send a double portion of everything, so that the receivers could return one portion to the sender, thereby fulfilling his or her own *mishloah manot* obligation.

Following the morning service, people would busy themselves with the preparations for *mishloah manot* and for the grand feast, *se'udat* Purim, that began in late afternoon, shortly after *minhah*, and lasted late into the night. It included many traditional courses for Purim, such as special Purim omelets, shad, chicken soup with egg noodles, chicken *tajine*, and a wide assortment of Moroccan salads. Rabbis composed special *piyyutim* for the *se'udah* and vied with each other over the number of courses they could weave into their rhymes.

Tish'ah be-Av. The fast of *shiv'ah 'asar be-Tammuz* (the seventeenth of Tammuz) was known in Morocco as the "small *Tish'a be-Av*." From the seventeenth of Tammuz until *Tish'ah be-Av* many Moroccan Jews would gather in the synagogue after the noon hour

to recite the *Tikkun Hatzot*. It is a short service that included the recitation of *ʿAl naharot
Bavel* (Ps. 137), *Mizmor le-Asaf* (Ps. 79), the
last chapter of Lamentations, and several
special *kinot* (lamentations) bemoaning the
destruction of the Temple and the suffering
endured in exile.

On *Tishʾah be-Av*, people would sit on the
floor during both the evening and morning
services. Before both services, they recited
many *kinot*, and the Book of Lamentations
is read at the end of both services. In some
communities, the *mappah* (covering) of the
Torah as well as the *parokhet* (ark curtain)
were turned inside out as a sign of mourning.
Many individuals would stay after the morning service to recite additional *kinot* written
by Moroccan rabbis in Hebrew, Aramaic,
and Arabic. These included several *kinot*
lamenting the expulsion of Jews from Spain
and Portugal. Several special *kinot* were
recited before afternoon worship as well.
Each one of the *kinot* had its own melody.
These many melodies constitute a veritable
repertoire of Moroccan liturgical music.

Popular Beliefs and Superstitions:
No description of Moroccan Judaism would
be complete without reference to the popular beliefs in demons, evil spirits (*mazzikim*
and/or *shedim*), and the evil eye (*ʿayin ha-
raʾ*). The belief in the evil eye in particular
had a strong hold on the imagination of
Moroccan Jews. While these beliefs were
rarely held by rabbis or learned individuals, they were widespread among the masses.
Although references to these beliefs abound
in Rabbinic literature, their pervasiveness
among Moroccan Jews was derived mostly
from the general cultural Arab milieu, which
was saturated with beliefs in the evil eye,
evil spirits, demons, and jinns.

To ward off the perceived harmful effect
of these evil forces, Moroccan Jews resorted
to various stratagems they believed provided
effective protection. These included wearing amulets prepared by self-proclaimed kabbalists, the performance of intricate rites at
the site where the suspected exposure to
the evil eye had taken place, and praying
at the gravesites of local saintly rabbis (*tzaddikim*). At times, people would leave a jug
of water at such gravesites overnight and
then drink the water or anoint themselves

with it. In the old Jewish cemetery in
Meknes, there was even a gravesite of a
tzaddik (known as Rabbi Solomon ben
Eliezer) renowned specifically for warding
off the evil eye.

As we have seen, keeping pieces of the
afikoman and the new salt from the *Omer* was
also meant as a *segulah* (protection) against
the evil eye. The fear of the harm caused
by such evil forces and spirits also informed
certain practices and customs associated with
births, weddings, and funerals, a description
of which is beyond the scope of this essay.

Conclusion: While far from comprehensive, this description of the practice of
Judaism in Morocco offered an overview of
some of the most important religious, cultural, judicial, educational, and communal
institutions of Moroccan Judaism. The focus
on many religious practices that are uniquely
Moroccan, such as the celebrations of the
Mimouna and *Hillula*, as well as the cultural
and literary traditions of *bakkashot* and *piyyutim*, capture the most characteristic features
of Moroccan Judaism as it was practiced in
Morocco and is still practiced in diasporic
Moroccan communities throughout the
world. It is a certain *joie de vivre* that permeates the entire spectrum of the Moroccan
Jewish experience.

We have also seen that some Moroccan
practices that are seemingly unusual, such
as the decoration of *lulavim* and the reading of the weekly Torah portion twice in
Hebrew and once in Aramaic, are inspired
by talmudic dicta, while others, such as the
Mimouna and *Hillula* as well as the water
games on Shavuot, have other religious
explanations. All in all, Moroccan Jewry
was a dynamic, well organized, and closely
knit community, united under its communal
and spiritual leaders, steeped in traditional
Judaism, and informed by its classical
sources. At the same time, it was full of a
zest for life, represented in particular in the
community's great love for music and *piyyutim*.

Bibliography
Hirschberg, H.Z., *A History of The Jews in North
Africa* (Leiden,1974-1981), 2 vols.
Toledano, Henry, "Rabbinic Education in
Morocco in the Nineteenth and Twentieth
Centuries," in *Les Juifs Du Maroc: Identité et
Dialogue* (Paris, 1980), pp. 203-221.

Toledano, Henry, "The Centrality of Reason and Common Sense in the Biblical and Talmudic Exegesis of R. Rephael Berdugo (1747-1821)," in Nash, Stanley, ed., *Between History and Literature: Studies in Honor of Isaac Barzilay* (Israel, 1997), English Section, pp. 171-205.

Zafrani, Haim, *Les Juifs Du Maroc: vie sociale, economique et religieuse- Etudesde Taqqanot et Responsa* (Paris, 1972).

Zafrani, Haim, *Mille Ans de vie Juive au Maroc: Histoire et Culture, Religion et Magie* (Paris, 1983).

HENRY TOLEDANO

P

PHENOMENOLOGY OF JUDAISM: Judaism has had a complex history and exists in many forms. In light of this diversity, some claim that there is no essential Judaism, that the religion is whatever any group of Jews, or individual Jews, say it is. This article, by contrast, argues that there is a normative Judaism, consisting of certain basic structures and values a religion must have for it to be called Judaism. To accomplish our goal, we must explain, first, what we mean by "normative." "Religion," too, needs clarification, there being a widespread tendency, particularly among those influenced by anthropology, to equate religion simply with a cultural-spiritual style, a way of feeling about the world and acting in it, a kind of mood or disposition. It will be suggested that while all these are important components of religion, they are not religion *per se*. Similarly, we will need to clear away the alien, often quite hostile, approaches to defining Judaism imposed on it by non-Jews, for whom Judaism was too important to permit Jews themselves to define Finally, an adequate definition of "normative Judaism" must not only show what Judaism is but also what it is not. The usefulness of the phenomenological definition proposed here will be tested by asking how it deals with three different kinds of marginal or ambiguous religious groupings: Christianity, Samaritanism, and Yiddishism, each associated with claims to be part of, continue, or fulfill Judaism.

What is "normative"? The term normative raises many issues that often are ignored when people make affirmations about "normative Judaism" or any other religion. On the one hand, "normative" may be understood to signify what almost all (or perhaps only some) members of a given religious tradition take to be its standard practices, institutions, and beliefs. What is normative in this sense can be discovered through an opinion survey of the religion's members. We may take this to express a view of religion as a folk culture, and indeed some religions do support such understandings.

On the other hand, normative may be defined as the religion's ideal-structure, those beliefs, practices, and institutions that uniquely define it. This would be how the religion authoritatively understands itself. Opinion surveys would not only not be the best way to discover this sense of normative, they could seriously mislead, since many or most members of a tradition may only know or follow it imperfectly. Instead, we need to turn to the religion's foundational writings, practices, and/or oral traditions. Whether or not the actual religious community preserves these archetypal structures is not directly relevant, unless this lack of observance is permitted or endorsed by the norms themselves.

A third way of understanding normative stresses what the elite members of the religion, those most immersed in its literature, teachings, and practices, hold to be essential. This allows for a mixture of sociological and archetypal approaches to what is normative. The problem is that what any given elite holds to be essential may be quite different from the views of the foundational sources, even though all elites legitimate themselves through (interpretations of) those sources. Over the centuries of a tradition, elite views change. In fact, how to define the elite will probably itself be debatable, with very different groups all claiming this status.

Still, since every elite claims legitimacy through the religion's foundational sources, those source's authority, at least, is clearly acknowledged on all sides. This means that only the archetypal approach offers a hope of surmounting the problems of the other two understandings of what is normative. Therefore, we proceed here on the assumption that normative religion refers to its ideal-structure, those beliefs, practices, and institutions that uniquely define it, which are authoritatively presented in its foundational sources. However, religions differ, and some center on changeable folk values; their sources arise from them and change with them. These pose special problems.

Folkist religions and scriptural traditions: While religions affirm moral, social, and theological norms, in many religions, these affirmations are mostly tacit and taken-for-granted. This holds for native religions, folk religions even in complex societies, and, in general, for religions whose members seldom come into contact with other religions and cultures. Only those religious communities that have extensive contact with others feel the necessity to make their own beliefs and norms explicit. We therefore find clear formulations of normative beliefs and practices chiefly in the religions of literate civilizations. In such civilizations, those norms are usually written down in texts ascribed a special sacrality, texts we commonly call "scriptures." Devotees use these texts to define themselves and may even feel forced to reform themselves, their moral behavior and socio-political structures if they find these to be out of conformity to the norms depicted in the texts.

Still, many religions, even of literate civilizations, may be called "folkist." Their scriptures arose and often continue to arise out of periodic attempts to articulate the divine reality acknowledged by the civilization. Thus these religions make explicit and raise to the highest honor what previously had been the implicit consensus in folk culture. It is important to emphasize that, in such cases, the culture is generally considered even by religious authorities to have preceded the actual revelation of the scriptures. The cultural universe is the foundation the scriptures explicate (even if the truths

presented in the scriptures are said to be eternal or timeless).

Since the underlying source of authority in these scriptures is the ongoing, tacit folk tradition itself, it is taken for granted that these scriptures can continue to develop and change, even coming to articulate fundamental religious norms radically contrary to earlier formulations. We find this, for example, in Hinduism, Shintoism, Asian Buddhism, and usually Taoism. In such cases, it is unlikely that these scriptures will become the basis for a normative reform of culture, to be used to protest the deviation of the present from the past.

Reformist scriptural religions and folkist tendencies: The scriptural traditions in Judaism, Christianity, and Islam arise out of critiques of folk culture, and the reformist potentiality is made explicit and central in them. If in all religions (as Clifford Geertz has observed) we find *models of* what is and also *models for* what should be, these reformist religions are grounded in a distinctive stress on the latter idea, religion as a model for what should be. What society ought to be is more important than what it is. The majority opinion does not rule, the norms do, and these are laid out in scriptures viewed as eternal and not subject to overturning by later revelations. These are book-religions in a special sense: their scriptures really do establish norms to which later forms of the religions must conform if they are to have legitimacy. For this reason, these religions are often grouped together as the "prophetic religions."

Of the three, the primacy of norms over general societal consensus is strongest in Judaism. Judaism therefore is different from the folkist religions and even from its daughter religions. It is the only religion in antiquity (or even in the modern period) to have arisen *de novo* by creating its own people and explicitly structuring the entire society in terms of religious norms. The ideals are at the source of the society, not the other way around. The people created by this religion had henceforth to measure up to those ideals, and it was affirmed explicitly in the originating covenant with God that folkist practices and norms were "idolatrous" and not to be accepted. The source of scriptural norms was therefore not the people but God and the one-time reveltion that created the people, preserved in Judaism's scriptures. This revelation is theological at root and is not merely to be determined by social-anthropological, historical, or other folkist criteria. Indeed, it is explicitly stated that only because of excessive accommodations that diluted the norms that the people were exiled from their land. They could now exist as a distinct community only if they strenuously conformed to scriptural norms.

It may be argued to the contrary that that ancient Judaism in fact was a product of the Jewish people, and that the Torah itself was produced over many centuries by the people to express their consensus understanding of their norms and worldview. This may or may not be so, and I will return to these questions below. But it is indisputable that the account given here is the way the scriptures of Judaism explain matters: this view therefore is normative from the start of Judaism. Whenever Judaism arose, this is how it defined itself, and a phenomenological approach must take this as its primary data. Moreover, this is the way the Jews have understood themselves through the ages. They did not and do not consider themselves to have existed as a people before the reception of Torah at Sinai. Moreover, for over 3,000 years, right up to the modern period, Jews have deemed folkist tendencies that contradict revelation to be impermissible. This remarkable and self-critical self-understanding radically affected their entire history. Without it they would not have been able to sustain their distinct character in either Canaan or the diaspora, so that there probably would have been no Judaism at all.

The impact of cross-cultural experience: Perhaps one cause for this extraordinary clarity of normative self-definition in Judaism is that specifically Jewish teachings and scriptures came into existence and persisted within a constant concourse of other cultures. Jews and Judaism did not emerge in an isolated region. On the contrary, Sinai and the land of Israel were the constant bridge and battlefield between the greatest and most self-absorbed cultures of the time, Babylonia/Assyria and Egypt.

That Judaism was formed out of a repudiation of these cultures is indicated in its own scriptures, which state that Judaism's original impulse was God's calling Abraham to leave the Babylonian cities (*Ur* literally means "City") and to become a wandering nomad. Moreover, the transformative revelation and covenant that created the people occurred in the Sinai desert to a "mixed multitude" of escaped slaves (most of them said to be Abraham's descendants) who had fled Egypt. Thus the two dominant powers of that era, Babylonia and Egypt, and indeed all pagan cultures, were rejected as models. That this astonishing repudiation was a considered one is also indicated by its qualifications: it was assumed that despite pagan cruelties and idolatries, the knowledge of God and righteousness was present in every culture from the time of Noah, and, therefore, there could be righteous people acceptable to God in any culture. Abraham hoped that even in Sodom and Gomorrah there might be such people. Other examples include Melchizedek, Jethro the Midianite (Moses' father-in-law), the Ninevites whom Jonah brought to repentance, and, perhaps most striking, Job, the model for Israel of godly righteousness, who the first sentence of the Book of Job and later Jewish tradition say was a pagan Arab. Furthermore, joining the Jewish people was presented by the Torah as always a possibility, as the mixed multitude at the time of the Exodus, Ruth, and many statements in Isaiah, Zechariah, and Micah show. The book of Jonah even indicates that entire pagan cultures can be acceptable to God if they repent of their idolatrous violence and injustice and return to God, whom they are presumed already to know. The prophets constantly come back to this affirmation and make it a cornerstone of their prophecies for the messianic era.

These ideas also underlay the self-critical emphasis of Torah tradition. It was explicitly affirmed that some Jews, even the majority in a given generation, might sin and pursue evil for the sake of convenience, to attain short-term goals, or to be like other nations. Idolatry was thought to be a temptation built into the human condition. For this reason, self-criticism was from earliest times an essential part of normative observance. There was a never-ending struggle to reform and perfect society as a whole, the prophets were enshrined in tradition as the most honored leaders, and repentance was a core value annually emphasized in festivals.

All of this suggests that a quite reflective and coherent view of other cultural options lay behind the self-definition of Judaism. And in any case, it certainly shows that biblical as well as post-Biblical Judaism rested on a normative core by which all forms of non-Jewish and especially Jewish religiosity could be measured.

The rise of folkist definitions of Judaism: How is it that a very different understanding of Judaism has gained currency even among many Jews in the past century? This understanding, especially current in academic treatments of Jewish history, assumes a folkist definition of Judaism and rejects the idea of a normative Judaism that disqualifies other forms. I believe these folkist and anti-traditional views are inseparable from, and directly indebted to, two chief sources: Christian "Old Testament" scholarship and secular, naturalistic, and anti-religious philosophies shaped by an anti-Jewish and anti-Judaic polemic in general Western culture. The two approaches, even if hostile to each other, have agreed on a hostility to Judaism and Jewish self-understanding. We need to have a clear grasp of the source of these views.

As is well-known, the modern secular understanding of biblical religion starts with the early modern polemics of Hobbes, Spinoza, Voltaire, d'Holbach, and other "enlighteners" against Judaism and its Scripture. Several factors operated in this polemic. One was simply the advocacy of egalitarian rationalism, which refused to accept the reality of cultural or ideological differences: all reasonable beings must think the same; therefore, all differences derived from irrational superstitions or dishonorable motives. The persistence of the Jews as a separate culture and society within Western societies was an offense to these thinkers, and they felt that the separatist foundations of Judaism must be undermined.[1] Strongly affecting this was the secularist attempt to replace revelation with the (modern and rational) state or the will of the people as the ultimate

authority. This rendered Judaism by definition a political or folk creation, and its separate persistence a merely social phenomenon, even an arrogance. Hobbes for example, who insisted that the state should have the power to determine its citizens' religious affiliations, included his critique of Scripture in the portion of his work dealing with political theory: he tried to show that the so-called Mosaic Scripture arose from the state to begin with, taking centuries to form—therefore the state had even then the final authority. Lying behind this viewpoint was a third factor affecting the secular understanding of biblical religion: "enlighteners" resented any suggestion that there might be other ways of understanding reality besides naturalistic reason. Here, too, Judaism was seen as a major offense, both in itself and because Christianity, the chief bulwark of medieval institutions, anti-rationalism and religious "superstition," arose from it. What was being attacked, then, was the very idea of "revealed religion" as such. Judaism was the safest target, since it was the religion of a despised minority, even if the implications of the anti-Judaic polemic obviously extended to Christianity as well. It is therefore not too much to claim that the debate about Judaism's definition and the nature of its normative and scriptural authority helped to lay the foundations for modern secularism. It was a momentous controversy.

It is important to realize that although early modern enlighteners wished to protest against traditional revealed religion, many of their ideas were modulations of and resonated with age-old anti-Judaic Christian polemics. This resonance helped strengthen their impact and win them greater acceptance.

For example, a guiding assumption of Christian theologies of redemption is the claim in the Gospels that the Jewish people preferred to worship its own collective self and material well-being rather than God, which is why they crucified Christ and refused to convert to Christianity (cf., John 8:47, Mark 12:1-9, Matt. 27: 25, Rom. 11, etc.). The religion of the Jewish people was thus folkist and particularistic. It consisted not of faithfulness to a transcendental God and the covenant with him but rather of devotion to "the Chosen People" and their worldly power and survival, even in defiance of God.[2]

But, as Hobbes and Spinoza show, something like this folkist explanation could also serve early modern secularists (Jewish or non-Jewish): Spinoza agreed with Hobbes that apart from the universal teachings that any reasonable person (such as himself) could live by without being Jewish, the Mosaic Scriptures chiefly consist of laws to ensure the successful socio-political organization of the Jewish people. These laws, the basis of normative Judaism, were compiled over many centuries and were therefore actually from the later Jewish people or at least their priests. The priests sought thereby to consolidate their own power; as Hobbes had already claimed, perhaps much of "Mosaic" revelation achieved final form at the time of Ezra. To Spinoza, then, the content and purpose of revelation, apart from some elementary universal truths, is oppressively chauvinistic priestly self-preservation and glorification. (Voltaire in turn made this a central theme in his secular anti-Semitism, and it was to echo down through the nineteenth and twentieth centuries in ever fiercer anti-Semitic tracts.)

Indeed, so successful were these ideas that they helped found modern Christian Old Testament scholarship. In another fruitful cross-current, this scholarship is now enshrined in the secular academies as the best authority on the rise of early Judaism. General academic introductions to the period of the Hebrew Bible structure their account around Old Testament research that emerged from Christian divinity school scholarship and agendas. It is precisely because of this that we must investigate that scholarship's assumptions before assessing its helpfulness in defining normative Judaism and before turning to clearly secularist anthropological perspectives.

"Judaism" and Old Testament Scholarship: Of course, as a broad field, many tendencies and viewpoints can be found in Old Testament studies, some more affirmative of Jewish values and others less so, some secularist and others pious. Still, its understanding of the history of Jewish religion and scriptures was deeply shaped both by traditional christian agendas and by the pioneering work of Hobbes, Spinoza, and other anti-Church enlighteners. As is the case with every academic discipline, the basic terminology of Old Testament studies gives important insights into what *Tendenz* underlies the entire field. Thus, it is striking how many terms, including those describing scripture itself, the God, land, people, and religion of ancient Israel are anachronistic and explicitly anti-phenomenological, ignoring and implicitly rejecting Judaism's values and normative self-understandings. Most of these terms first appeared in the context of early Christian theologies of history and polemical self-definition, and thus they are in the first instance Christian-referential. Taken together, they produce a radical de-Judaization of the religion, culture, and even people of ancient Israel, removing Jews and Judaism from their own formative religious history and replacing them with proto-Christians. Nothing like this can be found in the Western academic treatment of any other religion.[3] Judaism and Jewry, in this approach, become a late, degenerate, and perhaps even marginal development in their own tradition, while Christianity emerges as a reform movement reviving the earlier purer prophetic religion. For more liberal Christian scholars, these terms illustrate the evolution of Christianity out of a pagan Israelite religion, from which again Judaism and Jews are a late and questionable offshoot.

The agenda is clear in the very designation of the scriptures of Judaism as the Old Testament, which suggests that they were merely an early stage in the evolution of a clarified revelation and spirituality, leading inexorably to the New Testament. A common alternative designation, "Law," uses a key term from the Pauline epistles. But even Christian scholars acknowledge that this is not an accurate translation of the term found in the Bible itself, namely, *Torah*, which means "Teaching." To insist that Torah means "Law" not in a cosmic but a particularistic and punitive sense (as Paul constantly defines it) goes against the Hebrew and serves a polemic that separates "Law" from "Grace," particularism from universalism, and that attaches the latter in each case to Christianity. Thus it has much the same negative and subordinating implications as "Old Testament." Torah as "Law" sustains the assertion that Judaism is legalistic and priestly, external, socially oriented, and not spiritual or prophetic. Since 1945, some O.T. scholars have started to call their subject the "Hebrew Scriptures," but "Jewish Scriptures" is out of the question—for reasons directly related to our topic.

It is not surprising, then, that the god allegedly worshipped in the Old Testament is not familiar to later Jewry, either. Depending on the reconstruction, the Old Testament portrayed a God of vengeful wrath, and justice, whose nature was later refined in the New Testament's God of love. Alternatively the Jewish scriptures centered on a pagan and even polytheistic divinity, a national god called "Yahweh" allegedly identical to such other national gods as Chemosh of the Moabites. Not incidentally, even the seemingly minor terminological practice in Old Testament studies of constantly referring familiarly to *Yahweh* (not *Elohim*, "God," or even *Adonai*, "Lord"), violating the Ten Commandments' prohibition, bluntly rejects religious Jewish sensitivities and discourages their participation in the discipline.

However, according to Old Testament scholarly terminology, the very people of their study were not really Jews. So the objections of later Jewry are irrelevant. Actually and "objectively," it is said, there were only the "Israelites" or "Hebrews," who are best to be understood in terms of their neighbors—Canaanites, Moabites, Edomites, Babylonians or Egyptians, even modern Arab Bedouins—but not later Jews.

Not only were there no Jews, there was also no "land of Israel," Israel, or Judea that embraced all Israelites until the post-Exilic period. Not even the term "Canaan," used in the Bible, is preferred. The "Israelites" or "Hebrews" instead lived in a land called "Palestine," according to Old Testament scholarly convention. But this term, of later Greek not Hebrew derivation, was applied to Judea by the Romans in the second century C.E. to wipe out the memory of the over 1,400 years of Jewish occupation. It showed Roman hostility to Jewish self-determination, and was

so late and inauthentic the term "Palestine" is not even used in the New Testament itself.[4]

Since the Biblical people were not "Jews," naturally their religion could not be called "Judaism." This would be anachronistic, which is suddenly not acceptable. Instead, they followed "Israelite religion" (terms that also did not exist in pre-Exilic times either). This Israelite religion must have been similar to its neighbors (though strangely they had no Torahs nor Diaspora).[5] It is usually claimed that there was a gradual evolution from paganism to Judaism, contradicting the Torah's account of a radical break that occurred at Sinai. The strength of this consensus, despite the ambiguity or absence of evidence for it, contrasts oddly with the equally strong consensus that radical cultural and religious innovations associated with remarkable personalities certainly occurred in other cases, for example in ancient Greece, or in the rise and development of Christianity itself. (It also contrasts with the near silence in mainstream New Testament scholarship about pagan sources for the distinctive forms of earliest Christianity.) The consensus on gradualism and pagan influences in the case of ancient Israel therefore conforms to deeper paradigms controlling this field.[6]

So Judaism began only after almost the entire Old Testament was finished. It first appears at or following the Babylonian Exile in the sixth century B.C.E., or at the time of Ezra and his disciples of the fifth century, when the Pentateuch allegedly was finally redacted. A few scholars have even claimed that the entire Hebrew Bible is a work of fiction composed in the Hellenistic period.[7] Many add there was no agreed form of Judaism in the Second Commonwealth, so normative Judaism crystallizes fully only in Rabbinic circles around 200 C.E., post-dating Christianity. Thus Christianity is really a "sibling" religion, coeval with Judaism, not its offshoot. Christianity, then, has at least equal claim to represent and continue Israelite religion and the Old Testament.[8]

Most Old Testament scholars, however, still characterize "Judaism" as arising in the post-Exilic period. In consonance with this, it was common until quite recently to speak of "Early Judaism" as arising in Ezra's time but of "Late Judaism" as developed already by the end of the Second Commonwealth period (in "Pharisaism"). In this case, normative "Judaism" had at best only about five hundred years of real vitality. In the schema of many of these scholars, Jesus repudiated this Pharisaic Late Judaism in favor of the prophetic religion it had suppressed. Christianity, accordingly, is the legitimate successor to the prophetic-spiritual current of Israelite religion, a current crushed by Ezra and "Judaism."

None of this can be justified on any solid evidential basis, since even the hard evidence adduced by several generations of Old Testament scholarship need not lead to their conclusions, as just outlined. The radical and artificial separation between pre-Exilic religion and post-Exilic Judaism (and between "priestly Law" and "prophetic faith," etc.) is imposed on the material. The sources much more often depict continuities in these matters than discontinuities. The scriptural record gives the portrait of a single people, an ongoing tradition, and a single religion.

Long before the post-Exilic period, the prophets took for granted that the entire people understood that they had entered into a covenant with God, a covenant that detailed social, moral, and religious norms that applied to the society as a whole. Social legislation was a part of this from the beginning. This covenantal tradition in its fullness, already in the historical narratives and pre-Exilic prophets, called "the Torah of Moses" and "God's Torah" (1 Kings 2:3; 2 Kings 10:31; 14:6; 17:13; 21:8; 23:25; Is. 1:10; 2:3; 5:24; Jer. 8:8; 9:13; 44:23; Hos. 4:6; 8:1; Amos 2:4; etc.) was traced back to Sinai and celebrated in religious festivals. All of this remains the same after Ezra. From the start, the covenant was only with *Y-H-V-H*, by preference called *Adonai* and *Elohim*, to the exclusion of other divinities. This alone was specifically Israel's God. Whether at first henotheistically or otherwise, this God was praised by the prophets and priests as allpowerful creator of the universe, as shown among other things by his power over Assyria and Egypt: he could call upon and

remove his servants from those lands, overwhelming gentile rulers who resisted. That there was Jewish idolatry and assimilation to polytheistic practices emanating from other peoples in and about ancient Israel is emphasized in the Scriptures themselves, so the surprisingly slight archaeological or other evidences for such practices does not contradict the Scriptural version. If anything, it confirms that polytheistic practices were much rarer than the prophets might lead us to believe. That means that, whether pre- or post-Exilic, biblical Judaism is one continuous tradition. And it flows directly into post-biblical Judaism. Normative Judaism, in short, goes back to the early biblical period.

It is important to clarify just what is being claimed here. Samuel Sandmel, in his survey *The Hebrew Scriptures* (New York, 1978), after quoting the remark by "one Jewish scholar . . . that 'the Higher Criticism is higher anti-Semitism,'" goes on to defend Old Testament studies, saying that while some leading scholars in that field were "psychotic Jew-haters," they were few, and (p. 19):

> Higher Criticism is a process, not a conclusion. The discipline itself stands or falls on its rightness or wrongness, not on the personal foibles of its practitioners. . . . To label the Higher Critics anti-Semites is silly. Indeed, a more devastating judgment can be passed on the nineteenth century Higher Critics by demonstrating that their scholarship, however laborious and vaunted, was often shabby and that they were seldom able to rise above their own presuppositions and intellectual biases. Modern biblical scholarship, however, inevitably uses nineteenth-century scholarship as a point of departure. To ignore it is as grievous an error in judgment as never to depart from it.

All this is true. But it is superficial in one crucial respect. It fails to recognize how current understandings are still shaped by the earlier agendas. The issue goes beyond the anti-Semitism of many leading scholars (Sandmel trivializes that as "personal foibles"!). Fortunately, the pervasive anti-Semitism of the nineteenth century and first half of the twentieth century no longer dominates the discipline. The work today is informed by integrity, good will, and often astonishing industry and ingenuity. But most scholars have not and perhaps cannot escape the theological presuppositions laid down by earlier generations, for these presuppositions still provide the underpinnings for the entire discipline and have not really been questioned even today. The denegrating of all terms relating to the Jewish people is too consistent to be conincidental. It is these categories and their assumptions which are anti-Judaic.

The remarks made here do not call into question any particular findings of scholarship in regard to ancient Israel and its religion, insofar as these findings are substantive and not the product of bias. Nevertheless, the continuing acceptance of fundamental categories that de-Judaize the material cast into doubt the good faith of the entire enterprise and its most general conclusions concerning the history and nature of Judaism.

The reduction of religion to a cultural-spiritual style: Another major source of contemporary understandings of the nature of "Judaism(s)" is scholarship driven by a historicistic and relativistic outlook, which tends to reject talk of an underlying Judaism common to diverse historical contexts. Each context, instead, is said to dictate its own "Judaism," so that there are multiple Judaisms, not one overarching form. Of course, in making such a claim, this approach, which boasts a close attention to the actuality of each historical form of Jewish religion, actually denies the chief claim found in every one of them, namely, that each participates in the same transcendental realities and fundamental sources of Judaism that all other forms of Judaism share. Cultural relativism can often produce the antithesis of a phenomenological sensitivity to a group's actual religious interests and claims. But, in any case, the basic assumption of the secularist and relativist approach is that each cultural or spiritual style constitutes its own religion, and, since there have been many cultural-spiritual styles in the history of Judaism, it is concluded that there have been many Judaisms.

But a religion is not a cultural-spiritual style. That is an important component of religion, but by itself it does not constitute any particular religion. In fact, very often the same cultural style in a country or era may affect very different religions, sometimes in clear contradiction to their own basic beliefs and practices. Thus, the history of Judaism indicates that it, like other religions, has been deeply affected by the cultural-spiritual styles of its environment. For example, it is generally accepted that the almost pantheistic asceticism of the twelfth century German Hasidim, so different from the world-affirmations of Talmudic times or of modern Judaism, was strongly affected by a cultural mood dominant in that entire age, which also showed itself in Franciscan Catholicism, Albigensian Gnosticism, and in Sufi Islam. Rabbis in this period often praised other-worldly self-lacerating penitence and exemplary martyrdoms. Similarly, the changing cultural-spiritual style of modern Judaism very closely echoes the wider transformations of the secular-Protestant culture dominant in western lands over the past two centuries. The contemptuous treatment of Kabbalah by German scholars of the nineteenth century versus the reverential treatment of Kabbalah by American, Israeli, and other scholars in the late twentieth century are striking indices of the regnant cultural styles of wider society at those times.

Perhaps the tendency to confuse cultural-spiritual style with religion *per se* and to over-emphasize what are sometimes quite transient folkist understandings is to a degree the result of too uncritical an acceptance of contemporary cultural anthropological approaches to religion. Cultural anthropology has certainly greatly enriched our understanding of religious processes, but here we find the limitations of that approach. Cultural anthropology begins with a reduction of religion and spirituality to socio-cultural dynamics. It does not teach respect for the transcendental referent of religious worship; rather it attempts to supplant this with reference back to the believers themselves. Transcendence disappears in such a reduction. Let us take as an instance Clifford Geertz's justly celebrated definition of religion, which more than most other anthropological theories reaches toward a phenomenological appreciation of the specifically religious element in religion:

> A religion is a system of symbols which acts to establish powerful, pervasive, and long-

lasting moods and motivations in men by formulating conceptions of a general order of existence and clothing these conceptions with such an aura of factuality that the moods and motivations seem uniquely realistic.[9]

This definition replaces reference to reality with references to subjectivities: "conceptions" of existence given an "aura of factuality" that "seem . . . realistic" enough to create "moods and motivations." The subjective effect is the real object of religion, or culture as such. After all, what else could we expect "Religion as a Cultural System" (the title of Geertz's essay) to be? But if cultural moods are the essence of religion, and the specific beliefs, myths, and practices of a particular religion are merely symbols of those cultural moods, what is the difference between ancient Indo-European Zoroastrianism, Manichaeanism, central Asian Buddhism, medieval and modern Iranian Shi'ism? Very little, since the cultural moods and motivations are the same: there is only one Iranian religion despite various names and forms. How can we justly distinguish between German Hasidism, Franciscan Catholicism, and medieval Sufism, since they all share a similar symbolical mood? We cannot.

Or rather: the religions are in fact very different, and their members live for those differences. Each makes of their common mood something distinctive in the whole context of that religion, and the common mood can vanish while the religion continues on practically unchanged, to accommodate other moods or cultural-spiritual styles in other times or places. Geertz himself showed this in a brilliant contrast of the very different Moroccan and Indonesian cultural styles of Islam.[10] In the one cultural area (such as Iran), even the purpose to which the similar mood is put differs in accordance with the religion. Zoroastrianism elevated the farming life to cosmological and salvific dimensions. Manichaeism and Central Asian Buddhism valued celibacy and radical otherworldliness. Contemporary Shi'ite religion in Iran stresses nationalism and military aggression, even terrorism. Moreover, we can find quite different moods or cultural styles in different members of the same community (even sometimes in the same congregation or in the same person at different

times in her or his life). We cannot say that each mood or cultural outlook is a different religion. Religion is more than that. How then, if we want to understand "normative religion," are we to define "religion"?

A phenomenological definition of religion: Joachim Wach offers a useful starting point. His definition has the merit of taking seriously the specifically religious dimension of religion, that is, the realities the believers themselves hold to be central. It also hints at the dialogical way in which religious realities create or define believers, as much as believers create or define religious realities. Religion, to summarize Wach, is the total response to a reality apprehended as ultimate.[11] That reality is not only apprehended as ultimate and supreme but also as the source from which the religious person comes or that bestows identity and meaning. As such, the primal dialogue of self/group with the transcendental source engages and helps shape social, cultural, psychological, philosophical, and every other dimension of human existence, and brings those dimensions into connection with the fundamental realities apprehended as determinative. The term "apprehended" is meant to indicate that the response goes beyond a narrow intellectual belief or social datum: instead the reality is actually experienced as engaging multiple levels of personal and group existence. There are, then, three chief elements to religion: (1) ultimate and supreme reality, (2) those who apprehend this reality, and (3) the specific apprehension itself that engages the other two together in interaction.

Let us apply this to Judaism. The Jewish version of Wach's three chief elements are God, Israel, and the Torah covenant. The reality apprehended is God, the person(s) apprehending this reality is (are) Israel, and the medium and form of this apprehension or dialogue is Torah. Torah, (God's) "Teaching," is the most crucial element and the central pivot of Judaism, for it provides the framework for the interaction of the other two. It also defines the two partners in dialogue. It even presents and is the archetypal dialogue itself. As such it governs all later interactions between God and Israel. The adequacy of a given version of Judaism must be measured by its adherence to this Torah framework for dialogue between God and Israel.

Since this is what defines normative Judaism in the sources that guide each generation, we find that, down through history, all generally accepted forms of Judaism share this framework. This not only constitutes biblical Judaism (without distinction between pre- and post-Exilic forms), but also all post-biblical Judaism. We can go further: those forms that lack some element in this framework may make a claim to be Jewish but fail to persuade other Jews and soon either disappear or cease to be considered, even by their own adherents, Jewish or part of Judaism, the religion constitutive of Jewish identity. Thus the sociological dimension of Judaism ultimately follows the archetypal one, since every Jewish community has its final point of reference in the Torah that presents these archetypes. This is not a theological assertion but a phenomenological and historical one, even if the Torah, which is the touchstone, is a theological text.

The Torah as the core of normative Judaism: At the heart of the Torah is the covenant between God and Israel established at the start of the history of the Jewish people, at Sinai, and celebrated in its festival cycle. The Torah presents and constitutes this covenant in definitive terms.

Accordingly, Judaism arises in the course of a constructive dynamic that constitutes each partner for the other. At Sinai, the God of creation and history entered into a binding covenant with a "mixed multitude" who, through this covenant alone, became an actual and real people, the people Israel. Only through this covenant can Israel be a "blessing for the nations of the world." Without the covenant, as the Torah and the later prophets ceaselessly reiterate, Israel again disintegrates into a mixed multitude enslaved to the idolatries of the surrounding cultures. This means that Israel's essential identity is located in its covenant. The Torah consists not only of teachings about creation and the primal history of humanity, thus justifying the role of the people Israel, but it also elaborates this covenant into a vision of an entire society, indicating how the people Israel should comport itself in ethics, cult, and legal traditions. The explicitly nor-

mative commandments thereby create an entire society that is to be a "kingdom of priests." These commandments flesh out the covenant and constitute the people as the people of the covenant.

Such an understanding does not require us to posit that the Torah as we have it was all literally revealed at Sinai. It is quite possible to accommodate to this view the better established results of scholarship regarding the evolution of the Torah's text. For even if we suppose that the Torah as we have it took centuries to crystallize, the covenant is assumed even by Israel's earliest writings, and all the prophets certainly take for granted such a covenant with the entire Jewish people. The fact that they did not need to explain to their audience in much detail the basis of their appeals and demands shows that all understood their ancient covenantal context as axiomatic. The antiquity of the Sinai experience is also strikingly borne out by the festival cycle, which is structured as a single symbolic whole centered on the covenant. Although this was not adequately understood by earlier scholarship, even the number of days between the festivals testifies to their derivation at Sinai: they correspond exactly to the numbers of days that, according to the Torah, separate the crucial events of Exodus and revelation, stretching over some seven months. The annual cycle recapitulates and re-presents the Exodus-Sinai covenantal history precisely as given in the Mosaic books. This means the Torah did not reinterpret already fixed Canaanite folk celebrations piece-meal over many centuries. On the contrary, Israel's salvation-history provided their basic framework from the start.[12] In any case, as written down and crystallized in the Five Books of Moses, the Torah is Israel's covenant writ large, and it is this Scripture that will forever define both parties to the covenant, God and Israel.

As presented in the Torah, the revelation at Sinai is nothing less than the culmination of all history up to that point, the very purpose and fulfillment of the creation of the universe. It has truly ultimate status. No form of religion can be Judaism if this covenant-Torah and what follows from it for God and Israel are not given central authority.

We now turn to the "Israel" part of normative Judaism. It is necessary to underline that the covenant demands to be actualized within a real people. The people "Israel" is not in the first instance a metaphor or spiritual simile. It is a real people, which is why the commandments given at Sinai structure the civil and political structures of a society, not just individual pieties. This society, Israel, must be given its own land in which to live, the land of Israel, which is why entry into the land must follow after acceptance of Torah at Sinai. The land is also not first of all a symbol but a political reality. The prophets made their appeals to an entire society, calling not for individual reformation alone but above all for a more general social renewal. It is also because of this reality of an actual people in an actual land that Exile can take on such powerful meaning in later Judaism and that the hope for messianic peace builds explicitly on the restoration of the people to their land.

It is also because a real and actual people is involved that the Torah must from the start deal with the fact that not all Israel will be faithful to the covenant. This question of what to make of apostasy and falling away into the religious practices of surrounding cultures arises in the foundation era of the covenant itself, and the answers given there control later Jewish ways of dealing with internal diversities. The Torah presents a way not of sectarian extremes but of responsibility for a whole people. That is why the later prophets persist in addressing the entire people and their kings. They do not focus on an elite or the solitary contemplative. An entire people must be brought together in common responsibilities. This people was created by the Torah but once created takes its place among and is affected by other peoples. An ambivalent status of holy and profane therefore attaches to the people: when they live up to the covenant, they are truly a kingdom of priests and a chosen people (*am segulah*, treasured people); when they do not, they may be chastised by God even more strictly than non-Jews. Not every religious, ethical, or social practice of Jews can be called Jewish. The Torah is not a folkist document, to use our earlier terminology. But it addresses a folk and participates in their history. Even if individuals or groups fall away into the practices of the surrounding cultures, as the Torah says they will, they remain in some way part of the people Israel, sinners within the wider society of Israel. This conception of a faithful core and an errant periphery still tied to the core has extraordinarily important consequences for later understandings of Judaism and the Jewish people.

The historians and later priestly and prophetic writers whose works fill so many pages of the Hebrew Scriptures for the most part develop the implications of the normative core described here as already present in the Sinai covenant. They seek to show the validation of its clauses in the twists and turns of the post-Sinai history of Israel. The prophets apply the covenantal framework to the history of their own time and further elaborate on how the past promises will be fulfilled in a future messianic restoration of the people to their land, following the people's true repentance and reform. This does not modify the Sinai covenant or religion but merely supplements it, confirming its continuing centrality and application.

The distinction between foundation and superstructure: These are some of the chief characteristics of the normative structure of Judaism. One might suppose that because the covenant deals with all aspects of life, including the family, festivals, civil law, and priestly rituals, the forms the religion can take must be very limited. This impression, as history confirms, is mistaken. Rather, the normative core provides a firm foundation and a framework on which many different superstructures can be built. If we say that the normative structures provide a house within which Jews can live their Judaism, we still have many possibilities for how many floors there shall be, what the walls and ceiling will look like, what kind of roof will cover it all, and even how the façade will look. Ornamentation and extensions might be added or even whole wings. But these do not change the underlying structure even if they obscure it.

In fact, it is precisely due to faithful adherence to the underlying structure of tradition that the variations in superstructure occur. Were Judaism not to be faithfully practiced as a living religion, there would be no change in its contours. The same piety that insists on loyalty to the ancestral heritage guarantees its constant adaptation. The antithesis between continuity and change is in many ways a false one.

> There is an old story of an ax that had been in a family for many generations. Each generation inherited the axe, used it, and, as a cherished family heirloom, passed it along to the next generation. Recently, an old drawing of the ax was discovered, showing it as it had been originally. To the surprise of the current owners, the original was much smaller, perhaps one-half the size of what it is now, and with a smaller blade as well. Other records indicated that in the past two hundred years, the ax handle had been replaced ten times and the blade five times.[13]

Precisely because the ax continued to be used in actual life in devoted faithfulness to the functional role it played in former generations, it changed its outward form. Only if it had been put aside and never used would the axe have remained "precisely the same" as it had been formerly. If it had been put on a shelf to be worshipped together with the ancestors, or if it had been put into a museum, then it would have stayed superficially exactly the same axe for centuries. But in actuality, it would have ceased to be the family's axe and instead would have become an artifact of earlier ages, not this one, referring to the dead, not the living. Different outward forms over time thus need not mean that the normative core ceases to exist. The opposite may be true.

Applying these criteria, it will be seen that Ethiopian, Sadducean, and Karaite Judaism all conform to normative Judaism, as does, of course, Rabbinic Judaism. These forms of Judaism differ precisely because each has sought to be faithful to and to apply the normative core to their lives and environments. Naturally, divergences arise in different historical settings, reflecting the lives and real interactions involved. But all of them accept the three basic elements and make them the center of their religion and practice. Only the superstructure elaborates this differently. Rabbinic leaders, who created the historically dominant understand-

ing of Judaism, might cast doubt on the correctness of the other groups' Jewish observance and might set up barriers to marriage into them, but not even this has been consistent. In all three cases, the barriers to marriage generally proved to be permeable. Members of these groups were judged even by the rabbis to be part of the Jewish people, recipients of the commonly shared Torah, and therefore participants in the same religion. And these groups granted the same status to Rabbinic Jews, accepting that they shared a common heritage and peoplehood. The richness of Judaism in history arises from the faithfulness of Jews to the shared normative core.

Is Christianity a normative successor to biblical Judaism? Examples of borderline cases will clarify things and indicate the importance of the distinctions made above. Each is border-line in a different way. Our examples will be Christianity, Samaritanism, and Yiddishism. Each has been claimed to be a legitimate inheritor of biblical Judaism. Christianity is of course a distinct religion, with major indebtedness to Judaism but also many differences from it; Samaritanism is much more similar to Judaism and has had a much more ambiguous history of relationships with it; and Yiddishism may stand for the many forms of secular Jewish ideologies that have sprung up in the modern period, which some Jews have asserted are as much "Judaism" as traditional piety.

We take up Christianity first. At issue is how far we can distinguish Christianity from Judaism, either in Christianity's early forms or in the guise of "Messianic Judaism" or "Jews for Jesus" today. Is Christianity perhaps even a "sibling" of Rabbinic Judaism, with equal claim to inherit earlier biblical Judaism? Applying our criteria, the answer is clear. Christianity in none of its forms qualifies as either Judaism or its "sibling." While deeply indebted to biblical Judaism, Christianity so changes each of the three basic elements of normative Judaism that it is rightly viewed as a different religion.

First of all, the God is very different, a triune divinity, and one of the three modalities is a divine human being, something inconceivable within normative Judaism. The transcendent God found in the "Old

Testament," who created the universe, formed Israel, and bestowed the Torah, is generally identified by Christians with only one modality of the triune God, the one termed "God the Father," and God the Father has only secondary importance compared with God the Son, who became a human being, "died," and then was resurrected so as to become a universal savior. In this modality, God is allegedly revealed for the first time, or in perfected form, as filled with grace, love, and compassion, in contrast to the Old Testament God.

Salvation, according to Christianity, can be attained not through belief in God the Father alone, nor even in following the Torah commandments, but only through accepting Jesus Christ, God the Son, and acknowledging the atoning effect of his crucifixion and resurrection in divine form. Only then is there a saving experience of God the Holy Spirit. From a traditional Jewish perspective, all this is totally alien. There are no dying-and-rising gods, no divine humans, in the Torah. If we look for antecedents, however, it is evident that such a conception of God would have seemed natural within the pagan religions all around ancient Israel. Divinization of human beings was commonplace. Moreover, these religions were increasingly being refined into philosophical monotheism and had long known as their central revivifying drama the cycle of the dying and rising god.[14] It is significant that the mystery of the Mass, in which Christ via his death becomes wafer and wine, providing congregants a feast on the divine body through which eternal life is shared, has no parallels in Jewish ritual. Indeed, drinking any kind of blood and eating human flesh, whether actually or symbolically, or partaking of God in a feast, would be repugnant to Jewish values as laid down in the Torah. But the Mass shares a family resemblance with the central rituals of the mysteries of Isis and Osirus, of Demeter and Persephone, of Dionysius (who lives again in the wine), and of Mithras. Furthermore, until the Protestant Reformation, almost all Christians added to or associated with their incarnate but triune God the Virgin Mary, whose images were vehicles for prayer to her and worship.

Prayer to her was on a different, lower level of divinity from the Trinity, though higher than prayer to the saints. All of these phenomena quite obviously differ from the normative Torah view of God. In Christianity, then, we find an evident synthesis of pagan and Jewish ideas about God. This was explicitly asserted to be a novel revelation and essential to the "New" Covenant that bound Christians together. Only adherence to this new Covenant "saves."

Thus the view of Torah is also different from that of Judaism. The Torah in its fuller sense as Hebrew Scriptures is no longer the central framework within which all dialogue with God is conducted. Instead, the Torah is associated with another scripture, the "New Testament," just as in the Trinity the Jewish God is associated with a different kind of divinity. In both cases, the Jewish version becomes subordinated to the Christian one, which takes center stage. The "New Covenant" perfects, fulfills, and supplants the old Covenant at Sinai. Therefore the Torah's commandments, which flow from life with God, are no longer valid or efficacious. The age of Torah-piety is past. Christ came to free humanity from the "curse" of the Law, as also from sin and death: the antitheses are related together both by Paul and the later Church. This does not mean that "the Law" is to be entirely dismissed, according to Paul, for it was a necessary preliminary to the fuller revelation of the New Testament and still offers guidance and inspiration. Christian Jews might perhaps still hold to it (although Paul himself only does so among Jews, the better to win them over), but gentiles absolutely must not. They should not convert to it or become Jews. They should rather become members of a different group, that is, Christians.

In the light of this, we cannot be surprised that the third element of normative Judaism is also transformed: the people Israel. The New Testament makes much of breaking out of the concept of a particular people into a universal church (e.g., Gal. 3:28). The new Christian community is not part of the "children of Israel according to the flesh" (Rom. 9:8, cf., 8:3-9) but constitutes the "spiritual children of Israel," a community that rapidly becomes almost entirely gentile. This is seemingly an oxymoron: a gentile Israel? Nevertheless, Paul tells us, a gentile branch has been grafted onto the old tree trunk of Israel, establishing a universal community to which everyone must belong if they wish to be saved (Rom. 11:17-20; Gal. 3:29): this and this alone is the Christian "Israel" that will be rewarded by the messianic blessings promised in the Torah. The true Israel is a symbolic, transnational, cultic Church, not a real people, and it therefore must accept and accommodate the diverse social structures and laws of gentile nations. The old Israel, the Jewish people, insofar as it retains its integrity and its loyalty to the Torah and its God and refuses to merge with the Church community, may even be considered "enemies" of God (Rom. 11:28, but, cf., 11:11). It is the recipient of the old curses against errant Israel, while the universal Israel receives the blessings. The Jewish people are guilty of knowingly killing the messiah (Matt. 27:24-25; Luke 23; John 8: 37-44, 18:19-23, etc.): they are like greedy tenants who conspire together to murder the owner's son but by this lose their right to the vineyard (Matt. 21:33-46; Mark 12:1-12; Luke 20:9-19). The Christian "spiritualization" of Israel abolishes the need for a messianic restoration of Jews to the land of Israel. The home of Israel could be universalized and relocated in Rome, at the heart of the Roman Empire, or at Byzantium. In the End of Days, the last survivors of the Jewish people, the Old Israel, will convert and join the New Israel of the spirit. But, then, they shall be Christians of course.

We have, on the one hand, the one God, the actual Jewish people, and the Torah as the framework for their dialogue, in normative Judaism, and, on the other hand, in normative Christianity, a triune God who includes a dying-and-rising Christ, a gentile Church claiming to be the true, spiritual Israel, and a New Testament with Old Testament preliminaries as the framework for Church-God dialogue. The two religions clearly have different frameworks. They are not siblings, nor can it be said that Christianity arises out of but remains true to the framework of normative Judaism, whether biblical or post-biblical.

This conclusion throws light on the much debated issue of why and when Christianity became a distinct and separate religion. Many Christian scholars have assumed that the cause cannot be in Christianity, for it supposedly emerged organically and authentically out of Jewish religion. The separation, then, was brought about by Jewish persecution of Christians, as evidenced, for example, in the *birkat ha-minim*, the blessing against sectarians added to the worship service by the rabbis.[15] This assumes that without this "rejection," there would have been no separate Christian religion at all. But the logic of our discussion is that this was always impossible. The difference of Christianity from normative Judaism was too radical and too basic. A breakaway of Christians was inevitable, for internal Christian reasons. Paul, the final gentile additions to Matthew, and the Gospel of John all make this clear. If the Christian sectarians had really wanted to continue Judaism, and the supposed anathema had actually occurred, they could have formed their own synagogues and as such stayed Jewish sectarians. But they did not choose to do so, for good reasons. Instead they insisted on the distinctiveness of the new salvific doctrine and community of the "New Covenant," which excluded Jews and Judaism.

These comments do not apply to the Jamesian community in Jerusalem, whose main difference from other forms of Pharisaic Judaism seems to have been a conviction that the messiah had already arrived. Different opinions on the identity of the messiah have never been sufficient to violate the three basic elements in normative Judaism. Of course, the Jamesian community apparently did not believe that Jesus was God or that the Torah covenant was superseded, either of which would have put them outside of normative Judaism.

Samaritanism and normative Judaism: The Samaritans form another special case. While Christianity clearly changes all of the essential elements of normative Judaism, Samaritanism at first glance changes none. That is, it affirms the same God, as delineated in the same Torah, and acknowledges the same people. Yet appearances are not necessarily correct. After all, the Samaritan Torah is not quite the same: there are some three thousand divergences in it from the Jewish Torah. While these are mostly minor, the most crucial of them declares Shechem, not Jerusalem, the holy center of proper worship. As a consequence, the people of the covenant could be understood to be quite separate from the Jews. This crucial difference between the two communities eventually became decisive. It is relevant that 2 Kings 17 asserts that the Assyrians settled other peoples in the former kingdom of Israel, in Samaria, and these polytheists sought to placate "the god of the land," namely Israel's God. The Samaritans themselves are alleged to confess their alien parentage (Ezra 4:2; see also 4:8-10 and the possible Samaritan self-definition as non-Jews at 4:12). Whether or not this is factual, it is important that the Bible distinguishes Jews and Samaritans, suggesting that the Samaritans at first even misunderstood Israel's God. This means that in Samaritanism, all three essential elements—Torah, people, and possibly God—are modified.

The question of whether these modifications are so significant as to create a distinct religion was not answered definitively for many centuries. There has always been an ambiguity recognized by other Jews to the separate status of the Samaritans, even after the split became open and formal (probably in the second century B.C.E., the result of a war between Samaritans and Jews).[16] Although the separate status of their religion was affirmed, and notwithstanding continuing political, cultural, and other tensions, including warfare, positive statements about their piety can be found in the Talmud and later Rabbinic literature. The agreement of both the Jewish and the Samarian authorities that the Samaritans are a separate people placed them definitively outside of Judaism. But because they for the most part followed the same Torah, the communities never were seen as entirely unrelated. There remains a certain ambiguity to Samaritan status even today, and the Samaritans have accepted some intermarriage with Jews in Israel, although they are much less open to intermarriage with Muslims and Christians.

Yiddishism and normative Judaism: The case of Yiddishism is much easier. Like normative Judaism, Yiddishism includes a cultural world-view and way of life, and it defines "a new people Israel, this one a component in the united working people of the world."[17] But each of these differs from the essential elements in normative Judaism, namely, God (rather than a naturalistic or atheistic "world-view"), Torah (rather than a folkist eastern European "way of life"), and Israel (rather than the eastern European Jewish strand of the world proletariat). In Yiddishism, we find more of a cultural/spiritual folk style than with a religion *per se*. The "scientific socialist modernity" it espouses is generally understood by its advocates to be vehemently hostile to all religion, including Judaism. We might wish, despite this, to characterize the socialist outlook as a religion, but, if so, it is a different religion from Judaism, with a different set of adherents.

It has been argued that Judaism is not really a religion either: the very idea of Judaism as a religion emerged, according to this argument, from "a peculiarly nineteenth century and Protestant view of matters. . . . But that conception . . . imposes on Jews categories alien to their diverse historical cultural expressions."[18] These points correctly characterize certain aspects of the general contemporary understanding of religion. But their force in regard to Judaism is to a degree vitiated by the age-old Jewish insistence that God is the source of and is central to everything normative in the tradition, that from God, Torah and Israel gain their identities, and that all three together structure Jewish beliefs, practices and rituals, and Jewish peoplehood. These affirmations are not nineteenth century Protestant inventions but are authentic Judaic teachings common to all forms of Judaism up to the present time. When it exorcises God, and with God, of necessity the Torah, Yiddishism ceases to be part of normative Judaism, and this was recognized by the leading Yiddishists themselves.

Yet this does not mean that Yiddishists can escape the umbrella of Judaism, at least insofar as the teachings of normative Judaism are concerned. They remain "Jews" and share the fate and vocation of Israel, according to the normative Judaism that they themselves reject. Precisely because they cannot create their own Judaism, nor write their own Torah, they are impotent before the foundational sources of Judaism and its normative definitions. Those sources impute an identity that transcends even the Yiddishists own self-determination. And so we find that both Jews and non-Jews view Yiddishists within the larger Judaic context, often to the Yiddishists' own intense frustration. If there really were as many Judaisms as there are groups made up of Jews, or opinions held by individual Jews, the inability of any one group of Jews to actualize its own separate self-definition would be more of a puzzle than it is. This helps explain why groups of Jews who reject the foundational elements of Judaism have ended up either entirely fading away, or at least, being lost to Judaism and the Jewish people. This contrasts sharply with the astonishing tenacity of normative Judaism in its various forms.

Conclusion: A great deal is gained by the definition of normative Judaism outlined here. First and most important, it takes seriously what Jewish sources themselves say, and what Jews who have held to those sources have said in every form of Judaism up to (and including) the modern age. This approach, that is, is phenomenological rather than reductionistic. As such, it rejects definitions of Judaism that reflect alien and sometimes anti-Judaic agendas, whether Christian theological or secular relativist. Second, by virtue of the phenomenological approach, we can take seriously the transcendentalist, prophetic, book-centered, and reformist aspects of Judaism in a way that folkist, relativistic, and reductionistic definitions cannot.

Third, this approach reveals what all forms of Judaism hold in common. Ethiopian Judaism, Karaite Judaism, and Rabbinic Judaism are viewed as modalities of "normative Judaism." The same holds for contemporary forms, such as Orthodoxy, Conservatism, and liberal Judaism. Each must justify itself to the others in terms of the basic normative Judaism they all share. Our approach also demonstrates that fervent piety itself must lead to change (and divergence) in the superstructure of Judaism over time, without abandoning normative Judaism. The forms are divergent *because* of loyalty to normative Judaism. This is impor-

tant. It would be ironic if the very loyalty of Jews to Judaism and its ongoing vitality and persistence in different situations and ages were to be made evidence that there is no such thing as Judaism but only Judaisms.

Fourth, this approach allows us to understand how even Jews who follow non-Judaic forms of piety can be part of Judaism. The Torah sets at least some of the ground-rules for how to view diverse approaches to Judaism, so that this is part of the normative structure of Judaism itself. The primal Jewish sources explicitly critique folkist and paganist tendencies but nevertheless insist that all Jews are "Israel" and remain within the overarching community we call "Judaism" even if their own practice is idolatrous and not Judaism at all. The Torah therefore makes a distinction between what individual Jews acknowledge as their own religion and the religion mandated in the covenant; individual Jews may be part of Torah Judaism despite disaffiliating with it. The Israel of normative Judaism is genuinely a people, not a cultic community alone. This has the consequence that every variety of normative Judaism must acknowledge its continuing connection with the whole Jewish people for good or ill, even if other paths and Jews may be characterized as in error. Purely sectarian definitions of Judaism are discouraged, and if groups based on such definitions should arise, it is part of their schismatic logic (and redefinition of the people Israel) that if the groups are viable at all, they would soon be lost to Judaism and will cease to be seen as forms of Judaism. Perhaps this is what happened with early Christianity. Jewish identity thus is not simply a matter of religious affirmation or of self-determination; it is also an objective socio-religious category, reflecting the existence of an ongoing people.

A further advantage of this definition of normative Judaism is to make clear what Judaism is not, thus helping to resolve the egregious confusion over whether Christianity, for instance, is a form of Judaism. It also dissolves the fuzzy but common idea that merely ethnic affiliation or ethical behavior is all there really is to Judaism. A clear answer is given as well to the relativism especially seductive and commonplace among western Jews, which treats as Judaism anything anyone likes to affirm.

Finally, this definition highlights areas worthy of study when considering Jewish religious movements. Obviously, the ways the common elements of normative Judaism are articulated help distinguish various movements in the history of Judaism. But it is important to recognize also the common elements, so that we remain clear that we are dealing with an ongoing conversation about things transcending any particular time and place, the history of Judaism as it engages with universal concerns, and not the history of Judaisms, each limited to a particular period with its own situation, and its own group. That all movements share ideas about God, Torah, and peoplehood, and, as a result, generally celebrate the same festivals and even pray the same prayers is an essential datum. Each group sees itself within the fabric of the whole, as part of generations of Jews. Each sees itself as engaged on behalf of all Israel and even on behalf of humanity in general with universal and transcendental realities, which we tend to ignore when we relativize each group. A phenomenological understanding starts with the universals and the transcendental issues important to every religious Jew, in every age. Within that context, it is fascinating to see how different cultural-spiritual styles can arise and develop, producing qualitatively different ways of being Jewish. It is important to appreciate the enormous diversity possible in, as well as the clear normative limits of, the Judaic tradition. This speaks of the richness of that tradition. As in all great poetry, the most creative is spun out from the restraints of the normative structure, as that structure is brought into relationship with the realities of life.

Notes

[1] As Arthur Hertzberg has suggested, drawing on Jacob Talmon's research, the emphatically anti-Jewish themes in the "totalitarian democracy" advocated in the Enlightenment period were central enough to continue to be major obsessions in many modern forms of totalitarianism, both fascist and communist. See his *The French Enlightenment and the Jews: The Origins of Modern Anti-Semitism* (New York, 1970), pp. 363f. On Spinoza and his predecessor Hobbes, see Leo Strauss, *Spinoza's Critique of Religion*, trans. E.M.

Sinclair (New York, 1965). For a good analysis of the anti-Semitism of the most "liberal" Enlightenment figures, such as Goethe, Dohm, and Herder, see Isaac Eisenstein-Barzilay, "The Jew in the Literature of the Enlightenment," in A.G. Duker and M. Ben-Horin, eds., *Emancipation and Counter-Emancipation: Selected Essays from Jewish Social Studies* (New York, 1974), pp. 90-115.

[2] A memorable instance of this outlook is Martin Noth, *The History of Israel* (New York, 1960). His influential theory of the non-Sinaitic, Canaanitic source of Israel's religion leads directly to his conclusion (or starting point?) that the end of the history of Israel was signaled when the Jewish people rejected Jesus (i.e., universalism) and rose in a purely "national" rebellion against Rome (see his final chapter). The diaspora and Israel after 70 C.E. hardly exist in Noth's history.

[3] On the other hand, it is interesting to see how often western treatments of non-western religions have used the same triumphalist constructs first created to distort and Christianize the history of Judaism.

[4] David Jacobson, "When Palestine Meant Israel," in *Biblical Archaeology Review*, 27, no. 3 (May/June, 2001), pp. 42-47, 57, suggests that "Palestine" originally referred to *palaistês*, Greek for "wrestler," i.e., the equivalent of the Hebrew *Yisrael*, "God-wrestler." Josephus, Jacobson says, is the first author in antiquity to clearly link the name Palestine with the Philistines. Herodotus even asserts that the people of *Palaistinê* are circumcised—but the Philistines were uncircumcised.

[5] Julius Wellhausen bluntly insisted on this equivalence, as cited approvingly, by Robert Goldenberg, *The Nations That Know You Not* (Albany, 1998), p. 113, n. 20. As his title indicates, Goldenberg presents a negative view of his topic, to such a degree that he does not even discuss the two Biblical books that chiefly involve non-Jews, Job and Jonah, which assume a very different view of other cultures from that of his title.

[6] An excellent example of the alleged dichotomy between Israelite religion and Judaism is Johannes Pedersen's celebrated *Israel: Its Life and Culture* (London, 1926-1948): on the one side, we see the at least quasi-pagan and noble Arab-like Hebrews or Israelites, on the other—after the Babylonian Exile—the resentful, legalistic, particularistic Jews. At that point, Pedersen descends into anti-Semitic stereotype. This text is worth singling out as a still warmly regarded and studied classic and because it pretends to present a purely phenomenological and even philological analysis of the cultural history of ancient Israel. See similarly John Bright, *A History of Israel* (Philadelphia, n.d. [1959]), pp. 323, 413ff., 431, etc.

[7] For criticism of these "revisionists" on behalf of the consensus, see the strongly worded William G. Dever, "Save Us From Postmodern Malarky," in *Biblical Archaeological Review*, 26, no. 2 (March/April, 2000), pp. 28-69.

[8] So, for example, James H. Charlesworth, an author of unquestionable good will towards Judaism, has argued in his contributions to

H. Charlesworth, ed., *Jews and Christians: Exploring the Past, Present and Future* (New York, 1990). This idea even has been taken up by some Jewish scholars, e.g., Hayyim Goren Perelmuter, *Siblings: Rabbinic Judaism and Early Christianity at Their Beginnings* (New York, 1989).

[9] Clifford Geertz, "Religion as a Cultural System," in Michael Banton, ed., *Anthropological Approaches to the Study of Religion* (London, 1966), pp. 1-46, esp. p. 4. That symbols are basic to religion is surely correct, but the tendency to dismiss the actual referents of the symbols, what they mean for those who use them, and instead to stress the effects of these meanings on the believers, is at the root of the distortion we are here commenting on. Anthropologists (and other reductionists) patronize in their claim that they know better than the subjects themselves what the subjects mean by their words.

[10] Clifford Geertz, *Islam Observed* (New Haven, 1968).

[11] Joachim Wach, *The Comparative Study of Religion*, Joseph M. Kitagawa, ed., (New York, 1958), pp. 48-49 and *passim*.

[12] See my "Calendar of Judaism," in *The Encyclopaedia of Judaism*, vol. 1, pp. 32-50.

[13] M. Ethan Katsh, *The Electronic Media and the Transformation of Law* (Oxford, 1989), p. 3.

[14] Note that Ezek. 8:14 takes for granted that "weeping for Tammuz," a part of the Babylonian cult of a dying-and-rising god, is antithetical to Judaism. Cf., Jonathan Z. Smith, who argues against the consensus of previous scholarship that there was no dying-and-rising god complex in antiquity ("Dying and Rising Gods," in Mircea Eliade, ed., *The Encyclopedia of Religion* (New York, 1986), vol. 4, pp. 521-527). The claim is not persuasive. The Eleusinian mysteries, the Dionysian mysteries, and those of Attis, Mithras, and Cybele all explicitly pivot in one modulation or another around life's springing from death and eternal life attained through a bloody divine sacrifice. These were the most prevalent cults throughout the Roman world. Smith does not discuss the mystery cults in his survey. Nevertheless, their common stress on dying-and-rising gods means that they had to share a common indebtedness to earlier religious cults. We find their roots in Egypt, Asia Minor, Syria, and Mesopotamia.

[15] There was, however, no such anathema against Christianity in the *birkat ha-minim*. See Reuven Kimelman, "*Birkat Ha-Minim* and the Lack of Evidence for an Anti-Christian Jewish Prayer in Late Antiquity," in A.L. Baumgarten, et al., eds., *Jewish and Christian Self-Definition, vol. 2: Aspects of Judaism in the Graeco-Roman Period* (London, 1981), pp. 226-244.

[16] For a good overview of early relations and the split between the two religions, with bibliography, see Menachem Mor, "The Persian, Hellenistic and Hasmonean Period," in Alan Crown, ed., *The Samaritans* (Tübingen, 1989), pp. 1-18.

[17] Jacob Neusner, "Socialism-Yiddishism, Judaism and," in *The Encyclopaedia of Judaism*, vol. 3, pp. 1332-1342; cf., esp. pp. 1332f. and 1340f.

[18] Ibid., p. 1340. The claim that the very category of "religion" is a late medieval European Christian invention was forcefully made in Wilfrid Cantwell Smith, *The Meaning and End of Religion* (New York, 1963). Even Smith himself sometimes tends to reduce actual religions to "faiths," but we can be sure that Judaism was much more than that. This does not mean however that it was less than that!

EVAN ZUESSE

R

RABBINIC JUDAISM, SOCIAL TEACHING OF:

Israel forms God's kingdom on earth. Israelites in reciting the Shema ("Hear O Israel, the Lord our God, the Lord is One") accept the yoke of the kingdom of heaven and the yoke of the commandments, twice daily. That liturgical premise comes to realization throughout diverse halakhic formations. The basic theological conception concerning the kingdom of heaven is familiar and common to a number of Judaic religious systems, not only the Rabbinic. But for Rabbinic Judaism to be "Israel" means to live in God's kingdom, under God's rule, in a very particular way. It is the way that is set forth in the Torah, the written part as mediated by the oral part ultimately transcribed in the Mishnah-Tosefta-Yerushalmi-Bavli and related external traditions. That imperative addresses not individuals alone or mainly but, rather, corporate Israel, that is, the entire social order. It encompasses not merely feelings or attitudes but registers in the here of tangible transactions and the now of workaday engagements, not only in some distant time. The entire system of the halakhah of Rabbinic Judaism constitutes a practical response to Scripture's pronouncement: "You [plural] shall be holy, for I the Lord your God am holy" (Lev. 19:2). The halakhah in well-crafted, cogent category-formations spells out in vast detail what it means to form an abode for the indwelling God, creator of heaven and earth.

In the halakhic system, these theological affirmations, realized in practical law, make a tangible, palpable difference in the affairs of ordinary Israelites. We must therefore ask how a system for the social order, in very practical terms of conduct, not merely spiritual terms of aspiration, can accommodate the presence and intervention of God. That is a question especially because the very essence of a social order is regularity, order, proportion, stability, and certain reliability. God's sentient, effective presence, from beyond corporate Israel, then intervenes and interferes in that otherwise steady structure: charisma breaking into routine, so to speak.

The social teaching of Rabbinic Judaism takes up the narrative of the Torah and recasts it into an account of the norms of Israel's social order. Its recapitulation of the Torah's story regulates relationships between Israelites and corporate Israel, among Israelites in their units of propagation and production, and between corporate Israel and the ever-present, always-sentient God. The details coalesce to yield a clear picture of an entire social order, its relationships and its points of stability and order. To treat any detail apart from its larger context is to miss its point. That point is, Rabbinic Judaism undertakes to realize in the everyday and here and now of the Jews' communal existence the imperatives set forth in the Torah for the formation of God's abode on earth.

The Three Social Teachings of Rabbinic Judaism: Judaism sets forth three principal social teachings, which encompass the social thought of Rabbinic Judaism as categorically embodied by the halakhah in norms of public conduct. They concern the principal parts of the social order, in secular language, how they are defined, how they function, how they relate and cohere. These are as follows:

(1) the society viewed whole and in its constituents;
(2) the relationships within the society between its principal parts; and
(3) the setting of the society in the larger context of cosmos and history.

So we ask about how the social teachings afford recognition to the individual within the corporate society; how they mediate conflict between the smallest whole categorical aggregates of the Israelite social order; and how they embody the social results and effects of the conviction that God is everywhere present within Israelite society, through all of its transactions. Rules embody doctrines that hold together in topic and in proposition and in generative conception. In secular terms, that yields sociology, politics, and culture. But this is no secular system.

Important components of the halakhah viewed within the halakhic native categories contain the design of the relationships of individual to community, among the smallest social aggregates of that society; the Israelite households, among the intermediate aggregates; and between the entirety of corporate Israel and every Israelite, all together and one by one, and the ever-present God, for the largest. These three groups of native category-formations define the program. They supply its contents. They form the three teachings of Rabbinic Judaism about Israel's social order. It is a holy order, where the ubiquitous, commanding God enforces, but also is bound by, the rules he has given to shape that order. Marked by regularity and reliability, it is a society of proportion and order. It restores and maintains the stability of society partly through balances effected by humans, partly through interventions on the part of God. And it is a society so constructed as to afford a place worthy of God's perpetual presence. It aims at constructing out of Israelite society a suitable abode for God.

Genesis Rabbah I:1 teaches that God looked into the Torah and created the world in accord with the design found there. The Rabbinic sages looked into the Torah and created Israel as defined by the social teaching of Rabbinic Judaism. God's was a creative reading, and so was theirs.

Corporate Israel and the Individual Israelite: The Individual Finds Being within Corporate Israel, a Whole that Exceeds the Sum of the Parts: Rabbinic Judaism places corporate Israel at the apex of world and social order. It is a unique social entity, because it forms a society that, as a whole, bears moral responsibility before God for its condition and conduct. No other social entity ("nation," "people") compares. That is because Israel assembled collectively at Sinai and stated unanimously, in one voice, in response to God's self-manifestation in the Torah given by God to Moses, "We shall do and we shall obey." Individuals in that context are responsible for their own actions, but also for those of the community, Israel. And the entire community bears responsibility for the conduct of everyone in its midst. That is what defines its character as a moral actor, a moral entity without counterpart in humanity. That is why corporate Israel forms a whole that exceeds the sum of the parts. The parts, the individuals, attain individuation only on the terms dictated by the whole, "all Israel" viewed from God's perspective. Israel defines God's stake in humanity, as Scripture's narrative makes clear.

To corporate Israel the individual Israelite is subordinated. That is for taxic reasons to begin with: the one is a genus and unique, the other is a species of a genus. Thus in the hierarchical classification of the social order, the community of Israel is primary and autonomous, the individual Israelite secondary and contingent. Addressing the priority of corporate Israel over the individual Israelite, Rabbinic Judaism must mediate between the conflicting claims of community upon individuality. When, specifically, the individual's interests intersect with those of corporate Israel, the halakhah teaches that those of corporate Israel take priority. That accounts for the manifest policy that favors communitarian theories of stipulative proprietorship over absolute ownership. But the priority of corporate Israel, expressed in the imposition of heavy sanctions on the aberrant individual, requires explanation in its own terms. At just what turnings, for precisely what considerations, does corporate Israel find itself empowered to impose the interests of the community on the individual Israelite? The social teaching of Rabbinic Judaism evinces tolerance of individual deviation from the norm. But determinate considerations motivate the social order to intervene and sanction individual aberration.

Framing matters in this way—when the community imposes its collective will upon the individual, when not—does not mean to suggest that the system even acknowledges, let alone undertakes to resolve, tension between the individual and community. It does not address the matter in our terms. At issue for systemic construction is not finding a balance between the Israelite as an autonomous component of the social order and corporate Israel. The social teaching of Rabbinic Judaism does not recognize the radically isolated, autonomous individual, alone before God. It is, rather, articulating the hierarchical classification that places corporate Israel at the top, the individual Israelite beneath. For—as the matter of required martyrdom to avoid the public profanation of God's name indicates—no negotiation is possible when it comes to realizing the Torah's ultimate imperative for corporate Israel. The individual Israelite, whether by choice or by birth, never can claim utter personal autonomy, only limited individuality. He has no options in the Torah but to obey or to rebel. While the social policy recognizes and values the Israelite's individuality, embodying as it does the freedom of will and the free exercise of intentionality with which everyone by nature, at creation, is endowed, the Israelite subordinates his individuality to his place within corporate Israel. To revert to the formula at the head of this sub-division: the whole not only imparts its imprint upon the parts, the whole also exceeds the sum of the parts.

Between Israelites: Relationships of Balance and Stasis Are to be Restored and Maintained: The second teaching concerns resolving conflict within Israel in particular. "Israel in particular" refers to conflict defined in the context of corporate Israel: its public life and activities. At issue in that context is the social order that the halakhic system conceives corporate Israel to constitute. When, therefore, in the setting of the resolution of conflict we speak of "Israel in particular," that does not mean, the happenstance that two or more Jews (whether or not deemed "Israel" by the halakhah) come into conflict. Nor does that refer to two or more Israelites in random encounters, that is, episodic narratives of contention. To register, a conflict must be designated for conflict-resolution within the categorical-structure of the halakhic system. So at issue are two Israelites in conflict that the Halakhah deems of systemic interest, a conflict for which the halakhah legislates.

Only those conflicts between two, or among three or more, Israelites that engage the interests of corporate Israel define the principal parts of the halakhic categorical structure encompassing conflict-resolution. Other conflicts receive episodic attention to be sure, but that is ordinarily tangential to the main concern. It is not categorical, not comprehensive. Specifically, those conflicts in which corporate Israel recognizes no public interest—no pertinence to the commonwealth—gain only routine attention. They come to resolution, within the halakhah, in ordinary ways. This will happen by, e.g., invoking considerations merely of generic fairness or equity. They generate the amplification of no principal category-formations. Where equity, fairness, and similar universals define outcomes without the intervention of the distinctive considerations attendant upon the participation of corporate Israel, there the system speaks in banalities. Then the differentiation between Israelite and gentile prove a systemic anomaly: a distinction where there is no important difference.

The disputes that register are those between families or households; these are the social units conflict between which is resolved in the categorical formations of the halakhah. The halakhah elaborately explores the contentious relationships between husband and wife or co-wives or mothers-in-law and daughters in law (in Tractates Ketubot, Sotah, Qiddushin, Gittin, and Yebamot for example!)—but not between brother and sister, except as to estates. The latter's relationships, furthermore, do not define, but are subordinate and tangential to, the context in which they occur. They have to do with mainly the administration of estates and support of orphans. But the former—relationships between husband and wife—define their own categorical context(s). And these are elaborate, betrothals, marital relationships of property and personalty (wealth in the form of persons), and cessation of marriage through death or divorce, for

example. But even here, the possibilities—issues that can have arisen in imagination—are vastly outweighed by the actualities—the problems that do predominate for exegetical attention.

Providing for the stability of the household as the building block of the social order, the halakhah identifies those conflicts between, e.g., husband and wife, that demand attention. The halakhic category-formations as these are unpacked will define what is important about them, and will resolve matters in a way that is not only just and equitable, but that is systemically required and particular. The conception of justice and equity figures so far as it illuminates the systemic logic embodied, here as elsewhere, in the details. Then justice and equity give way, being too general to solve many critical problems.

We recall, in this connection, the critical position in the social order assigned to oaths, which invoke God's name and presence (not to be confused with vows). Oaths, in four classifications but for a single purpose, represent exceptional media for the resolution of social conflict. The oath of the judges, the oath of testimony, and the oath of bailment all serve to introduce the criterion of truth and to exclude the exercise of force. The claimant seeks a just restoration of his property or compensation for his loss, the defendant insists upon a fair adjudication of the matter. For that purpose, words backed up not by deeds but by divine supervision serves. But contention precipitates also the remaining classes of oaths: the taking of the vain and rash oath. The rash oath involves securing credence for a preposterous allegation—one that others deny. The vain oath asks people to believe one will carry out an implausible resolve, again bearing within itself the implicit motive to secure credibility where there is none. So one way or another, the oath serves, within the Israelite polity, to engage God's participation within the transactions of man, to involve God in Israel's points of inner conflict, to ask God to impart certainty to the points of stress and strain.

The upshot is readily apparent. It is God who keeps Israel's peace. That statement should be understood in concrete, not intangible ("spiritual") terms. The concrete fact emerges from the approach to resolving conflict between Israel's families and households. Heaven's heavy stake in family ties, God's engagement in securing truth-telling in response to the invocation of his name—these form the foundations of Judaism's theory of the social order, its social teaching. That is not always a paramount consideration, but it is everywhere potentially present. True, conflicts that pertain to restoring and maintaining the social order come to resolution within the this-worldly media of Israelite society in all but the single instance of oaths. But that instance tells the tale. The critical teaching of the social order is God intervenes in transactions that, in all other aspects, are guided by this-worldly rules and exchanges. That is because God is explicitly called to attest to the truth. Everywhere present, God knows the facts and "will not hold him guiltless who takes his name in vain" by swearing to the contrary. On what basis does the halakhic system of Israel's social order confidently call upon God to resolve Israelites' own conflicts? The written Torah answers that question, specifying the character of oaths in God's name and where they pertain.

God's Presence in Israel: Israel Lives in God's Ubiquitous Presence, Subject to God's Enduring Concern: Oaths form the bridge to the third and final social teaching of Rabbinic Judaism, that Israel is to form a society worthy of God's presence. A simple fact established in Scripture and instantiated in the halakhic system captures the palpability, the practicality, the physicality, of God's presence. Settling conflicts over ownership of a cloak or a plot of ground or an ox between Israelite householders under some circumstances requires God's direct intervention. A formula, the oath, invokes God's presence and settles the conflict over the cloak, land, or animal. That fact signals the fundamental social reality contemplated by Rabbinic Judaism: a social order in which God is ever engaged and everywhere present. As with the oath, so with much else, God dwells in the people of Israel. God's active presence affects time and space and brings about Israel's engagement both in Israel's households and in

God's House. That statement represents not a theological conviction alone. It also sets forth the principle of social organization that is outlined in Scripture's laws and realized and systematized in the Rabbinic halakhah.

What, precisely, does God's active presence mean in the system of the social order put forth by the Halakhah? The question divides into these principal parts:

(1) Where—locatively—does God's presence take effect?
(2) When—temporally—does God take place?
(3) Under what circumstance—occasionally—does God enter into the social order formed by corporate Israel, by its households, and, at the end, by even its individual participants?

The answers to these question then take the measure of God's presence within Israel's social order:

(1) location or space,
(2) occasion or time, and
(3) circumstance or transaction—hence the divisions of this part of the project.

In all these aspects of public life—time, space, circumstance—God plays a principal part. That presence—"residence" would be a more likely word—produces immediate and tangible results. To state the matter in negative terms: corporate Israel's social order cannot, and does not, function beyond the ken and concern of God in the here and now. That is categorically not a mere theological conviction, a colorful way of expressing an immanentalist doctrine concerning things spiritual. True, it represents an accurate description of the theological apologetics of the halakhah: it derives from the Torah revealed by God to Moses at Sinai, so the halakhah in general terms certainly represents God's will. But the argument here concerns not apologetics for a legal system viewed in general terms.

But God has given the rules that render his presence not disruptive but the opposite: reliable and predictable. God in Rabbinic Judaism cannot be characterized as "mysterium tremendum," intervening unpredictably and disruptively. On the contrary, the halakhah orders and regularizes relationships with him who says, "Your thoughts are not my thoughts." With the

Torah, God has made his thoughts accessible. Knowing the rules, Israel is able to think like God and abide confidently in God's presence. So even in matters of sanctification, for example, of time and space and circumstance, rationality governs. That is the gift of the halakhah. And that fact points to the question raised in an account of the social teaching of Rabbinic Judaism: how does the halakhah embody in social norms the reality of God's presence in Israel's social order? The answer is, by revealing in the Torah the governing principles of Israel's sanctification, God has laid the foundations for Eden: an Israelite social order that is perfect and eternal.

To state the whole at the outset: the social theory of Rabbinic Judaism sees God and Israel as enlandised, their relationship as a function of location. By "enlandisement," is meant the acts of relationship between Israel and God that take place in, and that are realized through, the situation of holy Israel within the actuality of the land of Israel. The presence of Israel upon the land affects the character of the land. That presence affects, also, the character of Israel's social order, and, as Scripture makes clear, the consequence for that social order, as to the future, of Israel's conduct. That explains why the union of Israel with the land imposes upon Israel occasions for a relationship with God that absence of Israel from the land prevents. How Israel conducts its activities in the land shapes Israel's relationship with God. And what matters then concerns how Israel cultivates the land, deriving its life from the land. God's presence among Israel in the land permits no alternative.

Israel conditionally got, through sin lost, and by repentance regained, the land: how many times more? Here the stabilizing power of the Torah and the sages' transformation of its cases into principles come to the fore. Moses has already stated the conditions for an enduring social order in the land. Israel's possession of the land is subject to the conditions of the covenant. So Israel's rendering to God what God requires as his share of the produce forms a principal expression of Israel's covenanted relationship with God, which takes place not only in, but also through, the land. With God as landlord, Israel's social order takes shape in the land held by Israel in the status of the sharecropper. Transactions in scarce resources—land, produce—are defined in part by the intervention of God's claim, in addition to the claims of the this-worldly participants.

God's presence in heaven as on earth shapes not only Israel's space but also marks its division of time. One day, one occasion is differentiated from another by reason of actions God has taken, and the media of differentiation extend deep into the Israelite household. Specifically, the rhythms of life lived in correlation with the movement of certain natural bodies—the moon's months, the sun's seasons—respond to God's imperatives for occasions defined by the positioning of those bodies in the Heavens. Days, weeks, lunar months, solar seasons—all bring along their particular imperatives. That is what is meant by finding God's presence in Israel not only in space but in time.

The meeting of Israel and God is both locative, focused as it is on the Temple, and utopian, taking place in Israelite households where they are situated. And, as a matter of fact, those very moments that find God welcoming Israel in that one place, the Temple, mark the time at which Israel in its households receives God. So encountering God *when*—not solely where—God may be found, the Israelite household matches God's House. The occasion of the arrangement of moon and solar seasons is matched by the earthly response: Israel's house is brought into alignment with God's. So eternal Israel on earth corresponds with the eternal movement of the moon and the solar seasons in heaven, world without end. That is what the halakhah brings into being: the realization of God's kingdom.

Rabbinic Social Teaching in Israelite Context: With this summary in hand, it is time to seek perspective. How do the Rabbinic sages see the social entity, Israel, that they propose through the halakhic norms to bring into being? The Rabbinic sages in their systematic halakhic writings rework the Torah's narrative into the norms of the Israelite social order. And no other encounter with those Israelite Scriptures so accurately and authentically retold the Pentateuchal story of Israel.

Social teachings of Rabbinic Judaism convey a vision of society seen whole but also embodied in detail. They take the form of both constitutive principles for the design of a social order and casuistic instruction on public virtue of a personal sort. Encompassed are both social thought on a grand scale, on the one side, and moral theology or ethics on the other. "You [plural] shall be holy" (Lev. 19:2) addresses the entirety of society, "Love [imperative, singular] your neighbor as yourself [singular you]" (Lev. 19:18), the individual and the occasion. The former—using the plural "you" of the Hebrew—addresses the social order, the latter—with the singular "you"—the personal attitude and condition. Teachings of a public, social character speak to the community as a working system, encompassing its parts. Those that concern social behavior, theological ethics, moral theology, and the like do not convey a vision of the whole. And the corpus of details holds together. Corporate Israel was the question, the individual Israelite was the given within the narrative of the Rabbinic construction of the Israelite social order. That is, if, like the rest of humanity, individuals are responsible to God for their actions and attitudes, why should corporate Israel form a moral entity encompassing all Israelites and making each responsible for the actions and attitudes of all?

We have, then, to wonder whence the conception of corporate Israel as a moral actor. Why should the Rabbinic sages have constructed out of the detailed laws of ancient Israelite Scripture, such as they cite start to finish, so magnificent vision of an entire society? My view is, they learned from the Torah of Our Rabbi, Moses. Specifically, Scripture itself provokes such a mode of thinking about the whole of the social order, not only about the details, corporate conduct, not only private behavior. It fosters the notion that the parts cohere, the details work together, above all, that the conduct of society as a whole shapes the fate of individuals therein, so that each is responsible for all, and all for each. Ancient Israelite society produced in the Pentateuch a remarkably coherent account of itself, its purpose and how through a narrative of the community's story the parts fit together

to attain that purpose. Scripture, then, told a single, unitary, continuous story of itself and encompassed within that narrative the entire corpus of its laws of the social order. The Pentateuch speaks of Israel as a whole and tells the story of how its social order is to realize God's plan. Rabbinic Judaism systematically states the result of profound reflection on that story and the plan it conveys—that and the determination to act upon the implications of the story and its plan.

Now the continuity of this society, called "corporate Israel" to distinguish "Israel" as the people from "Israel" as the individual Israelite, is not taken for granted as a given. It is portrayed as subject to stipulations, as a conditional gift. Moses and the prophets explicitly take the condition of Israel's society as indicator of Israel's relationship with God, who expresses intense concern for that matter. That fact explains why the Rabbinic sages, in the tradition of Moses and the prophets, set forth doctrines of public policy, not merely private conduct, beginning, as we have seen, with an account of the entire society, Israel. Theirs was a vision of the whole, a perspective from afar and not only from nearby. That fact explains why this inquiry into their social teachings identifies issues of considerable dimensions. That conception, thinking about society as a whole, in its largest components, then defines what is at stake in the Judaic teaching of the social order as undertaken by the Rabbinic sages. That is, to derive from Scripture not only details but large conceptions of a social character, not only rules for the construction of that "Israel" that Moses is commanded to bring into being, but also the principles that those rules adumbrate for situations undreamed of by Moses.

Specific social problems, e.g., the economy and the rational disposition of scarce resources, politics and legitimate violence, patterns of proper relationships among persons or classes of persons represent details. They produce an anthology of rules and sayings on contemporary concerns. But the context of those details, which imparts order, proportion, and meaning to them, will not have emerged. And the outcome would have been an account of how *our* contemporary category-formations impose themselves on a corpus of sayings that, while topically pertinent, are seen out of their own categorical context. But it is only in categorical context that a corpus of teachings pertinent to the social order transforms itself into a coherent doctrine of the social order. And that is precisely what we have in the Rabbinic system of the halakhah by its category-formations.

Seen whole, not only in its categorical components, Judaism starts with the Hebrew Scriptures of ancient Israel. That is a judgment of the whole, not only of the parts, some of which commence in statements of Scripture, some of which do not. It is a vision of the whole of Scripture's account of Israel that infuses the halakhic system, not only the stimulus of elements of that account in detail. Among the Scriptures, the Pentateuch, with its narrative formulation of the coherent design for the social order of the entire Kingdom of priests and holy people, enjoys privileged standing. Within the Pentateuchal narrative and laws, sages found the imperative to define the entirety of a social order worthy to serve as God's abode. There they identified as the moral actor in God's drama not Adam, the individual, but Israel, the corporate social entity—whether a family, as in Genesis, whether a kingdom of priests and a whole people, as in Exodus, whether a pilgrim people engaged in a common enterprise and responsible for its own fate by reason of its covenant with God, in Deuteronomy.

That is why, following the example of Moses and building upon the revealed Scripture, the Rabbinic sages proposed to identify the rules implicit in Scripture's stories and case-law. They thought deeply about the details of the laws, amplifying and extending them by defining the principles of right action exemplified therein. But theirs, then, was the task of global organization of the data, taken out of its narrative framework and placed into the systemic one of their own devising. So they made a unique contribution to the enterprise, in the definition of the large-scale category-formations that formed of stores and cases sustained and significant principles of an abstract character. The cases and rules of Scripture and tradition were treated as exemplary, surface-indicators of a deep structure of encompassing principles. Expressing the architecture through the detailed plan only, they set forth a system of law capable of imparting shape and structure anywhere, not bound to a particular culture or circumstance, time or place. And so it has worked out for Rabbinic Judaism for two millennia.

The upshot is clear. The social teachings form three large statements, spinning out the imperatives of a single logic. These statements in their necessary order speak, one on the social order formed by corporate Israel in its relationship to individual Israelites, the second on relationships between Israelites, and the third on relationships between Israel's society and the ever-present, ubiquitous one and only God who has taken up residence in the people, Israel. All three relationships—between Israel and the Israelite, Israelites by households or families, and all Israel and God—are defined by the pertinent category-formations of the normative halakhah.

JACOB NEUSNER

S

SERMONS IN MEDIEVAL AND EARLY MODERN JUDAISM: The sermon is here defined as an act of oral communication, ordinarily within the context of a public religious event, in which a selected individual expounds the meaning of a scriptural passage or some other classical Jewish text in a manner intended to address the intellectual or spiritual needs of the listeners. Secondarily, the sermon is a text that represents that act of communication in a form accessible to later readers.

The standard medieval Hebrew term for

this genre is *derashah*; the most common term for the one who delivers the sermon is *darshan*; the verb "to preach" is *li-derosh*. All three words are linked with the biblical root meaning "to seek, demand, investigate." The same root provides the word *midrash*, used in Rabbinic literature to indicate a mode of study focusing on careful interpretation of a biblical verse, the interpretation itself, and the literary work containing a collection of such interpretations. In the Middle Ages, two other related words came into use: *derash*, a level of biblical interpretation referring to the homiletical approach of the Rabbinic sages, and *derush*, a conceptual problem to be investigated in a sermon or philosophical text. A separate term for "eulogy," *hesped*, goes back to the classical Rabbinic literature.

Here we focus on sermons originating in Christian Europe from the thirteenth through the seventeenth century. While the tradition of Jewish preaching goes back at least two thousand years, the earliest extant texts of Jewish sermons date from the thirteenth century. This statement excludes the substantial corpus of literature known as midrash.[1] Although much of this literature was apparently based on sermons preached in the synagogue, and some of its most important homiletical collections were edited in the early Middle Ages, the midrashic literature should not be considered as a repository for the sermon in medieval Judaism.

The first reason is chronological. The sages whose biblical interpretations are recorded in the midrash lived in the period of antiquity, most of them during the first four centuries C.E. They were the contemporaries of the church fathers. Medieval Jews who were part of the dominant Rabbinic tradition (i.e., excluding the Karaites) all considered these sages to be in a different category from themselves, bearing a higher level of authority than their immediate predecessors. That the statements of these sages were redacted in early medieval texts does not make them medieval preachers. Of the anonymous material preserved in these collections, relatively little is datable to the Middle Ages.

Second, the "sermons" contained in the midrash are at best two or three times

removed from anything that was actually preached. The late Israeli scholar Joseph Heinemann sifted through the entire corpus of Rabbinic literature (Talmud and midrash) for an anthology entitled "Public Preaching in the Talmudic Period;" the result, including ample introductory material, was less than seventy-five pages.[2] More important, the passages in this anthology are clearly not transcriptions of sermons as they were preached. Some are too short: passages that could be read in less than a minute, these are perhaps only outlines of sermons. Others are too long: composites of homiletical material too disparate to have been used for a single sermon, these are the product of an editor composing a new literary form and do not represent the work of a preacher presenting a single, cogent address to a congregation.

Unlike the works of the church fathers, Rabbinic writing is entirely a corporate literature. No Rabbinic book from the classical period of late antiquity or the early Middle Ages is the teaching of an individual; rather, these collect the work of an entire class of scholars. We do not have preserved a single sermon of Aqiba or Yohanan ben Zakkai either written by them or recorded as it was preached and therefore comparable to the hundreds of sermons of Chrysostom, Augustine, and their colleagues. The midrash provides part of the content for the medieval Jewish sermon, as we shall see; it is not a record of medieval Jewish preaching.

As for the end of the period, a distinctively "modern" form of Jewish preaching is a product of the nineteenth century.[3] Still, here we consider material produced only through 1650, when the demographic and cultural center of Jewish life, and the most engaging examples of Jewish homiletical art, were shifting away from the Mediterranean basin to the Ashkenazic communities of central and eastern Europe. It bears noting that our focus is on Christian Europe rather than the sermons produced by Jews in North Africa and the Middle East. Although there is abundant evidence that preaching was a regular part of the religious life of medieval Jews in Muslim lands, investigation of the many manuscripts of Judeo-Arabic sermons in the collections of major libraries has barely begun.[4]

One type of text that raises an interesting taxonomic problem is the "conversionary" sermon, delivered by a Christian authority (sometimes a convert from Judaism) to a Jewish audience compelled to attend in order to be convinced about Christianity's status as the "true" faith.[5] Such texts have yet to be systematically studied; it remains to be determined whether in form and technique they are closer to the Christian or the Jewish homiletical tradition.

The Preaching Context: Jewish preaching is closely connected with the public reading from Scripture.[6] The annual cycle of readings from the Pentateuch and Prophetic books in the Sabbath morning worship service provided the structure for the most common form of preaching in medieval Jewish life, with the Sabbath sermon ordinarily delivered either immediately before or soon after the liturgical reading of Scripture. The most natural way for a Jewish preacher to organize a collection of his sermons would be to include one on each lesson for the year. Most of the extant medieval sermon collections are arranged in this manner.

In addition to the sermons for the ordinary Sabbath service, there were sermons associated with holidays, the Sabbaths immediately preceding the holidays, or the Sabbaths in the middle of the holiday weeks. These occasions had their own scriptural lesson independent of the weekly progression, and the sermons would be linked with the various themes of the festival or holy day. For example, the Sabbath between Rosh Hashanah and Yom Kippur was known as the "Sabbath of Repentance," and the sermon ordinarily dealt with this complex yet crucial theological doctrine and with actual shortcomings of the congregation in preparation for the approaching fast day.[7] The Sabbath preceding the holiday of Passover, known as the "Great Sabbath," was another extremely important preaching occasion, when the rabbi of the community would discuss the complicated laws of preparing the home for the holiday and the historical, philosophical, and ethical motifs of the Exodus and its cele-

bration.[8] Even rabbis who did not ordinarily preach each Sabbath were expected each year to deliver major sermons on these two occasions.

A third category of sermons are those related to liturgical events of the life cycle, especially circumcision, marriage, and death.[9] These were often delivered outside the synagogue: at the home, the place of a celebratory feast, or the cemetery. What makes them sermons is their connection with a public ritual and their link with the annual cycle of Torah readings. The aesthetic challenge was to take a verse from the week's Torah lesson and relate it to the occasion. In some cases, where circumcision, marriage, or death is mentioned in the Torah lesson, it was easy; in others, it placed considerable demands on the preacher's ingenuity.

The most important of these life cycle sermons were the eulogies. The tradition of delivering eulogies goes back to antiquity; unlike the other life cycle sermons, this has a clear status in Jewish law. There is ample evidence that eulogies were delivered throughout the Middle Ages. Yet apparently no actual eulogy written for a specific individual has been preserved from before the early fifteenth century.[10] Unlike the sermon at a circumcision or wedding celebration, this could not be merely a stereotyped model; it had to relate to the individual who had died. Only when the conception of a written sermonic text changed from that of a model for future use to a record of what had been said on a specific occasion (see below) did Jewish preachers begin to preserve texts of their eulogies for future readers. Once this occurred, the eulogy quickly developed into one of the most significant types of Jewish sermon texts.

The purpose of the eulogy was not to provide an obituary, a biography of the deceased, although on occasion it may provide important historical evidence for the contemporary image of a significant figure.[11] A few preachers have left moving personal records of their relationships with close members of their family who have died. But, mostly, these texts preserve evidence of religious and philosophical attitudes toward death and the afterlife (including the increasingly popular doctrine of reincarnation). We find in these sermons motifs about life and death familiar from the elegaic meditations of medieval Hebrew poetry. Some of the eulogies reveal that they were delivered in the cemetery, with the preacher (like his Christian colleague) using the physical presence of the body either near or within the grave to dramatize the inevitability of death and the deceptive vainglories of so many human aspirations. The ultimate purpose was to move the listeners to humility and repentance.[12]

A final category is occasional sermons, delivered on special moments in the life of the individual preacher or his community: at the dedication of a new synagogue building or the completion of a course of study; on a day of public fasting and penitential prayer because of some natural or historical calamity (a plague, a pogrom); at a celebration of a personal or communal milestone or triumph. Such sermons are often characterized by a stylized introduction in which the preacher seeks "permission" from God, the Torah, and the distinguished assembly to deliver his message, sometimes following a passage in which he explains why it would have been better for him to remain silent.[13] The texts of such sermons, increasingly common in the late medieval and early modern periods, do not always divulge as much explicit historical information as we might wish, but they are extremely important revelations of the mentality of an age.[14]

The fifteenth century was a dynamic period in the history of Jewish preaching; its major transformations may be noted, if not as yet adequately explained. First, there was a change in the conception of the nature and purpose of the recorded sermon text. Throughout most of the Middle Ages, the function of the written sermon was considered by Jews to be essentially utilitarian: to serve as a model usable in the future either by the preacher himself or by others seeking instruction, edification, or material for their own sermons.[15] These texts are without doubt considerably reworked, possibly including material from more than one sermon; the relationship to what was said on any particular occasion is problematic. Indeed, some texts in the sermon form may have been written by someone who had never stood in the pulpit but wished to provide model sermons for others to use.[16] Such "sermons" are purely literary texts, devoid of any direct connection with an audience of listeners, although this determination often depends on an argument from silence: the absence of external information that the author actually preached and the lack of internal indications of an oral delivery.

From the early decades of the fifteenth century, however, there is evidence for a new conception of the written text: a record of what was actually said. For the first time, we find details that bind the text to a specific occasion and that would serve no purpose in a sermon intended for use by others.[17] The writers of these texts evidently felt it important to preserve the content not of a model but of a unique discourse. Not coincidentally, the first texts of eulogies and of occasional sermons—two categories that by their nature are linked with a specific event and do not work well as models—date from this period.

There are also important structural changes, affecting the way in which the sermon is related to the scriptural text read in the worship service.[18] The older form, with roots in the classical texts of Rabbinic midrash, begins with a biblical verse from outside the Pentateuch—usually from the Hagiographa, most commonly from Proverbs, Psalms, or Job. Several different interpretations of the verse are given by the preacher, each one developed in its own way, before the preacher discloses a meaning that relates the verse to the week's lesson from the Torah.[19] Once the connection has been made, the preacher moves through a series of verses from the pericope, sharing the insights of the sages and responding to various exegetical issues in the passage, which are resolved in the course of the discussion. Sometimes ethical or religious "benefits" (*to'aliyyot*, cf., *utilitates*) are derived from the passage.[20] Sometimes the preacher will raise a series of questions about the section (*sefeqot*, literally, "doubts," cf., *dubitationes*) and resolve them in the course of his discussion of the verses.[21]

The newer form, first documented in the late fifteenth century, represents an innovation in Jewish homiletical art undoubtedly influenced by Christian preaching. Like the older form, this sermon begins with a biblical verse, but now the opening verse is taken from the Torah lesson itself. This verse is designated by the technical term *nosei*, "theme," clearly the equivalent of the analogous Latin technical term *thema*. There follows a passage from the Rabbinic literature (Talmud or midrash), the *ma'amar* or "dictum," sometimes obviously connected with the theme verse, sometimes bearing no apparent relevance. The ensuing sermon explores some conceptual problem (*derush*, equivalent to the Latin *quaestio*) in such a manner that the theme verse is eventually explicated, often in a novel way, and the Rabbinic passage is employed to illuminate some new aspect of the familiar verse. Jewish writers at the end of the fifteenth century will often reserve the term *li-derosh* ("to preach") for this new kind of formal thematic sermon, using a different term, *le-faresh*, akin to the word for a biblical commentary, to designate the more informal "homily" that proceeds verse by verse with no attempt at substantive unity.[22]

Perhaps the most striking formal innovation is the investigation of the theoretical problem in the form of a "disputed question," one of the characteristic modes of scholastic discourse. An example of this form, repeated in several sermons after its first appearance in a sermon for the Sabbath preceding Passover around 1400, explores the question "whether or not the miracle creates faith in the human soul without the concurrence of the will."[23] Another example, in a sermon for the Sabbath preceding Rosh Hashanah, is "whether God forgives the penitent;" we shall return to this sermon later. As in the Christian community, there was some controversy over the use of this form in public preaching, for it requires the preacher to defend a position that he will eventually repudiate as antithetical to the truth. At least one Jewish preacher felt compelled to justify the legitimacy of this mode of preaching, appealing to "precedents" in the classical literature and arguing that "truth becomes clear only through disputation."[24]

In addition to the texts of sermons, there are genres closely related to the sermon, of which isolated examples can be identified

in our period. The first is the "preaching aid," a collection of homiletical material, but not actual sermons, organized in a manner that will be useful to preachers. An example is *Kad ha-Qemah* ("The Jar of Flour," 1 Kings 17:14) by Bahya ben Asher of Saragossa (fl. ca. 1300). This is the first Jewish book to collect biblical and Rabbinic statements pertaining to discrete subjects, organized alphabetically, so that "whenever one is inspired and asserts himself in his desire to preach, he may find each commandment and each ethical quality under the appropriate letter."[25] Similar preaching aids, including selections from medieval literature, would be produced in subsequent centuries.

Some preachers recast their material to such an extent that it is no longer in the sermon form. Medieval Jews considered a biblical commentary to be a more substantial and prestigious work than a collection of sermons. Not a few individuals, well-known as preachers throughout their careers, failed to leave even a single sermon text behind. Some wrote nothing at all, but others collected the interpretations they had used in years of preaching, supplemented them in places, and produced a commentary on the Pentateuch or other biblical books.[26] That such commentaries draw on material once used from the pulpit is clear, but they should not be used for the same purposes as the sermon text recording an actual oral event.

Finally, there is the manual providing advice and instruction for the preacher. By contrast with the abundant Christian texts of this nature, the medieval Jewish material is limited: an anonymous early-fifteenth-century set of concise guidelines for preachers, and a work by the fifteenth-century Spanish scholar Joseph ibn Shem Tov that devotes considerable attention to homiletical issues.[27] No systematic *Ars praedicandi* is known to have been written by a Jew before the second half of the seventeenth century.[28]

Homiletical Geography: The Jewish communities of medieval and early modern Christian Europe can be divided into two broad categories: those of northern Europe, including northern France and Germany, with an offshoot (until the expulsion of 1290) in England and the burgeoning settlement in Poland; and those of the northern Mediterranean basin, including the Iberian peninsula, southern France, Italy, and the Byzantine realm. There is a striking disparity between these two groupings regarding the practice of preaching.

Although certain individuals in eleventh-century northern Europe were identified by the title *ha-darshan*, "the preacher," it seems fairly clear that the practice of a weekly Sabbath sermon was not commonly observed in these communities. One late medieval German rabbi contrasted the Jews of antiquity, who were "accustomed to sermons," with his contemporaries, who were "not accustomed to preaching."[29] Several short sermons from the thirteenth century intended for use at circumcision celebrations have recently been discovered in manuscript and published,[30] and extensive material from the holiday sermons of the early fifteenth-century rabbi Jacob Moellin has been preserved in the work of a faithful disciple. But the extant texts of Jewish sermons from pre-1600 northern Europe are meagre and mostly devoted to Jewish law. The creative arena for Jewish preaching during this period was in the Mediterranean communities that had more direct contact with the Jews living in Islamic lands.

Of these, the greatest number of texts dating from before 1492 come from the Iberian peninsula, the one region from which there is sufficient material from this period to venture preliminary conclusions about a distinctive homiletical tradition and its transformations. The great flourishing of preaching in Italy and the eastern Mediterranean began in the sixteenth century, in the wake of the immigration of Jews expelled from Spain and later fleeing from Portugal. One of the most important questions is how the Sephardic émigrés influenced the practice of preaching in Italy; unfortunately, there is simply not enough material of Italian provenance before 1500 to establish the "native" tradition and to respond with any measure of confidence.[31] The community composed of former Portuguese "New Christians" in Amsterdam starting in the early seventeenth century soon became another major center of homiletical excellence.[32] After 1650, the most dynamic examples of

Jewish homiletical art can be found among the rabbis and itinerant preachers of central and eastern Europe.[33]

Content and Historical Value: The content of the sermons was suggested by the scriptural lesson or the calendrical or special occasion of its delivery, as noted above, but these by no means restricted the preacher. Sermons on the same lesson, or for the same holiday, could differ dramatically in accordance with the predilection of the individual preacher and his judgment of the tastes and the needs of his listeners. Various types of material found in Jewish sermons may be quickly reviewed and the historical value of this material briefly assessed.

A. Biblical Exegesis: Traditional Jewish preaching is almost always anchored in the Bible. Exploring and probing the meaning of familiar Biblical passages for their listeners, the preacher mediated the tradition of biblical scholarship to the community as a whole. As noted above, many books eventually published in the form of commentaries were actually based on exegetical passages in sermons delivered by the author over many years and later recast into a different genre.

Not infrequently, preachers focus their discussion on the intricacies and ambiguities in a simple verse from the Torah lesson. Saul Levi Morteira of Amsterdam, for example, focuses on the problems in Gen. 32:14, which states that Jacob *took from what came into his hand*: "this indicates randomness and chance, namely, that he took from what happened to come into his hand. Yet according to the context, this cannot be . . .," for the rest of the narrative indicates the inordinate care taken by Jacob in his choice and arrangement of gifts. Morteira then invites his listeners to accompany him through his exegetical library, discussing the views of eight different commentators from Rashi to the preacher's older contemporaries, before he turns to his own explanation of the apparently simple yet tantalizingly elusive phrase. For the listeners, this would have been a crash course on one aspect of Jewish biblical exegesis.[34]

A simple verse from the Torah lesson could also be the trigger for a broad conceptual problem. The Spanish philosopher

Shem Tov ibn Shem Tov takes the verse "It is not good for man to be alone" (Gen. 2:18) as an occasion to examine whether human perfection is attainable only in isolation from others or whether human beings need society to reach their full potential. For the same preacher, God's statement to Abraham, "For now I know that you fear God" (Gen. 22:12), raises the question whether God did not know before the test how Abraham would respond, and whether indeed God's knowledge can contain something new.[35]

Preachers sympathetic to a philosophical exposition of Judaism regularly penetrated beyond the manifest, simple, contextual, surface meaning of the verses (*peshat, nigleh*) to what they claimed to be an esoteric meaning (*nistar*). Not infrequently, this mode of interpretation read the Bible as allegory (*mashal*), concealing a philosophical truth beneath narratives or assertions that appeared to mean something totally different. A straightforward example would be that Noah's ark with its three levels (Gen. 7:16) refers to the knowledge of the mathematical, physical, and metaphysical sciences that saves man from the stormy waters of destruction for the individual soul.[36] Including such interpretations in sermons became a matter of bitter controversy at times, especially if they were understood to repudiate rather than merely supplement the simple meaning of the biblical text.[37]

Another form of exegesis favored by Jewish preachers was typological, the technique that identifies biblical figures as prototypes for personalities or events that would occur subsequently in the history of the Jews, or were expected to occur in the future. This kind of exegesis is already used in the Rabbinic literature, and it stands to reason that preachers, who had to speak on the same narratives year after year, would be attracted to an approach that no longer consigned these narratives to the distant past but uncovered their relevance to issues facing the contemporary community and to their messianic expectations.

For example, Solomon Levi, rabbi and preacher in sixteenth-century Salonika, discussing Jacob's flight eastward from Esau's enmity to a new home with Laban, found in this story a model of Jewish experience that must have spoken to the children of those who fled from Christian Spain or Portugal to a haven in the Ottoman east:

> All this is an instructive sign that our people would be expelled and persecuted, moving from kingdom to kingdom, from one ruler who hates them to another. Within a relatively few years they would become more powerful and wealthier than the native inhabitants of the land, who would eventually come to despise them, so that they would have to flee from that land to yet another. Such would be the pattern until the messianic age. For God would arrange it that when they were persecuted by one who hated them, as was the case with Esau, they would find another who would welcome them warmly, as was the case with Laban.
>
> We learn also that the industriousness of our people, [enabling them] to earn money and acquire wealth, is similar to that found in our father Jacob.[38]

The biblical narrative provides insight into a pattern that structures the experience of Jewish history, rendering it less bewildering for the listeners.

B. Aggadic midrash: This refers to the corpus of classical Rabbinic homiletical comments on biblical verses of a non-legal character, as contained in the Babylonian Talmud and various collections dating from antiquity and the early Middle Ages. Since the sages had explored the biblical text in depth in order to unpack deeper levels of meaning and apply it homiletically to contemporary concerns, the dicta of the sages were the natural starting point for medieval preachers. Some seem to have viewed it as their fundamental task to present to their listeners the most important or intriguing Rabbinic comments of an exegetical, ethical, or historical nature; their sermons are major repositories of Rabbinic midrashim (some of them known from no other source).[39]

Especially after the Rabbinic dictum became a structural component of the sermon (late-fifteenth century), preachers began to devote considerable energy to the interpretation of the aggadah. Some of the well-known Rabbinic statements raised problems that required exegetical talent and conceptual ingenuity to resolve. One example would be the familiar statement of Yohanan (B. R.H. 16b):

Three books are opened on Rosh Hashanah, one for the wholly righteous, one for the wholly wicked, and one for the intermediates. The wholly righteous are at once inscribed and sealed for life; the wholly wicked are at once inscribed and sealed for death; and the intermediates are held suspended from Rosh Hashanah until Yom Kippur. If they are found worthy, they are inscribed for life; if unworthy, they are inscribed for death.

In their sermons for Rosh Hashanah, generations of preachers wrestled with the conundrum articulated by Moses ben Nahman: "How could R. Yohanan have said such a thing? Do all the righteous indeed live and all the wicked die [each year]?" The many solutions proposed to this conundrum suggest that it was a problem Jewish listeners wanted to hear addressed.[40]

C. Law: The other major category of Rabbinic literature was its legal material, halakhah. Learned discourses on abstruse problems of talmudic law were more in place in the academy than in the synagogue pulpit, but legal issues of practical significance would often find their way into sermons, particularly those intended for holidays. It was a complicated matter to prepare the home for Passover and to observe the festive meal according to the detailed requirements of Jewish law. Many rabbis therefore considered it their responsibility to use the sermon on the Sabbath preceding Passover to remind their listeners precisely what they were obligated and forbidden to do.[41] Since this discussion was intended to be not original but rather a reiteration of material well-known to educated Jews, there was little reason for the preacher to write it for posterity. An example of this is in an instruction apparently for future preachers in the sermons of the fourteenth-century Jacob ben Hananel of Sicily:

> From here you may begin to preach about the laws of the paschal lamb, and the search for leaven, and the supervision of the matzah. If you should want to refer to the *reason* for the prohibition of eating leaven, and the prohibition of benefiting from it, and the prohibitions "No leaven shall be seen [in all your territory for seven days]" (Deut. 16:4) and "No leaven shall be found [in your houses for seven days]" (Exod. 12:19), and the obligation of eating unleavened bread, refer to it. Reveal a little, and conceal a little.[42]

The halakhic content of the sermons tends, therefore, to be under-represented in the extant texts.[43]

D. Philosophy: Serious philosophical study of religious problems began among Jews in Islamic lands during the tenth century and reached its acme with Moses Maimonides in the late twelfth century. The works of these thinkers, translated from Arabic into Hebrew and eagerly read by Jews living in Christian Spain, southern France, and Italy, had a major impact on Jewish preaching. New kinds of questions were investigated in sermons on scriptural passages. Did the first chapter of Genesis really teach creation *ex nihilo*? How could God's hardening of Pharaoh's heart be reconciled with freedom of choice? Did Balaam's ass actually talk like a human being? Can human beings really effect a change in God through their repentance?

By the late Middle Ages, especially in Spain, material from the works of Aristotle was standard fare in Jewish preaching alongside Maimonides and other Jewish philosophers. Sometimes, the content might be quite technical, with specific references to Arabic philosophers and even Thomas Aquinas. Scholastic forms of argumentation, including the Aristotelian syllogism and the "disputed question," entered Jewish preaching, giving the sermon a structure quite different from the earlier homilies. The importance of the sermon as a vehicle for popularizing and diffusing philosophical ideas within the larger Jewish community cannot be over-emphasized.[44]

This innovation in the content of Jewish preaching aroused considerable resistance in some circles. The role of philosophical study in Jewish life was the subject of major strife among Jews as among their Christian neighbors. Preachers were bitterly attacked for disseminating philosophical views from the pulpit and for allegorical interpretations of narrative passages from the Bible that seemed to undermine the dignity of the biblical text (e.g., Abraham and Sarah are "form and matter").[45] Various efforts were made to set limits and control what could be said from the pulpit, both in the synagogue and at private occasions such as wedding feasts, but these were largely unsuccessful.[46]

E. Kabbalah: The medieval development of Jewish mystical doctrine (*Kabbalah*) began in twelfth-century southern France as an extremely esoteric doctrine; some of its early practitioners insisted that it be divulged only by teacher to disciple and were vehemently opposed to writing it, lest the text become accessible to an unqualified reader. The resistance to incorporating this kind of material into a sermon intended for the entire community must have been quite strong. Only one full collection of sermons before the late fifteenth century is known to contain Kabbalistic doctrines.[47] In the generation of the Expulsion, we find a Spanish Talmudist (with philosophical leanings) in a sermon for the Sabbath of Repentance providing a Kabbalistic explanation for why all ten days from the beginning of Rosh Hashanah to the end of Yom Kippur do not share a similar degree of sanctity.[48] After the printing of the Zohar and the general popularization of Kabbalah, opposition to the preaching of Kabbalistic material gradually diminished.

As Jews had no universally accepted credo or any centralized authority that could rule on acceptable theological doctrines, the sermon can serve as a test for the legitimacy of eccentric beliefs. The doctrine of the transmigration of souls, for example, had a questionable basis in authoritative Jewish sources. But once it began to appear in medieval Kabbalistic texts, some preachers recognized its usefulness as a solution to problems of theodicy such as the death of a young child. After a period of initial resistance to the practice of preaching about transmigration, the doctrine was eventually disseminated quite freely from the pulpit.[49]

F. Social Criticism: In addition to teaching the traditional texts, one of the functions of the Jewish sermon was that of *tokekhah*, rebuke of shortcomings or failures in the religious and ethical standards of the community. This was especially important around the Days of Awe with their theme of repentance. It is difficult to know how much time preachers devoted to this theme; because it purports to respond to the conditions of a specific community, they often thought it inappropriate to incorporate into a written text for wide dissemination. It is therefore probably under-represented in the extant texts. Although this does not seem to be the central concern of any known pre-eighteenth-century preacher, most collections of sermons contain some measure of criticism of contemporary Jewish society and practice, expressing the preacher's dissatisfaction with what he sees.

When allowance is made for certain *topoi* and conventions that can be documented in almost every generation, the sermons of rebuke may serve as important evidence for the tension points and fault lines in the community. One of the best medieval examples is a sermon delivered at Toledo in 1281 as part of a concerted effort by the Rabbinic leadership to inspire social, religious, and even institutional reform. Apparently the preacher was successful and changes were made—an unusual piece of evidence from the Jewish environment that sermons could on occasion make a dramatic difference.[50]

The homiletical oeuvre of Saul Levi Morteira provides abundant evidence of the rhetorical strategies used by a master preacher to attack behavior he considered inappropriate in the Amsterdam community. One sermon delivered early in his career is devoted to a powerful denunciation of Jews' displaying their newly acquired wealth through opulent living quarters, ostentatious clothing, and sumptuous banquets, thereby arousing the envy of their Dutch hosts and the anger of God, who prolongs the exile. This is rooted in his interpretation of a verse describing the behavior of the Israelites in Egypt in the period immediately before their enslavement.[51] Others of his sermons similarly draw from biblical or Rabbinic models to attack specific failings of the community, ranging from sexual licentiousness to shaving the corners of the beard.[52]

G. Polemic: The sermon also had the function of reinforcing the beliefs of the listeners against the challenges from the outside, particularly those of the Christian majority. Criticizing Christian doctrine from the pulpit could be dangerous, as it threatened the ground rules of Jewish toleration. Yet some of the references are quite sharp, to the point where they raise a question of the propriety of a Jewish preacher's saying such things in a vernacular address that might have been overheard by an outsider. Shem Tov ben Joseph ibn Shem Tov, for example, launches an attack against one who boasts that he proclaims new beliefs and laws out of prophecy, when he has really stolen them from someone else. "This is the religion of the gentiles. The ethical qualities and behavior of such a person should be investigated; indeed, he is the man who loved lechery more than any of his predecessors."[53] More often, implied polemic was expressed through the reassertion of crucial doctrines such as the immutability of the Torah, the permanence of God's selection of the Jewish people, and the ongoing validity of Jewish messianic hope. Sometimes we find a negative assessment of central Christian beliefs, or of new trends in Christian spirituality.[54] Especially interesting, because it is most characteristic of the specific genre of the sermon, are passages in which the preacher invokes a Christian doctrine or practice not primarily to polemicize against it but to attack a comparable phenomenon in the Jewish community.[55]

Once again, Saul Levi Morteira of Amsterdam left a prodigious number of sermon passages attacking various aspects of Christian (primarily Catholic) doctrine. An entire sermon responds to a claim that Christianity improved on Judaism in four realms: the ideals of poverty and chastity, the love of one's enemy, and the active pursuit of martyrdom. Christian doctrines of God, Torah, and the messiah are fiercely attacked; examples of distortion or intention falsification in Catholic biblical translation are exposed; such practices as the veneration of the bones of saints are held up to ridicule. While there were limits beyond which the preacher could not go, the texts of his sermons reveal a remarkable degree of freedom in seventeenth-century Amsterdam.[56]

H. Reaction to Historical Events: This category is also undoubtedly underrepresented in the extant texts. The more specific a sermon was in responding to an event with immediate and direct impact on the community, the more dated it would seem a decade or two later, and the less likely the preacher would be to deem it

important to preserve either as a model for other colleagues or as a record of what he had said. Often the references preserved are allusive and suggestive; they would have been clearly understood by all listeners when originally said, but are tantalizingly ambiguous to the historian today.

Nevertheless, some extant texts of medieval sermons explicitly respond to the historical challenges faced by the Jewish community, especially on occasions of suffering, whether from natural causes (plague) or human persecution. They provide dramatic evidence of how contemporary challenges were assimilated into the tradition. Central to most of these responses is the theological argument that God is in control of history and that Jews' suffering consequently serves a divine purpose—a theme reiterated so insistently that it bespeaks considerable doubts on the part of the listeners.[57]

An impressive example is the sermon delivered by Joseph ibn Shem Tov, courtier, physician, and philosopher (father of the Shem Tov cited above), who was sent by Prince Henry of Castile as a special emissary to the Jewish community of Segovia following an anti-Jewish riot beginning on Good Friday of 1452. The climax of the sermon comes when he turns to the question of Jewish responsibility for the crucifixion, undoubtedly the excuse for the riot. The preacher asserts that Jesus was put to death by the rightful Jewish authorities of antiquity in accordance with the biblical law of the "false prophet," but he insists that this is not the real reason why Jews are persecuted:

> He is a fool who says that had it not been for that incident [the crucifixion] those murders and conflagrations and forced conversions would never have befallen our sacred communities. Nothing prevents God from fabricating new causes and different libels to be directed against us as justification for the collection of His debt. . . . Look at the Jewish communities in Islamic lands. Murders and forced conversions have befallen them without any libels relating to the death of that man. Instead, we should look into our behavior, as individuals and as a community. This is why these tragedies occur.

The sermon does not provide us with detailed information about what actually happened. It does provide us with important insight about how spokesmen for the tradition responded to tragedy and attempted to interpret its significance for their listeners.[58] A comparable example of preaching in the face of catastrophe is the sermon delivered by Israel of Belzyce in the summer of 1648, after the Cossack attackers had decimated his community.[59]

Not all homiletical responses to historical events occurred in tragic times. In 1568, the Salonika rabbi and scholar Moses Almosnino delivered a monumental sermon at a community-wide gathering on the occasion of his triumphant return from Istanbul with a newly ratified charter of liberty for the community. The sermon, which describes the obstacles and temporary setbacks of the mission in exhaustive detail within an elaborate exegetical and homiletical framework, re-affirms the traditional doctrine of divine providence over even the smallest details of historical experience.[60] In a sermon delivered in early January, 1656, Saul Levi Morteira juxtaposed the tragic events that had recently befallen Jewish communities in Lublin and Recife with the joy of his own community at deliverance from the plague that had devastated Amsterdam during the previous half year.[61]

I. Entertainment: While never considered to be a primary function of the sermon, entertaining listeners was considered by some to be a legitimate subsidiary aspect of the preacher's role. The humorous interpretation of a biblical verse, which can be extensively documented in later Jewish preaching, was probably employed by some in the Middle Ages as well. More important was the use of the story, from external as well as Jewish sources, derived from folklore, popular literature, and serious intellectual texts, to illustrate and exemplify homiletical points. There was some controversy over the propriety of the use of such material by preachers, and some avoided it as a matter of principle as incompatible with the seriousness of their enterprise. But the popularity of this material guaranteed its continued use.

Most of the stories used were not original with the preachers but were taken from earlier, sometimes non-Jewish, sources. Their appearance in Jewish sermons is an important indication not only of the diffusion of literary motifs but also of the influence of spiritual aspirations. Here is an example used by an unknown Jewish preacher from a Christian country whose sermons are recorded in a manuscript of uncertain provenance, with an internal dating of 1425:

> A certain sage was once asked, "When was the happiest day in your entire life?" He responded, "Once I was on a ship with many gentiles. I was sitting in the most wretched place on the ship, among the sailors. I saw a certain gentile look arrogantly down at me. He exposed himself and urinated upon me. But I felt no urge to respond with anger." You can find this in Maimonides' [commentary upon] *Pirqei Avot.*

The passage indeed is taken from Maimonides' Commentary on the Mishnah; Maimonides himself claims to have read it in "one of the books of ethical literature." His source was a Muslim text, as this story is told of the well-known ascetic mystic Ibrahim ibn Adham. A strikingly similar motif appears in the *Fioretti* of Francis of Assisi, where St. Francis illustrates in detail how "perfect joy" is found in "conquering oneself and willingly enduring of insults, humiliations, and hardships for the love of Christ." This is, therefore, a narrative illustration of a theme found in all three religious traditions, incorporated by a Jewish preacher into the texture of Jewish sources—its Sufi origin obscured—and held up as a paradoxical ideal of humiliating self-abasement for his listeners to ponder.[62] The most aesthetically sophisticated use of such exempla or parables, however, would come in eighteenth-century eastern Europe, with the sermons of the Magid of Dubnow and his imitators.

The Problematics of Repentance in Late Medieval Sephardic Preaching: To illustrate in greater depth the value of the sermon as an expression of medieval and early modern Judaism, we focus on a central theme in the preaching of a critical period: the generation of the Expulsion from Spain. This is the theme of repentance, a significant homiletical motif in many collections of Jewish sermons, especially those delivered on the Sabbath of Repentance between Rosh Hashanah and Yom Kippur.

There seems to be no question of the importance of the doctrine of repentance, which leading Jewish thinkers describe as "the peg upon which redemption is hung, the cure for all ills and the repair of all curses."[63] Nevertheless, a reader is struck by the extent to which it appears to have become deeply problematic for late medieval Jewish preachers. Since repentance is understood to be one of the commandments of the Torah, it is certainly understandable for Jewish thinkers to ask whether it falls in Saadia Gaon's category of the rational or the traditional commandments, or whether God's acceptance of repentance is an act of justice or of totally unmerited divine grace. It seems, however, that the insistence by almost all Jewish preachers that the efficacy of repentance is *not* rational, *not* just, leaves them and their listeners in something of a quandary.

Thus, in the second of a recently-published series of sermons on repentance, the courtier-philosopher Joseph ibn Shem Tov insists that the atonement for sins sought from God "is not according to law and justice but rather total grace from God."[64] He sets out the arguments for this position in various ways, including the claim that, according to the standards of justice, for sins against God there "must be punishment for eternity, without any atonement; that is the law without doubt." Rational argument concludes that divine pardon due to repentance cannot be justified by the law and pure speculation, but only by divine grace and mercy. A considerable part of the sermon is devoted to presenting the argument against the rationality of repentance.[65]

A generation later, Joseph's son, Shem Tov ibn Shem Tov—like his father (and unlike his grandfather) deeply committed to the value of philosophy—wrote at least eight sermons on repentance. For him, the problem arises in a different way, through well-known Rabbinic aggadot, such as the statements that as a result of repentance, willful sins are transformed into merits (B. Yom. 86b), and "In the place where the penitent stand, the totally righteous cannot stand" (B. Ber 34b)—statements that he characterizes as "absolutely strange" (*be-takhlit ha-zarut*). Here is how he continues:

How can it be said that perversion and evil become virtues and merits? This is something difficult to say, all the more so to believe. And how can it be said that the stature of a man who has sinned is higher than one who never sinned throughout his life and who served God truthfully and faithfully? Human reason cannot tolerate the idea that a woman who has become degenerate and has betrayed [her husband], then returns in repentance, can sit with the righteous women and be of a higher level than they in holiness and purity? This is not right; it cannot be![66]

That does not sound like someone who is indulging in an intellectual exercise by making a case that he knows can be easily refuted. It sounds more like an anguished man wrestling with a real problem. After reviewing various attempts to answer this quandary by providing a plausible, rational exegesis of these statements,[67] he eventually gives up, throwing the matter back on tradition and faith:

What the sages said, they received from the prophets and the holy spirit. It is their *tradition* that the penitent is on a higher level than the righteous and than the ministering angels. But human intellect is unable to know this mystery. . . .

The one thing he insists is that the righteous who have no need for repentance will not be disenfranchised by the glorified status of the penitent: "There is no doubt that God will reward the righteous according to the fruit of their deeds."[68]

Isaac Arama discusses the aggadic dictum about "the place where the penitent stand" in a manner rather similar to Shem Tov, actually going further in specifying the conflict with philosophical tradition:

Now indeed this view conflicts with what is found in the writings of the Philosopher [Aristotle], in chapters 1 and 12 of the 7th book of the *Ethics* . . . and in chapter 11 of the first book. . . . Maimonides, in the 6th chapter of his introduction to Avot, mentioned this view [of Aristotle] and supported it with the following verse. . . . He then challenged [Aristotle] with the Rabbinic statements. . . . Then he reconciled the two positions. . . .[69]

But Maimonides' reconciliation is not satisfying to Arama, who ends—as does Shem Tov—unable to make peace between the two traditions: "Torah and philosophy are entirely different."[70] Unlike Shem Tov, Arama uses this conflict to expose the inadequacy for him of reason and philosophical analysis. Yet, for many, this discussion would have left the Rabbinic statement about repentance as puzzle and a problem.

Similar problems can be seen in the work of other preachers and commentators from the generation of the Expulsion. Isaac Caro, uncle of the celebrated author of the *Shulhan Arukh*, recapitulates the position we have heard from Joseph ibn Shem Tov:

> [The efficacy of repentance] is total grace. Why should it avail a murderer that he makes repentance? The soul of the dead person will not return to its body by means of this repentance! If one profanes the Sabbath, it will not return re-sanctified as a result of repentance! It is certainly nothing but total grace.[71]

Isaac Aboab, another of the leading Talmudists of the generation, raises the same issue in strikingly similar terms in one of his sermons. By rational legal standards, repentance should be of no avail.

> For what is the use of repentance made with the mouth for one who has denied God through his deeds? Furthermore, who can annul the reality of things that have already occurred? Who can set right what they have perverted? ... The sages taught ... that according to reason and strict justice, the sinner should not be able to achieve atonement through a verbal utterance.[72]

Finally, we have an extraordinary discussion of repentance from a preacher known only by the title of his manuscript sermon collection, "Dover Mesharim." The discussion is in the form of a "disputed question," one of the most characteristic modes of scholastic argumentation that increasingly found its way into fifteenth-century Spanish Jewish discourse. In this form, two antithetical positions on a theological question are supported with arguments from reason and authority, before a resolution is reached. Now our preacher realizes that this is a controversial preaching technique, as it requires him to defend a position that will ultimately be rejected, and he begins his sermon by justifying its use in the pulpit. Then he turns to the issue at hand: "Whether God for-

gives the penitent." Taking his cue from the theme verse of *Parashat Nitzavim*, "The Lord will not be willing to forgive him" (Deut. 29:19), the preacher goes on to bring an argument from "experience." We see in the example of Saul, that "even though he admitted his transgression and said 'I have sinned' several times, his repentance was not accepted." More provocative is the argument from reason:

> Assume that God decrees at the time of the commission of the sin that the evil person shall die, or given whatever punishment is appropriate. Then if it is true that afterward he decrees that the one who is supposed to die because of his sin will be accepted, and he removes from upon him what has already been decreed, the result is that God changes from wanting something to not wanting it. But whoever thinks this has thought something monstrously heretical, attributing a significant defect to God's stature.

This is followed by a straightforward philosophical argument: change entails movement, movement can occur only in time, if God changes, he must be subject to time, but that is false, as God created time. In conclusion, "the assumption that God accepts the penitent entails the conclusion that God changes, and this is total heresy. Therefore, we must necessarily conclude that God does not pardon and does not accept the penitent."[73] Of course the preacher does not leave it at this; he proceeds to argue the other side, and then to resolve the conflict. But why does he make such a strong argument against the efficacy of repentance to begin with?

Virtually alone, Abraham Saba insists the opposite: that the efficacy of repentance is totally rational. It seems as if he is arguing explicitly against the position we have seen:

> What you say—that once a person has sinned and transgressed there is no remedy for it—that is a lie. ... That was the position in which Adam erred ...; he had doubt about repentance, thinking that having sinned against God, there was no remedy ... but Cain did repentance [and Adam learned of its efficacy from Cain].[74]

He continues, "Therefore this passage [from *Nitzavim*] comes to remove this error from the hearts of people who think that repentance cannot benefit one who has sinned against God. . . . 'It is not distant' (Deut. 30:11) from reason, for reason requires that if one admits his sins, feels sorrow for them, and never repeats them, God will accept his repentance."[75] His very insistence on this matter indicates his recognition of a troubling problem.

What are we to make of this problematizing of repentance in the sermons and commentaries from the generation of the expulsion? What does it mean, as a cultural statement, to insist that the efficacy of repentance is irrational, in conflict with reason and justice? Following are some suggestions.

The material cited might serve as evidence for what Yizhak Baer and others, based on some contemporary sources, viewed as the corrosive effects of philosophical study on the foundations of Jewish belief. Philosophical analysis penetrates here into pulpit discourse that insists on using it as a touchstone; it thereby undermines the simple faith in one of Judaism's core values.[76]

Another possibility is that these passages reveal the power not of philosophy but of the Christian theology of grace. Some of these passage do, indeed, recall the classical Christian teachings denigrating the centrality of works as a means to salvation, insisting that sins against God cannot be atoned by finite human efforts, and promising to the sinner God's favor as an expression of totally unmerited love. Thus one influential fifteenth-century Christian preacher wrote, rather astonishingly,

> Even if you had committed a thousand mortal sins, if you had crucified Christ with your own hands, if you had killed all the apostles and martyrs, if you did not have a priest available, if you could not speak but could only think in your heart, "God, be merciful to me a sinner; I am sorry with my whole heart that I ever offended you," your soul would not descend into hell.

God's *greatest* wonder is *incarnation*, but the second—the preacher continues—greater even than creation of the world, is the *conversion of the sinner*.[77] If Christian theology could promise its sinners divine favor *beyond* what reason and justice could validate or explain, should Jewish teaching promise less?

A third context in which to evaluate this material is that of the *conversos*. Most discussions of repentance in this period have focused on this theme, analyzing the positions of Abravanel, Arama, and others on the relevance of repentance for those living as Christians.[78] Does this problem lurk in the background of our material as well? Is the emphasis on the irrationality of repentance a way of appealing to the *conversos*—perhaps through their familiarity with the Christian doctrine—by saying that even though it makes no apparent sense, God will accept your return? Or a way of addressing the Jews who may have been thinking, "It's not *fair* that we have continued to sacrifice to live as Jews, while *they* can be on the same level, indeed even a *higher* level, simply by a deathbed repentance"?

Finally, we should realize that repentance was not the only aspect of Judaism that was being problematized in this period. Virtually everything about the Bible and the aggadic literature was. Abravanel and Arama are well known for their exegetical technique of raising a series of "doubts" or intellectual problems with every passage they discuss and then resolving them. What is not as well known, as noted above, is that this technique was omnipresent in that generation, appearing in all of the cited writers, and many more, in contexts that have nothing to do with repentance. Apparently it was considered intellectually and aesthetically *de rigeur* to problematize the tradition in this way, so long as one could provide resolutions—despite the danger that the listeners or readers might remember the doubts and forget the resolutions. In this sense as well, the discussions of repentance would be part of a larger cultural trend.

Whatever may serve best to illuminate this puzzlement over repentance, it should not be understood to suggest that pulpit discourse was limited to the theory of repentance and overlooked completely its practical manifestations. It is fitting, therefore, to conclude with another brief passage from the philosopher Shem Tov ibn Shem Tov, which invokes repentance not as intellectual problem but as moral challenge. It is a sermon for Yom Kippur, and the preacher makes use of the Haftarah from Jonah. After discussing some conceptual and exegetical matters, he makes the application to his listeners: "And now you, O congregation of Israel, hear in how many ways the repentance of the nations is different from the repentance of Israel!" As expected in the tradition of the *tokhehah*, the Jews come off second best. Unlike the Ninevites, the Jews failed to repent despite many prophets; they insisted that their prophets bring signs of authenticity and that their prophets explicitly invoke God's name.

The preacher strikes home with his final contrast, no longer in the biblical past but in the present:

> Fourth, Israel repents only by fasting, and weeping, and affliction, but not by deeds. . . . No Jew has ever repented by returning that which he has stolen. But the nations, before anything else, made repentance and returned what they had stolen [*not in Jonah*]. No, *even on this sacred fast*, every Jew seeks out a place where he will be honored. In this way, our atonement needs atonement, and this Day of Atonement needs something that will atone for the sins and the transgressions that are performed on it![79]

No matter how problematic the theory of repentance may have become, it could still serve to inspire a primary function of the preacher—in the words of Is. 58:1: "to tell my people its sin."

Bibliography

Bettan, Israel, *Studies in Jewish Preaching* (Cincinnati, 1939).

Saperstein, Marc, *Jewish Preaching, 1200-1800* (New Haven, 1989).

Saperstein, Marc, *"Your Voice Like a Ram's Horn:" Themes and Texts in Traditional Jewish Preaching* (Cincinnati, 1996).

Notes

[1] On this literature as a whole, see Geoffrey Hartman, ed., *Midrash and Literature* (New Haven, 1986); Barry Holtz, "Midrash," in Barry Holtz, ed., *Back to the Sources* (New York, 1984), pp. 177-211; Jacob Neusner, *The Native Category-Formations of the Aggadah*, (Lanham, 2000). For general surveys of preaching during the talmudic period and the relationship between Midrash and Jewish sermons, see Leopold Zunz, *Die gottesdienstlichen Vorträge der Juden historisch entwickelt* (Berlin, 1832); Hebrew translation with additions by Hanokh Albeck and index: *Ha-Derashot be-Yisra'el* (Jerusalem, 1974); and Joseph Heinemann's work noted below.

[2] Joseph Heinemann, *Derashot ba-Tsibbur bi-Tequfat ha-Talmud* (Jerusalem, 1970) pp. 31-103. The material is available in English in Heine-

mann, *Literature of the Synagogue* (New York, 1975), pp. 113-196.

[3] For a convenient review of the problem of periodization, see Michael Meyer, "Where Does the Modern Period of Jewish History Begin?," in *Judaism*, 24 (1975), pp. 329-338. On the abandonment of the traditional preaching style, see Alexander Altmann, "The New Style of Preaching in Early Nineteenth-Century German Jewry," in *Studies in Nineteenth-Century Jewish Intellectual History* (Cambridge, 1964), pp. 65-116.

[4] For a welcome exception to the general neglect, see the bibliographical study by Ella Almagor, *The Manuscripts of David Ha-Nagid's Homilies* (Hebrew) (Jerusalem, 1995); Marc Saperstein, "Jewish Preachers and Their Literary Remains: A Review Essay," in *The Jewish Quarterly Review* 87 (1996), pp. 147-155.

[5] The first evidence for this practice dates from the middle of the ninth century; see S.W. Baron, *A Social and Religious History of the Jews* (Philadelphia and New York, 1952-1983), vol. 5, p. 55. For its cultivation in the high Middle Ages, see Jeremy Cohen, *The Friars and the Jews: The Evolution of Medieval Anti-Judaism* (Ithaca, 1982), pp. 82-84, and Robert Chazan, *Daggers of Faith: Thirteenth-Century Christian Missionizing and Jewish Response* (Berkeley, 1989), pp. 38-48.

[6] For a fuller discussion, see Marc Saperstein, *Jewish Preaching 1200-1800* (New Haven, 1989; henceforth: *Jewish Preaching*), pp. 26-44.

[7] The problematics of repentance will be discussed in greater detail later. For an example of part of a Sabbath of Repentance sermon from the fifteenth century in Germany, see S.Y. Agnon, *Days of Awe* (New York, 1965), pp. 27-30. For discussions of sermons for this Sabbath using motifs from the period of the Days of Awe, see Marc Saperstein, *"Your Voice Like a Ram's Horn": Themes and Texts in Traditional Jewish Preaching* (Cincinnati, 1996; henceforth, *"Your Voice Like a Ram's Horn"*), chapters 1, 4, and 15.

[8] See *"Your Voice Like a Ram's Horn,"* chapter 2. Cf., Dov Schwartz. "A Sermon on the Exodus from Egypt by Rabbi Vidal Joseph de la Caballeria" (Hebrew), in *Asufot*, 7 (1993), pp. 261-280; the preacher was part of a circle of Jewish neo-Platonists who flourished in Spain at the beginning of the fifteenth century. Also, Shaul Regev, "Sermons on the Passover Haggadah, for Festivals and Sabbaths: Remnant of a Manuscript by an Unknown Spanish Scholar" (Hebrew), in *Asufot*, 8 (1994), pp. 227-240.

[9] For a fuller discussion, see *Jewish Preaching*, pp. 36-37, 381-382, 200.

[10] "Sefer ha-Derashah," St. Petersburg Hebrew ms., First Series, num. 507, contains a wedding sermon and three eulogies, in only one of which, however, is the deceased identified by name. On this manuscript, see *"Your Voice Like a Ram's Horn,"* chapter 13.

[11] See Mordechai Pachter, "The Image of the Ari in the Eulogy Preached by R. Samuel Uceda" (Hebrew), in *Zion* 37 (1972), pp. 22-40.

[12] See the examples of eulogies in *Jewish*

Preaching, pp. 301-326 and *"Your Voice Like a Ram's Horn,"* chapters 16 and 17.

[13] See *Jewish Preaching*, pp. 76-77, and *"Your Voice Like a Ram's Horn,"* chapter 13.

[14] For a fine example of a Sabbath sermon prompted by a particular occasion, see *Jewish Preaching*, pp. 169-179 (from 1452). A selection from this sermon is discussed below.

[15] For an example of evidence for this, see ibid., pp. 156-157 (from the late fourteenth or early fifteenth century).

[16] See, for example, David Ruderman, "An Exemplary Sermon from the Classroom of a Jewish Teacher in Renaissance Italy," in *Italia* 1 (1978), pp. 7-38.

[17] The St. Petersburg manuscript (see above, n. 10) is critical for my revised dating of this shift, as its sermons reflect the new conception, referring to the occasion of delivery and to individuals in the audience. See the example in *"Your Voice Like a Ram's Horn,"* chapter 13. For more abundant evidence from the middle of the century, see *Jewish Preaching*, pp. 18-20.

[18] Cf., the fuller discussion in *Jewish Preaching*, pp. 63-79.

[19] This form is called the "proem," or, in Aramaic, *petihta*. See Joseph Heinemann, "The Proem in the Aggadic Midrashim: A Form-Critical Study," in *Studies in Aggadah and Folk Literature* (Jerusalem, 1971), pp. 100-122. For an example of a thirteenth-century sermon using this form, see *Jewish Preaching*, pp. 127-131.

[20] Ibid., p. 74.

[21] Ibid., pp. 74-75, especially n. 28; p. 181.

[22] Ibid., pp. 66-69, 75-76. The term *nosei*, meaning "subject" or "theme," comes from the Hebrew word meaning "lift, bear," producing the following etymology by a late-fifteenth century preacher: "Since the *nosei* is like *hyle*, the primal matter, which can receive any form, it is called 'that which bears,' for all parts of the sermon should be borne aloft by it" (p. 67 and n. 8).

[23] For a full analysis of this sermon and its parallels see Aviezer Ravitsky, *The Passover Sermon of R. Hasdai Crescas* (Hebrew) (Jerusalem, 1988); Ravitsky concentrates on the philosophical content of the material, not on the formal innovation. See also the discussion of this form in *"Your Voice Like a Ram's Horn,"* chapter 7, and the beautiful example in the sermon translated in chapter 13.

[24] See *Jewish Preaching*, pp. 395-398.

[25] The best Hebrew edition of the work is in Charles Chavel, ed., *Kitvei Rabbenu Bahya* (Jerusalem, 1970), pp. 17-462. This has been translated by Chavel as *Encyclopedia of Torah Thoughts* (New York, 1970). Cf., Israel Bettan, *Studies in Jewish Preaching* (Cincinnati, 1939; reprint, 1987), pp. 89-129. Bahya's book contains ten different model introductory passages that a preacher could use in asking "permission" from his listeners, and material appropriate for wedding, funeral, and holiday sermons as well as content for ordinary Sabbath preaching.

[26] Examples would be the Torah commentaries of Bahya ben Asher (whose interest in preaching is obvious, see previous note); Isaac Arama (ca. 1420-1494), whose *Aqedat Yitshaq* ("The Binding of Isaac") is a homiletical commentary, based on his preaching but not a record of his sermons (see *Jewish Preaching*, pp. 17-18, 392-393); Abraham Saba (fl. ca. 1500), whose commentary *Tseror ha-Mor* ("The Bundle of Myrrh," Song 1:13) contains frequent references to his own sermons and instructions for future preachers who wish to use the work; and Moses Alsheikh, known as one of the most popular preachers of the sixteenth century, who recast his sermons into biblical commentaries.

[27] For these two texts, see *"Your Voice Like a Ram's Horn,"* chapter 12, and *Jewish Preaching*, pp. 387-392.

[28] Henry Adler Sosland, *A Guide for Preachers on Composing and Delivering Sermons: The Or ha-Darshanim of Jacob Zahalon, A Seventeenth-Century Italian Preacher's Manual* (New York, 1987).

[29] Rabbi Jacob Moellin, quoted in *Jewish Preaching*, p. 27.

[30] Jacob Elbaum, "Shalosh Derashot Ashkenaziyot Qedumot mi-Q[tav] Y[ad] Beit ha-Sefarim," in *Kiryat Sefer*, 48 (1973), pp. 340-347.

[31] For an overview of Italian Jewish preaching, concentrating mostly on the period after 1500, see my essay in David Ruderman, ed., *Preachers of the Italian Ghetto* (Berkeley and Los Angeles, 1992), pp. 22-40, reprinted in *"Your Voice Like a Ram's Horn,"* chapter 8. Other essays in this book treat different aspects of Italian Jewish homiletics.

[32] Several of my articles on the sermons of Saul Levi Morteira of Amsterdam are cited below.

[33] See the material in *Jewish Preaching*, pp. 286-300, 327-373, 412-426; *"Your Voice Like a Ram's Horn,"* pp. 127-161, 445-484.

[34] Saul Levi Morteira, Budapest Rabbinical Seminary MS12, 5:51r, Sermon on Gen. 32:14.

[35] *"Your Voice Like a Ram's Horn,"* pp. 266-268.

[36] Jacob Anatoli, *Malmad ha-Talmidim* (Lyck, 1866), *Noah*, p. 12a.

[37] For a masterful discussion of allegorical exegesis, see Frank Talmage, "Apples of Gold: The Inner Meaning of Sacred Texts in Medieval Judaism," in Arthur Green, ed., *Jewish Spirituality from the Bible Through the Middle Ages* (New York, 1989), pp. 313-355.

[38] Solomon Levi, *Divrei Shelomoh* (Venice, 1596), p. 231a; see the fuller quotation in *"Your Voice Like a Ram's Horn,"* p. 29.

[39] Especially noteworthy in this respect is Joshua ibn Shueib. See S. Abramson's introduction to the reprint of his sermons, and Carmi Horowitz, *The Jewish Sermon in 14th Century Spain: The Derashot of R. Joshua ibn Shu'eib* (Cambridge, 1989), pp. 133-158.

[40] See on this *"Your Voice Like a Ram's Horn,"* pp. 37-44.

[41] See, for example, Joshua ibn Shu'eib, *Derashot R"Y ibn Shu'eib al ha-Torah u-Mo'adei ha-Shanah* (Jerusalem, 1952), pp. 402-414.

[42] Jacob ben Hananel of Sicily, *Minhat Bikkurim*, ed. S. Ben-Eliyahu (New York, 1954), p. 51. Cf., *"Your Voice Like a Ram's Horn,"* pp. 12-14.

[43] One manuscript of the sermons of Jacob Anatoli (Br. Mus. Add. 26,898) contains many similar statements indicating that the preacher may incorporate a discussion of appropriate legal material (see examples in *Jewish Preaching*, p. 16, n. 27). Cf., the statement cited in *Jewish Preaching*, p. 387, that the preacher should "speak of the laws relating to the Sabbath and the festivals." The extant texts of sermons from northern Europe were mostly delivered by rabbis in connection with holidays and were in large part devoted to legal material relating to their observance. For a confraternity sermon that reviews basic legal issues relating to the vow, see *"Your Voice Like a Ram's Horn,"* chapter 13.

[44] See *Jewish Preaching*, pp. 111-123, 386, n. 8; 392-393; 395-397, and *"Your Voice Like a Ram's Horn,"* chapter 7. Compare the example published by Dov Schwartz, "A Sermon on the Exodus by Rabbi Vidal Joseph de la Caballería: On the Influence of the Neo-Platonic Circle at the Beginning of the Fifteenth Century" (Hebrew), in *Asufot 7* (1993), pp. 261-280.

[45] See the texts in *Jewish Preaching*, pp. 80-83.

[46] See *Jewish Preaching*, pp. 56-57, 380-386, 390.

[47] Joshua ibn Shu'eib; see Carmi Horowitz (above, n. 39), pp. 159-170.

[48] *"Your Voice Like a Ram's Horn,"* p. 329; cf., also p. 318.

[49] See the striking example of this in the sermon by Elijah ha-Kohen of Izmir in *Jewish Preaching*, pp. 301-326.

[50] On the need for rebuke, see the source from Maimonides' code quoted in *Jewish Preaching*, p. 380. The Toledo sermon is described by Yitzhak Baer, *A History of the Jews of Christian Europe* (Philadelphia, 1961), vol. 1, pp. 257-261. See also Marc Saperstein, "The Preaching of Repentance and the Reforms in Toledo of 1281," in Beverly Mayne Kienzle, ed., *Models of Holiness in Medieval Sermons* (Louvain-la-Neuve, 1996), pp. 157-174.

[51] See Morteira, "The People's Envy," in *Jewish Preaching*, pp. 270-285.

[52] For examples, see Saperstein, "The Rhetoric and Substance of Rebuke," in *Studia Rosenthaliana* 34 (2000), pp. 131-152. For a discussion of sermonic material from late-eighteenth-century Prague, see *"Your Voice Like a Ram's Horn,"* chapter 10.

[53] *Derashot al ha-Torah*, Sermon on Yitro, p. 28d.

[54] See *"Your Voice Like a Ram's Horn,"* chapter 6.

[55] See the passage from Anatoli cited in *"Your Voice Like a Ram's Horn,"* p. 60, and the passage from a manuscript collection of sermons from ca. 1425 cited in Marc Saperstein and Ephraim Kanarfogel, "Byzantine Manuscript of Sermons" (Hebrew), in *Pe'amim* 78 (1999), pp. 173-174.

[56] On the presentation of Christianity by Morteira, see Saperstein, "Christians, Christianity, and 'New Christians,' in the Sermons of Saul Levi Morteira," in *HUCA* 70-71 (1999-2000), pp. 329-384.

[57] See *Jewish Preaching*, pp. 79-89.

[58] For the text of this sermon, see ibid., pp. 169-179.

[59] See the full text of this sermon, ibid., pp. 286-300.

[60] Ibid., pp. 217-239.

[61] According to the preacher, the Jews of Amsterdam emerged relatively unscathed from the plague, with only two infants dead during a period when hundreds of their Christian neighbors succumbed. Budapest Rabbinical Seminary Hebrew MS 12, vol. 5: 118r-v, *Va-Yiggash* on Gen 45:2. For Jacob Zahalon's preaching while the same plague ravaged the Roman Ghetto, see Sosland, *A Guide for Preachers* (above, n. 28), p. 26.

[62] Anonymous, Cambridge University Add. Ms. 1022, fol. 89b; Moses Maimonides, *Mishnah 'im Perush ha-RaMBaM* (Jerusalem, 1963), 4: 28; cf. A.S. Halkin, "Classical and Arabic Material in Ibn Aknin's 'Hygiene of the Soul,'" in *PAAJR*, 14 (1944), p. 67 and n. 1, which gives the Islamic sources. Cf., *The Little Flowers of St. Francis* (Garden City, 1958), pp. 58-60.

[63] Abravanel, *Perush al ha-Torah*, Deuteronomy, p. 283c; cf., Arama, *'Aqedat Yitzhaq*, chap. 100, Deut, p. 86c.

[64] Shaul Regev, "Sermons on Repentance by Rabbi Joseph ibn Shem Tov" (Hebrew), in *Asufot* 5 (1991), p. 191.

[65] Ibid., p. 193. This is taken up again in a later sermon: it is only "God's gracious compassion" that provides a way for human beings to return to their "pristine stature" following sin (p. 207). On grace, see also sources in *"Your Voice Like a Ram's Horn,"* p. 319, n. 104.

[66] Shem Tov ibn Shem Tov, *Derashot al ha-Torah* (Salonika, 1525, reprint: Jerusalem, 1973), p. 162b.

[67] For example, "Some say this is said homiletically, in order to motivate people to repent, but the truth is that level of the righteous is higher . . ." (p. 163a). But this approach—that the sages stated things they knew to be false in order to motivate Jews to act properly—is rejected.

[68] Ibid., p. 163b. This confession on the part of someone obviously committed to philosophy of an utter inability to comprehend or make sense of a Rabbinic statement that appears to be repugnant to reason, nevertheless reaffirming its validity as an authentic tradition, echoes skeptical formulations of Abraham ibn Ezra.

[69] *'Aqedat Yitzhaq*, chap. 100 (*Nitzavim*), pp. 83c-d. The reference in Maimonides is to the sixth of his "Eight Chapters:" see Isadore Twersky, ed., *A Maimonides Reader* (New York, 1972), pp. 376-379.

[70] Ibid., p. 84a: *"divrei Torah le-hud ve-divrei filosofiyah le-hud."*

[71] Isaac Caro, *Toledot Yitzhaq* (Riva di Trento, 1558), *Re'eh*, p. 103b.

[72] Isaac Aboab, Sermon for Sabbath of Repentance, in *"Your Voice Like a Ram's Horn,"* pp. 317 (English), 350 (Hebrew).

[73] On this sermon, see *Jewish Preaching*, pp. 395-398.

[74] Abraham Saba, *Tseror ha-Mor*, (Venice 1566, reprint: Tel Aviv, 1975), Deuteronomy, p. 27b.

[75] Ibid., pp. 27b-c; also 28a. Cf., Abraham Gross, *Iberian Jewry From Twilight to Dawn: The World of Rabbi Abraham Saba* (Leiden, 1995), pp. 121, n. 96, 159.

[76] This interpretation seems quite questionable. The scholars cited were not radical preachers devoid of grounding in traditional texts. Isaac Aboab and Isaac Caro were distinguished talmudists whose absolute commitment to Judaism is beyond question. Shem Tov ibn Shem Tov, while a strong defender of Maimonidean philosophy, was, as far as we know, not attacked for heretical philosophical doctrine in his sermons. The work of such preachers shows rather that Rabbinic leaders of the generation incorporated philosophy and rational categories into their sermons and commentaries without viewing it as a threat.

[77] See J.W. Dahmus, "*Dormi Secure*: The Lazy Preacher's Model of Holiness for His Flock," in *Models of Holiness in Medieval Sermons* (Louvain-la-Neuve, 1996), p. 308, on the German Franciscan Johannes von Werden.

[78] Netanyahu, *The Marranos of Spain*, chap. 4. Abravanel introduces this category explicitly into his discussions of repentance, speaking, for example, of "the victims of duress who have left the category of religion. Regarding these it is said, 'You shall take it to heart' (Deut. 30:1), for their repentance will be in the heart, not in the mouth, for they will not be able to proclaim their repentance and their faith publicly" (Abravanel: *Perush al ha-Torah*, Deuteronomy 30, p. 283a).

[79] Shem Tov ibn Shem Tov, *Derashot al ha-Torah*, p. 179a.

MARC SAPERSTEIN

SUPERSTITION IN JUDAISM: Superstitions may be categorized as folk religion, folk customs, and folklore. The concept of superstition thus emerges from the existence within religious traditions of powerful elites that determine a religion's official, normative content. Beliefs and practices found within the community that do not conform to this norm frequently are deemed superstition. In this way, religions, including Judaism, determine the way in which power over the individual is exercised by setting out norms that exclude and invalidate non-normative practice, defined as "false" or as "superstitious."

One may speak of a multitude of superstitions that find expression in Judaism. In every culture there is a diversity and a dialogue between different groups and value structures as well as between religious belief and superstition. There are many corresponding or parallel beliefs, concepts, ceremonies, practices, and rituals in each age's prevalent "normative" Judaism and in the Judaism of the common folk. Often, normative practice changes, and phenomena that contemporary practitioners view as superstitious were once commonly practiced and accepted. Superstitions are often related to *minhagim* (local customs), and some superstitious practices may eventually become accepted customs. Generally, superstitions in Judaism pertain to a realm of human belief and perception dominated by extra-religious powers or to a realm of spiritual experience that does not fully conform to the Rabbinic belief system, with its ambivalent attitude toward folk religion and remedies. Superstitions frequently are related to the supernatural and to theories and practices surrounding magic and medicine. Superstition is related to magic since both contend that certain actions can engender desired reactions or prevent undesirable occurrences (B. Shab. 67a). Practices intended to heal the sick or avoid disease thus were often practiced on the borderline between superstition/magic and what has been, since the Renaissance, characterized as early science.

Jewish superstitions appear in documents widely separated geographically, chronologically, and ideologically. There is no unifying perspective in Judaism in regard to superstitions, although the formative period of Judaism and the documents it produced lay the foundation for subsequent exchanges with superstitious practices. The Hebrew terms *emunah tefelah* and *emunat hevel* expresses the nullity of so-called superstitious beliefs, whereas the Hebrew term *mi-darkhe ha-emori*, the practices of the Amorite, views these as foreign beliefs to be rejected. In Judaism, superstitions relate to angels, demons, and spirits as manifestations or agents who cause harm and can be adjured to help. Superstitions also involve objects, such as metals, stones, and other substances that can cause or heal certain conditions. Superstitions relate to body parts (hands) and to specific locales (ruins, bathrooms, cemeteries) as well as time periods (*tekufot*), astrological influences, life cycle events (pregnancy, childbirth, wedding, death), and medical and psychic conditions. Biblical superstitions involved staffs, salt, plants, magical practices, omens, and dream interpretation. Hellenistic Judaism added its own realm of superstitions, absorbed from the Mediterranean cultural climate, including Egyptian, Greek, and Roman influences, in particular in the realm of magic. Talmudic literature shows influences from Babylonian and Persian practices.

A list of actions that could affect a person is found in T. Shab. 8:9; within this context, certain actions are categorized as "the practices of the Amorite" (T. Shab. 7 and 8). In regard to this category, B. Shab. 67a-b states:

> [Mishnah:] *As a prophylactic: This is R. Meir's opinion.*
> Abayye and Rava both maintain: Whatever is used as a remedy is not [prohibited] because of the Amorite ways. Then if it is not a remedy, it is prohibited because of the ways of the Amorites? It was surely taught: If a tree is losing its fruits, one paints it with *sikra* and loads it with stones. Now, as for loading it with stones, this is done to reduce its vitality [of overproducing], but painting it with *sikra*, what remedy does one gain? That is that the people may see it and pray for it. . . . A tanna recited the chapter of Amorite practices before R. Hiyya b. Abin. He said to him, All these are forbidden as Amorite practices except the following: If someone has a bone in his throat, he may bring of that kind, place it on top of his head, and say the following: One by one go down, swallow, go down one by one. This is not deemed to be "the practices of the Amorite." For a fish bone he should say the following: You are stuck in like a pin, you are locked up as a cuirass, go down, go down! Someone who says: Be lucky, my luck and tire not by day or night is guilty of Amorite practices.

In addition to early inner-Jewish contemplations and discussions of superstitions, the term was utilized in virulent anti-Jewish works as early as in Roman and Carolingian times. Horace, Plutarch and Tertullian applied the term *superstitio* to Judaism; Judaism was considered to be superstitious (Acts 17:22). The Archbishop of Lyon, Agobard (769-840), composed the work *De Iudaicis Superstitionibus* ("On the Superstitions of the Jews"), which intended to keep Christians from sympathizing with aspects of Jewish religious practice and thought.

Maimonides (1135-1204) dealt intensively with Jewish superstitions; his attitude can be summarized as ignoring previous talmudic laws associated with superstitions or finding rational explanations for the terms that he perceived to be based upon superstitions. For example, Maimonides cites B. Ber. 3a: "Our rabbis taught: There are three reasons one must not go into a ruin: because of suspicion, because of falling debris, and because of demons," but Maimonides omits the reasons mentioned in the Talmud, because they are based on superstitions (*Yad*, Hilkhot Tefillah 5:6); in another place (commentary on M. A.Z. 4:7), Maimonides mentions that a conversation with demons is impossible; or he mentions that the springs in Tiberias are hot because they run over a sulphurous source (commentary on M. Neg. 9:1), contrary to the talmudic claim that they are hot because they run over the entrance to Gehinnom (B. Shab. 39a). Maimonides was against astrological determination (*Letter on Astrology*).[1]

Terms and Realms of Superstitions—Amulets: Amulets have always been part and parcel of Jewish superstitions, either as inanimate objects, jewelry, or written texts. The *lehashim* in Is. 3:18 are interpreted as amulets; otherwise there are few instances of amulets in the Hebrew Bible. The talmudic *kame'a* is in all likelihood derived from *kam'a* (Arabic and Hebrew), "to bind, to master." The rites of transition observed during birth, coming of age, marriage, and death called for special ceremonies to protect people who were vulnerable to dangerous influences from demons, the evil eye, other people, the stars, and sickness. A special prayer and an amulet could be prepared for each of these life stages. Amulets are often mentioned in early Rabbinic literature (e.g., M. Shab. 6:2; M. Miq. 6:4; M. Kel. 23:9, B. Shab. 61b).

Amulets are often worn or carried on the body; sometimes they are hidden. Since the weak were more likely to suffer from the evil influence of witchcraft and demons than the strong, it was usually women and children who wore such means of protection (B. Qid. 73b). An amulet for a woman is mentioned in Pesikta Rabbati 5. Children wore small tablets on their chests inscribed with Scriptural verses or a proverb thought to have symptomatic meaning (Y. Hag. 15c). A similar custom was practiced by the Romans. Pendants worn by women are mentioned frequently. Sometimes women wore bells around the neck, on the chest, or on a belt. Pieces of jewelry were found on the forehead, or as pendants close to the heart or stomach. Some jewelry items had the form of a tiara, had pictures of cities (T. Shab. 4:5), and might have been worn for protective purposes. Amulets written on lead and silver in Palestinian Jewish Aramaic were utilized during the Byzantine period to cure illness by means of exorcising evil spirits that had invaded a person and had caused an illness. *Sefer ha-Razim*, which dates probably from the Byzantine period, is full of protective spells. While the Talmud generally lacks textual inscriptions found on amulets (B. Yom. 84a), some specific instructions concerning the writing of amulets are found in *Sefer Yetzirah*. Also *Sefer Razi'el* contains detailed examples of amulets and charms and instructions on how to fabricate them. The underlying principle in the writing of amulets was the belief in the power of God and the name of God, in particular the secret four-letter name of God. The work *Hurba de-Moshe* ("The Sword of Moses," Deut. 33:29) contains many mystical names; it further details a correspondence between parts of the body and a list of diseases and their treatments. The power of certain combinations of the letters of the Hebrew alphabet is a well-attested remedy and prophylactic against the forces of the dark; other letters were avoided because of superstitions. The medieval *Sefer Hasidim*, section 1154, states:

> Since the letter *peh* is found in the name of the destroyer angels, such as Aph Soaph Shezeph Ketzeph Nagaph Agaph Resheph, you will not find a *peh* in a prayer except in the *musaph* prayer, because you have to say, the *musaph* of such and such a day, we will worship you and sacrifice before you . . .

Maimonides was opposed to the use of amulets (*Yad*, Tefillin 5:4; *Guide* 1:61), whereas Nahmanides (1194-1270) and Adret (1235-1310) permitted them; also the Vilna Gaon (1720-1797) permitted the use of amulets.

Some laws in regard to amulets are discussed in the *Shulhan Arukh* (*Orah Hayyim* 301:24ff.; *Yoreh Deah* 179:12). A famous controversy between Jacob Emden (1697-1776) and Jonathan Eybeschütz (1690/95-1764), the rabbi of Hamburg, targeted amulets written by Eybeschütz. Emden claimed that Eybeschütz utilized the name of the seventeenth century false messiah Shabbetai Tzevi in his amulets.

Shapes of Amulets: The name of God is used in different permutations on amulets, often just *Shaddai* (the Almighty) is found. The Priestly Blessing (Num. 6:24-26) is also inscribed on many amulets. In addition to protective formulas and citations, amulets also show depictions or geometrical figures. Very often amulets display or are made in the form of a particular shape; among these are rectangles, squares, triangles, hexagrams (the Star of David), a *menorah*, or a hand. Some of the geometrical figures, such as triangles, reduce the evil spirit by first writing the full name and then reducing the number of letters. For example, the eye demon Shabriri is mentioned frequently (B. Pes. 112a; B. Git. 69a). A person in danger of becoming a victim of this demon is advised to say the following:

> My mother has told me to beware of
> SH-A-B-R-I-R-I
> .B-R-I-R-I
> ..R-I-R-I
> ...I-R-I
> ....R-I

The danger emanating from Shabriri is also discussed in B. A.Z. 12b, in the context of the danger inherent in drinking water at night. The reduction of the danger is equally present in the Abracadabra pattern:

> Abracadabra
> Abracadabr
> Abracadab
> Abracada
> Abracad
> Abraca
> Abrac
> Abra
> Abr
> Ab
> A

The same reductional procedure is found in the following (*Sefer Razi'el*):

KARGAMAN
ARGAMAN
RGAMAN
GAMAN
MAN
AN
N

In addition to the triangle achieved by the reductional pattern, many amulets are in the shape of a hand; although the protective hand is usually explained and understood to be the hand of Fatimah (Islam), one could assume that it is related to the blessings from the hands of Moses or the Aaronide priests.

The Book of Psalms in particular was a source of protective amulets. An often published booklet, *Shimmush Tehillim*, is a medieval compilation of Psalms and their uses in the cure and prevention of sickness, protection from animals, demons, street robbers, and many other real or perceived dangers. Texts such as these depend upon the notion that the entire Torah is based upon the names of God and that the text of the Bible can therefore save and protect humans. Parchments containing Psalms are also used for protective purposes. Ps. 121—"I will lift up my eyes unto the mountains" (esp. 121:6: "the sun shall not smite you by day, neither the moon by night")—is another inscription found on amulets. Some amulets (*Shiviti* amulets) are based on Ps. 16:8—"I will set the Lord always before me." These amulets contain Ps. 16:8 in combination with Ps. 67: "to the chief musician on Neginot, a psalm;" this latter verse is usually written in menorah form. These Shiviti amulets also have an inscription of Gen. 49:22, which protects against the evil eye.[2]

Particularly potent against demons are Pss. 3 and 91, the anti-demonic psalms from talmudic times (*shir shel-pega'im*). Amulets with exquisite calligraphy contain Psalms that are believed to ward off illnesses; among the life-preserving Psalms mentioned are 13:4; 30:4; 34:13; 91:16; for particular conditions, such as diseases of the bones, Ps. 6:3, and for fertility, Ps. 128:3, are utilized among many other inscriptions from Psalms.[3] Sickness and disease are understood to result from the negative influence of demons or an evil eye. The condition called *sira* (anxiety producing somatic symptoms) among

Moroccan Jews is believed to be caused by a demon. This particular demon, jinn, is harmed, and the ailment it produces is considered to be the jinn's retaliation.[4] *Segullot* ("letters from heaven") as folk remedies are often prepared by women and are available for purchase until this present day in Israel.

Demons: Demons were created on the eve of the Sabbath of creation; they have souls but are bodiless because the arrival of Sabbath interrupted their creation (Gen. Rabbah 7:7). There are additional legends and views dealing with demons and their creation (Gen. Rabbah 24:6; B. Erub. 18b); for example demons are the souls of the wicked (Zohar 3, 70a). Demons possess wings, but they do not cast shadows, and humans cannot see them, although they are numerous. Demons are threatening in part because they are invisible. Rabbis mention a reason for their invisibility and list a few of the problems they cause (B. Shab. 6a):

> It has been taught: Abba Binyamin says: If the eye had the power to see them, no creature could endure demons. R. Huna says: Everyone among us has a thousand on his left hand and ten thousand on his right hand. . . . Knee problems derive from them; wearing out of clothes of scholars is caused by them; brushing of feet is caused by them.

Demons that harm people with their stares have a cover over their eyes comparable to the cover that a miller's donkey wears. This is so that they do not inflict harm with their eyes at random. When the sins of a person are discovered and made known, the cover is removed, and the demons stare intensely at the wicked person and harm him or her with their eyes (Tanhuma, printed edition, *Mishpatim* 19). While demons are invisible to the human eye, certain preparations can make their footprints visible (B. Shab. 6a). There are different classes of demons, such as *mazzikim*, *shedim*, and *ruhot*. *Shedim* work at night; *ruhim* and *ruhot* are "lost souls;" *mazzikim* do a lot of damage. The Ashkenazic *Ma'aseh Bukh* contains a "demonology;" and many other Jewish sources warn against demons (*Brantshpigl*).

Much effort went into rendering demons powerless through prayers, amulets, *mezuzot*, and pharmacological procedures. The Shema has a long history in the protection from demons; Y. Ber. 1:1 states: "R. Huna in the name of R. Joseph [said], On what basis is one obliged to recite the Shema in one's house in the evening? So that one may chase away the demons." B. Ber. 5a relates: "R. Isaac says further: If one recites the Shema on his bed, the demons keep away from him.". *Sefer Hasidim* 235f. recommends spitting upon the demon of a dead person and saying: "Unclean one, go away from me." Spitting was generally applied in superstition to rid oneself of demons and dangers (*Sefer Hasidim* 326). Another method of protection was to conciliate the demons with gifts or offering a substitute to them.

The leader of demons is known as Ashmedai. Already the *Book of Tobit* contains a recipe to drive Ashmedai from the bedroom of Tobiah and Sarah: the heart and liver of a fish are burned. Extreme danger emanates from the female demon Lilith, the first wife of Adam, who snatches newborn babies and hurts their mothers. The Lilith legend is already present in the *Testament of Solomon* 5:7 and has many forms and contexts (*Alphabet of Ben Sira, Otzar Midrashim*, I:46). The Zohar 3, 77b, summarizes: "[Lilith] goes out into the world in search of infants, and when she sees human infants she attaches herself to them and tries to kill them in order to absorb the spirits of these infants." Lilith is believed to cohabit with men in their fantasies; she consorts with demons and takes on different shapes. Three angels, Sinoi (also called Sanvei), Sinsinoi (Sansenvei), Samengelof (Semangelof), overwhelmed her and, as a result, inscribing their names on paper or on the door of a room where a woman is in labor can serve as a protection. Lilith can also be trapped under an inverted bowl that is placed in the bed room.

Procreation: Superstitions regarding procreation and conception included a belief in spontaneous generation,[5] for example, that certain creatures, such as mice, come from the dust. The Babli offers a range of superstitions concerning human conception and pregnancy (B. B.M. 84b; B. Nid.16b); B. Nid. 38a states that sexual relations should take place on Wednesday or starting with Wednesday. B. Pes. 112b states: "He who

cohabits by the light of a lamp will have epileptic children." Objects seen or things said before and during conception confer their characteristics on the child. The Rokeah (Eleazar b. Judah) believed that the thoughts of a pregnant woman exerted a decisive influence upon a child. There are predictive signs that permit parents to tell the sex of the unborn child. If the belly of the pregnant woman aches, it is a girl; if her loins ache, it is a boy; certain actions by the mother and observations concerning her body also reveal the sex of the unborn (*Sefer Hasidim* 1141). If a pregnant woman sees a nut and does not consume it and scratches herself, the child will be marked at that spot; if a pregnant woman steps over nails, she will loose the child; a new mother puts a knife under her pillow for protection; if a rope is thrown at a pregnant woman, the child will be strangled; if a pregnant woman looks at terrifying things, the child will become stupid; if the wishes of a pregnant woman are not granted, mice will eat up the garments of the one who refused them; if you step over a child, it will not grow; if the child sneezes its growth will be stunted; a mother must slap a girl's face when she experiences menarche.[6] These superstitions show a belief in the power and sympathetic influences any behavior or occurrence might have over the fetus.

Birth: Amulets were used during pregnancy and childbirth, either worn by pregnant women or placed under the pillow and/or above the head of the woman in labor. As protective amulets or as remedies, we find child bed charms and parchments containing Psalms, as mentioned above. The *Kindbettzettel* (Yiddish: *kimpettzetl*; "child bed charm")—a text that is affixed in the location where labor takes place would often state the following (Germany, eighteenth century):

> In the name of the God of Israel whose name is great and awesome: Elijah the prophet, remembered for good, was walking and met Lilith and her cohorts and he said to Lilith the wicked, You are unclean with the spirit of contamination and all your group is unclean. And she said, No my lord Elijah. I am on my way to the house of the new mother N.N. to give her the sleep of death and take her newborn son, to drink his blood and extrude the marrow of his

bones, and to eat his flesh. And he answered her, Elijah the prophet, remembered for good, and he said to her, You are excommunicated from the Blessed Name and you will be like a stone, and she answered saying, Whenever the name will be revealed to me, I will flee and promise in the name of God to leave the paths of the mother and her son, and anytime I hear the name and whenever they are said neither I nor my cohorts will have evil power to enter the house and neither to cause harm. And these are my names: Lilith Abitu Abizu Amzarpohakash Odem Ikpoido Iyella Tatrutah Abanuktaw Shatrunah Kalikatizah Tilawtuy Pirtash Haw.[7]

The strong belief in the power of the word led to the practice of putting holy books, prayer books, and parchments into the cradle to protect the infant. Parchments containing Psalms (Yiddish: *shir hamalos tzetl*, based upon the Hebrew *Shir ha-ma'alot*, "the Song of Ascents") are used in the protection of the woman in labor, the child, or for general purposes. Moroccan Jews summon the teacher of children from the *heder* (school), and he reads "letters" (such as the Psalms) in order to chase away Lilith. Superstitious practices surrounding the dangerous time of childbirth are numerous. B. Shab. 129b, for instance, refers to hiding the afterbirth, "so that the infant may be kept warm." The Ashkenazic *Wachnacht* ("night of watching") is a vigil before circumcision.[8] This vigil is observed in the bedroom; Gen 48:16, from Jacob's blessing of Ephraim and Manasseh (May the angel who has redeemed me bless the boy . . ."), and the Shema (Deut. 6:4) are recited to protect the baby. Some Sephardic Jews use myrtle branches during a ceremony called *shadd-il-asse* to protect the child during the night before circumcision.

In the ceremony called *Hollekreisch* among German Jews, the newborn child is given a secular name on the fourth Sabbath after birth, possibly as protection against *Frau Holle*, a dangerous female figure in German folklore who is also mentioned as a child-snatching and snow-producing woman in the brothers Grimm's fairy tales. The derivation of the term *Hollekreisch* from the French expression for "up with the cradle,"[9] reflecting the fact that the child is lifted up in the air, is not convincing. Derivation of

the term *Hollekreisch* from the child eating *Frau Holle* is preferable.[10]

Wedding: Wedding preparations and the ceremony itself are dangerous periods of transition to which many superstitions pertain (B. Ber. 54a):

> R. Judah said, Three persons require guarding, namely, a sick person, a bridegroom, and a bride. In a baraita it was taught: A sick person, a midwife, a bridegroom, and a bride. Some add: A mourner. And some add: Scholars at night time.

Rashi comments that the people enumerated in this passage need to be guarded from evil spirits. Warding off an evil spirit before the wedding is accomplished by Sephardic Jews (Syrians) at a celebration that is held several days before the actual wedding. In the company of friends and relatives, including the mothers of the bride and groom, the bride is immersing in a *mikveh* to perform the requirement of immersion. This celebration is called *hamman el-arus* (the bath of the bride) and includes singing, ululations, and dancing. The ululations ward off evil spirits who might disturb the bride and interfere at the wedding ceremony. Gifts given to the bride during this celebration include henna (a red dye used to protect from the evil eye). Sometimes brides immerse in a ritual bath that contains some granules of henna, and some Moroccan Jews put henna on the hands of all participants in the party and adorn the bride with a *hamsa* (hand-shaped amulet). Covering the bride with a veil before the wedding of course has biblical reverberations (Leah and Rachel), but it may also have derived from a fear of the evil eye, which could only be avoided when the bride was covered. The groom veils the bride prior to the wedding ceremony ("checking the identity of the bride," *bodek et ha-kallah*; or the Yiddish/German *badekken/bedecken*, covering the bride). Not all Sephardic Jews perform this ceremony, but Ashkenazim do. The smashing of a glass at the end of the wedding ceremony has been compared to the smashing of clay pots containing excruciation texts (Ps. 2:9) and could be viewed as an attempt to smash the power of demons, although a new and distinctive meaning was attached to this practice with the idea that it symbolizes the destruction of the Jerusalem Temple. A belief that the husbands of certain women are doomed to die is called the "killer wife superstition;" this superstition is applied to more than twice-widowed women.[11]

Death and Burial: The angel of death is coming into town when the dogs are howling (B. B.Q. 60b). When a person dies, all the mirrors in a house are covered. It was the custom not to drink water that is standing in the home of the deceased at the time of his death. While preparing the deceased for burial, people in some Sephardic communities throw coins in four directions of the room or place them on the coffin while reciting seven times to ward off evil spirits (Gen. 25:6): "and to the children of Abraham's concubine he gave gifts." The reference to the "children of the concubines" is to the *mashhitim* (destroyers) or *shedim* who might have claims against the deceased person for having sinned on earth. The coins would satisfy them to release the dead person from their claims. Additionally, Pss. 90-100 are recited.[12] A grave that is dug may not lie open overnight, because it is believed that another death will occur (*Sefer Hasidim*). Sephardic Jews spell out the name of the deceased in verses taken from Ps. 119, the so called "Alfa Bet Psalm," so as not to invoke any living person with the same name. In some Moroccan communities, one does not mention the name of the deceased until after the seven day period of mourning. This is to prevent the name of the deceased's being overly carefully investigated in the heavenly court, which could bring about a harsh judgment for that person.[13] In Germany, after visiting a cemetery, one plucks some blades of grass and throws them behind one's back, supposedly as an offering to the demons dwelling among the tombs.

House: There are numerous superstitious practices surrounding the home; "R. Hanina said: One may not sleep in a house alone, and whoever sleeps in a house alone is seized by Lilith" (B. Shab. 151a). One leaves a small gap in the door and the windows and does not close them tightly in order to leave some opening for demons, because this is the only way for them to leave (*Sefer Hasidim* 1146). Sometimes the power of iron has to be invoked in an attempt to gain protection from demons: "If food and drink are under the bed, even if they are covered in iron vessels, an evil spirit rests upon them" (B. Pes. 112a; *Sefer Hasidim* 458). Protection from spirits or demons can also be accomplished by noise-making. In other cases, pieces of iron from utensils such as knives are placed into cradles or under the pillow of a woman in labor. Other effective means of protection are certain colors (M. Shab. 9:3).

Personal Names: Many superstitions and folk etymologies are involved in a person's given name; naming a newborn after a grandparent was followed already by Jews in Egypt in the fourth century B.C.E. as well as by Hillel. This may have been done in order to protect a newborn by covering her or him under the name of an older or distinguished person. However, nowadays very few Ashkenazim name a child after a living relative. Western Jews have a secular name in the vernacular in addition to their Hebrew name. These two names are purposely not alphabetically related in order to protect the child from child-snatching demons and the angel of death; by the vernacular name individuals are known to the community at large. This name is conferred to the individual during *Hollekreisch*, as mentioned above. Changing one's name was believed to confuse the angel of death. *Sefer Hasidim* 321 states: "changing one's name or one's residence brings about good luck, even if the luck does not do this since no luck (*mazal*, sign) rules over Israel." This is based on B. R.H. 16b; the passage in *Sefer Hasidim* demonstrates that multiple restrictions were placed upon "luck" and the influence of planets. On the other hand, changing one's name or utilizing an ugly name can deceive demons and evil spirits by disguising the individual.

Exorcism: Rabbis had the power to exorcise spirits. Exorcism by the *Hakham* (Sephardic) or the *Tzadik* (Ashkenazic) could remove spirit possession, such as a dybbuk (or *gilgul*, the belief in migrant souls that take possession of or seek refuge in the bodies of the living). There are souls condemned to wander for a time in this world (a person turned into a werewolf is mentioned in the *Ma'aseh Bukh*).[14] These souls are tormented by evil spirits that do not leave them alone and follow them everywhere. In order to escape from this torture, these wandering souls take refuge in the bodies of pious human beings, because the evil spirits have no power over the pious. The person who is possessed by such a soul endures great suffering, involving personality changes. The person to whom a wandering soul clings acts as if he or she were someone else. This person may be cured by a miracle working rabbi (*ba'al shem*), who performs rites of exorcism and uses amulets; often, the rabbi would recite Ps. 91 in the presence of ten observant men and adjure the soul in the name of God to leave the afflicted person. Exorcism is attested in many Jewish historical sources, Meir of Rothenburg used Ps. 91 for exorcisms. A rhymed Yiddish booklet entitled "The tale about a spirit in the holy congregation of Koretz" (ca. 1660) describes five futile and one successful attempt to exorcise the spirit that tortured this particular community. A case of exorcism is described in a source from seventeenth century Prague.[15] The exorcist, Eisik Bainish, had to deal with the following scenario: A man who was known as "the slanderer Trautsig from Prague" had been imprisoned by the community leaders in 1602; among these community leaders was the Maharal. This slanderer turned into a spirit and, as a dybbuk, he possessed people. The possessed victim functions as the medium through which the person turned into a spirit speaks.[16]

Chiromancy: Chiromancy and physiognomy deal with physical signs that are possible clues to the inner nature of a person.[17] Human palm- and face-lines are indications of strengths and can predict events in a person's life. Chiromancy is the determination of a person's future, health, and fate from the lines of the palm; the right hand is determining for males, the left for females. The main lines of the palm and certain parts of the hand are related to the seven planets and their influences; this astrological contemplation of chiromancy is found in *Merkavah* mysticism.

Astrology: The constellation of the stars and planets might affect a person's life and the events that occur naturally; astrology is the main discipline for the interpretation of time related constellations and planetary influences upon individuals. In the development from judicial astrology, the planets and stars were studied for horoscopes; the sky was divided into twelve realms ("houses"), corresponding to the signs of the Zodiac, each presided over by a planet. These celestial bodies gave astrological indications to the effect that a human being born on a certain day and under a certain sign or star would have a predetermined fate.[18] The month of Adar was considered lucky because Moses was born then. Further subdivisions determined favorable and unfavorable hours and days. For example: "He who is born in the sign of Libra on Sunday in (the station of) Jupiter or in (the station of) the moon, if he is born in (either of) these two hours, he will be short (?) and thin, and with a shining face (?). . . ."[19] Tuesday was considered a lucky day, whereas Monday and Wednesday were particularly unlucky (B. Pes. 112a):

> One should not go out at night . . . that is, on the nights of either Wednesday or Sabbath because Igrath the daughter of Mahalath (the queen of demons) and 180,000 destroying angels go forth, and each of them is permitted to wreak havoc independently.

The zodiacal signs are also considered in the Talmud (B. Shab. 156a), in a widely discussed and ambiguous passage that mentions that Joshua b. Levi had a notebook that contained the effect of the day of birth upon the person; Hanina refuted him and argued that not the sign of the day but the sign of the hour influenced a person's future:

> It was written in R. Joshua b. Levi's notebook, The person who [is born] on the first day of the week will be a person without anything in him. What is the meaning of "without anything in him"? Could we say, "without one virtue"? R. Ashi surely said, "I was born on the first day of the week." It must therefore mean "one vice." But R. Ashi surely said, "I and Dimi b. Kakuzta were born on the first day of the week, I am a king and he is the leader of a gang of thieves." Rather, it means either totally full of virtue or totally wicked. What is the reason? Because light and darkness were created on that [the first] day. A person born on the second day of the week will be bad-tempered. What is the reason?

Because the waters were separated [on the third day]. A person who is born on the third day will be rich and immoral. What is the reason? Because herbs were created [on the third day]. A person born on the fourth day of the week will be wise and have a good memory. What is the reason? Because the luminaries were hung on [that day]. Someone born on the fifth day of the week will act benevolently. What is the reason? Because the fish and the birds were created on [that day]. A person born on the eve of the Sabbath will be an explorer. R. Nahman b. Isaac made the following comment: "Someone who seeks good deeds." Someone born on the Sabbath will die on the Sabbath because the great day of the Sabbath was desecrated because of him. Rava b. R. Shila said, "He will be called a great and holy person." R. Hanina said to [his students], "Go and tell the son of Levi, 'Not the constellation of the day but that of the hour is the decisive influence.'" Someone born under the constellation of the sun will be an esteemed person, he will eat and drink of his own and his secrets will remain uncovered; if he is a thief, he will have no success. Someone born under Venus will be wealthy and immoral. What is the reason? Because fire was created in them. Someone born under Mercury will have excellent memory and be wise. What is the reason? Because it is the sun's scribe. Someone born under the Moon will suffer evil, building and destruction, destruction and building, eating and drinking what is not his own and his secrets will remain hidden; if he is a thief he will be successful. Someone born under Saturn will be a person whose plans will be stymied. Others say, "All designs against him will be stymied." Someone born under Jupiter will be someone who does righteous things. R. Nahman b. Isaac said, "Righteous in good deeds." Someone born under Mars will shed blood. R. Ashi said, "Either as a surgeon, a thief, a slaughterer or a circumciser." Rabbah said, "I was born under Mars." Abayye replied, "You too inflict punishment and kill." It was said, R. Hanina said, "The influence of the planets gives wisdom, and the influence of the planets gives wealth, and Israel is under the influence of the planets." R. Yohanan maintained, "Israel is immune from the influence of planets. . . ."

Astrological omen texts in Judaism often derived from the vast corpus of divination texts in Babylonia. A Jewish Palestinian Aramaic text recited for the sanctification of the New Moon of the month of Nisan mentions lunar omens:[20]

1. (If) when it rises, its horns are equal, the world is in danger. 2. If you saw the moon upright towards the south and its other horn inclined towards the north, let it be a sign for you: be careful of evil; trouble will go out from the north. 3. If you saw the moon pointing towards the north and its other horn inclined toward the South, (there will be) great joy for the entire royal court; cheap prices and plenty will be in the world. 4. (If the moon) is inclined toward the south, the sign is good. The year will be fat, and there will be plenty in the world. . . . 12. The moon is never eclipsed in Tishri. But if it is eclipsed, it is a bad sign for "the enemies of the Jews." Religious persecution will issue from the Kingdom and woeful destruction will be upon the Jews. . . .

Sefer Hasidim (1162) claims that every person has a star, and "one should be aware that the shadow that is thrown upon a wall and has the shape of a thief can be hit in the eye of the shadow and the eye of the thief will get hurt in its place." This theory of sympathetic magic holds that a representative, in this case a shadow, can be used to punish an absent individual. In present-day Israel, fortune-telling is still practiced through chiromancy, astrological charts, and cards.[21]

Tekufot: Certain times of the solar year are considered extremely harmful; the most dangerous time is the equinox or solstice (*tekufah*). This superstition is found in Hebrew literature as early as the ninth century.[22] Since, at the time of the *tekufah*, water was assumed to be poisoned by demons, drinking water during this period endangers one's life, in particular on the exact night of the *tekufah* and if the water is drawn from a fountain. There are four angels for each quarter of the year; these are appointed over the water and defend against demons. The angels change guard at the end of each *tekufah*, and the time between the watches is extremely dangerous. Iron wards off demons during the *tekufah*. Alternatively, it was believed that Cancer fought with Libra and drops of blood were spilled into water. To protect them, pieces of iron were placed on all water containers.

Other superstitions relate to the festivals. The ceremony for expiation of sin before Rosh Hashanah and Yom Kippur, the *Kapparah*, is deemed superstitious by some (to belong to "practices of the Amorite").

During this ceremony (Yiddish: *Kappore shlagn*), certain Psalms are recited while a chicken is swung around the head of a person three times. The chicken is believed to take on any misfortune that might befall a person. It is lucky if the shofar on Rosh Hashanah does not emit a sound; this signifies that Satan is caught in it (Hasidic) only by reciting Ps. 91 could Satan be exorcised and the shofar blown. This relating of the shofar and Satan is ancient.[23]

Adjuration: Help against the forces of the dark can be expected from angels, as in B. Ber. 60b:

> On entering a bathroom one should say: Be honored, holy honorable ones, servants of the Most High. Give honor to the God of Israel. Wait for me until I enter and do my needs and return to you. Abayye said: A man should not speak thus, lest they should leave him and go; he should say instead: Guard me, guard me, help me, help me, support me, support me, wait for me, wait for me until I enter and come out, as this is the way of humans.

Rashi explains that these words are directed to angels who accompany humans and that angels are especially needed in this situation. The adjuration of angels is often used in Jewish magic and in Jewish mystical texts. In addition to dark places and places of uncleanness, medieval Judaism expressed the belief that demons (*mazzikim*) dwelt on nut trees (*Sefer Hasidim*, 1153):

> Demons assemble in numbers of nine and the wild forest beings also in numbers of nine. And if you want to cure a person who has been harmed by a demon you have to pronounce the cure nine times, as they do in Ashkenaz, where they count nine knots or cure him with nine pieces of wood called *shtilotish* or *naven* and put into the waste of a sick person. One takes them from nine bridges or from nine city gates. . . . It is dangerous to sleep under a nut tree, as it is written: "I will also make it a possession for the bittern, and pools of water; and I will sweep it with the broom of destruction, says the Lord of hosts" (Is. 14:23), and every unclean thing that one sees at night, such as a dog, cat, mouse, which is born with its eyes closed, causes one not to be able to open one's eyes for nine days.

Divination: The Talmud is ambivalent: *lahash* is forbidden but *simanim* are permitted;

for example, incantations for wounds are forbidden (B. San. 90a). B. San. 101a mentions consulting demons and the spirits of oil or eggs. Active divination often involves calling up the dead (necromancy) by spending the night in a cemetery or by using incantations (*lahash*). The dead are believed to observe the actions of the living (B. Ber. 18a):

> R. Hiyya and R. Jonathan were once walking about in a cemetery and the blue fringe of R. Jonathan was trailing on the ground. R. Hiyya said to him, "Lift it up so that [the dead] should not say, 'Tomorrow they will join us and now they are insulting us.'"

Consulting the dead (B. Git. 56b-57b) and listening to their conversations (B. Ber. 59a) is wide-spread in Judaism. Some people fasted and spent the night in a cemetery in order to receive a visitation by the "spirit of uncleanness" and to find out the future or other hidden matters (B. San. 65b): "'One that consults the dead' (Deut. 18:11)—this means one who starves himself and spends the night in a cemetery, so that an unclean spirit may rest upon him." Rashi explains that this evil spirit refers to a demon. Ghosts from the cemetery visit the newer part of town, and there are haunted houses in the destroyed part of the town of Safed.[24]

Omens: Good or bad omens are perceived in almost any action, event, or matter. Many signs are listed by Maimonides (*Yad*, Hilkhot Akum 11:4). Some foods symbolize good omens and are consumed on certain festivals, such as sweet or round foodstuff as well as the head of a sheep or a fish on Rosh Hashanah; some people use new tableware on Rosh Hashanah for a good omen (*Kol Bo*, 41). Other foods are dangerous because an evil spirit rests upon them: "R. Simeon b. Yohai stated, 'There are five things that cause a person to forfeit his life and his blood is on his head . . . eating peeled garlic, a peeled onion, or a peeled egg'" (B. Nid. 17a).

The belief that keeping a peeled onion in the house brings on sickness is still found in Sephardic Judaism.[25] Omens are also read from bodily phenomena, such as sneezing (*Shulhan Arukh*, Orah Hayim 103:3), itching, or a particular manner of walking (B. Ber. 43b):

> Our rabbis taught: Six things are unbecoming for a scholar . . . some say that he should not take long strides . . . because a master once said, "Long strides diminish a person's eyesight by a five-hundredth part." What is the remedy? He can restore it by drinking the Kiddush wine on the eve of the Sabbath.

At the beginning and end of the Sabbath, there is a shift from the forces that have power on week-days and those that have power on the Sabbath. As soon as the Sabbath ends, a group of evil spirits ascends from Gehinnom, from the realm called Sheol. They strive to mingle among the Israelites and to obtain power over them. But when the Israelites perform the ceremonies of the myrtle and the cup of blessing and recite *havdalah*, these evil spirits leave and go to their place in Sheol, the region where Korah and his associates reside (Zohar I, 17b).

> Certain behaviors disclose a person's character (B. M.Q. 18a):
> Three things were said in reference to nails: One who buries them is righteous, one who burns them is pious, and one who throws them away is a villain. What is the reason? Lest a pregnant woman step over them and miscarry.

Many trivial actions or occurrences are considered good or bad omens (B. Ber. 51a):

> The following laws are stated: Do not take your shirt from the hand of your attendant when dressing in the morning; do not let water be poured over your hands by one who has not already washed his own hands; do not return a bowl of asparagus brew to anyone save the one who handed it to you; do not stand in front of women when they are returning from the presence of a dead person.

Some examples from the great variety of omens are the following: If a knife falls to the floor, one has to stop eating, or, in the Sephardic tradition, a visit is indicated. Brushing crumbs from the table with a broom will cause poverty; fish and milk eaten together are poisonous. It is unlucky to have a garment mended on a person, since this will sew up his memory as well; if a garment is put on inside out, bad luck will follow all day long. Forgetfulness may be caused by one's own actions, such as

placing one foot over the other while washing, eating certain foods, or drinking contaminated water (*Mahzor Vitry*, 720). The importance of water in superstition is often emphasized; for instance, it is considered dangerous to borrow water (B. Pes. 111a). One is to avoid a business loss in the morning (*Brantshpigl*); in the alternative, it is a bad omen to start the week with an unsuccessful business transaction. This led to the superstition of having to sell something to a customer on Monday; in Germany it was common knowledge that one would be able to obtain a bargain if one were the first customer on Monday morning. A Hebrew book's falling on the floor is a very bad omen; fasting is a remedy. Other omens involve animals (dogs, cats, pigs, and others); for example, a deer's crossing one's path (B. San. 65b) and *zugot*, anything that appears in pairs, were bad omens (B. Pes. 109b); thus: "He who drinks an even number should not say grace" (B. Ber. 51b). Anyone was in danger of becoming the prey of witchcraft in situations determined by constellations of two; witchcraft could be avoided if one avoided "pairs" (B. Pes. 110b-111a):

> Our rabbis taught: There are three who must not pass between two and one may not pass between them. These are: A dog, a palm tree, and a woman. Some say: Also a pig. Some say: Also a snake. If one passes between them, what is the remedy?
> R. Papa said: "[One recites a verse] commencing with *el* and ending with *el*; or commencing with *lo* and ending with *lo*. If a menstruant passes between people, she kills one of them if it is the beginning of her menses. And if it is at the end of her menses, she will cause a quarrel between them. What is the remedy? [One recites a verse] commencing with *el* and ending with *el*."
> If two women are sitting at a crossroad, one on one side and one on the other side, facing each other, they are certainly practicing witchcraft. What is the remedy? If there is another road, one uses this road. If there is no other road and if there is another man, the two men hold hands and pass through. If there is no other man, one says: *Igeret, Izlat, Azya, Belusya* have been slain with arrows.

We see that a protection against the evil eye, the danger emanating from certain "pairs," and certain animals or trees was the recitation of the name of God in certain Scriptural quotations. The avoidance of pairs is probably responsible for the admonition that sisters not get married on the same day and that brothers not marry sisters (*Sefer Hasidim*, 23). Other lucky and unlucky numbers involve even numbers, which are considered to be unlucky. However, it is lucky to be the tenth person in a prayer *minyan*.

Good or bad personal omens are also communicated through dreams, which need to be deciphered and interpreted by an expert (B. San. 30a; B. Git. 52a; B. Hor. 13b). Y. M.S. 4:9 states:

> A man came to R. Yose b. Halafta and said to him: "[In my dream I was wearing a crown of olive branches." [Yose] said to him: "You will soon be exalted."
>
> A man came and said to him: In a dream I was wearing a crown of olive branches. He said to him: "You will be flogged." The man said: "You told him that he would soon be exalted, but you told me I'm going to be flogged?" [Yose] said: "His [olives] were budding, while yours were ready to be harvested by beating the tree branches."
>
> A man came to R. Ishmael b. R. Yose and said to him: "In my dream I saw an olive tree that was watering the olive oil." [Ishmael] said to him: "May your soul expire, because you had sexual relations with your mother."
>
> A man came to R. Ishmael b. R. Yose and said to him: "In my dream I saw that [one of] my eye[s] kissed the other." [Ishmael] said: "May your soul expire, because you had sexual relations with your sister."
>
> A man came to R. Ishmael b. R. Yose and said to him: "In my dream I saw that I had three eyes." [Ishmael] said to him: "You will make ovens; two of the eyes are your own, and one eye belongs to the oven."
>
> A man came to R. Ishmael b. R. Yose and said to him: "In my dream I saw that I had four ears." [Ishmael] said to him: "You will be filling [casks]. Two of the ears are your ears and two ears belong to the cask."
>
> A man came to R. Ishmael b. R. Yose and said to him: "In my dream I saw that creatures were fleeing me." [Ishmael] said: "You will carry a thorny twig and people will run away from you."
>
> A man came to R. Ishmael b. R. Yose and said to him: "In my dream I saw that I was wearing a writing tablet with twelve plates." [Ishmael] said to him: "Your blanket has twelve patches."

The dream book in Y. M.S. contains numerous omens that have personal significance to the dreamer. The interpreters follow traditional procedures of onirology, the art of dream interpretation, to take into account the dreamer's occupation, background, gender, etc., in order to determine if the omen is good or bad. The correct interpretation of a dream has critical consequences and leads to the omen's being fulfilled. Separate dreams share the image of "a crown of olives." However, through Yose's interpretations the dreams are seen to contain distinct omens for different people.

Bibliography

Dobrinsky, H.C., *A Treasury of Sephardic Laws and Customs* (Hoboken and New York, 1986).

Josephy, M.R., *Magic and Superstition in the Jewish Tradition* (Chicago, 1975).

Schrire, T., *Hebrew Magic Amulets: Their Decipherment and Interpretation* (New York, 1982).

Trachtenberg, J., *Jewish Magic and Superstition. A Study in Folk Religion* (New York, 1982).

Notes

[1] See M.B. Shapiro, "Maimonidean Halakhah and Superstition," in *Maimonidean Studies* 4 (2000), pp. 61-108; T. Langerman, "Maimonides' Repudiation of Astrology," in *Maimonidean Studies* 2 (1991), pp. 123-158.

[2] T. Schrire, *Hebrew Magic Amulets. Their Decipherment and Interpretation* (New York, 1982).

[3] E. Davis, "The Psalms in Hebrew Medical Amulets," in *Vetus Testamentum* 42 (1992), p. 175.

[4] Y. Bilu, "Demonic Explanations of Disease among Moroccan Jews in Israel," (Hebrew) in *Jerusalem Studies in Jewish Folklore* 2 (1982), pp. 108-123.

[5] J. Trachtenberg, "Exorcisms in Prague in the 17th Century: The Question of the Historical Authenticity of a Folk Genre," (Hebrew) in *Jerusalem Studies in Jewish Folklore* 3 (1982), pp. 182f.

[6] W.D. Hand, "Jewish Popular Beliefs and Customs in Los Angeles," in R. Patai, F. Utley, and D. Noy, eds., *Studies in Biblical and Jewish Folklore* (New York, 1973), pp. 312f.

[7] M.R. Josephy, *Magic and Superstition in the Jewish Tradition* (Chicago, 1975).

[8] E. Horowitz, "The Eve of Circumcision: A Chapter in the History of Jewish Nightlife," in *Journal of Social History* 23 (1989), pp. 45-69.

[9] T.H. Gaster, *Customs and Folkways of Jewish Life* (New York, 1955), p. 37.

[10] Trachtenberg, "Exorcisms in Prague in the 17th Century," pp. 41ff.

[11] M.A. Friedman, "Tamar: A Symbol of Life: The 'Killer Wife' Superstitions in the Bible and Jewish Tradition," in *AJS-Review* 15 (1990), pp. 23-61.

[12] H.C. Dobrinsky, *A Treasury of Sephardic Laws and Customs* (Hoboken and New York, 1986), p. 80.

[13] Ibid., p. 82.

[14] M. Gaster, trans., *Ma'aseh Book of Jewish*

Tales and Legends Translated from the Judeo-German (Philadelphia, 1981), # 228.

[15] S. Zfatman-Biller, "'Tale of an Exorcism in Koretz:' A New Stage in the Development of a Folk Literary Genre" (Hebrew), in *Jerusalem Studies in Jewish Folklore* 2 (1982), pp. 17-65.

[16] See also Y. Bilu, "The Dybbuk in Judaism: Mental Disorder as Cultural Resource" (Hebrew), in *Jerusalem Studies in Jewish Thought* 2 (1983), pp. 529-563.

[17] G. Scholem, "*Hakkarat panim ve-sidre sirtutin*" (Hebrew), in *Simhah Assaf Jubilee Volume* (Jerusalem, 1953), pp. 459-495; Zohar, *Midrash ha-zohar* and *Raza de-razin*.

[18] I. Gruenwald, I., *Apocalyptic and Merkaba Mysticism* (Leiden, 1980), p. 219.

[19] J. Greenfield and M. Sokoloff, "Astrological and Related Omen Texts in Jewish Palestinian Aramaic," in *Journal of Near Eastern Studies* 48 (1989), p. 211.

[20] Ibid., p. 204.

[21] E. Aphek and Y. Tobin, *The Semiotics of Fortune Telling* (Amsterdam, 1989).

[22] I. Ta-Shma, "The Danger of Drinking Water during the *Tequfa*: The History of an Idea" (Hebrew), in *Jerusalem Studies in Jewish Folklore* 18 (1995), p. 26.

[23] On this superstition, see Trachtenberg, "Exorcisms in Prague in the 17th Century," p. 113; J.Z. Lauterbach, "The Ritual for the Kapparot Ceremony," in *Jewish Studies in Memory of George A. Kohut* (New York, 1935), pp. 413-422; H. Basser, "Superstitious Interpretations of Jewish Law," in *Journal for the Study of Judaism* 8 (1977), pp. 136f.

[24] A. Geva-Kleinberger, "Living Amongst the Spirits: Death and Superstition as Reflected in the Arabic and Hebrew Vocabulary of the Jews of Safed," in *Mediterranean Language Review* 12 (2000), pp. 16-38.

[25] Hand, "Jewish Popular Beliefs and Customs in Los Angeles," p. 314.

RIVKA ULMER

SURROGATE MOTHERHOOD: Despite the passage of time since the New Jersey case of Baby M[1] captured the attention of millions of Americans, both the human and legal questions posed by surrogate motherhood remain largely unresolved. Medically, the procedure is not at all complex and represents a simple method of coping with female infertility. A woman who is willing to serve as a surrogate, usually in return for a fee, is found and an agreement is reached. She is artificially inseminated with the semen of the infertile woman's husband, carries the baby to term, and subsequently surrenders the baby to the couple. In such cases, the husband is the biological father, but the wife has no natural relationship with the child. With the development of in vitro fertilization, it is now possible, in some limited circumstances, for the wife to be the biological mother as well.[2] If the wife's fertility problem is not related to production of ova, her own ovum can be fertilized in a petri dish with her husband's sperm and then transferred to the womb of the surrogate who serves as host for purposes of gestation. When all parties are content with the terms of the agreement, there is no occasion for pubic attention to be focused on the arrangement. But, at times, as was the case with regard to Baby M, the surrogate undergoes a change of heart and refuses to deliver the baby to the father and his wife or attempts to recover custody of the child after the child has been surrendered. In either event, the emotional turmoil is readily understandable and the legal dilemma is obvious.

Assuming the consent and desire of all parties, the permissibility of surrogate motherhood hinges upon resolution of a number of halakhic questions. Since surrogate motherhood involves insemination of a woman with the semen of a man who is not her husband, the first halakhic issue is identical to that involved in a far more common means of overcoming male, rather than female, infertility, *viz.*, AID, or artificial insemination using the semen of a donor. Surrogacy is essentially a form of AID, and utilization of a Jewish woman as a surrogate is proscribed.

Securing the services of a non-Jewish woman as a surrogate presents a different problem. For those authorities who maintain that only birth of children as a result of natural intercourse serves to fulfill the command to "be fruitful and multiply," permissibility of AID hinges upon whether non-coital ejaculation is permissible solely for purposes of fulfilling the commandment to "be fruitful and multiply"[3] or whether the goal of populating the universe (*shevet*), as expressed in Isa. 45:18 ("He created it not a waste; He created it to be inhabited"), is sufficient to legalize emission of semen.[4] Assuming that the sexual act is not a necessary condition of fulfillment of the commandment to "be fruitful and multiply" because a paternal-filial relationship exists even in the absence of a sexual act, some forms of non-coital ejaculation may be employed in order to fulfill the biblical command. However, ejaculation for the purpose of inseminating a non-Jewish woman does not serve to achieve that end. The issue of a Jewish father and a gentile mother, even if conceived in a normal, natural manner, is not regarded as the issue of the Jewish father for purposes of halakhah, and hence birth of such a child does not constitute fulfillment of the biblical commandment concerning procreation. Birth of such a child does, however, serve to populate the universe.

If, as is frequently the case, the surrogate is a non-Jewish woman, the child is obviously not Jewish and, presumably, if surrendered to the childless couple, would be converted to Judaism. Nevertheless, the father does not fulfill the commandment to "be fruitful and multiply" even upon conversion of the child. Hence, if non-coital emission of semen can be countenanced only for purposes of fulfilling the biblical commandment regarding procreation, impermissibility of semen procurement for insemination of a gentile woman would itself serve to bar a surrogate relationship with a surrogate who is not Jewish.

Once a child is born as a result of surrogate motherhood, may the identity of the mother be suppressed?

That question, too, has its counterpart with regard to children born as a result of artificial insemination. If, as the vast majority of Rabbinic authorities agree, a paternal-filial relationship does exist when a child has been born as a result of artificial insemination, is it necessary to disclose the identity of the father? As AID is customarily practiced in the United States, the donor is assured of anonymity and, in general, there is no way that the child can discover the identity of his or her father. In surrogate mother arrangements, sealing the records, if permitted, would have the same result.

Suppression of paternal identity is one of the considerations that led Rabbinic decisors to ban AID. Rabbi Moshe Feinstein, *Iggerot Mosheh, Yoreh De'ah*, I, no. 162 and *Even ha-Ezer*, I, no. 7, voices a similar concern in decrying sealed adoptions.[5] At least until recent years, adoption agencies and the American legal system joined forces in an attempt to prevent an adopted child from ever learning the identity of his or her natural parents. It would appear that *Iggerot Mosheh* regards any attempt to suppress the parental identity as a violation of a biblical commandment. Although polygamy is biblically permissible, B. Yeb. 37b, declares that a man may not maintain a wife in every port, i.e., he may not maintain multiple families and households whose members do not know of one another's existence. The concern is that, with the passage of time, children of the various households may grow to maturity and contract a marriage without realizing that they share a common father. In prohibiting such arrangements, the Gemara adduces the verse "lest the earth be filled with licentiousness" (Lev. 19:29) as the consideration upon which the ban is predicated. *Iggerot Mosheh* apparently asserts that the prohibition is not merely Rabbinic and simply reflective of the concern expressed in the cited scriptural passage; rather, the ban represents the instantiation of an actual biblical prohibition.[6] According to *Iggerot Mosheh*, any act carrying with it the potential for suppression of a familial relationship of a nature such that it may possibly lead to a consanguineous relationship is biblically proscribed. As such, suppression of the identity of natural parents in adoption proceedings, anonymous sperm donations, and surrogate relationships in which the identity of the mother is not disclosed are equally forbidden as a violation of "lest the earth will be filled with licentiousness."

Conception by means of artificial insemination presents halakhic problems with regard to the permissibility of the means utilized in causing pregnancy to occur in the context of surrogate relationships. Enforcement of the surrogacy contract providing for custody of the child presents an additional cluster of issues. Although the contract may provide for impregnation in a manner that halakhah regards as illicit, Jewish law does not regard illegal contracts as *ipso facto* unenforceable.

The enforceability of surrogate motherhood contracts in the American legal system is generally regarded as hinging in the first instance upon the question of whether the agreement is to be construed as a contract for the sale of a baby or as a contract for performance of personal services. Has the surrogate, who receives a fee for her services, simply agreed to make her uterus available for gestation of the fetus, or has she contracted for the sale of a baby upon birth? If the latter, not only is the contract unenforceable, but fulfillment of its terms constitutes a penal offense.[7] However, since baby-selling, while undoubtedly repugnant, is not a criminal act in Jewish law, the question of enforceability of the provisions of an illegal contract need not be addressed.[8]

There are nevertheless other considerations that serve to render surrogate motherhood contracts unenforceable in Jewish law.

Typically, for reasons that are obvious, the contract is executed before the woman is inseminated. At that point, the fetus is not yet in existence. Halakhah does not recognize the validity of the conveyance of an entity that is not yet in existence. Hence, were the contract to be construed as a sale, the sale would be void with the result that the woman has the prerogative of reneging on her undertaking. If, on the other hand, the agreement is to be construed as an employment contract that provides for compensation for services rendered, apart from the right of a worker to abrogate such a contract, provision of such services at the behest of the father does not serve to convey a proprietary interest in the child.

More significantly, children are not property and do not represent a property interest that can be transferred. Child custody, although often a matter of dispute between a couple no longer living together as man and wife, is regarded by Judaism primarily as an obligation rather than a right.[9] To the extent that child custody involves an issue of the rights of an individual, the rights involved are those of the child. The duty of a parent to care for and to support a child may be said to give rise to a concomitant right vested in the child to receive such care and support. Thus, although both conceptually and for certain aspects of Jewish law, there may well be a distinction between a duty and a resultant right, in general,

duties and rights may be regarded as two sides of the same coin.

Since determination of which spouse shall be the custodial parent is, in effect, adjudication of how a child's right can best be exercised, any contract between the parents must be regarded as a nullity if it in any way prejudices the rights of the child. It is self-evident that two contracting parties do not have the power to dispose of, or in any way prejudice, the rights of a third party who is not a party to the contract. For that reason, *Teshuvot Mabit*, II, no. 62, cited by *Be'er Heitev, Even ha-Ezer* 82:6, rules that a woman who, as part of a divorce settlement, enters into an agreement in which she renounces custodial prerogatives may subsequently renege and is not bound by her initial undertaking.[10]

Similarly, a surrogate contract providing for surrender of the baby by the natural mother represents an agreement by the natural mother not to seek custody. As such, it is unenforceable with the result that, if the mother declines to surrender the child voluntarily, the *Bet Din* must perforce treat the controversy as a dispute between two parents each of whom asserts a prerogative to custody of the child. Thus, the case before the *Bet Din* is not a contract dispute but a custody proceeding to be resolved on the basis of halakhic canons governing matters of custody.

Adoption of the policy inherent in the provisions of Jewish law with regard to child support and custody would have a chilling effect upon surrogate agreements. As recorded in *Shulhan Arukh, Even ha-Ezer* 82:5 and 82:8, a mother has the prerogative of refusing to accept custody. Hence, in a surrogate arrangement, if the neonate suffers from a congenital defect or abnormality, the mother may well decline to accept custody and thereby leave responsibility for the child entirely in the hands of the father. In every case, if the woman who has agreed to surrender the child as part of the surrogate agreement undergoes a change of heart and seeks custody, she may very well prevail. If awarded custody, she is entitled both to child support and to a fee for her services in rearing the child. As a result, a male contemplating such an arrangement has no guarantee that he will actually have a child to raise. However, he will be absolutely certain of incurring financial obligations to the child born to the surrogate as well as, should custody be awarded to the surrogate, of incurring an obligation for what constitutes, in effect, alimony payments to a woman who was never his wife. These prospects should be sufficiently onerous to discourage most people from pursuing such an agreement.

One further observation is in order. Surrogate relationships are often described as a modern-day counterpart of the concubinage that was prevalent in days of yore. There is no question that, in antiquity, and in the biblical period in particular, when a woman proved to be barren, her husband frequently took a concubine for purposes of procreation. The biblical narrative concerning Abraham and Hagar seems to be a case in point. Nahmanides, in his commentary on Gen. 16:2, offers the following observation:

"And Abraham hearkened to the voice of Sarah." Even now [Abraham] did not intend that he be fulfilled through Hagar by having progeny through her. Rather, his sole intention was to do the desire of Sarah so that she be fulfilled through [Hagar], that she derive happiness of spirit from the children of her handmaiden.

Hagar is here described as the surrogate who will bear the children while Sarah will experience the gratification and pleasure of raising those children.

Nahmanides, however, offers a second observation as well. Commenting on the verse "And Sarah oppressed her" (Gen. 6:6), he remarks: "Our mother [Sarah] sinned in this matter." Sarah is described as having desired to displace Hagar and to raise Hagar's child as her own. But, in practice, the arrangement does not succeed. The child is not Sarah's; it is Hargar's. People may believe they are capable of transcending biological realia but, in practice, they find that they cannot.[11] Despite the best intentions of all concerned, biological facts give rise to psychological consequences, and human beings frequently find it impossible to rise above, or to suppress, natural instincts and emotions.

The phenomenon of a mother who ren-

eges on a surrogate agreement should not be at all surprising. The woman may be a surrogate wife or a surrogate reproductive partner, but the term "surrogate mother" is a misnomer. There is nothing in the nature of surrogacy in her maternity; she is a natural mother, both biologically and psychologically. At the time when she enters into the contractual relationship, the surrogate may believe herself capable of renouncing her motherhood and surrendering the child. However, when confronted with the reality of her motherhood, she understandably may find herself incapable of doing so. Men and women are human, not superhuman, and should not be called upon sacrificially to deny natural human instincts and emotions.

Notes

[1] Matter of Baby, 217, N.J. Super. 313; 525 A.2d 128 (1987). *Aff'd in part and rev'd in part*, 109 N.J. 396, 537 A.2d 1227 (1988).

[2] The primary focus of this discussion will be upon surrogacy arrangements in which the gestational mother is the biological mother. The question of maternal identity in situations in which the gestational mother is not the biological mother is addressed in this writer's *Contemporary Halakhic Problems*, I (New York, 1977), pp. 106-109; II (New York, 1983), pp. 91-93; and IV (New York, 1995), pp. 237-272.

[3] Some few authorities maintain that AID does establish a paternal-filial relationship between the donor and the child born of such a procedure but that, since no sexual act is involved, the donor does not thereby fulfill his obligation with regard to procreation. See Rabbi Jacob Emden, *She'ilat Ya'avetz*, II, no. 97, sec. 3; Rabbi Chaim Joseph David Azulai, *Birkei Yosef, Even ha-Ezer* 1:14; *Maharam Shik al Taryag Mitzvot*, no. 1; *Bigdei Yesha*, no. 123; and *Bigdei Shesh, Even ha-Ezer* 1:11.

[4] Authorities who espouse the latter view include *Teshuvot Emek Halakhah*, I, no. 60: Rabbi Shlomoh Zalman Auerbach, *No'am*, I, 157; and Rabbi Judah Gershuni, *Or ha-Mizrah*, Tishri 5739, pp. 15-22, reprinted in *idem, Kol Tzofayikh* (Jerusalem, 5740), p. 367.

[5] See also Rabbi Shlomoh Goren, *Ha-Tzofeh*, 7 Adar I, 5744.

[6] Cf., however, *Bet Shmu'el, Even ha-Ezer* 13:1, who asserts that the ban against remarriage of a woman within three months of her divorce or of the death of her husband that is predicated upon the same consideration is Rabbinic in nature.

[7] See Matter of Baby, 109 N.J. at 422; 537 A.2d at 1240. See also Barbara Cohen, "Surrogate Mothers: Whose Baby Is It?" in *American Journal of Law and Medicine*, vol. X, no. 3 (Fall 1984), pp. 247-248; and Mark Rust, "Whose

Baby Is It? Surrogate Motherhood After Baby M," in *American Bar Association Journal*, vol. LXXIII (June 1, 1987), pp. 53-55. A number of states explicitly exempted surrogacy agreements from provision criminalizing baby-selling.

In one case brought by the attorney general of Kentucky to clarify the state's law on surrogacy, the Supreme Court of Kentucky found that surrogate contracts did not violate state baby-selling statutes because the child produced by the arrangement is the natural child of the father. See *Surrogate Parenting Ass'n* v. *Roman Com. Ex. Rel. Armstrong*, 704 S.W.2d 209 (1986). According to that reasoning, it would follow that, if the wife is the sole contracting party, the contract would be illegal. Similarly, if the surrogate was impregnated by donor sperm because of the husband's infertility, the contract would be illegal.

[8] See this writer's discussion in *Bioethical Delem-*

mas: A Jewish Perspective (Hoboken, 1998), pp. 256-258.

[9] Thus Rabbi Ben Zion Uzi'el, *Mishpetei Uzi'el, Even ha-Ezer*, no. 91, writes: "Neither the sons nor the daughters of a person are owned by him in the same way that he owns property or livestock . . . they are the inheritance of the Lord given to parents in order to receive an education in Torah *mitzvot* and daily life."

[10] See also *Osef Piskei Din Rabbaniyim*, ed. Z. Wahrhaftig (Jerusalem, 5710), p. 11 and *Piskei Din shel Batei ha-Din ha-Rabbaniyim be-Yisra'el*, III, 358; XI, 161; and XI, 172-173. See also *Pisket Din shel Batei ha-Din ha-Rabbaniyim be-Yisra'el*, XIII, 337.

[11] Cf., Nechama Leibowitz, *Iyyunim be-Sefer Bereshit* (Jerusalem, 5729), pp. 111-112.

J. DAVID BLEICH

T

TRADITION IN JUDAISM: Is Judaism a traditional religion? At stake is a long-term issue of culture, namely, the relationship, in the formation of the Judaic culture, between philosophical system and historical tradition. In its canonical documents beyond Scripture, which are the Mishnah, Talmuds, and Midrash, normative Judaism claims to present enduring traditions, a fundament of truth revealed of old—the oral component of the Torah of Sinai. Judaism appeals to literary forms and cultural media that accentuate the traditional character of the privileged writings, e.g., commentary-form, the master-disciple relationship for education. So normative Judaism in its authoritative canon presents itself as a traditional religion. But that same Judaism in its formative age, in the normative writings of the first six centuries C.E. also comes to realization in systematic, philosophical statements, which begin in first principles and rise in steady and inexorable logic to final conclusions: compositions of proportion, balance, cogency, and order. Unlike the traditionalist, the system-builder starts fresh to rationalize what is, in fact, the increment of the ages. The systemic statements address not only problems of thought but the structure of society, explaining why people conduct their lives in one way, rather than in

some other. Accordingly, the canonical writings speak not out of a hoary past but in the acutely present tense of a well-ordered, rational social construction. Tradition and change, inherited ideas in tension with reconstruction and re-visioning of a contemporary mind—these point to the ongoing relevance of the issue at hand: the place system-builders make for themselves within a traditional order.[1]

The Modality of Intellect: Philosophical-Systemic or Historical-Traditional?
The life of intellect may commence morning by morning. Or it may flow from an ongoing process of thought, in which one day begins where yesterday left off, and one generation takes up the truths and tasks left to it by its predecessors. A system by definition starts fresh, defines first principles, augments and elaborates them in balance, proportion, above all, logical order. In a traditional process, by contrast, we only add to an ongoing increment of knowledge, doctrine, and modes of making judgment. And, in the nature of such an ongoing process, we never start fresh, but always pick and choose, in a received program, the spot we propose to augment. The former process, the systematic one, begins from the beginning and works in an orderly, measured and proportioned way to produce a

cogent, and neatly composed statement, a philosophy for instance. The latter process is not that way. Tradition by its nature is supposed to describe not a system, whole and complete, but a process of elaboration of a given, received truth: exegesis, not fresh composition. And, in the nature of thought, what begins in the middle is unlikely to yield order and system and structure laid forth *ab initio*. In general terms, systematic thought is philosophical in its mode of analysis and explanation, and traditional thought is historical in its manner of drawing conclusions and providing explanations.

Systemic logic is philosophical, it generates syllogisms, well-crafted propositions, and it puts them together into a whole that neatly holds together all of the parts. The logic of coherent discourse of tradition is teleological and, at its foundations, in method and literary form it makes sense through narrative, defying the fallacy, *post hoc, ergo propter hoc*: first this, then that, therefore this comes prior to that. And system and tradition not only describe incompatible modes of thought but also generate results that cannot be made to cohere. For the conflict between tradition and system requires us to choose one mode of thought about one set of issues and to reject the other mode of thought and also the things about which thought concerns itself. And that choice bears profound consequences for the shape of mind.

So far as "tradition" refers to the matter of process, it invokes, specifically, an incremental and linear process that step by step transmits out of the past statements and wordings that bear authority and are subject to study, refinement, preservation, and transmission. In such a traditional process, by definition, no one starts afresh to think things through. Each participant in the social life of intellect makes an episodic and ad hoc contribution to an agglutinative process, yielding, over time, (to continue the geological metaphor) a sedimentary deposit. The opposite process we may call systematic, in that, starting as if from the very beginning and working out the fundamental principles of things, the intellect, unbound by received perspectives and propositions, constructs a free-standing and well-propor-

tioned system. In terms of architecture the difference is between a city that just grows and one that is planned; a scrapbook and a fresh composition; a composite commentary and a work of philosophical exposition.

The one thing a traditional thinker knows is that he stands in a long process of thought, with the sole task of refining and defending received truth. And, by contrast, the systematic thinker affirms the challenge of starting fresh, seeing things all together, all at once, in the right order and proportion. His goal is to produce for the social order a composition, not merely a composite, held together by an encompassing logic. A tradition requires exegesis, a system, exposition. A tradition demands the labor of harmonization and elaboration of the given. A system begins with its philosophical harmonies in order and requires not elaboration but merely repetition, in one detail after another, of its main systemic message. A tradition does not repeat but only renews received truth; a system always repeats because it is by definition encompassing, everywhere saying one thing, which, by definition, is always new. A system in its own terms has no history; a tradition defines itself through the authenticity of its history.

Judaism: Traditional or Systemic?
Now there can be no doubt that, from the Bavli (Talmud of Babylonia, ca. 600 C.E.) onward, the Judaic intellect is represented as flowing along traditional lines, making its contribution, from generation to generation, as commentary, not as fresh composition. Every available history of Judaic thought, academic and vulgar alike, every presentation of the religion, Judaism, concurs. Traditionality represents the principal modality of the Judaic intellect as the refinement, adaptation, or adjustment of a received increment of truth. And that is true even for what is new. However lacking all precedent, Judaic systems find representation as elaboration of the received Torah, imputed to verses of Scripture, and not as a sequence of fresh and original beginnings of systematic and orderly statements of well-composed and cogent principles. As between the fresh and perfect classicism of the well-proportioned Parthenon and the confused and disorderly alleyways of the streets below, the

Judaic intellect made its residence in the side-alleys of the here and now, in an ongoing, therefore by definition never-neatly-constructed piazza. The Judaic intellect carried on its work through receiving and handing on, not through thinking through in a fresh and fundamental way, the inheritance of the ages. It sought to preserve the sediment of truth and add its layer, not to dig down to foundations and build afresh, even bound to using the dirt removed in the digging.

But is that how things were in the classical age, when, from the formation of the Pentateuch to the closure of the Bavli, the normative Judaism was aborning? That is to say, was the Judaic intellect in that formative age fundamentally traditional and historical, or essentially systematic and philosophical? At stake in the answer to that question is our fundamental characterization of the Judaic intellect, in its successive writings, in ancient times. We shall know the answer in two ways, formal and conceptual.

The first, the merely formal, of course is the simpler. When an authorship extensively cites received documents and makes its statement through alluding to statements in those documents, then, on the face of it, that authorship wishes to present its ideas as traditional. It claims through its chosen form of expression (merely) to continue, (only) to amplify, (solely) to extend, in all, to apply truth received, not to present truth discovered and demonstrated in the philosophical manner. That authorship then proposes to present its ideas as incremental, secondary, merely applications of available words. Not only so, but that authorship always situates itself in relationship to a received document, in the case of all Judaisms, of course, in relationship to the Pentateuch. When an authorship takes over from prior documents the problem and program worked out by those documents, contributing secondary improvements to an established structure of thought, then we may confidently identify that authorship as derivative and traditional. We realize that that is how matters were represented, in theory at least, by the framers of tractate Abot, ca. 250 C.E., The Fathers, the opening statement of which is: "Moses received Torah at Sinai and handed it on to Joshua"—and onward to named authorities of the Mishnah in a process of oral formulation and oral transmission of tradition.

What tells us, second, that a piece of privileged, canonical writing is systemic and constructive, not traditional, not incremental, but composed in full rationality? The conceptual indicator is the more subtle but also the more telling. The formal side is easier to define. A systematic, and by nature, philosophical, statement or document presents its ideas as though they began with its author or authorship, rather than alluding to, let alone citing in a persistent way, a prior writing, e.g., Scripture. The form of a systematic statement ordinarily will be autonomous. The substantive side of systemic writing is more compelling. The order of discourse will begin from first principles and build upon them. The presentation of a system may, to be sure, absorb within itself a given document, citing its materials here and there. But—and this forms the indicator as to conception, not form alone— the authorship in such a case imposes its program and its problem upon received materials, without the pretense that the program and order of those inherited ("traditional" "authoritative" "scriptures") has made any impact whatsoever upon its presentation.

Yet there is more to the systemic medium of culture, a quite distinctive trait. It is the authorship's purpose and whether, and how, a statement serves that purpose. How do we know that a statement, a sizable composition for instance, is *meant* to be systematic? In a well-composed system, every detail will bear the burden of the message of the system as a whole. Each component will make, in its terms, the statement that the system as a whole is intended to deliver. In order to understand that fact, we have to appreciate an important distinction in the analysis of systems. It is between a fact that is systemically vital, and one that is inert. For the study of economics, this point has been made by Joseph A. Schumpeter as follows: "In economics as elsewhere, most statements of fundamental facts acquire importance only by the superstructures they are made to bear and are commonplace in the absence of such superstructures."[2]

That is to say, a religious system of the

social order, comprising a world-view, a way of life, and a definition of the social entity meant to adopt the one and embody the other, makes ample use of available facts. In order to make their statement, the authors of the documents of such a system speak in a language common to their age. Some of these facts form part of the background of discourse, like the laws of gravity. They are, if important, inert, because they bear no portion of the burden of the systemic message. I call such facts inert. Other of these facts form centerpieces of the system; they may or may not derive from the common background. Their importance to the system forms part of the statement and testimony of that system.

Now in a well-composed system, every systemically generative fact will bear in its detail the message of the system as a whole, and, of course, inert facts will not. Thus, it is clear to any reader of Plato's *Republic*, Aristotle's *Politics* (and related writings, to be sure), the Mishnah, or Matthew's Gospel, that these writers propose to set forth a complete account of the principle or basic truth concerning their subject, beginning, middle, and end. Accordingly, they so frame the details that the main point is repeated throughout. At each point in the composition, the message as a whole, in general terms, will be framed in all due particularity. The choices of topics will be dictated by the requirements of that prevailing systemic attitude and statement. We can even account, ideally, for the topical components of the program, explaining (in theory at least) why one topic is included and another not. A topic will find its place in the system because only through what is said about that particular topic the system can make the statement it wishes to make. Silence on a topic requires explanation, as much as we must supply a systemic motive or reason for the selection of, and substantial disquisition on, some other topic. Our criterion for whether a document is traditional or systematic, therefore systemic, therefore allows us to test our judgment by appeal to facts of verification or falsification.

For the importance of recognizing the systemically generative facts is simple. When we can account for both inclusion and exclu-

sion, answering why this, not that? we know not merely the topical program of the system but its fundamental intent and method, and we may assess the system-builders success in realizing their program. A well-composed system will allow us to explain what is present and what is absent. Consequently, we may come to a reasonable estimation of the system's coverage, its realization of its program and full, exhaustive, presentation of its encompassing statement. Not only so, but a well-crafted systemic statement will by definition form a closed system, and the criterion of whether or not a statement stands on its own or depends upon other sources, e.g., information not contained within its encompassing statement but only alluded to by that statement, serves a second major indicator for taxonomic purposes. Let me spell this out.

Some systems say precisely what they want on exactly those topics that make it possible to make its full statement. These are what we may call "closed systems," in that the authors tell us—by definition—everything that they want us to know, and—again, by definition—nothing that they do not think we need to know. They furthermore do not as a matter of systemic exposition have to refer us to any other writing for a further explication of their meaning (even though for reasons of argument or apologetic, they may do so). When an authorship sets forth a topic and completely and exhaustively expounds that topic, it has given us a systematic statement. The authorship has laid out its program, described the structure of its thought, given us what we need to know to grasp the composition and proportion of the whole, and, of course, supplied the information that, in detail, conveys to us the statement in complete and exhaustive form, thus, a closed system.

It has done more than simply add a detail to available information. Quite to the contrary, the authorship of a statement of a closed system will frame its statement in the supposition that that authorship will tell us not only what we need to know, but everything we need to know, about a given topic. And that is a solid indicator of a systemic statement. An open system, by contrast, requires the recipient of a statement to refer not only to what an authorship tells us, but also to what an authorship invokes. The program is partial, the statement truncated, the system incomplete and not in correct composition and proportion, if, indeed, there is a system at all. That will then mark a traditional, not a systemic, statement. A piece of writing that depends upon other writings, and that not occasioned by subjective judgment of the reader but by objective, if implicit, direction of the author, then forms part of an open system, or is not a systematic statement at all, but a fragment of thought.

Now in all that I have said, I have treated as an axiom the formal and putative autonomy of systemic thought, which is so represented as if it begins *de novo* every morning, in the mind, imagination, and also conscience, of the system-builders. But what about what has gone before: other systems and their literary, as well as their social, detritus? Let us turn to the relationships to prior writings exhibited by systematic and traditional authorships, respectively. How do we know the difference between a system and a tradition in respect to the reception of received systems and their writings? The criteria of difference are characterized very simply. A systematic authorship will establish connections to received writings, always preserving its own autonomy of perspective. A traditional authorship will stand in a relationship of continuity, commonly formal, but always substantive and subordinate, with prior writings. The authorship of a document that stands in a relationship of connection to prior writings will make use of their materials essentially in its own way. The authorship of a document that works in essential continuity with prior writings will cite and quote and refine those received writings but will ordinarily not undertake a fundamentally original statement of its own framed in terms of its own and on a set of issues defined separately from the received writings or formulations. The appeal of a systematic authorship is to the ineluctable verity of well-applied logic, practical reason tested and retested against the facts, whether deriving from prior authorities, or emerging from examples and decisions of leading contemporary authorities.

A traditional authorship accordingly will propose to obliterate lines between one document and another. A systematic authorship in the form of its writing ordinarily will not merge with prior documents. It cites the received writing as a distinct statement—a document out there—and does not merely allude to it as part of an internally cogent statement—a formulation of matters "in here." The systematic authorship begins by stating its interpretation of a received writing in words made up essentially independent of that writing, for example, different in language, formulation, syntax, and substance alike. The marks of independent, post facto, autonomous interpretation are always vividly imprinted upon the systematic authorship's encounter with an inherited document. Such a writing never appears to be represented by internal evidence as the extension of the text, in formal terms the uncovering of the connective network of relations, as literature a part of the continuous revelation of the text itself, in its material condition as we know it "at bottom, another aspect of the text." Not only so, but a systematic statement will not undertake the sustained imitation of prior texts by earlier ones. And even when, in our coming survey, we find evidence that, superficially, points toward a traditional relationship between and among certain texts that present us with closed systems and completed, systematic statements, we should, indeed, be struck by the independence of mind and the originality of authorships that pretend to receive and transmit, but in fact imagine and invent.

From the Pentateuchal statement of 450 B.C.E. to the Bavli of 600 C.E., we discern the paramount and definitive indicators of originality in nearly every document. We uncover few marks of imitation, but a vast corpus of indications of total independence, one document from the other—thus an imputed claim of essential originality. Accordingly, we proceed to further indicators of system as against tradition in the classification of writings and the minds that produced them. A traditional document (therefore the mind it represents) recapitulates the inherited texts; that defines the traditionality of such a writing. A systematic writing may allude to, or draw upon, received texts, but does not recapitulate them, except for its own purposes and within its idiom of thought. Traits of order, cogency, and unity derive from the governing modes of thought and cannot be imposed upon an intellect that is subordinated to received truth. A traditional writing refers back to, goes over the given. The system for its part not only does not recapitulate its texts, it selects and orders them, imputes to them as a whole cogency that their original authorships have not expressed in and through the parts, expresses through them its deepest logic. The system—the final and complete statement—does not recapitulate the extant texts. The antecedent texts—when used at all—are so read as to recapitulate the system. The system comes before the texts and so in due course defines the canon. The upshot is simply stated: the thought-processes of tradition and those of system-building scarcely cohere. Where applied reason prevails, the one—tradition—feeds the other—the system—materials for sustained reconstruction.

The statement of a system is worked out according to the choices dictated by that authorship's sense of order and proportion, priority and importance, and it is generated by the problematic found by that authorship to be acute and urgent and compelling. When confronting the task of exegesis of a received writing, the authorship of a systematic statement does not continue and complete the work of antecedent writings within a single line of continuity ("tradition"). Quite to the contrary, that authorship makes its statement essentially independent of its counterpart and earlier document. In a systematic writing, therefore, the system comes first. The logic and principles of orderly inquiry take precedence over the preservation and repetition of received materials, however holy. The mode of thought defined, the work of applied reason and practical rationality may get underway.

First in place is the system that the authorship through its considered, proportioned statement as a whole expresses and in stupefying detail defines. Only then comes that selection, out of the received materials of the past, of topics and even concrete judgments, facts that serve the system's authorship in the articulation of its system. Nothing out of the past can be shown to have dictated the systematic program, which is essentially the work of its authorship. The tradition is ongoing, and that by definition. Then, also by definition, the system begins exactly where and when it ends. Where reason reigns, its inexorable logic and order, proportion and syllogistic reasoning govern supreme and alone, revising the received materials and restating into a compelling statement, in reason's own encompassing, powerful and rigorous logic, the entirety of the prior heritage of information and thought.

The Mishnah: A Systemic Document of List-Making and System-Building: The framers of the Mishnah, a philosophical law code of the genre of Plato's *Republic*—a utopian design aimed at restoring the rationality and perfection of society—in ca. 200 C.E. presented to their "Israel" a proportioned, balanced, and fully exposed, closed system. They invoked a single logic throughout in the presentation of a tightly constructed structure, secure at all the joints of its frame. They set forth a freestanding document, with slight connection to any that had gone before, so that, within a generation, their heirs and apologists could assign origin of the whole to God's revelation of Torah, inclusive of orally formulated and orally transmitted tradition, to Moses at Sinai. But the Pentateuchal system—the written part of the Torah of Sinai within the Rabbinic myth of origins—and the Mishnaic system have virtually nothing in common. They exhibit shared preferences neither in form, nor in systemic statement and interest. Rhetorically, logically, and topically, they might as well have come down, each from its own universe of reference. The differences in language between biblical and Mishnaic or Middle Hebrew need not detain us and are, systemically, inert.

But the differences in logic, perspective, and focus will demand our attention. For they are fundamental. The Pentateuch tells a story and weaves all rules into that story. Its logic of coherent discourse is fundamentally teleological, and into that logic all its rules are fit. The Mishnah presents rules and treats stories (inclusive of history) as incidental and of merely taxonomic interest. Its logic is propositional, and its intellect does its work through a vast labor of classification, comparison, and contrast generating governing rules and generalizations. The Pentateuch provides an account of how things were in order to explain how things are to be, and set forth how they should be, with the tabernacle in the wilderness the model for (and modeled after) the Temple in the Jerusalem a-building. The Mishnah by contrast speaks in a continuing present tense, saying only how things are, indifferent to the were and the will-be. The Pentateuch focuses upon self-conscious "Israel," saying who they were and what they must become to overcome how they now are. The Mishnah understands by "Israel" as much the individual as the nation and identifies as its principal actors, the heroes of its narrative, not the family become a nation, but the priest and the householder, the woman and the slave, the adult and the child, and other castes and categories of person within an inward-looking, established, fully landed community. Given the Mishnah's authorship's interest in classifications and categories, therefore in systematic hierarchization of an orderly world, one can hardly find odd that (re)definition of the subject-matter and problematic of the systemic social entity.

Let us dwell on this matter of difference in the prevailing logic of coherent discourse. While the Pentateuch appeals to teleology expressed through narrative in order to draw together and make sense of facts, so making connections by appeal to the end and drawing conclusions concerning the purpose of things, the Mishnah's authorship knows only the philosophical logic of syllogism, the rule-making logic of lists. The Pentateuchal logic reached concrete expression in narrative, which served to point to the direction and goal of matters, hence, in the nature of things, of history. Accordingly, those authors, when putting together diverse materials, so shaped everything as to form of it all as continuous a narrative as they could construct, and through that "history" that they made up, they delivered their message and also portrayed that message as cogent and compelling. If the Pentateuchal writers were theologians of history, the Mishnah's aimed at composing a natural philosophy

for supernatural, holy Israel. Like good Aristotelians, they would uncover the components of the rules by comparison and contrast, showing the rule for one thing by finding out how it compared with like things and contrasted with the unlike.

Then, in their view, the unknown would become known, conforming to the rule of the like thing, also to the opposite of the rule governing the unlike thing. That purpose is accomplished, in particular, though list-making, which places on display the data of the like and the unlike and implicitly (ordinarily, not explicitly) then conveys the role. That is why, in exposing the interior logic of its authorship's intellect, the Mishnah had to be a book of lists, with the implicit order, the nomothetic traits, dictating the ordinarily unstated general and encompassing rule. And all this why? It is in order to make a single statement, endless times over, and to repeat in a mass of tangled detail precisely the same fundamental judgment. The Mishnah in its way is as blatantly repetitious in its fundamental statement as is the Pentateuch. But the power of the Pentateuchal authorship, denied to that of the Mishnah, lies in their capacity always to be heard, to create sound by resonance of the surfaces of things. The Pentateuch is a fundamentally popular and accessible piece of writing. By contrast, the Mishnah's writers spoke into the depths, anticipating a more acute hearing than they ever would receive. So the repetitions of Scripture reinforce the message, while the endlessly repeated paradigm of the Mishnah sits too deep in the structure of the system to gain hearing from the ear that lacks acuity or to attain visibility to the untutored eye. So much for the logic. What of the systemic message? Given the subtlety of intellect of the Mishnah's authorship, we cannot find surprising that the message speaks not only in what is said, but in what is omitted.

When we listen to the silences of the system of the Mishnah, as much as to its points of stress, we hear a single message. It is a message of a system that answered a single encompassing question, and the question formed a stunning counterpart to that of the sixth century B.C.E. The Pentateuchal system addressed one reading of the events of the sixth century, highlighted by the destruction of the Jerusalem Temple in 586 B.C.E. At stake was how Israel as defined by that system related to its land, represented by its Temple, and the message may be simply stated: what appears to be the given is in fact a gift, subject to stipulations. The precipitating event for the Mishnaic system was the destruction of the Jerusalem Temple in 70, but at stake now was a quite fresh issue. It was, specifically, this: what, in the aftermath of the destruction of the holy place and holy cult, remained of the sanctity of the holy caste, the priesthood, the holy land, and, above all, the holy people and its holy way of life? The answer was that sanctity persists, indelibly, in Israel, the people, in its way of life, in its land, in its priesthood, in its food, in its mode of sustaining life, in its manner of procreating and so sustaining the nation.

The Mishnah's system therefore focused upon the holiness of the life of Israel, the people, a holiness that had formerly centered on the Temple. The logically consequent question was, what is the meaning of sanctity, and how shall Israel attain, or give evidence of, sanctification. The answer to the question derived from the original creation, the end of the Temple directing attention to the beginning of the natural world that the Temple had (and would again) embodied. For the meaning of sanctity the framers therefore turned to that first act of sanctification, the one in creation. It came about when, all things in array, in place, each with its proper name, God blessed and sanctified the seventh day on the eve of the first Sabbath. Creation was made ready for the blessing and the sanctification when all things were very good, that is to say, in their rightful order, called by their rightful name. An orderly nature was a sanctified and blessed nature, so dictated Scripture in the name of the Supernatural. So to receive the blessing and to be made holy, all things in nature and society were to be set in right array. Given the condition of Israel, the people, in its land, in the aftermath of the catastrophic war against Rome led by Bar Kokhba in 132-135, putting things in order was no easy task. But that is why, after all, the question

pressed, the answer proving inexorable and obvious. The condition of society corresponded to the critical question that obsessed the system-builders.

Once we discern that message, we shall also understand the logic necessary for its construction and inner structure. For the inner structure set forth by a logic of classification alone could sustain the system of ordering all things in proper place and under the proper rule. The like belongs with the like and conforms to the rule governing the like, the unlike goes over to the opposite and conforms to the opposite rule. When we make lists of the like, we also know the rule governing all the items on those lists, respectively. We know that and one other thing, namely, the opposite rule, governing all items sufficiently like to belong on those lists, but sufficiently unlike to be placed on other lists. That rigorously philosophical logic of analysis, comparison and contrast, served because it was the only logic that could serve a system that proposed to make the statement concerning order and right array that the Mishnah's authorship wished to set forth. To the urgent question, what of the holiness of Israel after the destruction of the Temple in 70, therefore, the system of the Mishnah provided the self-evidently valid answer and gave that answer in ineluctable and compelling logical form. That sanctification, as a matter of fact, from the viewpoint of the system now endured and transcended the physical destruction of the building and the cessation of sacrifices. For Israel the people was holy, enduring as the medium and the instrument of God's sanctification. The system then instructed Israel so to act as to express the holiness that inhered in the people. This Israel would accomplish by the right ordering, in accord with a single encompassing principle, of all details of the common life of the village and the home, matching the Temple and the cult.

In the Mishnaic Judaism do we deal with a tradition or a free-standing system? The Pentateuchal authorship, we recall, made ample and continuous use of received materials. So too the authorship of the Mishnah exploited what they chose, out of a heritage of facts deriving from we know not where, those facts it required for its structure and composition. Most of the Pentateuch derives from writers prior to the compilation and formation of the Pentateuch as we have it, but the Pentateuch is an utterly new composition. And what is new in the Mishnah is the system of the Mishnah, not most of the facts upon which the document draws. What the framers do with those facts gives the system its proportion and character, its systemic definition, power, message. For the framers ask their questions when they deal with a fairly broadly familiar corpus of facts. What defines the Mishnah's system is the generative questions the framers addressed to those facts, the trait or characteristic, about a given fact, that drew attention, made a difference and demanded emphasis. When we know what the authorship of the Mishnah wanted to know about a given subject and why that point of interest commanded attention, we define the generative problematic that made everything new in what was, as a matter of fact, a collection of commonplaces. So we must appreciate the work of the authors of the document by appreciating the antiquity of many of the facts upon which they drew—beginning, after all, with Scripture itself. From Scripture onward, no other composition compares in size, comprehensive treatment of a vast variety of topics, balance, proportion, and cogency.

But the authors of the Mishnah reshaped whatever came into their hands. The document upon close reading proves systematic and orderly, purposive and well composed. Facts are formed into statements of sense and meaning, for the Mishnah is no mere scrapbook of legal data, arranged merely for purposes of reference. Each topic bears its point of interest, and that is what defines what the authorship wishes to tell us about that topic. The Mishnah is a systemic document that is meant to make a statement on virtually every page, a document in which the critical problematic at the center almost always exercises influence over the merely instrumental, peripheral facts, dictating how they are chosen, arranged, utilized. So even though facts in the document prove very old indeed, on that basis we understand no more than we did before we knew that

some of the document's data come from ancient times. True, law as the Mishnah presents law derives from diverse sources, from remote antiquity onward. But the law as it emerges whole and complete in the Mishnah, in particular, that is, the system, the structure, the proportions and composition, the topical program and the logical and syllogistic whole—these derive from the imagination and wit of the final two generations, of the authors of the Mishnah, that is, from ca. 140 to ca. 200. And through them the authorship delivers its message, asking its question by answering it again and again. But this answer comes only in picayune detail, as though the main issue were settled and beyond dispute, a remarkably powerful way of making one's main point.

Let me now spell out the basic statement that the document wishes to make. The Mishnah's system as a whole may be characterized in a simple way. Overall, its stress lies on sanctification, understood as the correct arrangement of all things, each in its proper category, each called by its rightful name, just as at the creation. Then everything having been given its proper name, God called the natural world very good and therefore blessed and sanctified it. This stress on proper order and right rule explains why the Mishnah makes a statement of philosophy, concerning the order of the natural world in its correspondence with the supernatural world.

The system of philosophy expressed through concrete and detailed law presented by the Mishnah, consists of a coherent logic and topic, a cogent world-view and comprehensive way of living. It is a world-view which speaks of transcendent things, a way of life in response to the supernatural meaning of what is done, a heightened and deepened perception of the sanctification of Israel in deed and in deliberation. Sanctification thus means two things, first, distinguishing Israel in all its dimensions from the world in all its ways; second, establishing the stability, order, regularity, predictability, and reliability of Israel in the world of nature and supernature in particular at moments and in contexts of danger. Danger means instability, disorder, irregularity, uncertainty, and betrayal. Each topic of the system as a whole takes up a critical and indispensable moment or context of social being. Through what is said in regard to each of the Mishnah's principal topics, what the system expressed through normative rules as a whole wishes to declare is fully expressed. Yet if the parts severally and jointly give the message of the whole, the whole cannot exist without all of the parts, so well joined and carefully crafted are they all.

The diverse topical program of the Mishnah, time and again making the same points on the centrality of order, works itself out in a single logic of cogent discourse, one which seeks the rule that governs diverse cases. And that logic states within its interior structure the fundamental point of the document as a whole. The correspondence of logic to system here, as in the Pentateuch viewed overall, hardly presents surprises. Seeing how the logic does its work within the document therefore need not detain us for very long. Let us take up by way of illustration a single pericope of the Mishnah and determine the logic that joins fact to fact, sentence to sentence, in a cogent proposition, that is, in our terms, a paragraph that makes a statement. Mishnah-tractate Sanhedrin, Chapter Two, sets forth the subtle way in which list-making yields a powerfully argued philosophical theorem. It shows us through the making of connections and the drawing of conclusions the propositional and essentially philosophical mind that animates the Mishnah. In the following passage, the authorship wishes to say that Israel has two heads, one of state, the other of cult, the king and the high priest, respectively, and that these two offices are nearly wholly congruent with one another, with a few differences based on the particular traits of each. Broadly speaking, therefore, our exercise is one of setting forth the genus and the species. The genus is head of holy Israel. The species are king and high priest.

Here are the traits in common and those not shared, and the exercise is fully exposed for what it is, an inquiry into the rules that govern, the points of regularity and order, in this minor matter, of political structure. My outline, imposed in italic type, makes the point important in this setting.

Mishnah-tractate Sanhedrin
Chapter Two

1. *The rules of the high priest: subject to the law, marital rites, conduct in bereavement*
2:1 A. A high priest judges, and [others] judge him;
   B. gives testimony, and [others] give testimony about him;
   C. performs the rite of removing the shoe [Deut. 25:7-9], and [others] perform the rite of removing the shoe with his wife.
   D. [Others] enter levirate marriage with his wife, but he does not enter into levirate marriage,
   E. because he is prohibited to marry a widow.
   F. [If] he suffers a death [in his family], he does not follow the bier.
   G. "But when [the bearers of the bier] are not visible, he is visible; when they are visible, he is not.
   H. "And he goes with them to the city gate," the words of R. Meir.
   I. R. Judah says, "He never leaves the sanctuary,
   J. "since it says, 'Nor shall he go out of the sanctuary' (Lev. 21:12)."
   K. And when he gives comfort to others
   L. the accepted practice is for all the people to pass one after another, and the appointed [prefect of the priests] stands between him and the people.
   M. And when he receives consolation from others,
   N. all the people say to him, "Let us be your atonement."
   O. And he says to them, "May you be blessed by Heaven."
   P. And when they provide him with the funeral meal,
   Q. all the people sit on the ground, while he sits on a stool.

2. *The rules of the king: not subject to the law, marital rites, conduct in bereavement*
2:2 A. The king does not judge, and [others] do not judge him;
   B. does not give testimony, and [others] do not give testimony about him;
   C. does not perform the rite of removing the shoe, and others do not perform the rite of removing the shoe with his wife;
   D. does not enter into levirate marriage, nor [do his brother] enter levirate marriage with his wife.
   E. R. Judah says, "If he wanted to perform the rite of removing the shoe or to enter into levirate marriage, his memory is a blessing."
   F. They said to him, "They pay no

attention to him [if he expressed the wish to do so]."

G. [Others] do not marry his widow.

H. R. Judah says, "A king may marry the widow of a king.

I. "For so we find in the case of David, that he married the widow of Saul,

J. "For it is said, 'And I gave you your master's house and your master's wives into your embrace' (2 Sam. 12:8)."

2:3 A. [If] [the king] suffers a death in his family, he does not leave the gate of his palace.

B. R. Judah says, "If he wants to go out after the bier, he goes out,

C. "for thus we find in the case of David, that he went out after the bier of Abner,

D. "since it is said, 'And King David followed the bier' (2 Sam. 3:31)."

E. They said to him, "This action was only to appease the people."

F. And when they provide him with the funeral meal, all the people sit on the ground, while he sits on a couch.

3. SPECIAL RULES PERTINENT TO THE KING BECAUSE OF HIS CALLING

2:4 A. [The king] calls out [the army to wage] a war fought by choice on the instructions of a court of seventy-one.

B. He [may exercise the right to] open a road for himself, and [others] may not stop him.

C. The royal road has no required measure.

D. All the people plunder and lay before him [what they have grabbed], and he takes the first portion.

E. "He should not multiply wives to himself" (Deut. 17:17)—only eighteen.

F. R. Judah says, "He may have as many as he wants, so long as they do not entice him [to abandon the Lord (Deut. 7:4)]."

G. R. Simeon says, "Even if there is only one who entices him [to abandon the Lord]—lo, this one should not marry her."

H. If so, why is it said, "He should not multiply wives to himself"?

I. Even though they should be like Abigail [1 Sam. 25:3].

J. "He should not multiply horses to himself" (Deut. 17:16)—only enough for his chariot.

K. "Neither shall he greatly multiply to himself silver and gold" (Deut. 17:16)—only enough to pay his army.

L. "And he writes out a scroll of the Torah for himself" (Deut. 17:17)

M. When he goes to war, he takes it

out with him; when he comes back, he brings it back with him; when he is in session in court, it is with him; when he is reclining, it is before him,

N. as it is said, "And it shall be with him, and he shall read in it all the days of his life" (Deut. 17:19).

2:5 A. [Others may] not ride on his horse, sit on his throne, handle his scepter.

B. And [others may] not watch him while he is getting a haircut, or while he is nude, or in the bathhouse,

C. since it is said, "You shall surely set him as king over you" (Deut. 17:15)—that reverence for him will be upon you.

The philosophical cast of mind is amply revealed in this essay, which in concrete terms effects a taxonomy, a study of the genus, national leader, and its two species, [1] king, [2] high priest: how are they alike, how are they not alike, and what accounts for the differences? The premise is that national leaders are alike and follow the same rule, except where they differ and follow the opposite rule from one another. But that premise also is subject to the proof effected by the survey of the data consisting of concrete rules, those systemically inert facts that here come to life for the purposes of establishing a proposition. By itself, the fact that, e.g., others may not ride on his horse, bears the burden of no systemic proposition. In the context of an argument constructed for nomothetic, taxonomic purposes, the same fact is active and weighty.

No natural historian can find alien the discourse and mode of thought at hand; it exemplifies the ordinary disposition of data in quest of meaning: making connections, drawing conclusions. For if I had to specify a single mode of thought that establishes connections between one fact and another, it is in the search for points in common and therefore also points of contrast. We seek connection between fact and fact, sentence and sentence in the subtle and balanced rhetoric of the Mishnah, by comparing and contrasting two things that are like and not alike. At the logical level, too, the Mishnah falls into the category of familiar philosophical thought. Once we seek regularities, we propose rules. What is like another thing falls under its rule, and what is not like the other falls under the opposite rule. Accordingly, as to the species of the genus, so far as they are alike, they share the same rule. So far as they are not alike, each follows a rule contrary to that governing the other.

So the work of analysis is what produces connection, and therefore the drawing of conclusions derives from comparison and contrast: the *and*, the *equal*. The proposition then that forms the conclusion concerns the essential likeness of the two offices, except where they are different, but the subterranean premise is that we can explain both likeness and difference by appeal to a principle of fundamental order and unity. To make these observations concrete, we turn to the case at hand. The important contrast comes at the outset. The high priest and king fall into a single genus, but speciation, based on traits particular to the king, then distinguishes the one from the other. In a treatise on government, organizing details into unifying rules, the propositions of the present passage will have been stated differently. But the mode of thought, the manner of reaching conclusions, above all, the mind-set that sees connections in one way, rather than some other, that draws conclusions in this wise, not in that—these will have found an equally familiar place in the mind of both philosophy, of Aristotle's kind in particular, and the Judaic intellect represented by the Mishnah.

The framers of the Mishnah have drawn together diverse materials in a single, nearly-seamless fabric. And in them they have made a single statement, many times over, in the setting of an extraordinarily vast range of topics. Once an authorship has registered the statement it wishes to make, it finds possible the expression of that same statement through what seems to me an unlimited range of topical media. That logic of list-making, which brings to the surface a deeper intellectual structure formed of comparison and contrast, classification and exclusion, predominates throughout. Accordingly, a single logic serves to make a single statement. That logic is the one of the philosophical syllogism for a statement made up of rules governing (or deriving from) a variety of cases.

What about the question of tradition versus system? The Mishnah's authorship sets forth a system, without laying claim to the authority of tradition, e.g., with a myth of origin at Sinai, with a routine invocation of proof-texts. And that is surely a trait of intellect of system-builders, so persuaded of the compelling character of their statement as to deny need to invoke the authority of tradition. Logic takes the place of tradition, argument and powerful rhetoric, of the argument of precedent and an authoritative past. In the face of the Torah of God revealed to Moses at Sinai, the Mishnah's system-builders set forth a system resting wholly on the foundations of logic and order. Theirs was a statement standing on the firm two feet of the systemic authorship itself. The authorship of the Pentateuch appealed to Sinai for authority. The framers of the Mishnah kept silent about why people should keep the rules of their document and so construct out of an inchoate and chaotic world that system that they set forth. The systemic statement contained its own authority.

Logic, compelling and uncompromising, sustained the system; an appeal to tradition would have contradicted that proud claim of the system-makers of the Mishnah, and it is a claim that they did not deign to put forth. True, others alleged in their behalf that their authority, if not their exact positions, set them into a chain of tradition commencing with Moses at Sinai. But that claim came only in the context of debates following the closure of the Mishnah and made necessary by the character of the Mishnah. To state the upshot simply, the framers of the Mishnah set forth a system that, in its very nature, demanded to be transformed into a tradition. And that demand would be met by the authorship of the Bavli, but there too, in terms defined by that authorship, and for purposes dictated not by tradition but by yet another system-making Judaic intellect, the last and best of the formative age of Judaism.

The Mishnah, then, utilized a single logic to set forth a system that, in form as in inner structure, stood wholly autonomous and independent, a statement unto itself, with scarcely a ritual obeisance to any prior system. As soon as the Mishnah made its appearance, therefore, the vast labor of not only explaining its meaning but especially justifying its authority was sure to get under way. For the Mishnah presented one striking problem in particular. It rarely cited scriptural authority for its rules. Instead, it followed the inexorable authority of logic, specifically, the inner logic of a topic, which dictated the order of thought and defined the generative problematic that instructed its authors on what they wanted to know about a particular topic.[3] These intellectual modalities in their nature lay claim to an independence of mind, even when, in point of fact, the result of thought is a repetition of what Scripture itself says. Omitting scriptural prooftexts therefore represents both silence and signals its statement. For that act of omission bore the implicit claim to an authority independent of Scripture, an authority deriving from logic working within its own inner tensions and appealing to tests of reason and sound argument. In that striking fact the document set a new course for itself. But its authorship raised problems for those who would apply its law to Israel's life.

From System to Tradition, From the Mishnah to the Bavli: The Bavli forms both a systemic statement and also a traditional document. Precisely in what sense? It is systemic in its consistent presentation of a closed system, a whole, proportioned, and well-composed statement, one that in vast detail blatantly and repetitiously delivers the same self-evidently true answer to the same ponderous and urgent question. But it is traditional in the very real sense that its authorship constantly quotes and cites received writings, laying out its ideas in the form of commentaries to two of those writings, Scripture and the Mishnah. That internal evidence is backed up by the mythic framework of the document, which is consistently represented as the oral part of the Torah in two media, written and the oral, respectively.

The particular way in which the authorship of the Bavli accomplished this feat—presenting its Judaic system in the garb of a tradition—is through a fresh conception of the logic of cogent discourse. Specifically, it utilized (1) philosophical logic for the for-

mation of propositions in sustained units of systematic discourse, that is to say, for the drawing of conclusions. But it also made ample and prevailing use of (2) the logic of fixed association—linking units of coherent discourse to one another only through positioning them as comments on a shared and common, prior text (the Mishnah, Scripture). Thus for the linking of one proposition to another, an other-than-philosophical medium for coherent discourse served. But the units of discourse themselves are analytical and syllogistic, in some cases even sustained exercises in dialectics. So, in a word: (1) in its syllogistic discourse the authorship presented the propositions that, all together, comprised its statement. And (2) in organizing that discourse within the discipline of the logic of fixed association, the authorship imparted to its statement the status of tradition, pretending that whatever it had to say constitute a mere clarification of the received Torah, whether oral, in the Mishnah, or written, in Scripture.

Let me amplify. One way by which intellectuals reframe received writings into a single, systemic statement is to adopt the form of a commentary for the presentation of what is, in fact, a free-standing composite, a statement of their own. In the case of the Bavli, by forming the final statement as a commentary on the Mishnah and on Scripture alike, the writers made a coherent and independent statement upon the entire received corpus. But to make their system look traditional, they attached it to the Mishnah or to Scripture. But in two fundamental ways, they took an independent stance of their own. Either of these ways suffices to justify characterizing the Bavli as systemic, not traditional. First, they made their own choices of passages of the Mishnah and of Scripture that required comment. So they reconfigured the entire topical program of the Torah as they portrayed it. And, second, they composed large-scale propositional composites, coherent through the logic of syllogism we have already encountered in the Mishnah. So they constructed compositions along philosophical lines. Since a superficially traditional form cloaked a deeply philosophical mode of discourse, the Bavli, critical to the development of Judaism henceforward, set the task. It was to innovate in a traditional framework. Viewed in relationship to its sources[4] the Bavli emerges through a set of purposive choices not dictated by the received canonical writings and therefore is simply not a traditional document. Most of what the Bavli's authorship says simply expresses, in a cogent and coherent way, the topical, rhetorical, and logical choices, forming the well-crafted statement and viewpoint, of its own authorship. Little of what the Bavli's authorship presents in a propositional form derives cogency and force from a received statement.

To substantiate these generalizations, three questions require answers. First, is the Bavli viewed whole an autonomous system or has its authorship produced merely a dependent commentary? In demonstrating the autonomy of the Bavli's statement, I set the stage for the argument that the Bavli's statement comes to us within the logic of cogent discourse imparted by argumentation for a theorem and other modes of propositional cogency. Second, does the Bavli utilize logic(s) congruent to its systemic program and purpose (if any)? Third, is the Bavli systemic or traditional (by the criteria already put forth), and how does the authorship of the Bavli represent its document in relationship to received writings, e.g., as tradition or free-standing? The proposition I advance then is simple: first, the Bavli makes a coherent statement, second, it forms a systemic document in traditional form, and, third, it utilizes a mixture of logics remarkably suitable to the task of doing just that. The argumentation for these propositions amply serves the task.

The Bavli as an autonomous system in command of the received tradition: The Mishnah in the Bavli: The Bavli takes an autonomous stance in relationship to the Mishnah. That is shown by a simple fact. The Bavli's authorship has picked and chosen among Mishnah-tractates those that it wished to highlight and amplify. It brought to bear on Mishnah-tractates its own, original analytical program, devising its own program of exegesis and its own agenda of problematics. On that basis it imputed to the Mishnah those meanings

that that authorship, on the foundations of its own critical judgment and formidable power of logical reasoning in a dialectical movement, itself chose to impute. Accordingly, the Bavli on the face of it presents a system, not merely an incremental tradition spun out of the Mishnah (and related compilations of Halakhah). The authorship's cogent, rigorously rational reading of the received heritage has demonstrably emerged out of the fresh and sustained, rigorous reflection of its own extended authorship. It did not grow in an organic way in a long process of formulation and transmission of received traditions, in each generation lovingly tended, refined and polished, and handed on essentially as received. The breaks are too sharp, the initiatives too striking, for us to imagine that it did.

Not only so, but at any point of entry into the Bavli, opening a page at random, we find ourselves directed by a purposive and well-composed program of inquiry. The authorship, standing at the outset of discourse, knows precisely what it wishes to find out in any passage of the Mishnah; it follows a clear-cut program, imposed throughout, a program to be discerned in devices of fixed rhetoric, persistent logical argument, and coherent analytical program, extending over the whole surface of the topical agenda that the authorship has selected. None of these traits of a coherent and cogent inquiry, so elegantly put together in a single formally-repetitive statement, can be located, in their present combination and structure, in any prior writing of Rabbinic Judaism or of any other Judaic system in antiquity. And the Bavli's original program did not even form a continuation of the exegetical tradition of the Mishnah formulated by the authorship of the Yerushalmi two hundred years earlier.[5]

The break with the Mishnah, moreover, is not only in rhetoric and logic and topic, as the most superficial glance shows. They are marked by a fresh systemic perspective, one that is quite different from that of the Mishnah's and as pervasive, for the Bavli, as the Mishnah's fundamental systemic statement is pervasive in the entirety of the Mishnah. For the Mishnah's authorship set forth a system of sanctification focused on

the holiness of the priesthood, the cultic festivals, the Temple and its sacrifices, as well
as on the rules for protecting that holiness
from Levitical uncleanness—four of the six
divisions of the Mishnah on a single theme.
The Mishnah's system stresses the issue of
sanctification, pure and simple. The Bavli's
authorship complemented the issue of Israel's
sanctification with the issue of Israel's salvation, making explicit that attainment of
the one would lead to the realization of the
other. That authorship worked out a system intersecting with the Mishnah's but
essentially asymmetrical with it, a system
for salvation, focused on the salvific power
of the sanctification of the holy people.[6]

The manifest shift from the Mishnah's to
the Bavli's systems shows us that the Bavli's
authorship has made up its own mind and
then imputed to a received documents the
consequence of its own independent thought.
And the Bavli's authorship accomplished its
own goals in its own way, making a statement independent of that of the Mishnah,
to which, in form, the Bavli's authorship
attached its statement. How then are we to
demonstrate the autonomous and fresh character of so protean a statement as the Bavli,
showing that that system is not continuous
with the one of the Mishnah, but only connected to it? A simple experiment will amply
prove the point. For the sake of argument
stipulating for the moment that the Bavli's
authorship has indeed made a systemic statement, let us ask ourselves whether, on the
basis of the system of the Mishnah, we can
have predicted through extrapolation from
the Mishnah's shape and structure the
important components of the statement of
the Bavli. The answer is partly affirmative,
partly negative—and therefore negative.

The affirmative side is merely formal and
so quite simple to delineate. With only the
Mishnah in hand, we can surely outline the
main principles of the normative rules that
the Bavli incorporates into, and utilizes as
the medium for, its systemic statement. But
if we knew only the Mishnah's program,
we would vastly overstate the range and
coverage of the Bavli's, which omits all reference to the Mishnah's first and sixth divisions (Agriculture, save only Blessings, and
Purities, except for the rules of Menstrual

Uncleanness). And that only suggests the
vast disproportions between the Mishnah's
authorship's estimates of the attention to be
paid to a given range of law, and the decision of the Bavli's authorship on those same
matters. The enormous volume of the Bavli's
discussion of the three tractates of the Civil
Law (Baba Qamma, Baba Mesia, Baba
Batra), is out of all proportion to the place
that those same tractates occupy within the
composition and proportion of the Mishnah.
The disproportions form only one indicator of the autonomous judgment exercised
by the Bavli's authorship. For once they
have chosen their own program of subjects
and determined the attention they wish to
devote to those subjects, they give evidence
of a set of priorities and concerns that are
their own and not inherited. Theirs is a
fixed and methodical analytical inquiry,
which wants to know the same thing about
all things.

**The Bavli's Logic of Coherent Dis-
course: Syllogism and Sustained Analytical Argument:** At the outset I pointed
out that the Bavli resorts to two distinct
logics of coherent discourse, syllogistic-propo-
sitional for its completed units of discourse,
fixed-associative for linking completed units
of discourse in a common document. Now
the question arises: Does the Bavli utilize
logic(s) congruent to its systemic program
and purpose (if any)? What then holds the
whole together? It is that logic of fixed association that effects the linkage between completed thoughts, fully spelled out, not in a
topical sequence established to argue for yet
larger propositions, but in a sequence defined
by an external connection, one with no
propositional substance whatsoever. Stated
simply for the case of the Bavli, we work
out our propositions as paragraphs of completed, syllogistic thought and argument.
But then we link one to the next by reference to the sentences of the Mishnah, read
one by one. So the cogent discourse at the
level of drawing conclusions is philosophical, while discourse is held together at the
logic of the large-scale making of connection through a fixed associations formally
extrinsic to discourse. Laying matters out
as a commentary to the Mishnah is the
result of this mixture of two logics. Let us

then consider the traits of the logic of fixed association, which serves our authorship so effectively in imparting the form of tradition to the structure of a systemic system they have composed for us.

The logic of fixed association connects into protracted statements of a cogent character otherwise unrelated sequential sentences, and also joins into sizable compositions entire paragraphs that on their own, through their own propositions, in no way coalesce. Among the documents that reached closure prior to the conclusion of the Bavli, few are wholly put together in such a way that the logic of fixed association prevails both in composing sentences into paragraphs and also in establishing the intelligible connection and order of large units of thought, that is, whole paragraphs, whether propositional or otherwise.

Let us rapidly review the criteria for recognizing the presence of the logic of fixed association. The negative criteria are, first, that read in sequence and proximity, the free-standing sentences, two or more, do not all together yield a statement that transcends the sum of the parts (e.g., a "paragraph"). Fixed associative compositions moreover do not gain cogency through statements of propositions. The sentences are cogent, but the cogency derives from a source other than shared propositions or participation in an argument yielding a shared proposition. The fixed association that effects connection for cogent discourse derives, it follows, from a "text" outside of the composition at hand and known to, taken for granted by, the composition at hand. True, that "text" may be a list of names; it may be a received document or portion thereof. But it is the given, and its cogency is the single prevailing premise that otherwise unrelated facts belong together in some sort of established sequence and order. While some of the sentences joined together in a statement the cogency of which appeals to fixed association may on their own make quite cogent points, and all of them are surely intelligible as discrete statements, the lot of them form a chaotic composite, except that the authorship of the document assigns them to the rubric defined by the named authority. Simple symbols here serve. The

logic of fixed association shows radical limitations characteristic of a mode of thought that joins A to 3 because both A and 3 refer back to a common point, represented here by the symbol #. That mode of thought is fundamentally alien to the orderly pursuit of logical inquiry familiar in the Western philosophical and scientific tradition, because, carried to its logical conclusion, that logic never requires its practitioner to make connections; these are invariably supplied, imputed, never discovered, never source of stimulus to curiosity.

This brings us to the demonstration of how the authorship of the Bavli has composed their document, in the making of medium- and large-scale logical connections, by resort to two distinct principles of cogent discourse. These are, first, the one of propositional connection within completed units of thought, a connection discovered through the pursuit of reasoned speculative inquiry, and second, the other of the fixed associative connection between and among those same completed units of thought, producing large-scale compositions. Sizable numbers of the completed units of thought of the Bavli find inner cogency through the development of a proposition concerning a given theme. Overall, these units of completed thought are linked to one another through the connections supplied for the Bavli extrinsically by both the Mishnah and Scripture. The framers of the Bavli had in hand a tripartite corpus of inherited materials awaiting composition into a final, closed document. First, they took up materials, in various states and stages of completion, pertinent to the Mishnah or to the principles of laws that the Mishnah had originally brought to articulation. Second, they had in hand received materials, again in various conditions, pertinent to the Scripture, both as the Scripture related to the Mishnah and also as the Scripture laid forth its own narratives. And that fact points to the way in which the logic of fixed association governed their work.

Let me now give an example of the way in which I conceive the Bavli's framers to have made use of the logic of fixed association in that dual way that involved appeal for cogency to both the Mishnah and Scripture. Once more I turn to a familiar item, namely, Mishnah-tractate Sanhedrin Chapter Two, now as the Bavli's authorship presents the matter. Since our interest is in identifying passages in which both the Mishnah and Scripture serve to hold together discrete compositions, ordinarily of a propositional character, I give only highlights. These will then illustrate the workings of the logic of fixed association in the Bavli. The numbers in square brackets refer to the Bavli's pagination.

BAVLI-TRACTATE SANHEDRIN TO MISHNAH-TRACTATE SANHEDRIN
THE MISHNAH: 2:3
A. [If] [the king] suffers a death in his family, he does not leave the gate of his palace.
B. R. Judah says, "If he wants to go out after the bier, he goes out,
C. "for thus we find in the case of David, that he went out after the bier of Abner,
D. "since it is said, 'And King David followed the bier' (2 Sam. 3:31)."
E. They said to him, "This action was only to appease the people."
F. And when they provide him with the funeral meal, all the people sit on the ground, while he sits on a couch.

THE TALMUD, UNIT I
A. Our rabbis have taught on Tannaite authority:
B. In a place in which women are accustomed to go forth after the bier, they go forth in that way. If they are accustomed to go forth before the bier, they go forth in that manner.
C. R. Judah says, "Women always go forth in front of the bier.
D. "For so we find in the case of David that he went forth after the bier of Abner.
E. "For it is said, 'And King David followed the bier' (2 Sam. 3:31)."
F. They said to him, "That was only to appease the people [M. 2:3D-E].
G. "They were appeased, for David would go forth among the men and come in among the women, go forth among the women and come in among the men,
H. "as it is said, 'So all the people and all Israel understood that it was not of the king to slay Abner' (2 Sam. 3:37)."

The Bavli's authorship now inserts a sizable exposition on David's relationship with Abner, and this goes its own way, without regard to the amplification of M. Sanhedrin 2:3D-E, cited just now. The following not-very-cogent unit of discourse makes no single point but holds together because of the

systematic amplification of the cited verses. No. II stands by itself and sets the stage for what is to follow.

THE TALMUD, UNIT II
A. Raba expounded, "What is the meaning of that which is written, 'And all the people came to cause David to eat bread' (2 Sam. 3:35)?
B. "It was written, 'to pierce David' [with a K], but we read, 'to cause him to eat bread' [with a B].
C. "To begin with they came to pierce him but in the end to cause him to eat bread."

THE TALMUD, UNIT III
A. Said R. Judah said Rab, "On what account was Abner punished? Because he could have prevented Saul but did not prevent him [from killing the priest of Nob, 1 Sam. 22:18]."
B. R. Isaac said, "He did try to prevent him, but he got no response."
C. And both of them interpret the same verse of Scripture: "And the king lamented for Abner and said, Should Abner die as a churl dies, your hands were not bound or your feet put into fetters" (2 Sam. 2:33).
D. He who maintains that he did not try to stop Saul interprets the verse in this way: "Your hands were not bound nor were your feet put into fetters"—so why did you not try to stop him? "As a man falls before the children of iniquity so did you fall" (2 Sam. 3:33).
E. He who maintains that he did try to stop Saul but got no response interprets the verse as an expression of amazement: "Should he have died as a churl dies? Your hands were not bound and your feet were not put into fetters."
F. Since he did protest, why "As a man falls before the children of iniquity, so did you fall"?
G. In the view of him who has said that he did protest, why was he punished?
H. Said R. Nahman bar Isaac, "Because he held up the coming of the house of David by two and a half years."

The framer reverts to the Mishnah-passage and proceeds. What we have now is the familiar program of Mishnah-exegesis: amplification of words and phrases in the instance of No. IV, of which I present only a few stichs.

THE TALMUD, UNIT IV
A. And when they provide him with the funeral meal, [all the people sit on the ground, while he sits on a couch] [M. 2:3F]:
B. What is the couch?

C. Said Ulla, "It is a small couch."

D. Said rabbis to Ulla, "Now is there something on which, up to that time, he had never sat, and now we seat him on that object?"

E. Raba objected to this argument, "What sort of problem is this? Perhaps it may be compared to the matter of eating and drinking, for up to this point we gave him nothing to eat or drink, while now we bring him food and drink . . . ."

The ongoing discussion of the matter provides a secondary development of the rules pertaining to the couch under discussion and need not detain us. Yet another example of a sizable composition appealing for cogency to Scripture is tacked on to M. 2:4A-D. Here is another composition that holds together solely because of reference to verses of Scripture. Specifically, 2 Sam. 13 forms the center, and the various sentences then are joined to that center, but not to one another:

THE TALMUD, UNIT V

A. Said R. Judah said Rab, "David had four hundred sons, all of them born of beautiful captive women. All grew long locks plaited down the back. All of them seated in golden chariots.

B. "And they went forth at the head of troops, and they were the powerful figures in the house of David."

C. And R. Judah said Rab said, "Tamar was the daughter of a beautiful captive woman.

D. "For it is said, 'Now, therefore, I pray you, speak to the king, for he will not withhold me from you' (2 Sam. 13:13).

E. "Now if you hold that she was the daughter of a valid marriage, would the king ever have permitted [Amnon] to marry his sister?

F. "But, it follows, she was the daughter of a beautiful captive woman."

G. "And Amnon had a friend, whose name was Jonadab, son of Shimeah, David's brother, and Jonadab was a very subtle man" (2 Sam. 13:3): Said R. Judah said Rab, "He was subtle about doing evil."

H. "And he said to him, Why, son of the king, are you thus becoming leaner . . . And Jonadab said to him, Lay down on your bed and pretend to be sick . . . and she will prepare the food in my sight . . . and she took the pan and poured [the cakes] out before him" (2 Sam. 13:4ff.): Said R. Judah said Rab, "They were some sort of pancakes."

I. "Then Amnon hated her with a very great hatred" (2 Sam. 13:15): What was the reason?

J. Said R. Isaac, "One of his hairs got caught [around his penis and cut it off] making him one whose penis had been cut off."

K. But was she the one who had tied the hair around his penis? What had she done?

L. Rather, I should say, she had tied a hair around his penis and made him into one whose penis had been cut off.

M. Is this true? And did not Raba explain, "What is the sense of the verse, 'And your renown went forth among the nations for your beauty' (Ez. 16:14)? It is that Israelite women do not have armpit or pubic hair."

N. Tamar was different, because she was the daughter of a beautiful captive woman.

O. "And Tamar put ashes on her head and tore her garment of many colors" (2 Sam. 13:19):

P. It was taught on Tannaite authority in the name of R. Joshua b. Qorhah, "Tamar established a high wall at that time [protecting chastity]. People said, 'If such could happen to princesses, all the more so can it happen to ordinary women.' If such could happen to virtuous women, all the more so can it happen to wanton ones!"

Q. Said R. Judah said Rab, "At that time they made a decree [21B] against a man's being alone with any woman [married or] unmarried."

R. But the rule against a man's being alone with [a married woman] derives from the authority of the Torah [and not from the authority of rabbis later on].

S. For R. Yohanan said in the name of R. Simeon b. Yehosedeq, "Whence in the Torah do we find an indication against a man's being alone [with a married woman]? As it is said, 'If your brother, son of your mother, entice you' (Deut. 13:7).

T. "And is it the fact that the son of one's mother can entice, but the son of the father cannot entice? Rather, it is to tell you that a son may be alone with his mother, and no one else may be alone with any of the consanguineous female relations listed in the Torah."

U. Rather, they made a decree against a man's being alone with an unmarried woman.

V. "And Adonijah, son of Haggith, exalts himself, saying, I will be king" (1 Kgs. 1:5):

W. Said R. Judah said Rab, "This teaches that he tried to fit [the crown on his head], but it would not fit."

X. "And he prepares chariots and horses and fifty men to run before him" (1 Kgs. 1:5):

Y. So what was new [about princes' having retinues]?

Z. Said R. Judah said Rab, "All of them had had their spleen removed [believed to make them faster runners] and the flesh of the soles of their feet cut off [Shachter, p. 115, n. 12: so that they might be fleet of foot and impervious to briars and thorns]."

What do I see in this abstract? It is that two principal sources of fixed associations served the Bavli's framers, the Mishnah and Scripture. The authorships of the tractates of the Bavli in general first of all organized the Bavli around the Mishnah, just as the framers of the Yerushalmi had done. Second, they adapted and included vast tracts of antecedent materials organized as scriptural commentary. These they inserted whole and complete, not at all in response to the Mishnah's program. They never created redactional compositions of a sizable order that focused upon given authorities, even though sufficient materials lay at hand to allow doing so. They joined the Mishnah to Scripture in such a way as to give final form and fixed expression, through their categories of the organization of all knowledge, to the Torah as it had been known, sifted, searched, approved, and handed down, even from the remote past to their own day. Accordingly, the Bavli's ultimate framers made the decision to present large-scale discussions along lines of order and sequence dictated not by topics and propositional arguments concerning them—as had Aphrahat, for instance, in his compelling Demonstrations. Rather they selected the two components of the one whole Torah, oral and written, of Moses, our rabbi, at Sinai, and these they set forth as the connections that held together and ordered all discourse. That is how they organized what they knew, on the one side, and made their choices in laying out the main lines of the structure of knowledge, on the other.[7]

Let me now generalize on the traits of the simple example just now reviewed. The Bavli is made up of sizable systematic statements of propositions, syllogistic arguments fully worked out and elegantly exposed. Accord-

ingly, two principles of logical discourse are at play. For the statement of propositions, sizable arguments and proofs, the usual philosophical logic dictates the joining of sentence to sentences and the composition of paragraphs, that is, completed thoughts. For the presentation of the whole, the other logic, the one deriving from imputed, fixed associations, external to the propositions at hand, serves equally well. The framers of the Bavli drew together the results of work which people prior to their own labors already had completed. Available as both completed documents and also sizable components, statements awaiting agglutination or conglomeration in finished documents, these ready-made materials were sewn together with only one kind of thread. Whatever the place and role of the diverse types of logics that formed the compositions circulating before and in the time of the Bavli—compilations of scriptural exegeses, the Yerushalmi, not to mention the exegeses of Pentateuchal laws in Sifra and the two Sifes, the Tosefta, The Fathers [Avot] and The Fathers According to Rabbi Nathan, Genesis Rabbah, Leviticus Rabbah, Pesiqta deRab Kahana, and on and on—the Bavli superseded them all and defined the mind of Judaism. It was through the Bavli that the entire antecedent canon reached the Judaism of the Dual Torah beyond the formative age.

The Bavli's Stance Vis-à-vis the Received Writings, Scripture and the Mishnah: Is the Bavli systemic or traditional (by the criteria already put forth), and how does the authorship of the Bavli represent its document in relationship to received writings, e.g., as tradition or free-standing? Were we therefore to enter into conversation with the penultimate and ultimate authorship of the Bavli, the first thing we should want to know is simple: what have you made up? And what have you simply repeated out of a long-continuing heritage of formulation and transmission? And why should we believe you? The authorship then would be hard put to demonstrate in detail that its fundamental work of literary selection and ordering, its basic choices on sustained and logical discourse, its essential statement upon the topics it has selected—that anything important in their document derives from long generations past.

Should they say, "Look at the treatment of the Mishnah," we should answer, "But did you continue the Yerushalmi's program or did you make up your own?" And in the total candor we rightly impute to that remarkable authorship, the Bavli's compositors would say, "It is our own—demonstrably so."

And if we were to say, "To what completed documents have you resorted for a ready-made program?" our *soi-disant* traditionalists would direct our attention to the Tosefta, their obvious (and sole) candidate. And, if they were to do so, we should open the Tosefta's treatment of, or counterpart to, a given chapter of the Mishnah and look in vain for a systematic, orderly, and encompassing discourse, dictated by the order and plan of the Tosefta, out of which our authorship has composed a sizable and sustained statement.

And when, finally, we ask our authorship to state its policy in regard to Scripture and inquire whether or not a sustained and on-going tradition of exegesis of Scripture has framed discourse, the reply will prove quite simple. "We looked for what we wanted to seek, and we found it." Traditionalists indeed!

These four loci at which boundaries can have merged therefore mark walled and sealed borders. A received heritage of sayings and stories may have joined our authorship to its teachers and their teachers—but not to that larger community of sustained learning that stands behind the entirety of the writings received as authoritative, or even a sizable proportion of those writings. The presence, in the ultimate statement of the Bavli, of sayings imputed to prior figures—back to Scripture, back to Sinai—testifies only to the workings of a canon of taste and judgment to begin with defined and accepted as definitive by those who defined it: the authorship at hand itself. The availability, to our authorship, of a systematic exegesis of the same Mishnah-chapter has not made self-evident to our authorship the work of continuation and completion of a prior approach. Quite to the contrary, we deal with an authorship of amazingly independent mind, working independently and in an essentially original way on materials on which others have handed on a quite persuasive and cogent statement. Tosefta on the one side, Scripture and a heritage of conventional reading thereof on the other—neither has defined the program of our document or determined the terms in which it would make its statement, though both, in a subordinated position and in a paltry limited measure, are given some sort of a say. The Bavli is connected to a variety of prior writings but continuous with none of them.

The upshot is simple. The Bavli in relationship to its sources is not a traditional document. That is because most of what it says in a cogent and coherent way expresses the well-crafted statement and viewpoint of its authorship in particular. Not only so, but the Bavli's authorship's cogent, rigorously rational reading of the received heritage has demonstrably emerged not from a long process of formulation and transmission of received traditions, in each generation lovingly tended, refined and polished, and handed on essentially as received. The program of the Bavli is uniform and consistently applied throughout; these are not marks of agglutination of a sedimentary tradition but of the imposition, all at once, upon diverse received formulations to be sure, of an igneous construction. A system of applied reason and sustained, rigorously rational inquiry cannot coexist with a process of tradition. No institutions of tradition can for very long impose the kind of intellectual structure and cogency that characterize the Bavli throughout.

At the outset I asked three questions, concerning (1) whether or not the Bavli makes a systemic statement on its own, (2) the definition of the logics of cogent discourse used by the framers, and (3) the classification of the Bavli's authorship's statement (if it was a statement) as systemic or traditional. We now recognize that (1) the authorship of the Bavli by the criterion of its teleological position assuredly made an autonomous statement of its own, one that, moreover, constitutes the statement of a system. That statement bore the marks of connection to, but not continuity with, the system of the Mishnah. While (2) the systemic statement bore its own distinctive message, however, it came forth in the form of a traditional and (merely) incremental account of how things had happened to attach themselves to received truth. And this leads us (3) to the final point of our inquiry: how does the authorship of the Bavli situate its statement in relationship to the received heritage identified by them as authoritative, meaning, in this context, to the Pentateuchal Judaism? System-builders prior to the Bavli had taken a position of benign neglect of their predecessors, if they acknowledged any.[8] The Pentateuchal case of course is extreme: reworking a vast corpus of received writing, the authorship acknowledged no past but the single point of origin at Sinai. But the Mishnah's, in context, is no less striking in its indifference to, e.g., supplying proof-texts from Scripture for more than a negligible minority of its statements.

On the surface, then, the Bavli's authorship broke new ground among system-builders by adopting the form of a commentary to the Mishnah and Scripture for its systemic statement. Implicitly, after all, the message was clear. The commentary-form bore the message that the Bavli's authorship stood in a line of continuing tradition, even while that authorship presented a systemic statement of its own shaping. How to accomplish, in form, precisely what, in intellectual substance, the authorship before us had in mind? The logic of fixed association is what permitted the Bavli's authorships to appeal to two distinct repertoires of sequential items, the Mishnah and also Scripture. The use of the logic of fixed association served a critical theological purpose, specifically, facilitating the linkage into a single statement ("the one whole Torah") of the two Torahs, oral and written, that is, the Mishnah and Scripture. That is the effect of the Bavli's layout as a commentary to the Mishnah or to Scripture. As between the two kinds of logic relevant in this context—propositional and fixed associative—the Bavli appealed for ultimate composition, for the deep structure and cogency of all learning, therefore all thought worth thinking, to the latter.

The Bavli defined the mind of Judaism and imparted to Judaic thought, inculcated in enduring institutions of learning but also in implicit patterns of public discourse, the logics that would predominate, both propositional and otherwise. The Bavli made all the difference, because made room for propositional discourse at that middle range of knowledge that made of the parts autonomous statements of one thing or another, then also put all knowledge together in its own rather odd way, by the imputed and extrinsic associations dictated by Scripture and the Mishnah. Judaic thought therefore yielded not a series of treatises on topics and propositions, but a series of medium-length discourses that gain cogency imposed only from without. The upshot for the Bavli's authorship was to yield a systemic statement in the form of a traditional document.

Is Judaism a Traditional Religion?
What happened then: is Judaism beyond its formative age traditional or systematic? The Bavli imposed its model upon the Judaic intellect for the next millennium and beyond. For the impact of this mixed logic of cogency upon the Judaic intellect was to stimulate one kind of thinking and not another. Propositional thought of a philosophical character could go forward. But in form, and therefore, in interior structure, propositional thinking standing on its own in the centers of Torah-study defined by the mind of the Bavli, would not—could not—yield sustained and coherent system-building of an abstract character. I refer to that kind of free speculation, independent of all connections except those implicit in interior propositions, those characteristic of philosophy, including natural philosophy. Skepticism would flourish, contention and criticism would abound. Dialectics would gather energy to itself. An intellectual world defined in this way found ample stimulus for speculation. But it was not going to be that kind of speculation that, to begin with, without a public agenda and without an a priori system would address the issue of connection between one thing and something else.

For Judaism, it would be the Talmud itself, or the Mishnah or Scripture, or even the lives and teachings of holy men, that would perpetually impart to two or more discrete facts that (self-evident) connection that led to the drawing of conclusions and the framing of theses for inquiry. But philosophical, even scientific, thinking did go forward. In the end the mode of systematic thinking of the Mishnah and the Bavli would make its mark even upon the tradition of Judaism.

Notes

[1] I amplify at great length in *The Making of the Mind of Judaism* (Atlanta, 1987), and *The Formation of the Jewish Intellect. Making Connections and Drawing Conclusions in the Traditional System of Judaism* (Atlanta, 1988).

[2] Joseph A. Schumpeter, *History of Economic Analysis*, p. 54.

[3] I have spelled these matters out for the second through the sixth divisions of the Mishnah in my *History of the Mishnaic Law* (Leiden, 1974-1985; Reprint: Binghamton, 2002) in forty-three volumes. For each tractate I show how the topic at hand was analyzed by the tractate's framers, proving that what they identified as the problematic of the topic instructed those writers on what they wanted to know about the topic and also on the correct, logical order in which they would state the results of their inquiry.

[4] See my *The Bavli and its Sources: The Question of Tradition in the Case of Tractate Sukkah* (Atlanta, 1987).

[5] See my *The Bavli's Unique Voice*. Volume Seven. *What Is Unique about the Bavli in Context? An Answer Based on Inductive Description, Analysis, and Comparison* (Atlanta, 1993).

[6] *Rabbinic Judaism. The Documentary History of the Formative Age* (Bethesda, 1994).

[7] My Academic Commentaries to the Bavli and the Yerushalmi through visual media present the units of discourse and how they relate to one another. I show what is inserted and what continues a line of established argument, indicate primary sources of formal coherence, and otherwise show the construction and dynamics of the two Talmuds, all semiotically. See my *The Talmud of Babylonia. An Academic Commentary* (Atlanta, 1994-1996, 1999); *The Talmud of Babylonia. A Complete Outline* (Atlanta, 1995-1996); *The Talmud of the Land of Israel. An Academic Commentary to the Second, Third, and Fourth Divisions* (Atlanta, 1998-1999); *The Talmud of the Land of Israel. An Outline of the Second, Third, and Fourth Divisions* (Atlanta, 1995-1996); and *The Two Talmuds Compared* (Atlanta, 1995-1996). These volumes are now published by University Press of America, Lanham, MD.

[8] The so-called "intra-biblical exegesis" is a case in point.

Jacob Neusner

W

WOMEN IN THE JUDAISM OF THE DUAL TORAH:

All forms of contemporary religious Judaism view themselves as the heirs to the Judaism of the Dual Torah, justifying their theologies and agendas by citing that Judaism's canon. Here we examine the Dual Torah's rulings regarding women and analyze how these rulings, and the values they represent, were applied in subsequent Rabbinic cultures. The extent to which the Dual Torah allowed women to have access to the Torah, permitted social integration with men, and offered them the right to participate in ritual provides a key to comprehending the Judaism of the Dual Torah.[1] How this Judaism's canon was appropriated by subsequent Judaic cultures similarly provides insight into the constructions of reality invented by those later cultures.

Women's access to Torah study: D. Boyarin maintains that "Talmudic Judaism denies women access to the most valued practice of the culture, the study of Torah."[2] While there are voices within the Dual Torah that were clearly uncomfortable with women's Torah study, a close reading of the actual norms indicates that women's learning was not explicitly forbidden.

Deut. 11:19 states that a father is obliged to "teach them," i.e., the Torah's words, to his sons. Sifre 46 glosses with the words, "and not to your daughters," which may be taken either to forbid women's Torah study or to make the more limited claim that the *obligation* to teach Torah falls upon men and not women.[3] Rabbinic law, for its part, legislates that the father *must* teach Torah to his sons, with no comment regarding daughters (B. Qid. 29b), and the putative learning of Zelofhad's daughters is praised (B. B.B. 119b). It is reported that Beruriah, the wife of Meir, was very learned

(B. Pes. 82b), and Yalta, the wife of the Amora Nahman, participated in halakhic debate (B. Hul. 109b). Women's learning was not protested in any of these reports. Women were required to attend the *Haqhel* convocation in order to hear the Torah being read (Deut. 31:12, B. Yom. 66b, and Mechilta *Bo Pisha 17*).

M. Sot. 3:4 and B. Sot. 20a report that Ben Azzai believed that women's Torah study is a source of merit, and hence permitted, while Eliezer contended that this merit is a mixed blessing, because it may enable an unfaithful wife to endure the ordeal of the bitter waters (Num. 5:12-31). Medieval decisors took Eliezer's comment as an implied prohibition.[4] But his actual observation, that teaching Torah to women is akin to teaching inappropriate sexual license, is *descriptive* rather than *prescriptive*,[5] and does not necessarily yield a Rabbinic restriction. Sifre 46 is also cited selectively in order to justify denying women access to Torah. Its second provision, that Torah instruction should take place using *leshon ha-Qodesh*, that is, sanctuary or Rabbinic Hebrew, is rarely cited or applied, because to do so would call attention to the distance between the Dual Torah's ruling and actual practice.

T. Ber. 2:12 explicitly permits women to study Torah, prophets, writings, and the oral Torah, without limitation, even during their menses. While B. Ber. 22a reports the Toseftan tradition without citing the Palestinian license for women's Torah study, the Bavli does not forbid the practice explicitly.[6] While the Babylonian tradition is clearly uncomfortable with women's Torah study, the discomfort was not expressed through an explicit prohibition.[7]

The Oral Torah's View of Women: J. Neusner holds that women are deemed a source of danger in Dual Torah Judaism and therefore need to be classified and controlled.[8] In this Judaism, women were not socially or religious equal to men. D. Boyarin states that women lacked autonomy and were subordinate to men but were not regarded as inherently evil.[9] The separation of the sexes that was grounded in ancient purity rules has more to do with mimicking the destroyed but imagined Temple and

does not necessarily refer to a diminished status of women. But the fact that Rabbinic law favors the life and property of a man over that of a woman (M. Hor. 3:7) confirms Boyarin's observation that women were subordinate in Rabbinic culture. Only if a woman were in danger of sexual violation would she be saved before a man. And if a man and woman were in equal danger of violation, the man is saved first (B. Hor. 13a). Since the Dual Torah assigns more commandments, which are the means of earning holiness and eternity, to men, men are more holy, and, therefore, more worthy than women in this Judaism.[10]

Synagogue seating: It is widely assumed that separate synagogue seating is a fundamental Jewish law. M. Feinstein claims that the Temple architecture, which to his view was revealed as prophecy and applies to the synagogue, is a divine law,[11] and J. Soloveitchik argues that the segregation of men and women in the synagogue "can never be abandoned . . . what is decreed by God can never be undone by human hand."[12] His opinion is "based" on the verse that requires that no unseemly thing (*ervat davar*) be seen in the Israelite camp (Deut. 23:16), the context of which refers to burying excrement, not segregation of the sexes. No statement within the early commentators provides precedent for this innovative interpretation.

The only statement in the Dual Torah canon that deals with a synagogue partition (*mehitsah*) actually refers to the segregation of the leper, who is a source of defilement (M. Neg. 13:12). In the Judaism of the Oral Torah, there is no mandate to segregate the sexes in the synagogue.

Since women may tempt men to sin, Rabbinic culture did discourage excessive intergender familiarity. While men and women are equally obliged to recite the invitation to join in the after-meal blessing, women may not join to enable men to form a group for this blessing, since propriety might be compromised (B. Ber. 45b). Excessive conversation between the sexes is also discouraged (M. Ab. 1:5). The rabbis discouraged, but did not generally forbid, men from engaging in trades that brought them into regular contact with women. There is, however, a restriction regarding teaching children, because a man would have to deal with the children's mothers (B. Qid. 82a). The medieval midrashic collection *Yalqut Shimoni* records that man and women ought not pray in proximity (*Yalqut Shimoni, Ki Tetsei* 934), because the sanctity of the camp would be undermined. This medieval sensibility is confirmed by Tosafot to B. Shab. 125b (s.v., *ha-kol modim*), who allow the erection of the partition because it is for conventional modesty. While this opinion may be the source of Soloveitchik's innovative interpretation, it is in fact consistent with the Dual Torah's attitude, cited above, that male/female segregation is a matter of propriety, but *not prohibition*. The great priest (B. Yom. 69a-b) and king (B. Suk. 41a) read the Torah in the women's section of the Temple without any mention of gender segregation.[13]

Intergender physical contact: While the Dual Torah is concerned with avoiding sin[14] and did not view women to be the religious equal of men, the rabbis were not prudes. Aha danced with a woman riding on his shoulders (B. Ket. 17a), a priest may support a woman's hand in ritual (Y. Sot. 3:1), a person who would allow a woman to drown rather than save her for fear that he might come to sexual arousal is ridiculed as a pious fool (B. Sot. 21a), and the exceedingly attractive Yohanan sat in front of the *miqvah*, where women who have immersed in order to be intimate with their husbands, did so with pure rather than improper intentions.[15] These citations posit that only *improper* intentions disqualify physical contact, while innocent contact is permitted.

Scripture forbids a man to approach a woman during the menses with the intent to "uncover nakedness" (Lev. 18:19), a euphemism for sexual intercourse. The halakhic midrash extends the "uncovering nakedness" prohibition to incest, the violation of which, like intercourse with a menstruent, carries the penalty of excision (M. Ker. 1:1). Sexual contact less invasive than intercourse is also forbidden in the Judaism of the Dual Torah (B. Shab. 13a) and is interdicted with the idiom "approaching" or "coming near," which refers to non-coital physical erotic contact. Sexual gestures that do not entail physical contact are forbidden by Rabbinic decree (Safra 13). Maimo-

nides codifies these rules at *Sefer ha-Mitsvot* Negative commands, 353, and *Hilkhot Issurei Bi'ah* 21:1-2.[16]

While 21:1 forbids erotic physical contact and 21:2 forbids erotic gestures without contact, intergender contact that is *not* erotic is *not* forbidden. Aha's dancing with a woman on his shoulders exemplifies this. According to the Amora Samuel, it is forbidden for a man to make use of a woman (B. Qid. 70a), but this prohibition is inapplicable when intentions are innocent, or "for the sake of heaven" (B. Qid. 71b). Only actions that lead to sin are sinful.[17] A menstrual wife may not wash her husband's hands and feet, mix alcoholic drink, or prepare the (conjugal) bed in his presence (B. Ket. 61a), regardless of intent, because of the explicit talmudic statute. The school of Samuel suggests that a woman other than a man's wife might be permitted to perform these services.[18] Because pious people may also succumb to sin (Y. Ket. 1:5, B. Ket. 13b), the sages tried to strike a balance between appropriate license on one hand and sinful temptation on the other.

Clandestine unions [*Yihud*]: The Judaism of the Dual Torah forbids *yihud*, or clandestine male/female unions where sexual intimacy might take place without notice by others. According to the sages, King David is the promulgator of this prohibition (B. A.Z. 36b). For Maimonides, this prohibition finds its source in "tradition" (*Issurei Bi'ah* 22:2).

According to Yohanan, the Tamar pericope provides an allusion to the prohibition of *yihud* in the Torah,[19] indicating that the prohibition itself is Rabbinic. In response to Amnon's rape of Tamar (2 Sam. 13:19), it is reported that a decree outlawing *yihud* was issued (B. San. 21a). The anonymous Talmud concludes that this prohibition is scriptural (*de-oraita*). Hence, the Tosafot, who lived in the orbit of Christianity, ruled that clandestine unions with women with whom sexual intercourse warrants the penalty of excision are forbidden by Scripture.[20] Since the *yihud* prohibition is not derived from the Pentateuch, its force is Rabbinic, the Tosafot's claim notwithstanding. Obadiah Yosef observes that on occasion the idiom *de-oraita* refers to Rabbinic legislation.[21]

Furthermore, this idiom is part of the anonymous Talmud, which might reflect a later post-Talmudic gloss. Unions with family members, with whom erotic intention is not present, do not fall under the ban (B. San. 103b).

Women's singing in the presence of men: Samuel's ruling that "the voice of a woman is *erva*" (B. Ber. 24a and B. Qid. 70a) has been taken to forbid women's singing in the presence of men.[22] But a close reading of the sources suggests a different set of values and religious propriety. Samuel also rules that the propriety of intergender activity depends upon moral intent (B. Qid. 71b), and his ruling regarding women's singing should be understood in this context, and not as a categorical prohibition. Hence, Samuel's putatively restrictive ruling goes uncited in al-Fasi's legal summary of the Talmud.

Scripture reports that Deborah and Barak sang together,[23] and the proof-text cited by Samuel defining women's singing as *erva*, "let me hear your voice because your voice is sweet and your countenance is pleasant" (Song 2:14) indicates that in biblical (Jer. 9:16) and Rabbinic writing (T. Yeb. 14:7, M. Ket. 4:4), a woman's singing voice may actually be solicited. The term *erva* in this context only disqualifies sacred activity when naked[24] and does not consider the state of nakedness to be inherently sinful. Thus, a menstruating woman is not sinning because she is menstruating, even though she is ritually impure. Like his ruling prohibiting suggestive non-contact gestures (*Issurei Bi'ah* 21:2), Maimonides only forbids women's singing when it is done with an erotic intent. Hence, Maimonides restricts women's singing when the words are immodest.[25]

After ruling that a man may not recite the *shema* in the presence of a woman who exposes hair or a body part that is usually covered (*Shulhan Arukh Orah Hayyim* 75:1-2), Caro ruled that he *ought to* avoid hearing a woman's singing voice during the recitation of the *shema*.[26] In his *Bet Yosef* (75), Caro states that he does not believe that Samuel's restriction is normative. J. David Bleich does not address this when citing, out of context, Caro's words as "a man may not listen to the voice of a female vocalist."[27] Maimonides maintains that the

phrase "it is forbidden hear the sound of *ervah*" (*Hilkhot Issurei Bi'ah* 21:2) refers to *singing* that is sexually arousing.[28]

Women's hair covering: Talmudic law prohibits a married woman from appearing in public with her head uncovered.[29] Whether this ruling is *dat Yehudit*, the conventional practice of Jewish women, or *dat Moshe*, the law of Moses, is unresolved. The anonymous Talmud glosses that this requirement derives from the Torah, like the case of clandestine unions. T. Sot. 5:9 states that a married woman's going bear-headed in public is grounds for divorce. The Bavli cites this view when ruling that one may divorce such a woman and that she forfeits her *ketubbah*, the monetary stipend normally hers upon divorce or her husband's death. In the Dual Torah, the woman's head covering seems to signify that she is married. The constant covering of the married woman's hair is described as an act of piety.[30] While M. al-Shaqer rules that a woman's head must be covered, her uncovered hair is not necessarily *erva*.[31] Following the Zohar,[32] M. Sofer[33] disallows women's uncovering any hair at all. Like M. al-Shaqer, M. Feinstein reads the talmudic text literally and concludes that the woman's head, but not every strand of hair, must be covered.[34] Because some, but not all,[35] post-talmudic Judaisms were so concerned with women's sexuality that they required women to cover all of hair, B. Shab. 84b's prohibition against wearing a wig on the Sabbath was suspended.[36]

Women serving in the Israeli army: According to the Talmud, men and women must serve in a war of conquest, as described at Josh. 1-11, or in a defensive war (*milhemet mitzvah*) in the land of Israel.[37] Exemptions only are granted for discretionary wars (*milhemet reshut*; Deut. 20:5-7). But discretionary wars, like the wars of King David, require the consent of the Great Sanhedrin (M. San. 1:5) consulting the Urim and Tumion (B. San. 16a), and the leadership of the king (M. San. 4:2). By imposing these conditions on discretionary wars, the rabbis effectively outlawed all political wars. Maimonides (*Hilkhot Melachim* 5:1-2) rules that any war that defends the Jewish polity is a defensive, or commanded, war.

In these wars, women *must be* conscripted. Like the case of the wig worn on the Sabbath, most later Rabbinic opinion either ignores the explicit talmudic law[38] or avoids the discussion altogether.

Women in leadership roles: According to the Bible, the people of Israel must appoint a king to rule the polity (Deut. 17:15). Sifre 157 glosses Scripture by requiring that the monarch be a man. Maimonides further glosses, adding that women may not be appointed to *any* leadership position (*Hilkhot Melachim* 1:5). While variant readings supporting Maimonides' ruling are extant,[39] M. Feinstein permits a woman to serve as a kashrut supervisor by regarding the standard Sifre reading to be binding and rejecting the restrictive Maimonidean gloss (*Iggarot Moshe Yoreh Deah* 2:44). J. David Bleich observes that "an impressive roster of authorities" rule that women ought not to be permitted to vote[40] and portrays M. Feinstein's perspective as a "somewhat equivocal but essentially negative view."[41]

Bleich apparently views the decisors to be the ultimate source of authority, as he did with regard to female vocalists. He does not explain whether Feinstein's opinion is grounded upon strict law, which he would cite if the statute were extant, or conditioned culture taste. For Bleich, the prohibition against allowing a woman to assume a leadership position "is a reflection of the religio-social ideal . . .' the entire glory of the king's daughter [Jewish women in general] is within" (Ps. 45:14). This rule represents, for Bleich, *tseniut,* or modesty,[42] which usually refers to submission and culture conformity. While Rashi to Ps. 45:14 associates this passage with modesty, B. Shab. 29b suggests that the verse does not indicate that women may not work outside of their domicile,[43] but by convention do not appear in court. Now, Rashi's medieval Ashkenazic Talmud commentary is an explanation of the Oral Torah and is not itself part of that canon. The canonical documents do insist that women "must" be modest, but the definition of modesty is left open.

Women in Ritual Life: While in general, women are exempt from fulfilling time-bound commandments, there are some such commandments that Rabbinic halakhah obliges them to observe,[44] such as reciting the blessing over wine that sanctifies the Sabbath (B. Ber. 20b), fasting on the Day of Atonement (B. Suk. 28b), attending the *Haqhel* convocation (B. Hag. 4a), and eating matzo on the first night of Passover.[45] By Rabbinic rule, women are also obliged to kindle the Hanukkah menorah (B. Shab. 23a), to drink four cups of wine on Seder night (B. Pes. 108a), and to read the scroll of Esther on Purim (B. Meg. 4a). Since prayer, at its origin, is not a time-bound commandment, women are also obligated to pray.[46] This principle is applied selectively in medieval Rabbinic culture, with women being restricted from those rites that offended male sensibility. By defending communally accepted practices that contradict the Dual Torah, medieval rabbis revealed the tension between their practice and what is explicitly required by the canonical texts.

Women's recitation of the invitation to the Grace after the Meal: Because women possess human intelligence, they are, in the Judaism of the Dual Torah, obligated to thank God through the Grace after Meals as well through participation in the invitation to the public recitation of the Grace.[47] While Maimonides is unsure whether women's obligation to recite the Grace derives from the Torah or Rabbinic law, his ruling follows the Talmud in requiring that three people who break bread together recite the invitation (*Hilkhot Berachot* 5:1). The Tosafot's response reveals a social, halakhic, and ideological distance from the earlier talmudic culture.[48] After claiming that women are permitted, but not required, to recite the invitation, note is made of Rabbenu Abraham's daughters, who recited the invitation. The Tosafot also concede that the plain sense of the Talmud requires the recitation. But the Tosafot also observe that the "world," that is, the living community of Northern European Jewry, does not observe this "custom," which the Talmud defines as law. The Tosafot are neither commenting on nor explicating the Talmud, nor are they suggesting that there exists an alternative tradition of equal antiquity, validity, or normativity to that of the Talmud. Instead, they justify the community's practice with the implicit claim that its existence invests it with a virtual canonicity equal to that of the talmudic text. By initiating the invitation to the Grace, a woman would be assuming a leadership role, which offends this Judaism's sense of propriety.

The right to perform kosher slaughter: The obligation to consume properly slaughtered meat (Deut. 12:21; B. Hul. 17a, 28a, 84a) *is not* conditioned by time and is a negative rather than positive command. Men and women therefore share an equal obligation (B. Ber. 20b). M. Hul. 1:1 accordingly explicitly rules that *everyone* who is technically competent is authorized to slaughter. In instances of determining whether particular meat is forbidden, an individual's testimony is accepted, and women are eligible to offer this testimony (B. Git. 2b). On this foundation, the Tosafot reject the view of *Hilkhot Erets Yisrael*, who denies women the license to slaughter because they are "light-headed."[49] However, the Talmud permits women to slaughter animals that have been dedicated to the altar (B. Zeb. 31a) and does not restrict women in general from observing this rite because they are "light-headed." The *Agor* (62) argues that 1) the decisors permit women to slaughter, 2) I never saw women slaughter, 3) *we* do not permit women to slaughter, 4) a custom [of a community] may nullify a law [recorded in the Talmudic canon], and 5) the custom of our ancestors *is* law [the legal equivalent of Talmudic law].

Sensing the implications of this ruling and its implied hermeneutic, Caro contends that for women's slaughtering to be forbidden by Rabbinic law, the talmudic rabbis would have issued a protest, which they did not do. Claiming that a license unused must be construed as a license withdrawn, the *Agor* insists that the fact that an act has not been done is sufficient to prohibit the act. Rabbinic Judaism rejects this reasoning by explicitly affirming the principle that an act is *not* forbidden simply because the license to perform it was not exercised in a given culture (M. Ed. 2:2, B. Zeb. 103b). The advancement of the argument from silence is, for Caro, an inadmissible assault upon the hermeneutic of Rabbinic discourse.[50] In the Judaism of the Dual Torah, acts are prohibited if and only if they are explicitly forbidden by legislation.

The right of women to recline at the Seder: B. Pes. 108b state that only "important" women *must* recline at the *Seder*.[51] In the absence of a formal prohibition, other women have the option but not the requirement to recline. Maimonides (*Hilkhot Hamets u-Matsa* 7:8) codifies the sages' ruling that only important women must recline at the *Seder* (see also *Shulhan Arukh Orah Hayyim* 472:4). *Bet Yosef* reports that Tosafot regarded all women to be important and permitted them to recline. Whatever "important woman" means in Talmudic context, for the Talmud, Maimonides, and Caro, some women are important while others are not. By claiming that all of his women are important, Tosafot is using the word "important" differently than the Sages. This Tosafist ruling is consistent with his view that permits women to recite benedictions before performing acts that for men, but not women, are commandments (B. Ber. 14a, s.v. *yamim*).

M. Isserles rules that women do not have the custom to recline in Eastern Europe, even though his women, like Tosafot's women, are "important."[52] Tosafot's claim that all women are important and may recline at the *Seder* redefines the Talmudic definition but does not conflict in practice with Talmudic requirements, because important women are reclining. Reclining at the *Seder*, like reciting blessings before observing rites that for the devotee are not commandments, are acts of personal rather than communal piety in this Judaism. M. Isserles's ruling that women do not recline, even if they are important, prevents women who, according to the Talmud, *are* important, from observing their religious requirements. The new "modesty" of Eastern Europe, which cannot tolerate women's observing public ritual, here abolishes a talmudic obligation.

Women's right to access of ritual objects. Phylacteries: Talmudic law does not forbid women's wearing of phylacteries, and it is reported that Michal bat Kushi, whom Rashi identifies with Michal bat Saul, wore phylacteries and "the sages did not protest."[53] By not protesting, sages imply that this act is acceptable but not required. Tosafot (B. Erub. 96a, s.v. Michal) claim that women may not don phylacteries because they are unable to insure personal hygiene. Now, if all of the women of Tosafot's time were indeed really "important," one would presume that they would be able to maintain personal hygiene. And given T. Ber. 2:12's ruling that menses do not restrict women from learning and since there is no unambiguous prohibition in the Talmudic canon, the Tosafists' restriction must be taken to be a local enactment, not a universal rule. Furthermore, subsequent Judaisms would then have the right to reconsider the localized Tosafists' restriction. However, M. Feinstein affirms their ruling, thus withdrawing a talmudic license given to women (even as he permits a male with an attached ostemy bag to don phylacteries; *Iggarot Moshe Orah Hayyim* 4:49 and 1:17).

Women's use of Tallit and Lulav. The *tallit* (prayer shawl) and the lulav used on Tabernacles are both-time bound rites from which women are exempt. According to B. Shab. 23a and B. Ber. 33a, only actual commandments may be introduced with a blessing. Consequently, Maimonides rules that such blessings may not be recited before one observes a custom (*Hilkhot Megilla ve-Hanukkah* 3:7). He explicitly permits women to observe both *tallit* (*Hilkhot Tsitsit* 3:9) and lulav rites, but, viewing their actions as not commanded, he denies them the right to recite the blessing that normally precedes the rite.[54]

Unlike the Talmud and Maimonides, Tosafot argue that one may recite a blessing on customs, and women may recite blessings for time-bound rituals.[55] The Asheri[56] contends that the talmudic *derasha*, or legal exegesis of Scripture, that forbids women's blessings is flawed and therefore rejects the rule generated by this exegesis. Since M. Isserles (gloss to *Shulhan Arukh Orah Hayyim* 38:3) accepted the Tosafists' dispensation, which was also validated by the Asheri, the right to recite a blessing before observing a custom became normative in Ashkenazic Judaism and is not subject to review, talmudic legislation not withstanding.

In contemporary Ashkenazic Orthodox Judaism, women are not granted access to phylacteries or the *tallit*. According to *Targum Yerushalmi* (in this literature, *Targum Yonatan*) on Deut. 22:5, a woman's wearing a *tallit*

violates the Torah's prohibition against a women's wearing men's clothing. Citing this ruling as normative, M. Feinstein permits a woman to wear a *tallit* if its style differs from men's.[57]

According to M. Meiselman, J. Soloveitchik permitted a woman to wear a *tallit* if and only if her intention was to observe the commandment to wear fringes.[58] But J. Soloveitchik does *not* demand this intention of women who wish to observe the lulav rite, even though there is a talmudic principle, rejected in Ashkenazic society, that disallows women's observing the lulav rite with a blessing. Neither J. Soloveitchik[59] nor M. Feinstein explain why Maimonides' logical reading of talmudic law is inadequate, why the Tosafists' restriction regarding phylacteries must be accepted uncritically, or how the Asheri's explicit rejection of a talmudic *derasha* and the law derived from it may go unchallenged.

Women's reading of the Scroll of Esther: Four sources in the Oral Torah, when read as a canonical statement, define the women's obligation to read the Scroll of Esther. According to the M. R.H. 3:8 (see B. R.H. 29a), only those obligated to observe a commanded rite may discharge that obligation on behalf of others. According to the Mishnah (B. Meg. 19b), everyone is obliged to read the Esther scroll, but T. Meg. 2:17, in a statement rejected by *Rashba* (at B. Meg. 4a), maintains that women have no obligation to observe this rite whatsoever. B. Ar. 2b-3a concludes that women are indeed obligated without any qualification that might impact the mandate of reading or the license to read for others.[60] After conceding that, according to talmudic statute, women are obligated to read the Scroll and "that they may indeed discharge the law for others," the Tosafot add that *Halakhot Gedolot* did not so rule.[61] The Tosafot then report *Halakhot Gedolot*'s ruling that a woman is obliged to *hear* but not to *read* the scroll. This means that the license to read the scroll on behalf of men is withdrawn. Both the Tosafot and *Halakhot Gedolot* hold that a post-talmudic sage is empowered to override talmudic law and to define new blessings and legal concepts.[62] The Tosafot analogize the withdrawing of women's license to read the scroll for men with the limited license of a woman to help an ignorant man recite the Grace after Meals (B. Ber. 45b), and consider women's ritual activity with men to be inappropriate because men are more important than women and because women's ritual activity cheapens the rite. In all, this Judaism treats women as "light-headed," holds that their activity cheapens rituals, and believes that they cannot be trusted to maintain proper hygiene. These sensibilities, which deny the full humanity of women, are present in medieval Ashkenazic Judaism but not in the Dual Torah.

Talmudic Judaism's cultural statement: Talmudic Judaism exhibits what may be called soft sexism.[63] Ultimately, women did not participate in the formulation of the Rabbinic canon and were believed by this canon to be less holy, but not less human, then men. In medieval Ashkenazic Rabbinic culture, women were permitted to recite the lulav blessing, possibly because their private rituals were not valued. But women were restricted from wearing a *tallit* or donning phylacteries, from publicly reading the Esther Scroll, and from studying Torah. In Eastern European Judaism, women were further restricted from slaughtering and reclining at the Passover *Seder*. The invitation to the Grace after Meals was downgraded from Rabbinic law to medieval custom. The common feature of the rites from which women were restricted was that they would have allowed women to express leadership and power over men.

Legitimation of the devaluation of women required a new reading of the talmudic canon. Avraham Grossman has shown that Ashkenazic sages cite appropriate precedents from the textual canon to validate practices that emerged as a new Judaism.[64] In this culture, custom may supersede the law whenever the community's sense of propriety is threatened.[65] This shift in focus from the sacred text of the past to the ideology of a person living in the present characterizes the legal thought of the Tosafot[66] as well as of contemporary Orthodox culture, which also appeals to contemporary Rabbinic intuition when forbidding activities that violate

the expectations of the present community.[67] Notably, in its growth, the medieval Jewish community was significantly affected by developments within Christianity. Thus Jane Tibbets Schullenberg has shown that in medieval Christianity from 500-1000 C.E., women's sexuality was "seen as a serious threat to male order or authority." Women were a "dangerous other" who "needed to be constrained, marginalized, or punished."[68] The sexual purity of women was a major concern of male power in this society.[69] The similarities are significant, even if, in contrast to Christianity, Rabbinic culture only marginalized illicit sex, not sex itself, as evil.[70]

The Evolution of a New Judaism: Just as Rabbinic Judaism emerged out of the religion of ancient Israel, medieval Ashkenazic Rabbinism evolved out of the Rabbinic Judaism of the Dual Torah. Taking the Rabbinic canon to be formative—providing the language of religious discourse—rather than normative[71]—actually recording the norms that oblige the community in practice—early Ashkenazic Judaism was so certain of its religious legitimacy that the tension between popular practice and canonical norms could be negotiated with ease. Ultimate normativity resided in the community and its validating rabbinate, with the Rabbinic canon being cited selectively, allowing women only to engage in private piety, like reciting the lulav blessing.

Public piety in Ashkenazic culture is reserved for men. The same Tosafist tradition that claimed, against the Talmud, that all its women are important, denied women the Talmudic right to read the Scroll of Esther on behalf of men, because men are more important. While the Tosafot permit women to slaughter animals and to recline at the Seder, these licenses were denied to women in Eastern European culture. The Talmudic canon claims that women are less spiritual and less holy because they observe fewer commandments. J. Soloveitchik, "Two Kinds of Tradition," describes medieval Ashkenazic rabbinism as well as his own Judaism. Hence, M. Meiselman reports that Soloveitchik opposed women's holding and dancing with the Torah on *Simhat Torah* as a prohibited change in etiquette.[72] Soloveitchik's student, Herschel Schachter, in turn claims that this change is forbidden because the great rabbis of our age, J. Soloveitchik and M. Feinstein, opposed it, and R. Tam, the leading Tosafist, claims that one may not disagree with the great sages of the age.[73] Schachter adds that Jewish law forbids any changes in synagogue customs.[74] Curiously, the Tosafists permit dancing and clapping on Jewish holidays, against the plain sense of the talmudic statute.[75] Soloveitchik cites with approval the oral tradition that Elijah b. Solomon, the Gaon of Vilna, danced on Simhat Torah.[76] Soloveitchik thus upholds the etiquette of his day, while ignoring an explicit violation of the Dual Torah.

In Ashkenazic culture, a talmudic statute may be ignored upon the authorization of a great sage, but etiquette must go unchallenged. Contemporary sages may not be challenged even with regard to canonical statutes. But Maimonides, *Mamrim* 2:2, rules that only a court greater in number and wisdom may reverse the legislation of an earlier court, and he permits individual post-talmudic rabbis to rule independently for their communities as long as they do not violate talmudic law. Both Tosafot's and Maimonides' positions are addressed in the Dual Torah. If a sage were to rule on the basis of charisma, intuition, and arbitrary authority, the sages invalidate the bona fides of the offending sage (B. B.M. 59b). Tosafot's view, that a great rabbi has a right to invalidate talmudic law on the basis of authority, charisma, and intuition, is not confirmed by the Dual Torah, but Maimonides' ruling that only a legal organ of equal authority and jurisdiction has a legal right to reverse an earlier court, is confirmed by M. Ed. 1:5, the very diction of which is cited by Maimonides as a reference marker. Ashkenazic culture cites the canon selectively, in order to give the impression that it preserves an old, sacred, and venerable tradition and that it is the sole legitimate heir of that Judaism. Since the actual practices of this Judaism, especially with regard to women, reflect a different Judaism with an alternative construction of reality, the living hermeneutic of culture supercedes the

Dual Torah's legal hermeneutic. The real life of the Jews is much too important to be left to the norms, values, and law of a bygone age, and the living sense of religious propriety is too sacred to be judged against the benchmark of an ancient canon. In the Judaism of the Dual Torah, God was revealed at Sinai, in the wilderness, and in the rulings of the Supreme Sanhedrin, the authorization of which is biblical. (Deut. 17:10-11, B. Sot. 17b) In subsequent Rabbinic cultures, God revealed the Torah *from* the moment of Sinai and that revelation continues in the intuition of those who sit in the seat of human authority.

Notes

[1] Sara Epstein Weinstein, *Piety and Fanaticism: Rabbinic Criticism of Religious Stringency* (Northvale and London, 1997), shows how the Dual Torah opposed excessive ritual piety as misplaced at best and arrogant at worse. Her claim, and the polemic of this paper as well, is that the Judaism of the Dual Torah has much to say about a particular issues. The Judaisms that evolved out of it are best understood when their positions are compared to those statements.

[2] *Carnal Israel*, p. 168.

[3] Ibid., pp. 174-1755, calls attention to these two possibilities.

[4] See Maimonides, *Hilkhot Talmud Torah* 1:13, who applies Eliezer's statement, and by implication Sifre 46, restrictively "because most women . . . will find in Torah fleeting value because of the poverty of their minds."

[5] See Alan J. Yuter, *"Nashim be-Talmud Torah: 'Iyyun halakhah tahbiri"* [Are women permitted to study Torah: a syntactic study of *halakhic* sources], in *Ha-Darom 61* (Elul, 5752). When writing this study, I was unaware of T. Ber. 2:12, discussed below.

[6] Boyarin suggests, plausibly but not necessarily, that the Bavli is here outlawing women's Torah study; *Carnal Israel*, pp. 180-181. Given the precedent of the Babylonian Yalta, cited above, the Bavli is uncomfortable with women's Torah study, but did not feel empowered explicitly to override the explicit Toseftan license.

[7] At *Liqqutei Halakhot Sotah* 21, Meir Kagan argues that women did not study in pre-modern times, but given the threats of enlightenment, emancipation, and assimilation, women's spiritual growth must be nourished by Torah information. However, when Elya Svei, Dean of the Philadelphia Yeshiva, posed the question regarding the propriety of women's study the Mishnah, M. Feinstein forbade the practice, citing Maimonides but not addressing T. Ber. 2:12. [*Iggrot Moshe Yoreh Deah* 3:87]. Svei's view of women is expressed in his comment that women's

public speaking is inherently immodest [*Jewish Observer* 26:10 (1994), p. 7].

[8] Neusner, *Judaism*, p. 143, and *Introduction*, pp. 106-107.

[9] *Carnal Israel*, p. 133.

[10] Y. Hor. 3:7. In contemporary Orthodox Judaism, this citation is suppressed, and instead it is argued that women are more spiritual and private than men. By declaring that women must be private beings, Meiselman, *Jewish Women in Jewish Law* (New York, 1978), p. 14, like Svei, subjected women to a control much more severe than that imposed by the Dual Torah. See Judith Plaskow, *Standing Again at Sinai*, who argues that in its classical and Orthodox formulations, Judaism is sexist and patriarchal (p. xiii), suppresses women's power (43), and cannot accept the "power of sexuality to overturn rules and threaten boundaries" (202).

[11] *Iggarot Moshe Orah Hayyim* 1:39. According to this view, 1 Chr. 28:19 reports that God revealed as divine mandate the actual architecture of the Temple, and the sin of *qallut rosh*, or undue sexual familiarity, is a of sufficient gravity for the rabbis to alter the divine blueprint.

[12] Cited in *Conservative Judaism* (Fall, 1956). For Soloveitchik, Torah law mandates the separation of the sexes in the synagogue, and Rabbinic law requires the segregation of the sexes with a partition.

[13] I. Weiss, *Minhat Ritzhaq* 2:20, concedes that no mention is made of a partition at the *Haqhel* convocation. He argues that sexuality is so powerful a force that a *mehitsa* "must" have used during the convocation. As noted above, conjectures like this are not normative in Dual Torah Judaism.

[14] Rabbinic decrees are designed to distance people from sin (B. Ber. 4b). When no sin is likely, the Dual Torah does not oppose interaction. Consider King David's relationship with Avishag, 1 Kings 1:3-4.

[15] B. Ber. 20a. Later Judaism, and not the Judaism of the Dual Torah, is anxious regarding women's bodies. See Boyarin, *Carnal Israel*, p. 106, and Weinstein, pp. 165-174.

[16] For Nahmanides' disagreement, see his gloss to *Sefer ha-Mitsvot* Negative Commands, 353. See also the discussion of Jose Faur, *Iyyunim be-Mishnah Torah le-ha-Rambam* (Jerusalem, 1978), pp. 25-27.

[17] B. Ber. 81a, B. Er. 18b, and B. B.B. 57b. Although Feinstein permits travel on New York subways during rush hour, because the contact between the sexes is not erotic, *Iggrot Moshe Even ha-Ezer* 2:14, and he concedes that pious men shake women's hands, he is unwilling to do so. Ibid., 1:56.

[18] *Bet Shemuel* to *Even ha-Ezer* 21:9. Moses Isserles, who occasionally waives talmudic requirements when the reason for their implementation is not readily apparent, rules that the only consideration is *hibba*, or physical affection. Note that *Bet Shemuel* here assumes that an act is permitted unless it is explicitly forbidden.

[19] "When you are enticed by your brother the son of your mother," Deut. 13:7.

[20] Tosafot to B. Sot. 7a, s.v. *niddah she-he*.

[21] *Yehavveh Da'at* 5:62, and Faur, pp. 17-19.

[22] J. David Bleich, *Contemporary Halachic Problems* II (New York: Yeshiva University and KTAV, 1983), p. 147.

[23] Jdg. 5:1. Bleich, p. 148, dismisses this text because *Eliyahu Rabbah Orah Hayyim* 75:5 "declares that this incident cannot be cited as supporting any point of normative halakhah, since it is to be viewed as an isolated occurrence that was divinely mandated." Why it is to be so viewed is not explained, and it is also unclear how Bleich knows that the duet was the result of a divine mandate, unreported by Scripture.

[24] As in donating *terumah*, B. B.M. 114b. *Shulhan Arukh Yoreh Deah* 1:10 rules that a slaughterer may not perform his profession naked, because he would not be permitted to recite the appropriate blessing. But the slaughtering act remains valid after the fact. J. Soloveitchik did not address this doctrine when he ruled that one must forgo the *shofar* ritual on Rosh Hashanah if one must attend a mixed seating synagogue to do so.

[25] Commentary to M. Ab. 1:6 and Responsa, n. 224. See also Boaz Cohen, "The Responsum of Maimonides Concerning Music," in *Law and Tradition in Judaism* (New York, 1959), pp. 167-181, who argues that the sages outlawed discretionary, but not sacred, singing.

[26] Ibid., 75:3.

[27] *Shulhan Arukh Even ha-Ezer* 21:1. By avoiding Caro's actual understanding of the law, which is consistent with a close reading of the Rabbinic canon, Bleich gives the impression that his approach is in fact the modesty discipline required by the Rabbinic canon. But Caro only rules that one may not hear *erva*." Since the idiom is Caro's, his definition should applied in this context.

[28] The contemporary Orthodox rabbi, Saul J. Berman, "*Kol Ishah*," in Leo Landman, ed., *Rabbi Joseph H. Lookstein Memorial Volume* (New York, 1980), argues that there is sufficient warrant in classical sources and compelling need in contemporary society to be lenient. Ben Cherney affirms the conventional Rabbinic consensus, which to his view is how the canonical materials must be parsed and applied; "Kol Ishah" in *Journal of Halakhah and Contemporary Society* 10 (Fall, 1985). The most thorough treatment of this subject is Jacob J. Weinberg, *Seridei Esh* 2:8, where he rules that Deborah's singing is indeed a precedent, that earlier great Ashkenazic rabbis, S.R. Hirsch and I. Hildesheimer, permitted the practice, and that the practice is consistent with the letter of Jewish law. Bleich dismisses Weinberg's responsum as "innovative," p. 149. Weinberg's appeal to Hirsch is rhetorical, because Weinberg disagreed strongly with Hirsch's parochialism and opposition to the critical study of Judaism. See Marc. B. Shapiro, *Between the Yeshiva World and Modern Orthodoxy: The Life and Works of Rabbi Jehiel Jacob Weinberg* (London and Portland, 1998), pp.

154-157. See also Yehuda Henkin, *Equality Lost: Essays in Torah commentary, Halachah, and Jewish Thought* (Jerusalem, 1999), pp. 66-75. Unnoticed in the literature are B. Meg. 3b and M. M.Q. 3:8, which rule that women sing mournfully even on the intermediate festival day, which corroborates the doctrine that women's singing for the sake of heaven was never banned. I thank my son, Joshua D. Yuter, for this insight.

[29] B. Ket. 72a. Obadiah Yosef, *Yehavveh Daat*, Rules of Talmudic exegesis 7 and Moses Isserlein, *Terumat ha-Deshen* 242, also understand the idiom *de-oraita* as a rhetorical hyperbole.

[30] B. Yom. 47a describes the practice of Qimhit, whose seven sons served as High Priests. But her behavior is not normative.

[31] Responsa *Maharam al-Shaqer* 35.

[32] *Parashat Naso*, s.v. *u-min he-'afar*. Even if Simeon were indeed the Zohar's author, the legal opinions recorded there are at best the views of individual sages and not really normative. Zoharic halakhah is taken to be normative by those who find Talmudic law socially or theologically insufficient.

[33] *Responsa Orah Hayyim* 36.

[34] *Iggarot Moshe Even ha-'Ezer* 1:58.

[35] See Obadiah Yosef, *Even ha-Ezer* 5:5, who argues that the fact that the wives of rabbis and Hassidic rebbes wear wigs proves nothing, and the wearing of the wig on the Sabbath is absolutely forbidden because of the talmudic restriction. Feinstein concedes that the woman's wig is legally problematic, but he defers to the many rabbis who are lenient, with women who rely on their view being "proper;" *Iggarot Moshe Even ha-Ezer* 2:12 and *She'elat Ya'avets* 1:9.

[36] See Moses Isserles, *Eben ha-'Ezer* 212, gloss, *ad. loc.* Obadiah Hodaya, *Yaskil 'Abdi* 7:16 and *Kaf-ha-Hayyim Orah Hayyim* 74:19 adopt the Ashkenazi view because of the contemporary rabbinic consensus. *Shiltei Gibborim* 375 argues that women's hair must be covered, but not the hair upon her hair, ignoring the plain sense of the Mishnah, which might permit the wearing of the wig only in a courtyard. While conceding that the woman's wig is problematic, Feinstein accepts the living rabbinic consensus. *Iggarot Moshe Even ha-Ezer* 2:12. Ironically, it is in his responsum on feminism that Feinstein rails against those who would violate the unchanging laws of the Torah and sages, but is much less vehement when justifying the *halakhic* changes of his constituent community. Ibid., *Orah Hayyim* 4:49.

[37] B. Sot. 44b. According to Yohanan, Judah's *milhemet hova* is a semantic variant of *milhemet mitsvah*.

[38] Abraham Karelitz, *Iggarot* I, no. 111, pp. 122-3, "Voluntary National Service for Girls: Compromise of a Nation's Purity," in *Jewish Observer* 4 (1971), p. 21, and Alfred Cohen, "Drafting Women for the Army," in *Journal of Halacha and Contemporary Society* 16 (Fall, 988), pp. 26-43.

[39] *Midrash Tannaim* 17:15 and a Sifre variant reported in by Louis Finkelstein, *Sifre Devarim* (New York and Jerusalem, 1993), p. 209.

[40] Bleich, 2:255.

[41] Bleich, *supra.*, *Iggarot Moshe Yoreh Deah* 2:44-45. Feinstein calls attention to Tosafot to B. Shab. 29b, s.v. *shevu'at ha-'edut*. Bleich does not distinguish between Feinstein's view of the pure law and his attitude toward the practice, but he piously emphasizes what he takes to be negative.

[42] Bleich, *supra*, 266.

[43] B. Git. 12a. Bleich concedes that women are not barred from seeking a "career outside the home."

[44] B. Ber. 20b. While Caro obliges women in reciting *havdalah*, *Orah Hayyim* 296:8, M. Isserles claims that women do not have this obligation and ought to hear *havdalah* from men. See Abraham Gumbiner, *Magen Abraham*, ad loc. n. 11, who realizes that women's license in Ashkenaz, to recite the *lulab* blessing, to be discussed below, is inconsistent with Isserles' restriction regarding women's *havdalah*. M. Kagan cites the custom of I. Horowitz, *Shenei Luhot ha-Berit Masekhet Shabbat*, end, that women do not drink the wine because the tree which brought sin into the world is, according to legend, the grape vine. Note that a folklore custom overrides what may be a statutory obligation, because one remembers the Sabbath with both *qiddush* and *havdalah*. See B. Pes. 106a-107a.

[45] B. Pes. 43b. Technically, *hag ha-matsot*.

[46] The anonymous statement at B. Ber. 20b suggests that women are required to pray because they are in need, like men, of divine mercy;. See Maimonides *Hilkhot Tefillah* 1:1-2, Exod. 23:28, and B. B.M. 107b. Note that Maimonides is aware of two conflicting Talmudic voices, and rules according to what is clearly Amoraic, and ignores the *setam*.

[47] *Nashim hayyabot be-birchat ha-zimmun*, B. Ber. 45b and B. Ar. 3a.

[48] Tosafot to B. Ber. 45b. s.v., *sha'ani hatam*.

[49] Tosafot to B. Hul. *2a*, s.v., *ha-kol*. The term *qallut rosh*, light-headed, has negative sexual connotations. M. Feinstein considers the mingling of the sexes to be an instance of light-headedness; *Iggarot Moshe Orah Hayyim* 1:39, 41. B. Meg. 9a forbids eating and drinking in the synagogue—but not separate pews—because of light-headedness. Maimonides deems light-headedness the opposite of wise activity; *Hilkhot Deot* 7:4, which includes, but is not restricted to, improper intergender activity. Maimonides' view reflects T. Ber. 3:21. On lightheadedness as referring to improper sexual familiarity, see T. Suk. 4:1 and B. Suk. 51a. Ironically, Feinstein invokes lightheadedness to outlaw mixed pews, an idea unsupported in the canonical texts, but he justifies eating in the synagogue (*Iggarot Moshe Orah Hayyim* 1:45), which the texts explicitly forbid (see B. Meg. 28b, Maimonides, *Hilkhot Tefillah* 11:6).

[50] This principle is an instance of what H.L.A. Hart calls a "rule of recognition," whereby members of a legal community are empowered to determine whether a given rule is part of the legal order. See Hart's *The Concept of Law* (Oxford, 1979), pp. 97-107.

[51] The Vilna edition reports that a woman with her husband is not required to recline. Joseph Kapih notes that the words "next to her husband" are probably a gloss.

[52] *Shulhan Arukh Orah Hayyim* 472:4, gloss. An anonymous rule at B. A.Z. 27a states that a non-Jew may not perform the operation on a Jew. One possibility is that a woman, like a non-Jew, does not circumcise. The Asheri (*ad loc.* 11) permits a woman to circumcise only if no trained male is present. Shulhan Arukh *Yoreh Deah* 264:1 and Maimonides, *Hilkhot Milah* 2:1, rule that anyone, including women, may perform the circumcision rite, but Isserles, *ad loc.*, and Shabbatai Kohen rule restrictively.

[53] B. Erub. 96a. Only at Y. Ber. 2:3 do we find the minority view of Hezeqiah, who claimed that the rabbis indeed protested. Jewish law follows the Bavli over the Yerushalmi and the majority view over the minority view. See Rashi to the Bavli, *ad loc.*

[54] *Hilkhot Lulav* 6:3. I suspect that Maimonides, following the Talmud, holds that only the legally authorized norm-creating body may initiate a rite with the status of "commandment." See *Hilkhot Abodah Zarah* 1:1-2, Tsebi Hirsch Chayyes, *Ma'amar al bal Tosif, Kol Kitvei Maharits Chayyes* (Tel Aviv, 1958), p. 81. M. Feinstein chooses not to cite Maimonides regarding women's wearing of *tsitsit*, but cites him to forbid their learning Torah (*Iggarot Moshe Yoreh Deah* 3:87).

[55] Tosafot to B. Ber. 14a, s.v. *yamim*, and to B. Qid. 33a. B. Men. 43a states, "Everyone is obliged to wear *tsitsit*: priests, Levites, Israelites, converts, women, and slaves. Simeon exempts women because it is a positive command conditioned by time ... from which women are exempt." Neither *Targum Yonatan/Yerushalmi* nor Tosafot are part of the Rabbinic canon, but B. Men. 43a most assuredly is. The minority view comports with a later Judaism's taste, and, with time, assumed *de facto* normativity.

[56] *Pesaqim* to B. Qid. 1:49. On the role of exegesis in Jewish law, see Menahem Elon, *Ha-Mishpat ha-'Ivri* (Jerusalem, 1973), pp. 243f., and Faur, pp. 19-32. By making this innovative claim, the Asheri implies that his charismatic intuition suffices to supercede the Dual Torah. Similarly, in his critical note on Maimonides' *Sefer ha-Mitsvot*, Negative Commands, 353, Nahmanides rejects Maimonides' ruling that the Rabbinic interpretation of B. Shab 13a represents a normative prohibition against erotic physical contact, claiming that the *derashah* need not be taken seriously.

[57] *Iggarot Moshe Orah Hayyim* 4:49, who also cites the *Targum, supra*. The Targumic literature is not generally taken to be part of the halakhic canon.

[58] M. Meiselman, "The Rav, Feminism, and Public Policy," in *Tradition* (Fall, 1998), 33, pp. 1, 10.

[59] In his "Two Kinds of Tradition" [Hebrew], in Isador Twersky, ed., *Shiurim le-Zecher Abba Mari* (Jerusalem, 1983), p. 228, Soloveitchik claims that in Judaism a legal tradition is subject to dialectic review while a folk tradition, like the oral ones that come from Sinai, are not. Soloveitchik here concurs that the blue thread (*tekhelet*) may not be restored to the *tallit* because the "tradition" he received from his father did not know what *tekhelet* was. Soloveitchik identifies the folk tradition of his ancestors with the tradition from Sinai. According to Maimonides, laws that are conceded to stem from Sinai are not subject to dispute; *Introduction to Pirush la-Mishnah*. But he believes that only rulings of a *bet din* accepted by all Israel, but not one's family tradition, fall within this rubric. Since women's wearing *tallit* or mixed seating violate inherited folk sensibilities, which are for Soloveitchik an unbroken tradition from Sinai, he opposes these changes not on legal or dialectical, but on cultural, grounds.

[60] This law is codified by Maimonides, *Hilkhot Megillah* 1:1, *Kesef Mishnah, ad loc.*, and *Shulhan Arukh Orah Hayyim* 689:1.

[61] B. Suk. 38a, s.v. *be-emet ameru*, and B. Ar. 3a, s.v., *le-attuyei nashim*.

[62] *Halakhot Gedolot* also invents others benedictions, like the one for a groom upon discovery that he has indeed married a virgin. See Ruth Langer, *To Worship God Properly: Tensions between Liturgical Custom and Halakhah in Judaism* (Cincinnati, 1998), p. 7.

[63] See Daniel Boyarin, *Unheroic Conduct: The Rise of Heterosexuality and the Invention of the Jewish Man* (Los Angeles, Berkeley, and London, 1997), pp. 127f.

[64] Avraham Grossman, *The Early Sages of France: Their Lives, Leadership, and Works* (Jerusalem, 1966) (Hebrew), p. 450.

[65] Israel M. Ta Shma, *Minhag Ashkenaz ha-Qadmon* (Jerusalem, 1994) (Hebrew), pp. 86-87. Langer, p. 98, observes that in Ashkenazic Judaism, "precedence [is] given to *minhag* [custom] over theoretical [canonical Rabbinic] halakhah."

[66] Jose Faur, "The Legal Thinking of Tosafot," in *Dine Israel* 6, 1975, pp. 43-72.

[67] Aaron Cohen, "Women Reading Megillah for Men: A Rejoinder," in *Torah u-Madda Journal* 9, 2000, pp. 248-259, claims that, in spite of the talmudic license, women are prohibited from reading the Scroll of Esther for men because post-talmudic rabbis have imposed conditions to prevent a violation of communal sensibility. Hershel [Tsevi] Schecter *"Tsei lach be-'Iqvei ha-Tson*, in *Be-'Iqvei ha-Tson* (Jerusalem, 1997), pp. 21-36, argues that changes in accepted practice violate "tradition." Logic does not avail when great rabbis have issued rulings, p. 36. M. Twersky, "A Glimpse of the Rav," in *Tradition* 30:3 (Summer, 1996), articulates this position eloquently: 1) J. Soloveitchik, his grandfather, is so great that lowly successors should not cheapen his legacy (pp. 79-80); 2) the proof offered by R. Tam does not derive from "textual analysis, rather it flows from his Torah intuition," (p. 82); 3) *Gedolei Torah* who will take their place in the chain of tradition ... "possess a sharply honed Torah intuition," (p. 93). This intutional tradition reflects J. Soloveitchik's second sense of tradition, which is not subjected to analysis or

review, especially by those who have not become members of the canon of communal greats.

[68] Jane Tibbets Schulenburg, *Forgetful of Their Sex: Female Sanctity and Society, CA. 500-1000* (Chicago and London, 1998), p. 2. See also Georgees Duby, *Women of the 12th Century* (Chicago, 1997), vol. 1, p. 101.

[69] Ibid., p. 138.

[70] Boyarin, *Carnal Israel*, pp. 82-83.

[71] Moshe Halbertal, *People of the Book: Canon, Meaning, and Authority* (Cambridge and London, 1997), p. 3.

[72] Meiselman, "The Rav," p. 16.

[73] Herschel Shachter, "In the Heels of the Sheep" [Hebrew] (Jerusalem, 1997), pp. 21, 29. See Tosafot to B. B.B. 51b, s.v., *beram*. If this rule was operative in Rabbinic Judaism, there would be no Rabbinic dispute.

[74] Ibid., p. 32.

[75] B. Bet. 30a., Tosafot, s.v. *tenan ein*.

[76] Joseph Soloveitchik, *Halakhic Man* (Philadelphia, 1984), p. 77.

ALAN J. YUTER

GENERAL INDEX
(Volumes I-IV)

INDEX OF TEXTUAL REFERENCES
(Volumes I-IV)

1. *Jewish Bible*

2. *Anonymous and Pseudepigraphical Jewish and Christian works closely related to the Jewish Bible*

3. *Qumran Writings, except lemmata Dead Sea Writings and Dead Sea Writings, the Judaisms of*

4. *New Testament*

5. *Ancient Writings (a. Jewish, b. Christian, c. non-Jewish, non-Christian)*

6. *Rabbinic Literature*